THE LOGIC OF POLITICAL SURVIVAL

THE LOGIC OF POLITICAL SURVIVAL

Bruce Bueno de Mesquita, Alastair Smith,
Randolph M. Siverson, and James D. Morrow

The MIT Press
Cambridge, Massachusetts
London, England

This book was set in Times Roman by SNP Best-set Typesetter Ltd., Hong Kong
Printed and bound in the United States of America.

Library of Congress Cataloging-in-Publication Data

The logic of political survival / Bruce Bueno de Mesquita ... [et al.].
   p. cm.
   Includes bibliographical references and index.
   ISBN 0-262-02546-9 (hc. : alk. paper)
   1. Heads of state—Succession. 2. Heads of state—Term of office. 3. Political planning.
I. Bueno de Mesquita, Bruce, 1946–

JF285.L64 2004
320′.01′1—dc21

2003045943

10 9 8 7 6 5 4 3 2 1

To Our Winning Coalition:
Arlene
Fiona
Suzanne
Karen

Contents

Preface

The Logic of Political Survival is our collective effort to solve a fundamental political puzzle: why are leaders who produce peace and prosperity turned out of office after only a short time, while those who produce corruption, war, and misery endure in office? In trying to solve this puzzle we have developed a theory about political selection that is surprisingly broad in its implications. The theory focuses on how two factors that govern the selection of leaders influence taxing and spending decisions, leadership turnover, social welfare, and institutional change. The two factors relate to what we call the *selectorate*—the set of people with a say in choosing leaders and with a prospect of gaining access to special privileges doled out by leaders—and the *winning coalition*—the subgroup of the selectorate who maintain incumbents in office and in exchange receive special privileges. Our theory challenges Hobbes's view that an absolute sovereign—the Leviathan—is the best form of governance, while also probing and questioning the perspectives of Machiavelli, Hume, Madison, Montesquieu, and other democratic theorists about the virtues of republics.

This project, begun a decade ago, started as a narrow investigation of the consequences of war for the political survival of regimes and leaders. It has grown into a theory of how political leaders allocate resources, with allocation decisions assumed to be made with an eye toward enhancing incumbents' prospects for remaining in office. From there it spread to assessing the relationship between institutions for selecting leaders and such factors as economic growth, corruption, property rights, patterns of population migration, coups d'état, war aims, war outcomes, revolution, health care, regime change, oppression, imperial expansion, foreign aid, civil liberties, trade policy, the quality of drinking water, the demise of monarchy, the endurance of democracy, apparent civic-mindedness, selection of core institutions of governance, and much more. All of these and many other central economic, social, and political variables are shown to share common explanations in the theory we propose.

We have endeavored to provide a general theory coupled with specific formal models from which we deduce our central claims. The political intuition underlying the models is explained plainly and nontechnically in the body of the text, buttressed by formal proofs in chapter appendixes. More technically inclined readers may wish to read the appendixes immediately after chapters 3, 6, and 9, while just skimming the intuitive explanation in the body of those chapters. Following the presentation of the basic model in chapter 3, subsequent chapters expand applications through related models that form part of the same theory and by relaxing assumptions to evaluate the theoretical, as well as empirical, robustness of the theory. We test most of the theory's implications on a broad body of data, sometimes spanning a period as long as nearly two centuries. The central propositions are evaluated with extensive control variables representing alternative explanations as well as exogenous factors that might lead to spurious associations between our predictions and observations.

Many results are probed further by close examinations of case histories, both to illustrate the workings of our theory "on the ground" and to evaluate the similarity between our theory and real-world politics. The combination of formal logic, statistical testing, and case histories provides a basis for evaluating the credibility of the theory's explanation as a significant part of the story of political survival and, indeed, much else in politics. The tests also help separate standard claims about democracy, autocracy, and monarchy from the argument we offer regarding the role played by coalition size and selectorate size in central aspects of politics. Ultimately, of course, this theory—like any theory—can only be judged through the development of still more demanding tests, better indicators, and the extent to which its core arguments prove consistent with the empirical record, past, present, and future.

If we can summarize our results in one sentence, it is that we have provided an explanation of when bad policy is good politics and when good policy is bad politics. At the same time, we show how institutions for selecting leaders create incentives to pursue good or bad public policy, with *good* and *bad* referring to governmental actions that make most people in a society better off or worse off. In that regard, we offer policy prescriptions in the closing chapter, being careful to base those prescriptions on what we believe has been demonstrated theoretically and empirically. Others, of course, will prove far better judges of what we have done and what we propose than we can be.

In the course of writing this book, we have collectively and individually amassed many debts of gratitude that we are happy to acknowledge here. We thank Ray Wolfinger for the use of his office at Berkeley as a central meeting place. We benefited greatly from the able advice, guidance, and insights of David Austen-Smith, (the greatly missed) Jeffrey Banks, Marcus Berliant, Ethan Bueno de Mesquita, Larry Diamond,

George Downs, Yi Feng, Robert Jackman, Kenneth Judd, Tasos Kalandrakis, Robert Keohane, Jacek Kugler, David Laitin, Dimitri Landr, Fiona McGillivray, Stephen Morris, Thomas Nechyba, Robert Powell, Adam Przeworski, Thomas Romer, Hilton Root, John Scott, Kiron Skinner, and Paul Zak, as well as many other colleagues at the University of Arizona, University of California, Cato Institute, University of Chicago, Claremont Graduate University, University of Colorado, Columbia University, Harvard University, Hoover Institution, University of Michigan, Michigan State University, New York University, Princeton University, University of Rochester, Rutgers University, Yale University, and elsewhere where portions of our research were presented, discussed, and critiqued. Portions of this research were kindly and generously funded by the National Science Foundation, grants SBR-9409225 and SES-9709454. Other portions were supported by our respective universities and departments. We particularly thank The Hoover Institution and its Director, John Raisian, for its exceptional support of this project. Beyond the support of two of us as fellows of the Institution, visiting fellowships at Hoover greatly assisted the development and writing of this book by allowing us to work together for extended periods of time. Only our own pigheadedness has led to the errors and deficiencies that remain.

I A THEORY OF POLITICAL INCENTIVES

1   Reigning in the Prince

Thomas Hobbes, writing in 1651, observed of life in the state of nature that it is "solitary, poore, nasty, brutish and short" (Hobbes [1651] 1996, chap. 13, p. 89). *The Leviathan's* concern is to investigate what form of government best improves that state of affairs. After so many centuries we might pause to ponder how much progress, if any, humankind has made in the quality of life and how such improvements relate to alternative forms of governance. Certainly life on our crowded planet is not solitary, though whether people are more engaged in supportive and protective communities—Hobbes's notion of escaping a solitary life—is an open question. Improvements in sanitation, nutrition, and medicine ensure that life is considerably longer than it was in Hobbes's day, but not everyone has shared in these improvements equally. For some it is less poor, though oppressive poverty remains the everyday circumstance for many people. As for life being nasty and brutish, progress is regrettably mixed. Today, despite various waves of democracy, much of the world's population continues to live under the yolk of nasty, brutish regimes.

Hobbes's remedy for the war of all against all is the absolutist Leviathan state. In this view, monarchy is the ideal form of sovereignty because

in monarchy the private interest is the same with the publique. The riches, power, and honour of a monarch arise only from the riches, strength, and reputation of his Subjects. For no king can be rich, nor glorious, nor secure, whose subjects are either poore, or contemptible, or too weak through want, or dissension, to maintain a war against their enemies. (Hobbes [1651] 1996, chap. 19, p. 131)

A century and a half earlier, Niccolò Machiavelli pondered similar questions, arriving at rather different answers. Though best known for his advice in *The Prince*, especially his observation that a ruler is better off being feared than loved, Machiavelli favored the individual liberty provided by a republic over the corruption of monarchy. His lament was that few places had either sufficient people of probity and religious conviction or institutions to foster competition across classes so that liberty and law could coexist "in such a manner that no one from within or without could venture upon an attempt to master them" (*Discourses* I; Machiavelli [1531] 1950, chap. 55, p. 253). He reasoned that Germany in his day was unusually successful in sustaining republics because the Germans engaged in little commerce with their neighbors and because

Germans maintained equality among the people, rather than permitting the emergence of what today we might call "the idle rich"—that is, those gentlemen as he called them "who live idly upon the proceeds of their extensive possessions, without devoting themselves to agriculture or any other useful pursuit to gain a living" (*Discourses* I; Machiavelli [1531] 1950, chap. 55, p. 255).

In Machiavelli's view,

whoever desires to establish a kingdom or principality where liberty and equality prevail, will equally fail, unless he withdraws from that general equality a number of the boldest and most ambitious spirits, and makes gentlemen of them, not merely in name but in fact, by giving them castles and possessions, as well as money and subjects; so that surrounded by these he may be able to maintain his power, and that by his support they may satisfy their ambition, and the others may be constrained to submit to that yoke to which force alone has been able to subject them.... But to establish a republic in a country better adapted to a monarchy, or a monarchy where a republic would be more suitable, requires a man of rare genius and power, and therefore out of the many that have attempted it but few have succeeded. (*Discourses* I; Machiavelli [1531] 1950, chap. 55, p. 256)

We share Hobbes's concern to explain when the public's interests are most advanced and Machiavelli's to comprehend when a republic is most likely to succeed. We will argue that Hobbes's confidence in monarchy was mistaken in logic and in fact and that Machiavelli's perspective that a republic is best for promoting freedom and institutional stability is correct. Indeed, this book can be construed as an investigation of the accuracy of the above-quoted suppositions of Hobbes and Machiavelli about the ties between civic-mindedness (i.e., probity), public well-being, private gain, the security of leaders in office, and alternative institutions of government. We will suggest that the appearance of honest, civic-minded government is a consequence of key features of republican political institutions and that corruption and political security are consequences of parallel features in monarchy and autocracy. On the basis of our analysis, we propose ways of reigning in not only Hobbes's Leviathan, but Machiavelli's well-advised Prince as well.

Three Puzzles

The alternative to the poor, nasty, brutish life in the state of nature envisioned by Hobbes is a life of peace and prosperity. It is easy to agree with

Hobbes that governments that provide for the peace and prosperity of their citizens are successful governments. Indeed, we might naturally expect that leaders who promote peace and prosperity are effective and so deserve long terms in office. Who, after all, does not desire a leader who knows how to provide peace and prosperity? The trouble is, as Machiavelli so aptly observed, that these two enviable qualities are not necessarily conducive to political survival. In fact, just the opposite may be true. Democrats offer their citizens more peace and, by some accounts, more prosperity than autocrats. Yet autocrats last in office about twice as long, on average, as do democrats.[1] Why is this so?

This first puzzle motivates part of our work. To seek an answer, we propose to identify political decisions that are incentive compatible with particular institutional constraints. We identify two basic institutions of governance that together expose generic differences between democracy, monarchy, military junta, autocracy, and other forms of government. We use these institutions to explain why poor policy performance is incentive compatible with many forms of nondemocratic governance, while good policy performance is induced by democratic institutions even in the absence of a population that is particularly honest, forthright, or civic-minded. In the process of doing so, our analysis will indicate that the institutionally appropriate choice of policy performance—good or bad—enhances the prospects for political survival (Robinson 1998).

A second puzzle that motivates this book revolves around the selection of governing institutions. People are said to be creatures of habit. Yet, in politics, they often deviate from past practice when the opportunity arises to alter the rules by which they are governed. Consider, for instance, the Bolshevik revolutionaries in Russia who—having defeated the czar and the Kerensky government—launched a social and political experiment of monumental proportions. Their social experiment included the implementation of an entirely new form of command economy based on the labor theory of value. Centuries of evolution in the ideas of property rights were set aside. In one fell swoop almost all property belonged, at least in principle, to everyone. The social and economic changes wrought by the Bolsheviks were accompanied by profound political changes as well. Vladimir Ilyich Lenin promulgated a political system grounded in democratic centralism. At first blush, it does not appear to be that different from the czarist system of concentrated authority. Once a decision was taken, all those close to the seat of power were expected to adhere to that decision; there was no room for dissent. Such a principle required that only a small group could influence the actions of the central authorities, a characteristic that typified most of the reign of Czar Nicholas. Lenin's principle of democratic centralism left no room for democratic competition of the sort known in the United States at the time. However, while keeping the reigns of real power in the hands of a small group, the Bolsheviks pursued an innovative experiment in the design of their political system, an innovation that made their government different structurally from the Romanov monarchy. They produced one of history's first universal adult suffrage voting systems when they held an election in December 1917. Of the 41.6 million votes cast, the Bolsheviks received about 25 percent (<http://kuhttp.cc.ukans.edu/kansas/cienciala/342/ch2.html>). The set of people with an ostensible say in choosing the government had been tiny during the Romanov dynasty. Under the Bolshevik system, it was very large indeed.

The experiment with universal suffrage leaves us with a puzzle. Why would any authoritarian state adopt universal adult suffrage as part of its political system? What possible value could leaders, elites, and ordinary citizens derive from rigged elections that everyone recognized as meaningless? Surely the government could gain little, if any, legitimacy from the charade of such elections. Yet there must have been a reason behind decisions to deviate from the standard monarchical approach that relied on noble birth or the military model relying just on the control of guns to decide who has even a nominal say in choosing leaders.

Equally puzzling are institutional innovations adopted by the early English settlers of North America. Just as the Bolsheviks had lived under the repressive regime of the czar, the early English pilgrims had endured and fled the religious oppression of Britain's monarchy. These pilgrims certainly oppressed those who did not share their religion, but theirs was a government starkly less dictatorial than the monarchy they fled. They built a system in which many had a say about the actions of the government and many had a say in choosing the leaders of that government. Elections were on a fixed and frequent schedule, sometimes with a secret ballot, and open to many. Why did these English settlers, no less so than Lenin and his followers, devise a form of government different from the one they had previously experienced? It has been observed that "those who are conquered always want to imitate the conqueror in his main characteristics" (Hochschild 1999, 304). Certainly, neither Lenin nor the English settlers in North America fit easily into this description. Those who had long subjugated them ruled on the basis of principles different from the principles chosen by the Bolsheviks or the pilgrims, and these two groups chose principles quite different from each other. How are we to square each of these choices about what government institutions to erect when none comport with the previous experience of those making the choice? What leads to the selection and maintenance of democracy in some places, autocracy in others, military juntas in still others, while others choose monarchy or some other form of governance?

A third puzzle arises out of the study of war. At the end of World War II, the victors deposed the leaders in many of the vanquished states. What is more, they toppled the institutions of government and replaced them with others more to their liking. The Americans, with the support of the British and the French, imposed democracy on Germany and Japan, going so far as to write their constitutions for them. Yet at the same time these very countries heartily resisted the creation or promotion of democratic institutions in their own colonial territories and frequently backed and bolstered dictators in Africa, Latin America, and elsewhere. These observations raise questions. When and why do victors in war impose new forms of government on the vanquished and when and why do they sometimes choose to leave the institutions of government as they found them? Does democracy emerge out of monarchy, autocracy, or military junta as a consequence of peaceful domestic transitions? Is democracy or autocracy imposed on the vanquished by foreign victors? Are there sustainable paths from monarchy or autocracy to democracy? Are there, we must alas ask, sustainable paths back to monarchy or autocracy? Finally, can the choice to produce peace and prosperity or war and misery be shown to follow from the same factors that influence preferences for government institutions and the length of time leaders survive in office?

The Essence of the Argument

Political leaders need to hold office in order to accomplish any goal. Every leader answers to some group that retains her in power: her *winning coalition*. This group controls the essential features that constitute political power in the system. In democracies the winning coalition is the group of voters who elect the leader; in other systems it is the set of people who control enough other instruments of power to keep the leader in office. If the leader loses the loyalty of a sufficient number of members of the winning coalition, a challenger can remove and replace her in office.

Leaders make three related sets of decisions. First, they choose a tax rate that generates government revenue and that influences how hard people work. Second, they spend the revenue raised in a manner designed to help keep incumbents in office, particularly by sustaining support among members of their winning coalition. Finally, they provide various mixes of public and private goods. Private benefits are distributed only to members of the winning coalition and diminish in value to individual coalition members as the size of the group expands. Consequently, as the size of the coalition increases, leaders are expected to shift their effort to the provision of public goods that benefit all in society.

Coalition members are drawn from a broader group: the *selectorate* (Shirk 1993). The incentive to defect from the incumbent to a challenger depends on the prospects of being included in the challenger's winning coalition if he should replace the incumbent. The larger the selectorate relative to the winning coalition, the smaller the chance that a given member of the current leader's coalition will be included in the challenger's new winning coalition and so continue to receive private benefits. In political systems characterized by small winning coalitions and large selectorates—as is common in many rigged-election autocracies—supporters of the leader are particularly loyal because the risk and cost of exclusion if the challenger comes to power are high. Conversely, in political systems characterized by large coalitions and large selectorates—as is common in many democracies—supporters of the leader have weak bonds of special privileges and so are more willing to defect.

Organization of the Investigation

Our starting point is that every political leader faces the challenge of how to hold onto his or her job. The politics behind survival in office is, we believe, the essence of politics. The desire to survive motivates the selection of policies and the allocation of benefits; it shapes the selection of political institutions and the objectives of foreign policy; it influences the very evolution of political life. We take as axiomatic that everyone in a position of authority wants to keep that authority and that it is the maneuvering to do so that is central to politics in any type of regime. When we say it is central, we mean that all actions taken by political leaders are intended by them to be compatible with their desire to retain power (Downs 1957; Black 1958; Wintrobe 1998). For us, the critical question in politics is how political institutions shape the goal of some leaders to produce peace and prosperity, while for others, institutional arrangements do not discourage war, misery, and famine. This is, of course, a topic also of considerable interest to economists who are concerned with how institutions influence economic growth (Olsen 1993; Niskanen 1997; Acemoglu and Robinson 2000) and with why institutions emerge in particular forms in different places (Engerman and Sokoloff 1997; Feng and Zak 2002; Acemoglu and Robinson 2001). These are the central themes we investigate.

The study is organized in three parts. The first three chapters develop a theory of institutions, leadership incentives, and governance. The second part of the book, which consists of four chapters, presents the empirical evidence regarding the theory's predictions about taxing and spending decisions by government, policy choices, war behavior, and the impact of these decisions on leaders' longevity in office. The third part of the book, made up of the final three chapters, evaluates the implications of the findings in the first two parts for the development of preferences over institutions that shape political selection and the actions that lead to institutional change. In the next section of this chapter we briefly present the main contours of our analysis.

A Theory of Political Incentives: Part I

In part I we construct a theory that addresses how institutions for selecting leaders, which we call *selection institutions*, shape the incentives leaders have to promote or inhibit social welfare. Our theoretical account examines how political-selection institutions influence the prospects that political leaders will survive and shows that different institutions create different imperatives of action for politicians who want to remain in office.

In developing what we call the *selectorate theory*, we build on important research by many others. Our theory depends partially on an understanding of coalition politics, and so we extract insights from the literature that ties coalition strategies to officeholding. Anthony Downs (1957) and William Riker (1962) draw attention to winning office as a central goal of each politician. Coalitions are built to maximize the prospect of winning and retaining office. We share that view, while also agreeing with Riker—who departs in this regard from Downs—that, subject to winning, political leaders want to maximize their control over policy choices and minimize the price they must pay to their coalition members and so build minimal winning coalitions when possible. Because the size of a winning coalition influences the price that must be paid to assemble it, we believe that the minimal coalition size required in a polity is itself a fundamental institutional aspect of governance that leads to structure-induced allocation decisions (Shepsle and Weingast 1981). Indeed, one of our main purposes is to develop a better understanding of how basic coalitional institutions shape allocation decisions.

Studies of voting and political succession inform our thinking about mechanisms by which leaders construct governments. The literature draws sharp distinctions between authoritarian and democratic regimes, particularly with regard to what is maximized through government choices. We suggest a theoretical approach intended to offer an integrated explanation of the differences that persist across nominal regime types. In designing our theoretical approach it is important, of course, to capture the regularities already identified in the literature. There is, in fact, a rich literature on authoritarian rule and a separate, rich literature on democratic governance. Of course, others have followed this path before. At least since Hannah Arendt (1951)—not to mention much earlier research starting with Thucydides, Aristotle, Sun Tzu, and Kautilya—scholars have been concerned to understand authoritarian and totalitarian forms of government. Ronald Wintrobe's (1990, 1998) influential political-economy account of dictatorship draws attention to rent-seeking behavior as a crucial characteristic of such regimes (Krueger 1974; Buchanan, Tollison, and Tullock 1980). Mancur Olson (1993, 2000) expands on Wintrobe's work, identifying factors that encourage despots to become territorial, thereby leading to the creation of authoritarian states. The theory we propose, therefore, must explain the rent seeking common in authoritarian states, while still accounting for its lower frequency and intensity in more democratic polities.

Kenneth Arrow (1951), William Riker (1982, 1996), Richard McKelvey (1976, 1979), and Norman Schofield (1978) focus on democracy, drawing attention away from rent-seeking behavior and toward the pursuit and selection of policy outcomes and their linkage to maintaining oneself in office or throwing the rascals out. Gary Cox (1997) carefully demonstrated how electoral rules influence policy outcomes even if voter preferences are fixed, providing a coherent basis for distinguishing among different forms of democracy. We try to build on those insights, expanding them beyond the democratic setting while also noting how differences among various forms of democracy are distinguished within the selectorate theory.

Studies of autocracy and democracy naturally contributed to the rise of investigations concerned with endogenous institutional change. Douglass North and Barry Weingast (North and Weingast 1989; Weingast 1997) help inform our thinking about what allocation decisions leaders can credibly commit to and how allocation choices and revenue needs influence institutional change. Their attention is particularly drawn to periods of economic crisis such as arise following war or internal insurrection. We attempt to generalize their ideas to allow us to theorize about commitment issues, both during crises and in more everyday political circumstances. A related literature, exemplified by the work of Stanley Engerman and Kenneth Sokoloff (1997) and Daron Acemoglu and James Robinson (2000), addresses additional questions regarding endogenous institutional change. These studies point theoretically and empirically to the close relationship between economic shocks and political transitions. We build on their models to endogenize the ties between the economy and political institutions so that economic crises are themselves a product of choices regarding governing institutions. In this way, we try to add to the predictability of economic setbacks, placing them within their political context.

Having incorporated ideas from many research programs, the selectorate theory weaves these insights together to facilitate the derivation of both well-established empirical regularities and new propositions regarding governance and political economy. Our theory is, then, a natural amalgamation and extension of previous studies. While it provides new ideas about a variety of political subjects, it remains a primitive theory in need of enrichment with more institutional details and improved measurement. Nevertheless, it affords a way to integrate seemingly disparate aspects of politics and is amenable to testing and falsification. In fact, parts II and III are devoted to those tasks.

The institutions we examine are shown to create norms of conduct that influence the welfare of political leaders and that shape the policies those leaders pursue. These norms take various forms, which might be called political culture, civic-mindedness, oppressiveness, venality, and the like. We will argue theoretically that institutional arrangements strongly influence whether civic-mindedness or oppression, transparency or corruption, prosperity or poverty, war or peace are rewarded politically. We also provide extensive empirical evidence that encourages us to believe that the account offered by the selectorate theory is consistent with real-world politics. We offer an explanation of why some polities pursue successful policies while others do not.

Part I is organized so that this first chapter sets out the empirical puzzles we hope to solve. It also explains the organization of the book. Chapter 2 provides detailed definitions of core concepts in the selectorate theory. The third chapter then presents a model of domestic politics and a general statement of the theory. Subsequent chapters extend the basic model laid out in chapter 3 and modify it to account for important phenomena—including uncertainty—temporarily put aside in that chapter. As the subsequent chapters unfold, we begin to relax assumptions made in chapter 3. By relaxing assumptions we are able to assess the robustness of core results, and we are also able to explain the deposition of leaders and differences in political survival rates.

Policy Choice and Political Survival: Part II

While part I suggests propositions about norms of conduct and about taxing and spending decisions, part II investigates the extent to which those propositions are supported by the empirical record. The selectorate theory provides a coherent explanation for many aspects of political, economic, and social life. Logical consistency, however, is not enough to establish that a theory is useful. Confidence in a theory is built by failed but demanding attempts to falsify its predictions. The second section of the book attempts just this. Having developed measures for the key theoretical concepts of the selectorate and winning coalition, we show that they help explain a broad array of social phenomena in a manner consistent with the theory.

Chapter 4 analyzes core aspects of the theory. In particular it examines taxation, the willingness of individuals to participate in economically productive activities, the creation of wealth and economic growth, government expenditure levels, kleptocracy, and societal welfare. Chapter 5 then examines specific policy provisions. These analyses encompass such seemingly diverse phenomena as the protection of civil liberties, levels and changes in per capita income, the quality of drinking water, access to health care, educational opportunity, and black market exchange rates.

Chapter 6 expands the domestic selectorate model, producing a comprehensive account of the known empirical regularities collectively called the *democratic peace*. Additionally, chapter 6 evaluates the empirical evidence regarding novel deductions from the dyadic version of the selectorate theory. Chapter 7 assesses the impact that public-goods and private-goods allocations have on the prospects leaders have of remaining in office. Here we draw out further theoretical implications of the selectorate theory—including new ideas about the life-cycle survival prospects of leaders and the impact of term limits on the behavior of incumbents—and test core predictions about how variations in selection institutions systematically influence a leader's longevity in office. In chapter 7 we relax several assumptions of the basic model presented in chapter 3, bringing the model closer to the details of politics, and we develop and test extensions of and additions to our core hypotheses. We conclude that bad policy is good politics under some political arrangements, while being disastrous for political survival under other arrangements.

Choosing Institutions for Political Selection: Part III

The third part takes the lessons learned from our comparative analysis and applies them to the development of a theory of endogenous selection of institutions. If leaders want to survive in office, they must have an interest in choosing institutional arrangements that insulate them from threats of removal. We identify the most desirable political systems from the perspective of ruling elites, political challengers, key backers of the incumbent, ordinary citizens, the disenfranchised, and foreign conquerors. We lay out how the choice of systems and adjustments to political-selection institutions is linked to political survival within the theory's context. Chance circumstances in history may seemingly influence who gets to define a political system, but the alteration of political systems is also subject to strategic considerations well within the control of the competitors for and subjects of political authority (Acemoglu and Robinson 2001; Feng and Zak 1999; Tilly 1978).

Part III begins with chapter 8. In that chapter we look at institutional preferences and their ties to different segments of a country's population. Through use of these institutional preferences, we extend the selectorate theory and move toward a theory of endogenous institution selection. We evaluate the motives for oppression, term limits, and immigration and emigration, as well as the conditions that make revolutions, civil wars, coups, and other antigovernment activities likely. Our analyses will test the empirical relationship between the predictions of the selectorate theory and each of these phenomena, including the consequences that follow from successful changes in institutions. We also provide an explanation of a significant political puzzle identified by Adam Przeworski (2001), namely, the seeming immunity of wealthy democracies from coups, revolutions, and other actions that lead to the collapse of democracy. Chapter 9 extends the investigation from chapter 8 by inquiring about the conditions under which military conquest is likely to lead to institutional change and the circumstances of conquest under which the institutions of the vanquished state are expected to remain the same. The chapter focuses on how selection institutions influence war aims, particularly with regard to why democracies seem more inclined to depose defeated foreign foes than are autocrats. It also offers a theoretical and empirical way to think about nation building as a consequence of the deposition of leaders, either by foreign rivals or by domestic challengers in the context of the nation's war experience. Again extensive empirical tests are presented to evaluate the accuracy of the model's predictions. The final chapter, chapter 10, returns to Hobbes's view of life in the state of nature. We develop the Hobbes Index to assess how far each country has come from life in the state of nature—that is, life that is solitary, nasty, poor, brutish, and short. We use the Hobbes Index in conjunction with insights suggested by the selectorate theory to provide policy suggestions that, if implemented, might result in improved quality of life around the world.

Why Focus on Political Survival?

This book investigates comparative domestic politics, economics, and foreign affairs as well as the interplay among them. Naturally, in covering so much territory, we necessarily leave out much of the important detail of daily political life. Our objective is to set out and test a basic theory with the hope that it will be elaborated in the future, filling in the details that for now are absent.

We discuss several vital problems in politics and how they are tied to the quest for political survival. For instance, it will be seen that the policies and programs necessary to ward off domestic and foreign threats to a leader's survival vary dramatically under different institutional arrangements. Sometimes policies and programs that promote general welfare also trigger the deposition of leaders by political rivals. Sometimes it is impossible for leaders to simultaneously satisfy critical domestic constituents and advance social well-being. In such cases, politicians must gamble on how far they can go in distorting the national economy for the benefit of a small group of cronies. If they choose incorrectly— either providing too much social welfare or not enough—they face defeat.

Our main subject of investigation is selection institutions and their effect on domestic and foreign affairs. Why, then, do we place so much emphasis on political survival rather than just addressing institutions? The answer is simple: different circumstances influence the choice of political-selection institutions, but in each case we believe that such choices are motivated by the interest politicians have in holding onto office.

Since the earliest polities, leaders have worried about their hold on power. In ancient Assyria, Ashurbanipal had been named crown prince by his father, King Esarhaddon, making him coregent and future king. Although he received the oath of loyalty from the nobles, still he worried about his security:

Is danger to be anticipated from the bearded chiefs, the King's Companions, his own brother and the brothers of his father, the members of the royal family? He doubts the loyalty of his charioteer and of his chariot attendant, of the night-watch, of his royal messengers and of his body-guard, of the officers in the palace and those on the frontier, of his cellarer and baker. He fears for what he eats and what he drinks, he fears by day and by night; in the city and without, there is danger that a revolt against him will be undertaken. (Olmstead [1923] 1975, 396)

Ashurbanipal was skilled at discerning and thwarting the multitude of threats to his power; he ruled Assyria as king for forty-one years (668–627 BC).

This belief in the desire to hold power leads us to theorize about the interdependence between institutions of governance and questions related to political survival, a topic that has received limited attention in the literature on political institutions. A brief outline of how we think about these relationships may be helpful.

All Incumbents Have Rivals

The competition for political office has always been fierce. In modern democracies, the battle for the highest of offices is frequently punctuated by vicious personal attacks, by acrimonious charges of personal corruption, indecency, and incompetence. As Franklin Roosevelt and Richard Nixon learned, the attacks may even extend to questions about their pet dogs. No democracy, however, ever lacks people eager to be candidates for office.

Even more puzzling is the surfeit of candidates for the highest offices in autocracies and monarchies. In these political systems, defeat often has meant imprisonment and even death. When King Richard I of England died on April 6, 1199, for instance, he left vague the succession to the crown. Like the Holy Roman emperor and so many other medieval monarchs, the English king was elected, a tradition that was still strong at the time of Richard's death (Painter 1949). To be sure, the great barons tended to follow feudal hereditary customs, but they were not above deviating from those norms. How else can we explain the competing, simultaneous elections of Canute (by the witenagemot—an assembly of thanes or nobles) and Edmund Ironside (by the citizens of London) as king of England, or the choice of Hugh Capet over Charles of Lower Lorraine in France?

English custom, like French custom, dictated that only one of noble birth could be king and hence hereditary claims imparted an advantage.

But English custom, like French custom, also dictated that anticipated competence be taken into account in selecting among those who could be or would be king. The "magistrates," in whom the right to choose eventually came to reside, had both the right to reject hereditary priority and subsequently to depose whomever they had chosen if the king proved wanting. In Northumbria shortly before the Norman Conquest, for instance, thirteen of fifteen elected kings were subsequently deposed (Taylor 1889, 109, 175–176, 215–217). In France in 987, Hugh Capet was elected over the hereditary heir to Charlemagne's throne because, in the words of Archbishop Adalbero, "In him [Hugh Capet] you will find a defender, not only of the state, but also of your private interests" ("The Election of Hugh Capet," <http://www.fordham.edu/halsall/source/987/capet.html>).

Two claimants were put forward on King Richard's death. John Lackland was Richard's only surviving brother and King Henry II's only surviving son. Arthur, John's (and Richard's) nephew, was the surviving son of an older brother (Geoffrey) who died before their father, King Henry II. It might also be noted that Queen Eleanor, Henry II's wife, was still alive and might herself have made a claim to the throne. She was the duchess of Aquitaine, representing a significant portion of the Angevin empire. She preferred to support John. In any event, Arthur and his backers were not reluctant to press his case although the risks were great. As (bad) luck would have it for Arthur, he lost. What was Arthur's fate? After Arthur failed in attempting to raise a rebellion with French support, John had him taken prisoner and (probably) murdered, thereby protecting himself from a potential political rival. Arthur paid the ultimate price as part of John's struggle for political survival. John ascended to the throne, but he did not free himself of political rivals. Years later, of course, he faced the famous barons' revolt that led to the Magna Carta.

Arthur's fate is hardly unusual. During the Safavid dynasty in Persia (1502–1736) it was a virtual custom for the successor to the throne to engage in the wholesale execution of brothers, sons, and other nobles who might represent rivals for the crown. Ismail II (1576–1578), Shah Abbas I (1588–1629), Shah Safi (1629–1641), and Shah Mahmud (1722–1725) were especially noteworthy for their penchant for killing prospective rivals among their own close relatives (Langer 1980, 565–657). The excesses of the Safavids might strike us as ancient history. But we cannot forget that Lavrenty Beria, a contender to succeed Joseph Stalin, was executed shortly after Stalin's death in 1953 or that General Sani Abacha in Nigeria in the late 1990s kept Moshood Abiola imprisoned rather than allow him to become president, an office to which he was duly elected. Abiola was eventually murdered while in prison. General Abacha himself also appears to have been murdered by political opponents. King Hassan of Morocco, who died in 1999, enjoyed a reputation as a progressive Muslim monarch, yet he is reputed to have had his political rivals flown out to sea in helicopters and dumped overboard. Saddam Hussein in Iraq is alleged to have personally shot members of his own cabinet when they questioned his policies. The list hardly needs further enumeration to make the point. Political succession is a risky business, yet there is no shortage of people willing to take even life-and-death risks in seeking high office.

Civic-Mindedness

It is pleasant to think that the brutish behavior of a King John or a Genghis Khan, his approximate contemporary, is a thing of the past, a relic of a less civilized age. It is pleasant to think that most contemporary political leaders are motivated by high ideals in their pursuit of office; that the opportunity to do good works—not the quest for power—is more prominent a motive today than it was centuries ago. We are agnostic on the question of whether modern-day leaders are more high-minded than their predecessors. We prefer simply to enumerate the benefits of office and to note that apparent civic-mindedness by leaders appears to be strongly influenced by selection institutions, so that institutions shape the behavior of leaders as much as leaders shape institutions. Certainly we are not among the first to make this observation. David Hume, writing more than 250 years ago, noted:

It is true, those who maintain that the goodness of all government consists in the goodness of the administration may cite many particular instances in history where the very same government, in different hands, has varied suddenly into the two opposite extremes of good and bad. . . . But here it may be proper to make a distinction. All absolute governments must very much depend on the administration, and this is one of the great inconveniences attending that form of government. But a republican and free government would be an obvious absurdity if the particular checks and controls provided by the constitution had really no influence and made it not the interest, even of bad men, to act for the public good. Such is the intention of these forms of government, and such is their real effect where they are wisely constituted; as, on the other hand, they are the source of all disorder and of the blackest crimes where either skill or honesty has been wanting in their original frame and institution. (Hume [1742] 1985, chap. iii, p. 16)

One might well think of this study as a somewhat more rigorous theoretical and empirical elaboration on Hume's contention. We reach conclusions remarkably similar to Hume's and for similar reasons. Our analysis indicates that leaders operating under certain institutional arrangements closely associated with republican government or democracy emphasize good public policies rather than establishing secret Swiss bank accounts because good policy—that is, policy that satisfies their crucial supporters—is essential to their personal political welfare. We also show that leaders working under institutional arrangements correlated with authoritarianism are wise to establish special privileges for their backers like the special stores party members enjoyed in the Soviet Union. Doling out special privileges often is vital to their political survival. Autocrats can be forgiven bad policy, but they are not likely to survive the elimination of patronage or the corrupt benefits of cronyism. For autocrats, what appears to be bad policy often is good politics. It is no coincidence that a market exists for secret bank accounts.

Our agnosticism with regard to the civic-mindedness of leaders is part of what distinguishes our undertaking from the views of many contemporary economists. Economists share with us a concern to explain such important phenomena as economic growth and the elevation of human capital. Many economic theorists, however, departing now from a Machiavellian viewpoint, assume that leaders are benign at least when it comes to economic policies. For many economists, leaders are *assumed* to be interested in enhancing the welfare of their citizenry. Failure to do so is thought to be a product of ignorance or the result of constraints beyond their control that prevent them from implementing the necessary economic reforms.[2] Such distinguished and influential economists as Joseph Stiglitz or Paul Krugman focus on the failure of governments to apply the central principles of economics to their formation of public policy. They see the failures of growth as being explained by the mistaken policies followed by national governments. James Robinson (1998, 13), for instance, quotes Paul Krugman as saying, "It makes considerable sense for the World Bank . . . to push very hard for liberal policies in developing countries, given their [i.e., developing countries'] demon-strated tendencies to engage in economically irrational interventions." Our departure from accounts by some economists does not lie in any dis-agreement on the principles of economics, but rather on the focus of how to fix the problem.

We do not subscribe to the notion that government leaders fail to understand what policies represent good applications of the economic principles that lead to growth. Rather, we share the concern of many political scientists and economists to understand how political in-stitutions influence economic growth and social welfare. Persson and Tabellini (2000), for instance, find that parliamentary democratic systems tend to be more corrupt than presidential systems. We argue that this is related to the vote total required to form a wining coalition in these two different types of democracy. Acemoglu and Robinson (2000) investigate the dependence between income inequality and the expansion of the voting franchise. They maintain that societies with high inequality are likely to be politically unstable, while societies that achieve relative income equality through redistribution tend to consolidate their hold on democracy. This view is broadly consistent with that expressed by Robert Barro (1996, 1997) or Adam Przeworski et al. (2000), each of whom con-tends that democracy satisfies the wants of the median voter, producing stability and a decline in growth rates. The median voter has a below-average (mean) income and so is more likely to support redistributive policies than growth-oriented policies. We contend that political insti-tutions significantly influence income levels, income distribution, and growth rates and that a large winning-coalition structure is particularly conducive to income growth. Other aspects of democracy may work against growth, but not coalition size. Further, we model economic per-formance as an endogenous product of political institutions and then suggest how institutionally induced economic performance influences subsequent institutional or political stability. Thus, we offer an account of the causes and consequences of coups, revolution, and institutional change that is complementary to but also different from that suggested by others (Jackman 1978; Muller and Seligson 1987; Londregan and Poole 1992). At the same time our model agrees with the findings of William Niskanen (1997), Mancur Olson (1993), Ronald Wintrobe (1998), and David Lake and Matthew Baum (2001) that rent seeking is more common in autocracy than in democracy. We derive this distinction while assuming that all political leaders, regardless of their institutional setting, have a common utility function that emphasizes first holding onto (or gaining) office and second maximizing their personal income while in office.

Our focus is on political incentives and institutions that encourage or discourage leaders from promoting economic policies conducive to growth and general social welfare. We assume that political leaders are self-interested and that their actions are chosen to be politically beneficial to themselves. Bad economic policies are not, in our view, obviously irrational; rather they are a phenomenon to be explained by a process of rational decision making by self-interested leaders. The explanation we offer leads to some surprising conclusions that suggest a departure from the policy recommendations following from theories focused on economic rationality alone. Those theories ignore and therefore fail to incorporate political rationality into their construction of policy recommendations.

In our undertaking, leaders are interested in enhancing their own welfare and so seek to produce what their supporters want. The phrase "their supporters," however, is not shorthand for the citizens of the state. The behavior of leaders arises from their own self-interest in holding their positions. If that coincides with or is compatible with the welfare of the citizenry, many will benefit. If the welfare of a leader and the welfare of the society are at odds—and our theory and data will indicate that they often are—it is more likely to go well for the leader than for society.

High political office provides two primary paths by which leaders can derive satisfaction. Leaders may be motivated by a desire to pursue public policies they sincerely believe will enhance the public welfare. We think of such an orientation in leaders as being civic-minded, and perhaps it is. Abraham Lincoln's declaration that "in giving freedom to the slave we assure freedom to the free,—honorable alike in what we give and what we preserve" is an apparent instance of such high-mindedness (Abraham Lincoln, Second Annual Message to Congress, December 1, 1862; in Lincoln [1862] 1991, 79). However, so too was Winston Churchill's wartime declaration that he had not become the king's first minister to preside over the dissolution of the British empire. And he was right. The British people swept the hero of World War II out of office at the first opportunity and replaced him with a prime minister,

Clement Atlee, who decidedly would and did preside over the dissolution of that empire.

High office not only provides an opportunity to do good works. High office also holds out the prospects of great personal aggrandizement. Few, even among those who profess and demonstrate a strong commitment to the public welfare, leave office alive less well off personally than they had been when they came to power. Indeed, the quest for personal benefits seems to be a substantial motivation behind the competition for high office. Napoleon Bonaparte, for one, accumulated a personal treasury of 200 million francs at the height of his power, an immense fortune at the time (Schroeder 1994, 399). Unfortunately for him, he was not allowed to take it with him to St. Helena. Napoleon's fortune should not be surprising. When the risks are large, so too must be the prospective compensation. Otherwise, who would take the risks? Still, however rational it may be from a cost-benefit perspective to pursue personal gain while in office, many tend to think of this as low-minded and base. Leaders interested in holding onto office can and do adjust their relative emphasis on personal aggrandizement and the national welfare in accordance with the requirements of the moment. We hope to demonstrate logically and empirically that a significant factor in those requirements emanates from the structure of institutions for selecting political leaders.

The theory proposed in the next two chapters emphasizes the circumstances under which leaders realize personal gains, promote public benefits, and create special benefits for their political allies. The degree to which they choose to emphasize one form of benefit over another is shown to depend on the selection institutions under which they operate. We are less interested in their personal inclinations to trade between the public good and their personal well-being than we are in identifying how selection institutions shape the profitability of such trades. After all, if particular institutions can ensure that even the most venal leader will nevertheless pursue the public welfare, then recognizing what those institutions are can make an important contribution to improving the quality of life around the world. At the same time, we recognize that even some autocrats can care enough about public policy to use the rents they extract to advance their own public policy vision. That is, while most autocrats are likely to use their office to benefit themselves and their backers, some—Lee Kwan Yew of Singapore is an exemplar—may choose to use the resources available at their discretion to advance public welfare. Nikita Khrushchev's agricultural policies in the Soviet Union and Mao Zedong's economic and cultural policies in China may be examples of such well-intentioned—but in these instances disastrous—uses of personal control over national resources for personal pet public policy projects.

We treat political survival as a necessary, but not a sufficient, condition for leaders to achieve other personal objectives, whether those other objectives involve policy goals, personal venality, or whatever. That is not to say that leaders cannot prefer to lose office, nor is it to say that leaders who want to hold onto office can always do so. Losing office is easy to do. It is especially easy for those who do not value holding onto office in the first place. We have no doubt that many people value other things above political survival. It is just that such people are not likely to find themselves in high office and so need not overly occupy our interest.

Threats to Political Survival

Political survival can be threatened in three distinct ways. These include domestic challenges to leadership, revolutionary challenges to individual leaders and the political systems they lead, and external threats in the form of military attack by foreign adversaries. Leaders can sometimes face these in combination. The basic tools to cope with each of these challenges are, we believe, the same, but the strategic responses by leaders (and followers) differ depending on the source of the threat.

Our central concerns here are with domestic challenges and external threats to political leadership. Although they represent less of our focus, we also address several features of revolutionary politics. Our approach provides an explanation of revolution and provides a partial explanation for institutional changes brought on by revolutions, a topic addressed in chapter 8. Indeed, we think of change as falling along an evolutionary/revolutionary continuum rather than thinking of revolutions as categorically different from slower or subtler political changes (see Haber and Razo 2000 for a similar view). We offer an explanation of, for instance, the conditions under which monarchies become democracies or democracies revert to authoritarianism. We also provide an explanation for civil war and uprisings by the disenfranchised in which the existing political order is overthrown. In our perspective, the processes of revolution or civil war are not very different from the process of foreign intervention that results in the overthrow of a government and perhaps a change in its institutions. Additionally, we suggest that the motivations for emigration and revolution are similar. We also offer a tentative and partial explanation for why some successful revolutionaries select authoritarian rule while other successful revolutionaries adopt democratic principles of governance.

We propose a comparative theory of political-system change motivated by the notion that leaders want to keep their positions of power and privilege. Our focus differs in a subtle but important way from many historical treatments that view the gradual emergence of representative institutions as being the product of efforts by wealthy individuals to constrain the confiscatory, predatory inclinations of monarchs (Schultz and Weingast 1998) or as chance, path-dependent developments (Moore 1966; Tilly 1978; Skocpol 1998). Our approach also contrasts with those who view the emergence of political institutions primarily in terms of wealth-maximizing or rent-seeking behavior by political leaders, or in terms of differences in the motivations of democrats and autocrats (Olson 1993; Lake 1992; Niskanen 1997).

Notwithstanding our comments above about the venal, self-seeking behavior of some leaders, we assume that leaders care about both policy and personal aggrandizement. Leaders generally care to keep themselves in office so that they can allocate goods and, when possible, retain resources for their discretionary use. To stay in office, they must be attentive to the pressures they face from the institutions within which they operate and they must, when they can, adjust those institutions to suit their interests. Institutions change in response to events serious enough to threaten the political survival of leaders, and leaders choose actions to avoid or eliminate such political circumstances.

Because we focus on selection institutions and political survival, our analysis is concerned to explain how selection institutions shape the incentives and actions of leaders. This focus leads to an important departure in our study from previous efforts to account for the ties between politics and economic choice (e.g., Schumpeter 1942; Moore 1966; Olson 1982, 1993; McGuire and Olson 1996; Wintrobe 1990; Niskanen 1997; Przeworski 2001). Other political-economy accounts of institutional politics tend to assume a different set of values for leaders in democracies and autocracies or investigate a decision-making process that is not strategic and that ignores political competition.

Niskanen (1997), for example, assumes autocracies are led by an individual who wants to maximize the difference between government revenue and spending, with the remainder being available to the leader for personal use. He assumes that the "leader" in a democracy is the median voter and that the median voter is someone with an about-average income who wants to maximize the difference between income and taxes paid. Acemoglu and Robinson (2000) make similar assumptions in distinguishing between systems in which elites choose policy and democratic systems in which average citizens shape policy in the guise of the median voter.

Olson (1993) and McGuire and Olson (1996) present a model that produces results similar to ours with regard to taxing and spending decisions, but they do not include fundamental features of politics, most notably competition over office. Rather than explicitly modeling political competition and the survival of leaders, the McGuire-and-Olson model asks what policies and tax rate maximize the welfare of the leader's coalition in the absence of a challenger. In contrast, we propose that a leader need not always spend all available resources in order to match the best possible challenge a rival can offer. Additionally, we draw out the strategic dependence between taxing and spending decisions, tenure in office, and preferences over governing institutions. In this way, the selectorate theory extends the political-economy view of institutions proposed by Olson and McGuire and Olson.

Acemoglu and Robinson (2001) explain allocation decisions by leaders in a manner close to the selectorate view of politics. They argue that "the gains to an extractive strategy may depend on the size of the ruling elite. When the elite is small, each member would have a larger share of the revenues, so the elite may have a greater incentive to be extractive" (Acemoglu and Robinson 2001, 1376). This insight guides their empirical study of economic development (2001) and also helps inform their views on tax rates and political stability (2000). They do not, however, develop an equilibrium account in which economic performance, tax rates, institutional stability, and leadership survival are endogenous. Instead, they treat autocrats and democrats as having different, exogenously given utility functions driven, in the first instance, by personal wealth, and in the second, by the median voter's preferences.

In the selectorate theory, we try to endogenize these features of politics while attempting to articulate a theory that can be applied to any form of government, not just autocracy or democracy.

Still others distinguish the utility functions in autocracies and democracies in other ways, but in each case the problem is attacked by assuming a fundamental difference in the interests of leaders in different types of regimes or by overlooking political competition. We suggest that the variation in actions in different political systems can be explained as a result of a common utility function or set of objectives for all leaders, with all political leaders embedded in an institutional environment that includes constraints on coalition size, selectorate size, and rivals for office who cannot credibly commit to give all necessary individuals access to a future stream of private goods in exchange for their current political support. Given these conditions, the selectorate theory indicates that selection institutions—the mechanisms that determine how leaders are chosen or deposed—explain the differences in policy choices across all regime types. Our analysis will show, for example, that it is an equilibrium property of autocracies that leaders achieve a large difference between government revenue and expenditures, as *assumed* by Niskanen. We also show that it is an equilibrium property of democracies that citizens pay low taxes while the national leader fails to control a large amount of resources, as observed by Lake and Baum (2001) and others.

Challenges to Political Survival

Political survival is put at risk whenever leaders lack the resources to maintain the support of essential backers. Likewise, survival is tenuous when incumbents possess the necessary resources to retain office but misallocate funds. We now briefly consider how these factors impinge on political survival and, therefore, on policy choices.

Financial Crisis = Political Crisis

The survival of leaders and of the institutions or regimes they lead is threatened when they are no longer able to provide sufficient resources to sustain political support. The vast literature on revolutions focuses on moments of crisis—usually economic—when competing elites have incentives to come together to manage their collective survival (Moore 1966; Tilly 1978; Olson 1982; Goldstone 1991; Skocpol 1998). North, Summerhill, and Weingast (2000) point to such moments of crisis as stimulating the emergence of a shared mindset or collective new belief system. In these moments of crisis, as characterized by the Glorious Revolution, as well as by the American, French, Russian, and Chinese Revolutions, new ideas and institutions are accepted by people who earlier were competitors for political authority. These former competitors coordinate with one another to solve a shared problem: the (usually financial or military) crisis of confidence encourages them to cooperate for the moment, putting aside their divergent concerns in the interest of preserving or creating a political setting in which they can in the future return to competing over the distribution of valuable goods. Their incentive to cooperate at a moment of crisis exceeds their divergent interests. Those divergent interests loom larger when resources are sufficient to fight over the distribution of the pie.

Sometimes, in moments of crisis, the emerging consensus of beliefs fosters lasting changes that channel future competition in socially productive directions. This seems to have been the case for the Glorious Revolution and the American Revolution. Other times, the solutions adopted in response to the momentary crisis fail to remove the incentives for destructive forms of competition in the future. In those cases, the divergent interests of competing elites over the future allocation of resources are put on hold during the crisis, then reemerge.

Once a sufficient fix is put in place to restore growth to the total amount of resources, the interests in coordination fall by the wayside and institutions to protect some competitors at the expense of others reemerge. This seems to have been what happened over the decades following the French, Russian, and Chinese Revolutions. This is also a common pattern in the post–World War II years as agencies like the World Bank and International Monetary Fund provide aid during financial crises. By bailing out leaders during such crises, these organizations may unwittingly hinder political reforms that would reduce the odds that the countries in question will experience future economic calamities (Easterly 2001; Bueno de Mesquita and Root 2002). Instead, these international financial institutions may provide the help needed to keep corrupt or incompetent leaders in office. We address these issues and suggest remedies in chapter 10. In examining these issues, we offer a partial explanation for the emergence of "shared mindsets" by demonstrating how selection institutions shape incentives among different parts of a society to come together in an effort to alter the institutions of governance.

Coordination and Distribution Issues

Some earlier theories of institutional change during crises emphasize the coordination issues that can help promote new political arrangements (Linz and Stepan 1978; Haggard and Kaufman 1995; North, Summerhill, and Weingast 2000). These theories draw our attention to important but inherently rare events. The theory we suggest complements the focus of others on coordination during crises by addressing the problems associated with the distribution of valuable resources during ordinary times. Most politics and much political change do not take place during a crisis, but rather reflect slower evolutionary change. We try to fill in the gap by looking at distribution issues as well as coordination issues in politics.

Leaders in any political system face the more-or-less continuous threat that they will lose the support of key backers. Democracies somewhat ameliorate this threat by providing for fixed terms. Of course, they also generally provide mechanisms to shorten the fixed term. That is exactly the purpose of votes of no confidence (Huber 1996), the right to call early elections (Smith 1996, 2004; Gallego 1999, 2001), and impeachment. If leaders in any political system lose the support of key backers, the incumbent—and perhaps the regime—is turned out of office. In a democracy, the incumbent lives to run again another day. In many authoritarian systems defeated incumbents are lucky if they can retreat into exile. Sometimes their loss of office is accompanied by the loss of their life (Werner 1996; Goemans 2000).[3] Even the pope must maintain support among core constituents (usually a set of bishops) and can be forced from office if he fails to do so. Pope Celestine V (1294) "voluntarily" resigned his office, an action unprecedented in Church history. It is widely believed that Celestine was forced to leave office by Boniface VIII, elected as his successor eleven days after Celestine's resignation. Indeed, after Celestine V resigned, Boniface sentenced him to death and had him imprisoned in Castel Fumone, where he died in 1296 (Schimmelpfennig 1992, 195). Boniface's apparent motive was to prevent a resurgence of support for his rival.

Make no mistake about it, no leader rules alone. Even the most oppressive dictators cannot survive the loss of support among their core constituents. Hitler was well aware of this fact. Members of the German army, for instance, plotted against Hitler in 1938 and attempted to assassinate him in 1942 and 1944. Following the 1944 attempt, Hitler ordered the deaths of thousands of military and intelligence officers, including Erwin Rommel, one of his best and most popular generals. Earlier, Hitler suspected Ernst Röhm of being a rival for power and had him murdered.

Public Goods and Private Goods

Regardless of the structure of the political system, leaders have a relatively small set of instruments available to promote their political survival. They can promulgate general public policies that satisfy the desires of their supporters and perhaps the desires of others among the citizens of the state, and they can dole out private benefits to purchase the continued support of their critical backers. We have in mind that public policies, or at least identifiable components of them, approximate the characteristics of classic public goods, being nonexcludable and nonrival (Olson 1965; Bergstrom and Goodman 1973; Cornes and Sandler 2001).[4] Private goods, of course, are excludable and rival.

Examples of public and private benefits abound in politics. On the foreign policy side of the ledger, public goods include the promotion and exportation of a state's religious or cultural beliefs or the enhancement of national security. In the domain of domestic politics, the public-goods component of policies include the rule of law, transparency and accountability, even-handed police services, general access to education, a level commercial playing field, antipollution legislation, parkland preservation, communication and transportation infrastructure, and the like. Private goods are similarly widespread in the domains of domestic and foreign policy. For example, they could encompass the booty or rents that are distributed only among supporters of the regime (Wintrobe 1990; Lake 1992), favorable tax policies, subsidies to special interests, trade or tariff policies that especially benefit domestic supporters (McGillivray 1997, 2003), or, according to Hobson ([1902] 1945), British imperialism, a policy that, at the same time it was a burden to the entire state, greatly benefited a narrow segment of the population.

These two types of benefits, and their mixtures, are by no means new. Consider the benefits provided or promised during the medieval crusades against Islam. All of Christendom—then the pope's citizenry—was promised a public good in the form of the advancement of what was thought to be the one true religion. Kings who provided sufficient support for the crusades were promised indulgence for their sins and were thus assured entry into heaven. Kings, in turn, promoted the crusades among their subjects by promising to advance Christendom, understood as a public good, and by forgiving individual debts, a private benefit. Today private benefits may be more likely to take the form of tax forgiveness, protective tariffs, or special trade privileges for key supporters than they are indulgences, but the forgiveness of past political sins is no less prominent today than it was hundreds of years ago.

Naturally, all the residents of a state enjoy the benefits (or costs) of public policies regardless of their support for the regime. Conflicting attitudes toward these policies are one basis on which erstwhile supporters might defect to a domestic challenger. One reason George H. W. Bush lost votes to H. Ross Perot and the presidency to Bill Clinton in 1992 is that substantial numbers of voters from Bush's 1988 electoral coalition were displeased with a tax increase he fostered, as well as with his international free trade orientation. Conflicting attitudes toward policies are one source of threat to political survival. Essential domestic backers must be kept satisfied to prevent their defection to a rival. The threat to survival arising from policy differences is not, however, restricted to the loss of domestic constituents.

Policy differences can also be a core source of danger in terms of threats from external rivals. Foreign policy differences clearly can lead states into rivalry. Indeed, the security dilemma is just one example of such a clash over the provision of a public good, the security of the state (Jervis 1978). If the leader of one state pursues the enhancement of national security—a policy that provides a public good for his citizens—the leader of another state and its citizens may feel threatened because the means of providing enhanced national security in the first state involves encroachment on the security of the second. This too is a common motivation behind revolutions. Those benefiting from the policies of the government often pay for the benefits they derive by disproportionately taxing citizens who lack a say in governance. The latter, such as the peasants and working class in France in 1792, feeling encroached on, make revolutions if they are able to organize and mobilize enough resources (Moore 1966; Tilly 1978; Olson 1982; Goldstone 1991; Root 1994; Skocpol 1998). Private goods differ from public policies in that they can be limited to a select set of citizens, in this case those who support the regime.

In reality it is often difficult to distinguish between public policies and private benefits since these can be, and usually are, mixed.[5] Goods fall along a continuum from pure public goods to pure private goods. The rule of law and the provision of national security are close to being pure public goods, though lawyers and generals certainly enjoy private gains when the rule of law and national security are promoted. The rule of law and national security are possibly the most important public goods leaders can provide to encourage peace and prosperity. The right to steal the nation's treasure and sock it away in a secret bank account surely is a pure private good. Most corrupt practices tend to fall nearer to the private-goods end of the spectrum, though, as Samuel Huntington (1965, 1968) argued, limited representation and corruption might sometimes be the means to grease the wheels of progress. Empirical research by economists contradicts this claim (Kauffman and Wei 1999).

Antipollution policies have a public-goods character to them in that everyone breathes the same air or drinks the same water. Yet antipollution policies also have a private-goods side. Some businesses or industries bear a heavier burden in literally cleaning up their act than do others. This differential burden could be used as a political instrument to punish firms or industries that are not supporters of the incumbent while benefiting those that are. Still, many public policies can be distinguished from pork barrel legislation, patronage, or simple theft of the public treasure. In our model we think of allocations between public and private goods either as readily discerned and distinguished or as the selection of goods with varying mixes of public and private components. By attending to allocation decisions involving public and private goods, we hope to show a number of interesting and surprising political consequences that follow from the basic desire of leaders to retain their offices.

Easy Answers, Inadequate Answers

Many answers come naturally to mind to explain why leaders perform differently in different political systems. Given the availability of common answers, why have we chosen a different approach? To answer this, we consider some accounts of the variations in political life that seem to advantage dictators and disadvantage democrats.

Autocrats often are oppressors. They sometimes stay in power because they do not hesitate to repress opposition and oppress their citizens. True though this is, it cannot explain the significant survival advantages of dictators nor the policy advantages of democrats. This is so because oppression is itself a phenomenon requiring explanation. When is oppression an effective strategy to deter challenges? When do leaders have the incentive to do anything to hold onto power? Where do leaders find those willing to carry out oppressive measures? How does oppression intimidate challengers? The effectiveness of oppression and the reasons autocrats last so long can be traced to the same causes. Oppression is a byproduct of the political arrangements that ensure longevity. We address this issue in chapter 8.

Before accepting oppression as the explanation for the political viability of dictators, we must confront difficult problems. Why can dictators marshal the support of those who control their society's guns while democrats cannot? If control over guns is all it takes to stay in office, why are there civilian dictators? Such civilian leaders as Joseph Stalin (USSR, 26 Years), Adolf Hitler (Germany, 12 years), Francis Joseph (Austria, 67 years), Wangchuck Jigme (Bhutan, 26 years), Tsendenbal (Mongolia, 30 years), or Mobutu Sese Seko (Zaire, 32 years) had no special military skills. Why are military leaders loyal to them rather than setting themselves up as rivals for power? Why can't democrats rely on the loyalty of the military and just stay on after their term in office expires? Some apparently elected leaders—Hitler comes to mind—do. Having been elected to government, he maneuvered himself into the chancellorship and used the advantages of office to secure the loyalty of the military (in part by assassinating rivals in the *Sturmabteilung* or storm troops), and he then ended democracy.

Why, if oppression is the solution to political longevity, are there long-lasting autocrats who avoid extreme oppressiveness and who, instead, provide peace and prosperity? Lee Kwan Yew held power in Singapore for twenty-six years before voluntarily stepping aside. His rule was certainly not democratic and it did engage in subtle forms of oppression, but it just as certainly never rivaled the oppressiveness common in Cambodia, China, Uganda, the Soviet Union, or so many other countries.

One ready alternative to oppression as an explanation of autocratic longevity is an appeal to civic-mindedness. Good fortune, serendipity, or the "right" political culture may be the reason that some societies are ruled by civic-minded leaders and others by ogres. Surely some people are more civic-minded than others. Perhaps democracies have the good fortune of having a disproportionate share of the world's civic-minded leaders or of honest citizens. A pleasant thought but almost certainly false. If civic-mindedness is defined by what leaders do, it appears that democrats are more civic-minded than autocrats. However, we will see that the differences in the performance of political leaders can be explained without any appeal to civic-mindedness or national character or culture. In doing so, we will suggest why Leopold II, as king of the Belgians, was at the forefront of promoting economic growth, educational reform, and other successful policies at home in the emerging Belgian democracy while, as the personal owner of the Congo, he simultaneously promoted unspeakable oppression and exploitation in his dictatorship. We will suggest that he had no change of heart, no change in culture, no change in civic-mindedness; he did have a change in fundamental political realities, and those changes altered his behavior.

Another alternative explanation for the manifest differences between democratic and nondemocratic rule may be the existence of competitive elections. Electoral politics certainly are closely associated with institutional arrangements that ensure a large winning coalition, but elections are neither necessary nor sufficient to account for differences in political survival or in fundamental allocation decisions. We can certainly point to examples of electoral systems that nevertheless encourage rent-seeking behavior. India unfortunately fits this bill, as did Mexico at least until 2000 or Tammany Hall in the late nineteenth and early twentieth centuries. Rigged electoral systems, of course, encourage universal suffrage and often permit rival candidates. They just cheat on how votes are counted or count honestly but stifle *competent* rivals. The presence of elections is not sufficient to explain political choices in those societies. They have a large selectorate, as we will see, but a small coalition. On the other side of the ledger, we must explain the successful performance of Hong Kong prior to its return to China. For most of Hong Kong's modern history it was a crown colony of Great Britain. There were no elections, yet its government produced high-quality public policy and extremely low levels of corruption or other forms of private-goods, rent-seeking behavior. Singapore has also provided substantial public benefits and relatively few private goods, yet for much of its history it has been subject to what nominally might be called autocratic rule. The absence or presence of elections is inadequate to explain these variations.

Then, also, we should recognize that single-member district parliamentary political systems, presidential systems, and proportional-representation or multiple-member district systems all engage in competitive electoral politics, yet they perform differently in their provision of public and private goods and in the longevity in office of their leaders (Alesina and Rosenthal 1995; Knack and Keefer 1995; Cox 1997; Persson and Tabellini 1999). The selectorate theory offers an account that is consistent with these examples and others but that is also generally consistent with the idea that elections are usually emblematic of—though not determinative of—a regime that produces relatively few private goods and many public goods.

An Incomplete Theory of Institutional Political Laws

We begin with a simple, skeletal theory—one without bureaucrats, without subunits of the polity, without explicit political parties or ideology—in the hope that others will find it of sufficient interest to participate in efforts to elaborate and build on it. This is a step along the way, not an end. It is a step that relies on and builds on much previous political-economy research. We illustrate the broad applicability of the generalizations we deduce by combining three modes of analysis: formal, deductive logic grounded in game theory; statistical analysis of propositions derived from the assumptions behind our theory; and flesh-and-bone case histories designed to illuminate, probe, and illustrate the workings of the theory. The statistical analysis will encompass events spread over the past 200 years. The case histories are drawn from ancient Greece and Rome, as well as from medieval, Renaissance, and modern events. The use of formal modeling is to ensure logical consistency and to help tease out nonobvious implications that can be deduced from our assumptions. We will call attention to particularly surprising deductions and to novel hypotheses generated by the theory, as well as to its reiteration of things already known empirically about politics. We are encouraged by David Hume's observation regarding political institutions that "so great is the force of laws and of particular forms of government, and so little dependence have they on the humors and tempers of men, that consequences almost as general and certain may sometimes be deduced from them as any which the mathematical sciences afford us" (Hume [1742] 1985, chap. iii, p. 15).

2 The Theory: Definitions and Intuition

This chapter introduces the basic components of the selectorate theory. The theory consists of a family of closely related models, each of which produces the same core insights. In the next chapter we offer the basic model of the selectorate theory. After exploring some implications of this model, we expand on it in later chapters to include models that integrate aspects of international affairs into a theory of domestic politics. We also relax assumptions and investigate what the model indicates about the political-survival prospects of government leaders.

We begin by describing relevant sets of people within any polity. Nested within the *residents* of all polities is a *selectorate* and within that there is a *winning coalition*. *Leaders*, all of whom face *challengers* who wish to depose them, maintain their coalitions of supporters by *taxing* and *spending* in ways that allocate mixes of *public* and *private goods*. The nature of the mix depends on the size of the winning coalition, while the total amount spent depends both on the size of the selectorate and on the winning coalition. More specifically, leaders who depend on only a few to keep them in office, especially when they are drawn from a large pool of potential supporters, engender loyalty among their backers by providing them with access to ample personal, private benefits they would not otherwise have if they were not in the coalition. All else constant, with many supporters demanding rewards, the costs of personal benefits required to keep their loyalty are just too high. Instead, whether leaders are civic-minded or not, those who rely on a large coalition emphasize the production of goods that benefit everyone in their society.[1] Because of the *loyalty norm*, leaders who rely on a broad-based coalition to remain in office cannot keep their supporters from defecting to a rival by offering substantial private benefits. Because of *affinity* between leaders and followers, not all members of the selectorate are equally attractive as members of the winning coalition.

This chapter provides detailed definitions of the principal concepts of our theory presented in italics in the previous paragraph. Chapter 3 uses those definitions in setting out the basic selectorate model, exploring the logic of the argument in careful but nontechnical form. A more detailed, formal mathematical account, along with logical proofs, is found in the appendix to that chapter.

The Elements of the Polity

All polities consist of three nested and changeable groups, as well as a national leadership and prospective substitute leaders, referred to here as the *challenger*. The largest of the three nested groups is the set of all residents within the state. Within this set of people there is a smaller group that has a formal role in expressing a preference over the selection of the leadership that rules them, though their expression of preference may or may not directly influence the outcome. We call this group the *selectorate* (Shirk 1993). Each member of the selectorate has some chance, albeit the probability may be small, of becoming an essential supporter of the incumbent. We call the subset of the selectorate whose support is essential if the incumbent is to remain in power, the *winning coalition*. When we say these backers of the leadership are essential, we mean that they control the resources vital to the political survival of the incumbent. If enough members of the winning coalition defect to a rival politician, the incumbent loses office. The smallest set of individuals is the *leadership*, which actually makes decisions about gathering and allocating resources. Because these different groupings of people are so important for our theory, we elaborate on each.

The Leadership (*L*) and Challenger (*C*)

Every polity has one or more central individuals with the authority to raise revenue and allocate resources. These are the criteria that define what we mean when we refer to a country's political leadership or leader (*L*). Although we generally speak as if the leadership is a single individual, nothing in our theory imposes that requirement. In an absolute monarchy or an absolutist tyranny of any sort, a single individual may hold the necessary authority or power to raise revenue through taxes and to allocate revenue to public works, to benefits for supporters, and to personal accounts. In other forms of government, the leadership may rely on several people who collectively have the authority over taxing and spending. In the United States, for instance, legislation setting policy requires the approval of a simple majority in the House of Representatives and in the Senate, as well as the approval of the president. Or, in the face of a presidential veto, the two legislative houses require a two-thirds majority in each. One might, loosely speaking, think of the leadership in the United States as the president, speaker of the House, and majority leader in the Senate. This of course is only an approximation, but it helps capture the central defining component of our use of the term *leader* or *leadership*: those who have the authority to raise taxes and allocate government funds to pursue chosen policies, including private uses of the monies as well as uses aimed at the general welfare.

Leaders are drawn from the selectorate, defined below. So too are political rivals who compete for leadership positions within the bounds of the polity's structural arrangements. Later we expand the theory to examine the emergence of new leaders from outside the selectorate. At that time we discuss an endogenous account of institution selection and institutional change. Until then, however, we use the term *challenger* (*C*) to refer to an individual or would-be leadership group attempting to depose the incumbent leader within the "rules" or norms of transition in the existing system so that the challenger can gain control over policy choices regarding taxing and spending.[2] Of course, in some forms of government the standard rules or norms for transitions include coup d'état, execution, and the like, so that the theory is not restricted to orderly transitions.

Although leaders and challengers are members of the selectorate, not all members of the selectorate are necessarily eligible to be the leader. We only assume that there is a pool of potential leaders, all of whom are members of the selectorate.

Challengers differ from incumbents primarily in terms of the information available to them. When we define the term *affinity* below we make clear the informational advantages that incumbents have relative to challengers. Other than the informational differences between those at the head of a government and those who aspire to that position, challengers and leaders can be thought of as otherwise equivalent so that one can substitute for the other. Indeed, the primary problem an incumbent faces in the selectorate theory is to figure out how to prevent being replaced by a challenger.

The Residents (*N*)

A defining characteristic of every polity is the identification of the set of its members. The group of members or residents can be subdivided along a critical dimension: those in the selectorate, defined below, and those not in the selectorate. The latter are disenfranchised. They have comprised the vast majority of people throughout human history. They often are the cannon fodder of revolutions and wars. Typically, one goal of revolutions is to replace members of the selectorate with individuals from the disenfranchised group, or to add this group to the selectorate. Politics appears to be evolving so that the selectorate, roughly the citizenry, gradually expands to take in more and more members, thereby reducing the size of the disenfranchised group.

Human history is a mix of evolutionary change punctuated with revolutions. Slaves, always in the disenfranchised group, have largely disappeared as an identifiable category of people. In ancient Greece almost no one was a member of the selectorate; almost everyone was a slave or nearly so. By the Middle Ages, feudal customs had greatly eroded the ancient sense of slavery. Still, the disenfranchised group remained overwhelmingly large, being the great majority. Serfs and free men may not have been true slaves, but they were not participants in the choice of leaders and they had no prospect of becoming leaders themselves so long as the existing political arrangements remained unaltered.

One revolutionary feature of the Magna Carta (1215), or Castile and León's Espéculo forty years later, was that each suggested the extension of consequential political rights—including due process of law—to all free men. Here was a proposal that held out the prospect of an evolutionary expansion of the selectorate so that more and more members of the society would also become part of the political process. This idea, however, was set aside in England when King John, with the pope's support, reneged on the Magna Carta's major proposals for political change. Likewise, the Espéculo was observed more in the breach than in reality in the Spanish kingdoms. Some of the ideas in these important documents returned with greater force in 1297 when England's King Edward I reluctantly signed *Confirmatio Cartarum*, promising to bind himself and future kings to seek the approval of the commons before levying new taxes. Similar ideas are found even earlier, perhaps as early as 1255, in Castile and León, and soon followed suit in many other kingdoms of Europe (O'Callaghan 1989). Though a beginning, still many centuries passed before the commons or the townspeople truly were incorporated into the group of people—the selectorate—who have a prospect of rising to positions of influence in government or of gaining access to the private largesse that governments dole out.

By the seventeenth century—if not earlier—the proportion of the population that was disenfranchised began to shrink noticeably as propertied people increasingly gained access to participation in government. Birth into the nobility was no longer the only—perhaps not even the main—source of access to the selectorate in some parts of the world. Still, the vast majority of residents in each polity remained disenfranchised. The American Revolution represented an early experiment in the further expansion of the selectorate and the reduction in numbers of the disenfranchised, though still the majority of any nation's residents remained outside the selectorate. In the late nineteenth and early twentieth centuries, as democracies extended the vote to women and with the virtual universal elimination of property tests for voting, at least some political systems made the transition to a condition in which the disenfranchised included basically only children. No political system has yet expanded the citizenry to include children, so that those roughly under eighteen—even fifteen in Iran—appear to be the final bastion of the disenfranchised in contemporary democracies. In some parts of the world, the disenfranchised remain the largest group of people as the seemingly evolutionary process of enfranchisement continues.

The consequential effect of N in the selectorate theory is to establish the scale of each polity. The scale has two important effects in the models. The larger the scale of a society, the higher the absolute cost of providing public goods. For example, it costs considerably more, even taking economies of scale into account, to educate 100 million people than 10 million. Additionally, the society's scale sets the number of people who can be taxed by the state and therefore the magnitude of resources that could be extracted through taxation.

For the purposes of our analyses we essentially normalize the scale effects by fixing N in the theoretical analysis. This is intended to emphasize that the size of the coalition and the selectorate must be evaluated relative to the size of the total population. Thus, while the winning coalition, defined below, in contemporary China includes many more people than does the winning coalition in Belgium, still Belgium's winning coalition, as a proportion of the population, is vastly larger than China's.

The Selectorate (*S*)

Politics involves a seemingly infinite variety of institutional details. Though we commonly speak of only a handful of regime types, such as democracy, monarchy, autocracy, junta, or oligarchy, no two political systems are identical.[3] We believe, however, that the infinite variety of real-world institutional arrangements can be distilled into just two critical dimensions: the selectorate and the winning coalition. By mapping a diverse set of political considerations onto the two dimensions of selectorate size and winning-coalition size, we sacrifice detail and precision, but gain the possibility of explaining a rich variety of political phenomena with a relatively simple theoretical structure. We also gain the possibility of mapping all nominal regime types onto a continuous two-dimensional space, creating an opportunity to integrate insights from democratic theory and from theories of autocracy, totalitarianism, monarchy, and military rule into a single analytic framework.

Though members of the selectorate (denoted S) have a government-granted say in the selection of leaders, this is not their most important or meaningful characteristic. It is, however, their most easily discerned characteristic. The important aspect of being in the selectorate is that membership conveys the opportunity to become a member of a winning coalition. To be sure, membership in the selectorate does not necessarily make the prospects of joining a winning coalition good, but it does raise those prospects above zero and, in democracies, up to levels as high as 50 percent.

We define the selectorate as the set of people whose endowments include the qualities or characteristics institutionally required to choose the government's leadership and necessary for gaining access to private benefits doled out by the government's leadership. All selectorate members within a polity, therefore, share certain common characteristics. Those characteristics, however, can differ across political systems, so that an individual can qualify for selectorate membership in one polity and yet have no possibility of qualifying in another.

Polities can be characterized by more-or-less formalized mechanisms that allow some people to have the prospect of gaining access to valued goods dispensed by government while excluding others from even the chance of such access. Access to such valued goods is a fundamental quality of membership in the winning coalition, a concept we define and discuss in the next section. Membership in the selectorate is a necessary condition for membership in a winning coalition.

One function of political rules and institutions is to distinguish the subset of residents who possess the characteristics required for membership in the selectorate. More loosely, selectorate membership identifies those who meet the polity's criteria for enfranchisement or, still more colloquially, citizenship. The qualities generally used to sort people into and out of the selectorate vary in terms of their inherent scarcity and in terms of the extent to which they can be created, transferred, or assigned to people, so that their scarcity is subject to political manipulation. That is, scarcity can be a function of insurmountable barriers, like birthplace, or of artificial barriers, like restricted entry into certain professions. The greater the scarcity of a required quality, whether that scarcity is natural or artificial, the smaller will be the selectorate. We suggest a list of such qualities and discuss their inherent or politically manipulated scarcity. The qualities we identify have found common usage throughout history, but they may not be exhaustive. It is sufficient for our purposes to identify these few key qualities so as to clarify what we mean by the selectorate.

Virtually all societies throughout human history have sorted people into and out of the selectorate based on different combinations of at least four defining categories of personal characteristics. These defining characteristics include (1) personal origin: birthplace and lineage; (2) special proficiency: skills, beliefs, and/or knowledge; (3) wealth; and (4) gender and/or age.

These dimensions clearly differ in their inherent scarcity and in the social prospects of altering their scarcity. Selectorates have been defined to include only one or any mix of these four elements.

Personal Origin: Birthplace and Lineage

The birthright to participate in choosing and maintaining leaders and to gain access to the largesse of the incumbent leadership divides along at least two important dimensions. One is place of birth. Until relatively recently, birth within a polity's territorial boundaries was, in many instances, necessary but not sufficient for membership in its selectorate. With the advent of naturalization it has become possible to overcome the failure to be born in a polity. The ease with which birthplace can be overcome as an impediment to entry into the selectorate varies greatly across modern societies. Some countries, such as the United States or Canada, provide easy access to citizenship. Others, like Japan and Saudi Arabia, remain more exclusionary. Birthplace by itself does not create great scarcity as a quality for selectorate membership. Throughout most of history almost everyone lived in the society in which they were born.

Although mass migrations have occurred—for instance, the movement of people out of the Asian steppes and into Europe—individuals moving from one society to another in large numbers is a recent phenomenon. To the best of our knowledge, no society defines selectorate membership only in terms of birthplace, though many make birthplace a necessary condition.

The second birthright dimension is lineage—that is, membership in selected "aristocratic" families. The right lineage is sufficient in some societies for entry into the selectorate. Any eldest surviving son—and sometimes daughter if there was no son—of a twelfth-century English baron, for example, was assured of selectorate membership on his father's death. Any Romanov could be in the Russian selectorate under the czars, whereas being a Romanov was a guarantee of exclusion from the Bolshevik selectorate.

Acceptable lineage is an extremely restrictive, exclusionary condition of birth. As such, it is exceedingly scarce. It is inheritable but, barring unusual circumstances, cannot be assigned or transferred to others. One either is born of the "right blood" or not. The pool of people with the designated lineage can grow within a strictly hereditary system only by procreation or, in rare instances, by adoption or recognition of illegitimate children. Polities, like hereditary monarchies, that rely on lineage as a critical characteristic required of those who can influence the selection or deposition of leaders necessarily have a small selectorate. Many societies that relied on lineage gradually adapted their requirements for entry into the selectorate to include substitute characteristics—including, for instance, wealth or military prowess—thereby expanding the possible pool of selectorate members. If other criteria were added while maintaining the requirement of acceptable lineage, the selectorate would be even smaller.

Special Proficiency: Skills, Beliefs, and/or Knowledge

We group skills, knowledge, and beliefs together into a single category of special proficiency. We do so because these have in common the possibility and incentives for creating artificial scarcity through regulation. This category plays a central and special role in the size of winning coalitions, especially in recent history, and has played a prominent part in determining selectorate size across much of human history. This class of attributes refers to possession of or control over such characteristics as presumed spiritual or magic powers, ideological or religious calling, military prowess, or technical knowledge. Expertise of this sort sometimes is sufficient for selectorate membership. More often it is necessary but not sufficient, and sometimes it is only contributory. These special attributes often are added to broader criteria in narrowing the choice of selectorate members forming the winning coalition.

Using criteria that focus on proficiencies of the sort just enumerated is associated with, for example, tribal societies, religious movements, theocracies, revolutionary ideologies, military regimes, and university administrations. Religious beliefs and powers, for instance, have sometimes facilitated the efforts of clerical leaders to coerce the civilian society into accepting their political leadership. The Catholic Church achieved this level of authority during the high Middle Ages, thanks to its skillful use of its exclusive right to provide religious sacraments and its related influence over salvation. The pope may not have had an army, but the Catholic clergy has the exclusive authority to grant absolution or condemn people to the threat of eternal damnation, a powerful prerogative in societies that subscribe to Catholic beliefs. So powerful was the Church's sway that for several centuries no European king could be legitimately crowned without the Church's blessing, making the pope personally a member of the selectorate in many European kingdoms. By carefully guarding and limiting the right to acquire religious mastery, the Catholic hierarchy created an artificially restricted selectorate within its domain. With the success of Protestant reformers, that restriction on selectorate size quickly diminished in Europe following the Thirty Years War. Similar accounts are given for the power of the priesthood among the Maya (Gallenkamp 1985, 108, 112, 115), as well as in Pharaonic Egypt and many other ancient civilizations.

Other forms of proficiency have played a role comparable to that of religious authority. Hunter-gatherer societies, for example, favored skilled hunters by giving them a prominent role in choosing tribal or clan chiefs (Diamond 1997). Skilled hunters were revered because they could resolve a fundamental social problem, providing an adequate supply of food, just as clergy members were sometimes revered for resolving another fundamental social problem, providing spiritual assurance. Like theocracies and hunter-gatherer societies, universities also emphasize special proficiency in choosing their selectorate. They grant a say to professors (and wealthy or influential alumni and dignitaries—that is, the board of trustees—and more occasionally to students) in choosing their leadership and only rarely to secretarial or maintenance staff. The apparent notion is that the special skills and knowledge possessed by professors (and trustees or students) make them better able to determine who should lead the university. Knowledge-based selectorates, as in universities, are much less common than theocratic or weapons-based selectorates. Theocratic societies coerce their way into political control through the threat of damnation. Weapons-based selectorates, starting with early hunters and continuing on to modern military regimes, coerce their way into political control through their domination over the means of taking lives.

Not surprisingly, military prowess is among the most common special skills used to determine selectorate membership. Possession or control over arms is a special type of expertise that continues to play a crucial role in governance in many societies. Whether one looks to the Indian caste system or the European system of estates, one sees the clergy (religious proficiency) and the military (arms proficiency) singled out for special recognition. Military prowess and control over arms is a proficiency that can offer its owners the opportunity to provide counsel to civilian leaders. Beyond counsel, military skills also can be used to coerce others into accepting the military leadership as the political leadership.

The military skills of the selectorate play an important role in warding off threats to the leader from the disenfranchised. Revolutionary challenges, taken up in chapter 8, can be resolved as a conflict between the military might of members of the selectorate and those among the disenfranchised who are mobilized to fight on behalf of the revolutionary challenger. Leaders then have an incentive to increase the collective military prowess of the selectorate as a way to ward off revolution. They can do so either by including those with military talent in the selectorate or by encouraging the members of the selectorate to develop such skills.

The importance of military prowess or control has waxed and waned in its centrality throughout human history. The Roman Republic allowed entry into the selectorate based on land ownership—a broader category than military might—only to be turned aside later by dictators who used their special skills in arms and military command—a narrower category—to redefine the selectorate to include only military leaders, giving the world early versions of military juntas. During the Empire the selectorate in Rome consisted variously of the army, the Senate, and occasional others. But a subset of it, the Praetorian Guard, in fact, was so powerful that following their assassination of the emperor Pertinax they auctioned off the vacant throne. The winner was Didius Julianus, who offered 25,000 sesterces to each member of the guard and was confirmed by the Senate (Grant 1999, 281). He lasted sixty-six days. His successor, Lucius Septimius Severus, disbanded the guard and replaced it with his own men. While Septimius broke the Praetorian Guard's power, it is noteworthy that years later his dying advice to his sons was: "Do not disagree with each other, enrich the soldiers, despise everyone else" (Grant 1999, 290).

Special proficiency, whether in knowledge, beliefs, the use of arms, or other skills, generally is not directly inheritable, though such abilities can be taught. These skills can readily be assigned, spread, or transferred through apprenticeship. The set of people with special proficiency can grow, but the political or social value of such abilities diminishes as it shifts from possession by a small community to expansion into common knowledge. The "specialness" depends on maintaining scarcity of supply. Consequently, the spread of expertise or military prowess has often been carefully guarded and regulated. That is why entry into guilds, military academies, civil services, religious orders, or political parties in some one-party states has so often been severely restricted.

The selectorate is typically small in polities, like theocracies or military juntas, that define selectorate membership along the dimension of one or more special proficiencies. Conversely, as we will see, some societies define the selectorate broadly, but then require possession of one or more special proficiencies in order for a selectorate member to enter the winning coalition. This distinction reemphasizes the point that selectorate membership is necessary but not sufficient for membership in a winning coalition. The key in such cases—usually rigged electoral systems—is that the pool of people with the potential to be granted access to special proficiency—those who are in the selectorate—can be enormous, while the supply of people allowed to acquire special skills, beliefs, and knowledge can be made artificially small, thereby ensuring that the winning coalition is a small portion of the selectorate.

Wealth

Wealth has been central to gaining the rights of citizenship or selectorate membership in many polities. In ancient Greece and Rome, for instance, wealth was necessary, though not always sufficient, for citizenship. Without sufficient wealth to support banquets, Spartan citizens could not maintain their rights, as we explain in chapter 5. Spartan citizens who no longer had sufficient wealth were compelled to leave the selectorate, losing their right both to choose leaders and to become leaders.

Throughout history wealth has been calibrated along diverse dimensions. Land ownership was a requirement for membership in the selectorate of Sparta and also for membership in the community of prospective voters in the early days of the United States. Throughout the Middle Ages, land ownership was a means of sorting people into and out of the selectorate despite equal wealth. Rich merchants, for instance, had no prospect of entering the selectorate in King John's England, though poorer landowners might be barons with the right to choose the king. Part of what makes Edward I's acceptance of *Confirmatio Cartarum* important is that it fostered the expansion of the English selectorate. Though the expansion took centuries, *Confirmatio Cartarum* and numerous subsequent concessions by the crown gradually expanded access to the selectorate to rich merchants. Slowly but surely, money as well as land became a basis for entry into the selectorate.

Land, of course, is inherently scarcer than forms of wealth based on entrepreneurship. Except under unusual circumstances, land cannot be created and, as such, it is a relatively fixed resource. Because it is naturally scarce, societies that require substantial landholdings in order to achieve membership in the selectorate ensure that they have a smaller selectorate than those that grant membership to people possessing sufficient wealth regardless of its source. Wealth-based selectorates, however, typically are larger than those that rely on designated lineage or some special proficiency. Riches beyond land, of course, can grow through industry and entrepreneurship. Those riches can be transferred, divided, and assigned so that access to them is much less restricted than is wealth in land or than is lineage. As with expertise or special proficiency, those in possession of wealth have long recognized that their assets can be dissipated through division among heirs. This is a primary reason for the development of primogeniture as a social means of preserving scarcity of wealth.

Gender and/or Age

Gender requirements throughout much of history typically eliminated about half of the population, while age requirements eliminate an additional indeterminate number of people from membership in the selectorate. Yet even in the Middle Ages, some societies did not restrict selectorate membership based on either gender or age. The medieval period in Europe, for instance, provides numerous examples of child kings and governing queens and female regents. Of course it is also true that many monarchies restricted selectorate membership to males even though a female could ascend to the throne.[4] It is noteworthy that it is only in modern times that polities began removing all restrictions of lineage, special proficiencies, or wealth as qualifications for entry into the selectorate. The recent world provides the bulk of examples of truly large selectorate systems.[5] These include both liberal democracies and many rigged electoral systems. Understanding how they differ institutionally requires that we also elaborate on the concept of a winning coalition. As this discussion implies, the size of the polity within which the selectorate is embedded can itself sometimes prove important in our considerations. We now turn to this subject.

The Size of the Polity

The size of the selectorate is highly variable across states and time. In a democracy with universal suffrage, it is approximately equal to the total population of (adult) citizens. This means that the ratio of the selectorate to the residents is not so variable across contemporary democracies, but the actual size of the selectorate is.

Although the focus of the selectorate theory is the size of S and W relative to N, rather than the overall magnitude of a polity, we pause to consider the impact of overall size. James Madison, among the founding fathers in the United States, argued vigorously (though his views changed as he aged) that the size of a republican polity matters. In *Federalist* 10 Madison asked "whether small or extensive Republics are most favorable to the election of proper guardians of the public weal: and it is clearly decided in favor of the latter" (Madison [1787] 1961, 62). His conclusion, not easily reached because he was vexed by concerns over factions and the tyranny of the majority, is at odds with that of Montesquieu, who maintained that "in a large republic the public good is sacrificed to a thousand views; it is subordinate to exceptions; and depends on accidents. In a small one, the interest of the public is easier perceived, better understood, and more within the reach of every citizen; abuses have a lesser extent, and of course are less protected" (Montesquieu [1748] 1977, book VIII, chap. 16, p. 176).

The selectorate theory identifies conditions when a larger or smaller state ameliorates or exacerbates deviations from the public weal. Factions, the tyranny of the majority, and other departures from the common welfare are not always avoided by having a larger polity (including a larger selectorate), nor are they inherently prevented by smaller units. There is, in the logic of the selectorate theory, a natural tension between public welfare and the combination of the absolute size of the winning coalition and the ratio of the winning-coalition size to the size of the selectorate. In passing in chapters 5 and 10, we evaluate the size of republics and public welfare, taking into account specific aspects of institutional arrangements, including the relationship between coalition size and selectorate size and the choice between unitary or federal government and between parliamentary, mixed, and presidential democracy. We do so in a skeletal, simplified way, and are mindful that institutional setups and federalism have many characteristics and almost infinite variation. That institutional variation makes the division of a large unitary state into several smaller, partially self-governing federal entities only one important characteristic of governance. Still, the distinctions we draw allow us to reach general principles that distinguish expected policy choices in monarchies, juntas, rigged-election autocracies, list-voting proportional-representation systems, single-member district parliamentary systems, multimember district systems, and many presidential systems, while further distinctions can be drawn between unitary states and federal republics.

For some institutional arrangements a large size facilitates promoting the common good (conceived of here as the promotion of peace, freedom, and prosperity, as detailed in subsequent chapters), but for others, an expanded selectorate is predicted to diminish the public well-being. Factionalism can be promoted when the selectorate is small or large, though how it is promoted depends on the relationship between such institutions as the selectorate and winning coalition, on the one hand, and the pool of resources available to the government, on the other.

One proposition we deduce and evaluate empirically notes that the larger the winning coalition, the more inclined are its leaders to provide public policies that satisfy the welfare of their winning-coalition members, a group that typically represents a substantial portion of the society. But we will also see that special conditions can arise in which leaders in large states are liberated by a big selectorate to pay less attention to the public well-being than when the state's selectorate was smaller. That is, the selectorate theory suggests an explanation for the different conclusions reached by Madison and Montesquieu. The evidence from history will allow us to assess this debate and our claims.

The Winning Coalition (*W*)

The winning coalition is defined as a subset of the selectorate of sufficient size such that the subset's support endows the leadership with political power over the remainder of the selectorate as well as over the disenfranchised members of the society. How many supporters are required to form a winning coalition depends on the mix of qualities required for membership in the winning coalition and on the degree to which those qualities relate to lumpy or broadly distributed characteristics within the selectorate. In exchange for their support, members of the winning coalition receive a share of whatever private benefits the incumbent doles out to her supporters.

In a hereditary monarchy, the lineage required for selectorate membership occurs among a defined subset of the population: the aristocracy or nobility. Anyone in that subset, by definition, is adequately endowed with the quality of lineage. Therefore, loosely speaking, the winning coalition must include approximately a simple majority of those with the necessary lineage. That is, a majority of the relevant aristocracy's support is sufficient to ensure that an individual becomes or remains a monarch in a *strictly* hereditary system. Thus, both the selectorate and the winning coalition are small, with the ratio of the coalition to the selectorate being approximately one-half.

In a system that depends in part on control over weapons, by contrast, the requisite quality—arms—may be distributed unevenly. For example, election of the king of England in the twelfth century required support among the barons and was not determined purely by heredity. To be sure, noble birth was a requirement for membership in the selectorate, but it was not the only requirement for selection of the winning coalition, whose support was needed to elect and sustain the king. At the time John Lackland was elected king of England (1199) there were 197 lay barons and 39 ecclesiastical barons. These nobles (including some women, such as Constance, countess of Richmond) had the sole authority to vote for the king. To be king required support from a majority of them, or at least a majority of the knights fees they controlled, and, of course, the endorsement of the pope. Knights fees provide a useful albeit imperfect index of the wealth of each baron (or baroness) and of his or her ability to muster military might in support of his or her candidate for the crown. In a contested election for king—and John's election was contested—control over a majority, or even supermajority, of knights may have been essential. The winning coalition, then, consisted of a subset of the barons such that the subset controlled a sufficient number of knights. Control over knights, however, was not evenly distributed. John, for instance, in his capacity as the earl of Gloucester, held 300 knights fees. Others held nearly as many, but still other barons held only a handful. Aubrey de Vere, earl of Oxford, held only 30 knights fees yet was still among the more influential barons. Just how many barons were needed depended on the specific mix included in the winning coalition. To illustrate this point we construct an example based on the situation in England in 1199.

England's 236 barons collectively controlled 7,200 knights fees in 1199. Sidney Painter (1949, 19–24) notes that just 60 lay baronies held 4,632 knights fees, while 15 ecclesiastical baronies accounted for another 820. Indeed, 75 percent of the knights fees belonged to barons who held 30 or more. The 10 most powerful barons collectively possessed around 1,850 knights fees. The 20 most powerful barons collectively had approximately 3,000 knights fees. With fewer than 60 barons, the king could muster support from two-thirds of the knights fees. With that much backing, he could be confident of military victory if the remaining barons and their knights opposed him.

The election of John Lackland, earl of Gloucester, as king of England shows that political domination may require control over a majority or even supermajority of the requisite qualities, but those qualities may fall within the hands or under the control of a subset of the selectorate that is much smaller than a majority of individual members. In modern times military juntas illustrate the same principle. That is, the selectorate is small and the winning coalition often requires support from among fewer than half of the senior officers who collectively control a majority or more of the nation's soldiers and arms.[6]

To further illustrate the point that a coalition can be considerably less than half of the selectorate, consider the size of a winning coalition in a rigged electoral system, like the systems that have operated in Iraq, Kenya, and many other places, including the Soviet Union. In the Soviet Union, as in many other similar systems, the selectorate arguably consisted of as many as all adult citizens. That is, selectorate membership was determined solely by age and birthplace/naturalization criteria. The winning coalition, however, consisted of the subset of people who met the selectorate-membership criteria and, in addition, who possessed a defined special proficiency or quality, including critically membership in the Communist Party. Party membership was emblematic of acceptance of a set of beliefs and principles without which one could not be in a winning coalition.

Lenin specifically defined the Communist Party as the vanguard of the proletariat—that is, a small contingent within the broader selectorate, a contingent that was not susceptible to trade unionism and that would accept the principle of democratic centralism. In *What Is to Be Done?* (1902), Lenin argued that

revolutionary experience and organizational skill come with time only if there is a desire to cultivate the necessary qualities, and if there is a consciousness of one's shortcomings which in revolutionary activity is more than half-way towards their correction. . . . A small, tight, solid nucleus of the most dependable, experienced and hardened workers having trustworthy representatives in the main regions and connected by all the rules of secrecy with the organization of revolutionaries can quite capably, with the widest support of the masses and without any formal organization, fulfill all functions of a professional organization, in a manner desirable to a Social-Democratic movement. . . . The moral from this is simple: if we begin with a solid foundation of strong organization of revolutionaries, we can guarantee the stability of the movement as a whole and realize the goals of Social-Democracy and of trade unions. If we, however, begin with a wide workers' organization, supposedly the most accessible to the masses (but in fact is the most accessible to the gendarmes, and makes revolutionaries most accessible to the police) we shall not achieve one goal nor the other.

Communist Party membership was made artificially scarce, generally representing less than 10 percent of the population and often much less. Party membership in 1988, for instance, was about 19.5 million as against a population of 281 million, according to the 1987 census in the USSR. Before Stalin's purges, party membership was 3.5 million, dropping to only 1.9 million by 1938.[7] Anyone in the selectorate had the potential to become a party member, but only a few were chosen. The incumbent needed about half of the party membership to ensure maintenance in office, so that while the pool of potential members was huge (recall that the selectorate arguably equaled the adult population of citizens), the winning coalition consisted of no more than 3 to 5 percent of the population and perhaps much less. This small group was given access to special privileges not granted to the rest of the selectorate, as Georgi Arbatov (1992, 225–228), an influential scholar and advisor within the Soviet system, observed:

During the stagnation years nomenklatura was finally separated into a special caste. Theirs was something akin to an aristocracy—a life peerage associated with honors, with a high standard of living and a good assortment of privileges. . . . The number of people who received various perks grew constantly under Khrushchev and Brezhnev, keeping up with the growth in sheer numbers of the apparat. People abused these privileges shamelessly, even flaunted them. They lived with an incredible extravagance and a luxury that bordered on the absurd.

All rigged electoral systems create artificial scarcity in some designated proficiency, typically in membership in the single approved political party, thereby guaranteeing that membership is valuable. As in the Soviet system, so too in virtually all rigged systems, any selectorate member could be granted the opportunity to gain the requisite additional qualities to make it into the winning coalition, but to protect the value of those additional qualities, only very few actually are given that opportunity. The consequence of this choice of selectorate members for entry into a winning coalition is that many people are candidates for entry into the winning coalition, but only a tiny subset is chosen. Thus, rigged electoral systems have a large selectorate and a small winning coalition.

Liberal democratic presidential systems differ, in part, from rigged-election systems in that they do not create an artificial scarcity in the qualities required for access to the winning coalition. A characteristic of competitive democratic presidential political systems is that universal suffrage makes the selectorate very large, and majority rule makes the winning coalition equal to about half of the selectorate.[8] Not all competitive electoral systems are alike in the required size of the winning coalition. First-past-the-post parliamentary systems, for instance, require a winning coalition equal to only about one-quarter or less of the selectorate. If such a system has only two political parties and the prime minister requires support from half of the legislators in order to remain in power, and each legislator needs approximately a simple majority to be elected, then the prime minister needs support from one-half of the legislators, each of whom needed support from one-half of his or her constituents in order to be elected. Thus the prime minister only needs support from one-fourth of the voters. If there are more than two viable political parties, then the prime minister needs an even smaller percentage of the selectorate in order to remain in power. In many proportional-representation systems the size of the winning coalition can be sub-stantially smaller than one-quarter.[9] This is one noteworthy respect in which we can see how coalition and selectorate size provide the possibility of a more nuanced understanding of political dynamics than is achieved through the use of categorical regime labels like *democracy*, *junta*, *autocracy*, or *monarchy*.

Illustrative Examples of Small, Restrictive Winning Coalitions

To illustrate how a winning coalition can be much smaller than a majority of the selectorate and still determine who the national leadership will be, we offer an extreme example of a system that condoned fraudulent vote counting. Consider a case that took place during an election in Kenya in 1989.

The Kenyan government introduced what it called a queue voting system in 1986. Under these rules, instead of using a secret ballot, voters lined up publicly behind a representative of the candidate they supported. If a candidate was deemed to have received 70 percent or more of the vote, the candidate was elected. Otherwise a runoff was held by secret ballot. Many of these queuing elections were rigged by the simple mechanism of lying about how many people lined up in favor of this or that candidate. The ruling party ensured victory by cheating in about one-third of the elections. The case that is of particular interest is striking because of its egregious nature. In it the winning coalition—all the votes it took to elect an official—appears to have been just *one* man.

In a by-election on February 1, 1989, in Kiharu, one candidate— Dr. Julius Kiano—was a former government minister who was highly regarded by the citizens of Kiharu. He was, however, distrusted by the ruling party because of his independence. Indeed, that was why he had been dropped from the government. He was opposed in the by-election by a relatively unknown and inexperienced man named Mweru. A local reporter happened to photograph a chalkboard with the tally of votes: 9,566 (92.46 percent) for Kiano and 780 (7.53 percent) for Mweru. The Returning Officer, charged with responsibility for determining and reporting who won the election, returned vote totals of 2,000 for Kiano and 9,000 for Mweru. Mweru won based on the support of a winning coalition of one man, the Returning Officer (Throup and Hornsby 1998, 42–45). Of course, the winning-coalition size for the whole country—where the same electoral procedure was used—was larger. It surely included at least one individual from each constituency and probably considerably more people whose loyalty to the ruling government was not in doubt. As surely, winning coalitions in any district did not need to meet the test of majority rule, let alone the 70 percent stipulated for queuing elections.

The example from Kenya is far from unique. Ebenezer Foote, a Federalist Assemblyman from upstate New York reporting on the election of 1792, observed that

the Clintonian [i.e., Governor George Clinton's] Party in the assembly have by a damned Maneuvre got the better of us in appointing Canvassers for the next Election. We, as honest men, agreed to vote for a part of their List, and they agreed to vote for half of ours. We kept our word and they, as usual, disregarded theirs. In Consequence of which, they have Got every one of the Committee on their Side. Thus you see, we are Duped & fooled every way and shall Continue so to be as Long as we act honestly and Candidly in anything which concerns them. (Taylor 1996, 177)

Not only the size but also the characteristics required for membership in S and W can be quite idiosyncratic. In monarchies, as we have indicated, having "blue blood," as a member of the nobility, was the apparent requirement for membership in the winning coalition. Earls were valuable backers by mere happenstance of birth. During the English civil war in the thirteenth century, following the issuance of the Magna Carta, for instance, King John sought the loyalty of Henry fitz Count by offering to consider making him earl of Cornwall. Henry was the illegitimate son of Earl Reginald of Cornwall and was, by the happenstance of his birth, precluded from succeeding his father in that position. Yet Henry, an able combatant, had considerable standing. King Richard had given him two manors in Devonshire and John had given him authority over the escheated barony of Bradninch. What is more, he was a well-respected captain who had done much to help King John against the rebellious barons in 1215. With his loyal service in mind and with John desperate for help against the rebellious barons, on September 15, 1215, "John appointed Henry sheriff of Cornwall with the promise that when peace was restored he would investigate his rights to the earldom. As Henry clearly had no rights, this promise had little real meaning .... As it was he was removed on November 16 and replaced by Robert de Cardinan, the most powerful of Cornish barons" (Painter 1949, 358–359). Despite his military prowess, personal wealth, and loyalty to John, Henry's illegitimate birth precluded his becoming an earl and, thereby, a prospective essential member of a winning coalition. He could be attached to a member of such a coalition and derive benefits through that attachment, but he could not himself be essential.[10] Henry fitz Count surely understood that the accident of his birth precluded his becoming a member of King John's postrevolt winning coalition. John could not credibly promise to provide Henry with private benefits beyond the crisis during which his help was needed, but he could pay him handsomely during the crisis and he did.

Henry obviously was happy about the rewards he received during John's difficult period, and John was happy about Henry's support during the crisis. Beyond the birthright problem Henry faced, this example illustrates an additional important aspect of the selectorate theory, namely, that challengers cannot guarantee that everyone who participates in their transition coalition will be a long-term member of their winning coalition when they come to power. We return to this issue when we discuss the role of affinity in our theory.

Of course, if England's political institutions were changed, the criteria for membership in the winning coalition might have been altered, fundamentally changing Henry fitz Count's prospects. Indeed, one feature of the Magna Carta was that it extended political rights to all free men, not just the nobility. Had the Magna Carta been fully enacted, this might have dramatically changed the size of W and S in England as early as 1215.

Sources of Risks and Rewards

In our earlier discussion we referred to leadership decisions regarding the allocation of resources to public and private goods. Before turning to our model in the next chapter, it is appropriate to elaborate a bit on these and related concepts, providing definitions and explaining their role in the selectorate theory.

Taxing and Spending

In the theory, leaders maintain themselves in office by raising taxes and then spending some portion of government revenue on public and private goods. Public goods are indivisible and nonexcludable: they benefit everyone in the society, including the disenfranchised. In contrast, private goods generated by government go only to members of the winning coalition, and not everyone enjoys their benefits. We assume that the public and private goods produced by the leader are normal goods for all actors; more is always better.

For purposes of our theory it is not critical that any good meets the definition of a pure public good or a pure private good. We are concerned with how much a leader spends on each type of good. Equivalently, the selectorate theory can be thought of as addressing the allocation of a bundle of mixed goods, with the relative weighting of the mix between private benefits and public benefits being the estimated quantity in the theory. For instance, when spending on the military, to what extent do leaders emphasize creating an effective fighting force and to what extent do they reward cronies with lucrative government procurement contracts? Since even the most public of goods are often private in their production (Aranson and Ordeshook 1985), defense policy must contain aspects of both public and private rewards. Our question is how selection institutions shape the balance between public and private goods.

A leader will make efforts to ensure that his supporters understand that they receive private goods because of his efforts. The Byzantine emperor made sure that his *strategoi*—agents responsible for military and civil affairs within a district—understood who buttered their bread. To quote Samuel Finer (1997, 631), "Once a year, their [the militarily and politically critical Asian districts'] *strategoi* filed in order of precedence past a long table covered with sacks of gold coins, and took their salary from the emperor's own hands."

How much a leader allocates to public and private benefits depends in our theory on institutional constraints and, of course, on how much revenue is available to spend. The revenue available for allocation is determined by the tax policy of the government. Taxation rates, which are endogenous in the theory (as are allocations to public and private goods), equal a percentage of total economic resources extracted by the government from the N residents (Feldstein 1974; Judd 1985). The resources extracted through taxation are the product of the labor effort of the population. In the model, tax rates, not surprisingly, shape the effort the population puts into productive work and the amount it puts into personal consumption. When people work more and engage in leisure less, per capita incomes rise, as does the gross domestic product, making a larger gross amount of money available for taxation. This creates a tension between the tax rate and the GDP. When the institutional arrangements are such that leaders expropriate any surpluses through high taxes and corruption, individuals prefer more leisure activity rather than high productivity. Consequently, high-tax-rate systems take a larger portion of GDP, but, all else being equal, can generate lower government revenues than do polities with low tax rates. For those who tax at a high rate, however, this potential loss of revenue is partially offset, as we will show, by a diminution in the amount that must be spent by the leadership to keep any member of the winning coalition from defecting to a challenger. Once we develop the selectorate theory, it will become evident why societies with larger winning coalitions tend to be richer than societies with smaller winning coalitions.

The Challenger's Commitment Problem

Leaders use the combination of public and private goods they produce to hold the loyalty of their winning coalition. To depose an incumbent, a challenger needs to convince a sufficient number of members of the current winning coalition to defect to him. On the surface this appears to be a relatively easy task. All the challenger has to do is to promise these members of the existing coalition more rewards than they currently receive. Unfortunately for the challenger, such a promise lacks long-term credibility.

The supporters of the current leader know that they receive private goods only because they are members of the current winning coalition. They also understand that should the challenger come to power, they will continue to receive private goods only if he includes them in his new winning coalition. How does a defector know that the challenger will continue to reward him with private goods if he helps the challenger replace the current leader? Although the challenger can promise defectors that he will continue to reward them for their aid in bringing him to power, he cannot bind himself to carry out this promise. The inability of the challenger to guarantee that the prospective defectors will always be members of his winning coalition is a substantial advantage for the incumbent leader.

History is littered with examples of challengers who, once in control, pushed aside those who helped them come to power. Franz von Papen of the Centre Party recommended to President Paul von Hindenburg that he call on Adolf Hitler, leader of the Nazi Party, to become chancellor and form a new German government in January 1933. Papen expected that he and other relative moderates could control Hitler and use him to continue their role in the government. Instead, Hitler cut out the other parties as he subverted the Weimar constitution. Indira Gandhi did much the same in September 1969 when she wrested control of India's Congress Party from the so-called Syndicate, who backed her rise to become prime minister under the mistaken idea that they would then be able to control her politically.

The incumbent leader does not face this problem of credibility as severely because her current supporters understand that they will continue to receive private benefits as long as they remain loyal. When leaders purge their coalition, they push out those they suspect of disloyalty, not their faithful followers. Mao Zedong did turn on Lin Piao, his right-hand man and comrade from the Long March, but he did so out of the suspicion that Lin was conspiring to replace him.

The challenger's inability to commit to prospective defectors is central to understanding the stability of winning coalitions over time. Members of the current winning coalition have greater confidence that they will be in the winning coalition, and so will receive private goods, in the future under the current leader than under the challenger. To represent this commitment problem and the relative advantage of incumbents in solving it, we introduce the concept of *affinity*.

Affinity

Affinity is the idea that there are bonds between leaders and followers that both can use to anticipate each other's future loyalty. Members of the selectorate are not perfectly interchangeable from the point of view of an incumbent. While everyone prefers to be in the winning coalition rather than excluded from it, there is greater affinity between leaders (or challengers) and some members of the selectorate than others (Enelow and Hinich 1984; Hinich and Munger 1994; Harding 1997; E. Bueno de Mesquita 2000). The factors that influence affinity may be clustered, as in ethnic or religious preferences, or they may be tied to tastes about personality, ideology, political-party identification, experience, family ties, charisma, or what have you.

For purposes of our basic model the nature of the affinity does not matter. Affinity is simply a preference for one individual over another, independent of the policies of the individuals. This is to say, even if in the 2000 presidential election Al Gore and George W. Bush had offered completely identical policy platforms, some voters would have preferred Gore and some voters would have preferred Bush for purely idiosyncratic reasons. For the purposes of the selectorate theory, affinities need not be large. Indeed in the mathematical model, affinities are only used to break ties when all other considerations are identical.[11] Further, we assume that affinities are not so large that they ever overwhelm the importance of public and private goods in the decisions of leaders, challengers, or members of the selectorate. In our theory, affinity cannot lead followers to prefer a sitting leader over a challenger who is expected to produce a higher value of goods in the long run, even after accounting for the commitment problem.

Although affinities might reflect small idiosyncratic tastes, as a practical matter they shape coalitions. All else being equal, leaders prefer to form coalitions with people they like rather than dislike and they also prefer to form coalitions with people who inherently like them. As a broad categorization, from an incumbent's point of view, the members of the selectorate can be divided into three general categories: those about whom it can confidently be said that they feel a strong idiosyncratic attachment to the incumbent (or the challenger); those about whom it can confidently be said that they do not feel a strong idiosyncratic attachment to the incumbent; and the individual who defines the boundary between these two groups—that is, the pivotal supporter needed as the Wth member of a winning coalition of size W. From a challenger's point of view there also are three groups, but the boundaries between them are less well known. Thus, challengers may be able to identify some in the selectorate who are clearly "above the line" and some who are clearly "below the line," but others will remain about whom the challenger is unsure. In particular, the challenger is unsure who the crucial person is who ranks Wth in affinity for him—that is, the lowest-affinity person whose support is needed to sustain a long-term coalition.

Specifically, we assume that the leader evaluates the three groups we described based on affinity, learns who the marginal selector is in terms of affinity, and has a strict preference for including that marginal selector as a member of the winning coalition (Diermeier and Feddersen 1998). In other words, all else being equal the incumbent chooses a coalition of those selectors from whom she expects the highest affinity. However, she will always form the cheapest coalition possible. Affinity considerations are very much secondary in magnitude.

Members of the posttransition winning coalition then know that the ties of affinity between the current leader and themselves will continue to bind them together because they are members of that coalition. They can anticipate that the current leader will continue to reward them with private goods in the future.

The challenger has a similar ordering over who he wishes to include in his coalition; however, the identify of the marginal-affinity member whose support he needs to retain power at the lowest cost remains unknown until after the challenger comes to office. Prior to gaining office, the challenger will accept support from any quarter in his efforts to topple the incumbent. The challenger's first order of business is to come to power. He actively pursues that goal while sorting out his affinities for selectors and their affinity for him. He is especially concerned about coming to power because if he fails, having once challenged the incumbent, in our model he is eliminated from the prospective future role of challenger.

Members of the selectorate then cannot be certain that the challenger seeks their aid because of their mutual affinity or simply as a means to come to power. Potential defectors from the winning coalition feel this uncertainty most deeply. They understand the bonds of affinity with the current leader but cannot be certain about those with the challenger. The challenger has every incentive to tell potential defectors anything if it will encourage them to defect and help him topple the sitting leader. Only if the challenger comes to power will he reveal his true affinities when he is free to place those he likes—as opposed to those he needed to come to power—in favored positions.

This difference in the shared knowledge of affinities between leaders and followers creates an incumbency advantage, an advantage that may be large or small depending on how valuable membership in the winning coalition turns out to be. That value depends primarily on the size of the coalition and the size of the selectorate, not on affinity.

The degree of the heterogeneity of affinity within a society can be thought of as a measure of the distribution of values. Societies with homogeneous cultures, for instance, are likely to have less variance than others in the affinity ordering from one political leader to the next simply because the homogeneous culture probably creates a selection effect. Individuals without the socially preferred set of characteristics are unlikely to be contenders for high office. In heterogeneous societies candidates probably are more diverse in their appeal to individual choosers and so feel different degrees of affinity for different sectors of the society. In that sense, affinity is more dispersed in such environments, so that once challengers gain a secure hold on office, they are likely to assemble their winning coalition from a quite different group of people than did the erstwhile incumbent.

In our model, decisions are made based on affinity only if everything else is exactly equal. In other words, the affinity effects are very small in magnitude. The proofs we offer in the appendix to chapter 3 are based on the convenient assumption that affinities are smoothly distributed across selectors. That is not necessary for the theory, but it does make the mathematics much simpler. We also make affinity a property of leaders for followers rather than one of followers for leaders. Although we believe that bonds of affinity flow in both directions, our assignment of affinity to leaders simplifies the mathematics of the model without altering its conclusions. We digress now to offer some conjectures about what we believe happens if affinities are distributed in a lumpy or correlated way. Since they do not influence our analysis, we leave efforts to evaluate these conjectures to future research projects.

In societies that have many substantial groups, affinity is likely to be lumpy in its distribution. Here we have in mind that leaders may choose to reward potential followers on the basis of bloc identity, creating ethnic, religious, or other forms of group "voting" of the sort that characterizes elections in many Indian states, or voting in the days of New York's Tammany Hall or Mexico under the PRI, with its close ties to the labor movement. Of course, such lumpy affinities are also especially common in rigged electoral systems such as prevail in Iraq or Zimbabwe. Lumpiness in affinity may have the potential to create what are effectively small winning-coalition systems even though the legal or constitutional system dictates majority rule. The idea is that a few key individuals—members of the winning coalition—can deliver bloc votes, much as the Returning Officer did in the Kenyan example offered earlier. In a similar way, labor union leaders in Mexico, the United States, and France for long periods could muster the support of the vast majority of their membership for whichever national candidates they endorsed. Recall that the loyalty norm approximates W/S as the number of essential coalition members approaches zero. However, as the proportion of coalition members who are "essential" increases, then even though the nominal size of W might be large, the effective size is smaller. This is, we believe, the key characteristic of lumpy or correlated affinities. They create bloc leaders—essential coalition members—who collectively deliver the requisite number of nominal coalition members—who reduce the size of the actual winning coalition.

If affinities are highly correlated across individuals within groups, the candidate's selection by a single member of the group can serve as a signal to all members of the group. Members of the group follow the lead of their bloc leader in choosing how to vote. This means that a candidate who can gain a group leader's support can count on the group leader to deliver a bloc of votes, a phenomenon especially common in settings in which patron-client relations are strong. Such a circumstance makes it relatively inexpensive to buy support among a few members of large groups, thereby ensuring the reality of a small winning coalition with the appearance of dependence on a large coalition. Generally, such bloc affinities are based on clearly known social categories, such as ethnicity or union membership, so that potential followers know who will be included in the winning coalition if their bloc comes to power. In this way, blocs can reduce the commitment problem that the challenger faces.

It is important to note that the selectorate theory does *not* require the affinity variable. We can and have constructed models of the theory that do not include affinity (Bueno de Mesquita and Siverson 1997; Bueno de Mesquita et al. 1999). These models lead to the same fundamental insights, though the mathematics can be more complicated than when affinities are included. However, we include affinity because it serves two purposes in our model.

First, it serves a technical convenience that simplifies solving the game. The theory depends on members of the incumbent's winning coalition having a higher probability of being in the winning coalition in the future than do members of the challenger's coalition or any other members of the society. That is, while the incumbent can credibly commit to continue to maintain the composition of her winning coalition once she is ensconced in power, the challenger cannot credibly commit to keep everyone in his transition coalition. As he learns about affinities, he rebuilds his coalition to include the highest-affinity individuals because he can credibly commit to retain them once he is ensconced in power. Affinity sharpens this distinction by allowing us to fix the probability as W/S that an individual will make it into the permanent winning coalition if the challenger wins office, while fixing the probability of continuing in the incumbent's winning coalition if one already is in it at 1.0. We do not require this stark a difference and it does not produce any of our results. The results depend on the latter probability being higher than the former without regard to how much higher it is.

Second, affinity also plays a substantive role. It allows us to capture the idea that the coalition that sweeps a new leader into office rarely is the same as the coalition that the leader uses to stay in power. We represent this switch between a transition coalition and the subsequent permanent coalition in the stylized form of revelation of affinities. Additionally, we believe, as suggested earlier, that alternative assumptions about how affinities are distributed can expand the generality of our theory to encompass important features of ethnic, religious, labor union, or other group politics. This permits us to explain why some apparent democracies—like New York City under Tammany Hall, Mexico under the PRI, or India with patron-client voting—engage in corruption and other activities more characteristic of autocracies than democracies.

The Loyalty Norm (W/S)

The selectorate theory suggests a link between the number of people who make up the winning coalition or the selectorate and an incumbent's prospects of political survival. The theoretical link relates to the risk to coalition members of exclusion from future winning coalitions. One result derived from the selectorate theory indicates that each member of the selectorate has an equal probability of being in a successor winning coalition, with that probability equal to W/S. Although we have not yet presented our theory, we briefly explain the intuition behind this condition since it generates the loyalty norm, which plays so central a role in understanding leadership incentives and the behavior of different sectors of a polity.

Suppose that a sufficient number of members of the current winning coalition defect by switching allegiance to a rival of the incumbent so that the incumbent is removed from office. Because members of W have defected, the incumbent's political challenger now has the opportunity to form a new government. The challenger must draw W members from the available S members of the selectorate. Since W is less than S, the defectors cannot be certain of being included in the new winning coalition. Many of the defectors may be eliminated, proving to be inessential to the formation of a new winning coalition even though they participated in the transition from one incumbent to the other. Since only W individuals out of a pool of S candidates are needed to form the new winning coalition, there is a risk and a cost associated with defection, as well, of course, as benefits. The benefits come in the form of immediate payment for the defector's support. The risk involves the chance of exclusion and the cost entails being cut off from the future stream of private goods, which occurs if the defector is excluded from the successor winning coalition. As the size of the winning coalition becomes smaller, or the size of the selectorate becomes larger, challengers are less likely to need or use the support of any particular individual when forming their winning coalition. Hence, if either the size of the winning coalition shrinks or the size of the selectorate grows, defecting becomes riskier.

The risk of exclusion from a challenger's long-term winning coalition drives loyalty to the current leader. Not surprisingly, leaders have tried to choose followers with the greatest risk of exclusion because they are the most loyal. Finer (1997, 788) stresses exactly this point in his discussion of why Chinese emperors during the Tang dynasty came to rely on eunuchs:

In these circumstances [after the rebellion of An Lu-Shan from 756 to 763 AD], the emperors could look for loyal service to one source and one alone—their eunuchs. For eunuchs were absolutely and unconditionally loyal to the emperors. This indeed is true, not only for the Chinese Empire, but for all the others that used the services of eunuchs—Persia, late Rome, Byzantium. Eunuchs had neither lands nor fortunes nor families to fall back upon. To the generals they were half-men, to the mandarins guttersnipes with neither the breeding nor the education of a gentleman. The Emperor, therefore, was their sole support and they lived or died, rose or fell, entirely by his favour.

Further, eunuchs could not usurp the emperor because they could not father sons to establish dynasties; they could be members of a winning coalition, but never leader. Not surprisingly, some Chinese parents castrated their sons and sold them to the authorities so that they might rise to a powerful position (Finer 1997, 787).

The risk of exclusion is central to the selectorate theory. In the context of our formal mathematical model, we derive the probability that a selector is included in future coalitions to be precisely W/S; hence the risk of exclusion and the concomitant loss of future private goods is $(1 - W/S)$. The key to deriving the selectorate theory is that the probability of inclusion increases as W increases and as S decreases—that is, as leaders pick more from a smaller pool. In reality, we might imagine there is considerable heterogeneity in the probability with which each member of the selectorate makes it into future coalitions. Although we picked up on this issue in our discussion of affinity, there is logic to the W/S formulation.

Suppose for a moment that there is heterogeneity in the probabilities of inclusion in future coalitions. In particular, suppose there is some selector—we will call this individual Pat—who has a greater probability of inclusion in future coalitions that other selectors. Since Pat anticipates being included in future coalitions, the deposition of the incumbent is less likely to interrupt Pat's access to private goods than it would for other members of the winning coalition. Since Pat's risk from defecting is low, in order to maintain Pat's loyalty the incumbent must offer Pat more private goods—personal benefits—than must be offered to someone who has a lower expected value for receiving private benefits under a new leader in the future. Since leaders supply Pat with additional private benefits, it is more costly to include Pat in their winning coalition, and the leader prefers to form the winning coalition exclusively from the other members of the selectorate. However, this violates the initial supposition that Pat is included in coalitions at a higher rate, and so it follows that the probability of being in a successor coalition equals W/S.

The loyalty norm shapes political survival, and hence the actions a leader must take if she wants to remain in power. The smaller W/S is (and hence the larger the risk of exclusion from a future coalition, $1 - W/S$), the less inclined any member of the coalition is to put private benefits at risk by giving support to a political opponent of the incumbent. Thus, when the coalition is especially small and the selectorate is especially large, as in many rigged-election autocracies, the loyalty of coalition members to the incumbent is especially high. From the perspective of the leader, this is one of the beauties of a rigged electoral system.

Universal suffrage provides a mechanism through which practically anyone can be brought into the coalition and everyone is replaceable. Returning to a different aspect of the Kenyan elections, we see even basic numeracy was not a requirement of coalition membership. Charles Rubia, an independent-minded member of Parliament, was "defeated" by Kiruhi Kimondo, who reportedly received 70.5 percent of the first-round votes: "According to reports, the Returning Officer announced two different sets of results until Rubia intervened to point out that the officials had miscalculated and Kimondo's vote was still less than 70 percent [required for a first round victory under Kenya's queue voting system]. Rubia then suggested that they change the result yet again in order to spare him the farce of having to contest an equally rigged secret ballot" (Throup and Hornsby 1998, 43).

In chapter 8 we expand our discussion of the selectorate theory to address the endogenous selection of institutions. At that time, we will show that political leaders are best off if W/S is small, as in a rigged-election system. In contrast, members of the current winning coalition prefer systems in which the ratio of coalition size to selectorate size is large, though, depending on circumstances, they can prefer the ratio to be large by shrinking the selectorate relative to coalition size or by expanding the coalition relative to selectorate size. Those not in the winning coalition, especially those who are disenfranchised and so have no prospect of being in a winning coalition, will be shown to prefer governments in which the ratio W/S is large and in which the winning coalition's absolute size is large. The ratio of coalition size to selectorate size, therefore, will prove to have important implications for population migration, revolutions, coups d'état, and a host of other factors.

The Replacement or Deposition Rule

Since our theory focuses on the actions leaders take to stay in office, we need to define the circumstances that result in their being deposed. We identify two different deposition rules, but focus only on the first. The second produces similar analytic results. The rules emphasize different thresholds that challengers must pass to come to power. Two plausible deposition thresholds are what we label (1) the constructive vote of no confidence and (2) simple deposition.

A constructive vote of no confidence is the more demanding of the two illustrative deposition rules.[12] It gives the incumbent an advantage. Under this rule, the challenger must attract enough supporters away from the incumbent so that the incumbent no longer retains backing from W members of the selectorate. In addition, the challenger must have the endorsement of a coalition at least of size W to take over. That is, the constructive vote of no confidence indicates that if no one currently controls a coalition of size W, the incumbent remains in office. In a parliamentary democracy this is equivalent to the survival of a prime minister who only retains a minority coalition so long as no opponent assembles a majority coalition (Strom 1990).

The simple-deposition rule relaxes one restriction; specifically, the challenger simply has to pull off sufficient supporters from the incumbent's chosen set of backers. If fewer than W members remain loyal to the incumbent, she is deposed and the challenger enters office. Under this rule if the incumbent loses control of a coalition of size W, the default favors the challenger. Although other deposition rules are plausible, for the sake of continuity and clarity, here we will use only the constructive vote of no confidence rule.

Political Systems: Analogies But Not Equivalence

The size of the winning coalition and the selectorate can be readily related to conventional labels for describing different political systems. As we have already intimated, in modern presidential democracies with nearly universal suffrage, S is about equal to N and W is typically a simple majority of S. In such systems, citizenship automatically holds out the prospect of benefits, both in terms of public policies and in terms of private benefits. In our framework, leaders, as agents of the selectorate, choose policy positions that they believe will satisfy those who keep them in power. They do not necessarily choose the policies most desired by the citizenry or even by their backers. Leaders may have their own policy preferences, after all. Still, since any citizen in a democracy can be a member of the winning coalition, the policy preferences of all citizens must be considered by leaders as they formulate the public policies they pursue and the private goods they allocate. In addition to the consumption of public policies by all citizens, any enfranchised resident in a democratic system with direct election of a president as chief executive has about a 50 percent chance of obtaining some, probably very small, private benefits through membership in the winning coalition.

In nondemocratic political systems, the picture is different. In a single-party dictatorship, for instance, S may not be equal to N. S may be only 10 or so percent of the total citizenry, as was common in some communist and fascist states. S might be much smaller than that. It might consist of a tiny minority of citizens. Authoritarian regimes run the gamut in terms of the size of the selectorate. When the selectorate is small, this means that the policy preferences of the vast majority of residents $(N - S)$ can be ignored as a part of daily, routine politics.[13] Only the preferences of the citizens in S need attention. For the citizens in the selectorate, then, there is a chance of gaining access to private benefits in the future and there is a current influence on policy choices. For the disenfranchised set of people, $N - S$, neither of these benefits exists. For the members of W there is influence on current policy and there are immediate private gains to be had. In universal-suffrage democracies, W is large. In single-party dictatorships, even if S is universal, W is small. Communist Party membership in Vietnam, for example, is only about 3 percent of the population and only a fraction of that 3 percent are needed to keep the leadership in office.

Monarchies have still different characteristics. In a typical monarchy, only a very small number of people have a routine prospect of becoming members of the winning coalition. Recall that King John's England had 236 barons who comprised the entire selectorate. Of course, they had their own followers who were likely to be rewarded by them for their good service, but only supporters among these barons were really vital to the king's election and survival in the face of rivals. In traditional monarchies, the selectorate is small. The winning coalition, W, is naturally even smaller because it is a subset of S. In some monarchies the value of W is determined by a very limited-franchise majoritarianism and in others it is not. We have already mentioned examples of elective monarchies. Some had even smaller selectorates than those we have mentioned. The Holy Roman emperor, for instance, was chosen by a majority vote among seven electors, a very tiny group indeed (Eulau 1941).[14] These few constituted S.

Monarchies were sometimes only nominally majoritarian; still, many did function at least in a quasi-majoritarian manner. Without the support of a majority of the royal family it was often difficult for an individual to become a monarch or to remain as the leader. During the Merovingian, Carolingian, and Capetian dynasties in France, for instance, it was not automatically the case that the king's eldest son succeeded him. Rather, there was a quasi-electoral process and a clear requirement that the future king have support among a significant proportion of the royal family and other influential individuals. Indeed, this was a central concern in the early years of the reign of Philip Augustus (1179–1223) in France, who, unlike many of his predecessors, was designated by his father to succeed to the throne (Baldwin 1986). His father did so out of fear that Philip would otherwise not be selected by the nobles. Even with his father's endorsement, there was controversy surrounding Philip's ascent to the throne. Similar patterns of election and competition for kingship can be found in the history of the monarchies of medieval Castile, León, England, and elsewhere. Indeed, recognition of this essential fact is at the heart of William Shakespeare's *Hamlet*.

Sometimes majoritarian monarchies expanded the selectorate beyond the royal family. At least since 1295, the king of England depended partially on majority votes by the House of Lords in Parliament to retain many of the privileges of office. These lords were drawn from a somewhat broader set of people than the few barons on whom earlier English kings depended. Chapter 8 explains the specific conditions under which kings had incentives to increase the size of the selectorate and to increase (or at least to accept an increase in) the size of the winning coalition.

Like monarchies, military juntas include very few people. Typically, a military junta depends on a handful of colonels or generals to form the selectorate, and some small fraction of those are in the winning coalition. Juntas, like monarchies, need not be majoritarian within their very limited selectorate.

Though it is simple enough to relate W and S to well-known regime types, we make a conscious effort to move away from categorical discussions of political systems. The links between the size of W and S and regime types like democracy, autocracy, monarchy, and junta are useful as heuristic devices, but no two democracies are alike, nor are any two autocracies, monarchies, or juntas. Inevitably, categorical discussions of regime types lead to the construction of arbitrarily drawn boundaries. That, of course, is why there are so many different ways that people define democracy.[15]

The two institutional variables on which we focus are theoretically much more finely calibrated than broad classifications such as democratic, autocratic, monarchic, and so on, and they encompass *all* nominal regime types. Though W and S are difficult to estimate in practice, in large part because little effort has been put into their measurement to date, they are conceptually continuous variables rather than categorical or ordinal. This means that they have both conceptual properties and mathematical properties that facilitate drawing generalizations about the marginal impact of even small changes in their values on important political factors. This is not true of the more common focus on regime typologies. Therefore, we believe that as we learn more about estimating the values of W and S we will learn more about politics than is possible by focusing on categorical schemes for defining regimes.

There is an additional reason to distinguish between institutional variables like the selectorate and the winning coalition on the one hand, and typologies of regimes on the other. While most systems with large winning coalitions and large selectorates are democratic, *a large selectorate and a large coalition do not in themselves define democracy.* Of course coalition size and selectorate size are not equivalent to what people seem to have in mind when they speak of democracy. We have already indicated, for example, that the voting rules in presidential systems and list-voting systems more strongly imply the necessity of a larger minimal winning coalition than do single-member district parliamentary systems, yet each of these three types are routinely categorized as equally democratic by typological or categorical methods. To be sure, democracies require larger coalitions than autocracies or monarchies, but different forms of democracy may produce substantially different coalition sizes. Within our model those differences imply variation in tax rates, corruption, immigration, and other important political concerns across the broad nominal category of democratic governments. Likewise, all modern democracies surely have large selectorates, but then so do many rigged-election systems that are patently autocratic. Thus there is likely to be important variation in patterns of behavior across democratic systems, variation that depends on differences in the ratio of coalition size to selectorate size, just as there are likely to be important variations in behavior across all regime types because of variance in the absolute sizes and ratios of W and S.

Democracy is generally associated with a variety of characteristics, of which coalition size is but one. These characteristics include, among others, an independent judiciary, free press, civil liberties, legal constraints on leaders, norms of conduct, and reliance on law. Rather than defining coalition size, as we will show, many of the features that contribute to definitions of democracy are themselves expected, endogenous policy *consequences* that follow from having a large winning coalition and a large selectorate. Equivalently, though autocracy is not defined by corrupt politicians whose actions imply indifference to the public welfare, we will show that such behavior is an expected consequence of having a small winning coalition and a large selectorate. Therefore, we make an effort to integrate core ideas of democratic theory (Downs 1957; Dahl 1999) and of autocratic theory (e.g., Wintrobe 1998; Olson 2000) into a theory of leadership incentives driven by selectorate size and coalition size. As part of our empirical effort, we try to parse out the impact of coalition size and selectorate size from other attributes of regimes that lead to their classification along a democracy-autocracy continuum. To do so, we suggest operational indicators for W and S in chapter 4, and we calculate the residual variance in a standard indicator of democracy or autocracy that is not explained by W and S. Then we can conduct tests to ascertain the independent effects of coalition size, selectorate size, and other unrelated institutional aspects of nominal regime types. This permits us to evaluate our theory within the broader context of theories of democracy and autocracy. Because particular institutional configurations seem to be necessary but not sufficient conditions for defining democracy, autocracy, military junta, or monarchy, we should expect that the empirical implications of the theory will hold when we relate winning-coalition size and selectorate size to an array of dependent variables, but they may not always hold when relating the residual institutional effects of standard measures of democracy, autocracy, and so on to the same dependent variables.

What Is Missing from Our Theory

Our theory has broad applicability across political systems. Nevertheless, we have excluded important elements of politics. These simplifications of reality are necessary to produce a simple but powerful model. To include all of them would move us from having a simple theory of politics to a description of the politics of every specific polity. Still, we think it important to highlight key simplifications for the reader.

First, we assume that the leader acts as an individual with sole control over policy. Although we have discussed the idea of treating groups of political actors as "the leader," as in our example of the United States, we will talk about the leader as an individual. Even if we think of the leader as a group in a polity, we will not consider the internal politics of that group. Questions of separation of powers and checks and balances among powerful actors in a government lie outside our theory.

Second, we assume that the implementation of policy is never problematic (except in the case of policy imposed on a foreign rival). The leader collects taxes, allocates resources, and produces public and private goods without concern for inefficiencies in provision. If such inefficiencies exist, it is because they are in the leader's interest as a way to reward followers. Special exemptions from taxes and corruption are examples of these inefficiencies. Questions then of how to organize bureaucracy to provide government services most efficiently lie outside our theory, except to the extent that one thinks of efficient organization as itself being a public good.

Third, we assume public goods are normal goods. No one disputes the fact that more public goods are better, nor is there any differentiation in the range of public goods that could be provided where the actors might disagree about which public good should take priority. This assumption places questions of ideological competition, which are central to spatial models of electoral competition, outside our model. Ideology appears in our model only to the extent that affinity captures ideological similarity between leaders and followers.

Fourth, we assume that all members of our groups—leaders and challengers, coalition members, the selectorate, and the disenfranchised—are identical except for their affinities for one another. Questions of individual competence or particular interests (beyond an interest in more private goods) are not covered in our model. Representation, as it is generally understood to concern how differences in opinion or interest are represented, does not occur in our model. Of course, the leader does represent the interests of her winning coalition to the extent that she provides public and private goods to them.

Having acknowledged these assumptions, we add that our theory leads to important insights into all of these questions. Representation can be thought of as a problem of layers of winning coalitions within one political system. The representative has a winning coalition in his district that elects him, and, in turn, is a member of the selectorate of the executive in parliamentary systems with a vote of no confidence by virtue of his role in making and breaking prime ministers. We do not pursue such elaborations of our theory to address these questions, because doing so would take us too far from our goal of developing our argument, deducing its consequences for a wide range of government actions, and then testing those conclusions. We hope to pursue some of these possibilities in future research and invite others to do so as well.

Conclusion

We have defined the key players in our view of politics, how they are chosen, and what they do. Polities consist of leaders who try to stay in power. They always face challenges to that objective. Leaders stay in power by raising government revenue through taxation and then spending that revenue, dividing it between public-goods allocations that benefit everyone in the society and private rewards that go only to members of the winning coalition. To remain in office, leaders need to protect themselves against defections by members of their winning coalition. The coalition's members are a subset of the selectorate, with members of the selectorate having the prospect of becoming members of a future winning coalition. Those in the current coalition are chosen, in part, based on their affinity. At the outset, when they back a would-be leader, they cannot be sure that once in power, the challenger will keep them on. The risk that they will be replaced increases as the selectorate gets larger and as the required coalition gets smaller. Those who are in the winning coalition beyond the transition period—that is, those in the coalition once the challenger is ensconced as the new incumbent—can be confident of remaining in the leader's long-term coalition, since they were chosen because of their high affinity for the leader. Their primary benefit is the private rewards doled out to coalition members. Those who are neither the leader nor members of the winning coalition derive benefits only to the extent that the government provides public goods. They enjoy none of the private benefits that coalition members get.

Building on the relationship between coalition size and selectorate size, we develop a model that suggests a way to explain whether people face high taxation, receive many public benefits, live under the yoke of poverty, corruption, and rent seeking, or live in peace and prosperity.

3 A Model of the Selectorate Theory

In the previous chapter we introduced the core features of the selectorate theory. Here we put these components together in a rigorous mathematical manner to explain how selection institutions shape the political incentives. The mathematical structure of our theory forces us to be explicit about assumptions and logic. Although mathematical inference prevents us from making logical errors in our reasoning and allows others to see exactly where our deduction is wrong if we have erred, it does necessitate a substantial amount of mathematical notation. We have endeavored to minimize the mathematical presentation in the text by providing a formal appendix for the model at the end of the chapter. But we think it necessary to fully describe the model before explaining its logic in prose.

The selectorate model is an infinitely repeated game, meaning that leaders, selectors, and residents engage in the same form of political interaction over an indefinite series of rounds. We describe a single round here. The incumbent leader (denoted L) is kept in power by a winning coalition of W members of the selectorate, where each member of the selectorate has equal weight in contributing to the winning coalition. We denote the members of the incumbent's winning coalition W_L. The incumbent always faces the prospect of being deposed by a challenger, denoted C.

A round begins with the incumbent picking a coalition, W_L, of size W.[1] A challenger is then randomly selected. Both the incumbent and the challenger simultaneously propose tax rates and the allocation of revenues between public and private goods. Additionally, the challenger selects a coalition, W_C. Proposed expenditures can be less than tax revenue, but, by assumption, cannot exceed tax revenue. Later we investigate a conjecture about what happens if the budget constraint is relaxed and deficit spending is permitted. Any revenue raised through taxation that is not spent on providing public and private goods remains as funds available for the discretionary use of the leader. After the incumbent and challenger announce their tax proposal and their spending program, all members of the selectorate choose between the incumbent and the challenger. The incumbent is removed and replaced by the challenger if and only if the challenger receives the support of at least W members of his nominated coalition (W_C) and the incumbent retains fewer than W supporters from within her coalition (W_L). Each member of the society (N) allocates his or her personal resources (including time, energy, skills, money, and so on) between economically productive activities and leisure. Finally, the chosen leader's policies are implemented.[2]

We define r, subscripted with L or C as appropriate, to represent the tax rate proposed by the leader (L) or the challenger (C), while public goods are denoted x and private goods g, again with the appropriate subscript to indicate that the allocation was proposed by the leader or challenger. Leisure activity for individual i is said to equal l_i with l_i falling between 0 and 1, including 0 and 1 respectively. Productive activity equals $(1 - l_i)$. For convenience, we refer to $(1 - l_i)$ as labor, although it can be thought of as any kind of economic input.

Economic Activity, Policy Provision, and Payoffs

As mentioned, each citizen chooses to allocate resources between leisure and economic activity. While the nature of these resources could be viewed quite generally, for simplicity we do not differentiate types of economic activity or leisure, referring instead just to labor or leisure. If an individual chooses l_i leisure, she contributes $(1 - l_i)$ units of labor effort to economic activity. Given a tax rate of r, each individual retains $(1 - r)$ percent of the product of her economic activity. This means that an individual's total retained level of personal economic product is equal to $(1 - l_i)(1 - r)$. We sometimes denote this quantity y. Given each individual's leisure-versus-labor decision, the overall level of economic activity in the society is equal to

$$E = \sum_{i \in N} (1 - l_i)$$

and so government revenue (R) equals rE.

When leaders or challengers propose the provision of public and private goods they take into account the cost of each type of good. The cost of public-goods provision is stipulated to equal p, while private goods have unit cost and all members of the coalition receive the same level of private goods. Consequently, the size of a leader's coalition effectively acts as a price for private goods. That is, the cost to purchase a unit of private goods for her supporters is proportional to the number of people who must be rewarded: the size of the winning coalition.

The incumbent's cost for providing x_L public and g_L private goods, given a coalition W_L, is $px_L + |W_L|g_L$, where the notation $|W_L|$ means the size of the set W_L—that is, how many people are in the incumbent's coalition. Rewards to the N residents in a society can come from four sources, although how much anyone receives from each source, if anything at all, varies with whether they are in the winning coalition or not. Everyone receives the benefits derived from the public goods provided by the government (x), while members of the winning coalition get their share of government-provided private goods (g) as well. Everyone enjoys the returns derived from the untaxed portion of their personal economic activity (y) and from leisure (l). Each individual's utility function depends on these four components (x,g,y,l), and the utility function is posited to be an additively separable, smooth, twice-differentiable function, which is increasing and concave in each component. That is, the more of each component an individual gets, the greater that individual's well-being. The more one gets, the less the additional increment to total utility, so that the function is increasing at a decreasing rate.

We assume that everyone shares a common discount value (δ) in calculating the worth of future benefits.[3] Those not in the winning coalition receive no private goods, while those in the coalition each receive the same share of private goods.[4] We focus on the following specific utility function—$V(x,g,y,l) = x^{1/2} + g^{1/2} + y^{1/2} + l^{1/2}$—for numerical examples, but in the appendix we do not assume such a specific form.[5]

The incumbent leader receives a payoff of $\Psi + R_L - M_L$, where R_L represents total government revenues collected during the current period under the incumbent's leadership and M_L represents the incumbent's total expenditures on public and private goods ($M_L = px_L + |W_L|g_L$) in that period if she survives in office. The incumbent's payoff if she fails to retain her office is 0. The inherent value of holding office is $\Psi \geq 0$. This term plays no consequential role in any of our general results, but it does play some part when we turn to analyzing an important linkage between domestic politics and foreign affairs. For now, we note that the value of office in our model can be 0, though it cannot be negative. That is, all else being equal, leaders want to be in office. The intrinsic value of office (Ψ) reflects the idea that some people derive psychological or symbolic value simply from being in power.

The important aspect of the leader's utility in terms of the results from our theory is the term $R - M_L$. This term reflects the surplus resources the incumbent can keep for her own discretionary use. These slack resources can be thought of as the opportunity the incumbent has to engage in kleptocracy—that is, theft of the state's wealth for personal use—or as the cushion the incumbent has against challenges by political rivals. This surplus can be used for any purpose the incumbent chooses. Public-spirited leaders might spend the surplus on pet projects designed to enhance public welfare, or they might retain the surplus as insurance against the chance of political trouble if they risk losing support from members of the winning coalition. Additionally, they might place the surplus in an offshore account to provide for their own personal welfare.

If the challenger succeeds in coming to power, his payoff in the initial, transition period in power equals $\Psi + R_C - M_C$, where

$$R_c = r_c \sum_{i \in N} (1 - l_i) \qquad \text{and} \qquad M_c = p x_c + |W_c| g_c$$

In subsequent periods after the transition, the challenger becomes the new incumbent, and so his payoff is as specified above for the incumbent leader. If the challenger fails to attain office his payoff is 0. Finally, the leader, whether she be the former incumbent or the newly acceded challenger, learns her affinity for members of the selectorate. Of course, if it is the incumbent who survives, she already had this information. In contrast, this information is useful for a former challenger, who having emerged from a position of obscurity, has not had past opportunities to learn who he would ideally like in his future coalitions. With these payoffs in mind, the time line of a round of the leadership selection game is given in box 3.1.

Equilibria of the Selectorate Model

We now describe a Markov perfect equilibrium (MPE; see Fudenberg and Tirole 1991, chap. 13) in which the incumbent always survives in each period, with the incumbent choosing the selectors for whom she has the highest affinity to be members of her coalition. Of course we could introduce uncertainty into the model so that the incumbent would not necessarily be reselected. We do just that in chapter 7 when our attention turns to what leaders do to improve their prospects for political survival. For now, however, our primary interest is in identifying the optimal policy choices—tax rates, public-goods provisions, private-goods provisions, total spending levels, and individual labor efforts—that result from

Box 3.1
The time line

---

1. The incumbent leader picks a coalition, W_L, of size W from the members of the selectorate: $W_L \subset S$.

2. A challenger is randomly chosen, and then simultaneously both the incumbent and the challenger propose tax rates and policy provisions. Specifically, the challenger proposes his coalition, $W_c \subset S$, a tax rate r_c, and a provision of x_c public and g_C private goods. The incumbent proposes a tax rate r_L, and policy provisions of x_L public and g_L private goods.

3. All selectors choose between the proposal of the challenger and the incumbent. The incumbent is removed and replaced by the challenger if and only if the challenger receives the support of at least W members of his nominated coalition (W_c) and the incumbent retains less than W supporters from within her coalition (W_L).

4. Each citizen allocates his or her resources between economically productive activities and leisure: $l_i \in [0,1]$, where l_i refers to individual i's leisure and $(1 - l_i)$ refers to each individual's level of economic activity, which we refer to as labor.

5. If the chosen leader's policy provisions can be implemented, then they are. Otherwise a caretaker policy is implemented that gives everyone in the game a reservation payoff of v_0. By "can be implemented" we mean that revenues are sufficient to finance the proposed policies. Specifically, assuming the incumbent leader is retained, then saying that a proposed resource allocation can be implemented implies that

$$r_L \sum_{i \in N} (1 - l_i) - p x_L - |W_L| g_L = 0$$

Players receive payoffs, and the affinity preference ordering of the chosen leader is revealed.

---

the leader's efforts to stay in office. It is easy enough to see how an incumbent might lose office by spending too much or too little on public or private goods or by taxing at the wrong rate. It is harder to see how the optimal tax rate and spending allocations relate to coalition and selectorate size. We will show how these optimal levels depend on the size of the winning coalition, the size of the selectorate, and the ratio between the two.

In MPE, players condition their strategy on a state variable. In the current context, the state variable is the incumbent's preference ordering over selectors—that is, the incumbent's affinities. In addition to the standard equilibrium requirement that each player's strategy must be utility maximizing given the strategy of the other players, the Markovian aspect of MPE insists that players condition their strategies only on the state variable—the incumbent's ordering over selectors—and on no other aspect of the history of the game. In the MPE we characterize, this means leaders pick the selectors for whom they have the highest affinity when forming their coalitions. MPE also requires subgame perfection within a round.

There is an important difference between being in an incumbent's winning coalition and being in a challenger's first-period, transition coalition. The challenger does not know his affinity for individual supporters at the time he assembles his transition coalition. Of course this can be stated in a less stylized, more realistic way. The incumbent, who has had a greater opportunity to interact with and learn about the selectors than has the challenger, is more confident about her affinity toward selectors than the challenger since he is relatively unknown. From a modeling perspective, we sharpen this distinction by assuming a leader's affinity ordering is unknown prior to coming to office but is fully revealed on coming to office. As we will see in chapter 7, relaxing this assumption so as to allow affinity to be learned gradually over time or to be known by both the challenger and the incumbent from the outset has important implications for the survival of leaders.

Before learning about his affinity, the challenger and each selector start off with the belief that all possible affinity orderings are equally likely. Since all affinity orderings are equally likely, a selector's probability of being one of the challenger's W highest-affinity selectors is equal to W/S. This means that each selector, including those in the challenger's transition coalition, have a $(1 - W/S)$ probability of being excluded from the challenger's winning coalition if and when the challenger passes beyond the transition period and becomes the new incumbent.

One implication of MPE is that the challenger must be expected to switch to the incumbent's political strategy after the transition period if he is selected as the leader. That is, once he is leader and learns his affinities for the selectors, he, like his predecessor, chooses a coalition that includes only the W highest-affinity selectors to be in his long-term coalition. Clearly, the challenger's decision in forming the transition coalition is a matter of doing whatever he credibly can to gain office in the current round, because he will be removed from the game if he fails to do so. He is not bound in future rounds by any actions he takes now to gain power. Thus, there is a $(1 - W/S)$ chance that members of the transition coalition will enjoy private goods for one period and then will be dropped from the coalition and get no future private goods. So, the expected cost for someone in the incumbent's winning coalition who switches to backing the challenger depends on three factors: the degree to which future rewards are discounted (δ) (i.e., the individual's patience), the quantity of private goods provided to members of the winning coalition, and the probability $(1 - W/S)$ of being excluded from the challenger's permanent coalition if the challenger succeeds in coming to power.

Members of the incumbent's winning coalition, having survived the transition period, know that they are among the W highest-affinity members of the incumbent's coalition. They know, therefore, that they will continue to receive private goods as long as the incumbent's affinity for them does not change. For the sake of simplicity we assume that affinities are fixed once learned. Our results do not require fixed affinities. We only require that a member of the current coalition has a greater probability of being in future coalitions under the incumbent than if the challenger should come to power. That is, before being secure in office, a challenger cannot credibly commit to retain anyone who helps him come to power. This is surely true in real-world politics.[6]

Because of the credible promise of a future flow of private goods, loyalty to the incumbent is induced among members of the winning coalition. That loyalty is not absolute. It varies depending on the prospects a defector has of making it into the challenger's posttransition coalition and on how valuable the flow of private benefits is. Specifically, the larger the risk of future exclusion following a defection to the challenger $(1 - W/S)$, the more loyal a member of the winning coalition is inclined to be. This is what we call the *loyalty norm*. Our subsequent analysis focuses on how the loyalty norm affects taxation and policy provision as institutions vary. We now discuss our main proposition, from which our main results follow. A formal statement of our main proposition and its proof are presented in the appendix. Here we focus on describing the properties of our main proposition.[7]

PROPOSITION 1   If $W \leq (S + 1)/2$, then there exists a Markov perfect equilibrium to the game in which the equilibrium level of taxation, public- and private-goods provision, and leisure activity are optimal, where the optimization depends on the size of the winning coalition and the size of the selectorate.

A more extensive description of proposition 1 depends on the solutions to six equations. The substantive implications of these equations are summarized below and are fully developed in the appendix:

1. *Incumbency condition.* The incumbent matches the challenger's best possible offer regarding taxation as well as public- and private-goods expenditures.

2. *Budget constraint.* Expenditures by government are restricted so that they do not exceed revenue.

3. *Incumbent's policy.* The incumbent's policy choice is the optimal mix of public and private goods, given the institutional constraints and the available budget.

4. *Challenger's policy.* The challenger also makes the optimal policy choice to attract supporters.

5. *Incumbent's tax rate.* The incumbent chooses the tax rate optimally.

6. *Challenger's tax rate.* The challenger makes an optimal tax-rate choice.

Of course, the interesting question is what the optimal choices are that form the MPE of the selectorate game. We start by contemplating what the leisure-and-labor decision is expected to look like for each of the N residents of the polity.

Leisure-and-Labor Decision

Once the selectors choose a leader, be it the previous incumbent or the challenger, the residents know which tax and spending policies will prevail for the current period. In our model the tax rate determines the proportion of their economic enterprise that they get to keep. Consequently this affects how hard they work. When the government takes nearly everything, residents have little incentive to work. In contrast, when the tax rate is low, residents get to enjoy more of the fruits of their labor and so work harder. The higher the tax rate the greater the proportion of their time residents dedicate to leisure and the less they dedicate to economic activity.

We let the function $l(r)$ represent the amount of leisure citizens choose when the tax rate is r. For the specific illustrative utility function we focus on, the relationship between leisure and tax rates is $l(r) = 1/(2 - r)$. Under this precise functional form, when the tax rate is zero individuals split their time evenly between labor and leisure. As the tax rate increases residents reduce their labor, until at the point of 100 percent taxation residents do no work. Lower taxes yield greater economic activity, and this is true in the model for any set of tax rates and policy allocations.

Having said that, it still remains for us to show how the choice of tax rates relates to the size of the winning coalition and the size of the selectorate. We defer this until we present the core implications of the theory.

Selectorate's Choice: *L* or *C*

Members of the selectorate calculate their payoff if the incumbent survives and likewise calculate their payoff if they choose the challenger instead. At the time they make these decisions, they know what tax rates, public-goods expenditures, and private-goods expenditures can credibly be offered by the two candidates. Of course, having this information, they also know how much productive economic effort they will make and how much of their available resources will go instead to leisure activity. Given this information, each resident can calculate his or her welfare under the leadership of both the incumbent and challenger and choose whomever they wish to be leader. Yet, while all residents have a preference, only the choice of certain individuals is relevant to who is chosen as leader. In particular, if fewer than W members of the incumbent's coalition support her and at least W members of the challenger's coalition support him, the incumbent is deposed; otherwise the incumbent survives. Hence the number of individuals whose choice actually matters is never greater than $2W$, which for many systems, particularly those with small W, is much smaller than the selectorate. Consequently, while S selectors have a nominal say in the choice of leader, under many political systems the choice of many of these selectors is irrelevant and never consequential to the outcome. This is especially true in rigged electoral systems, as are operated throughout the communist world and still operate in parts of Africa, the Middle East, and elsewhere.

The institutional setup of society (i.e., the size of W and S) influences how residents weigh the policies offered by the incumbent and the challenger. In addition to what is offered today, citizens must consider their rewards in future periods. The size of S and W influence these choices since selectors know that their chance of being in the challenger's winning coalition past the transition period is W/S. Those currently excluded from the winning coalition know that if the incumbent remains in office they will receive the benefits that can be derived from the current and future flow of public goods and that they will get no private goods from the government now or in the future. Those in the incumbent's winning coalition know the worth of their current and future flow of public and private goods if they stay with the incumbent. Likewise, everyone knows whether they have been chosen to be part of the challenger's transition coalition in the event that the selectorate chooses the challenger over the incumbent. Those so chosen know they will get a one-time private-goods reward and then only a probabilistic continuation of a smaller quantity of private goods in the future, with that probability depending on the ratio of coalition size to selectorate size.

Members of the selectorate decide between the incumbent and the challenger by assessing their personal welfare as a function of their coalition membership(s), the incumbent's affinity for them, the proposed tax rates and expenditure allocations between public and private goods by the incumbent and the challenger, and their own leisure-versus-labor decision. Each selector chooses L if his or her utility is expected to be at least as high under L's continued leadership as it is if a switch is made to the challenger. We now examine how the competition for supporters between challenger and incumbent shapes policy choices.

Challenger's Coalition, Tax, and Policy Choices

To depose the incumbent the challenger needs the support of at least W selectors. He also needs to attract a sufficient number of the incumbent's supporters that she retains the support of fewer than W members of her coalition. To achieve these goals the challenger forms a coalition of size W that includes at least one individual who is also in the incumbent's coalition.[8] If he picks a smaller coalition he can never gain enough support. In contrast, if he increases his coalition size by adding surplus supporters, he only reduces the level of rewards he can supply to his existing coalition. As we might expect, individuals who are only in the challenger's coalition support the challenger. Similarly, individuals who are only in the incumbent's coalition support the incumbent. Thus, who comes to power depends on the individuals who are members of both W_L and W_C. Only by offering these individuals a package of policies worth more than they expect to receive by remaining with the incumbent can the challenger gain office. Therefore, the challenger's decision problem can be reduced to finding the tax and spending policies that maximize the welfare of his coalition. We now turn to this problem, and to the issue of how W and S influence it.

The challenger needs to provide greater expected benefits than the incumbent to those key supporters in both L and C's coalition. We analyze how institutional features affect the greatest possible offer C can make. First, any such offer involves C spending all the resources at his disposal, $R_C = M_C$.

Second, the larger W is, the more the challenger focuses his policy provisions on public goods. When W is small he concentrates instead on private goods. When W is small the challenger can greatly enrich his coalition through private goods, since he only has to divide his resources between a small number of individuals. As W increases, his available resources become more thinly spread and public goods become a relatively cheap way to reward supporters and, coincidentally, often the rest of society as well. This relationship between coalition size and the relative importance of private versus public goods in policy provisions is a key, perhaps the key, result in our theory.

Third, the challenger chooses the tax rate that, if implemented, maximizes the welfare of his coalition. In resolving which tax rate is optimal, he faces two competing incentives that can perhaps be best explained by considering the limiting cases. Suppose W is extremely small relative to N. To maximize the benefits for his coalition, the challenger wants to raise as much revenue as possible to allow him to lavish huge rewards on them. To a certain extent the high tax rate required to generate such large revenues hurts his own supporters, since it discourages them from productive enterprises that they would otherwise undertake. However, since the challenger has only a few supporters, he can easily compensate them for these lost opportunities with private goods. In contrast, when the coalition is large, each individual's rewards are small. As a result the challenger cannot compensate each of them sufficiently for economic opportunities they have forgone as a result of high taxation. Hence leaders with large coalitions choose lower levels of taxation.

Incumbent's Tax and Spending Choices

For the incumbent to stay in office she needs to at least match the value of the challenger's best possible offer to members of her coalition. The key to characterizing the incumbent's strategy is to find the tax and spending choices that maximize the incumbent's discretionary income subject to the constraint that she provides her supporters with at least the same level of rewards as the challenger's best possible offer. Such policies exist, and so in the equilibrium the incumbent can always survive in office and retain some resources for her discretionary use. The key to understanding why the incumbent can always offer the same level of rewards to her supporters as the challenger can and yet spend less relies on the ability of the incumbent to credibly promise future private goods, while the challenger can only offer access to such private goods probabilistically.

Given that the challenger attempts to pick off some of the incumbent's supporters, to survive in office the incumbent needs at least to match the best possible offer the challenger can make. While doing so she also wants to maximize the amount of her discretionary funds. Consequently, while ensuring that she provides funds that at least match the challenger's best possible offer, she chooses the tax and spending policies that most efficiently reward her supporters. These optimal policies reflect many of the same themes just discussed with respect to optimal policies for the challenger. For instance, as W increases, the effective price for private goods increases and so the incumbent switches to a greater share of public goods in her policy provisions. The incumbent wants to maximize revenue since this increases the pool from which she draws her discretionary funds. Yet as the tax rate rises, the incumbent must increasingly compensate supporters for forgone economic opportunities, which means spending more. When W is large, the increase in spending required to compensate a large number of supporters for lost opportunities overwhelms the extra revenue earned from a high tax rate. As a consequence, as W increases, incumbents reduce tax rates. We now turn to the final question, which is the first move in the game, L's choice of coalition.

Incumbent's Choice of Coalition

The incumbent forms her coalition with W selectors for whom she has the highest affinity. This is the coalition that, for any given set of policies, maximizes the incumbent's welfare. In every period the incumbent picks this same coalition of supporters. These supporters know they will be in the incumbent's coalition in every period, and this is what makes them loyal. While in equilibrium the challenger offers them more rewards today, they have only a W/S chance of getting private benefits in the future. By sticking with the incumbent they guarantee themselves private-goods access in every future period.

If the incumbent attempts to choose supporters for her coalition today that she would not include in her future coalitions (i.e., selectors for whom she does not have the highest affinity), she will be deposed. This is because such supporters know that their access to private goods today from the incumbent is a one-time benefit and that in future periods they will be excluded from access to private goods. In contrast, should the challenger come to power then, in addition to receiving benefits today, these individuals also have some, albeit small, chance of inclusion in future coalitions under the challenger. Since this W/S chance is better than no chance, such individuals readily defect to the challenger. The incumbency advantage is predicated on supporters anticipating being in future coalitions and receiving future private goods. Switching coalition membership away from core supporters is, therefore, political suicide.

We have now characterized the taxing and spending policies of the incumbent and challenger and the leisure-versus-labor decision of selectors such that all are best responses given the strategies of every player. The equilibrium policies therefore satisfy the conditions for proposition 1 to be true. In the appendix we also present a second proposition that shows why, even if we relax the assumption that the incumbent's coalition is restricted to size W, the incumbent maintains coalitions of that size. Here we simply point to the intuition. It is straightforward to see why the incumbent never wants to reduce the size of her coalition below W. Doing so allows the challenger to form a coalition of disgruntled selectors who are outside the incumbent's coalition. The challenger would not need to attract supporters away from the incumbent to come to power. Expanding the coalition is also unattractive. As described above, the challenger forms a coalition of size W, which includes some members of L's coalition. However, C only needs to reduce L's number of backers to less than W. This means if $|W_L| = W$, then provided the challenger succeeds in attracting one member of W_L to his coalition, he does not care what the remaining $W - 1$ individuals do. Now suppose L expands her coalition, but less than doubles it. In response suppose C picks a coalition composed of W members of W_L. Since $|W_L| < 2W$, there are fewer than W members of W_L who are not also in W_C. The challenger has not altered the size or reward of his coalition but the incumbent has taken on additional members, forcing her either to dilute the rewards she provides to each member or spend more resources. Only when the incumbent increases her coalition beyond $2W$ might the challenger be forced to add additional members to his coalition. As shown in proposition 2 in the appendix, the incumbent already has weakened her position by having to support an additional $W - 1$ more supporters than the challenger. Consequently, she prefers the minimal winning coalition (Riker 1962).

Alternative Equilibrium

As a consequence of what we have shown above, it is evident that the incumbent's choice to pick a minimal-sized coalition is driven by the constructive vote of no confidence deposition rule and the assumption that $W \leq (S + 1)/2$. In the appendix we discuss equilibria under the simple deposition rule. With the exception that coalitions are oversized, the results change little. The rule that $W \leq (S + 1)/2$ relates to all political systems in which incumbency is maintained with a simple majority or less. This includes virtually all extant forms of democracy, autocracy, monarchy, and military junta, and any and all other political arrangements that do not require a supermajority of the selectorate. Here we do not explicitly model super-sized coalitions, although in a related model of the selectorate theory we have done so (Bueno de Mesquita et al. 2002). In this alternative model, when $W > (S + 1)/2$, rather than form a coalition of size W, the incumbent forms a coalition of size $S - W + 1$. Under the constructive vote of no confidence deposition rule this forces the challenger to form a coalition of size W, which is larger than the incumbent's coalition, while still trying to attract supporters away from the incumbent's coalition.

In perhaps the most extreme example of an oversized-coalition system, eighteenth-century Poland, we can see the results. Under the Polish constitution every member of the Diet possessed *liberum veto*, the right to veto any legislation. Hence any bill to change laws or rules or depose the monarch could be halted by the veto of a single individual. The Polish state was, as a consequence, extremely weak and dominated by foreign powers, particularly Russia, who having gotten its puppet elected as the Polish monarch could easily maintain his position, needing to buy off only a single member of the Diet (McKay and Scott 1983). Since we think such systems are extreme rarities, we do not consider them further here.

How Institutions Structure Incentives

Incumbents want to keep their jobs. To do so, they must generate revenues through taxes and allocate a sufficient amount of the revenues as public and private goods to retain the loyalty of their winning coalition. Now we investigate how the incumbent's policy provisions and taxation policy depend on selection institutions.

For any given level of spending, M_L, by the incumbent leader, she wants to maximize her supporters' rewards by optimizing her provision of public goods (x_L) and private goods (g_L). The size of the incumbent's coalition (W) effectively determines the price the leader must pay for private goods. Hence, as coalition size increases, so does the effective cost of private goods. In response, leaders switch to more publicly oriented policies—that is, as the size of the winning coalition increases, leaders reduce their provision of private goods in favor of the now relatively cheaper public goods. Consequently, under optimal spending provisions, the larger the incumbent's coalition, the greater her reliance on public goods and the less her reliance on private goods to reward her coalition, provided she wants to stay in office. This result is the driving motivation behind most of our subsequent results. While we present these results in terms of the incumbent's decision process, the same implications hold for challengers trying to form a winning coalition.

The incumbent's optimal choice over the allocation of revenues involves two calculations: how much must be spent on the winning coalition in toto and, of the amount spent, how much should go to public goods and how much to private goods. The solution to the second calculation is fundamental to the welfare of members of the winning coalition. The solution to the first calculation determines the leader's welfare. Those outside the winning coalition, of course, derive government-provided welfare only from the leader's provision of public goods. They receive no private benefits from the government. Therefore, those inside the winning coalition always enjoy higher welfare than those outside the coalition. How big the welfare advantage is from membership in the winning coalition, however, depends on the configuration of the polity's institutions.

Recall that the challenger is inherently disadvantaged in the provision of private goods. Under the incumbent's leadership, members of the current coalition are guaranteed private goods, being among the highest-affinity types around whom the incumbent built her own posttransition coalition. These individuals know that the incumbent will keep them in the coalition over the long run. The challenger might offer much higher rewards than an individual is currently receiving from the incumbent, but such a large reward can only be credible for the transition period during which, so to speak, the new winners get to raid the palace. Immediately after the transition period is over the value of private goods can be expected to drop off, falling to zero for those individuals not retained in the long-run coalition of the now new incumbent. Their expectations for what the challenger will do if he gains power match those expressed by The Who in their antirevolutionary anthem "Won't Get Fooled Again": "Meet the new boss/Same as the old boss." Even those retained in the posttransition coalition get fewer private goods than during the transition because those who are retained are the more loyal individuals who cannot easily be bribed away. Therefore, less goes into the pool reserved for the coalition and more shifts to the pool for the incumbent's discretionary use.

When W is small, so that more valuable private goods are provided, the winning-coalition members receive a far higher level of rewards than do those outside the coalition. However, as the coalition becomes larger, the relative difference in the value of goods received between those in and those outside the coalition becomes smaller. This is true for two reasons.

First, the value of private benefits to members of the winning coalition shrinks as W increases because the pool of private goods is divided over W members. Second, when W is large, the proportion of spending allocated to private goods is smaller compared to the proportion so allocated when the coalition is smaller. Instead, more resources are put into providing the relatively cheaper public goods, which benefit insiders and outsiders equally. Thus, the relative importance of private goods as a source of rewards declines, thereby reducing the difference in welfare between outsiders and insiders. This result indicates that the value of membership in the winning coalition increases as the size of the winning coalition decreases. As the winning coalition increases in size, the access to private goods that is bestowed on coalition members decreases in value. This relationship, in conjunction with the size of the selectorate (S), helps drive what we identified earlier as the loyalty norm.

The loyalty norm is, we believe, a central principle of politics. As a first view of its importance, consider which nominal type of government is most likely to have a strong loyalty norm and which a weak norm. The loyalty norm is strongest when the winning coalition is small and the selectorate is large. Autocracies with rigged electoral systems like Iraq, China, or Egypt fit this mold. By contrast, democracies usually require a relatively large winning coalition and a large selectorate, with the winning coalition often needing to be near to half of the voting selectorate, depending on the exact institutional rules in place. Thus, autocracies have institutional structures that promote loyalty to the incumbent leader among the privileged few in the winning coalition. Democracy promotes more disloyalty to the incumbent. In democracies, the weak loyalty norm encourages defection from the winning coalition so that the norm is "throw the rascals out." Within democracies, variations in the size of the winning coalition further point to subtle differences in loyalty. For instance, as noted earlier, single-member district parliamentary governments require a smaller winning coalition than most presidential systems do. This means that loyalty is expected to be higher in such parliamentary systems as compared to, for instance, presidential systems. One manifestation of this loyalty may be the stronger party discipline generally observed in parliamentary governments than in presidential systems.[9]

Thus, the selectorate theory indicates that—operating within their budget constraint—leaders of systems with a strong loyalty norm spend less on the coalition and retain more for their own use or to salvage their incumbency if they find themselves at risk of being deposed. We offer a conjecture that expands on this claim. If we relax the budget constraint so that deficit spending is possible, then the incumbent's promised policies can always be implemented provided the government has sufficient credit to borrow. In that case, we speculate that leaders will have two avenues to increase their discretionary opportunities for personal gain and their chances to survive a crisis: by spending less than they raise in tax revenues or by spending less than they raise in tax revenues, foreign aid, and sovereign debt.[10] By borrowing, they can expand the pool of available resources relative to expenditures so that some of the money borrowed by their government ends up under their personal control. In chapter 4 we will test this conjecture as well as the theory's prediction that government spending in large-coalition systems comes closer to equaling the budget constraint than does spending in small-coalition systems, whether from above or below the budget constraint.

We have utilized the size of the incumbent's coalition and the size of the selectorate to show how loyalty is induced and to show what this loyalty implies about leadership tenure. Further, we have demonstrated that the relative allocation of private and public benefits is directly dependent on the size of the winning coalition, as is total expenditures. Now we turn to an assessment of coalition size and individual welfare.

High taxes make sense when a leader needs to redistribute substantial resources from one set of people to another. When a leader returns tax revenues to the populace in the form of public goods, it makes sense only to tax enough to provide beneficial services that individuals find difficult to provide for themselves (e.g., rule of law, protection of property rights, national defense) plus some small quantity of private goods that go to the members of their large coalition. To meet these needs, taxes need not be especially high. Indeed, the theory shows that the larger the coalition, the lower the tax rate in equilibrium.[11] When a leader survives in office by providing private benefits to her small coalition, plus still having to provide some few public goods and having the opportunity to create a very large slush fund for herself, she has incentives to tax at a relatively high rate. That way she can raise enough revenue to have sufficient resources to redistribute from the general population to the few key supporters needed to keep her in office (and, again, to herself). Of course, the leader is constrained not to tax so much that labor effort falls to such a low level that she cannot meet her private-goods obligations. If that happens, she is in grave danger of being deposed by a challenger.

Leaders in small coalitions must curb their tendency to expropriate resources because residents otherwise will simply refuse to work. However, this need to allow people to retain part of their income so as to keep them working is reduced when the polity possesses abundant natural resources. When states are rich in natural resources such as oil, leaders do not have to rely on the economic activity of residents to provide the resources they need to reward their supporters as much as when such resources are absent. Without the need to hold in check their desire to expropriate income, leaders dependent on small winning coalitions can attempt to seize all of the pie. This has disastrous economic and social consequences, as witnessed by the experience in Nigeria and elsewhere (Sachs and Warner 1995, 1999; Lam and Wantchekon 1999; Leite and Weidmann 1999). The economic and social consequences of resource abundance depend on political institutions. For example, the discovery of oil in the North Sea has not harmed the economy in either Britain or Norway; in fact, the contrary is the case.

In large winning-coalition systems, leaders set low taxes to avoid inhibiting the private economic activity of individuals while furnishing sufficient government revenues to provide public goods. The addition of rents from natural resources enables leaders to provide these public goods and reduce taxes. The weak loyalty norm of such systems prevents leaders from expropriating the resource rents for themselves. In contrast, when W is small and the loyalty norm is strong, leaders expropriate societal resources, pay off their coalition primarily with private goods, and keep the rest for themselves. This predatory behavior is held in check only by the desire to keep residents economically engaged. Resource abundance diminishes this restraint.

Our theory leads to the expectation that tax rates are inversely related to coalition size, while per capita income—a function of the leisure-versus-labor choice in our model—is directly related to coalition size. Large-coalition polities, therefore, are expected to produce higher per capita incomes and lower taxes than are small-coalition systems (Buchanan 1985; Rabushka 1985; Tullock 1986; Barro 2000). Figure 3.1

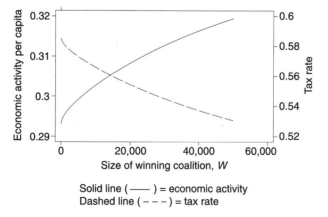

Solid line (——) = economic activity
Dashed line (– – –) = tax rate

Figure 3.1
Coalition size, economic activity, and tax rates

depicts the deduced functional relationship between tax rates, economic activity per capita, and coalition size. The figure is based on simulated estimates derived by applying the model's equations to hypothetical data. The scales, consequently, are arbitrary, while the shapes of the functions faithfully reflect the logic of the model. In the next chapter we will see whether these and other expectations are fulfilled in reality.

The incumbent wants to maximize her discretionary resources. To do so, she minimizes expenditures by reducing M_L until she spends just enough to match the expected value of the challenger's promised expenditures to the pivotal member of the selectorate. Since continued access to private goods is assured to the members of the current winning coalition and since they only gain access to such goods probabilistically if they defect, the incumbent can spend less than the challenger and still equal the expected value of defection for members of her coalition. If she spends less than that expected value, she is deposed. If she spends more, she wastes resources that she could have taken for her discretionary use.

The optimal level of spending has interesting characteristics. Not only do public goods make up a larger proportion of policy provisions, as noted earlier, but as the winning-coalition size increases, in order to survive, incumbents must spend a higher proportion of the available resources. The size of the winning coalition affects policy provision along two dimensions. First, the larger W is, the weaker the loyalty norm and hence the greater the quantity of resources expended on the coalition. Second, as W gets larger, so does the relative importance of providing public goods compared to private goods. Thus, as W gets larger, incumbents spend more within their budget constraints (i.e., come closer to balancing expenditures and revenue) and, of the amount they spend, more goes to providing public goods relative to private goods. So, an increase in W has two competing effects on the welfare of the winning coalition. First, the increase in W means that each member's share of rewards is diluted since the overall number of people who receive rewards has increased. This effect reduces welfare. Second, the increase in W reduces the loyalty norm and therefore forces leaders to spend more resources on keeping their coalition loyal. Such an increase in expenditures improves the welfare of members of the winning coalition. Which of these two effects predominates depends on the specific conditions.

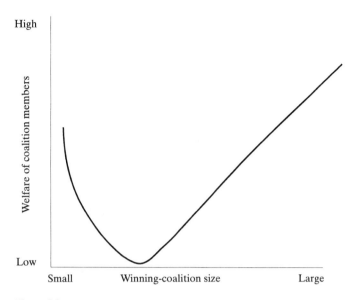

Figure 3.2
The winning coalition's welfare

Figure 3.2 shows a plot of the winning coalition's welfare as a function of the size of the coalition (W). It describes an asymmetric, nonmonotonic function that looks much like a check mark, a j-curve, or a swoosh like the Nike logo. This pattern is indicative of the incentives held by members of the winning coalition. When W starts off small, increases in coalition size diminish the rewards received by individual members of the winning coalition. Beyond a turning point, as seen in figure 3.2, further increases in W improve the welfare of members of the winning coalition, although at a diminishing marginal rate. This happens because the increases in W from this point forward improve the odds of being in a successor coalition faster than they decrease the value of private goods. As the probability of being in a successor coalition improves and policy switches away from private and toward public goods, the loyalty norm is weakened and so the incumbent must try harder, spending more to satisfy her supporters. The precise location of the turning point in the figure depends on all of the parameters in our model, but the general shape is robust and worth noting. Later we test whether the shape of this function is observed in our data, and we draw out the implications this function has for the occurrence of coups d'état and for the conditions under which large-coalition democracy is "locked in" as a long-term, stable form of government. The latter question, taken up empirically in chapter 8, represents, we believe, an important novel implication of the selectorate theory for democratic stability (Przeworski 2001).

Selectorate size also influences total expenditures on public and private goods. As S increases leaders reduce their expenditures (other than for their own discretionary purposes), although the strength of this relationship depends heavily on the size of the winning coalition. Selectorate size does not influence the relative importance of public or private goods in determining the policy mix that the incumbent provides, but it does help determine the risk of exclusion from future coalitions.

Remember that the probability of inclusion in the long-term coalition of the challenger is equal to W/S, and so as S increases, each individual's chance of gaining access to future private goods declines. When W is large most rewards are provided via public goods and so exclusion from a future coalition is not too costly. Under this circumstance, an increase in S has only a modest effect on loyalty. When W is small, more rewards are private in nature and the relative difference in welfare between those inside and those outside the coalition is large. In this case, exclusion from future coalitions is extremely costly and, therefore, increasing S sharply increases loyalty, allowing leaders to skim off more resources for themselves.

Increasing the selectorate size strictly diminishes the welfare of the incumbent coalition. Increasing S reduces the effort the incumbent needs to make in order to maintain the support of her coalition. This is true because an increase in the selectorate size diminishes the chances that current members of the winning coalition would be in a successor coalition. This operates to strengthen their loyalty to the incumbent, which reduces the amount the incumbent must spend to keep them loyal.

The size of government revenues and the relative patience of the citizens also influence the effort level of the incumbent. The more resources that are available, the greater the challenger's best credible offer and, therefore, the more the incumbent must offer to meet the conditions for retaining incumbency. Consequently, when the resource pool is larger, so is the total expenditure on the optimal mix of private and public goods. This implication—that rich societies enjoy higher levels of policy provisions from the government than do poor societies—is unsurprising. More surprising is the result that the more patient citizens are (i.e., the larger

δ is), the lower the level of policy provisions they receive. This result is best explained by reference to the criteria for sustaining incumbency.

In equilibrium, the incumbent spends an optimal amount of resources on the coalition in each period. In making his best credible bid for power, the challenger offers to spend everything in the first period. Of course in subsequent periods, if he comes to power he behaves as the current incumbent does, spending the same amount of resources on a coalition of size W. When individuals choose between leaders, they are uncertain as to whether they will be included in the challenger's postcompetition coalition. Therefore, the incumbent can credibly promise more future payoffs than can the challenger. The discount factor weights the importance of these future payoffs relative to payoffs today. When citizens are patient (high δ), the incumbent's inherent advantage in providing future private goods weighs heavily in a current supporter's calculations. This means that in the current period the incumbent can offer only a low level of reward relative to what the challenger is currently offering and still look like the more attractive leader. When citizens are impatient (low δ), heavily discounting future rewards as compared to current ones, incumbents must spend more to survive in office and so can keep less for themselves. In this circumstance, the incumbent's inherent advantage in providing private goods in the future is worth less relative to rewards in the current period. As a result, the incumbent must spend more resources in order to match the challenger's offer. This deduction stands in contrast to much of the literature on cooperation and regimes (Axelrod 1984, 1986), while paralleling an important result by Robert Powell (1999) that shows when costs endured today presage larger benefits later, patient decision makers are less likely to choose a cooperative path than are impatient decision makers. In our case, the cost endured in the short term is a reduced quantity of private goods by remaining loyal rather than defecting. The long-term benefit is the future stream of private goods gained through continued loyalty to the incumbent.

Further Implications

We touched on several implications of our model as we developed our argument. Here we present and discuss briefly the implications of the model with respect to the tenure of leaders, the provision of public policy and private goods, economic growth, and corruption.

The Tenure of Leaders

Our model, as modified in chapter 7, indicates that leaders in systems with small winning coalitions and large selectorates (e.g., autocracies) find it easier to survive in office after the initial transition period than do leaders of systems with large coalitions and large selectorates (e.g., democracies). This is true even though small-coalition leaders are expected to produce less public welfare than their large-coalition counterparts. Further, in the context of our model we can account for finer differences between the survival of leaders in democratic and autocratic regimes. The difference in survivability between autocracy and democracy stems from differences in the relative importance of private and public goods. In large winning-coalition systems, leaders must compete over the provision of public goods. Although the incumbent is privileged in the supply of private goods, her advantage is small since political competition centers around the ability to produce public goods. Democratic politics becomes an "arms-race" competition over who, in the minds of the electorate, has the best public policy ideas.

In contrast, in autocratic systems the small winning-coalition size means political competition is focused on the provision of private goods. Once the incumbent has identified the members of the selectorate for whom she has the highest affinity, she finds satisfying the requirements of incumbency relatively easy. She can credibly commit to include these individuals in every future coalition, while the challenger can offer them access to future private goods only probabilistically. For the purposes of parsimonious modeling we assume affinities are fully revealed when a new leader arises. Yet realistically the learning process takes years. Until it is over, members of the winning coalition cannot be certain of inclusion in future coalitions. This implies that initially an autocrat's coalition is relatively unstable since members fear exclusion. However, as the learning process continues, it becomes increasingly unlikely that supporters will be replaced, and so their fear of exclusion diminishes and the loyalty norm strengthens. In contrast to democrats, for whom the hazard rate always remains high, the risk of removal from office theoretically diminishes over time for autocratic leaders.

Within democratic regimes, we can make some further distinctions. In electoral systems in which the chief executive is chosen more or less by national vote, as in many presidential systems, the coalition is larger than in a comparably sized single-member district parliamentary system. So, the hazard rate for survival should also be higher in presidential systems than it is in parliamentary systems with single-member districts. These parliamentary systems should induce less loyalty than in autocracies, but more loyalty among coalition members than is true in presidential systems. It remains for later chapters to see whether these implications for political survival are borne out.

The Provision of Public Policy and Private Goods

Our main deductive predictions relate to the quantity of public policy and private goods provided by government. In particular, because polities such as democracies rely on relatively large winning coalitions, they must provide more public goods than those that depend on small winning coalitions. Indeed, David Lake and Matthew Baum (2001) extensively survey the literature on this issue and examine a wide variety of public policy issues. They conclude that democrats provide significantly more public goods than autocrats. Gary Cox's (1987) study of nineteenth-century British electoral reform provides a specific illustration. At the beginning of that century many electoral districts were small, some districts having only a handful of voters. In fact, fifty constituencies had fewer than fifty voters. The major business of the House of Commons at that time was bills proposed by private members on behalf of specific constituents. Much of the population remained unrepresented. By the end of the century, various reform acts, through redistricting of rotten boroughs and the enlargement of the franchise, produced large, much more evenly sized, electoral districts. The effects on British politics were profound. With more equal, larger districts, members of Parliament could no longer adequately reward individual constituents with private goods. Both bribery of the electorate and private members' bills declined, to be replaced by government-initiated public policy. In chapter 5 we will probe these conclusions further to see whether the size of the winning coalition is a major feature of democracy that helps to account for important public-goods provisions beyond those explained by other characteristics of democratic polities.

Economic Growth

The policy differences between alternative institutional configurations carry implications about economic growth. We will show that, consistent with much of the literature, aspects of democracy that are independent of coalition size do not help explain differences in growth rates, but that the size of the winning coalition contributes to such an explanation.[12] If our expectation is borne out, we can conclude that definitive features of democracy other than the winning-coalition size act to partially nullify the benefits for growth implied by having a large winning coalition. Such a result could have important implications for policies oriented toward encouraging institutional, political changes in countries with poor records of growth.

Since we expect low tax rates and the provision of such public goods as protection of property rights, the rule of law, transparency, protection of human rights, national security, and education to promote economic growth and greater national prosperity, we also expect large winning-coalition systems to be richer and to experience higher average growth (Barro 1991; Rebelo 1991; Benhabib and Spiegel 1994; Hanushek and Kimko 2000; Przeworski et al. 2000; Easterly 2001). We also anticipate that systems with larger winning coalitions produce higher educational levels, freer trade systems, smaller black market premiums over official exchange rates, less corruption, less kleptocracy, less oppression and repression, and better-balanced budgets than their smaller winning-coalition counterparts. Just as large coalition size is expected to promote prosperity, so too is it expected to promote a peaceful, secure environment. Major types—but not all types—of violent international conflict should be a less common experience in large-coalition systems than in small-coalition systems.

Corruption

Our theory yields clear expectations with regard to corruption. Naturally, to some extent corruption persists in all polities. Yet the extent to which leaders attempt to detect and eradicate corruption depends on institutional arrangements (Campos and Root 1996). The selectorate model suggests three motives for corruption, all of which are encouraged by small winning-coalition systems. The survival of leaders in small winning-coalition systems depends on their ability to provide private goods to their supporters. To the extent that eliminating corruption and encouraging the development of institutions that promote the rule of law are public goods, leaders with small winning coalitions have few incentives to find and eliminate corruption. Hence small W encourages complacency. In addition to failing to root out corruption, leaders with small winning coalitions might endorse corruption as a way of rewarding supporters. In small-coalition systems, leaders can provide private benefits by granting supporters the right to expropriate resources for themselves. Consequently, some authoritarian leaders might encourage corrupt practices as a reward mechanism. A final form of corruption predicted by our model is kleptocracy (i.e., ruling to steal) (Grossman 1999; Fan and Grossman 2001). As discussed above, small winning coalitions and large selectorates allow leaders to syphon off resources for pet projects, which might include private bank accounts. Indeed, some, like Ferdinand Marcos or Mobutu Sese Seko, stole so much that one might say they belong in the "Haul" of Fame.

Within small-coalition settings that are coupled with a large selectorate, the extra value—through private rewards—from coalition membership as compared to exclusion from the coalition is very large. Because the value of continued coalition membership is great and loyalty to the incumbent is strong, it is easier for incumbents and coalition members to engage in oppressive and repressive measures designed to prevent others from reducing their corrupt privileges. Consequently, such systems can be expected to engage in a variety of practices contrary to the promotion and protection of civil liberties and freedom of expression.

The selectorate theory suggests, as conjectures, additional predictions about expected degrees of corruption across different types of democracy and between unitary and federal republics. As argued earlier, parliamentary systems (with single-member districts) can have smaller winning coalitions than presidential systems. They are, therefore, expected to manifest greater corruption than presidential systems, albeit still having much lower levels of corruption than would be typical for autocracies (Kunicova 2002). Holding the particular type of democracy constant (that is, the specific ratio of coalition size to selectorate size), we also expect levels of corruption to rise as one moves down the ladder from the central government to state or provincial governments and on down to city, town, and village governments. Each successive layer relies on a smaller coalition and so provides more incentives to turn to private rewards rather than public goods as the means of maintaining loyalty. That incentive may be partially offset by the central government's incentives to protect the rule of law, one of the central public goods it can be expected to provide.

Bridging from Theory to Testable Hypotheses

The selectorate theory is not sufficiently sophisticated at present to predict which specific bundle of public or private goods will be emphasized in different societies. Therefore, our predictions about specific public goods (e.g., education, national security, economic growth, low tariffs, high productivity, and so on) or private goods (e.g., high premium for black market exchange, general corruption, and so forth) are made with less confidence than our prediction that the overall quantity of public goods will increase with W and that the overall quantity of private goods will decrease with W. Further, whatever mix of goods goes into the overall bundle of coalition benefits, we predict that the value of the bundle—per capita expenditures by the government—will reflect the asymmetric, nonmonotonic swoosh function suggested in figure 3.2. We also expect that the total value of private goods will be higher in the initial period of incumbency—the transition period from one leader to another—than in subsequent years and that the overall size of the winning coalition will shrink after the transition period. All of these expectations, though made with greater or lesser confidence, are testable. They are the subject of the empirical portions of our study.

Conclusion

We have set forth a theory of how institutions influence policy and political survival.

The institutional features of the winning coalition and the selectorate influence a plethora of political phenomena, including taxation, government expenditure, choice of government policies, economic productivity, and political survival. Through the use of mathematical modeling we have rigorously shown how W and S shape politics.

The size of the winning coalition determines whether policies have a public or private focus. When the coalition is small, as is the case in a monarchy, in a junta, and in autocracies, leaders focus on providing their small number of essential supporters with private benefits. In contrast, when the coalition is large, leaders have insufficient resources to reward their supporters with high levels of private goods and so must switch to policies with a public focus if they want to survive.

Coalition size fundamentally affects the types of policies leaders enact. When W is small, members of the winning coalition (who receive private goods) are much better off than those outside the coalition who must rely exclusively on public goods, of which there are few. However, as the coalition's size increases, the differences between the welfare of these groups diminish because leaders rely more on public goods and less on private goods to reward their supporters. Combined with the loyalty norm (W/S), the size of W influences many diverse aspects of political life, such as how much the leader spends and the welfare of the winning coalition.

When W is small, its members fear the deposition of the incumbent since this jeopardizes their access to future private goods. The cost of losing this privilege is high when W is small and hence rewards are predominantly private in nature. If a challenger comes to power, he cannot credibly promise to maintain the coalition that brought him to power, preferring instead to readjust his coalition to include those with whom he shares greater affinity. This creates a risk of exclusion. This risk increases as the number of supporters a leader needs (W) diminishes and as the pool of potential supporters (S) grows. When W is small and S is large, supporters are particularly likely to be loyal since both the cost of exclusion and the risk of exclusion are high. Once established in power, leaders in such systems, which often take the form of rigged electoral systems, find it easy to stay in power and can skim off societal resources for their own aims. These leaders are able to do so because of their advantage in private-goods provision over challengers. When the value of the challenger's best possible (credible) offer is low, leaders do not need to expend many resources to match such an offer. In contrast, in large-W, large-S systems, such as democracies, leaders have little advantage in the provision of private goods since these goods are relatively unimportant contributors to overall welfare for any individual. As a result, incumbents must work hard, spending nearly all of the resources they collect, in order to match the best offer of challengers.

Institutions also create an incentive to tax, with leaders from small-coalition systems taxing at higher rates than leaders from large-coalition systems. In small-coalition systems leaders tax at close to income-maximization rates. Although this high level of appropriation discourages economic activity, the revenues enable the leader to adequately compensate her small coalition with private benefits and retain resources for herself. Such a tax policy is political suicide in a large-coalition system. Taxing at high levels discourages economic activity that residents would otherwise have undertaken. A small-coalition leader can easily compensate her supporters for these lost opportunities, but when the coalition is large it simply requires too many resources. If a large-coalition leader taxes too highly, a challenger can offer a reduced tax rate, just sufficient to provide the public goods that citizens demand and a few private goods, and can depose the incumbent. As a result, large-coalition systems encourage economic activity, and, by extension, economic growth, through their relatively low tax rates and provision of public goods. In contrast, small-coalition systems discourage productive enterprise and promote personal consumption rather than investment.

Despite the sparse, skeletal character of the selectorate theory, it generates numerous predictions about a variety of political, economic, and social phenomena. We now set out to see if these theoretically deduced claims are true.

Appendix

This appendix formally describes the game and characterizes the equilibrium discussed in chapter 3. Since we anticipate that those who read this appendix will read little of the text and vice versa, we replicate many of the points addressed in the text—although in a more concise manner.

The Model

The game is infinitely repeated, and we show only a single stage here. Payoffs in each round are discounted by a common discount factor δ.

Time Line

1. The incumbent leader picks a coalition, W_L, of size W from the members of the selectorate: $W_L \in S$.

2. A challenger is randomly chosen,[13] and then simultaneously both the incumbent and the challenger propose tax rates and policy provisions. Specifically, the challenger proposes his coalitions, $W_c \subset S$, a tax rate r_c, and a provision of x_c public and g_c private goods. The incumbent proposes a tax rate r_L, and policy provisions of x_L public and g_L private goods.

3. All selectors choose between the proposals of the challenger and the incumbent. The incumbent is removed and replaced by the challenger if and only if the challenger receives the support of at least W members of his nominated coalition (W_c) and the incumbent retains less than W supporters from within her coalition (W_L).

4. Each citizen allocates his or her resources between economically productive activities and leisure: $l_i \in [0,1]$, where l_i refers to individual i's leisure and $(1 - l_i)$ refers to their level of economic activity, which we will refer to as *labor*.

5. If the chosen leader's policy provisions are feasible, they are implemented; otherwise a caretaker policy is implemented that gives everyone in the game a reservation payoff of v_0.[14] By *feasible*, we mean that revenues are sufficient to finance the proposed policies. Specifically, assuming the incumbent leader is retained, feasibility implies

$$r_L \sum_{i \in N} (1 - l_i) - p x_L - |W_L| g_L \geq 0$$

Players receive payoffs, and the affinity preference ordering of the new leader, B—whether it is the former incumbent or the former challenger—is revealed.

Affinity

We assume the leader has a strict lexicographic preference over who is in her coalition (i.e., the same assumption made by Diermeier and Feddersen (1998)). Let B_L represent the incumbent's strict preference ordering over who she prefers in her coalition, and we refer to individuals according to their position in this ordering. For example, selector $i = 1$ is the individual for whom the incumbent has the highest affinity, and selector $i = S$ is the individual for whom the incumbent has the lowest affinity. The challenger has a similar ordering over who he wishes to include in his coalition, B_c. However, this orderings remains unknown unless the challenger comes to office. All possible preference orderings are equally likely—that is, $Pr(B_c = b) = Pr(B_c = b') = (1/S!)$ for all b, b'. Throughout we use the notation $X \backslash Y$ to refer to elements that are in set X but not in set Y, $\{i | i \in X, i \notin Y\}$.

Economic Activity, Policy Provision, and Payoffs

Each citizen chooses to allocate his or her time and resources between leisure and economic activity. If an individual chooses l_i leisure, she contributes $(1 - l_i)$ units of effort toward economic activity. This effort can be thought of quite generally as any kind of investment or economic activity, but we refer to it simply as either effort or labor. Given a tax rate of r, each individual retains $(1 - r)$ proportion of her economic activity. Hence an individual's retained level of economic rewards is $(1 - l_i)(1 - r)$. Given each individual's leisure/effort decision, the overall level of economic activity is

$$E = \sum_{i \in N} (1 - l_i)$$

and government revenues are rE. Throughout we use the subscripts L and C to associate tax rates and policies with the incumbent and challenger, respectively.

Leaders propose provisions of public and private goods. Public goods benefit all members of society, while private goods benefit only those in the leader's coalition. The cost of public-goods provision is p. Private goods have unit cost, and all members of the coalition receive the same level of private goods. Hence the size of a leader's coalition effectively acts as a price for private goods. The incumbent's cost for providing x_L public and g_L private goods, given a coalition W_L, is $M_L = px_L + |W_L|g_L$.

Citizens receive payoffs from four sources: government-provided public goods (x), government-provided private goods (g), returns from economic activity (y), and leisure (l). Each individual's utility function is $V(x,g,y,l)$, where $V(\ )$ is an additively separable, twice-differentiable function that is increasing and concave in each component. If the incumbent survives in office with policies r_L, x_L, and g_L and individual i chose leisure l_i, then i's payoff for that period is $V(x_L,(l_{WL,i})g_L,(1 - r_L)(1 - l_i),l_i)$, where $(l_{WL,i})$ is an indicator function that takes the value 1 if i is a member of W_L and is 0 otherwise.[15] In particular we focus on the following specific utility function, $V(x,g,y,l) = \sqrt{x} + \sqrt{g} + \sqrt{y} + \sqrt{l}$, and set the value of the caretaker policy as $v_0 = 0$.[16]

To reduce redundancy, we will abuse notation and exploit the additive separability of $V(\ )$, so for example we will write $V(x)$ to refer to the value of public goods without specifying the other arguments of $V(\ )$.

The incumbent leader receives a payoff of $\Psi + R_L - M_L$, where R_L represents total government revenues and M_L represents her total expenditure $(M_L = px_L + |W_L|g_L)$, if she survives in office, and 0 otherwise. $\Psi > 0$ represents the inherent value of holding office and $R_L - M_L$ is the surplus resources the incumbent can keep for her own discretion. If the challenger succeeds in coming to power, his payoff in that period is $\Psi + R_c - M_c$, where

$$R_c = r_c \sum_{i \in N}(1-l_i) \qquad \text{and} \qquad M_c = px_c + |W_c|g_c$$

In subsequent periods he becomes the incumbent. If the challenger fails to attain office his payoff is 0.

Markov Perfect Equilibrium

Initially, the game form restricts the incumbent's choice of coalition size to W. In proposition 2, we relax this assumption and show that there is no utility-improving defection for the incumbent, who consequently always prefers the minimal coalition of $|W_L| = W$. In each period the strategy of the incumbent is a choice of coalition: $W_L \subset S$. On observing this choice of coalition, the challenger's strategy is a choice of coalition, $W_c \subset S$, a tax rate, $r_c \in [0,1]$, a public-goods provision, $x_c \in \Re^+$, and a private-goods provision, $g_c \in \Re^+$. The incumbent's strategy is a tax rate, $r_L \in [0,1]$, a public-goods provision, $x_L \in \Re^+$, and a private-goods provision, $g_L \in \Re^+$. Given the announced coalition, tax rates, and policies, all selectors choose between the incumbent and the challenger. To avoid the problem of all selectors voting for the same alternative, we assume the selectors' choices are weakly undominated strategies (i.e., selectors vote as if their choice matters). Following the choice of leader, each citizen selects a leisure/effort level: $l_i \in [0,1]$.

We characterize a Markov perfect equilibrium (see Fudenberg and Tirole 1991, chap. 13) in which the incumbent survives in every period, forming the coalition W_L from her most preferred selectors in the ordering B_L—that is, $W_L = \{1, \ldots, W\}$. In this equilibrium in each period the taxation and policy provisions of the incumbent and the challenger are (r_L^*, x_L^*, g_L^*) and (r_c^*, x_c^*, g_c^*), respectively, and in each period each citizen's leisure/effort choice is l^*. In a Markov perfect equilibrium players condition their strategy on a state variable. In the current context, the state variable is the incumbent's preference ordering over selectors. Hence in addition to the standard equilibrium requirement that each player's strategy must be utility maximizing given the strategy of the other players, the Markovian assumption of MPE insists that players condition their strategies only on the state variable—the incumbent's ordering over selectors—and on no other aspect of the history of the game.

In this MPE the overall level of economic activity is $E = N(1 - l^*)$. The government's revenues are $r_L E$. Given this equilibrium, if the incumbent survives, then the continuation value (the value of the game starting in the next period) for the selectors is

$$Z_{L,i} = \frac{1}{1-\delta} V(x_L^*, (1_{\{1,\ldots,W\},i}) g_L^*, (1-r_I^*)(1-l^*), l^*)$$

where $(1_{\{1,\ldots,W\},i})$ is an indicator function that takes the value 1 if i is one of the selectors for whom L has the highest affinity defined by B_L (i.e., $i \in \{1,\ldots,W\}$) and is 0 otherwise. Since all affinity orderings are equally likely, for each selector, the probably of being one of the challenger's W highest-affinity selectors is (W/S). With the complementary probability, $(1 - (W/S))$, each selector will be excluded from the challenger's coalition in all future periods. Hence the continuation value associated with the challenger deposing the incumbent is

$$Z_{c,i} = \frac{1}{1-\delta}\left(\frac{W}{S} V(x_L^*, g_L^*, (1-r_L^*)(1-l^*), l^*)\right.$$
$$\left. + \left(1-\frac{W}{S}\right) V(x_L^*, 0, (1-r_L^*)(1-l^*), l^*)\right)$$

A key intuition for our argument arises from the result that for $i \in \{1,\ldots,W\}, Z_{L,i} > Z_{c,i}$. That is, the incumbent can credibly promise members of his coalition private goods in every future period, while the challenger can only offer future private goods probabilistically. Our analysis focuses on how the loyalty norm derived from this result affects taxation and policy provision as institutions vary. We now state our main results.

DEFINITION   The function $l = l(r)$ describes the value of l_i that satisfies the following equation:

$$-(1-r)V_y(.,.,(1-r)(1-l_i),l_i) + V_L(.,.,(1-r)(1-l_i),l_i) = 0$$

In addition,

$$\frac{dl}{dr} = \frac{V_y((1-r)(1-l)) + (1-r)(1-l)V_{yy}((1-r)(1-l))}{(1-r)^2 V_{yy}((1-r)(1-l)) + V_{ll}(l))}$$

For our specific utility function, this implies $l = 1/(2 - r)$ and $dl/dr = 1/((2 - r)^2)$.

PROPOSITION   If $W \leq (S + 1)/2$, then there exists a Markov perfect equilibrium to the game in which the equilibrium taxes and policies, (r_L^*, x_L^*, g_L^*) and (r_c^*, x_c^*, g_c^*), and leisure/effort (l^*) decision solve the following six equations (we use the labels to provide intuition as to the origin of each equation):

1. Incumbency condition (incumbent matches the challenger's best possible offer)

$$I1 = V(x_c, g_c, (1-r_c)(1-l_c), l_c) - V(x_L, g_L, (1-r_L)(1-l), l) - \delta Z_{L,i} + \delta Z_{c,i} = 0$$

where $Z_{L,i} = (1/(1 - \delta))V(x_L, g_L, (1 - r_L)(1 - l), l)$ and

$$Z_{c,i} = \frac{1}{1-\delta}\left(\frac{W}{S}V(x_L, g_L, (1-r_L)(1-l), l) \right.$$
$$\left. + \left(1 - \frac{W}{S}\right)V(x_L, 0, (1-r_L)(1-l), l)\right)$$

and l equals $l(r)$ evaluated at r_L and l_c equals $l(r)$ evaluate at r_c.

2. Budget constraint

$$I2 = r_c N(1-l) - px_c - Wg_c = 0$$

3. Incumbents optimal policy choice

$$I3 = pV_g(x_L, g_L, (1-r_L)(1-l), l) - WV_x(x_L, g_L, (1-r_L)(1-l), l) = 0$$

4. Challenger's optimal policy choice

$$I4 = pV_g(x_c, g_c, (1-r_c)(1-l_c), l_c) - WV_x(x_c, g_c, (1-r_c)(1-l_c), l_c) = 0$$

5. Incumbent's optimal tax choice

$$I5 = -\frac{dl}{dr_L}r_L N + N(1-l) + \frac{p}{V_x(x_L)}\left(\left(-(1-l) - (1-r)\frac{dl}{dr_L}\right)\right.$$
$$\left. V_y((1-r_L)(1-l)) + \frac{dl}{dr_L}V_l(l)\right) = 0$$

6. Challenger's optimal tax choice

$$16 = -\frac{dl}{dr_c} r_c N + N(1-l) + \frac{p}{V_x(x_c)}\left(\left(-(1-l)-(1-r_c)\frac{dl}{dr_c}\right)\right.$$
$$\left. V_y((1-r_c)(1-l)) + \frac{dl}{dr_c} V_l(l)\right) = 0$$

Intuition Behind Equilibrium

We believe the inherent logic behind the above proposition is straightforward, although checking all the conditions makes the proof tedious. Therefore, prior to launching into the proof we intuitively explain the logic behind the six equations above. We subsequently provide a proof of the proposition.

Using the logic of backward induction, we start with the last decision in the stage game, the choice of effort level.

Effort Level

The definition $l(r)$ ensures that, given the policies of the leader, residents all choose the optimal effort levels. The definition of $l(r)$ follows from the first-order condition from each resident's programing problem of $\max_{li \in [0,1]} V(x,g,(1-r)(1-l_i),l_i) + \delta Z_i$, where x, g, and r are the policies of the chosen leader and Z_i is i's continuation value associated with the chosen leader. Note that since i picks an effort level in each period, her continuation value is unaffected by today's effort choice. Neither is her continuation value affected by her current effort level.

Best Possible Offer by the Challenger

To attract supporters we characterize the best possible offer any potential challenger could offer a supporter. Dropping the subscript on the effort level, which is given by $l = l(r)$, the challenger's programming problem is to maximize the reward level he offers his coalition members: $\max_{rc \in [0,1], gc, xc} V(x,g,(1-r)(1-l),l) + \delta Z_{c,i}$ subject to the budget constraint that

$$R_c = r_c \sum (1-l_i) = M_c = px_c + |W_c|g_c$$

This offer represents the very best possible offer a challenger could ever credibly make. The first-order conditions for this maximization problem ensure that the challenger picks the optimal ratio of private to public goods (equation 4) and the optimal tax policy (equation 6), and does not violate the budget constraint (equation 2).

Incumbent's Policies

To ensure that no members of her coalition defect to the challenger, the incumbent must match the best possible offer of the challenger, and she does so using the policies that maximize her discretionary resources:

$$\max\nolimits_{r_L \in [0,1], g_L, x_L} r_L \sum_{i \in N} (1 - l_i) - p x_L - |W_L| g_L$$

subject to the budget constraint (which does not bind) and the constraint of matching the challenger's best possible offer $V(x_L, g_L, (1 - r_L)(1 - l), l) + \delta Z_{L,i} = V(x_c, g_c, (1 - r_c)(1 - l_c), l_c) + \delta Z_{c,i}$. If the incumbent fails to match the challenger's best offer, she is deposed. If she provides a greater level of rewards than the challenger can credibly offer, she wastes resources that she could have retained for her own discretionary use. Hence the incumbency constraint (equation 1) is satisfied with equality. Equations 3 and 5 derive from first-order conditions that ensure that in satisfying the incumbency constraint, the incumbent uses the optimal mix of private and public goods and the optimal tax rate to maximize her surplus resources.

Proof of Proposition 1   Given that the equilibrium path in all future period will be given by (r_L^*, x_L^*, g_L^*), (r_c^*, x_c^*, g_c^*), and l^*, and hence the associated continuation values $Z_{L,i}$ and $Z_{c,i}$, we characterize best responses for each player at each choice node in the current period. Given the sequential nature of moves, we work backward though the moves in the current period calculating optimal strategies for each player given how players will behave in every future period, namely, (r_L^*, x_L^*, g_L^*), (r_c^*, x_c^*, g_c^*), and l^*.

Leisure/Effort Level

Given the tax rate and policies of the leader (r, x, g), be they the incumbent or the challenger, the citizens choose a leisure level to maximize their welfare. For instance, if the incumbent is retained, then $l_i \in$ argmax $U_i(L|W_L, W_c, B_L, r_L, x_L, g_L, r_c, x_c, g_c, l_i)$. Supposing the policy is feasible, then the FOC implies

$$-(1-r_L)V_y(X_L,(1_{wL,i})g_L,(1-r_L)(1-l_i),l_i)$$
$$+V_L(X_L,(1_{wL,i})g_L,(1-r_L)(1-l_i),l_i)=0^{17}$$

We define the function $l=l(r)$ as the leisure level that satisfies this equation for a given tax rate. Note that given the additively separable utility function, l does not depend on x or g: specifically, $l=1/(2-r)$. Further, by implicit differentiation,

$$dl/dr=-V_y((1-r)(1-l))+(1-r)(1-l)V_{yy}((1-r)(1-l))\big/(1-r)^2$$
$$V_{yy}((1-r)(1-l))+V_{ll}(l)=1\big/(2-r)^2$$

Thus far we have assumed the policy is feasible if all citizen-choice leisure $l_i=1$. If $rN(1-l)-px-gW+l<0$, then the strategy $l_i=l(r)$ is a best response for all citizens since no single deviation makes the policy feasible. If $rN(1-l)-px-gW<0<rN(1-l)-px-gW+(1-l)$, then the citizens' strategy is for $N-1$ citizens to choose $l_i=l(r)$ leisure and a single citizen to choose leisure $l_i=r(N-1)(1-l)-px-gW-1$. For convenience, suppose that the individual who contributes extra effort is an element of $W_L \cap \{1,\dots,W\} \cap W_c$ if this set is nonempty and is a member of $W_L \cap W_c$ otherwise.

This defines the leisure/effort choice for any set of tax rates and policies.

Selectorate's Choice

If the incumbent survives, then i's payoff is

$$U_i(L|W_L,W_c,B_L,r_L,x_L,g_L,r_c,x_c,g_c,l_i)=$$

$V(x_L,(1-r_L)(1-l_i)+g_L(1_{w_L,i}),l_i)+\delta Z_{L,i}$	if	$r_L\sum_{j\in N}(1-l_j)-px_L-|W_L|g_L\geq 0$
$v_0+\delta Z_{L,i}$	if	$r_L\sum_{j\in N}(1-l_j)-px_L-|W_L|g_L<0$

If the challenger defeats the incumbent, then i receives

$$U_i(C|W_L,W_c,B_L,r_L,x_L,g_L,r_c,x_c,g_c,l_i)=$$

$V(x_c,(1-r_c)(1-l_i)+g_c(1_{w_c,i}),l_i)+\delta Z_{c,i}$	if	$r_L\sum_{j\in N}(1-l_j)-px_c-|W_c|g_c\geq 0$
$v_0+\delta Z_{c,i}$	if	$r_L\sum_{j\in N}(1-l_j)-px_c-|W_c|g_c<0$

Let $\Xi_i(W_L,W_c,B_L,r_L,x_L,g_L,r_c,x_c,g_c,l_i)$ be selector i's strategy mapping taxes, coalitions, affinities, and policies into a choice for either the incumbent or the challenger. Undominated best responses require i chooses L if

$$U_i(L|W_L,W_c,B_L,r_L,x_L,g_L,r_c,x_c,g_c,l_i) > U_i(C|W_L,W_c,B_L,r_L,x_L,g_L,$$
$$r_c,x_c,g_c,l_i)$$

and i chooses C if

$$U_i(C|W_L,W_c,B_L,r_L,x_L,g_L,r_c,x_c,g_c,l_i) > U_i(L|W_L,W_c,B_L,r_L,x_L,g_L,r_c,$$
$$x_c,g_c,l_i)$$

To avoid the need to introduce an epsilon solution concept, we split indifferences on the basis of whether C spends all his possible resources. Hence if

$$U_i(L|W_L,W_c,B_L,r_L,x_L,g_L,r_c,x_c,g_c,l_i) > U_i(C|W_L,W_c,B_L,r_L,x_L,g_L,r_c,$$
$$x_c,g_c,l_i)$$

or

$$[U_i(L|W_L,W_c,B_L,r_L,x_L,g_L,r_c,x_c,g_c,l_i) = U_i(C|W_L,W_c,B_L,r_L,x_L,$$
$$g_L,r_c,x_c,g_c,l_i) \quad \text{and} \quad M_c = r_c E]$$

then

$$\Xi_i(W_L,W_c,B_L,r_L,x_L,g_L,r_c,x_c,g_c,l_i) = L$$

Otherwise i supports

$$C, \Xi_i(W_L,W_c,B_L,r_L,x_L,g_L,r_c,x_c,g_c,l_i) = C$$

Challenger's Coalition, Tax, and Policy Choices

To depose the incumbent, the challenger needs to win the support of at least W selectors from his coalition (W_c) and must attract a sufficient number of the incumbent's supporters that she retains the support of less than W members of her coalition. Specifically, (1) $|\{i \in W_c| \Xi_i(W_L,W_c,B_L,r_L,x_L,g_L,r_c,x_c,g_c,l_i) = C\}| = W$, and (2) $|\{i \in W_L| \Xi_i(W_L,W_c,B_L,r_L,x_L,g_L,r_c,x_c,g_c,l_i) = L\}| < W$.

Given the incumbent's coalition, W_L, and supposing the incumbent's strategy is r_L,x_L,g_L and the citizens' leisure are l_i, we characterize best responses for the challenger.

LEMMA

A. Coalition Choice

Case 1 If $W_L = \{1, \ldots, W\}$ then W_c contains one individual, k, from W_L and any other $W - 1$ individuals: W_c such that $|W_c| = W$ and there is some $k \in W_L \cap W_c$.

Case 2 If $|W_L \cap \{1, \ldots, W\}| < W$ then W_c ($|W_c| = W$) contains at least one individual, k, from $W_L \backslash \{1, \ldots, W\}$ and $W - 1$ other individuals none of whom are in $W_L \cap \{1, \ldots, W\}$ and none of whom are in $\{1, \ldots, W\} \backslash W_L$ if for $j \in W_L \backslash \{1, \ldots, W\}$ and $j' \in \{1, \ldots, W\} \backslash W_L$, $U_j(L|.) < U_{j'}(L|.)$.

B. Tax and Policy Choice

If feasible, then the challenger's strategy is $(r_c, x_L, g_L) \in \text{argmax}_{rc \in [0,1],}$ $_{xL \in \Re+, gL \in \Re+} r_c N(1 - l_i) - px_c - Wg_c$ subject to $U_k(L|W_L, W_c, B_L, r_L,$ $x_L, g_L, r_c, x_c, g_c, l_i) = U_k(C|W_L, W_c, B_L, r_L, x_L, g_L, r_c, x_c, g_c, l_i)$, where individual k is the selector identified in A above. If no such feasible strategy exists, then

$$(r_c, x_L, g_L) \in \text{argmax}_{rc \in [0,1], xL \in \Re+, gL \in \Re+}$$
$$U_k(C|W_L, W_c, B_L, r_L, x_L, g_L, r_c, x_c, g_c, l_i)$$

such that the policies are feasible.

Proof We start with the observation that given the strategy profile (l_i, x_L, g_L, r_L), either the challenger cannot depose the incumbent or the constraint

$$U_k(L|W_L, W_c, B_L, r_L, x_L, g_L, r_c, x_c, g_c, l_i) = U_k(C|W_L, W_c, B_L, r_L, x_L, g_L, r_c,$$
$$x_c, g_c, l_i)$$

binds for some individual $i \in S$. In the former case any strategy, including those described, are best responses. The latter case is true, since if it were not true the challenger could always reduce his expenditure and still defeat the incumbent. Therefore we focus on the latter case and characterize best responses for the challenger to any policy provision by the incumbent. This is more than required, since we only need to show that C's strategy is a best response to L's equilibrium strategy. Since the challenger's payoff is

$$\psi + r_c \sum_{i \in N} (1 - l_i) - px_c - |W_c| g_c$$

if he deposes the incumbent and 0 otherwise, his programming problem is

$$\max\nolimits_{W_c \subset S, r_c \in [0,1], x_L \in \Re_+, g_L \in \Re_+} \psi + r_c \sum_{i \in N} (1 - l_i) - px_c - |W_c|g_c$$

subject to (1) $|\{i \in W_c| \ \Xi_i(W_L, W_c, B_L, r_L, x_L, g_L, r_c, x_c, g_c, l_i) = C\}| = W$, and (2) $|\{i \in W_L| \ \Xi_i(W_L, W_c, B_L, r_L, x_L, g_L, r_c, x_c, g_c, l_i) = L\}| < W$. Note the first constraint implies $|W_c| = W$. Since $|W_L| = W$, to satisfy the first constraint the challenger needs to attract the support of at least one member of W_L.

First we show that the constraint $U_i(L|.) = U_i(C|.)$ does not bind only for $i \in W_c$, nor does it bind only for some $j \in W_L$. Suppose the challenger forms coalition W_c', with policies (r_c, x_c, g_c), such that constraint $U_i(L|.) = U_i(C|.)$ binds for some set of individuals A. If A such that $i \in A$ implies $i \notin W_c$, then there exists another coalition W_c'' that differs from W_c' in that $|A|$ members of the original coalition are replaced by A. If C implements the same policies (r_c, x_c, g_c), then all $i \in A$ who were previously indifferent between L and C now prefer C (strictly prefer providing $g_c > 0$). But since the constraint $U_i(L|.) = U_i(C|.)$ is relaxed, C can reduce expenditure. Hence either $g_c = 0$, or the constraint $U_i(L|.) = U_i(C|.)$ binds for some $i \in W_c$. Given the interior solution assumption, $g_c > 0$, so $U_i(L|.) = U_i(C|.)$ binds for some $i \in W_c$. Repeating this proof by contradiction with $j \in A$ implies $j \notin W_L$ proves $U_j(L|.) = U_j(C|.)$ binds for some $j \in W_L$.

Second, for any strategy profile (r_L, x_L, g_L), $U_i(L|W_L, W_c, B_L, r_L, x_L, g_L, r_c, x_c, g_c, l_i)$ is greatest for $i \in W_L \cap \{1, \dots, W\}$, and least for $i \notin W_L \cup \{1, \dots, W\}$. The ordering for the remaining possibilities $i \in W_L \backslash \{1, \dots, W\}$ and $i \in \{1, \dots, W\} \backslash W_L$ depends on the precise parameters. Suppose $W_L = \{1, \dots, W\}$ (case 1). To satisfy the second constraint (i.e., leave L with fewer than W supporters), C includes $k \in W_L \cap \{1, \dots, W\}$ in his coalition. The argument follows directly from above: If k were excluded from W_c, then C could substitute some member of this coalition for k and then reduce expenditure. Given that $k \in W_L \cap \{1, \dots, W\}$, then $U_i(L|.) = U_k(L|.)$ for $i \in W_L$, for all W_L that include k. Since $U_i(C|.)$ is the same for all $i \in W_c$, if $\Xi_k(W_L, W_c, B_L, r_L, x_L, g_L, r_c, x_c, g_c, l_i) = C$, then $\Xi_i(W_L, W_c, B_L, r_L, x_L, g_L, r_c, x_c, g_c, l_i) = C$ for $i \in W_c$, for all W_c that include k.

Suppose $|W_L \cap \{1, \dots, W\}| < W$ (case 2), then $i \in W_c$ implies $i \notin W_L \cap \{1, \dots, W\}$. Suppose not: C forms a coalition W_c' with policy provisions

(r_c, x_c, g_c) such that $\{i \in S : i \in W_L \cap \{1, \ldots, W\} \cap W_c)\} \neq \varnothing$. Next consider the alternative coalition, W_c'', constructed as follows: W_c'' contains $W_L \backslash \{1, \ldots, W\}$ plus $W - |W_L \backslash \{1, \ldots, W\}|$ individuals from $S \backslash \{1, \ldots, W\}$. Since $W \leq ((S+1)/2)$, such a coalition can always be formed. Since $\max_{i \in WC'} U_i(L|.)$ $> \max_{i \in WC''} U_i(L|.)$, forming coalition W_c'' enables C to lower his expenditure and still depose the incumbent. Hence $W_L \cap \{1, \ldots, W\} \cap W_c$ $= \varnothing$.

Third, the above results show C forms a coalition of size W, which includes the individual $k \in W_L$ with the lowest value for $U_i(L|.)$ for the individuals within W_L. If k prefers C to L, then so do all other members of W_c, and hence C receives the support of W members of W_c and L is left without W supporters from W_L. Hence C's programing problem reduces to attracting individual k. This implies the programing problem in B.

The challenger's program is $\max_{rc,xc,gc} R - M_c = r_c E - p x_c - W g_c$ subject to

$$U_k(C|W_L, W_c, B_L, r_L, x_L, g_L, r_c, x_c, g_c, l_i, k) - U_k(L|W_L, W_c, B_L, r_L, x_L, g_L, r_c, x_c, g_c, l_i, k) = 0$$

and

$$r_c \sum (1 - l(r_c)) - p x_c - W g_c = 0$$

We start by examining the condition when the first constraint alone binds. Forming a Lagrangian,

$$L = r_c \sum (1 - l(r_c)) - p x_c - W g_c + \lambda(V(x_c, g_c, (1 - r_c)(1 - l_k), l_k) + \delta Z_{c,i} - U_i(L|.))$$

the first-order conditions are

$$L_{x_c} = -p + \lambda V_x(x_c) = 0$$

$$L_{g_c} = -W + \lambda V_g(g_c) = 0$$

$$L_\lambda = V(x_c, g_c, (1 - r_c)(1 - l_i), l_i) + \delta Z_{c,i} - V(x_L, g_L, (1 - r_L)(1 - l_i), l_i) - \delta Z_{L,i}$$
$$= 0$$

and

$$L_{rc} = N(1-l) - r_c N \frac{dl}{dr_c} + \lambda\left(\left(-(1-l) - \frac{dl}{dr_c}(1-r_c)\right)V_y((1-r_c)(1-l))\right)$$
$$+ \lambda \frac{dl}{dr_c} V_l(l)$$

if $r_c N(1 - l) - px_c - |W_c|g_c \geq 0$ and $L_{rc} < 0$

if $r_c N(1-l) - px_c - |W_c|g_c + l \geq 0 > r_c N(1-l) - px_c - |W_c|g_c$

The FOC L_{rc} requires further explanation. If $r_c N(1 - l) - px_c - |W_c|g_c = 0$, then should the challenger come to power, each citizen will do $(1 - l)$ work. However, given the citizens' strategy, above, the challenger can stretch the budget constraint by l, since rather than accept the caretaker policies, a single citizen forgoes her leisure (l) to make C's policies feasible. This occurs when $r_c N(1 - l) - px_c - |W_c|g_c + l \geq 0 > r_c N(1 - l) - px_c - |W_c|g_c$. However, since the citizen who undertakes this extra work is the selector critical to the deposition of the incumbent, and giving up leisure makes her worse off, the challenger prefers not to stretch the budget constraint.

Rearranging these equations implies *I4* and *I6*. These equations characterize optimal tax rates and policies for the challenger that allow him to depose the incumbent.

Incumbent's Tax and Policy Choices

We define r_c, x_c, g_c as the challenger's best responses as described in lemma 1, which, if C deposed L, would provide members of W_c with a payoff of $U_i(C|.) = V(x_c, g_c, (1 - r_c)(1 - l_i), l_i) + \delta Z_{c,i}$. Given $\Xi_i(W_L, W_c, B_L, r_L, x_L, g_L, r_c, x_c, g_c, l_i)$, provided L offers payoffs larger than this (or equal to this if $r_c E - px_c - Wg_c = 0$) to all her coalition members, then she survives. Let k represent the individual in W_L with the lowest value for $U_i(L|.)$. This is a member of $W_L\backslash\{1, \ldots, W\}$ if this set is nonempty and is a member of $W_L = \{1, \ldots, W_L\}$ otherwise.

The incumbent's programming problem is

$$\max r_L \sum (1 - l(r_L)) - px_L - |W_L|g_L$$

subject to

$$V(x_c, g_c, (1-r_c)(1-l_i), l_i) + \delta Z_{c,k} - V(x_L, g_L, (1-r_L)(1-l_i), l_i) - \delta Z_{L,k} = 0$$
$$\text{and} \qquad r_c E - px_c - Wg_c = 0$$

This constraint can be rewritten as $V(x_L, g_L, (1 - r_L)(1 - l_i), l_i) + \delta Z_{L,i} - v - \delta Z_{c,i} = V(x_L, g_L, (1 - r_L)(1 - l_i), l_i) + Y = 0$

where $v = V(x_c, g_c, (1 - r_c)(1 - l_i), l_i)$ when $r_c N(1 - l(r_c)) - p x_c - W g_c = 0$.

The appropriate Lagrangian is

$$K = r_L N(1 - l(r_L)) - p x_L - W g_L + \tau(V(x_L, g_L, (1 - r_L)(1 - l_i), l_i) + Y)$$

which implies the following first-order conditions:[18]

$$K_{xL} = -p + \tau V_x(x_L, g_L, (1 - r_L)(1 - l_i), l_i) = 0,$$
$$K_{gL} = -W + \tau V_g(x_L, g_L, (1 - r_L)(1 - l_i), l_i) = 0,$$
$$K_{rL} = N(1 - l) - r_L N(dl/dr_L) + \tau[-(1 - l)V_y((1 - r_L)(1 - l)) - (1 - r_L)(dl/dr_L)$$
$$V_y((1 - r_L)(1 - l)) + (dl/dr_L)V_L(l)] = 0, \qquad \text{and}$$
$$K_\tau = V(x_L, g_L, (1 - r_L)(1 - l_i), l_i) + Y = 0.$$

Therefore $\tau = (p/V_x(x_L, g_L, (1 - r_L)(1 - l_i), l_i))$ and so K_{xL} and K_{gL} imply

$$I3 = p V_g(x_L, g_L, (1 - r_L)(1 - l), l) - W V_x(x_L, g_L, (1 - r_L)(1 - l), l) = 0$$

K_{rL} implies

$$I5 = -(dl/dr)r_L N + N(1 - l) + (p/V_x(x_L))((-(1 - l) - (1 - r)(dl/dr))V_y)$$
$$((1 - r_L)(1 - l) + (dl/dr)V_L(l)) = 0$$

and K_τ implies

$$I1 = V(x_c, g_c, (1 - r_c)(1 - l), l) - V(x_L, g_L, (1 - r_L)(1 - l), l) - \delta Z_{L,i} + \delta Z_{c,i} = 0$$
$$\text{and} \qquad I2 = r_c N(1 - l) - p x_c - W g_c = 0$$

Incumbent's Choice of Coalition

The incumbent chooses $W_L = \{1, \ldots, W\}$. Since $Z_{L,i}$ is greater for members of $\{1, \ldots, W\}$ than other selectors, it is easier for the incumbent to maintain the support of these rather than other selectors. Hence the strategies (r_L, x_L, g_L), (r_c, x_c, g_c), and l_i are best responses given the strategies of every player. Thus there exists a MPE in which the incumbent survives in every period and in which the equilibrium policies satisfy equations $I1$ through $I7$.   QED.

Limiting Cases

In the chapter we calculate optimal tax rates and policies for a numerical example. Here we derive the corresponding policies for two limiting cases, which we will refer to as the revenue-maximizing scheme and the utilitarian welfare-maximizing policies. These extreme cases represent the limiting behavior. As coalition size shrinks, leaders' choices tend toward revenue maximizing. In contrast, as W grows, policies move toward utilitarian welfare maximizing.

1. Revenue-maximizing case
Since $l(r)$ is increasing in r, then the revenue-maximizing program is $\max_{r \in [0,1]} R(r) = rN(1 - l) = rN(1 - (1/(2 - r)))$. Hence the revenue-maximizing tax rate is $r = 2 - \sqrt{2} \approx 0.58579$.

2. Utilitarian welfare-maximizing case
$\max_{i \in N} V(x,g,(1 - r)(1 - l),l)$ subject to the budget constraint. The solution is to have a coalition of size N, and $\max V(x,g,(1 - r)(1 - l),l)$ s.t. $Nr(1 - l) - xp - Ng = 0$.

For the numeric example of $N = 100,000$, $p = 10,000$, this implies a tax rate of $r = 0.508412$, public-goods provision of $x = 1.52327$, and private-goods provision of $g = 0.01523$, which provides each citizen with a welfare level of 2.57893.

Robustness

The key to the equilibrium is that L picks the same set of W individuals in each period. Hence there are $S!/(W!(S - W)!)$ related equilibria, each corresponding to a different choice of W selectors. However, we focus only on the focal coalition of L picking her most preferred selectors ($\{1, \ldots, W\}$).

Nonconstructive Deposition Rule

Our model assumes the challenger can only depose the incumbent if he attracts sufficient members of the incumbent's coalition and forms a coalition of W supporters. We refer to such a deposition rule as a constructive vote of no confidence deposition since it requires the specification of a successor coalition. One might legitimately argue that deposition only requires the removal of the incumbent's supporters and not the constructive aspect. Under such a nonconstructive deposition rule, we conjecture that a series of equilibria exist in which the incumbent forms a coalition of size $|W_L| > W$, and chooses the optimal tax and policy provisions given a coalition of this size. In response the challenger forms a coalition of size $|W_L| - W + 1$, providing the highest possible rewards to this coalition given the budget constraint. We conjecture that the equilibrium policies under such conditions satisfy the following equations, similar to those specified in proposition 1:[19]

1. Incumbency condition
$H1 = V(x_c,g_c,(1 - r_c)(1 - l),l) - V(x_L,g_L,(1 - r_L)(1 - l_i),l_i) - \delta Z_{L,i} + \delta Z_{c,i} = 0$, where $Z_{L,i} = (1/(1 - \delta))V(x_L,g_L,(1 - r_L)(1 - l),l)$ and $Z_{c,i} = (1/(1 - \delta))(((|W_L|/S)V(x_L,g_L,(1 - r_L)(1 - l),l) + (1 - (|W_L|/S))V(x_L,0,(1 - r_L)(1 - l),l))$.

2. Budget constraint
$H2 = r_c N(1 - l) - px_c - (|W_L| - W + 1)g_c = 0$

3. Incumbent's optimal policy choice
$H3 = pV_g(x_L,g_L,(1 - r_L)(1 - l),l) - |W_L|V_x(x_L,g_L,(1 - r_L)(1 - l),l) = 0$

4. Challenger's optimal policy choice
$H4 = pV_g(x_c,g_c,(1 - r_c)(1 - l_i),l_i) - (|W_L| - W + 1)V_x(x_c,g_c,(1 - r_c)(1 - l),l) = 0$

5. Incumbent's optimal tax choice
$H5 = -(dl/dr_L)r_L N + N(1 - l) + (p/(V_x(x_L)))((-(1 - l) - (1 - r)(dl/dr_L))V_y((1 - r_L)(1 - l)) + (dl/dr_L)V_L(l)) = 0$

6. Challenger's optimal tax choice
$H6 = -(dl/dr_c)r_c N + N(1 - l) + (p/(V_x(x_c)))((-(1 - l) - (1 - r_c)(dl/dr_c)V_y((1 - r_c)(1 - l)) + (dl/dr_c)V_L(l)) = 0$

Oversized Coalitions

In the initial game form we restricted L's coalition choice to size W. In the following proposition we derive sufficient conditions to ensure that even if this restriction were dropped, L never benefits from adding additional members to her coalition. We consider the modified game where at stage 1 L's decision is whether to add addition members of the selectorate to the coalition $\{1, \ldots ,W\}$.

Define $v(w,a)$ as the best possible offer that a leader can make to a coalition of size w that leaves a budget surplus of a—that is, $v(w,a) = \max_{x,g,r} V(x,g,(1 - l)(1 - r),l)$ subject to $Nr(1 - l) - xp - wg = a$. Hence on the equilibrium path the challenger's greatest possible offer is $v(w,0)$. Define $u(w,a)$ as the payoff from receiving the public but not the private goods associated with the policies of $v(w,a)$. Define the budget surplus associated with providing a coalition of size w a reward level of q as $K(w,q) = \max_{r,x,g} rN(1 - l) - xp - gw$ subject to $V(x,g,(1 - l)(1 - r),l) = q$.

PROPOSITION 2   In the modified game, either of the following conditions is sufficient to ensure that the incumbent never benefits from adding additional members to her coalition:

1. $K(W,(v(W,0) + \delta(Z_{c,i} - Z_{L,i}))) = K(S,(v(S - W + 1,0) + \delta(Z_{c,i} - Z_{L,i})))$, where $i \in \{1, \dots, W\}$.

2. There exists x_c, g_c, and r_c such that $r_c N(1 - l) - px_c - Wg_c = 0$ $V(x_c, g_c, (1 - r_c)(1 - l), l) = v(2W, k) + \delta(Z_{c,i} - Z_{L,i})$ for $i \in \{1, \dots, W\}$ and $V(x_c, 0, (1 - r_c)(1 - l), l) = v(2W, k) + \delta(Z_{c,j} - Z_{L,j})$ for $j \notin \{1, \dots, W\}$, where $k = K(W, v(W,0) + \delta(Z_{c,i} - Z_{L,i}))$.

Proof of Proposition 2   Suppose $|W_L| < 2W$. Deposition requires that the challenger form a coalition of size W, and attract enough of L's supporters that L is left without W supporters. Suppose C plays the strategy described above in proposition 1, forming W_c, which includes $k \in \{1, \dots, W\} \cap W_L$ and additional members of W_L. Given the results in proposition 1, if k supports C, then so do all other members in $W_c \cap W_L$ and hence $|W_c| = W$ is sufficient to ensure both conditions for deposition. Providing $|W_L| < 2W$, C does not need to enlarge his coalition to counter L's oversizing of her coalition. Since $K(w,q)$ is decreasing in w, enlarging her coalition, when it does not force C to alter his coalition or policies, harms L's welfare.

Suppose $|W_L| \geq 2W$. If L remains on the equilibrium path described in proposition 1, her payoff is $K(W,(v(W,0) + \delta Z_{c,i} - \delta Z_{L,i})) = K(W,(v(W,0) - (\delta/(1 - \delta))((W/S))V(g_L^*)))$. Unfortunately, characterizing C's best responses to oversized coalitions in a general setting is difficult. Instead we examine two possible strategies by the challenger. First, the challenger enlarges his coalition in response to increases in the incumbent's coalition. In particular, given the incumbent's coalition of size $|W_L|$, the challenger forms a coalition of size $|W_c| = |W_L| + 1 - W$. Second, the challenger does not enlarge his coalition. Instead he overproduces public goods such that members of the incumbent's immediate coalition who do not anticipate being members of future coalitions $(W_L \backslash \{1, \ldots, W\})$ prefer the challenger despite the incumbent's offer of private goods. While the challenger might have a better strategy than these, he can never do worse than play one of these strategies. We derive conditions under which the incumbent is worse off if she enlarges her coalition if the challenger plays one of these strategies. If the incumbent is worse off defecting against either of these strategies, she could do no better against the challenger's best reply. Let the incumbent's coalition be of size w.

STRATEGY 1   The challenger forms a coalition of size $|W_c| = w - W + 1$. Given this coalition, the challenger's best possible offer is $v((w - W + 1), 0)$. To match this best possible offer, the incumbent's policies leave her with a budget surplus of $K(w, (v(w - W + 1, 0) + k))$, where $k = \delta(Z_{c,i} - Z_{L,i})$, the difference in the discounted continuation values. Since $dK(w, (v(w - W + 1, 0) + k))/dw > 0$, L benefits from enlarging her coalition.[20] However, if condition 1 of proposition 2 holds, then even the largest possible coalition is suboptimal relative to a minimal winning coalition.

STRATEGY 2   Suppose the challenger plays a strategy of $|W_c| = W$ but C overproduces public goods. Specifically, the incumbent's policies satisfy $\min_{r_c, x_c, g_c} r_c N(1 - l) - p x_c - W g_c$ subject to

$$V(x_c, g_c, (1-l)(1-r_c), l) - V(x_L, g_L, (1-r_L)(1-l), l) + \delta Z_{c,i} - \delta Z_{L,i} \geq 0$$
   for $i \in \{1, \ldots, W\}$ and

$$V(x_c, 0, (1-l)(1-r_c), l) - V(x_L, g_L, (1-r_L)(1-l), l) + \delta Z_{c,j} - \delta Z_{L,j} \geq 0$$
   for $i \notin \{1, \ldots, W\}$.

Noting that $Z_{L,i} > Z_{c,i} = Z_{c,j} > Z_{L,j}$, there are two cases: (1) Only the first constraint binds. In this circumstance the surplus members of L's coalition prefer C to L, and hence increasing her coalition size can only hurt the incumbent. (2) Both constraints bind, which implies that unless C overproduces public goods (relative to the case in proposition 1 when $|W_L| = W$), then the surplus members of L's coalition support L and C cannot depose her.

Given a coalition of size w, the incumbent's maximization problem is $\max_{r_L, x_L, g} r_L N(1 - l) - p x_L - w g_L$ subject to $V(x_c, g_c, (1 - l)(1 - r_c), l) - V(x_L, g_L, (1 - r_L)(1 - l), l) + \delta Z_{c,i} - \delta Z_{L,i} = 0$.

Forming a Lagrangian for these two problems and taking the FOC yields the following set of equations in much the same manner as those derived in proposition 1. To simplify the mathematics we assume the challenger fixes his tax rate, and does not change it in response to increasing coalition size. Note that such a restriction can only hurt him and make it easier for the incumbent to survive. Hence relaxing this assumption would make it even harder for the incumbent to retain office. The FOC for these maximization problems imply the following equations:

$$J1 = V(x_L, g_L, (1-r_L)(1-l), l) - V(x_c, g_c, (1-r_c)(1-l), l) + \delta(1/(1-\delta))$$
$$(1-(W/S))V(g_L^*)$$

$$J2 = r_c E - p x_c - W g_c = 0$$

$$J3 = p V_g(x_L, g_L, (1-r_L)(1-l), l) - w V_x(x_L, g_L, (1-r_L)(1-l), l) = 0$$

$$J4 = V(x_L, g_L, (1-r_L)(1-l), l) - V(x_c, 0, (1-r_c)(1-l), l) - \delta(1/(1-\delta))$$
$$((W/S))V(g_L^*) = 0$$

$$J5 = -(dl/dr)rN + N(1-l) + (p/(V_x(x)))((-(1-l)-(1-r)(dl/dr))V_y$$
$$((1-r)(1-l)) + (dl/dr)V_L(l)) = 0$$

Equation $J1$ refer to the incumbency constraint (i.e., the equivalent of $I1$), $J2$ is the budget constraint ($I2$), $J3$ implies optimal policy choice for the incumbent ($I3$), $J4$ implies that C overproduces public goods such that surplus members of L's coalition still prefer to support the challenger rather than the incumbent, and $J5$ implies optimal tax rate for the incumbent ($I5$).

Below we calculate the partial derivative for these equations:

$$J1_{xL} = V_x(x_L) = a, J1_{gL} = Vg_L(g_L) = (w/p)V_x(x_L) = (w/p)a,$$

$$J1r_L = -((1-l)-(1-r_L)(dl/dr))V_y(\ ) + (dl/dr)V_L(\cdot) = A,$$

$$J1_{xc} = -V_x(x_c) = -b, J1_{gc} = -V_g(g_c) = -c, J1_w = 0,$$

$$J2_{xL} = 0, J2_{gL} = 0, J2_{rL} = 0, J2_{xc} = -p, J2_{gc} = -W, J2_w = 0,$$

$$J3_{xL} = -w V_{xx}(x_L) = wd, J3_{gL} = p V_{gg}(g_L) = -pf, J3_{rL} = 0, J3_{xc} = 0,$$

$$J3_{gc} = 0, J3_w = -V_x(x_L) = a,$$

$$J4_{xL} = V_x(x_L) = a, J4_{gL} = V_g(g_L) = (w/p)V_x(x_L) = (w/p)a,$$

$$J4_{rL} = -((1-l)-(1-r_L)(dl/dr))V_y(\ ) + (dl/dr)V_L(\cdot) = A,$$

$$J4_{xc} = -V_x(x_c) = -b, J4_{gc} = 0, J4_w = 0,$$

$$J5_{xL} = -\left((pV_{xx}(x))\big/((V_x(x))^2)\right)\left((-(1-l)-(1-r)(dl/dr))\right.$$
$$V_y((1-r)(1-l))+(dl/dr)V_L(l))$$
$$= -\left((pV_{xx}(x))\big/((V_x(x))^2)\right)A = ((pdA)/(a^2)), J5_{gL} = 0,$$

$$J5_{rL} = \text{SOC} = -B < 0, J5_{xc} = 0, J5_{gc} = 0, J5_w = 0$$

By Cramer's rule $dx_L/dw = -N_x/D$, where

$$D = \begin{vmatrix} J1_{xL} & J1_{gL} & J1_{rL} & J1_{xc} & J1_{gc} \\ J2_{xL} & J2_{gL} & J2_{rL} & J2_{xc} & J2_{gc} \\ J3_{xL} & J3_{gL} & J3_{rL} & J3_{xc} & J3_{gc} \\ J4_{xL} & J4_{gL} & J4_{rL} & J4_{xc} & J4_{gc} \\ J5_{xL} & J5_{gL} & J5_{rL} & J5_{xc} & J5_{gc} \end{vmatrix} = \begin{vmatrix} a & \frac{w}{p}a & A & -b & -c \\ 0 & 0 & 0 & -p & -W \\ wd & -pf & 0 & 0 & 0 \\ a & \frac{w}{p}a & A & -b & 0 \\ \frac{pdA}{a^2} & 0 & -B & 0 & 0 \end{vmatrix}$$

and

$$N_x = \begin{vmatrix} 0 & \frac{w}{p}a & A & -b & -c \\ 0 & 0 & 0 & -p & -W \\ a & -pf & 0 & 0 & 0 \\ 0 & \frac{w}{p}a & A & -b & 0 \\ 0 & 0 & -B & 0 & 0 \end{vmatrix}$$

There are similar expressions for dg_L/dw and dr_L/dw. The incumbent's payoff is $r_L N(1-l) - px_L - wg_L$, which is decreasing in w since $d(r_L N(1-l) - px_L - wg_L)/dw = acpwAd((-Na + Nal + Nar_L(1/(1-\text{r}_L)^2) - pA)/((Ba^3cfp^2 + A^2cdfp^3 + Ba^3cdw^2))) - g_L < 0$.

Therefore, if the challenger plays strategy 2, then as L increases her coalition size she reduces her payoff. Hence, if against strategy 2 defecting to coalition of size $|W_L| = 2W$ reduces L's payoff, then so does defection to any larger coalition. Suppose the incumbent forms a coalition of size $2W$ and proposes retaining the equilibrium budget surplus, k—that is, $k = K(W, v(W,0) + \delta(Z_{c,i} - Z_{L,i}))$, where $Z_{L,i} - Z_{c,i} = (1/(1-\delta))(1 - (W/S))v(g_L^*)$ for $i \in \{1, \ldots, W\}$ and $Z_{L,i} - Z_{c,i} = ((-1)/(1-d\delta))((W/S))V(g_L^*)$ for $i \notin \{1, \ldots, W\}$. If there exists x_c, g_c and r_c such that $r_c N(1-l) - px_c - Wg_c = 0$ $V(x_c, g_c, (1-r_c)(1-l), l) \geqslant v(2W, k) + \delta(1/(1-\delta))(1 - (W/S))v(g_L^*)$ and $V(x_c, 0, (1-r_c)(1-l), l) \geqslant v(2W, k) - (1/(1-\delta))((W/S))v(g_L^*)$, then for the incumbent, enlarging her coalition is not utility improving. This is condition 2 of proposition 2.

II POLICY CHOICE AND POLITICAL SURVIVAL

4   Institutions for Kleptocracy or Growth

In aristocracies those who wish to get to the head of affairs have great wealth at their disposal, and as the number of those by whose assistance they rise is comparatively small, the government is in a sense up for auction. In democracies those who intrigue for power are hardly ever rich, and the number of those who help to give it to them is very great. Perhaps there are just as many men for sale in democracies, but there are hardly any buyers; besides, one would have to buy too many men at the same time to attain one's end.
—Alexis de Tocqueville, *Democracy in America*

In the epigraph, de Tocqueville succinctly notes the differential opportunities to realize personal pecuniary gain afforded by autocracy and democracy, and he ties this difference directly to the number of people "by whose assistance they rise"—that is, the size of the winning coalition. There is no doubt that de Tocqueville was a careful and perceptive observer. But whether his general claim regarding greed and governance can withstand scrutiny across time and place is an empirical question. In this chapter we try to provide that scrutiny through systematic analysis. We examine the implications of the selectorate theory regarding taxation, labor, leisure, and total spending and we assess the implications of the theory regarding personal income, economic growth, and kleptocracy, one form of the venality of concern to de Tocqueville. In the next chapter we turn our focus to the theory's predictions about decisions to spend on public and private goods and the implications selection institutions have for corruption, another form of the greed that de Tocqueville attributes to autocratic rule.

According to the basic selectorate model, the size of a polity's winning coalition and selectorate contribute to the tax rate leaders impose and to the degree to which citizens apply themselves to productive labor or to leisure activity. The theory further suggests that the ratio W/S influences the magnitude of any leader's discretionary budget. Specifically, the selectorate model leads to the expectation that tax rates drop as coalition size increases and as selectorate size decreases; labor effort, and other productive activities, increase in response to a reduced tax rate. When the tax rate is high and residents anticipate any surplus they make will be expropriated, they choose not to engage in productive enterprise, preferring leisure activities instead. The smaller the ratio W/S, the greater the degree of loyalty to the incumbent that is induced and, consequently, the less the incumbent must spend to stay in power. Therefore, a small coalition combined with a large selectorate provides the foundation for

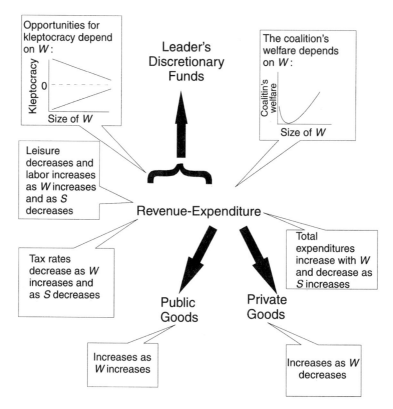

Figure 4.1
Core predictions of the selectorate theory

kleptocracy. Conversely, a large ratio of *W/S* provides a weak basis for leaders to be corrupt, especially when *W* is large. Leaders in this latter setting must work hard and dedicate the revenues they collect to improving the lot of society in general rather than spending them on personal aggrandizement.

The theory also implies that the welfare of members of the winning coalition first decreases as *W* rises from a very small size and then, following a turning point, the coalition's welfare increases as *W* gets larger. How this nonmonotonicity result influences institutional transitions, the risk of coups, and the stability of democracy is discussed in chapter 8. Figure 4.1 summarizes the main predictions of the theory. Most elements in figure 4.1 are investigated empirically in this chapter, with those pertaining to public- and private-goods spending being assessed in the next chapter.

Variations in economic growth rates is one of the more difficult topics occupying the attention of those who study political economy. The causes of variations in growth rates across space and time are undoubtedly complex and multifaceted. The selectorate theory is far from a comprehensive account of such variation, but it does have something to add to the debate. There is general agreement that rule of law, free trade, transparency in government, and low taxes contribute to high growth rates (see, among many other sources, North and Weingast 1989; Campos and Root 1996; Barro 1997; Bueno de Mesquita and Root 2000; Przeworski 2001). The core considerations—rule of law, free trade, transparency in government, and low taxes—all involve public policies that benefit everyone in society. They are all thought of as public goods in this study, and the provision of each is therefore expected to increase as the size of the winning coalition increases. Although in general we use the next chapter to explore the relationship between public goods and coalition size, here we consider the impact of these core public goods on economic growth. To the extent that W helps shape the four core public goods and W/S contributes to lower tax rates, the selectorate theory predicts that growth accompanies systems with large coalitions and a high ratio of W to S.

Also following from the selectorate theory's hypotheses about taxing and spending decisions are predictions about kleptocracy. Kleptocracy is not mere corruption, but rather the outright theft of a nation's income by its leaders.[1] The opportunity to engage in kleptocracy—while still retaining one's position as an incumbent—is determined by the difference between the revenue available to a government and the expenditures made by the government. Whatever is left over between those two quantities is money available for the discretionary use of incumbent leaders. As we argued theoretically in chapter 3, when tax rates are low, people work hard and so produce more income per capita than when tax rates are high. Unable to benefit from the fruits of their own labor, in the latter scenario people engage in leisure rather than labor. The selectorate theory predicts that tax rates are low when the size of the winning coalition is large and, relative to the coalition, the selectorate is small. The theory also predicts that leaders must spend more of the revenue they raise on providing rewards for their supporters when the ratio of the coalition to the selectorate is large, than they have to spend when W/S is small. As a result, when W/S is large, there is little opportunity for kleptocracy, government spends amply on public goods, people work hard, they produce higher incomes, and, as they continue to work productively, they are likely to stimulate greater economic growth than when W/S is small. This leads to the somewhat paradoxical inference that in societies where loyalty to incumbents by coalition members is strong (i.e., W/S is small), leaders are better able to engage in kleptocracy, reserving money against future uncertainty. They also spend less to maintain coalition support, they produce relatively poor public policy, including especially low economic growth rates, and, on average, they keep their jobs longer than when W/S is large.

Measurement Issues

Reducing any political system to only its winning coalition and selectorate obviously simplifies reality. Polities are more complex and more nuanced than such a reduction implies. We are well aware of these complexities and do not claim that the factors in the selectorate theory *alone* explain the major features of governance. However, we think it unlikely that anyone will successfully build a general theory of politics by starting with an all-inclusive model and gradually whittling down the number of variables that need to be addressed. We prefer to start with a fairly simple, skeletal view of politics, such as is described in chapter 3, and build up toward greater inclusiveness and complexity as required to account for important phenomena. Therefore, our purpose is not to maximize the variance explained for any dependent variable, but rather to assess the extent to which the selectorate model contributes meaningfully to a general understanding of a broad palette of economic, political, and social factors. We start by examining the performance of citizens in pursuing leisure or labor and of leaders in spending government revenue. We then consider the consequences of both of these factors for economic growth and individual prosperity. To explore these issues, we must first specify how we estimate the dependent and independent variables relevant for the selectorate model. In doing this we describe our data set and the procedures by which we estimate personal leisure and labor, government spending, opportunities for kleptocracy, and, most important, the sizes of W and S. In the next chapter, we explain our procedures for estimating the provision of specific public and private goods.

The unit of analysis in our data set for this chapter is a country-year. The data are organized around up to 192 different countries, spanning the years 1816–2000. Although we have data on at least some variables for the entire period, we nonetheless face substantial amounts of missing data. For most performance variables examined in this chapter, our data cover the period 1950–1999. For some variables, the data go back to 1960, or sometimes only to 1970. When we discuss issues of leadership tenure in a later chapter, our data extend back over all or almost all of the nearly two centuries covered by at least some variables. The dataset and ".do" files that replicate our statistical results using the program Stata are available on our website, <http://www.nyu.edu/gsas/dept/politics/data/>. Using the program Stata, anyone can replicate or modify what we have done.

Institutional Variables

The measurement of selectorate size and winning-coalition size, especially in nondemocratic states, is in its infancy. This means the approximations we propose are crude and primitive. They should, however, be adequate to evaluate whether the central tendencies of politics are aligned with the expectations that follow from the selectorate model. We repeat that our objective is to evaluate the general tendency for the predictions of the selectorate model to be a significant component of a broad array of phenomena, not to maximize the variance explained for any dependent variable. The indicators of W and S are much too crude for us to focus on variance explained. Having said that, we will explain as little as 1 percent of the variance for some dependent variables and as much as 70 or 80 percent for a few others. We believe it is better to test a theory with crude data than not to test it at all. It is possible, however, that others may have too little confidence in our approximations of the size of a winning coalition or the selectorate to accept the empirical results that rely on those variables. We hope that such disagreement will motivate the search for better ways to estimate the institutions with which we are concerned. The theory, of course, stands on its own merits, rising or falling in its explanatory power as a function of its logical implications and the precision and stringency of empirical assessments.

The POLITY IV collection of data plus Arthur Banks's cross-national time-series data include a number of institutional variables, four of which provide an approximation of an index of the size of *W* for the years through 1999.[2] New data to update the estimate of *W* are reported annually. We use another POLITY variable, Legislative Selection (*LEGSELEC*), as an initial indicator of *S*.[3] We discuss the latter first.

LEGSELEC measures the breadth of the selectiveness of the members of each country's legislature. POLITY codes this variable as a trichotomy, with 0 meaning that there is no legislature. A code of 1 means that the legislature is chosen by heredity or ascription or is simply chosen by the effective executive. A code of 2, the highest category, indicates that members of the legislature are directly or indirectly selected by popular election. The selectorate theory is not focused on legislative selection per se, but the selection mechanism for the legislature seems to us a reasonable, albeit crude, indicator of the inclusiveness of the polity's selectorate. We believe it is evident that the larger the value of *LEGSELEC*, the more likely it is that *S* is large. We divide *LEGSELEC* by its maximum value of 2 so that it varies between 0 and 1, with such normalization being a practice we observe with many variables to help facilitate comparisons. This normalized variable, referred to as *S*, provides a rough indication of the order of magnitude of the selectorate. It should also be evident that in reality the size difference between a selectorate with a score of 0 and a selectorate with a score of 0.5 is smaller than the size difference between a score of 0.5 and a score of 1.

The current indicator of *S* can be thought of as a logarithmic scale of the magnitude of a polity's selectorate. In the future we hope to improve on this indicator by obtaining data on enfranchisement rules in each country and across time. Unfortunately, current data on enfranchisement are typically focused on democratic societies with free, competitive elections. The selectorate theory requires a comparable indicator for all types of political systems and not just for democracy.

We estimate the size of *W* as a composite index based on the variables *REGTYPE*, taken from Banks's data, and *XRCOMP*, *XROPEN*, and *PARCOMP* from the POLITY IV data. When *REGTYPE* is not missing data and is not equal to code 2 or 3, so that the regime type is not a military or military/civilian regime, we award one point to *W*. Military regimes are assumed to have particularly small coalitions and so are not credited with an increment in coalition size through the indicator of *W*.

When *XRCOMP*—that is, the competitiveness of executive recruitment—is larger than or equal to code 2, another point is assigned to *W*. An *XRCOMP* code of 1 means that the chief executive is selected by heredity or in rigged, unopposed elections, suggesting dependence on few people. Code values of 2 and 3 refer to greater degrees of responsiveness to supporters, indicating a larger winning coalition. *XROPEN*, the openness of executive recruitment, contributes an additional point to *W* if the executive is recruited in a more open setting than heredity (that is, the variable's value is greater than 2). Executives recruited in an open political process are more likely to depend on a larger coalition than are those recruited through heredity or through the military. Finally, one more point can be contributed to the index of *W* if *PARCOMP*, competitiveness of participation, is coded as a 5, meaning that "there are relatively stable and enduring political groups which regularly compete for political influence at the national level" (POLITY II; Gurr 1990, 18). This variable is used to indicate a larger coalition on the supposition that stable and enduring political groups would not persist unless they believed they had an opportunity to influence incumbent leaders—that is, they have a possibility of being part of a winning coalition. No one variable in our index alone indicates a large coalition size, but polities that meet more of the criteria seem to us more likely to have a larger coalition than polities that meet fewer criteria, because the criteria speak directly to dependence on more or fewer people in gaining and holding office. As with the selectorate indicator, *S*, we divide by the maximum value of the *W* index, which is 4. The normalized minimum value, then, is 0 and the maximum is 1. And again it is evident that the progression from 0 to 0.25 to 0.50 to 0.75 and up to 1.0 is not linear. Like *S*, the indicator of *W* is more likely to be logarithmic in its reflection of order-of-magnitude changes in coalition size. Given the crudeness of the indicators and the breadth of the dependent variables we examine, as well as subtle functional forms, any significant central tendencies for the data to support the theory's implications are a source of encouragement that with better indicators the theory might perform better.

Coalition size, selectorate size, and their combination as the loyalty norm (*W/S*) are the pertinent institutional factors for hypotheses about labor, leisure, taxation, and economic growth explored in this chapter. We therefore construct a variable, which measures the strength of the loyalty norm, by dividing *W* by $(\log((S + 1) * 10))/3$. For convenience, we refer to this variable as *W/S*. We make this transformation of *S* to avoid division by zero and to ensure that the index for *S*, for this calculation, is never smaller than *W*. In this way we preserve observations without altering results, because this construction is almost perfectly correlated with a construction that did not transform *S*, though for a smaller sample size due to division by zero.[4]

Earlier we argued that not only do the relative sizes of *W* and *S* matter, but that the total magnitude of *W* sometimes also matters, taking population size into account. To assess this possibility we evaluate tests that control for the logarithm of each state's population. We use the logarithm under the supposition that there is a marginally decreasing impact of each added individual in a country as the total population of the country increases. That is, in a country of one million people, growth to two million has a bigger impact than is true in a country that adds a million people to a base population of 100 million. The variable *Log(Pop)* is our measure of the logarithm of population.

To alleviate the problem that our results might be the consequence of spurious temporal or spatial effects, in every cross-sectional, time-series analysis we include the interaction of geographic region and year as a set of fixed-effect dummy variables. Thus, each analysis includes a variable for Europe in 1950, Europe in 1951, North America in 1950, North America in 1951, and so on. We include these fixed effects because there may be spatiotemporal dependence in our data resulting, for instance, from factors that influence fluctuations in economic growth rates or health care or other factors in particular parts of the world in particular years. In this way we recognize that environmental factors outside any government's control, such as drought or the business cycle (and a host of other factors) have an exogenous impact on government performance at different times in different places.

We specify six geographic regions: Europe, South and Central America, North America and the Caribbean, Asia, the Middle East, and Africa.[5] We have also tested our theory against alternative regional specifications that are less geographic and more cultural, economic, or political. Of course, since we are interested in political effects, it makes little sense to reduce political factors to fixed effects. In any event, our results are substantively the same across widely used means of specifying regions. We generally do not discuss the fixed effects in the text, because they are strictly statistical corrections of no substantive interest regarding the tests of our theory. Their presence, however, makes our tests especially demanding, since we have removed any temporal and spatial factors that might be the actual explanation for shifts in the values of our dependent variables. The number of fixed-effect variables can be large, so success at finding substantively and statistically significant institutional effects provides considerable encouragement for further refinement and testing of the selectorate theory.

We have argued that large winning coalitions are a part of, but are not equivalent to, democracy. Likewise, small winning coalitions with large selectorates are expected to be correlated with, but are not by themselves equivalent to, autocracy. Small coalitions and small selectorates are associated with, but do not define, military juntas and monarchies. We use a well-established measure of regime type, which we call *Democracy*, to facilitate separating the impact of W and S on governance from the effects of other aspects of democracy, autocracy, and so on. The POLITY data contain a democracy scale and an autocracy scale, each ranging between 0 and 10. We subtract the autocracy score from the democracy score, as is common in many other studies (Maoz and Russett 1993; Gleditsch and Ward 1997). This yields a variable that ranges between -10 and $+10$. We add 10 to the score and divide by 20. Thus, our variable *Democracy* varies between 0 and 1, with scores closer to 0 reflecting more autocratic governments and scores closer to 1 reflecting more democratic governments. To assess the independent impact of democracy on our dependent variables, we create a variable called *WS:DemRes* by regressing W and S on *Democracy* and then saving the residuals, they being the portion or characteristics of a country's degree of democracy or autocracy not endogenous to W and S.

Tests including *WS:DemRes* allow us to separate the effects of selection institutions from other aspects of democracy, autocracy, and so on, thereby facilitating an evaluation of the independent effects of these different aspects of political institutions. If the theory is borne out, the results will suggest subtle differences between policies aimed at promoting democracy and policies oriented toward promoting specific institutional configurations that are conducive to what most people think of as good government—that is, peace and prosperity.

As a further check on the institutional account offered by the selectorate theory, we also examine where appropriate the theory's predicted variation in effects strictly within large-coalition, democratic systems.

Recall our conjecture that parliamentary systems require a smaller winning coalition than do presidential systems. Alvares and colleagues (1997) provide a variable called INST that receives a code of 0 for dictatorships, 1 for parliamentary democracies, 2 for mixed democratic systems, and 3 for presidential systems. We construct a variable called *Parl_Pres* that takes on the value of INST/3 when *Democracy* is at its maximum score of 1.0 and otherwise takes the value 0. *Parl_Pres*, then, is normalized to fall between 0 and 1, just as are *W* and *S*. Likewise, we estimate a variable we call *ParloverS* as $Parl\_Pres/(\log((S+1)*10))/3$ so that it is analogous to *W/S*.

We also construct a control variable called *WS:IncomeRes*. This is the residual components of real per capita income (a variable documented in the next section) that is independent of the selection institutions *W* and *S*. *WS:IncomeRes* is created to be analogous to *WS:DemRes*. That is, its values are the residuals that remain after calculating the regression analysis for *Income* as the dependent variable and *W* and *S* as independent variables.

WS:IncomeRes permits us to separate the effects of political institutions from wealth effects that cannot be attributed to those institutions. Tests that include *Parl_Pres* permit us to evaluate our conjecture that parliamentary systems behave as if they have smaller winning coalitions than do presidential systems. These tests are far from perfect, because some parliamentary systems include list voting, which does not require the same minimal winning coalition as a single-member district, first-past-the-post parliamentary system. Consequently, *Parl_Pres* only roughly approximates the conditions of our conjecture and is used only when the conjecture is the right setting for a test. If the conjecture is correct, more fundamental public goods should be produced in presidential systems than in parliamentary democracies and more private goods in parliamentary systems than in presidential ones, all else being equal. Results on this issue, however, are not central to our theory, because the argument regarding parliamentary systems and presidential systems is a conjecture that is not thoroughly worked out yet in the selectorate model.

Before returning to the development of the selectorate theory, we offer a few examples that highlight differences between the measurement of coalition size and at least one standard assessment of "democraticness" (drawn from the POLITY data set: Gurr 1990; Jaggers and

Gurr 1995). In doing so, we emphasize a general principle: At the extremes of democracy or autocracy when *Democracy* equals 0 or 1, there is an almost perfect correlation (0.97) between our indicator W of coalition size and the type of regime ($N = 3{,}225$). In the interior of the indicator of coalition size, however, the correlation drops to 0.61 (*W*, *Democracy*, $N = 10{,}562$). While this is still a high correlation, it indicates that on the interior, W and *Democracy* only have 37 percent of their variance in common.

Kristian S. Gleditsch and Michael D. Ward (1997) explore the properties of the commonly used measures of democracy and autocracy, as well as their differences. They demonstrate that these scores depend primarily on one indicator, the degree of decisional constraints on the executive (XCONST in POLITY III). Gleditsch and Ward (1997, 380) write that "although the degree of executive constraints accounts for only 4 of the possible 10 democracy scale points, all of our analyses point strongly to the conclusion that this variable virtually determines the democracy and autocracy scale values." Our measure of W does not use the XCONST variable and so taps into dimensions of the nature of political competition that the commonly used measures of democracy do not utilize. The correlation between W and XCONST is 0.30 ($N = 14{,}422$) in our data set; the correlation between *Democracy* (i.e., our measure, meaning the difference between democracy and autocracy scores) and XCONST is 0.90 ($N = 13{,}940$).[6] We stress, then, that W is not just *Democracy* with a different name. Rather W is one important feature of governance that helps distinguish democratic rule from other forms of government, virtually all of which involve a smaller winning coalition combined in different ways with the selectorate.

It is in the subtleties of nearly democratic (or only partly autocratic) systems that the indicators and concepts of coalition size and democracy diverge most. We illustrate this point with examples:

• Gorbachev's Soviet Union earned a score of 0.75 on our coalition-size indicator (W) in 1990. On the measure of *Democracy* (described above), his regime scored only 0.50 in 1990 but 0.90 a year later (revised downward by POLITY to 0.80 in subsequent editions). Apparently, the indicator of coalition size captured the change in Soviet political arrangements more quickly than did the standard democracy index.

- Prior to the presidency of Ulysses S. Grant, the United States generally scored 0.95 on *Democracy* and 0.75 on coalition size. The coalition indicator does a better job of capturing the restricted American franchise before the Civil War than does the *Democracy* indicator.

- Lee Kwan Yew's Singapore (1965–2000) scored 0.75 on the coalition index, but only 0.40 on *Democracy*. The higher score for coalition size can be read as either indicating a more broadly based government than Lee and his party actually had or, alternatively, as capturing a breadth of necessary popular support for his government and its programs that is missed by the *Democracy* score.

- Taiwan also had a larger coalition score (0.25) than *Democracy* score (0.10) during Chiang Kai-shek's rule. Both scores are low (indicating little democracy and a small coalition), but still the relatively larger coalition score favors somewhat more public-spirited, less corrupt policy than does the democracy-autocracy indicator.

- Even more dramatically, the scores for Cambodia have moved in opposite directions in the 1990s. In 1993–1994, for instance, Cambodia's coalition score was 0.75 and its *Democracy* score was 0.55. In 1998–2000, W had dropped to 0.25 while *Democracy* increased to 0.60. Obviously, the two are measuring different aspects of the Cambodian system.

Later, we return to these differences in indicators and discuss the example of India to illustrate how coalition size and other aspects of democracy differ in practice.

The correlation between W and S is 0.43 ($N = 12,462$). Clearly the selectorate indicator and the coalition indicator measure different characteristics of political systems. When we regress W and S against *Democracy* we find an R^2 of 0.69 ($N = 10,866$). Most of the explained variance is contributed by coalition size. The probability that the association with S is a chance relationship is fairly substantial ($p = 0.18$), probably because many rigged-election autocracies have a large selectorate.

Measurement of Labor, Leisure, and Taxes

Residents of a state are expected to select their leisure and labor levels in response to the taxing and spending policies proposed by leaders and challengers. When leaders expropriate, residents are reluctant to invest their energies in productive ventures. To test the model's expectations regarding leisure and labor, we offer estimates of these choices. Once we establish how we approximate leisure and labor, we turn to a discussion of the problems inherent in measuring tax rates and to the solutions we propose.

We approximate labor (and other economically productive) activity indirectly in three different ways. First, we assess the impact of selection institutions on real per capita income. Our presumption is that people's incomes rise with economic effort and that, therefore, all else being equal, real per capita income is a good proxy for economic effort. We use the World Bank's real GDP per capita in constant 1995 U.S. dollars to evaluate per capita income. These data are observed for between 97 and 169 countries (depending on the year) for the period 1960–1999. We call the variable *Income*. For most tests we transform this variable into the logarithm of real per capita income (*LogIncome*) to reflect magnitudes under the assumption that marginal dollar increments in income add less and less value the higher an individual's income is.

Second, we approximate economic activity with an estimate of the per-centage of each polity's GDP that is invested. Investment reflects confi-dence that the government will not confiscate unconsumed wealth, while also reflecting long-term confidence in the performance of the national economy. Taken from the World Bank data, the variable we call *%Invest* is referred to by the Bank as GrossDomInvest.

Third, we examine a variable from the same data set that reports the percentage of GDP saved (i.e., the World Bank's GrossDomSaving). Like investment, saving displays confidence that governmental policies will not lead to expropriation or to excessively high taxes on the uncon-sumed portions of a person's income. This variable is called *%Save*. The variables *%Invest and %Save* are observed for the years 1960–1999 and, in most years, for more than 100 countries. The correlation between *LogIncome* and *%Invest* is 0.24 ($N = 4,187$), between *LogIncome* and *%Save* is 0.51 ($N = 4,659$), and between *%Invest* and *%Save* is 0.26 ($N = 4,286$). Each measures a different aspect of economic activity.

Our estimate of leisure activity is the percentage of a polity's GDP spent on private consumption. This is the proportion of national income channeled into consumption rather than economic production by indi-vidual citizens. We recognize that this is an imperfect translation of the concept of leisure into an observable quantity. Leisure can and often does arise without consuming goods, and consumption by one person can, of course, be productive economic activity for another. However, personal leisure is not easily measured by a direct indicator available across many countries for many years and is especially difficult to assess in the Third World, other than to relate anecdotes about the number of able-bodied people seen strolling the streets and occupying coffee shops during the workday. Thus, we choose personal consumption as a reasonable proxy for leisure. The data for this variable, called *Consumption*, are taken from Alvares et al. (1997), who refer to it as PRIVCON. This variable is measured for up to nearly 100 countries for the years 1970–1990.

Tax-rate estimates are somewhat more problematic than estimates of labor or leisure activity. The World Bank collects data from individual countries regarding their tax revenue as a percentage of GDP. At first blush, these data might seem like a reasonable surrogate for tax rates. It might appear straightforward that the higher the percentage of GDP reportedly paid in taxes, the higher the tax rate must be. This, however, is almost certainly not true.

Recall that the theory predicts that labor decreases and leisure increases as tax rates rise. High tax rates, therefore, are expected to lead to low incomes. Further, high rates of taxation encourage citizens to hide labor activity, income, and assets. Under these conditions, high-tax-rate polities are likely to find it difficult to collect tax revenue. As incentives rise for people to avoid labor and to hide whatever economic activity they engage in, the cost of tax collection must go up. A simple calculation serves to illustrate the problem of collecting taxes. In 2000 it cost the U.S. government 37 cents to collect every $100 of tax revenue (see <www.irs.gov>). Given that U.S. per capita income is about $30,000 (1995 constant dollars) and that tax revenues are approximately 20 percent of GDP, as a very rough approximation the Internal Revenue Service spends $22 to collect taxes from the average person. In 1999 Ethiopia's GDP was a mere $122 per capita. If Ethiopia used the same tax-collection efficiency as the United States, it would cost nearly 20 percent of GDP to simply collect the taxes, pushing many people into starvation. While this calculation assumes Ethiopia collects taxes as efficiently as the IRS, an even larger difference lies in the incentives to hide income. Paying taxes in Ethiopia literally means taking food out of your children's mouths. It is likely, therefore, that governments that maintain high-tax-rate policies generate relatively low revenues through direct taxation because people focus on leisure at the expense of labor and because people try to hide the labor effort they make as much as they can so as to avoid being taxed. We believe that this results in two effects.

First, government reporting of tax revenue to the World Bank is likely to be biased, so that small-coalition societies with the concomitant high tax rates are especially unlikely to report tax revenue fully or even at all.

Second, since, as we will demonstrate below, this expectation turns out to be correct, we can only reliably observe variation in tax revenue as a percentage of GDP for democratic societies. This means that we can test the relationship between tax revenue as a percentage of GDP (a variable called *TaxGDP*) and selection institutions reliably only within the largest-coalition societies. Thus, we use *TaxGDP* to measure tax revenue, but we test it against *Parl_Pres* and *S* rather than *W* and *S*, because the theoretically implied bias is observed in the data. *TaxGDP* is also tested against the effects of *ParloverS* to assess the impact of the loyalty norm on taxes in the face of the selection bias anticipated for *TaxGDP*.

Evidence: Labor or Leisure

An implication derived from the selectorate theory maintains that individuals choose to allocate time, energy, and resources between productive economic activities (i.e., labor) and leisure depending on the policies proposed by incumbent leaders and their political rivals. The content of policy proposals depends theoretically on the size of the winning coalition, on the size of the selectorate, and on the loyalty norm (W/S). Labor effort increases as coalition size goes up, as selectorate size decreases, and as the loyalty norm weakens (so that W/S increases). The predicted effects of these selection institutions on leisure are opposite to their effects on labor.

In testing the predictions, we generally report results for four different models. The independent variables for these models are:

Model 1: *W, S*, fixed effects

Model 2: *W, S, WS:IncomeRes, WS:DemRes, Log(Pop)*, fixed effects

Model 3: *W/S*, fixed effects

Model 4: *W/S, WS:IncomeRes, WS:DemRes, Log(Pop)*, fixed effects

Table 4.1
Summary of institutional effects on labor and leisure

β_w, t, R^2 β_s, t, N	W, model 1 S	W, model 2 S, WS:DemRes	W/S, model 3	W/S, model 4 WS:DemRes
LogIncome	2.58, 37.23, 0.38 −0.84, −15.07, 4,867	2.51, 33.85, 0.40 −0.76, −12.13, 4,255 0.34, 3.90	2.05, 34.37, 0.35 4,867	2.04, 32.42, 0.37 4,255 0.67, 8.04
% Invest	1.73, 2.91, 0.03 2.85, 5.97, 4,150	1.79, 2.84, 0.09 1.28, 2.50, 3,570 −5.40, −7.64	3.60, 7.14, 0.03 4,150	2.59, 4.89, 0.09 3,570 −5.84, −8.56
% Save	4.53, 4.70, 0.04 1.84, 2.44, 4,649	12.63, 13.55, 0.32 −1.42, −1.91, 3,942 −7.74, −7.43	5.71, 7.15, 0.04, 4,649	11.79, 15.17, 0.32 3,942 −7.03, −7.05
Consumption	−8.63, −5.59, 0.08 −4.83, −4.26, 1,872	−23.71, −14.26, 0.29 0.83, 0.70, 1,609 1.52, 0.92	−12.30, −9.96, 0.07 1,872	−23.19, −18.16, 0.29 1,609 0.86, 0.55

Note: *WS:IncomeRes* is not included in the tests of models 2 and 4 when the dependent variable is *Income*. Cell entries in the first row of each cell are the coefficient and *t*-statistic for *W* (or *W/S*), and R^2 for the regression analysis. The second row in each cell shows the coefficient for *S*, its *t*-statistic, and *N*. The third row, where appropriate, shows the coefficient and *t*-statistic for *WS:DemRes*, the effects of aspects of democracy that are independent of *W* and *S*.

In addition to these four "standard" models, our website programs at <http://www.nyu.edu/gsas/dept/politics/data/> provide tests of numerous other specifications as well as affording the opportunity for those who so desire to conduct other tests. Table 4.1 provides a summary of the four standard models in the context of labor and leisure. As a benchmark for assessing the information in this and other tables, *t*-statistics of about 2.00 (regardless of sign) or more are significant at least at the 0.05 level, and *t*-statistics of about 1.65 or more are equivalent to one-tailed significance at the 0.05 level. Naturally, the larger the *t*-statistic (or *z*-statistic in maximum-likelihood estimations), provided it is in the direction predicted by the theory, the greater the confidence we can have that the statistical test reflects a relationship consistent with the expectations of the selectorate theory. The note accompanying the table explains what each value represents.

As table 4.1 shows, the expectations regarding coalition size and leisure and labor are matched by the empirical record. Per capita income increases sharply with coalition size ($p = 0.000$) and decreases with increases in the size of the selectorate ($p = 0.000$, $N = 4,867$), with 38 percent of the variation in real per capita income accounted for by these two institutional factors based on an analysis with region-year fixed effects. Indeed, the coefficient associated with coalition size (2.58) relative to the logarithm of per capita income—ignoring other effects for the moment—tells us that a shift from the smallest-coalition system to the largest results in a more-than-tenfold increase in per capita income. This is partially offset by the expected accompanying large selectorate, whose coefficient is –0.84. The impact of the coefficient of W alone captures the expected impact on income from a shift from a rigged-election autocracy to a large-coalition democracy, since S is large in both these cases. In fact, a regression analysis of the impact of the lagged size of W ($L3.W$) and of S ($L3.S$) measured three years prior to the assessment of $LogIncome$, combined with measures of the change in W ($DW30$) and in S ($DS30$) over the three-year period from when the lagged institutions were evaluated to when $Income$ is evaluated, not only shows that big-coalition systems are strongly associated with higher incomes. It also demonstrates that changes in political institutions that move a polity from a small coalition to a large coalition dramatically increase subsequent income levels. The coefficients are 2.97 for $L3.W$ ($p = 0.000$), –1.04 for $L3.S$ ($p = 0.000$), 1.39 for $DW30$ ($p = 0.000$), and –0.41 for $DS30$ (0.000), with 42 percent of variance explained based on 4,658 observations and with 268 fixed effects.

Adding a control for the independent impact of democracy ($WS:DemRes$), we find that both coalition size and the independent effects of democracy have strong beneficial effects on the magnitude of per capita income. Shifting from the smallest to the largest coalition size continues to yield about a tenfold increase in income, while greater democracy adds about another 40 percent to per capita income. Comparable results are found when we substitute W/S for W and S.

The second indicator of economically productive activity is the percentage of GDP that goes into investment. Again the results strongly support the expectation that large-coalition systems encourage productive economic activity. The t-statistic between coalition size and %$Invest$ is 2.91 ($N = 4,150, p = 0.004$). The effects of S, however, are positive and significant rather than negative as predicted by the selectorate theory. Closer inspection of the data, though, reveals that this result is actually consistent with the theory. Reportage of investment in the data set is biased. Large-coalition systems disproportionately report investment information. A Heckman selection analysis to see if there is a bias in reporting investment based on W yields a z-score of 12.71 for W *as a selection variable* with the selection coefficient being 0.63. In other words, the sample of variation we observe for selectorate size is biased in favor of large-S systems because all large-coalition systems must, by definition, be large-selectorate systems. Those with the opportunity to have more variance in their selectorate size—the small-coalition systems—tend not to report investment data (presumably because they experience little investment). Finally, we note that W/S produces very strong, positive results (coefficient = 3.60, $p = 0.000$, $N = 4,150$), reinforcing the theory's expectations.

The analysis of savings (%*Save*) leads to results comparable for those observed regarding %*Invest*. W and S both are significant and have positive coefficients, and a Heckman selection analysis supports the contention that there is a selection bias in reporting %*Save*. Small-coalition systems (with the opportunity for more variance in selectorate size) are substantially less likely to report savings than are large-coalition systems. In the selection equation, the coefficient for S becomes insignificant but with a negative sign associated with it. These selection effects are equally robust if we evaluate the selection bias in terms of *Democracy* rather than W. The analysis of savings rather than investment even more sharply highlights the importance of coalition size relative to democracy. Again, W/S is highly significant and in the predicted direction when %*Save* is the dependent variable, with the t-statistics varying between 7.15 and 15.17 depending on the specific control variables included in the test.

Substantively, model 2 suggests that the largest coalition size increases savings by about 12.6 percent of GDP compared to the smallest. Investment as a percentage of GDP rises by 1.79 percent as we move from the smallest- to the largest-coalition systems after controlling for the residual effects of democracy, income, population size, and region-year fixed effects. These substantive effects are dramatic. As the theory suggests, when political institutions are such that expropriating resources harms a leader's survival, residents are far more likely to invest and save.

Economically productive activity is apparently higher in polities that have a larger winning coalition. The first part of the leisure/labor equation is reinforced by the evidence. Is personal, private consumption diminished as coalition size rises? The evidence summarized in table 4.1 supports the contention that it is. Large-coalition, large-selectorate polities spend 23 percent less of GDP on personal consumption than do polities with the smallest coalitions, according to model 2's results.

Democracy does not have a significant independent influence on consumption after we extract aspects of democracy explained by coalition size and selectorate size. Interestingly, democracy's independent impact on investment and savings as a percent of GDP is significant and negative. That is, the attributes of democracy that are not explained by or that do not share variation with the size of the coalition and the size of the selectorate, tend to retard investment and savings. This may help explain the frequently replicated finding that democracy, per se, does not appear to contribute to economic growth. Savings and investment are important contributors to growth—effects that we demonstrate empirically later in this chapter—and now we see that the aspects of democracy that are not explained by W and S set savings and investment rates back. Perhaps the other aspects of democracy contribute more to income redistribution than does the impact of coalition size combined with selectorate size. Whether this is so will be evaluated when we turn to an examination of economic growth rates.

Evidence: Taxation

We noted earlier that we do not have data on tax rates but that we do have data on tax revenue as a percentage of GDP, which, of course, is readily translated as the average tax rate. In discussing the variable *TaxGDP*, we argued that whether the data are reported or not is itself a strategic decision for governments and that this decision is expected to be influenced by the size of the polity's winning coalition. In the next chapter, when we test our hypotheses regarding transparency, it will be evident that our expectation of a bias in reporting tax information is strongly supported by the evidence. Because of this bias in reportage on tax revenue, we only test the taxation aspect of the selectorate argument within the confines of democratic states.[7]

In chapter 3 we set out the conjecture that parliamentary systems, on average, require a smaller winning coalition than do presidential systems. With that in mind, we test the relationship between *TaxGDP* and *Parl_Pres* rather than W. Since the test is only within the confines of the most democratic states (i.e., *Democracy* = 1), there is no variation in S

Table 4.2
Effect of selection institutions on tax revenue as a percentage of GDP in democracies

	Coef. (Std. Error)	t-stat. (Prob.)	Coef. (Std. Error)	t-stat. (Prob.)
Parl_Pres	−21.08 (1.73)	−12.18 (0.000)	−23.75 (1.69)	−14.05 (0.000)
Log(Pop)			−1.54 (0.21)	−7.17 (0.000)
WS:IncomeRes			1.54 (0.49)	3.13 (0.002)
Constant	40.29 (0.84)	48.07 (0.000)	64.78 (3.46)	18.74 (0.000)
Summary statistics	F = 148.41 R^2 = 0.19	N = 447 F.E. = 88	F = 80.90 R^2 = 0.35	N = 426 F.E. = 88

and so we exclude the indicator of selectorate size from the tests (and, of course, *ParloverS* for the same reason). With these substitutions in mind, we examine two regression analyses. The first assesses the impact of *Parl_Pres* while controlling only for fixed effects. The second adds controls for each country's population size (i.e., *Log(Pop)*) and for the impact of per capita income.[8] *WS:DemRes* is excluded because it falls out of the equation, since we are looking only at democratic states because of the previously discussed selection bias in reporting tax revenues. Table 4.2 reports the findings. The expectation is that tax revenues as a percentage of GDP decline as we move up the democratic coalition ladder from parliamentary to mixed to presidential systems.

The evidence in table 4.2 is consistent with the conjecture. In these data presidential systems have lower tax rates than mixed parliamentary/ presidential systems, and those have lower tax rates than purely parliamentary systems. For instance, during the years for which the data are available—1970 to 1990—the average tax revenue as a percentage of GDP among presidential systems was 19.2 percent. For mixed systems, the average was 29.8 percent, while for parliamentary systems, it was 32.9 percent. The highest presidential tax rate in the data set—for Costa Rica in 1983—was just 24.2 percent, while the highest rate among parliamentary systems in the data reached 53.2 percent: Luxembourg in 1987. From this tentative evidence among democracies, smaller-coalition systems take a higher proportion of GDP in taxes than do larger-coalition systems.[9]

Thus far we have seen that core economic decisions are substantially influenced by political institutions that shape leadership selection. Economic activity—indexed by income, savings, and investment—increases as coalition size increases and as the loyalty norm weakens (so that W/S increases). Spending on leisure activity increases as either the coalition size decreases or as the loyalty norm grows stronger. Whatever aspects of democracy (or autocracy) arise that are independent of the size of W and S generally have little or a reversed impact on these core economic activities. These results suggest that a key characteristic of democracy—dependence on a large coalition—promotes economically productive activities, while a key characteristic of autocracy—dependence on a small coalition—promotes leisure and retards economically productive activity. These are some of the central effects that advantage democracy according to democratic theorists. Our findings point to these effects being due to selection institutions rather than to other aspects of democratic governance.

Economic Growth

Leaders foster an environment that can be conducive to economic growth by promoting savings and investment. Many have also argued that a promising environment for growth is fostered when governments protect civil liberties, political rights, and transparency in government (North and Weingast 1989; Campos and Root 1996; Barro 1997). Now we ask directly whether institutional arrangements influence variation in economic growth. In doing so, we assert for now that extensive civil liberties, assured political rights, and transparency in government are all endogenous products of large-coalition systems. In the next chapter we offer evidence that these core public goods are substantially promoted by larger-coalition systems and discouraged in polities that depend on smaller coalitions. This assertion means that when we control for the effects of civil liberties, political rights, or transparency in subsequent analyses, we look at the residual effects of these factors that are independent of the selection institutions W and S.

Economic growth is one of the most widely studied phenomena related to nations. Robert Barro's (1996, 1997, 2000) analysis and research by Adam Przeworski and Fernando Limongi (1993) are probably among the best-known studies showing empirically that democracy does not necessarily lead to a high economic growth rate.[10] The selectorate theory

Table 4.3
Large coalitions help make people richer

	GDP per capita (1995 U.S. dollars)	
W	Mean	Std. dev.
0 ($N = 434$)	2,306	6,537
0.25 ($N = 734$)	2,891	5,375
0.50 ($N = 1,374$)	1,345	1,555
0.75 ($N = 1,617$)	3,147	4,303
1.00 ($N = 1,086$)	16,180	10,556
Coalition size in democracies		
Parliamentary ($N = 505$)	15,557	7,798
Mixed ($N = 71$)	16,868	6,016
Presidential ($N = 95$)	19,161	14,433

suggests that governments with small winning coalitions, like many autocracies, redistribute wealth from the relatively poor to the relatively rich, but is agnostic with regard to redistribution from the rich to the poor. The selectorate theory does, however, predict that systems with large winning coalitions emphasize policies favorable to economic growth. High savings and investment rates, coupled with a smoothly functioning civil society, favor economic growth.

We have shown that variation in per capita income across countries depends to a substantial degree on institutional arrangements. Table 4.3 reiterates this point by showing, in the upper half of the table, the mean and variance of per capita income (in 1995 constant U.S. dollars) in relation to the five levels on our indicator W of coalition size. This part of the table is important in understanding how we structure some tests linking growth to institutions. The table reinforces our earlier conclusion that coalition size helps shape the *level* of income. Thus, large-coalition systems are expected, on average, to have already reached high incomes, which means that they have already experienced considerable growth. The question posed in the upper part of table 4.3 is extended further in the lower half of the table. There we evaluate whether our conjecture about variation in coalition size *within democratic institutions* also leads to variation in per capita income, with residents in presidential systems (i.e., larger-coalition democracies) enjoying higher incomes than those in mixed or parliamentary systems.

Per capita income not only rises significantly as *W* increases, but also as we move up the coalition ladder within democracies. The statistical association is so strong that, even after controlling for fixed effects, the regression coefficient for the impact of *Parl_Pres* on the logarithm of per capita income is 1.38 and the *t*-statistic is 9.97. This observation plus the mean scores in table 4.3 indicate support for our conjecture and, therefore, also support the notion that coalition size is a central aspect of governance that varies *across and within* nominal regime types and that contributes to the explanation of fundamental aspects of government taxation and personal efforts to be productive. What is more, the result is robust. One might speculate that the beneficial effect of presidential systems merely captures the high per capita income in the United States. However, even if we introduce a dummy variable coded as 1 for the United States and as 0 for all others, the effect of *Parl_Pres* remains strong. It is also equally strong if we split *Parl_Pres* into dummy variables to represent its constituent parts.[11]

Our first set of tests on growth examine the level of income as measured by the logarithm of per capita income as the dependent variable against the direct and indirect effects of selection institutions while controlling for the lagged logarithm of per capita income. The expectation is that increases in coalition size, decreases in selectorate size, or weakening of the loyalty norm contribute to that growth. When we complete these analyses, we examine an alternative measure of growth, defined as the annual percentage change in GDP. There, as in the analyses of income level while controlling for prior income level, we examine the effect that institutional change has on subsequent growth, capturing the idea that change in income depends on change in institutions.

Models 5 and 6 calculate the effect of coalition size on growth. The logarithm of per capita *GDP(LogIncome)* is the dependent variable. We control for the lagged logarithm of per capita GDP (*Lagged LogIncome*), *W* and *S* in model 5. *WoverS* substitutes for *W* and *S* in model 6. In both models, we also control for *Log(Pop)*, the residual impact of civil liberties (*CL:Res*), political rights (*PR:Res*), investment (*Invest:Res*), and savings (*Savings:Res*) independent of the direct effect *W* and *S* have on these goods, as well as *WS:DemRes*, and our standard fixed effects.[12] Table 4.4 reports the results.

The variance explained (it is over 0.99) is not reported, because it is artifactual since lagged income is extremely highly correlated with

Table 4.4
Economic growth and coalition size: dependent variable is *LogIncome*

Variable	Coef., (std. error) t-stat., (prob.)	Coef., (std. error) t-stat., (prob.)
Lagged LogIncome	0.998, (0.001) 811.48, (0.000)	0.998, (0.001) 829.56, (0.000)
W	0.029, (0.006) 4.73, (0.000)	
S	−0.006, (0.004) −1.38, (0.167)	
W/S		0.024, (0.005) 4.67, (0.000)
Log(Pop)	0.002, (0.0007) 2.33, (0.020)	0.002, (0.001) 2.34, (0.019)
CL:Res	0.001, (0.001) 0.62, (0.538)	0.001, (0.001) 0.69, (0.491)
PR:Res	0.004, (0.002) 2.66, (0.008)	0.004, (0.002) 2.50, (0.012)
Invest:Res	0.002, (0.0001) 12.53, (0.000)	0.002, (0.0001) 12.46, (0.000)
Savings:Res	0.0001, (0.0001) 1.63, (0.103)	0.0001, (0.00008) 1.47, (0.141)
WS:DemRes	−0.005, (0.008) −0.70, (0.487)	−0.003, (0.007) −0.34, (0.737)
Constant	−0.010, (0.014) −0.70, (0.485)	−0.015, (0.014) −1.12, (0.262)
Summary statistics	$N = 2,931$, F.E. = 179 $F = 148,469, p = 0.000$	$N = 2,931$, F.E. = 179 $F = 166,923, p = 0.000$

current income. That fact makes the variance explained uninteresting, but it makes the tests extremely demanding. Growth here is assessed as the proportionate change in income or, in other words, the difference between the current *LogIncome* and *LogIncome* one year earlier. The structure of these tests makes achieving significance a challenge for any of the independent variables. The models, of course, also include our standard fixed-effect controls for region-year, further compounding the difficulty of achieving significance for any of the substantive independent variables.

Models 5 and 6 provide support for the contention that large coalition size fosters growth. *W* and *W/S* are significant in their independent impact. What is more, the coefficients associated with coalition size vary between 2.9 and 2.4 percent, indicating that regimes with a coalition requirement at the upper bound of W's scale enjoy an ample annual growth advantage over their smaller-coalition counterparts. To appreciate how large this advantage is, consider the impact on real per capita GDP growth over a 10-year, 20-year, 50-year, and 100-year period depending on whether W equals 0 or 1.0.

Assume that per capita income equals $2,000 at the start of the period and hold the real value for small-coalition polities equal to that amount (that is, zero real growth). What is the difference in real per capita incomes for the largest-coalition polities as time unfolds, assuming that their growth rate is 2.5 percent? Recall that the coefficient associated with W is 2.9 and with W/S 2.4, indicating the growth-rate advantage is between 2.4 and 2.9 percent. After ten years, the large-coalition polity's income rises from $2,000 to $2,560, putting it more than 25 percent ahead of its small-coalition counterpart. After twenty years, the difference rises to nearly $1,300 ($2,000 compared to $3,277), a more than 60 percent advantage for the large-coalition polity. Fifty years from the start, the large-coalition polity enjoys a real per capita income of $6,874, or 3.9 times higher than the small-coalition state. A century of institutional difference results in the large-coalition system enjoying a real per capita income of $23,627, compared to $2,000 in real per capita income for the small-coalition society. These differences are so large that one might almost say that institutional differences by themselves seem sufficient to account for the disparities in real per capita income between otherwise seemingly comparable societies like North and South Korea, the former East and West Germany, or present Southern California and Northern Mexico.

Shifting to an alternative approach to economic growth, we turn now to growth rates measured as percentage changes in real per capita income. We already anticipate that large-coalition societies have achieved growth through their institutional setup. That this is so is apparent from the evidence already presented. Large-coalition societies become rich because they have institutions that create incentives for leaders to promote labor effort over leisure activity. Given the importance of economic growth, next we examine the issue of growth with greater detail and a wider array of models than the standard specification we present for other variables.

To evaluate the impact of political institutions as well as the impact of changes in these institutions on growth, we must consider several factors.

The selectorate theory implies that growth rates should be responsive both to the institutional setup in a polity and to changes in that setup. Changes can be expected to have two independent effects. Any change in political institutions represents a major alteration in how a state is governed. As such, institutional change probably is indicative of general unrest in the society and probably reflects a heightened degree of uncertainty about where the society is headed. Institutional change in and of itself is likely to impose a short-term decrease in a nation's rate of growth. However, over time, some changes should bolster growth while others retard it. Specifically, institutional changes that increase coalition size and/or weaken the loyalty norm (i.e., increase W/S) should, according to the selectorate theory, lead to better policy choices that help foster economic growth. Policy responses to a reduced coalition size and/or to a strengthened loyalty norm are likely to promote kleptocracy and corruption, which stymie growth.

Our tests below consider three ways political institutions influence growth. First, as we discussed above, we anticipate that any kind of institutional change, whether it increases or decreases W, increases uncertainty, which leads to a short-term decline in growth. We construct a variable called *PoliticalChange*. This variable is the squared difference in the coalition size W, compared with the coalition size W two years earlier. By squaring the change in W over this two-year period, we evaluate the impact of institutional change regardless of its direction. This variable is intended to capture the uncertainty provoked by change and is expected to predict a reduction in growth rates.

Second, although political change disrupts the economic status quo, creates uncertainty, and alters economic expectations, the selectorate theory suggests that institutional changes that increase coalition size and reduce the loyalty norm induce leaders to try harder on behalf of their supporters. Hence, when institutional changes increase coalition size relative to the selectorate, economic actors should anticipate that future governments will generate policies more conducive to economic activity. While any change might create uncertainty, changes that enlarge W/S are more likely to have positive short-term economic effects than changes that reduce W/S. To test whether the direction of institutional change does indeed have the predicted effect on economic growth, we create another variable $\Delta W/S_{t0-t-2}$, which is the change in W/S (i.e., the loyalty norm) compared with the same variable two years earlier. When either the coalition size increases or the selectorate decreases, this variable is positive and indicates a move toward institutions that are predicted to enhance economic activity. If $\Delta W/S_{t0\text{-}t\text{-}2}$ is positive, indicating a decline in the strength of the polity's loyalty norm, we expect that growth should increase, offsetting and perhaps even improving on the immediate uncertainty created by institutional change. If $\Delta W/S_{t0\text{-}t\text{-}2}$ shows decline, meaning that the loyalty norm is getting stronger, the uncertainty associated with institutional change is also expected to be reinforced by a shift to policies not conducive to growth.

Third, the previous variables focus on the short-term effects of institutional change on growth rates; they assess the extent to which institutional changes over the last two years influence growth. Our final set of variables, W and S, assess the long-term, or steady-state, impact of political institutions. That is, over the long run, do nations with larger or smaller coalitions grow fastest?

Using these three sets of variables, we measure the short-term impact of institutional change, the short-term directional effect of institutional change, and the long-run effects of institutional configuration on economic growth rates. We determine economic growth using the World Bank's measure of annual economic growth in GDP measured in constant (1995) dollars. Table 4.5 presents three analyses to evaluate institutional effects on growth. The first evaluates the impact of institutional change and of the steady-state institutional configuration on economic growth. The second repeats this test, but adds a control for the country's population. The third adds controls for the residual impact of civil liberties, political rights, investment, and savings that are independent of W and S. In each case, the expectation is that higher values on *Political Change* dampen growth, higher values on $\Delta W/S_{t0\text{-}t\text{-}2}$ and W improve growth, and higher values on S diminish growth.

Even after taking the residual effects of civil liberties, political rights, investment, and savings into account, the model only accounts for about 5 percent of the variance in growth rates. Still, table 4.5 strongly supports the predictions of the selectorate theory. First, the coefficients on W and S indicate that it is indeed large-coalition, small-selectorate systems that achieve higher long-term rates of growth. Second, the models show that political change impedes economic growth over the following two years, but third, this effect is largely offset when the institutional change is toward a larger value for W/S. These results prevail even in the presence

Table 4.5
Economic growth, institutional change and the new institutional configuration

	Coef., (std. error) t-stat., (prob.)	Coef., (std. error) t-stat., (prob.)	Coef., (std. error) t-stat., (prob.)
W	1.354, (0.498) 2.72, (0.007)	1.156, (0.505) 2.29, (0.022)	1.720, (0.624) 2.76, (0.006)
S	−0.240, (0.346) −0.69, (0.489)	−0.222, (0.346) −0.64, (0.521)	−0.471, (0.430) −1.10, (0.274)
$PoliticalChange$	−1.182, (0.358) −3.30, (0.001)	−1.175, (0.358) −3.28, (0.001)	−1.251, (0.454) −2.76, (0.006)
$\Delta W/S_{t0\text{-}t\text{-}2}$	1.001, (0.623) 1.61, (0.108)	1.132, (0.625) 1.81, (0.070)	1.813, (0.762) 2.38, (0.017)
$Log(Pop)$		−0.164, (0.071) −2.32, (0.021)	0.059, (0.099) 0.60, (0.552)
$CL{:}Res$			0.207, (0.174) 1.19, (0.234)
$PR{:}Res$			0.114, (0.162) 0.70, (0.482)
$Invest{:}Res$			0.130, (0.016) 8.00, (0.000)
$Savings{:}Res$			0.012, (0.009) 1.39, (0.163)
Constant	3.361, (0.283) 11.87, (0.000)	5.990, (1.169) 5.13, (0.000)	2.013, (1.656) 1.22, (0.224)
Summary statistics	$N = 3{,}619$, F.E. = 262 $F = 7.96, p = 0.000$	$N = 3{,}614$, F.E. = 262 $F = 7.44, p = 0.000$	$N = 2{,}313$, F.E. = 181 $F = 11.73, p = 0.000$

of a host of control variables often thought to be associated with economic growth. Before we discuss the impact of these controls, we pause to clarify what the analysis says about the role of institutions in influencing economic growth. For this we focus on the third model, although the results are very similar across all three model specifications.

The coefficients of 1.72 on W and −0.47 on S indicate that large-coalition systems have higher growth rates than small-coalition systems, and the smaller the selectorate, the faster the rate of growth. To give this some substance we compare two systems, both of which have a large selectorate ($S = 1$) but one with a large coalition ($W = 1$) and the other a small coalition ($W = 0$). On average the large-coalition system grows 1.72 percent faster than the small-coalition system. If instead of a large selectorate, the small-coalition system also had a small selectorate ($W = 0, S = 0$), then the large-W, large-S system still grows faster—1.25 percent faster on average. The long-run advantages of a large-coalition system for promoting economic growth must by now be obvious. However, in terms of institutional design, do these long-run benefits justify the short-term costs?

The coefficient of -1.251 on the political-change variable is statistically significant and indicates that for each of the two years following institutional change from the highest to lowest W, or vice versa, economic growth declines by 1.25 percent. Although the uncertainties created by institutional change appear to adversely affect economic conditions, the direction of the institutional change alters the economic impact of political change. The statistically significant coefficient of 1.81 on the $\Delta W/S_{t0-t-2}$ variable shows that if a large-selectorate system moves from the smallest-W category to the largest-W category, then the short-term impact of the political change over the next two years is positive.[13] Indeed, such an institutional change should induce a temporary boost of 0.56 percent in addition to the long-run advantages of a large-W system. In contrast, if the change occurs in reverse, from large W to small W, then the institutional change reduces growth rates by about 3 percent in each of the next two years, in addition to the long-term movement to an institutional arrangement that retards long-term growth.

At least from the perspective of the economic welfare of the average resident, the policy prescription is clear. In the short term, the enlargement of the winning coalition has on average either very mild negative consequences or positive benefits, and in the long run its growth advantages lift a country's residents out of poverty. Despite these obvious benefits, in chapter 9 we will show that it is not always to the benefit of leaders in large-coalition systems to foster democracy abroad. Paradoxically, although it would vastly improve the lot of people abroad, democratic nation builders do not, except under special circumstances, wish to promote the expansion of the winning coalition abroad.[14]

We provide one final, extremely demanding test. Earlier we noted that tax rates, transparency in government, openness to trade, and rule of law are each thought to contribute to economic growth. The tests in table 4.5 control for some but not for all of these factors. Our final test includes all of the variables in table 4.5, but adds several other controls. We include the residual effects of the tax rate (measured as the percentage of GDP that goes to taxes) not explained by W and S, as well as the effect of openness to trade that is independent of W and S. Additionally, we include the independent effects of transparency (measured by whether or not tax revenue is reported by the government) not explained directly by W and S, as well as *WS:DemRes* and *WS:IncomeRes*. Inclusion of so many factors greatly reduces the sample size but controls more thoroughly for rule of law (*WS:DemRes* in addition to *CL:Res* and *PR:Res*), transparency (*TaxYN:Res*), tax rates (*TaxGDP:Res*), and openness to trade (*Open:Res*).

The empirical results, based on 917 observations with 114 fixed effects, indicate that the impact of transparency, tax rates, trade openness, and democracy or autocracy that is independent of coalition size and selectorate size fails to meet conventional standards of statistical significance (i.e., the probability that the results are due to chance for these variables ranges between 0.111 and 0.580). The residual effect of civil liberties also fails to satisfy conventional views of significance ($p = 0.386$), as does population size. Selectorate size has a negative effect on growth, as predicted, and is significant with a one-tailed test ($p = 0.046$, one-tailed). The effect of coalition size is highly significant ($p < 0.01$) and positive, as anticipated by the theory. The coefficient of 3.20 suggests a substantial substantive effect of large coalition size on growth as well. Change in the loyalty norm improves subsequent growth, though the effect is statistically weak ($p = 0.154$ or 0.077 one-tailed). The measure of political change continues to have a debilitating effect on growth, though the effect is statistically attenuated ($p = 0.166$ or 0.083 one-tailed).[15]

Political rights help promote growth ($p < 0.05$), though the size of the coefficient (0.56) is much smaller than the size of the effect from coalition expansion. Higher-income societies also enjoy higher growth rates according to this analysis (coefficient of 1.02, $p = 0.00$). Thus, even after taking a host of important political and economic factors into account, coalition size remains a substantively and statistically meaningful contributor to economic growth.

The statistical results indicate that institutional change contributes to growth, but does growth contribute to institutional change (Jackman 1974; Burkhart and Lewis-Beck 1994)? In the following test we examine whether the growth rates in each of the four preceding years lead to an institutional change in W. We find that the cumulative effect of prior growth is not significantly related to changes in governmental inclusiveness ($N = 4,597, p = 0.479$). Interestingly, prior growth is significantly associated with *PoliticalChange*, the variable that measures institutional upheaval regardless of its direction ($N = 4{,}395, p = 0.000$). Thus it appears that growth fosters institutional instability but does not systematically encourage development of a more inclusive coalition structure.

With or without additional control variables, lagged growth does *not* significantly influence subsequent changes in the size of the winning coalition. Growth apparently does not cause consistent institutional changes, at least with regard to the institutions on which we focus. This finding must be discouraging for policymakers who think that economic growth leads to democratization. This claim, often made specifically in the context of policy debate about China's political future, is not warranted by the record of history. Economic success does not, by itself, induce political change favoring more inclusive institutions.

We close this discussion with a caveat about the well-known and important nonlinear association between democracy and growth uncovered by Barro (1996, 1997). Barro's result points to a debilitating characteristic of democracy. Because the median voter's income is generally well below the mean income of all the voters, democratic societies tend to favor redistributive policies that shift resources from the relatively wealthy to the relatively poor. This may be to the good socially, but it apparently produces a marked diminution in growth rates, as reported by Barro.

Indeed, Barro's contention that the median voter's interests can lead to debilitating effects for growth is made in a broader context by a number of development theorists. Some make the case that democratization (or, implicitly, institutional development) is an endogenous product of economic development or, alternatively, that development is retarded by high levels of democratization (Lipset 1959; Jackman 1974; Wittman 1989; Sirowy and Inkeles 1990; Przeworski and Limongi 1993; Burkhart and Lewis-Beck 1994; Barro 1996; Feng 1997; Feng and Zak 1999). Yi Feng and Paul Zak (2001, 4) sum up the debate by observing that "the resolution of this puzzle is that democratic transitions occur both in economies that are economically successful as well as those that are economically unsuccessful so that no unambiguous cross-sectional correlation between democracy and growth should be evident."

We are agnostic with regard to whether economic development causes aspects of democratization other than winning-coalition size and selectorate size. Recall that neither the size of the winning coalition nor the size of the selectorate alone matches any prominent definition of democracy or autocracy or any other categorical regime type. By controlling for the independent contributions of democracy (and of income), we can see the separate contribution made by coalition size or the loyalty norm to major political decisions and outcomes on economic and social policy.

If we add either the residual or total effects of *Democracy* and *Democracy* squared to the regression results reported in table 4.5, we do not find the significant downturn reported by Barro and others. More important, we do find that the effect of coalition size on the growth rate remains robust with regard to significance and the size of the coefficient. Thus, the effect of coalition size is robust and independent of other characteristics of democracy that may themselves dampen growth or have no consequential impact on growth. Institutional engineers in the World Bank, the IMF, and elsewhere would do well to consider this distinction when helping poorer countries reform their political institutions.

Of course, most societies cannot and do not constantly shift their institutional arrangements, now expanding the size of the coalition and later contracting it.[16] So we must also ask what happens to the predictability of growth once a government achieves a coalition requirement of any particular size. The survival of leaders who rely on large coalitions is hypothesized to depend on their public-goods performance. Therefore, leaders in such systems endeavor to maintain consistently high growth. In contrast, economic growth is a theoretically less important determinant of political survival in small-coalition systems.[17] Although all else being equal, small-coalition leaders prefer growth, their survival does not hinge on it and so it is not their central policy focus. While sometimes a small-W leader's policies coincide with policies that promote growth, this is not always the case. The promotion of growth is more erratic in small-W systems than in large-W systems. The theory anticipates that variance in growth shrinks when the coalition is large, and expands when the coalition is small. The evidence strongly reinforces this expectation. For model 1 (now being able to return to our standard models), the t-statistic between coalition size and *VarGrow*—our indicator of variance or uncertainty about growth rates, measured as each country's variance in growth rate from year to year—is −12.87 and for S it is 2.72. Both are significant and each is in the direction predicted by the selectorate theory, with an R^2 of 0.15 ($N = 5{,}287$). Models 2, 3, and 4 produce comparable findings. Their respective t-statistics for W or W/S are −6.59, −13.14, and −8.73. R^2

for these models varies between a low of 0.14 and a high of 0.25. Societies with larger winning coalitions have more predictable, less uncertain growth rates than do societies with smaller coalitions. Low variance in growth is an attractive feature of a polity that makes it ripe for high rates of investment and savings, which encourage still further growth in the future.

All of the analyses undertaken thus far have provided encouragement for the belief that the large size of democratic coalitions is central to the success of this form of government in promoting labor over leisure, low taxes, high per capita incomes, and high economic growth rates. Other aspects of democracy so far have proven less consequential and less consistent in their beneficial effects. Autocratic structures that favor a small coalition and strong norms of loyalty to incumbent leaders have been seen to promote low incomes, low growth, high taxes, and leisure over productive labor. These analyses have all helped point the way toward understanding variation in government revenue and in economic growth. Now we turn to the other side of the macrogovernment ledger, namely, expenditures and their relationship to political institutions.

Government Expenditures, Expenditures Per Capita, and Opportunities for Kleptocracy

According to the selectorate theory, spending decisions are strategic. While leaders want to retain as many resources as possible for their own discretionary use, institutional arrangements influence their ability to do so without jeopardizing their tenure in office. Because the loyalty norm created by the focus on private goods and the risk of exclusion from future coalitions is strong in small-coalition systems, leaders can provide low levels of rewards and still adequately match the best possible offer of a challenger. Leaders in such systems need not spend much to survive.

This is not true for those who head large-coalition governments with their concomitantly weak loyalty norm. Leaders in such systems need to work hard to provide benefits for their supporters and cannot afford to skim off resources if they wish to survive. Ignoring for a moment the possibility of deficit spending, these incentives mean that when the coalition is small, government expenditures are expected to be relatively small, and when the coalition is large, so are government expenditures. Small-coalition leaders can survive spending a smaller quantity of what they collect than can large-coalition leaders. This creates the opportunity for kleptocracy.

In practice, many governments engage in deficit spending. Although in our formal model such a possibility was ruled out, we conjecture that small-coalition leaders are more likely to engage in such behavior than are large-coalition leaders. By funding their discretionary pet projects, or rewarding cronies with lucrative government contracts, deficit spending allows leaders to skim off resources. However, in the case of deficit spending the resources are skimmed off of future revenues rather than current revenues. Small-coalition institutional arrangements make both forms of misappropriation (that is, stealing from funds collected or spending resources yet to be collected) easier for leaders. Leaders in large winning-coalition systems need to work hard to provide rewards for their supporters; they have far less scope to direct funds away from policies that optimally reward their coalition. Leaders in such systems are more likely to run budgets that are close to balanced. Small-coalition leaders can either steal funds collected, leading to what from an accounting viewpoint looks like a budget surplus, or overspend on discretionary projects, which leads to a budget deficit. Of course, small-coalition leaders might actively engage in both behaviors and so make expenditures and revenues appear to balance. This possibility makes the tests to follow extremely demanding. While large-coalition leaders cannot steal on either end, small-coalition leaders can potentially steal on both ends. Our tests focus on showing that large-coalition leaders remain closer to a balanced budget than small-coalition leaders do.

If the theory is borne out, we should observe positive associations between W and *Expenditures* and a tendency to spend approximately all of revenue, not much more or less, when W is large. When W is small, expenditures are predicted to be smaller and there is expected to be more imbalance between revenue and expenditures, so that more is available for the kleptocratic leader.

Revenue and *Expenditures* are measured as a proportion of GDP. The data are assembled by the World Bank and currently cover the years 1970–1999. *Revenue* is assessed as tax revenue (TaxGDP). The variable *Kleptocracy* is measured as the absolute value of the difference between revenue and expenditures (i.e., |TaxGDP-*Expenditure*|). The absolute value is used so that in cases of deficit spending we can evaluate our conjecture, while also testing the derived hypothesis that the gap between revenue and expenditure is greater when W is small and S is large than when their sizes are reversed.[18]

Expenditures

The four standard models, summarized in table 4.6, all show a significant increase in government expenditures as one moves from the smallest-coalition systems to the largest-coalition systems. Societies with large populations appear to enjoy economies of scale that help hold expenditures down, while societies with high per capita incomes spend more. However, even after controlling for these effects (or the independent, positive, and significant impact of democracy), large coalition size and a weak loyalty norm are still powerful indicators of higher government spending. But on the negative side, models 1 and 2 show that S also has a significant positive impact on government expenditure. The theory, though, leads to the expectation that as selectorate size increases, the loyalty norm is strengthened and so spending should decrease. The tests in models 3 and 4 assess the impact of W/S, and the effect is as predicted. This leads us to infer that the positive independent effect of S is possibly an artifact of selection bias in the reportage of government expenditures. To assess this possibility, we construct a dummy variable called *ExpendYN*. It is coded 1 if *Expenditure* is not missing data and is coded 0 if *Expenditure* is missing data. A logit analysis of *ExpendYN* as the dependent variable, with W and S as independent variables, shows a strong selection effect in favor of large-W systems ($z = 16.14$, $p = 0.000$, $N = 12,462$) and insignificance for S ($z = 0.20$, $p = 0.841$). The data on government expenditures disproportionately reflect information about

Table 4.6
Summary of institutional effects on expenditures

β, t, R² β, t, n β, t,	W, model 1 S	W, model 2 S WS:DemRes	W/S, model 3	W/S, model 4 WS:DemRes
Expenditures	3.77, 2.95, 0.02 2.78, 2.63, 2,703	2.32, 2.33, 0.18 3.10, 3.66, 2,373 2.83, 2.46	5.62, 5.31, 0.02 2,703	4.37, 5.33, 0.25 2,373 1.55, 1.42

large-coalition polities. These polities, of course, must have a large selectorate as well.[19]

Government spending, in the aggregate, is consistent with the expectations derived from the selectorate theory. Though the variance explained is small, still the central tendency—as measured by statistical significance—shows that large-coalition, weak-loyalty-norm polities spend more. Is it also true that they leave less over for kleptocrats, or do they just have more to spend? We answer this question in the next section.

Kleptocracy

Kleptocracy plays a more complicated role in our model than any of the other factors we have thus far examined. The opportunity for the incumbent leadership to steal from the state depends on how much must be spent on keeping the loyalty of the coalition. The theory indicates that the more that is available for a corrupt leader to take, the greater the private-goods focus and the less the total expenditure by the government relative to revenue. Our tests reflect the expectation that the opportunity for theft of the state's wealth diminishes as W increases and as S decreases. Having said that, we recognize that some leaders are personally civic-minded. Such leaders can take the discretionary funds that constitute their opportunity for kleptocracy and spend them on projects that enhance general welfare in the society; they are not inclined to steal from the state. Our theory does not include an independent assessment of each leader's degree of civic-mindedness, though we do not deny its existence. The selectorate theory does suggest that selection institutions create strong incentives for leaders who are interested in keeping their job and that such incentives dampen the personal spirit of civic-mindedness when the winning coalition is small, especially if the selectorate is large.

The theory leads us to expect that large coalition size favors a reduction in the opportunity for kleptocracy. That is, the theory favors a *Kleptocracy* score tending toward zero as W gets larger (and as S gets smaller). Figure 4.1 shows a graphic representation of the expected pattern. As noted earlier, we measure *Kleptocracy* as the absolute difference between revenue and spending to facilitate an evaluation of the propensity for political systems to keep expenditure and revenue in balance, in which case the indicator *Kleptocracy* = 0. We evaluate the

Table 4.7
Kleptocracy and political institutions

β, t, R^2 β, t, n $\beta, t,$	W, model 1 S	W, model 2 S $WS{:}DemRes$	W/S, model 3	W/S, model 4 $WS{:}DemRes$
Kleptocracy	−5.26, −3.16, 0.03 3.70, 2.69, 1,489	−5.60, −6.86, 0.10 2.62, 3.70, 1,356 −3.18, −3.61	−2.42, −1.90, 0.01 1,489	−3.77, −5.97, 0.09 1,356 −3.77, −5.97

theory's predictions first with our four standard models, as summarized in table 4.7. Then we turn to more elaborate tests that take into account sources of government revenue other than taxes.

The results for the four standard models are consistent with those anticipated from the theory. W (or W/S) is negatively signed and S is positively signed and each is significant. The spread between what government takes in and what it spends grows larger as winning coalitions get smaller and as the selectorate gets larger. Other characteristics of democracy also substantially diminish the opportunity for kleptocracy. The opportunity for kleptocracy apparently is maximized in rigged electoral autocracies—that is, regimes with small W and large S and other autocratic characteristics.

With the results from our standard models in mind, we now look at *Kleptocracy* while taking into account other sources of government revenue besides taxes. We add controls for government debt as a percentage of GDP and per capita foreign aid received. Debt and aid, of course, provide two other opportunities to direct funds toward kleptocratic uses. Indeed, we find that the gap between revenue and expenditure rises with debt and with foreign aid per capita, while continuing to rise significantly as the size of the winning coalition diminishes. As Easterly (2001) outlines, foreign aid has not been a panacea for economic development. Our analyses suggest that this is because the aid is not allocated toward the policy goals for which the donor hoped. Table 4.8 shows the results of two regression analyses for which *Kleptocracy* is the variable to be explained. The first looks at the independent effects of W and S, while the second evaluates the impact of W/S, in each case controlling for the effects of democracy and per capita income that are independent of coalition size and selectorate size. We control as well for the size of each country's population and for its per capita foreign aid receipts and

Table 4.8
Kleptocracy, institutions, debt, and aid

	Coef., (std. error) t-stat., (prob.)	Coef., (std. error) t-stat., (prob.)
W	−3.90, (1.13) −3.44, (0.001)	
S	0.20, (0.77) 0.26, (0.794)	
W/S		−3.73, (0.95) −3.93, (0.000)
Log(Pop)	−0.67, (0.15) −4.45, (0.000)	−0.66, (0.15) −4.43, (0.000)
WS:DemRes	1.02, (0.96) 1.19, (0.235)	0.91, (0.84) 1.07, (0.284)
WS:IncomeRes	−0.98, (0.26) −3.71, (0.000)	−0.97, (0.26) −3.81, (0.000)
%Debt	0.06, (0.004) 14.09, (0.000)	0.06, (0.004) 14.22, (0.000)
Aid per Capita	27.68, (4.68) 5.92, (0.000)	27.73, (4.68) 5.93, (0.000)
Constant	14.17, (2.80) 5.05, (0.000)	14.17, (2.83) 5.99, (0.000)
Summary statistics	$F = 76.48, p = 0.000$ $N = 547$, F.E. = 95	$F = 89.16, p = 0.000$ $N = 547$, F.E. = 95

its debt as a percentage of GDP. The overall variance explained is 45 percent in each model. In these tests, coalition size continues to exert a substantial effect in reducing the threat of kleptocracy. The independent effect of other aspects of democracy is no longer visible once we add controls for foreign aid and debt as sources of money for leaders. These other sources of money do not dampen the opportunity leaders have to create a large gap between tax revenue and spending. Quite the contrary, these other sources of money simply bolster the kleptocratic opportunity, a fact that aid donors and those who advocate debt forgiveness might wish to keep in mind.

Illustrating Kleptocratic Politics

The statistical evidence lends credence to our hypotheses linking political institutions to opportunities for kleptocracy. The results proved robust even after correcting for the independent effects of income and of other aspects of democracy or autocracy besides coalition and selectorate size, and even after taking the impact of foreign aid and indebtedness into account. Now we illustrate the workings of the theory with a brief case history, one that is elaborated further later in this book.

Those of us fortunate enough to live in large-coalition systems are disturbed by stories of political corruption and sleaziness. While stories of politicians mishandling public funds are unfortunately all too commonplace, the scale of theft relative to national income in Western democracies is but a drop in the ocean compared to the level of kleptocracy in some small-W, large-S systems. The *Guinness Book of Records 1999* (p. 84) records former Philippine President Ferdinand Marcos as guilty of the largest-ever theft, $860.8 million in 1986. He is estimated to have stolen between $5 and $10 billion during his thirty-one-year reign. This is comparable to Mobutu Sese Seko, former leader of Zaire (now Congo), who is alleged to have amassed a personal fortune of over $4 billion (*Facts on File*, May 22, 1997, p. 351) during his years in office. Of course, by its very nature, the true extent of theft in such kleptocratic regimes is likely never to be fully known. In comparison, former German Chancellor Helmut Kohl's mishandling of party funds or questions about former U.S. President William Clinton's removal of furniture from the White House pale into insignificance. While the excesses of contemporary leaders like Ferdinand Marcos and Mobutu Sese Seko are horrendous, in a historical context many appear little more than petty criminals.

The caliphate established by the Arabs following the death of the Prophet Muhammad shows the extent to which leaders can extract discretionary resources. Finer (1997, 675) describes the caliphate as

a Palace polity. It was a government by tribal Arab chieftains superimposing themselves as an exclusive racial/religious military caste on pre-existing administration and living as parasites on the population. . . . It was a more than commonly exploitive empire, where "exploitive" means taking in from subjects more than is handed back to them. The principal motivation of Arab tribesmen in following leaders was booty, and this was immense. . . . The taxation system they introduced was deliberately designed to keep the Arab extractors apart from the subjects, the providers. Little of this taxation came back to the subjects in the way of public works.

The vast Umayyad and Abbasid dynasties of the caliphate, which stretched from Spain through North Africa and much of the Middle East, were the epitome of a small-W, large-S system. Their political structure and operations appear to have been designed to redistribute wealth from the poor to the rich through taxation. It was a system in which kleptoc-racy was an essential characteristic of rule.

Effectively, the selectorate in the caliphate dynasties were the Arab nomads, whose number varied from 100,000–200,000 at the time of Muhammad's initial conquest to several million in later dynasties. To attain and keep office, the caliphs required support from two groups. The first group consisted of the leading provincial governors, senior admin-istrators, and senior generals. Given the pool of at least several hundred thousand potential supporters, the caliphs rarely had problems filling such positions. In addition to relying on these secular supporters, the caliphs depended on a religious group, the Ulema, for their legitimacy. Unlike its contemporary Byzantine rival, the Islamic religious organiza-tion was decentralized, and while the caliphs needed approval by a pro-portion of the Ulema, they were free to pick supporters from within the Ulema. Competition within the Ulema to join the coalition meant caliphs never had problems attaining the requisite religious endorsement. In contrast, to be crowned Basileus in Constantinople required the support of the head of the Orthodox church. While both Byzantium and the caliphate were small-coalition systems, this difference in selectorate size—that is, between needing the support of *the* religious leader in one case, and needing the support of *a* religious leader in the other—pro-foundly altered the functioning of these polities. The larger selectorate in the caliphate led both to a lower turnover of leaders and to a greater number of rebellions in the caliphate as compared to Byzantium (see Finer's comparison of the stability of the two systems on pp. 702–704).

The kleptocratic ability of the caliphate was truly staggering. Finer (1997, 724) reports central government revenues for 918–919 as 15.5 million dinars, of which a colossal 10.5 million was spent on the caliph's household. It appears the luxurious excesses of the *Arabian Nights* were no exaggeration (Mather 1947). While it is hard to scale the value of 15.5 million dinars, it must have been a massive amount given the sheer size of the empire and the extraordinarily high taxes imposed. Truly, the caliphate epitomized the high-taxation, high-kleptocracy approach indicative of a small-coalition, large-selectorate political system.

Per Capita Expenditures

One empirical regularity from figure 4.1 remains to be tested in this chapter, with the remaining hypotheses about public- and private-goods expenditures being the subject of the next chapter. Per capita government expenditure approximates our theory's prediction of the welfare of the individual members of the winning coalition. That welfare is a mix of private and public benefits, with public benefits being increasingly dominant in the overall welfare of coalition members as coalition size increases. Of course, those public benefits also uplift the welfare of everyone else in society. Because they improve everyone's welfare, per capita government expenditure is, except in extremely small coalition settings, a reasonable proxy for coalition welfare. Remember, the government spends more as coalition size expands and particularly as the loyalty norm weakens.

The selectorate model implies a specific, subtle, surprising, and demanding prediction regarding the welfare of members of the winning coalition. As can be seen in figure 4.1, the expectation is that the size of the winning coalition has a nonmonotonic, asymmetric relationship to coalition welfare. Increasing the size of the coalition from a very low level diminishes the welfare of the coalition's members because private goods drop off faster than the decrease in the loyalty norm bolsters spending. Beyond a turning point, however, the beneficial effects of the loyalty norm kick in as the coalition gets larger and the incumbent is forced to spend more on the coalition (and less on herself) and more on public goods in particular, thereby improving the welfare of the coalition's members and all others in society. The predicted pattern also has significant implications about aspects of politics other than the welfare of coalition members. In particular, it leads to predictions about the conditions under which, once established, large-coalition, inclusive democracy is expected to persist and when societies can be expected to churn through governments as a consequence of recurring coups d'état. These issues, however, are best left for later chapters. In this chapter we are interested in whether the predicted asymmetric, nonmonotonic functional relationship between per capita government expenditures and coalition size is observed.

In fact, the check-mark-like swoosh relationship between per capita government spending and coalition size emerges from the data. Based on 2,694 observations (with 207 region-year fixed effects), covering the years 1970–1999, we find that W has a slope, measured in constant 1995 U.S. dollars, of $-\$7,888$ ($p = 0.001$) and W^2 has a positive slope of $\$10,599$ ($p = 0.000$). The turning point at which the welfare of the coalition

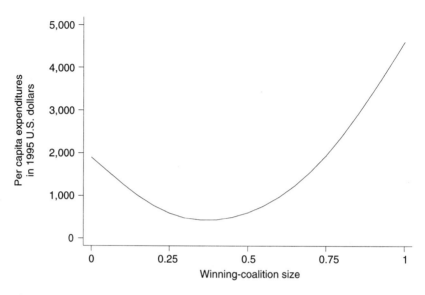

Figure 4.2
Coalition welfare and coalition size: the empirical relationship

members begins to improve occurs when W equals 0.37, with welfare improvement continuing through to the top of W's range ($W = 1$). Forty-three percent of the variance in government per capita expenditures is explained just by the effect of coalition size and the square of coalition size. Figure 4.2 shows the shape of the observed association. It looks like the functional relationship depicted in figure 4.1 that reflects the expectation deduced from the selectorate theory.

It is noteworthy that theoretically and empirically, the maximum welfare derived by coalition members in small-coalition systems (consisting of more than one person) is always less than the maximum available as the coalition's size expands beyond some threshold (0.37 in our data) toward infinity. This means—at least for polities with substantial populations—that inclusive, democratic governance is more likely to enhance welfare than is a small-coalition, autocratic form of government. In the next chapter we return to this theme by examining the propensity of regimes to provide different mixes of public and private goods as a function of coalition size.

Conclusion

Two of the most important decisions governments make concern how much to tax and how much to spend. Citizens, in turn, make choices about how hard to work or play in response to government taxing policies. The selectorate theory suggested that tax rates drop as governments become more inclusive and rise as they become more exclusive. As a consequence of tax-rate decisions, the theory led us to predict that economically productive activity would be greater in large-coalition democracies than in small-coalition autocracies, juntas, and monarchies. Conversely, more leisure consumption was predicted for small-coalition polities, especially those with a large selectorate. These results together imply higher per capita incomes in large-coalition systems than in small-coalition structures, again especially those rigged-election autocracies characterized by large selectorates and small coalitions. Together these claims imply higher growth rates in large-coalition polities and less opportunity for kleptocracy. Finally, we examined how per capita government expenditure responds to coalition size, testing the prediction that the relationship would be asymmetric and nonmonotonic, with coalition welfare falling and then rising as coalition size increases.

We undertook extensive empirical tests of the hypotheses concerned with taxing, spending, kleptocracy, and growth. We provided a set of demanding models that include region-year fixed effects and that isolate the effects of W and S, as well as other remaining, independent effects of democracy or autocracy, and of income. We also offered tests of our most important propositions that provided controls for such factors as savings and investment rates, civil liberties, political rights, and other relevant factors. Despite the demands of these tests and the crudity of our indicators for coalition size and selectorate size, the evidence consistently provided encouragement for the view that the selectorate theory offers a plausible account of the ties between governance structure and key aspects of economic and political performance.

Institutions, Peace, and Prosperity

The selectorate theory proposes that small winning coalitions encourage leaders to use public resources to provide private goods to their supporters at the expense of public welfare. This effect is exacerbated when the selectorate is large. Large winning coalitions, by contrast, diminish loyalty to the incumbent, resulting in an increase in expenditures and in the provision of public welfare. Before examining the statistical evidence for the relationships between public- and private-goods expenditures and selection institutions, we illustrate the workings of our theory with a brief example from the history of the Greek city-state of Sparta. Then we report the more systematic tests of the relationship between winning-coalition size, selectorate size, and the production of public and private goods that are part of the core of the selectorate model. This chapter closes with an investigation of the pattern of governance of Leopold II. He was simultaneously king of Belgium and the ruler of the Congo Free State, providing a natural experiment with which to evaluate the selectorate theory.

The Shift from Public to Private Goods in Sparta

In 404 BC, Sparta defeated Athens in the Peloponnesian War and entered its era of glory. That golden era ended just thirty-three years later on the battlefield of Leuctra, where Thebes crushed the Spartans, killing many members of the oligarchy who were the heart and soul of the previously undefeated Spartan army. Later we show how the earlier success of Sparta contained the seeds of its own destruction. Here we focus on how Spartan policy changed in response to a contraction in the size of the winning coalition and selectorate following the Peloponnesian War. We begin with a brief review of the unusual political organization of the Spartan city-state from the late fifth century BC to the reign of King Agis IV (244–241 BC).

Sparta's citizens, the Spartiate, formed the backbone of its army. Indeed, one of the privileges of being a male Spartiate was the right to provide Spartan security through service in the military. The Spartiate constituted the selectorate. Their numbers never exceeded 9,000 out of a population of more than 225,000 Spartans, including Lacedaemonians and subjects. That is, at the beginning of the period we discuss, Sparta had a small selectorate, with the winning coalition constituting a relatively large proportion of the selectorate. It was a system that produced both public and private goods, with private goods greatly advantaging all in the Spartiate.[1] Following the Peloponnesian War, the number of Spartiate fell more or less continuously, as the impoverishment of many of its members resulted in their inability to meet their obligation to contribute to the costs of the syssitia, which, as we explain below, was the social organization primarily responsible for the distribution of benefits.[2] So too did the size of the winning coalition decline, seemingly at a faster rate than the selectorate, as some citizens became wealthier and more influential compared to others. This change introduced into Spartan politics the pattern our model predicts for systems with small winning coalitions. Specifically, politicians curried favor with prospective backers through the provision of private benefits to those who supported them.

Membership in the Spartiate required membership in a syssition, a unit of fifteen men that formed the basis of the army. Members of each syssition were required to contribute dues to its common benefit, most notably the monthly common mess or banquet (see Finer, 1997, 336–340, on Spartan institutions). All citizens partook in the benefits offered by the syssitia, including the installation of common values, education, and the distribution of food through the common mess.[3] These benefits acted as public goods within the Spartiate in the sense that the distribution of these benefits—clearly acting as private benefits not enjoyed by those outside the Spartiate—were intended to diminish or eliminate competition among Spartiate members, treating each equally.

The syssitia was introduced to Sparta by Lycurgus (about 800 BC) with the intention that it would help diminish reliance on wealth as a means of judging citizens, thereby promoting greater equality, much as his land reforms, educational policies, and other programs were designed to do. The syssitia was cast as an instrument for providing a sense of community among the Spartans. The rich and proud and the poor and humble among the Spartiate (and others) were all offered identical, modest fare through the syssitia, thereby giving us the modern meaning of the word *Spartan*. Beyond its role as a means of redistributing wealth (a private good), it also promoted education (through the Agoge) and common values or norms of conduct. Additionally, the syssitia was central to the extraordinary security against foreign invasion provided by the Spartan military, with such security being a crucial public good.

By 418 BC the male Spartiate population fell to around 3,600. After the defeat at Leuctra in 371 BC, the Spartiate consisted of fewer than 1,000 men. By the middle of the third century BC, it is estimated to have been below 700 (Fornis and Casillas 1997). This steady decline was to contribute to a dramatic change in Spartan policy and in the welfare of its people.

Sparta was ruled by three groups, consisting of a pair of hereditary kings who led the army, a body of twenty-eight elders aged sixty or more, known as the gerousia, and five administrators called ephors. The gerousia and ephors were elected by the Spartiate in assembly (the ecclesia), the former for life and the latter for a single one-year term. The elections were held with a form of what today is called approval voting by a semisecret ballot. Judges listened to the applause and shouts of support as each candidate silently walked across the assembly. The judges were sheltered from view and so could not see and presumably did not know who the candidate was at any given moment. The voters, of course, knew who cheered for whom. Those deemed by the judges to have received the most enthusiastic support were elected. In essence, a candidate achieved a winning coalition among the Spartiate selectorate by receiving sufficient support to rank among the top n candidates, with n equal to the number of positions to be filled. For the ephors, of course, this was always five positions, but for the gerousia it depended on how many died in a given year. A winning coalition, then, did not require more than a majority and could be a significantly smaller plurality (Plutarch, n.d.).

Each of the leaders exerted different aspects of control. The kings had primary responsibility for military affairs, providing the public good of security. The gerousia set the legislative agenda, while the ephors exerted financial, judicial, and administrative authority not only over the Spartiate, but also over the gerousia and the kings. To them fell primary responsibility for ensuring the rule of law. It is noteworthy that the ephors and the gerousia could overrule the kings either directly (the ephors) or indirectly through the exercise of a veto over the assembly (the gerousia) (see <http://www.csun.edu/~hcfl104/sparta-c.html>). In that sense, the Spartan system provided some separation of powers among the leadership institutions.

At the time of the Peloponnesian War, with the Spartiate consisting of about 3,600 members, a winning coalition required not more than 1,800 members. Given the voting system, it could have required even a smaller number in a hotly contested election. After the disaster of Leuctra, the winning coalition had diminished to less than 500 members, perhaps much less. A century later the winning coalition was reduced to fewer than 350 members, again possibly much less. This diminution in the size of the winning coalition should have produced an increasing emphasis on the provision of private goods according to the selectorate theory. Such a shift toward private goods did follow.

Victory in the Peloponnesian War and the Spartan dominance that followed led to a period of military adventures that provided vast new wealth to the city-state. This new wealth was concentrated in the hands of those Spartiate who obtained political and military commands throughout Sparta's newly enlarged empire, breaking down the earlier Spartan emphasis on relative equality.

The infusion of wealth raised by the externally secured resources of Sparta had two broad political effects.[4] First, the demands of wealth in supporting the syssitia forced poorer members of the Spartiate to drop out of their syssition and so to lose their rights as citizens, thereby diminishing the size of the selectorate and the winning coalition. Second, ambitious men too young to be elected to the gerousia embarked on careers as independent military commanders to gain wealth for themselves and their followers. They often gained the opportunity of foreign command through favoritism or cronyism (Fornis and Casillas 1997).

The demands of wealth and the corrupted opportunity to gain wealth through military command caused Spartan politics to shift from the provision of general benefits to all the Spartiate and to many in the lower classes to a system that provided personal benefits to a few wealthy and powerful men. Stephen Hodkinson (2000, 167) describes the shift as follows:

The development of foreign commands was . . . an oligarchic trend which worked against the cohesion of the citizen body. The traditional ambition of leading the gerousia must have restrained their behavior toward ordinary citizens, since it was upon such men that their election depended. The ambition for foreign commands, however, made no such demands, but depended rather upon the possession of influence or a patron's goodwill. There was less need for moderate behavior toward ordinary Spartiates; on the contrary, there was a built-in incentive for would-be commanders and patrons to increase their personal status through the acquisition of additional property, often at the expense of poorer citizens.

The infusion of wealth that accompanied victory in the Peloponnesian War, concentrated in the hands of a small subset of the Spartiate, plus the substantial diminution in the selectorate and the winning coalition size, changed the substance of Spartan politics. Following institutional change there was a diminished emphasis on public goods and an intense competition over private goods produced from empire.

Both the growth in resources and the shrinkage of the Spartiate produce this shift from public to private goods. The ratio between resources and the size of a winning coalition drives the focus of leaders on either public or private goods; the greater the ratio, the more attractive the provision of private goods to selected supporters becomes because there is more money for fewer hands. In the end, this competition for power through the provision of personal wealth to supporters led some Spartan factions to plan revolution against their system (e.g., the conspiracy to overthrow the government led by Cinadon in 398 BC) while, shortly after its greatest triumph, the system met its fate on the battlefield of Leuctra.[5]

The decline in the Spartiate eroded Sparta's position. The elevation of private benefits over public goods following the victory in the Peloponnesian War weakened the city-state, diminished the Spartiate, and caused an unprecedented emphasis on wealth within the city's ruling circles. Sparta's philosophical foundation lay in the belief that spare living and severe training prepared male Spartiate members for battle. It was thought that great wealth promoted an easy life that made men weak, jeopardizing "national" security. Whether such increased weakness contributed to Sparta's defeat at Leuctra we cannot say for sure, though Xenophon, a Spartan sympathizer, provides hints that this was the case. We know that the army of General Epaminondas, the brilliant leader of Thebes's military campaign, was greatly outnumbered by the Spartan army under King Cleombrotos. Xenophon observes of the contending cavalries (where Thebes had a numerical advantage) that

the Theban horses were in a high state of training and efficiency, thanks to their war with the Orchomenians, and also their war with Thespiae; the Lacedaemonian [i.e., Spartan] cavalry was at its very worst just now. The horses were reared and kept by the richest citizens; but whenever the levy was called out, a trooper appeared who took the horse with any sort of arms that might be presented to him, and set off on an expedition at a moment's notice. These troopers, too, were the least able-bodied of the men—just raw recruits simply set astride their horses, and wanting in all soldierly ambition. Such was the cavalry of either antagonist. (Xenophon, *Hellenica*, book VI, chap. IV; downloaded from <http://www.fordham.edu/halsall/ancient/371leuctra.html>)

In this account wealth contributed to a reluctance to risk the best horsemen and horses,[6] and that wealth brought a shift in loyalties and an emphasis on private goods as the means of currying favor with a few key individuals rather than maintaining the support of a broad base of ordinary citizens. So diminished was Sparta that by the reign of King Agis IV the society was in need of political transformation, which he tried to provide through radical constitutional reforms.

With the experience of Sparta as an illustration of some of our claims, we turn now to a systematic investigation of the relationship between selection institutions, public goods, and private goods. In the discussions that follow, we evaluate the hypotheses that as coalition size increases, public-goods provision increases and private-goods provision decreases.

Rather than burden the reader with a plethora of statistical tables, we summarize the results in the text using the four standard models introduced in chapter 4—minus the variable S, because selectorate size does not directly influence public- and private-goods provisions according to the selectorate theory—whenever appropriate. We incorporate a fifth model that adds *Parl_Pres* to the effects of W, *Log(Pop)*, *WS:DemRes*, and *WS:Income* in the case of the public goods that we treat as core elements for any successful polity. These are, as explained below, civil liberties, political rights, transparency, and peace.

Given the sheer number of analyses reported here, we will generally report only the impact of the key selection institutions. For instance, for model 1 we will typically only report the coefficient and t-statistic for the variable W, and the summary statistic of R^2 and the number of observations. The typical models presented are:

Model 1: W, fixed effects

Model 2: W, *WS:IncomeRes*, *WS:DemRes*, *Log(Pop)*, fixed effects

Model 3: W/S, fixed effects

Model 4: W/S, *WS:IncomeRes*, *WS:DemRes*, *Log(Pop)*, fixed effects

Model 5: *Parl_Pres*, W, *WS:IncomeRes*, *WS:DemRes*, *Log(Pop)*, fixed effects

For those who are interested in more of the details regarding our tests, we provide, as noted earlier, the data and Stata .do program files on our website so that the tests reported here can be replicated and other tests performed. When it is essential, we provide a fuller statistical description in the body of the text. As appropriate, we comment near the end of the chapter on the independent impact of the size of each polity, based on the logarithm of its population. This provides a partial way to address the debate referred to in chapter 2 between Montesquieu and Madison over the relative merits of large and small republics.

Empirical Assessments: Core Public Goods

The selectorate theory draws our attention to the provision of public and private goods, but it does not instruct us as to which particular public or private benefits will constitute the bundle of goods offered by any leader. The specific bundle of goods presumably depends on the personal tastes and needs of the winning coalition, selectorate, and leadership. Therefore, we test the theory against a broad array of such goods. However, a small set of core public goods appear to be of universal importance.

Civil liberties, political rights, transparency, peace, and prosperity are among the most important public welfare enhancements that any government can provide (among other sources, see North and Weingast 1989; Campos and Root 1996; Barro 1997; Bueno de Mesquita and Root 2000; Przeworski 2001). The welfare of citizens is enhanced when their government provides ready access to information about how and what the government is doing, when citizens are secure against domestic tyranny (i.e., they have assured civil liberties), when they are protected against foreign threats (i.e., peace rather than war), and when property is secured against the confiscatory whims of the state (i.e., political rights). Further, when a polity provides an environment that secures its citizens against domestic abuses and war, it establishes the foundations for economic growth, an argument for which we provided evidence in chapter 4. Whatever else is found in the basket of public goods provided by government, the benefits of civil liberties, political rights, transparency, peace, and growing prosperity seem to be of universal desirability among residents of a state. Therefore, we treat civil liberties, political rights, transparency, and peace as core public goods. We have already seen that selection institutions promote high per capita incomes and growth, so we already know that prosperity is associated with a large-coalition, democratic governing structure.

Civil Liberties and Political Rights

Freedom House has devised a widely used seven-point scale to assess civil liberties and another seven-point scale to assess the protection of political rights. These data are available for about 140 countries spanning the years 1972–1999. In the Freedom House data, higher values are associated with lower levels of civil liberties or protection of political rights. To avoid confusion, we reverse the direction of these variables by subtracting their scores from 8. This ensures that higher scores are associated with higher levels of political-rights protection and civil liberties. The variables are identified, respectively, as *Civil Liberties* and *Political Rights*.

Transparency is, by its nature, difficult to measure. Transparency concerns the extent to which governments make crucial information readily available for inspection and evaluation (Root and Nellis 2000; Barro 2000). Access to information permits citizens, prospective domestic and foreign investors, and others to make informed judgments. Naturally, government leaders will not be keen on transparency if they are heavily engaged in rent seeking, kleptocracy, or other corrupt practices. These are the behaviors predicted by the selectorate theory to be among the bread and butter of leaders who depend on a small coalition. We capitalize on the incentive for obfuscation to develop indirect indicators of transparency.

The World Bank, United Nations, and other international agencies routinely ask governments to report critical economic indicators. Two such indicators are our variables *Income* and *TaxGDP*, with the latter assessing tax revenue as a percentage of GDP.[7] We believe that information on per capita income and on the government's tax revenue are important in helping people formulate views on how hard to work and how much they should count on the government to provide policies that are broadly beneficial to the society. Government failure to report this information may reflect a government's strategic interest in hiding just such information. With that in mind, we estimate transparency with two dichotomous variables: *TaxYN and IncomeYN*.

We assign a country a score of 1 on *TaxYN* each year for which the variable *TaxGDP* is not missing data for that country. In all other years for which we have data on at least one country for *TaxGDP* between 1970 and 1990, a given country receives a score of 0 on TaxYN if for that country that year *TaxGDP* is missing data. Since the World Bank has no incentive to hide the data, we work on the premise that the data are missing because the government failed to report them. *IncomeYN* is measured in an equivalent way based on whether real per capita income data were or were not provided by the country in question during the years 1960–1999. We now evaluate the variation in performance on these variables as a function of institutional setting.

The statistical results of our analyses are summarized in table 5.1. Both civil liberties and political rights show extraordinary dependence on coalition size. The larger the coalition or the weaker the loyalty norm, the stronger the society's commitment both to civil liberties and to political rights. The residual portion of *Democracy* also remains strongly associated with these two central benefits. What is more, the variable *Parl_Pres* also shows a significant association with the extension and protection of civil liberties and a respectable, though decidedly weaker, association with political rights. That is, within the realm of systems generally considered democratic, presidential systems (with their larger coalition requirements) do better at advancing civil liberties and somewhat better at protecting political rights than parliamentary systems (with their

Table 5.1
Civil liberties, political rights, and coalition size

	W model 1	*W* model 2 *WS:DemRes*	*W/S* model 3	*W/S* model 4 *WS:DemRes*	*W* model 5 *WS:DemRes* *Parl_Pres*
Civil Liberties	4.11, 53.78, 0.55 4,078	4.37, 70.18, 0.78 3.56, 44.31, 3,223	4.19, 54.11, 0.55 4,004	4.41, 70.30, 0.78 3.60, 44.83, 3,223	3.88, 46.81, 0.82 3.45, 35.95, 1,906 1.08, 9.53
Political Rights	5.49, 72.90, 0.67 4,078	5.85, 102.02, 0.87 4.07, 55.04, 3,223	5.56, 72.27, 0.67 4,004	5.87, 99.76, 0.86 4.12, 54.74, 3,223	5.52, 71.93, 0.88 3.67, 41.29, 1,906 0.15, 1.45

Note: The reported values in the first row of each cell are *W*'s (or *W/S*'s) coefficient, *t*-statistic, and R^2. The second row displays the coefficient for *WS:DemRes* and its *t*-statistic, as well as *N*. The third row provides the coefficient and *t*-statistic for *Parl_Pres*.

smaller coalition requirements). Eighty to ninety percent of the variance in these two fundamental benefits of a civil society is explained by institutional arrangements. Income also contributes strongly to the degree to which a society is characterized by civil liberties and political rights, but neither income effects nor the effects of democracy notably diminish the impact that coalition size has on these public goods. The t-statistics for W (or W/S) in association with civil liberties varies in the five models between a low of 47 and a high of 70. When we switch to a focus on political rights, the t-statistic varies between a low of 72 and a high of 102! The substantive impact, revealed through the regression coefficients, is even more impressive. A shift from a score of 0 to a score of 1 on the indicator of coalition size, W, implies a four- to six-point jump on the seven-point civil liberties and political-rights scales.

Transparency

Government failure to report tax revenue data to international organizations like the World Bank, the United Nations, and so forth could plausibly be the consequence of at least two considerations. Because of poverty, the government may not have sufficient resources to collect the necessary information and so it remains unreported. Additionally or alternatively, the government may have political incentives to hide the truth and may find this easiest to do by just not reporting information. The former explanation argues that the failure to achieve transparency through reportage is an endogenous consequence of income effects. This account is benign. The latter explanation depends on selection institutions and the incentives to hide reliable information. Hiding such information—thereby producing a selection effect in the data—is decidedly not benign. It is a way to protect the vices of leaders: corruption, cronyism, and kleptocracy. Separating the two explanations, therefore, is important in helping us reach conclusions about the degree to which the lack of transparency reflects simple cost considerations and the extent to which it reflects governments that have something to hide.

The evidence regarding transparency in tax-revenue reporting, shown in table 5.2, supports both explanations. That is, there is some truth to the argument that poor societies fail to report tax revenue, presumably because they just cannot afford to gather the information. However, there is also evidence that some do not report the information because of their institutional makeup. For instance, some very poor countries, like

Table 5.2
Transparency in governance and coalition size

	W for model 1	W for model 2 WS:DemRes	W/S for model 3	W/S for model 4 WS:DemRes	W for model 5 WS:DemRes Parl_Pres
TaxYN	3.21, 20.54, 493 3,981	2.89, 12.97, 208 1.03, 4.06, 2,168	2.20, 11.36, 206 2,491	2.87, 12.81, 203 1.06, 4.16, 2,168	2.28, 9.23, 148 0.57, 2.16, 2,055 1.08, 2.49
IncomeYN	3.07, 24.60, 685 7,168	3.63, 17.48, 541 2.77, 11.75, 3,910	2.47, 17.92, 345 5,386	3.70, 17.67, 551 2.83, 11.95, 3,910	2.19, 7.09, 205 1.28, 3.93, 2,490 5.34, 3.89

Note: The coefficient and z-statistic for *W* (or *W/S*) and χ^2 for the logit analyses regarding *TaxYN* and *IncomeYN* are in row 1 of each cell. The second row, as apropriate, reports the coefficient and z-statistic for *WS:DemRes* and the number of observations (*N*). The third row, when appropriate, reports the coefficient and z-statistic associated with *Parl_Pres*.

Papua New Guinea, Botswana, and Sri Lanka, with fairly large coalition governance structures, have managed for years to report their tax revenue. Poverty did not serve as an insurmountable impediment for them. At least on this dimension, they appear to be more transparent in their revenue structure than, for example, such small-coalition, undemocratic, relatively high income societies as Iraq and Saudi Arabia, which in the past have routinely failed to report tax revenues. The pattern of tax reportage in relation to governance institutions is strong and systematically consistent with expectations across the range of regime types. Even within democracies, as *Parl_Pres* shows, tax reportage is significantly more likely in larger-coalition voting systems than in smaller-coalition democratic systems. What is more, while coalition size is by far the most powerful institutional effect measured, the other remaining characteristics of democracy or autocracy also contribute significantly to the likelihood that a government reports tax revenues. Less democratic, smaller-coalition systems consistently engage in less transparent governance, as assessed by the tax-reportage indicator. The effects of coalition size are not only stronger than those for other political institutions, but they are also stronger than the independent impact of income on transparency, as assessed through tax-revenue reportage.

Turning to our second indicator of transparency—*IncomeYN*—we find a similar pattern to that reported for tax transparency. Of course, when evaluating transparency based on reportage of per capita income data, we cannot control for the level of income in the society, since income is missing data by definition when the *IncomeYN* indicator equals zero. The results even more strongly support the expectation that transparency is enhanced by large coalition size when *IncomeYN* is evaluated, although, as we have seen, *TaxYN* shows very strong associations. Once again, the effect of selection institutions on transparency is found to hold across the range of regime types. *Parl_Pres* is highly significant. In fact, while democracies are overwhelmingly likely to report per capita income data, we find that all presidential and mixed parliamentary/presidential systems in our data report such income information, while a small, but statistically significant, set of parliamentary regimes do not. Additionally, as with *TaxYN*, the residual characteristics of democracy not captured by coalition and selectorate size also exert a positive influence on transparency, though once again the effect of coalition size is substantially larger than the effect of other aspects of democratic or authoritarian governance. In short, we find strong evidence for the contention that small-coalition systems are systematically less likely to have transparency in governance, at least as evaluated through reportage of tax revenues or per capita income data.

War or Peace

Chapters 6 and 9 are devoted to investigating how coalition size and selectorate size influence different aspects of war-and-peace decisions. Chapter 8 looks at how institutional factors influence the risk of civil war and other forms of domestic unrest. Here we only touch briefly on the subject by looking at the likelihood that a country becomes enmeshed in war—whether interstate or civil—as a function of its institutional composition. We estimate peace by using the Correlates of War indicator of a country's involvement in an interstate war and/or the presence or absence within a country's territory of civil war (Singer and Small 1994). This is a dummy variable called *War*; it is coded 1 for years in which the country was engaged in either international or civil war and coded 0 otherwise. For the analysis of *War* we switch from region-year fixed effects to country fixed effects. The reason for the switch is straightforward. War, other than civil war, inherently involves more than one state. Most wars are fought between neighboring states (Vasquez 2000, 1995; Huth 1996). Therefore, they occur within the specific context of a region-year. By controlling for region-year fixed effects in the case of *War* we remove, by construction, all of the variance of interest. Therefore we control instead for each country, thereby controlling for any general characteristics of the country that might independently influence its propensity to engage in war.

One topic of heated debate among international relations researchers centers on the question of whether democracies are less prone to war than other types of regimes. That democracies are more pacific toward one another is widely accepted, but not the claim that democracies are inherently more peaceful or more averse to war in general. The evidence from our analyses reinforces the uncertainty about whether *Democracy* makes states more pacific. We do not find a consistent pattern across the three models that control for *WS:DemRes*. The coefficients for *WS:DemRes* with *War* are negative, as expected by those who maintain that democracies are more pacific than autocracies. In two of the three models that include control for *WS:DemRes*, the coefficient is not only negative, but it is statistically significant, adding further support to the claim for democratic pacifism. In model 5, which controls for *Parl_Pres*, the coefficient is insignificant. Thus, no firm inference can be reached regarding democratic pacifism based on these tests.

No such ambiguity attaches to the coalition variable *W* or to the loyalty norm, *W/S*. Whether alone, in concert with *WS:DemRes*, or in conjunction with *WS:DemRes* and *Parl_Pres*, large coalition size and a weak loyalty norm significantly reduce the probability of war. These results, though far from conclusive, reinforce the notion that it is the influence of coalition size—more than other characteristics of regime types—that promotes peace over war. Table 5.3 summarizes the results regarding war.

Table 5.3
Institutional effects on the likelihood of war

	W for model 1	*W* for model 2 *WS:DemRes*	*W/S* for model 3	*W/S* for model 4	*W* for model 5 *WS:DemRes* *Parl_Pres*
War	−1.17, −8.79, 79 12,871	−2.11, −3.25, 18 −1.24, −2.37, 1,613	−1.06, −8.59, 75 8,537	−2.60, −3.70, 21 −1.40, −2.63, 1,613	−1.61, −1.92, 43 −0.12, −0.16, 941 −102.64, −0.00

Note: Cell entries for the logit analyses regarding *War* are the coefficient, *z*-statistic for *W* (or *W/S*), and χ^2 in row 1; coefficient and *z*-statistic for *WS:DemRes* in row 2 as well as *N*. Row 3, when appropriate, presents the coefficient and *z*-statistic for *Parl_Pres*.

Summary for Core Public Goods

The core public-goods predictions based on the selectorate theory pertain to the promotion of civil liberties, political rights, transparency, peace, and prosperity. The previous chapter investigated the relationship between selection institutions and prosperity. Thus far in this chapter we have reported test results that evaluate the relationship between coalition size and civil liberties, political rights, war or peace, and two indicators of transparency in government. All of the statistical results have proven consistent with the selectorate theory. Most have also reinforced our conjecture regarding differences between parliamentary, mixed, and presidential democratic systems. The aspects of democracy or autocracy not accounted for by coalition size and selectorate size—except for one test regarding war—also significantly enhance the prospects that a government performs well in producing core public goods. However, in every instance, the strength of association between coalition size and the provision of core public goods is stronger than the strength of association tied to other characteristics of a regime's institutions. Apparently, democracy, and in particular dependence on a large winning coalition, makes polities more responsive to the natural interests of citizens in ensuring their civil liberties, securing them within safe and peaceful borders, protecting their political rights, and making the workings of government transparent. Much still remains to be discussed about other public and private goods, but the core results are in and they are encouraging.

General Public Goods

As noted earlier, we believe most people share a common desire to be governed by a regime that is attentive to providing the core public goods we have discussed. Other goods that potentially enhance the common welfare are more likely to be subject to variation in tastes and needs as we move from society to society. Some will prefer to emphasize education, others health care, and still others social security and so forth. We turn our attention now to alternative baskets of public benefits that government might provide to see whether, in general, the provision of a variety of public goods is associated with coalition size and other aspects of governing institutions.

Education

Education certainly is a primary area for government investment in the current and future welfare of its citizenry. At least some previous research bolsters the view that selection institutions influence education levels, rather than causality operating in the other direction. As Peter H. Lindert (2001, 21) notes,

Most countries with high voting shares got them long before they attained anything like the schooling levels they had reached in, say, 1880. In fact, the rise of primary schooling came from public funding, which in turn came from critical votes. In most cases those critical votes took place within a context of widespread suffrage. The great rise of French enrolments in the 1870s and the 1880s was preceded by the jump to near universal adult male suffrage in 1848. England's catch-up after 1891 was preceded not on[ly] by the Fees Act of 1891 and the Forster Education Act of 1870, but by the extension of suffrage in the first three Reform Acts.

With Lindert's observations in mind, we evaluate governmental commitment to education through statistical tests of the first four models applied to core public goods.[8] We assess education based on four distinct indicators. Our first indicator of education is the percentage of GDP spent by the central government on education. Drawn from the World Bank, the variable is called *EducExpend* and it evaluates the government's overall financial commitment to the advancement of education. A second indicator, also derived from the World Bank, called *Illiteracy*, measures the percentage of the population over the age of fifteen that is illiterate. Here we evaluate in part the government's success in promoting at least basic educational attainment. The third, which we label *EDT*, measures the cumulative years of education for the average member of the labor force and is taken from Fischer 1993.[9] This variable provides insight into the government's success at developing human capital as a fundamental input for economic productivity. The final indicator, referred to as *FemSec*, evaluates the percentage of secondary school students who are female. This indicator speaks both to the general availability of education and to societal efforts to promote approximate gender equality.

Table 5.4 displays the bivariate correlations (with *N* in parentheses) among the four education indicators. As is evident, *Illiteracy* is strongly and negatively correlated with the educational level of the labor force

Table 5.4
Correlations among education indicators

	EducExpend	EDT	Illiteracy
EDT	0.40 (1,676)		
Illiteracy	–0.20 (2,725)	–0.86 (1,513)	
FemSec	0.40 (1,005)	0.64 (369)	–0.75 (917)

and with the percentage of secondary school students who are female. The remaining correlations are modest in magnitude, indicating that these variables capture meaningfully different aspects of a polity's record on education.

The results of our analysis are summarized in table 5.5. The assessment of spending on education as a proportion of GDP reveals that large-coalition governments commit greater resources to education than do small-coalition polities. On its own, W has a substantial statistical and substantive impact on educational spending. The smallest-coalition systems, for instance, spend on average just 2.67 percent of GDP on education. Those with slightly larger coalitions ($W = 0.25$) raise average spending to 3.41 percent. This is almost exactly the same amount spent on average by polities with a coalition score of 0.50. Those polities edging in on being truly democratic, with coalition scores of 0.75, spend 3.54 percent of GDP on education on average, while the largest-coalition systems ($W = 1.00$) spend on average 4.8 percent of GDP on education.

Adding controls for population, income, and the residual effects of democracy-autocracy, highlights the substantial impact that coalition size has on education spending. Although income substantially increases spending on education, as do the remaining aspects of democracy not accounted for by selection institutions, still the impact of W is statistically and substantively the largest effect we observe. Apparently, societies either enjoy economies of scale in education spending or countries with larger populations systematically undervalue education. National scale, as assessed by population, is inversely associated with educational spending. These results, consistent as they are with the selectorate theory, also reinforce theoretical deductions by John Roemer (2001). Roemer concludes that democracy inherently promotes education. Like Lindert, we have seen that it appears specifically to be the coalitional feature of democracy that most helps explain higher educational spending, though the residual effects of other aspects of democracy contribute as well to a boost in such spending.

It is, of course, one thing to spend on education and another thing to spend effectively. The illiteracy rate in a country is a reasonable approximation of the gross effectiveness of educational spending. Coalition size proves to be a very strong indicator of a country's illiteracy rate. A shift from the smallest to the largest coalition structure produces a 20 to 40 percent reduction in the illiteracy rate among those fifteen years old or older. The residual effects of other aspects of democracy are insignificant, while income effects, not surprisingly, also contribute significantly to a reduction in illiteracy. An order-of-magnitude increase in real per capita income, independent of selection institutions, reduces illiteracy by another 10 percent. Perhaps most informatively, even if we control for government spending on education—itself a powerful predictor of reduced illiteracy—the impact of coalition size remains statistically and substantively more important than does spending. A 1 percent increase in government spending on education as a share of GDP results in a 10 percent drop in illiteracy on average, while with this control in place (plus controls for *WS:IncomeRes*, *WS:DemRes*, and population), a shift from the smallest-coalition to the largest-coalition category accounts for a 36 percent drop in illiteracy, with 54 percent of the variance in illiteracy explained.

In our data, government spending on education, especially in large-coalition societies, reduces illiteracy. What is the effect of coalition size, however, on the average educational attainment of the labor force? Again the evidence provides substantial encouragement for the view that governments whose leaders depend on large coalitions are governments that foster relatively high educational attainment. The largest coalition size adds between three and four years, on average, to the cumulative education of the labor force. Democracy, presidentialism (as seen on our website), and high per capita income also significantly help to improve the educational preparedness of workers, though the magnitude of these effects are much smaller than the effects of *W*. This remains true even if we add a control for educational expenditures. The selection institutions that we hypothesize influence leadership incentives to spend on public goods or private goods seem to foster significant improvements in average education levels. Concretely put, a three- to four-year increase in the average cumulative education of the labor force is equivalent to the difference between workers who go through eight years of school and workers who complete high school.

Our final educational indicator helps evaluate a society's commitment to equal opportunity between males and females. The greater the deviation in the percentage of secondary school students who are female from 50 percent, the greater the inequality in gender treatment. Since more than twice as many country-years fall below 50 percent as above, it is clear that on average high school–aged girls are discriminated against and high school–aged boys advantaged in most societies. Thus, the variable *FemSec* helps us evaluate the extent to which educational opportunity is provided equally as a function of institutional arrangements.

The political institutions examined in the selectorate theory have a profound impact on the opportunities females have to gain equal access to secondary education. All the standard model specifications we use point to a 5 to 9 percent improvement in secondary school access for female students in the largest-coalition arrangements as compared to the smallest. Income also contributes significantly to equal opportunity education, though the independent impact of income separate from the selection institutions is decidedly smaller than is the effect of coalition size. The residual impact of democracy is negative and borders on one-tailed significance. That is, the characteristics of democracy or autocracy (as measured by POLITY) that are not captured by W and S have a tendency to harm equality of educational opportunity at the secondary school level.

The beneficial impact of a large-coalition system is seen more dramatically by stepping beyond our standard models. We calculated the impact of coalition size on *FemSec* in two more ways while continuing to control for population, *WS:IncomeRes*, and *WS:DemRes* (as well as our standard fixed effects, of course). In one test, we investigated the effect only for cases for which *FemSec* is less than 50 percent. These are societies that by our measures to a greater or lesser extent underrepresent females in their secondary schools. We replicated the analysis, but this time only for cases for which *FemSec* was greater than 50 percent, meaning that females appear to be overrepresented in secondary schools. If equal treatment is a cornerstone public good of a "just society," we should expect that as W increases, the effect on *FemSec* is to move it toward equality of representation among the genders. Thus, the first of these analyses should show a strong positive effect from W on female representation in secondary school; the second test should show a significant negative coefficient for W, indicating that the system is moving to reduce the percentage of females as compared to the relatively underrepresented males in secondary school.

In fact, we observe the predicted reversal in signs for W. In places where females are underrepresented, the coefficient associated with coalition size is 6.10 ($p = 0.000$, $N = 744$), while the residual effects of other aspects of democracy (or autocracy) partially offset this benefit from large coalition size (coefficient = -5.14, $p = 0.000$). When females are relatively overrepresented in secondary schools, the coefficient for W is -3.13 ($p = 0.000$, $N = 335$), with the remaining impact of democracy again acting to offset the benefits from dependence on a large coalition ($WS{:}DemRes$'s coefficient is 2.21, $p = 0.066$). In each of these regression analyses, the residual impact of income helps reinforce the equality-promoting aspects of a large coalition, yielding a significant improvement in equality in the majority of societies in which female students are underrepresented in secondary school.

The results for education are robust in the face of a host of economic, political, and social factors that can be introduced as control variables. There can be little doubt that coalition size and the loyalty norm are important contributors to government support for education. Table 5.5 summarizes the essential results.

Table 5.5
Summary of institutional effects on education

	W for model 1	W for model 2 $WS{:}DemRes$	W/S for model 3	W/S for model 4 $WS{:}DemRes$
EducExpend	1.96, 18.94, 0.12 3,402	2.20, 20.20, 0.22 0.52, 3.66, 3,083	1.89, 17.80, 0.12 3,313	2.25, 20.50, 0.22 0.55, 3.88, 3,083
EDT	3.34, 25.44, 0.35 2,900	4.71, 37.15, 0.64 1.73, 10.46, 2,415	3.34, 25.34, 0.34 2,900	4.85, 38.23, 0.65 1.80, 11.00, 2,415
Illiteracy	$-19.08, -16.32, 0.19$ 3,904	$-36.40, -28.10, 0.49$ $-10.23, -30.93, 2,709$	$-21.06, -17.49, 0.20$ 3,512	$-37.73, -28.99, 0.34$ $-1.18, -0.81, 2,709$
FemSec	4.90, 6.58, 0.15 1,375	6.48, 7.73, 0.24 $-1.63, -1.35, 1,079$	5.69, 7.67, 0.17 1,324	6.68, 7.92, 0.24 $-1.59, -1.32, 1,079$

Note: Entries in first row of each cell are the W (or W/S) coefficient, t-statistic, and R^2. The second row is the coefficient and t-statistic for $WS{:}DemRes$ plus N.

Health Care and Social Security

General health care is a valuable public benefit. We are concerned here with its availability and quality as a function of coalition size and as a function of other aspects of democracy or autocracy. To evaluate the health of a society, we turn to eleven different indicators, most of which have self-explanatory names. These are *LifeExp*, *DeathRate*, *InfMort*, *HealthEXP*, *Doctors*, *Beds*, *LowBirth*, *ImmuneMEASLES*, *ImmuneDPT*, *Water*, and *GXPDSSEC*. All but the last are taken from the World Bank, although the World Bank has now discontinued collection of the variable *Water*, which measures the percentage of the population with access to safe drinking water covering the years 1970–1995. The indicator for government expenditures on social security (*GXPDSSEC*) is taken from the data set amassed by Alvares et al. (1997) and is available for the period from 1970 to 1990.

The first three indicators (*LifeExp*, *DeathRate*, and *InfMort*) evaluate overall health. Clearly, a populace is healthier and better off if life expectancy is long, the death rate is low, and the infant mortality rate is low. These indicators cover the years 1960–1999. *HealthEXP* is the percentage of GDP spent on health care, reflecting the societal commitment to advancing good health. Data on this variable only encompass the years 1990–1999. *Doctors* and *Beds* evaluate the number of doctors and hospital beds per thousand people, and each covers the time span from 1960 to 1999. *LowBirth* measures the percentage of births that are low-birthweight babies. Because low birth weight is a major theat to infant survival, keeping this percentage as low as possible is highly desirable. Data for this variable also span the years from 1960 to 1999. Additionally, it is desirable to immunize young children against the measles, diphtheria, pertussis, and tetanus (the last three are commonly given together in one immunization referred to as DPT). The two immunization indicators reflect the percentage of children under the age of twelve immunized for the measles and for DPT respectively. The measles-immunization variable covers the years 1975–1999, while the DPT indicator encompasses 1974–1999.

Table 5.6 summarizes the results regarding health care and social security. Before discussing these results, it is noteworthy that half of the fifty-five bivariate correlations among the eleven health indicators are less than |0.50| and only eight are at least as large as |0.70|. That is, the indi-

Table 5.6
Health, social security, and coalition size

	W for model 1	W for model 2 WS:DemRes	W/S for model 3	W/S for model 4 WS:DemRes
LifeExp	11.31, 26.61, 0.28 3,193	13.45, 32.78, 0.68 2.76, 5.02, 2,042	11.99, 26.41, 0.33 2,701	13.66, 33.25, 0.68 2.89, 5.29, 2,042
DeathRate	−3.09, −13.94, 0.12 4,015	−3.74, −15.08, 0.25 −0.16, 0.47, 2,624	−3.65, −15.65, 0.14 3,435	−3.77, −15.12, 0.25 0.13, 0.38, 2,624
InfMort	−44.53, −24.82, 0.29 3,825	−52.32, −29.18, 0.62 −7.13, −2.93, 2,596	−48.42, −25.76, 0.33 3,377	−53.11, −29.52, 0.62 −7.52, −3.10, 2,596
HealthEXP	2.33, 8.99, 0.20 1,251	2.83, 10.42, 0.36 0.29, 0.78, 1,049	2.44, 9.09, 0.22 1,206	2.84, 10.44, 0.36 0.28, 0.77, 1,049
Doctors	0.05, 0.52, 0.11 2,003	0.51, 5.34, 0.31 −0.33, −2.60, 1,373	0.41, 4.95, 0.20 1,710	0.51, 5.30, 0.31 −0.33, −2.56, 1,373
Beds	2.45, 3.31, 0.04 1,436	3.53, 8.06, 0.39 0.28, 0.49, 962	3.71, 9.30, 0.24 1,158	3.55, 8.06, 0.39 0.32. 0.55, 962
LowBirth	−4.77, −4.38, 0.07 687	−7.92, −6.17, 0.32 4.23, 2.58, 535	−5.40, −4.78, 0.08 649	−8.16, −6.34, 0.32 4.24, 2.59, 535
Immune MEASLES	12.86, 8.13, 0.10 2,795	13.65, 7.54, 0.13 −8.99, −3.93, 2,029	13.14, 8.19, 0.10 2,687	13.25, 7.27, 0.13 −8.95, −3.91, 2,029
ImmuneDPT	21.51, 14.10, 0.15 2,981	23.13, 13.30, 0.25 −5.35, −2.45, 2,139	22.21, 14.31, 0.15 2,857	22.85, 13.03, 0.24 −5.23, −2.39, 2,139
Water	23.95, 7.07, 0.16 535	35.53, 9.99, 0.56 9.85, 2.31, 426	23.08, 6.72, 0.16 521	36.22, 10.16, 0.56 10.50, 2.47, 426
GXPDSSEC	2.10, 4.92, 0.29 1,238	4.02, 8.06, 0.54 2.07, 3.36, 1,075	2.13, 4.95, 0.29 1,238	4.16, 8.27, 0.54 2.14, 3.48, 1,075

Note: First-row cell entries are the coefficient and *t*-statistic for W (or W/S) and R^2. The second row displays the coefficient and *t*-statistic for *WS:DemRes* and shows N.

cators tap a diverse set of characteristics that measure variation in the health of a society's populace.

Life expectancy at birth is probably the single best indicator of the overall health of a population. In this regard, our use of region-year fixed effects makes tests of the relationship between selection institutions and life expectancy particularly tough, because the fixed effects are likely to soak up gross environmental factors like climate and regional economic development, which undoubtedly influence health and well-being. Nevertheless, the impact of coalition size or the loyalty norm on life expectancy is dramatic. Average life expectancy rises steadily as we move up the coalition ladder from W of 0 through W equal to 1.00. The average life expectancies are fifty-one years ($W = 0$, $N = 233$), fifty-six years ($W = 0.25$, $N = 437$), fifty-eight years ($W = 0.50$, $N = 1,104$), sixty-four years ($W = 0.75$, $N = 809$), and seventy-three years ($W = 1.00$, $N = 610$). Even after controlling for other aspects of governance (*WS:DemRes*) and the noninstitutionally induced effects of per capita income on health (*WS:IncomeRes*), living in a polity that depends on the largest-size coalition contributes nearly 13.5 more years of life than does living in a society that relies on the smallest-size coalition. The remaining aspects of democracy or autocracy add nearly another three years as one moves from the otherwise most autocratic to the most democratic regime. Income adds three more years. The impact of selection institutions is much more substantial than is the independent effect of income. With around 70 percent of the variance explained by our standard models, it is clear that the rules of governance are important for improving the prospect of a long life.

Across our data set, the crude death rate averages more than 11 per 1,000 people. The smallest-coalition polities average 16 per thousand, while the largest-coalition societies average a substantially lower 9 to 9.5 deaths per thousand. Here too we see that life holds out better health prospects in large-coalition settings than in small-coalition settings. The aspects of governance not captured by W and S (i.e., *WS:DemRes*) generally have an insignificant, marginal effect on death rates.

The average country-year rate of infant deaths per thousand live births in the data set is a bit over 57. In the smallest-coalition systems it is a depressing 111.5 per 1,000 live births. While still too high, in the largest-coalition systems the average is reduced to 17.1. Indeed, the coefficient for W with infant mortality in model 2 (which controls for population size, for other aspects of governance, and for independent income effects) is −52.3 (the *t*-statistic is −29.18), while residual income effects also reduce the infant mortality rate substantially (the coefficient is −13.6 and the *t*-statistic is −31.15), as do the residual effects of governing institutions other than W and S (the coefficient for *WS:DemRes* is −7.1, with a *t*-statistic of −2.93). Infants have a vastly better prospect of surviving and going on to live a long, prosperous life if they are born in a democratic, large-coalition society than if they are born anywhere else.

As is evident from table 5.6, similar findings obtain for each of the eleven indicators of health and social security. Large-coalition, weak-loyalty-norm selection institutions, independent of wealth, are associated with substantial increases in spending on health care, and the increased spending seems to deliver better health. Low-birth-weight babies are vastly less common in large-coalition polities than in small-coalition autocracies. Safe drinking water is far more available in large-coalition societies even if they have relatively low per capita incomes, while quality drinking water is relatively scarce in societies in which the government relies on a smaller coalition. Jamaica and the Dominican Republic, for instance, report per capita incomes of about $1,500 in the late 1980s or early 1990s, have relatively high scores on W (between 0.75 and 1.00), and are well above average in access to safe drinking water. Conversely, Lebanon and Oman during the same years report per capita incomes of between $5,000 and $10,000, low scores on W ($W = 0.25$), and relatively poor average access to safe drinking water.

The association between the number of doctors per thousand people and W by itself is not significant—thus far the only insignificant association between W and a public-goods indicator—though W or W/S is significant in all the other standard models when regressed against the number of doctors. Otherwise, W is significantly associated in each case with the health indicators. Interestingly, the same cannot be said for the characteristics of governance that are independent of W and S. $WS{:}DemRes$ is insignificant in the three models that control for it when it comes to health expenditures; it is insignificantly associated in two out of three models that include it when regressed against death rate or hospital beds; and most disturbingly, $WS{:}DemRes$ is significant in the wrong direction in the cases of doctors per 1,000 people, low-birth-weight babies, and the two immunization indicators. Here we see disturbing evidence that democracy per se is inadequate to ensure good health. The key factor appears to be the leadership's dependence on a large winning coalition, with other aspects of democracy either being inconsequential or, in some cases, acting to offset the benefits derived from a large-coalition structure.

Foreign Policy

Our public-goods indicators include two foreign policy measures. One—the variable called *War*—was introduced earlier. Now we introduce a variable called *Trade*. *Trade* is the variable Open found at the website for the Penn World Tables (<http://datacentre.chass.utoronto.ca:5680/pwt/docs/subjects.html>). The data for this variable cover the period from 1950 to 1992. *Trade* evaluates the openness of each country's economy to foreign imports and exports. The consequences of individual trades are, of course, private goods; they are both divisible and excludable (Conybeare 1984). However, a policy that promotes openness to trade is a public good in that it redounds to the benefit of all in society. It ensures consumers—and everyone is a consumer—that they can have access to quality goods at competitive prices rather than be limited to access to government-propped up industries that are likely to be inefficient (otherwise they would not require government protection from imports) and overpriced relative to the world market price for comparable quality.

An environment receptive to trade is generally accepted by economists as an environment that fosters greater national prosperity. Extensive trade usually indicates a society with low tariffs and few nontariff barriers to foreign competition. An economy open to trade typically offers little protection to inefficient domestic businesses faced with strong foreign competition, instead encouraging such competition. This means that citizens can choose to buy the products that fill their needs at the best price, whether those products are foreign or domestic. As a result, people can buy more goods, stimulate the economy, and help promote growth in the import, export, and domestic-production sectors of the economy. An economy open to imports and exports willingly exposes itself to efficiency-inducing competition.

Restrictions on the flow of imports and exports are generally motivated by political rather than economic considerations. Protecting the jobs of voters in democracies or protecting political cronies in authoritarian states helps leaders stay in office (Lohmann and O'Halloran 1994; McGillivray 1997). Politicians in any political system can be motivated to satisfy the needs of those who suffer adverse consequences from foreign competition. They are less interested in helping those who enjoy diffuse benefits from trade. Helping those who bear the brunt of the costs of trade means the politician is more likely to stay in office.

For leaders who rely on a small winning coalition, such as many authoritarian leaders, little meaningful offsetting pressure exists to get them to sacrifice their political cronies to enhance, on average, national economic performance. As long as they can keep the members of the winning coalition happy, these politicians are secure in office. The economic drag of restrictive trade policies need not burden such leaders.

We note in passing that the above observation explains the historical policies of mercantilism and import substitution. Mercantilist policies blocked imports and encouraged exports as a way of strengthening the national economy, according to the theorists of mercantilism. Of course, those policies did nothing of the kind; instead, they made domestic producers richer by reducing competition by imports and subsidizing export business. Such producers typically held monopolies granted by the king or were protected from domestic competition by royal policy. These restrictions made royal control into a private good that the king could grant to his supporters. Similarly, import substitution created protected industries whose control could be used as a political reward by the leader of the state. Once again, we see that policies that hurt the economy as a whole are politically advantageous to leaders who answer to a small winning coalition.

Leaders who require a large winning coalition, in contrast, face two problems when they pursue policies aimed at closing their country's economy to trade. First, the votes of producers who gain concentrated benefits from the absence of trade rarely add up to enough votes to provide the support needed to form a large winning coalition. Leaders in need of a large coalition must look beyond this small group, which means they must attract support from voters who do not gain from cutting the economy off to trade. Second, political opponents always look for ways to oust the incumbent at the next opportunity. In systems that rely on a large coalition, the quality of public policy looms large in the minds of voters and therefore looms large in an incumbent's prospects of reelection. Consequently, challengers work at persuading voters that conditions will improve under new leadership. One way to make things better for lots of voters is to allow competition from overseas goods, not just in one or two industries but in virtually all industries. In this way the benefits of trade will be dispersed across all voters. To counteract such a policy challenge, incumbents must improve their economic policies or face defeat. Receptive trade policies help them to do so nationally, though they may work against the politicians' interests in localized regions or districts (McGillivray 2003). In fact, others have already shown that democracies engage in trade with fewer barriers than do their autocratic counterparts (Mansfield, Milner, and Rosendorff 1998). Now we see how trade openness reacts to winning-coalition size.

Trade is promoted by a large winning coalition. The effects of W and W/S are consistently significant across our main models. The residual impact of democracy dampens openness to trade, while high per capita

Table 5.7
Summary of institutional effects on openness to trade

	W for model 1	W for model 2 WS:DemRes	W/S for model 3	W/S for model 4 WS:DemRes
Trade	18.20, 7.92, 0.01 4,784	15.81, 6.94, 0.34 −19.51, −6.66, 3,138	24.25, 10.53, 0.02 4,355	16.70, 7.25, 0.34 −19.25, −6.57, 3,138

Note: Cell entries in the first row are the coefficient and *t*-statistic for *W* (or *W/S*) and R^2. The second row, when appropriate, is the coefficient and *t*-statistic for *WS:DemRes* and *N*.

incomes also sharply improve receptivity to trade. Table 5.7 summarizes the effects of coalition size and the loyalty norm.

Public-Goods Summary

The evidence supports the contention that the size of a government's winning coalition is a significant factor promoting public-goods production. The effects are generally substantively, as well as statistically, meaningful. Correlation, however, is not causation. Of course, the fact that we have provided a deductive basis for the expectations fulfilled thus far by the empirical record elevates correlation to a plausible argument for causation on logical grounds. The evidence is considerably more mixed when it comes to aspects of governance that are independent of coalition size and selectorate size. The effects of these other characteristics sometimes reinforce the benefits of a large coalition, but at other times they are inconsequential or even act to countervail the societal gains from dependence on a large coalition.

Thus far we have analyzed twenty-one different public-goods indicators. These are in addition to our assessment in chapter 4 of hypotheses about per capita income, savings, investment, taxation, economic growth, government spending, and opportunities for kleptocracy. Now we ask how the scorecard looks with regard to the effects of coalition size, other aspects of democracy or autocracy, and the independent effect of income on public-goods provision.

More than 98 percent of the associations between *W* and the twenty-one public-goods measures (that is, sixty-two out of sixty-three associations) are statistically significant and in the predicted direction, based on the three standard models that include *W* as an independent variable.

One hundred percent of the associations between the public-goods indicators and W/S, our indicator of the strength of the loyalty norm, are significant and in the predicted direction. This is also true for the residual impact of income independent of selection institutions. Although income is consistently beneficial, its effects are almost always weaker than the direct effects of coalition size on public-goods provision.

The scorecard for the residual effects of *Democracy* is not nearly as impressive. The effect of democracy that is independent of W fails to meet conventional standards of statistical significance in 19 percent of the cases. In another 24 percent, there is a significant relationship, but its sign indicates a diminution in the provision of public goods. The remaining 57 percent are significant and reinforce an improvement in the provision of public goods. So much research has focused on categorical regime types like democracy or autocracy that these findings are worthy of great emphasis. Apparently the socially beneficial effects of democracy consistently come from requiring a large winning coalition and a weak loyalty norm (W/S). Whatever else characterizes democracy beyond a large coalition and a weak loyalty norm does not consistently contribute to the promotion of public welfare.

The most uneven results concern our conjecture that presidential systems provide more public goods than mixed systems, with these, in turn, providing more public goods than parliamentary systems. As we noted at the outset, our indicator *Parl_Pres* is far from adequate. Specifically, it fails to distinguish between parliamentary systems with proportional representation or multimember districts and those with single-member district, first-past-the-post electoral systems, although their coalition-size requirements vary markedly. With this caveat in mind, our results indicate that *Parl_Pres* is significant, in the predicted direction, in 43 percent of the cases. Another 43 percent are insignificant, with the remaining 14 percent being significant in the wrong direction. The poor showing highlights the importance of improvement in the estimation of coalition size in different democratic systems, as well, of course, as across all categorical political systems. On the plus side, recall that for core public goods, the distinction between parliamentary and presidential governance fared much better. Those core goods represent a bundle of public policies that the vast majority of people desire. The other public goods we evaluated are clearly important to most people, but they are more likely to vary in their significance than are the core goods.

Empirical Assessment of the Provision of Private Goods

Having established strong ties between coalition size, the loyalty norm, and the provision of public goods, we now direct attention to an examination of private goods. Do large coalitions also discourage the production of private goods by government, or do large coalitions just generally promote the production of every sort of benefit, public and private? Does democracy retard the provision of private benefits? Three factors—black market exchange-rate premiums, corruption, and construction—form the core of our assessment of the relationship between institutional arrangements and private-goods allocations to members of the winning coalition.

While we analyze three indicators of private goods, we note in passing that the variable *Consumption*, introduced earlier as an indicator of leisure, also has the characteristics of a private good, though not one directly allocated as part of the policy package proposed by an incumbent or challenger seeking office. Likewise the absence of transparency could be taken as indicating that private goods are being hidden from the light of day. It is, after all, hard to see why a government would want to hide its provision of public goods if it is doing a good job on this dimension. We focus on the three indicators *Black Market*, *Construction*, and *Corruption*. The first is measured as the average black market exchange-rate premium compared to the official exchange rate each year for each country.[10] This variable is available only for the years 1961–1988. Fischer (1993) presents it as one plus the logarithm of the premium above the official exchange rate paid for currencies. We use his formulation of the variable, although analyses using the unmodified premium directly lead to the same conclusions.

Black market exchange-rate premiums are not themselves the private goods that governments generally dole out. Rather, we believe a high black market exchange-rate premium is indicative of a polity that supports rent-seeking opportunities, because black markets can be made more-or-less accessible depending on how closely tied one is to the ruling elite. Additionally, opportunities to exchange currencies at the official rate are often restricted to government officials and the businesses they favor. These beneficiaries can then profit from arbitrage between the official and black market rates.

Construction is the sum of three variables derived from the World Bank. The three are residential, nonresidential, and other construction as a percentage of per capita capital stock in 1985 international prices. One of the easiest ways for leaders to hide misspent funds is on construction projects (Root and Nellis 2000). By spending large quantities of resources on construction, leaders create an opportunity to hide graft and corruption. Naturally, some large construction projects are perfectly legitimate, but the pathology of shoddy work and theft in construction is well known worldwide. Although the indicators we have do not directly address misappropriation of funds, we nevertheless treat the total percentage of capital stock per worker allocated to construction as a broad indicator of opportunities for corruption. *Construction* and *BlackMarket* share a correlation of 0.032 ($N = 612$).

We only have estimations of our third indicator of private-goods allocations, *Corruption*, for 1980, 1988, and 1995 through 1999. Our data on corruption come from Transparency International. They describe perceived corruption in varying numbers of states each year. The information in the data set is the result of tabulating questionnaires from surveys of businesspeople who have dealings in various states. Because countries receive relative corruption scores and different countries are covered by Transparency International's survey each year, the scores are not strictly comparable from year to year. We have, therefore, analyzed the data each year. The detailed results are found on our website. Since the association between selection institutions and a country's corruption ranking does not vary meaningfully from year to year, in the body of the text we report the associations after having pooled the time series together. Higher scores indicate little corruption, while lower scores reflect greater amounts of perceived corruption. The corruption scale runs from 0 (the most corrupt states) to 10 (the least corrupt states). We expect a positive association between coalition size and *Corruption*.

Black Market Rates

Black markets spring up when government restricts access to particular goods. Foreign economic sanctions promote black markets, for instance, by restricting the importation of contraband items. Domestically, black markets are stimulated by bans on the production or sale of certain goods, or as a consequence of restrictions on the use or conversion of currency. Regulators may censure particular books or access to news, for example, leading to a black market in those books or news media. When Galileo's *Dialogue* was banned because the Catholic Inquisitor deemed it heretical in its teaching that the earth moved and was not at the center of the universe, a vibrant black market emerged, pushing the price of the book up eightfold above its publication price (Sobel 1999). A similar black market growth in price within Muslim communities could be seen in the 1990s when Salman Rushdie's books were deemed heretical by Iran's clergy.

Black markets provide leaders with a golden opportunity to reward key constituents at the expense of the society in general. International economic sanctions essentially shut down Iraq's open economy throughout the 1990s. Yet it is widely rumored that Saddam Hussein's son Uday grew rich selling smuggled goods, particularly pharmaceuticals. Ordinary Iraqi citizens lack the same opportunity. Saddam Hussein used access to the black market as a private benefit to his loyal supporters. In the Soviet Union, members of the Communist Party were rewarded for their loyalty with access to special stores that sold goods not available to common citizens (Smith 1983). Many of the purchases from these stores found their way to resale on the black market, thereby providing a means to further enrich loyal members of the government's winning coalition, they being the only ones with access to the special stores.

The black market premium over the official exchange rate paid to obtain dollars, yen, or pounds reflects the restricted opportunity citizens have to convert their rupees, yuan, or rubles to hard currency. The government frequently looks the other way as these black marketeers ply their trade. Our indicator *BlackMarket* evaluates the average premium over the official exchange rate for each country's currency each year. This reflects the opportunity the government leadership has to distort the economy to favor cronies in the winning coalition at the expense of ordinary citizens. As such, it is probably strongly associated with the provision of private benefits. The question is, does this provision vary with the size of the winning coalition? To answer this question, we test private-goods provision against our standard models. The test results based on these models for *BlackMarket*, and also for *Corruption* and *Construction*, are summarized in table 5.8.

Based on 1,642 observations, we find that increasing W from its minimal value to its maximum alone can be sufficient to reduce the black market premium statistically by about 40 percent ($p = 0.000$), though only about 2 percent of the variance in black market exchange-rate premiums is explained by selection institutions. The marginal effect is magnified in model 2, which controls for population size and for the residual effects of income and democracy, though again with little variance explained. Shifting from the independent effects of autocracy to democracy, separate from the impact of selection institutions, further reduces the expected size of the black market premium, although not to the extent that coalition size does. Likewise the independent effect of income also reduces black market premiums.

Corruption

Corruption is a fact of life in many political systems, as the following quotation illustrates:

In November [1998], the state of Punjab, India, announced that its 18-month search for its most honest government officer (which carried an award of more than $2,000) was over, because they couldn't find anyone worthy. However, as part of the same program, the government revealed that it had found 300 corrupt officers worthy of prosecution.
<www.downhomer.com/webmay/1999/9904/page28.html>

At one time corruption was argued to be beneficial to economic and political development (Leff 1964; Huntington 1968). Despite this perspective, the large majority of those who have studied corruption now regard it as something to be eliminated or at least reduced.[11] This is so because it is thought, among other things, to have negative consequences for both economic growth (Mauro 1995; Knack and Keefer 1995) and the distribution of wealth across the state's population (Gupta, Davoodi, and Alonso-Terme 1998). In fact, recent evidence demonstrates that corruption has a staggering impact on investment in states pursuing centrally designed industrial policies (Ades and Di Tella 1997a). There is now a consequential literature on the negative economic effects of corruption.[12] Despite a growing literature on corruption, little by way of theoretically informed, cross-national analysis exists (see, however, Ades and Di Tella 1997a, 1997b, 1999; Triesman 2000). The selectorate model proposes a theoretical explanation for variation in the incentive of leaders to permit and even foster corruption. As noted in an analysis of corruption by Tanzi (1998, 30–31),

To a large extent it is the state that through its many policies and actions creates the environment and the incentives that influence those who pay bribes and those who accept or demand them. It is the state that influences the relationship between the briber and the bribee.

We believe the state creates these rent-seeking incentives by promoting loyalty to the leader through a small winning coalition and a large selectorate, since the former provides substantial access to private goods and the two together promote the loyalty norm. We test the idea that political leaders with small winning coalitions buy their continuation in office with permissive policies toward corruption by examining Transparency International's ranking of states on corruption. As is evident in table 5.8, the effects of selection institutions on corruption are substantial, both statistically and substantively.

It is sometimes argued that corruption is caused by poverty within a state. From the perspective of the selectorate model, poverty and corruption are both consequences of the same cause. However, given the prominence attached to this factor as an explanation, we cannot dismiss it in preference to our explanation without an empirical assessment of the effect of the political variables in the presence of poverty. Without control for income, population, and democracy, W or W/S alone explains close to 40 percent of the variance in corruption. The addition of $WS{:}Income$ and the other control variables increases the variance explained to just over 70 percent. Virtually all of the marginal increase in explanatory power comes from the independent effects of income, with population also making a meaningful contribution. $WS{:}DemRes$ is not significant in any of the models that include it. But even after taking the separate impact of income into account, W and W/S remain substantively and statistically highly significant. The provision of private benefits associated with corruption varies in accordance with the expectations derived from the selectorate model. If the political-selection institutions are configured to promote corruption, then crime does indeed pay. As former President Mobutu Sese Seko of Zaire (now Congo) declared to his supporters at a political rally, "Those of you who have stolen money, and used it to build homes here and not abroad, I congratulate you" (1996, 53).

Construction

The ease with which graft can be hidden in construction projects makes this industrial activity unusually attractive as a way for leaders to indulge

Table 5.8
Summary of institutional effects on private goods

	W for model 1	W for model 2 WS:Demres	W/S for model 3	W/S for model 4 WS:DemRes
BlackMarket	−0.292, −6.17, 0.019 1,642	−0.343, −6.36, 0.037 −0.214, −3.09, 1,254	−0.291, 6.14, 0.019 1,635	−0.353, −6.47, 0.0371 −0.218, −3.14, 1,254
Corruption	5.84, 11.76, 0.37 438	4.87, 12.58, 0.71 0.22, 0.46, 407	6.11, 11.95, 0.39 431	4.92, 12.72, 0.71 0.25, 0.52, 407
Construction	−9.77, 3.02, 0.01, 1,558	−12.36, 3.49, 0.01, 1,471	−9.83, 3.02, 0.01, 1,551	−12.49, 3.50, 0.015 −8.43, 0.076, 1,471

Note: Cell entries in the first row are the coefficients and *t*-statistics for *W* (or *W/S*), and R^2. The second row, when appropriate, shows the coefficient and *t*-statistic for *WS:DemRes* and *N*.

in cronyism and nepotism. Every society requires construction, of course, and not all of it involves the misappropriation of funds. But there is sufficient anecdotal evidence to suggest that construction involves an unusual degree of corrupt practices. We test the relationship between our indicator *Construction* and the effects of *W* and *W/S* using our standard models. The selectorate model performs well when it comes to assessing *Construction*, though the substantive impact is more modest than for corruption. *W* by itself is significantly associated with a dampening of construction projects and remains significant after we control for other factors. *WS:Income*, in contrast, turns out to contribute significantly to increasing construction. Rich societies build more—not surprisingly—and they do so especially if they have a small-coalition system with a strong loyalty norm. The general results are summarized in table 5.8.

Private Benefits and Violence: Sparta Reprised

When the coalition is small and corruption and black marketeering are rampant, it is also likely that government officials and coalition members engage in oppression and repression to prevent rebellions that would threaten to deprive the incumbent and her supporters of their access to the privileges of private gain. We illustrate this point by returning briefly to our earlier discussion of the history of Sparta. A more extensive and systematic discussion of oppression, repression, and suppression is reserved for chapter 8.

Following the defeat at Leuctra, Sparta continued a spiral of lost influence. With only about 700 Spartiate members by around 245 BC, reform was desperately needed. King Agis IV rose to the occasion and tried to return Sparta to the values expressed by its founder, Lycurgus. Agis pursued policies designed to restore Sparta's tradition of military training, redistribute land, equalize wealth, and relieve the severe burden of indebtedness suffered by many former citizens and others within the Spartan domain. He proposed canceling debts. He also proposed dividing Sparta's homeland into 4,500 lots for its citizens. Because the Spartiate had shrunk to 700, Agis proposed expanding it by granting full citizenship to many free men (the perioeci) and to some foreigners. Another 15,000 lots of land were to be distributed to the remaining voteless free men who were not to be offered citizenship. Had his reforms succeeded, Agis would have increased the size of both the selectorate and the winning coalition. The fear that his reforms would shift Sparta from its focus on private privilege back to a concern for public welfare lay at the core of why the reforms did not survive political contestation.

Agis received support for his proposals from many within his own influential family and from at least one ephor (Lysander) in 243. His supporters gave up their land to be part of Agis's program. But Agis IV shared kingship with Leonidas II, who, together with his wealthy backers, opposed the proposed reforms. Following Leonidas's successful effort to defeat the reforms, King Leonidas II was himself deposed. The new crop of ephors serving in 242 attempted to return Leonidas to the throne but were defeated. They were themselves replaced by a group led by Agesilaus, Agis's uncle. So, in 242 it appeared that Agis IV had secured his hold over government and was poised to alter Sparta's institutions in such a way that it might have returned to its old traditions and days of glory.

Agis had begun to implement his reforms when he was called away from Sparta to assist an ally enmeshed in war in 241. During his absence, Leonidas regained power with the aid of mercenaries bent on gaining private benefits for themselves. Leonidas's supporters captured Agis, tried him, and executed him along with his mother and grandmother, both of whom had actively supported his reform program. Agis was executed to prevent the erosion of privilege that was the cornerstone of Leonidas's hold on power. Agis IV clearly was the more public spirited of the two kings. He was inclined to restore Sparta to its earlier glory by reviving the institutions and practices that had ensured Sparta's earlier focus on public goods. Faced with the possible loss of their land and claims on debts, Leonidas II and his mercenary coalition rid themselves of the threat that Agis represented. Because their private benefits were so valuable, they engaged in no less than murder to protect their access to corruption and cronyism. Sparta's prospects for revival largely died along with Agis IV.

Montesquieu, Madison, Population, and Public Welfare

Before closing the statistical portion of our discussion of public and private goods, we digress to review briefly the effect that population size has on the variables we have assessed. In this way we can reflect, albeit inconclusively, on the debate over whether small or large republics are more conducive to social welfare.

We focus only on the effect of population in the context of our fourth model—which controls for income, democracy, and the loyalty norm—and in a separate set of analyses that only examine states whose coalition size equals 0.75 or greater on our index, W. The latter tests specifically examine the question in the context of large and small *republics*.

Either set of tests tells essentially the same story. Governments with large populations, whether found in polities in general or in republics in particular, tend to provide fewer public goods than their smaller-population counterparts. Civil liberties especially tend to be much weaker in large states. Likewise, efforts to promote education and health care are reduced, and per capita government expenditures plummet. On the plus side, large populations in republics encourage lower taxes as a percentage of GDP and also stimulate savings, though not investment. Apparently, in some areas larger polities enjoy economies of scale, but certainly such economies are not manifested across the board. Among the republics in our database, large-scaled populations contribute to a diminution in the provision of public goods in three out of every four such goods evaluated here. The results regarding population, on balance, favor the view expressed by Montesquieu. Recall that he maintained that "in a large republic the public good is sacrificed to a thousand views; it is subordinate to exceptions; and depends on accidents. In a small one, the interest of the public is easier perceived, better understood, and more within the reach of every citizen; abuses have a lesser extent, and of course are less protected" (Montesquieu [1748] 1977, book VIII, chap. 16, p. 176).

At the same time, our statistical findings hint at important merits in Madison's views on size and politics. Federalism is a means of creating many smaller states within a large state. Our results, though from a different perspective, reinforce the notion that federalism is conducive to social welfare and that federalism provides an institutional design whereby the benefits of a large polity can be complemented by the advantages of a small polity. Weingast and his colleagues (Montinola, Qian, and Weingast 1995; Qian and Weingast 1996; Ferejohn and Weingast 1997) have argued that market-preserving federalism advances social welfare. Federalism does so, in part, by promoting competition. The federal structure of the United States coupled with the commerce clause in the American constitution has proven especially effective at promoting economic efficiencies through competition (North, Summerhill, and Weingast 2000). Additionally, it appears that simply being of a smaller scale fosters improved public spiritedness, at least within large-coalition, republican governments. This suggests that among formerly autocratic polities, populous countries like Russia or China will have a harder time shifting their norms of governance from a focus on private goods to public goods than will Hungary, Poland, the Czech Republic, and others.

Leopold II: An Illustration

Leopold II was king of Belgium from 1865 until his death in 1909. He also was the personal owner and ruler of the Congo Free State from 1885 to 1908. King Leopold is a member of a tiny group consisting of people who led more than one country. Leopold did so simultaneously, while others, such as Chiang Kai-shek (twenty years in China and twenty-five in Taiwan) or Boris Yeltsin (albeit extremely briefly), did so sequentially. This club provides a superb opportunity to investigate the role of institutions in the behavior of leaders. In each case, factors of culture, religion, language, ethnicity, and so forth are held constant. In Leopold's case, the one to which we draw attention, even personal history is held constant because he ruled both countries at the same time. This makes his experiences ideal for purposes of illustrating the importance of political-selection institutions in shaping policy incentives, since in one country he was a revered leader and in the other he was a despot.

When Leopold II succeeded to the Belgian throne, Belgium was already a constitutional monarchy. Still, the king had substantial authority, considerably more than in most constitutional monarchies. His father, Leopold I, had skillfully maneuvered within constitutional constraints. As Margot Lyon (1971, 46) notes, "By appointing and dismissing ministers, indefinitely delaying his signature to bills he disliked, and dissolving the Chambers when he thought fit, he gradually came to possess more power than the drafters of the constitution had envisaged. Through his position as commander-in-chief of land and sea forces Leopold I became his own Minister for War." Leopold II was equally skillful in using his constitutional authority. Twice, for instance, he succeeded in removing legitimate cabinets because he disapproved of their policies (Emerson 1979, 129).

King Leopold II, and the governments over which he presided, depended initially on a fairly large selectorate for its day, though the franchise was still greatly limited, consisting of 137,000 out of a population of nearly six million (Lyon 1971, 54). During his reign, recognizing the constraining political reality of his circumstance as a constitutional monarch, he even helped promote the adoption of universal adult male suffrage in free, competitive elections, thereby greatly expanding the selectorate as well as the winning-coalition size. This suggests an emphasis on—if not a personal taste for—public goods in his domestic Belgian context.

By general account, Leopold II, though regretful that he did not have the authority of the absolute monarchs of old, was an excellent leader of Belgium (Lyon 1971; Emerson 1979; Langer 1980). Early in his reign he declared:

The new administration will exercise the utmost economy in the use of governmental funds, at the same time taking great care not to disrupt the functioning of established public services. It will study the best way to make use of our increasing financial resources; it will extend public works programmes but at the same time will seek means to reduce taxes on basic food stuffs. (quoted in Emerson 1979, 123–124)

Leopold was true to his word. Belgium experienced remarkable economic growth and rapid industrialization. Fueled by a free trade economy, imports and exports expanded at a remarkable clip and coal production was almost equal to that of the much larger French Republic. Belgium was, however, particularly vulnerable to a downturn in the business cycle, which began to have severe effects in 1873. Working conditions, especially for urban workers, were abysmal even by the standards of the day. Already in 1866 Leopold had declared his intention to improve the lot of the working class. International threats to Belgian security (first the Seven Weeks War of 1866 and then the Franco-Prussian War of 1870–71) deflected attention from domestic social issues, but with the resolution of the Franco-Prussian War and the global economic downturn, attention was returned to the domestic plight of workers. In 1873, workers were given the right to strike and other pro-labor reforms were instituted (Emerson 1979, 131). These reforms were progressive for their day and represented a dramatic change over Belgian policy before Leopold.

The impetus for reform did not end. In 1886—while already engaging in atrocities within his Congo fiefdom—Leopold strongly supported a huge public works program that included road and railway construction designed to alleviate unemployment, promote urbanization, and enhance commercialism. In 1889, again with the king's support, legislation was passed to protect women and children. The law of 1889 protected children by forbidding their employment until they turned twelve and then limited their workday to twelve hours (Emerson 1979, 133). By modern standards this may seem modest, but in the context of the times it was a progressive move.

Leopold was instrumental in promoting numerous additional reforms within Belgium, including the introduction of widespread improvements in education, introduction of universal suffrage, proportional-representation voting, the signing of treaties with Britain, Prussia, and France guaranteeing Belgian neutrality during the Franco-Prussian War, and efforts to improve Belgian defenses against threats to Belgian neutrality and sovereignty from France and Germany. As Emerson, in a study generally (and understandably) hostile to Leopold II, observes, "Throughout his life the king's attitude to social questions changed little: he favoured the alleviation of misery in a spirit of benevolent paternalism" (p. 131). However monstrous he was in his leadership of the Congo, a place where he showed no hint of benevolence and where he fostered unspeakable misery, it is evident that he worked hard as king to promote the delivery of public goods to the mass of the Belgian population. He did so before and during his personal reign over the Congo Free State.

Leopold rose to the throne at a time when many states in Europe were building empires on the backs of colonial labor. He aspired to be a member of that club. After several aborted efforts in various parts of the world, he finally succeeded in acquiring vast tracks of land in Africa's interior. Unlike Britain's, France's, Spain's, or others' colonies, however, the Congo Free State was not acquired by a colonizing sovereign state, but rather as Leopold's personal property. In ruling Belgium, he depended on the largesse of a popularly elected government; he depended, in other words, on a large winning coalition. The Belgian leadership included not only Leopold, but the prime minister and cabinet, whose choice depended on popular support within a selectorate that had been greatly enlarged by Leopold. In ruling the Congo, Leopold relied only on himself and the (quite literally) hired guns who went to the Congo in support of his objectives. The Congo winning coalition was minuscule. Therefore, the selectorate model suggests that in the Congo Leopold would turn his efforts to generating private goods for his backers and opportunities for kleptocracy for himself. He did exactly that.

As liberal, progressive a reformer as Leopold was in the Belgian context, he was a monstrously cruel and greedy leader of the Congo. There, through his surrogates (Leopold himself never set foot in the Congo), Leopold ruled for the purpose of making himself and his key backers rich. Slave labor extracted the rubber that fueled Leopold's kleptocracy and the corrupt gains of his overseers. Congolese who failed to meet their quotas were beaten, maimed, and often killed. As many as ten million may have been killed so that Leopold and his cronies could become rich (Hochschild 1999; Forbath 1977; Emerson 1979; Conrad 1903).

At first, Leopold used his authority over the Congo to exploit it for ivory. Later, as demand for rubber grew, the Congo became a major source of rubber throughout the world. Extracting the rubber was a tedious, labor-intensive undertaking. To ensure that demand was met, Leopold's government included the creation of the notorious *Force Publique*. This "police" force was paid a low salary but augmented its wages with commissions. Leopold imposed rubber quotas, and the *Force Publique* saw to it that they were fulfilled. Unrestricted by any law governing their conduct and provided with a huge financial incentive through the commission system, the "police" used whatever means they saw fit to meet the quotas. These means included torture, chopping off right hands, and murder. Hands were cut off as proof of how many antigovernment rebels they killed. The rebels were more often than not no more than locals resisting forced, slave labor. The "police" were rewarded for killing antigovernment rebels and so quickly took to indiscriminate mutilation as a means of boosting their hand count and thereby their fees. An eyewitness account by a Danish missionary reports:

If the rubber does not reach the full amount required the sentries attack the natives. They kill some and bring the hands to the Commissioner. That was about the time I saw the native killed before my own eyes. The soldier said, "Don't take this to heart so much. They kill us if we don't bring the rubber. The Commissioner has promised us if we have plenty of hands he will shorten our service." These were often smoked to preserve them until they could be shown to the European officer. (Forbath 1977, 374)

An American eyewitness noted:

Imagine them returning from fighting rebels; see on the bow of the canoe is a pole and a bundle of something on it. These are the hands of sixteen warriors they have slain. "Warriors? Don't you see among them the hands of little children and girls? I have seen them. I have seen where the trophy has been cut off, while the poor heart beat strongly enough to shoot the blood from the cut arteries at a distance of fully four feet." (Forbath 1977, 374)

One prominent officer in the *Force Publique*, Captain Léon Rom, was reported to have decorated the outer perimeter of the flowerbed in front of his house with more than twenty human heads.

Leopold and his supporters in the *Force Publique* grew fabulously wealthy off of the ill-gotten gains from the Congo Free State. Virtually nothing was invested in improving conditions in that hapless land. Roads were built only where they facilitated moving rubber to market. Laws protecting women and children or worker rights to strike were unheard of in the Congo Free State, even as Leopold promoted just such legislation in Belgium. Much as Leopold worried about protecting the security of his Belgian subjects, he worked to undermine the security of his Congolese subjects. Virtually the only items exported to the Congo Free State were weapons for the *Force Publique*, while vast riches were imported to Belgium. Indeed, it was this extraordinary imbalance in trade that eventually led to the discovery by outsiders, especially Edmund Morel, that Leopold was growing rich on the use of slave labor. Eventually, in 1908 the evidence of atrocities reached such a level that they could no longer be denied and Leopold, with great reluctance, was forced to cede his control to the Belgian government. They certainly did not rule well by contemporary standards, but compared to Leopold's rule, the Belgians were a significant improvement.

Who was the real Leopold? Was he the civic-minded king of Belgium or the murderous ruler of the Congo Free State? We must conclude that the latter comes closer to the mark. In Belgium Leopold operated under the institutional constraint of a large winning coalition. He did not select such a system—he inherited it—and he acted in accordance with the incentives created by such an institutional framework. In the Congo, Leopold was free to choose whatever institutional arrangements he wanted. No precedent or inherited institutions precluded his choosing a system that offered incentives to rule in the interest of public welfare. Finding himself unconstrained, he chose to focus on providing private goods for a small coalition and vast opportunities for kleptocracy for himself. In each case his actions were consistent with the institutional incentives he faced, and therefore his behavior was radically different in Belgium from what it was in the Congo.

Conclusion

Thus far we have investigated the relationship between the size of the winning coalition, the degree of democracy, and the loyalty norm (W/S), as well as offering a gross assessment of the impact of population size on more than thirty different dependent variables. These variables are, for the most part, only modestly correlated with one another. They represent an unusually wide array of policy areas, including many means of providing both public goods and private goods. The selectorate model makes a clear prediction in each case, sometimes anticipating a positive effect, sometimes a negative effect, and sometimes a specific nonlinear effect. Many tests were replicated with controls for the impact of factors that in other tests were themselves variables postulated to depend on winning-coalition size. All tests included controls for regional and temporal fixed effects. The evidence is consistent with the predictions deduced from the selectorate model.

Our tests were designed to show the independent effects of democracy and income that cannot be attributed to coalition size. Characteristics of democracy that are independent of W and S prove to have much less consistent relationships with the dependent variables assessed here than does coalition size or the loyalty norm. Neither democracy nor income effects are sufficient to explain the specific predicted impact that coalition size and the loyalty norm have on policy choices. The size of a polity's selectorate and winning coalition appears to be consistently consequential in influencing the decisions by leaders over how much to spend and on what to spend government resources. Public goods that enhance social welfare are especially emphasized by leaders who depend on a large coalition. Such goods are much less likely to be provided by those who rule with the support of a small group of cronies.

The institutions of coalition size and selectorate, mediated through the loyalty norm, consistently shape incentives for good governance. The incentives created by a large winning coalition foster what most people think of as good government. A small winning coalition, especially combined with a large selectorate, helps foster governance that seems indifferent to producing income for its citizens within a secure environment. Instead, such governments promote corruption, black marketeering, and cronyism. We have seen this in our statistical tests and also in our illustrative case histories of Sparta, Belgium, and the Congo Free State.

Our tests provide hints regarding the relationship between the size of a polity and its performance in enhancing the welfare of its residents. These tests, however, are only preliminary. Future studies will need to look more closely at evidence regarding the debate between Madison and Montesquieu. For now, we close this part of our study encouraged by the consistency with which the predictions of the selectorate model have thus far been supported.

War, Peace, and Coalition Size

Two-thousand five hundred years ago, Sun Tzu, a general in the service of King Ho Lu of Wu, wrote *The Art of War* (Sun Tzu 1983). On November 28, 1984, Caspar Weinberger, Secretary of Defense in the service of U.S. President Ronald Reagan, pronounced his doctrine for waging war. These two doctrines, separated by two and a half millennia, one prepared for a leader dependent on a small winning coalition, the other for a leader dependent on a large winning coalition, are remarkable in their similarities and their fundamental differences. Each is concerned with the conduct of warfare that best achieves the objectives of the incumbent leader. Each reaches different conclusions about when to fight, what to fight for, and how hard to fight. Each in specific and in important ways describes the expectations that follow from the selectorate theory.

Sun Tzu (1983, 9–14) wrote:

> The art of war is governed by five constant factors, all of which need to be taken into account. They are: The Moral Law; Heaven; Earth; the Commander; Method and discipline. . . .
>
> These five factors should be familiar to every general. He who knows them will be victorious; he who knows them not will fail. . . .
>
> When you engage in actual fighting, if victory is long in coming, the men's weapons will grow dull and their ardor will be dampened. If you lay siege to a town, you will exhaust your strength, and if the campaign is protracted, the resources of the state will not equal the strain. Never forget: When your weapons are dulled, your ardor dampened, your strength exhausted, and your treasure spent, other chieftains will spring up to take advantage of your extremity. . . .
>
> In all history, there is no instance of a country having benefitted from prolonged warfare. Only one who knows the disastrous effects of a long war can realize the supreme importance of rapidity in bringing it to a close. It is only one who is thoroughly acquainted with the evils of war who can thoroughly understand the profitable way of carrying it on.
>
> The skillful general does not raise a second levy, neither are his supply wagons loaded more than twice. Once war is declared, he will not waste precious time in waiting for reinforcements, nor will he turn his army back for fresh supplies, but crosses the enemy's frontier without delay. The value of time—that is, being a little ahead of your opponent—has counted for more than either numerical superiority or the nicest calculations with regard to commissariat. . . .
>
> Now, in order to kill the enemy, our men must be roused to anger. For them to perceive the advantage of defeating the enemy, they must also have their rewards. Thus, when you capture spoils from the enemy, they must be used as rewards, so that all your men may have a keen desire to fight, each on his own account.

In a speech on November 28, 1984, Caspar Weinberger articulated the Weinberger Doctrine. He indicated:

First, the United States should not commit forces to combat overseas unless the particular engagement or occasion is deemed vital to our national interest or that of our allies. That emphatically does not mean that we should declare beforehand, as we did with Korea in 1950, that a particular area is outside our strategic perimeter.

Second, if we decide it is necessary to put combat troops into a given situation, we should do so wholeheartedly, and with the clear intention of winning. If we are unwilling to commit the forces or resources necessary to achieve our objectives, we should not commit them at all. . . .

Third, if we do decide to commit forces to combat overseas, we should have clearly defined political and military objectives. And we should know precisely how our forces can accomplish those clearly defined objectives. And we should have and send the forces needed to do just that. . . .

Fourth, the relationship between our objectives and the forces we have committed—their size, composition, and disposition—must be continually reassessed and adjusted if necessary. Conditions and objectives invariably change during the course of a conflict. When they do change, then so must our combat requirements. . . .

Fifth, before the US commits combat forces abroad, there must be some reasonable assurance we will have the support of the American people and their elected representatives in Congress. . . . We cannot fight a battle with the Congress at home while asking our troops to win a war overseas, or, as in the case of Vietnam, in effect asking our troops not to win, but just to be there.

Finally, the commitment of US forces to combat should be a last resort. (Caspar Weinberger, speech to the National Press Club, Washington, DC, November 28, 1984; available at <http://www.pbs.org/wgbh/pages/frontline/shows/military/force/weinberger.html/>)

Sun Tzu's perspective can coarsely be summarized as follows: (1) satisfying moral law ensures domestic support; (2) war must be swift; (3) resources should be sufficient for a short campaign that does not require reinforcements or significant additional provisions from home; and (4) distributing private goods is essential to motivate soldiers to fight. Sun Tzu says that if the army initially raised proves insufficient or if new supplies are required more than once, the command lacks sufficient skill to carry the day, implying that perhaps the fight is best given up rather than risk exhausting the state's treasure and giving additional advantages to rival chieftains. Indeed, his advice is rather specific: "If equally matched, we can offer battle; if slightly inferior in numbers, we can avoid the enemy; if quite unequal in every way, we can flee from him" (Sun Tzu 1983, 16).

Weinberger's fifth point agrees with Sun Tzu's emphasis on moral law, but for the rest, there are important differences. Weinberger's doctrine does not emphasize swift victory, but rather a willingness to spend however much victory requires. He contends that if the United States is not prepared to commit resources sufficient to win, it should not get involved at all. Here he argues for great selectivity in choosing when to risk war. At the same time he recognizes that once committed, victory may take a long time and that, therefore, there must be regular reassessment of objectives in light of evolving circumstances. He endorses a preparedness to raise a larger army and to spend more treasure if warranted by subsequent developments.

Sun Tzu emphasizes the benefits of spoils to motivate combatants ("when you capture spoils from the enemy, they must be used as rewards, so that all your men may have a keen desire to fight, each on his own account"). Weinberger emphasizes the public good of protecting vital national interests. For Sun Tzu, the interest soldiers have in the political objectives behind a fight or their concern for the common good is of no consequence in determining their motivation to wage war. That is why he emphasizes that soldiers fight, "each on his own account."

Sun Tzu's attentiveness to private rewards and Weinberger's concentration on the national interest represent part of the great divide between small-coalition and large-coalition regimes. This chapter elaborates on that difference in the context of war. It also shows, within the context of the selectorate theory, that Weinberger's emphasis on committing however many resources victory requires or else not fighting are logical consequences of dependence on a large coalition. Sun Tzu's emphasis on an initial levy and then, if circumstances indicate this is insufficient, cutting losses, is the effort level that follows as a logical consequence of dependence on a small coalition. The remainder of this chapter is concerned with establishing that these and other principles that distinguish the war-fighting strategies of large-coalition and small-coalition systems follow logically from the selectorate theory.

The Democratic Peace

There are few widely accepted generalizations about politics. One such generalization, sometimes even asserted to be a law (Levy 1988), is that democracies do not fight wars with one another. The empirical evidence for this claim is, in fact, quite strong (Maoz and Abdolali 1989; Bremer 1992; Oneal and Russett 1997; Ray 1995). Recent efforts to cast this empirical observation in doubt notwithstanding (Layne 1994; Spiro 1994; Farber and Gowa 1995; Schwartz and Skinner 1997), extensive, rigorous statistical tests all show a significant propensity for democracies to have been virtually immune from wars with one another (Maoz and Russett 1993; Russett 1995; Maoz 1998). Associated with this observation of what has come to be termed the *democratic peace* are six additional empirical regularities that relate war-proneness and democracy. These are the data-based observations that democracies are not at all immune from fighting wars with nondemocracies (Maoz and Abdolali 1989);[1] democracies tend to win a disproportionate share of the wars they fight (Lake 1992; Reiter and Stam 1998); when disputes do emerge, democratic dyads choose more peaceful processes of dispute settlement than other pairings of states do (Brecher and Wilkenfeld 1997; Dixon 1994; Mousseau 1998; Raymond 1994); in wars they initiate, democracies pay a smaller price in terms of human life and fight shorter wars than nondemocratic states (Bennett and Stam 1998; Siverson 1995); transitional democracies appear to fight one another (Mansfield and Snyder 1995; Ward and Gleditsch 1998); and larger democracies seem more constrained to avoid war than are smaller democracies (Morgan and Campbell 1991).

Although these observations about democracy and war are part of an important pattern, they lack a coherent explanation. Several possible explanations have been put forward, but none has gained broad acceptance. Here we propose that the domestic selectorate model, introduced in chapter 3, suitably modified to deal with the dyadic aspect of international conflict, may help elucidate the causal mechanism governing the seven regularities mentioned above, as well as other regularities that follow from the dyadic view of the selectorate theory. This chapter demonstrates that the selectorate theory offers a logically coherent account for the empirical record regarding:

1. The tendency for democracies not to fight with one another

2. The tendency for democracies to fight with nondemocracies with considerable regularity

3. The tendency for democracies to emerge victorious from their wars

4. When disputes do occur between democracies, the tendency for them to use conflict-management processes that reach peaceful settlements

5. The tendency for democracies to experience fewer battle deaths and fight shorter wars when they initiate conflict

6. The tendency for transitional democracies to be more likely than democracies to fight one another

7. The tendency for major-power democracies to be more constrained to avoid war than less powerful democracies.

The selectorate account of the "democratic peace" is neither an endorsement nor a rejection of the pacifying role or normative superiority of democracy as compared to other forms of government. As we observed earlier, neither a large coalition nor a large selectorate by itself defines democracy. Whereas other discussions of the democratic peace attribute moral superiority to democracy over other regime types because of the seeming peacefulness of democracies, the selectorate model casts doubts on this interpretation. We will, for instance, show that large-coalition systems, while manifesting the pacific behavior mentioned earlier, also provide incentives for leaders to pick on much smaller rival states, including small democracies. Large coalitions, a characteristic shared by democracy, foster special reasons to find opportunities to engage in wars of colonial and imperial expansion and, in a sense, to be bullies. These hardly seem like attractive norms of conduct, but like the regularities already mentioned, they form part of the democratic, large-coalition "selectorate peace."

In the discussion that follows, we sometimes slip casually between use of the awkward phrase "large-coalition systems" and of the more common term *democracy*. In doing so, we do not intend to equate the two, but merely note that they are correlated. A large coalition may well be a necessary characteristic of democracy, but it is insufficient to capture conventional meanings of the term. We use the awkward coalition construction when it is critical to distinguish between coalition size and other characteristics of democracy.

The Debate

The current debate over the war behavior of democratic states, and particularly the democratic peace, centers on whether a normative or an institutional explanation best accounts for the known facts. Normative accounts postulate several different assumptions about democracies. One such supposition is that they share a common value system, including respect for individual liberties and competition. As William Dixon (1994, 17) states,

International disputes of democratic states are in the hands of individuals who have experienced the politics of competing values and interests and who have consistently responded within the normative guidelines of bounded competition. In situations where both parties to a dispute are democracies, not only do both sides subscribe to these norms, but the leaders of both are also fully cognizant that bounded competition is the norm, both for themselves and their opponents.

A closely related contention is that citizens in democracies abhor violence or at least prefer negotiation and mediation to fighting and so prevent their leaders from pursuing violent foreign policies. As succinctly explained by T. Clifton Morgan and Sally H. Campbell (1991, 189), "The key feature of democracy is government by the people and ... the people, who must bear the costs of war, are usually unwilling to fight." However, adherents of these perspectives also argue that democracies are willing to set aside their abhorrence of violence or their respect for other points of view when they come up against authoritarian states because the latter do not share these values. For instance, Zeev Maoz and Bruce Russett (1993, 625) contend, "When a democratic state confronts a nondemocratic one, it may be forced to adapt to the norms of international conflict of the latter lest it be exploited or eliminated by the nondemocratic state that takes advantage of the inherent moderation of democracies."

We believe that any explanation of the empirical regularities collectively known as the democratic peace must satisfy two criteria. First, it must account for the known regularities. Because explanations are generally constructed in response to the observed regularities, the ability to explain the known patterns helps build confidence that the account is not simply an ex post rationalization of a few patterns of behavior. Clearly, the more patterns that are explained, the more credible the explanation, provided that it does not come at the expense of parsimony. Second, a credible explanation should also suggest novel hypotheses that do not form part of the corpus of the democratic peace. If these novel hypotheses are borne out by systematic evidence, that adds further credibility to the overall explanation. The existing norms-based and institutional-constraints arguments fail these tests. The selectorate theory provides an explanation of the seven known regularities enumerated earlier. It also suggests novel hypotheses that we test here, as well, of course, as providing an account for the host of factors investigated in chapters 4 and 5.

Norms-based arguments have two difficulties. First, they appear ad hoc. The presence and substance of norms are established in the literature on the democratic peace solely by reference to the outcomes of conflict between democratic states. What the international and domestic norms are is induced from the observed patterns of behavior in international conflicts that these arguments seek to explain. That democracies abandon their normative commitment to resolve disputes peacefully in the face of threats to their survival by foes who do not adhere to those norms is entirely plausible. However, that assertion must be derived independently of the observation, either from prior axioms or from unrelated empirical evidence, in order to qualify as an explanation of the observation. Otherwise, we cannot know what the argument predicts about seemingly contradictory patterns of evidence. For instance, analyses of covert operations suggest that, provided they can escape public scrutiny, democratic leaders often undertake violent acts against other democracies (James and Mitchell 1995; Forsythe 1992). Does such evidence contradict a norms-based argument, or do the norms apply only to interstate conflict at the level of crises and war?

A related difficulty is empirical. The historical record is replete with examples of democratic states that followed policies at variance with the norms argument. That argument contends that when democracies confront one another they eschew violence. It suggests that they adopt the anticipated conduct of authoritarian states to ensure their own preservation in disputes with such states. Yet there are clear instances of democracies adopting violent dispute-resolution methods in opposition to adversaries who could not be a consequential threat to the democracy's survival. In particular, democratic states pursued imperialistic policies and in the process of building their empires engaged in numerous wars that were about subjugation rather than self-protection. It may be correct to argue that democratic states resort to realist strategies in the face of a powerful nondemocratic opponent who threatens their existence, but too many democratic wars have been against significantly weaker states for this argument to be sustained as an explanation for the democratic peace. It is difficult to reconcile such a pattern with notions of a democratic political culture that abhors violence or that endorses mediation and negotiation. The selectorate model, by contrast, provides an explanation of the willingness of democracies to pursue imperialistic or colonial conquest. This observation is the sort of novel fact for which an explanation of the democratic peace should account. We return later to our explanation of imperial wars by large-coalition systems and test the predictions from the dyadic selectorate theory on a broad database that includes such wars.

Theories about institutional constraints offer alternatives to the normative accounts. A version of the institutional-constraints argument holds that democracies are more deliberate in their decision making because their procedures preclude unilateral action by leaders. This is thought to raise the costs of violence. Maoz and Russett (1993, 626) make this point clearly:

Due to the complexity of the democratic process and the requirement of securing a broad base of support for risky policies, democratic leaders are reluctant to wage wars, except in cases wherein war seems a necessity or when the war aims are seen as justifying the mobilization costs.[2]

This latter argument seems, however, to suggest that democracies should be unlikely to wage war generally and not just against other democracies. The empirical record does not support such a conclusion.[3] Rather, it shows that democracies do not fight wars against one another, but do indeed engage in wars with authoritarian regimes.[4] The claim based on the cheapness of expressing opposition seems stronger than other putative institutional explanations, but it too has shortcomings, one of which is that it fails to account for the well-known rally-round-the-flag effect observed in democracies at the outset of crises and wars (Mueller 1973; Norpoth 1987). This effect suggests that there is not an inherent abhorrence of violence in democracies. Most importantly from a theoretical position, none of the institutional-constraints arguments has a sufficiently well developed theory of how and why democratic institutions constrain leaders in the particular way that produces the seven regularities that have been observed while other institutional arrangements do not. Rather, these arguments generally assert that democratic leaders are more constrained than autocrats, so that the constraints are taken as exogenous rather than as endogenous properties of equilibrium.

Bueno de Mesquita and Lalman's signaling explanation accounts for three of the seven observed regularities (Bueno de Mesquita and Lalman 1992). But they did not, for instance, explain why democracies win a disproportionate share of their wars or why their costs are lower. Bueno de Mesquita and Siverson's model accounts for these regularities, but not for the failure of democracies to fight one another (Bueno de Mesquita and Siverson 1995). Both Bueno de Mesquita and Lalman's signaling explanation and Bueno de Mesquita and Siverson's model have in common the assumption that democracies are more constrained than autocracies. For reasons of theoretical parsimony, we prefer that this be a deductive result of a general model, rather than an assumption. That is, we wish to account for the several empirical regularities without assuming that one type of political system is more constrained than another. Instead, we demonstrate that a dyadic model of the selectorate theory explains how institutional arrangements produce different levels of constraint in different political systems and what effect those institutional arrangements have on behavioral incentives and the empirical generalizations of interest.

The explanation we offer shows that the behavioral incentives (perhaps these could be called norms) are themselves endogenous to certain institutions' arrangements and the interests that sustain them. As with the domestic model elaborated in chapter 3, we make no assumptions about the citizens' abhorrence of violence or even the ease with which they might protest governmental policies. Neither do we assume that large-(or small-) coalition systems have a shared set of values or culture. Instead, we continue to assume that political leaders in any and all forms of government are motivated by the same universal interest: the desire to remain in office. We make no normative assumptions about differences in the values, goals, or civic-mindedness of democratic leaders or their followers as compared to authoritarian leaders or their followers. We do, however, propose a model that offers an explanation of the known regularities and that suggests new hypotheses regarding the democratic peace.

The Dyadic Selectorate Model

Building on the model in chapter 3, we continue to assume that incumbent leaders (as individuals or as a governing coalition) select and implement public policies. These public-policies inevitably have public-goods components and private-goods components. Leaders have only a scarce amount of resources to allocate to different policy goals and to help keep them in office. They can put everything into public policy that benefits everyone in the polity, everything into private goods that are consumed only by members of the winning coalition, or any mix in between. Naturally, if they spend resources on, for instance, providing defense for the citizenry (a public good), they cannot use those same resources to provide special privileges to the members of the winning coalition. If they buy national defense only from insiders in the winning coalition, the reduced competition to provide defense will likely result in an inefficient provision of that public good while political backers skim money off the top for their personal gain. Scarcity requires leaders to make choices over just how much to focus resources on providing generally beneficial public policies and how much to concentrate on satisfying the wants of their core supporters.

A formal representation of the dyadic selectorate model is found in the appendix for this chapter. Here we describe the basic structure of our model and outline the intuition that leads to the democratic peace results and to novel hypotheses. Then we provide a more detailed explanation of the logic behind the dyadic selectorate game that leads to the conclusions.

Assume two nations, A and B, are engaged in a dispute. The national leaders must decide whether they are prepared to start a war in the hope of achieving their objectives or rely instead on a negotiated settlement. If one side initiates a war, then both leaders must decide how much of an effort to make to achieve military victory in the war. By this we mean the proportion of available resources a leader is prepared to allocate to the war effort rather than to other purposes. Obviously, leaders who dedicate large quantities of resources to the war are more likely to win, but at the cost of not having those resources available to reward themselves or their supporters. The citizens receive payoffs based on the outcome of the crisis—be it a war or a negotiated settlement—and the rewards that accrue from resources not consumed in the war effort. Given these payoffs, the winning coalition decides whether they would be better off retaining their current leader or whether they would be better off replacing her.

A polity's institutional arrangements shape the selection criteria that supporters use to determine whether to retain the incumbent. Hence political-selection institutions determine which outcomes allow a leader to keep her job and which do not. As we will see, these differences profoundly influence the policies that leaders choose during international conflicts. Those like Sun Tzu's King Ho Lu, who depend on a small coalition, are best off saving resources for their backers rather than spending the national treasure on the pursuit of war aims. Those like Caspar Weinberger's President Ronald Reagan, who depend on a large coalition, are best off making an extra effort by shifting additional resources into pursuit of their war aims.

Recall that all citizens enjoy the benefits of public policies whether they belong to the winning coalition or not. The advantage members of the winning coalition have is that they also enjoy a share of whatever private goods are allocated by the leadership. Earlier we established that if the winning coalition gets larger, each member's share of private goods decreases. This makes public policy benefits loom larger in the overall utility assessment of members of the winning coalition in more democratic, large-coalition polities as compared to more autocratic, small-coalition states. One consequence is that large-coalition leaders, being just as eager to retain office as their small-coalition counterparts, must be especially concerned about policy failure. To reduce the risk of policy failure and subsequent deposition, they make a larger effort to succeed in disputes. This means that they are willing to spend more resources on the war effort to avoid defeat and only engage in fights they anticipate winning, as articulated, for example, in the Weinberger Doctrine quoted above. In contrast, leaders with small winning coalitions reserve more resources for distribution to their supporters in the form of private goods, as stated by Sun Tzu. As long as they can provide substantial private goods, they are not at such a high risk of being deposed as are their larger-coalition counterparts, who, perforce, cannot give large amounts of such benefits to each member of their winning coalition.

Because of their dependence on a large coalition, democratic leaders are more likely to try hard to win their wars than are autocrats. If they do not expect to win, they try to avoid fighting. This implies that they pick and choose their fights more carefully (Reiter and Stam 1998). This has several consequences. Democrats who are dependent on a large coalition are more likely to win wars than autocrats who depend on a small coalition, for two reasons. First, *if they need to*, democrats try hard, spending resources on the war to advance their public policy goals. Second, fearing public policy failure, democrats try to avoid contests they do not think they can win. Since two leaders of large-coalition systems— loosely democrats—in a dispute both try hard, both can anticipate that, if they go to war, each will spend lots of resources in a risky situation where they are not disproportionately advantaged by their great effort. This is shown to incline such leaders to negotiate with one another rather than fight (Lake 1999; Stam 1996, 176–178). By contrast, those who depend on a small coalition—loosely termed autocrats—typically reserve their resources for domestic uses, because their political survival depends on satisfying a few key constituents through the distribution of private goods. Autocrats do not have a great need to produce successful public policies. Consequently, autocrats try less hard than democrats in war, but still sometimes fight in wars where their chances are poor because defeat does not so greatly affect their prospects of political survival at home. Democrats, by their superior level of effort, more often defeat autocratic foes and achieve successful policy outcomes. This helps enhance their reselection.

Structure of the Dyadic Selectorate Game

Our modified model examines the fundamental decisions that national leaders make under the contingency that they are engaged in an international dispute. In the game, leaders choose to fight or to negotiate a settlement. If the choice is to fight, leaders decide how many of their available resources they are prepared to commit to the war effort. In reality, of course, either side in a dispute can resort to war. However, we consider the restricted game in which the leader in nation A chooses between the use of force and a negotiated settlement. The question of whether nation B wants to initiate is answered by simply flipping the labels A and B. If the leader of A decides to attack, then she also picks an effort level, by which we mean she allocates some proportion, g_A, of her available resources, R, to the conduct of the war. Once attacked, the leader in nation B also picks an effort level, g_B. If nation A decides not to attack, the dispute is settled peacefully through negotiations.

The war's outcome is partially a function of the relative effort by each side. That is, who wins depends in part on how leaders choose to allocate their scarce resources. When the dispute is settled, either through negotiation or war, the domestic audiences in A and B then decide whether to retain their leader or to depose the incumbent (Fearon 1994; Smith 1998b; Schultz 1998, 2001; McGillivray and Smith 2000). To make this decision, they evaluate their payoffs under each contingency and decide whether they are better off remaining in the incumbent's winning coalition or defecting to a prospective new leader.

Settling Crises by War

We model war as a costly lottery (Smith 1998a; Wagner 2000) in which each player's expected utility from the war depends on the probability that its side wins or loses and on the utilities associated with each possible outcome. In this section we develop our notions regarding the probability of victory (and defeat) and the attendant utilities.

The values of victory and defeat are normalized to 1 and 0, respectively. In addition, players pay a per capita cost, k, associated with the war's destruction and the risks of fighting. Therefore, the utility of victory equals $1 - k$ and the utility for defeat is $-k$.

Many factors shape the outcome of a war. Observable military capabilities certainly play an important part. So do short-term shifts in government priorities, by putting more national resources behind a war effort (Organski and Kugler 1980; Kim and Morrow 1992; Powell 1996b). The probability of victory is presumed to be increasing as the total military advantage dedicated to the war effort of one side grows relative to the other side. Therefore, if a war occurs the victor is more likely to be the nation with the most military capabilities dedicated to the war effort. We consider two types of military capabilities: the military balance before the onset of fighting, M, and the proportion of additional national resources committed to the war effort, g_i. (The subscripts below will refer to nation A or B, as appropriate.) The military balance, which takes values between 0 and 1, represents the ratio of observable military assets of the two sides. M, therefore, is treated as common knowledge. Additional resources dedicated to the war effort by either country are drawn from the R_i resources each leader has at her disposal. By choosing to devote the proportion g_i of R_i to the war effort, she generates an additional $g_i r$ military assets, where r represents the exchange rate between resources and military capability.[5]

The probability that A wins in a war is increasing in military balance, M, and in A's effort, g_A, and is decreasing in B's effort, g_B. The probability that B wins is $1 - p_A$, with p_A being the probability that A wins. We stipulate that the probability that side A wins is an increasing function of $M - \frac{1}{2} + g_A r - g_B r$, or in words, A's military advantage or disadvantage $(M - \frac{1}{2})$ adjusted for the relative additional effort made by the rival sides.

Settling Crises by Negotiations

When nations enter negotiations, we assume they have expectations about the likely outcome of the bargaining process. In particular, we assume that the expected rewards for A and B from a negotiated settlement are χ and $1 - \chi$, respectively. We might suppose this deal, χ, reflects the military balance, M, but it need not. Other factors can also be influential. As Morrow (1985) shows, the importance of the issue at hand to each party and the willingness of each side to suffer the material costs of war also affect what bargain the parties expect from negotiation.

Reselection

Following the international dispute, the leaders in each nation face reselection. The members of the selectorate evaluate the payoff they received under the incumbent leader. They compare this payoff with what they expect to receive if they depose the incumbent and choose a domestic challenger instead. Deposing the incumbent is not simply a matter of concluding that she has done a poor job during the dispute. Rather, it is a question of whether the members of the winning coalition believe they will be better off under alternative leadership.

Incumbents are deposed when they can no longer convince enough members of the selectorate to support them. If the package of benefits an incumbent offers to her supporters is better than the rewards any challenger can credibly offer, then the incumbent can find W members of the selectorate who will retain her in office. If, however, the incumbent fails to provide benefits to the winning coalition in excess of what a challenger can credibly promise to provide, then the incumbent can no longer garner enough support to form a winning coalition. At this point, supporters defect and the incumbent is ousted. Recall that the decision to defect is not simply a choice about which leader is better. Defection is risky, since there is a W/S chance of being essential to the new leader if the current incumbent is deposed. Failure to make it into the post-transition winning coalition of a new leader means losing an assured flow of private goods if one is a member of the current coalition. The loyalty norm, induced by the size of the risk of defection (W/S), when strong (i.e., W/S is small), encourages coalition members to stick with an incumbent who is doing a poor job for the nation as a whole.

Like the incumbent, the challenger proposes a mix of public- and private-goods allocations. Of course, the selectorate does not know what the challenger can or will actually deliver. In contrast, they have observed the performance of the incumbent. The observed performance or competence of the incumbent substitutes in the dyadic selectorate model for the concept of affinity used in the basic selectorate model. As we noted in chapter 2, affinity is a convenience rather than a necessity for the selectorate theory. We could continue to use affinity here, but choose to substitute prior performance by the incumbent as an alternative. We do so for two reasons. First, in the context of war, expectations about competence seem especially important. Second, we wish to demonstrate that affinity is not essential. Indeed, as noted in chapter 2, neither affinity nor competence is essential. We only require a condition that gives members of the current winning coalition a better chance of being in the incumbent's future coalition if they remain loyal than of being in the challenger's long-term coalition if they defect. Those who prefer the idea of affinity to competence can assume affinity is correlated with the prospective ability or competence of the challenger.

The selectorate must infer the ability of or their affinity for the challenger. That, of course, is the inherent feature of any political campaign, whether the society is democratic or autocratic. If the challenger performs well during the campaign—that is, appears competent—we expect that he will perform well once in office (Riker 1996). At the time the incumbent leader makes her choices about fighting or negotiating and how to allocate resources, she is uncertain of the qualities of a prospective domestic rival. We represent the distribution of the possible challengers the incumbent may face by using the cumulative density function, and, for technical convenience, we assume the distribution of challengers is exponential.

What can a challenger credibly offer the selectorate? The challenger cannot make credible promises regarding how he will perform during a dispute or on other policy questions. Knowing this, the selectorate's members focus on the reservation value they expect if they choose a new leader. Incumbents can anticipate what they must give to supporters in order to defeat challengers. They simply must provide more utility for their coalition members than that offered by the challenger. The utility coalition members receive depends, in part, on the outcome of the policy of the leader in the international dispute. The proportion of resources reserved for distribution as private goods to the winning coalition after spending g_A on the war effort is $1 - g_A$. Of course, if there is no war, then $g_A = 0$. The total pool of resources (R_A) is diminished by whatever portion has gone to the war effort, if any. What remains is distributed evenly to the members of the winning coalition. Of note is that members of the winning coalition receive their share of private goods for sure if they stick with the incumbent, while only receiving such goods probabilistically if they defect. Additionally, neither the incumbent nor the challenger can promise to distribute any resources destroyed or lost by the state during a war. This proves important later in understanding why small-coalition leaders like autocrats or kings do not make the same allocation decision as do large-coalition leaders like democrats.

Probability of Reselection

Leaders want to remain in office. At the time leaders choose their actions, including whether to wage war and how to allocate resources, they cannot be certain of the quality of prospective political rivals. However, given the distribution of possible challengers, the incumbent can assess how outcomes influence her prospects for reselection.

All else being equal, leaders who generally perform well on domestic issues of the sort examined in chapter 5, and those with large selectorates, find it easiest to remain in office. Good performance on domestic issues becomes a liability, however, when good performance costs resources that are needed as private rewards to retain coalition loyalty.

The size of the leader's incumbency advantage depends on the configuration of the polity's institutions. The smaller the selectorate, the greater the future private benefits that members of the current winning coalition can expect from any challenger and, therefore, the greater the private benefits the incumbent must provide to remain in power. Similarly, as the size of the required winning coalition decreases, the number of people with whom private benefits must be shared decreases, making the value of the benefits to each member that much greater. Therefore, as the winning coalition becomes larger, the incumbency advantage diminishes because the value of the private benefits to individual members of the winning coalition gets smaller. When the winning coalition is small and the selectorate is large, supporters of the incumbent jeopardize much of their welfare if they defect to a political rival of the incumbent, since they face a high risk of being cut off from private benefits under the new leader. The risk of being excluded from the private payoffs of future coalitions grows as the size of the selectorate increases and as the size of the winning coalition decreases. Thus the risk is greatest, speaking somewhat loosely, in autocracies and smallest in democracies.

The incumbent has a selection advantage over the challenger. The incumbent is advantaged in her ability to supply private goods because current members of the coalition are sure of receiving them. Given her advantage in private goods, the incumbent survives provided she does not do such a poor job on public policy that she is judged grossly incompetent as compared to the challenger. What constitutes sufficient policy incompetence by the leader so that she gets deposed, however, depends on the structure of the polity. If the leader has a huge advantage over the challenger in her ability to supply private goods, she can survive disastrous policy outcomes. Although leaders from systems with large winning coalitions have some advantage in the supply of private goods, the magnitude of this advantage is small, and so these leaders cannot tolerate policy failure as well as autocrats or even monarchs can (Bueno de Mesquita and Siverson 1995; King, Tomz, and Wittenberg 2000).

To summarize, during a dispute, leader A decides whether to fight, and if so, how hard to try. If attacked, leader B chooses an allocation of resources to dedicate to the war effort. Following the end of the dispute, members of the winning coalition decide whether to remain loyal or to defect, thereby retaining or bringing down the incumbent leadership. This is the sequence of play in the game. With the utilities all specified, we can now turn to solving the game.

Solving the Game

We solve the game by finding subgame perfect equilibria. Using backward induction, the analysis at each stage of the game ensures knowledge of actors' anticipated responses to subsequent decisions. Having already examined reselection above, we move to the preceding decision: the level of resources dedicated to prosecuting the war.

If attacked, the leader of nation B chooses how many of her available resources, R_B, to dedicate to the war effort. The advantage of spending more on the war is that she improves B's prospects of victory. However, trying hard also involves risks. By trying harder, B's leader reduces the amount of resources available to reward her supporters through private goods. Political-selection institutions influence the effort decision because they determine the relative importance for political reselection of saving resources to use as private goods versus increasing the odds of military victory by spending those resources on the war effort.

Leaders choose the effort level that maximizes their expected payoff. In general, the larger the winning coalition, the greater this optimal effort level. This leads to our substantive conclusion that democrats try harder in wartime than do autocrats.[6] Before explaining the origins of this result, it is important to add a qualifier. In some cases, the outcome of the war is so important for political survival relative to private goods that all leaders, whatever their domestic political institutions, try all out to win the war. For example, in a war like World War II where the survival of sovereignty was at risk, militarily defeated incumbents could be nearly certain of losing their jobs (and perhaps their lives) no matter what.[7] At the other extreme, the salience of the war might be sufficiently low that no political arrangements induce additional effort. This might be true, for example, in wars against such weak rivals that there is virtually no chance of defeat. Wars of colonial and imperial expansion against largely unarmed or underarmed indigenous adversaries may fit this category. However, between these extremes, it is large winning coalitions that induce high effort levels and small winning coalitions that induce the hoarding of resources for subsequent distribution as private rewards to the winning coalition.

The game reveals that large winning coalitions encourage leaders to dedicate additional resources to the war effort. As with all the technical results, the formal proof is contained in the appendix. The key insight concerns how coalition size influences the importance of private goods as a means of rewarding supporters. As leaders increase their level of effort during a war, they increase the probability of victory. A military victory benefits everyone in nation B, including members of the winning coalition. Since the difference in utility between victory and defeat was normalized to one, the marginal benefit of increased effort is one multiplied by the marginal impact of effort on the probability of victory. Quite simply, the value of trying harder is the extent to which extra effort improves the prospects of winning. The marginal benefit of increased effort is independent of political institutions since everyone benefits from the policy success, be they leader, member of the winning coalition, member of the selectorate, or part of the disenfranchised portion of society. Thus, victory itself is not more-or-less beneficial politically for one regime type as compared to another. All leaders prefer to win wars in which they are engaged. However, increased effort to win comes at the expense of having fewer resources with which to provide private goods for supporters. No leader wants to spend so much on the war effort that her chances of being deposed are increased.

Resources not spent on the war effort go to the winning coalition in the form of private goods. As we established in chapter 3, the value of these private goods depends on how many people must be rewarded. As the leader allocates resources to the war effort, she reduces the private-goods rewards for her supporters. The rate at which increased effort diminishes supporters' benefits depends on the size of the coalition sharing private goods. When the winning coalition is small, each member's share of the resources is high. Given these concentrated benefits, increased war effort drastically reduces the utility of members of the winning coalition. In contrast, when the coalition is large, each of its members receives only a small share of the private goods in the first place. Thus, when the winning coalition is large, the reduction in supporters' utility from having resources channeled into the war effort, instead of being retained as private benefits, is small. It is incentive compatible with a leader's goal of remaining in office to maximize her supporters' utility. In terms of the supporters' rewards, the cost of improving the probability of victory increases as the winning coalition gets smaller. The marginal benefit of increased effort—the increase in the probability of victory—is independent of institutional arrangements, but the cost of increased effort is dependent on those institutions. To make the institutional comparison as stark as possible, consider the following limiting case.

Suppose a leader chooses between making an all-out effort that guarantees victory and making no additional effort at all, even though this makes defeat in war inevitable. Consider the effects on the prospects of reselection. In terms of direct rewards, an all-out effort gets the leader a payoff of $1 - k$ (i.e., the utility of victory). With no additional effort there is a direct payoff of $-k + R/W$, where $-k$ is the cost of fighting and R/W is the unspent per capita share of resources that remain available for private goods (or for kleptocracy). Clearly, if the winning coalition (W) is larger than R, then the leader makes an all-out effort, because then $1 - k > R/W - k$. While the direct benefits are illustrative of why leaders with large W try hard, we think of our argument as predominately reselection driven. The reselection-related rewards associated respectively with all-out effort and with no additional effort, as shown in the appendix, again favor all-out effort when $1 > R/W$. Again, in the limiting case, leaders make an all-out effort to win only when $W > R$. Otherwise leaders hoard their resources for private-goods provision and make no additional effort even though military defeat is inevitable. Such leaders could improve their chances of victory by trying harder, but this is not incentive compatible with their desire to stay in office.[8]

Thus far we have shown how selection institutions affect the amount of resources dedicated to the war effort for B. Similar logic applies for A. Although A's decision calculus is slightly more complicated because she must anticipate B's effort level, the same motivations persist. The larger A's winning coalition, the less important private goods become relative to foreign policy success. Therefore, all else being equal, the larger the winning coalition, the more resources A dedicates to the war effort.

The game shows that democratic leaders, because they depend on large winning coalitions, try harder in war than do autocrats, who only need support from a small coalition to stay in office. One might think that autocrats have an interest in fighting hard to protect the pool of resources they need to distribute as private goods. However, to stay in office, they must only provide more than their challenger can credibly promise. The challenger cannot promise to distribute any resources that have been lost as a consequence of defeat in the war. Therefore, the incumbent autocrat's comparative advantage in distributing private goods and in reserving resources for that purpose remains unaltered following military defeat.[9]

The deduction from our model that democratic leaders try harder in wars than autocrats is, we believe, a novel theoretical result. It is interesting to note, therefore, that others have reported illustrative empirical evidence that fits our deduction. Rosenthal (1998)

> finds a "selection effect": parliamentary governments, for example, fight fewer wars. They are only willing to fight wars that are profitable, and they are more willing to adequately finance, and therefore more likely to win, the wars they choose to sponsor. His conclusion is reinforced by the argument of Levi (1998), who explores the impact of increased democratization and industrialization upon military mobilization. Faced by an increase in both variables, she argues, governments have to invest more in convincing their populations of the importance of the war and in winning their consent to fight. (in Bates et al. 1998, 7)

That is, democratic leaders invest their effort and resources in mobilizing their societies to produce the public good of victory in war, as predicted. Lamborn (1991) presents additional direct evidence for the deduction that democracies try harder in war. He shows that before World War I, Germany devoted a larger percentage of its GNP to the military than did Britain or France. Nevertheless, the latter countries defeated Germany in the First World War—that is, they mobilized greater resources once the war began because they were better able than the Germans to increase revenue extraction for the war effort. Below we provide large-N empirical tests of this proposition to go beyond the case-history evidence to see if the pattern indicated by the theory holds in reality across many countries, leaders, and years.

We have demonstrated that the incentives of leaders in war differ as a function of their institutional arrangements. Although we have explained the reasoning in the special case where all prospective private goods are either spent on the war effort or are saved to pay off supporters, it should be evident that the logic holds in the more general setting. In chapter 9 we exploit this difference again to show that the war aims of leaders vary systematically with the size of the coalition to which they answer. We have also focused our attention on conditions under which institutional differences cause democrats (due to their large coalitions) and autocrats (due to their small coalitions) to behave differently. There are also conditions under which both try hard or neither tries hard. All of these are documented in the appendix. The general conclusion is clear. All else being equal, institutional arrangements provide large-coalition leaders with greater incentives to try hard relative to small-coalition leaders. To show how this influences the empirical regularities associated with the democratic peace, we now assess the incentives to negotiate rather than fight.

The Decision to Fight or to Negotiate

We now know how national leaders are expected to behave once a war starts. A democrat's dependence on a large coalition makes the value of the improved prospects of victory from trying hard worth more than the lost benefit, or cost, arising from taking private benefits away from the winning coalition. The opposite is true for autocrats because of their dependence on a small winning coalition. This result is crucial to understanding the decision to fight or to negotiate.

Leaders in states with large winning coalitions cannot easily compensate for policy failure by doling out private goods. They need to succeed in foreign and domestic policy. Leaders in systems with small winning coalitions can more readily compensate for policy failure by providing private benefits to their few key backers. Therefore they do not try as hard in wars as do their more democratic counterparts. A consequence of this is that democracies are less attractive targets of war than are autocracies. By the same token, democracies are not eager to pursue wars they do not expect to win. Their leaders are at great risk of political defeat at home from failed policies. Autocrats are not.

It follows that democratic leaders, because of their dependence on a large coalition, generally attack only if they anticipate victory. They are highly selective; they prefer to negotiate when they do not anticipate military success. This does not imply that they are reluctant to fight. Democracies, because of their propensity to try hard, can often overwhelm their foe. This carries an important implication for the type of foe they can fight and defeat. Autocrats do not try as hard in war and so make attractive opponents for democracies. In contrast, democracies are unlikely to be willing to fight each other. Since both try hard, each minimizes, to the extent possible given resource endowments, the chance that the other will win. Since democrats, as we will show, need to be overwhelmingly confident of victory, it is difficult to satisfy the conditions necessary for democracies to fight each other. The reason is directly tied to coalition size and not to other characteristics of democracy.

Autocrats, being at the helm of small-coalition governments, do not depend on military victory to keep their jobs to the same extent as do democrats. Of course, autocrats prefer winning to losing, but their political (and personal) survival is primarily a function of satisfying their small band of supporters with private goods rather than providing their citizens with successful policies. They are more willing to gamble on war than their democratic counterparts are. Thus, the required chance of success in war under which an autocrat will take the risk is considerably lower than it is for a democrat. The latter's political survival is more likely to be on the line; the former's is not. It is straightforward to see that democracies and autocracies can fight wars against each other and that autocracies can afford to fight one another.

Above we characterized optimal effort decisions for A and B once war occurs. All else being equal, the larger W_i, the harder nation i tries. If A initiates conflict with B, then A's payoff is its chance of winning multiplied by its utility for winning plus the chance it loses multiplied by its utility for losing, plus the value of the private goods retained after choosing a level of war effort. A only initiates conflict when the benefit of doing so exceeds what she expects from a negotiated settlement. The more likely A is to win, the more likely it is that this condition is met. Given their institutional arrangements, A and B exert effort levels g_A and g_B respectively. These effort levels influence the probability of A being victorious. In addition to structuring how hard A and B try, selection institutions also influence whether leaders want to initiate conflict, given knowledge of the effort levels that will follow in any subsequent war.

We present examples for both autocrats and democrats to illustrate how institutions structure the conditions under which leaders choose war rather than negotiations. These standard cases show how autocrats and democrats differ in their decisions to initiate conflict. Generally, an autocrat's survival depends on her ability to distribute private goods. Provided she does not expend resources on the war effort, she typically survives whether she wins, loses, or negotiates. Since, except in the extreme cases discussed earlier, her survival is not strongly influenced by the war outcome, an autocrat's initiation decision resembles a standard realist calculation of benefits and losses. For a democrat the situation is different. Given the large number of supporters she must appease, she cannot buy political loyalty with private goods alone, relying instead on public policy success. For her, military defeat equates with political defeat, and so, where possible, she avoids fighting when defeat is a significant possibility.

Autocrats initiate conflict when the expected gains of conflict exceed what they expect to obtain through negotiations. The decision to fight is largely a secondary consideration that is not driven by an autocrat's primary objective—to stay in office. As such, conflict initiation depends on an assessment of the expected value of war relative to negotiations. As we saw theoretically, autocrats find it easier to retain office than do their democratic counterparts. Autocrats have an advantage over challengers in their ability to provide private goods. Since private goods figure predominantly in the rewards given to supporters in autocratic systems, supporters risk much if they desert the incumbent. This incumbency advantage in the supply of private goods means that as long as autocratic leaders retain resources to provide private goods for their supporters, they survive domestic challenges.[10] Hence, as shown above, provided she makes little additional effort, a leader in autocracy A survives in office.

Knowing that A makes no additional effort and typically survives whatever the outcome of conflict, A's expected value of fighting approximately reduces to $p_A - k - R_A/W_A + \Psi$ where Ψ is the leader's utility for remaining in office and p_A is A's probability of victory given no additional effort. Negotiated settlements leave A's resources untouched and available for distribution as private goods. Again, having the incumbency advantage of guaranteed private-goods provision, the typical autocrat also retains office via negotiations. An autocrat's expected value for negotiations reduces to approximately $\chi + R_A/W_A + \Psi$. Therefore, an autocrat's decision resembles that of a standard unitary-actor model. An autocratic leader typically initiates fighting when $p_A > \chi + k$: the expected benefits of conflict outweigh the expected value of negotiations.

Unlike autocrats, leaders with large winning coalitions have only a small incumbency advantage in the supply of private goods. As we have already shown, this makes their survival in office harder and more contingent on their public policy performance. Knowing that the survival of democrats depends on their public policy performance, we now construct a stereotypical example to demonstrate how institutions structure the conflict decision of leaders in large winning-coalition systems. Having examined this archetypal case, we analyze the limiting mathematical case. Although we believe the stereotypical case is generally appropriate, there are plausible conditions under which the results we generate from this example break down. These conditions are important because they predict the domestic political circumstance when democrats become belligerent and when war between democracies is most likely. Rather than interrupt the flow of our general argument by continually referring to these exceptional circumstances, which resemble those of gambling for resurrection under the diversionary-war hypothesis (Downs and Rocke 1995; Levy 1989; Smith 1998b; Werner 1996; Goemans 2000; Richards et al. 1993), we consider them separately.

As we have already demonstrated, leaders in systems with large winning coalitions have only a small incumbency advantage in the provision of private goods. Instead, leaders survive on the basis of their public-goods performance. This led to the earlier result that large-coalition (democratic) leaders retain few resources for private goods, and instead pump resources into the war effort to help ensure a successful resolution of the conflict. With their sensitivity to public policy provision in mind, we construct our stylized case by assuming that defeat means near-certain removal and victory means near-certain retention. Therefore, the expected payoff for a democratic leader from initiating conflict is approximately $p_A(1 - k + \Psi) + (1 - p_A)(-k) = -k + p_A(1 + \Psi)$, where p_A is the probability of victory for A given the effort each side makes. If instead of fighting A negotiates a settlement, then her expected payoff is approximately equal to $\chi + \Psi + R_A/W_A$.[11] We know that democratic leaders are sensitive to policy failure, and supporters' rewards from negotiations are generally closer to those of success than failure since conflict is inefficient. An additional, although small, benefit from negotiation is that leaders can allocate private goods. So as an initial working supposition, we assume that negotiations also give leaders a significant probability of retaining office.

Democrats, naturally enough, initiate conflict when the expected utility from doing so exceeds the expected utility from negotiation—that is, $-k + P_A(1 + \Psi) > \chi + \Psi + R_A/W_A$, which can be rewritten as $P_A > (\chi + \Psi + k)/(1 + \Psi) + R_A/(1 + \Psi)W_A$. Given the large winning-coalition size of a democracy, the latter term, $R_A/(1 + \Psi)W_A$, is small. The magnitude of the former term, $(\chi + \Psi + k)/(1 + \Psi)$, depends on the value of holding office. As the value from holding office becomes substantial (large Ψ), this term becomes close to 1. This indicates that large-coalition, democratic leaders who value officeholding need to be near certain of victory before risking war. They are highly selective about the wars they are prepared to fight, preferring negotiation if the odds of their victory are not overwhelming.

In constructing this stylized example we made suppositions about the probability of reselection associated with each outcome. Later we explore the robustness of our results in light of variation in these conditions. By looking at the limiting case of an extremely large winning coalition, we see justification for this working assumption. As the winning coalition expands, each supporter's private-goods allocation becomes vanishingly small. Under this contingency, private goods have no value to leaders either in terms of personal or reselection benefits. Hence leaders allocate all available resources to extra war efforts. If, as we believe, the reselection motive is primary, then given our technical assumptions of concavity and an exponential distribution of challenger types (see the appendix), this means that leaders in systems with large W must be more certain of winning before they would attack than is true for their autocratic counterparts.

As an aside, it is interesting to note what the above theoretical result implies about the willingness of democratic leaders to use violence as the means to advance their objectives. Autocracies may engage in imperialist expansion, for instance, out of a quest for additional private goods. Democracies can also be expected to participate in imperialist expansion according to our model, provided that doing so enhances (or at least does not diminish) the survivability of incumbents. The targets during wars of colonial and imperial expansion typically are very weak states or peoples who can easily be defeated. While the norms-based argument that democracies use violence to protect their survival against nondemocratic foes who do not share the abhorrence of violence might account for some democratic-autocratic wars, it seems to be contradicted by wars of colonial or imperial expansion by democracies. Certainly the weak foes in such wars did not threaten the survival of the democratic belligerent. Yet the dyadic selectorate model shows that such extremely weak opponents readily fulfill the requirements to be targets of democratic initiations of violence, even when the extremely weak target is democratic. Democracies, according to the selectorate model, only initiate fighting when officeholding is especially highly valued and their prospects of victory are a near certainty. So, democracies, like autocracies, are not immune from the temptations of colonial and imperial expansion according to the model. Near certainty of victory, not normative commitment to peaceful resolution of disputes, describes when large-coalition polities (democracies) go to war.

Later in this chapter, using data from the nineteenth and twentieth centuries, we show that democracies engage in colonial wars and imperial war against much weaker adversaries. This is not just a recent phenomenon. Throughout history democracies and other large-coalition systems have shown a propensity to use violence against weaker states. For example, having repulsed the Persian attack on Greece in 479 BC, Athens took the lead in the Delian League, an alliance formed primarily of eastern Greek city-states, for the purpose of gaining compensation from Persia (Buckley 1996; Fine 1983). By the symbolic act of dropping iron into the sea the allies signaled the permanence of their agreement. They set up a treasury, initially located on Delos, but subsequently moved to Athens in 454 BC. Each ally was expected to contribute to the league either by providing ships or by paying phoros (essentially tribute) into the treasury. While initially many allies provided ships, gradually nearly all shifted to phoros contributions that were used to pay for Athenian ships.

The Greeks were militarily successful. As the Persian threat diminished many of the allies no longer saw the need for the alliance and became discontented, particularly with Athens' high-handed approach. Even after peace was negotiated with Persia (c. 449 BC), Athens maintained the league. Naxos was the first city to rebel, in 471 BC. In response, the Athenians besieged the city, removed its autonomy, and reduced it to a subject, tribute-paying ally. Athens continued this policy of crushing allies who revolted, using its superior military strength, which was in part paid for by the allies. Through this process the allies lost their autonomy and the Delian League became the Athenian empire. Like European democracies in the nineteenth and twentieth centuries, Athens used force against inferior states. Indeed this case provides an even stronger rejection of normative arguments than European colonialism, which might be dismissed on racial grounds. The Athenians and many of the Ionian cities of the Delian League shared the same heritage. Relatively democratic Athens showed itself willing to suppress its owns kinsmen when its own security was not threatened.

The propensity of regimes with large coalitions, like democracies, to try hard makes it difficult for either side of a democratic dyad to overwhelm the other. Being unable to guarantee victory, both sides of a democratic dyad seek to avoid what is likely to be a bloody and protracted conflict. The exception to this claim arises when one party in the dyad is much weaker than the other. In that case, large democracies (because of coalition size) are not immune from attacking small democracies, but small democracies (again because of coalition size) are expected to sue for peace rather than fight back. This follows in the model because democracies, being large-coalition systems, need a high probability of victory in order to fight. Therefore, large democracies are prepared to fight weak adversaries, including democracies, but the weak democrats, having a low probability of victory, are unwilling to fight back. They prefer to negotiate. This results in cases of low-level, one-sided attacks by big democracies against small ones (e.g., the United States attacked the Dominican Republic in 1965), a phenomenon widely observed in the historical record. This also accounts for the proclivity of democracies to have been imperialist powers.

While democrats generally need to be more certain of victory than autocrats before they attack, this is not to say that democratic states are necessarily more dovish than autocratic states. Although democratic states must be confident of victory before initiating conflict, their increased effort means that they can often overwhelm other states. In the appendix we formally show that the size of a negotiated settlement sufficient to buy off A and prevent A from attacking is not a simple monotone in the size of the winning coalition. Because democrats are more selective in their conflicts, this does not always make them less aggressive. Rather, whether large or small winning-coalition systems are more aggressive is a function of the specific conditions. Under some circumstances autocrats might be more dovish, under other conditions they might be more hawkish. Our institutional explanation has two components pulling in opposite directions. First, leaders with large winning coalitions typically try hard during conflict, dedicating additional resources to the war effort and allowing them to overwhelm other states. Second, leaders with large winning coalitions need to be more certain of victory than their small-coalition, autocratic counterparts before initiating conflict. Given these two competing influences, we cannot say whether in general democrats are more hawkish or dovish. However, the combination of these two effects leads to the implication that democratic nations generally do not fight each other. It also implies that when democrats initiate wars, they are unusually likely to win. Reiter and Stam (1998) report that 93 percent of wars initiated by democratic states are won by them. In contrast, only about 60 percent of wars initiated by non-democracies are won by the initiator.

The Selectorate Peace: Interaction of Polities

Thus far, we have shown that political-selection institutions help shape war-fighting incentives. We found that a large winning coalition has two effects: it makes states try harder if there is a war and it makes leaders more selective about the disputes they are prepared to escalate to warfare. We now explore how these effects shape the possibility of conflict between different combinations of polities.

CASE 1   A is autocratic and so is B. In this case, neither tries hard if there is a war. A attacks if it believes that on average it can get more from conflict than from negotiations. A may believe, for instance, that the expected settlement through negotiations underestimates A's relative war-fighting ability. B presumably does not share this belief. If the leader in B did, then the negotiated settlement proffered by B would reflect that fact. Because the war's outcome is not critical to A's (or B's) political survival, the decision to fight is more easily influenced by secondary factors—such as uncertainty, rally-round-the-flag effects, a leader's idiosyncratic desires, and so on—not assessed in our model.

CASE 2   A is autocratic, but B is democratic. Despite the fact that A's institutions place few constraints on the decision to fight, A is generally reluctant to attack a democracy if it anticipates that the democracy is prepared to reciprocate with force. Democracies try hard. Therefore, the leader in A knows that her state is likely to lose any such war. However, since B is reluctant to engage in a war unless nearly certain of victory, B is likely to offer concessions to achieve a peaceful resolution when its capabilities are insufficient to make it sufficiently confident of military victory even with its extra effort. Therefore, A is likely to make demands, precipitating disputes, when B is a democrat without sufficient expected certainty of victory. This means that there will be many disputes initiated by autocrats against democrats, but only a small proportion of such disputes will escalate to reciprocal violence. A larger proportion of disputes between two autocracies are expected to escalate to reciprocal violence than is true for disputes initiated by autocracies against democracies.

CASE 3   A is democratic, but B is an autocrat. A's selection institutions make her reluctant to attack B unless military victory is highly likely. Yet A is prepared to put more effort into the war (if there is one) than will the autocratic B, making A more likely to win the conflict than, for instance, the prewar military balance alone suggests. Thus, democracies are willing to fight autocrats so long as the prewar military balance plus the democracy's additional effort give A a substantial probability of victory. Autocrats, depending on the risks to them from the war, are more willing to fight back under these conditions because victory is not essential for their political survival.

CASE 4   A is democratic and so is B. A will attack B only if B is sufficiently weak so that B will prefer to negotiate rather than fight back, taking both the prewar military balance and effort levels into account. Since B will also try hard if it chooses to fight back, A must either have a great prewar military advantage or a great advantage in overall resource endowments that can be put to use in the war effort. Or A must be confident that B's resources are insufficient for B to believe it can have a near certainty of victory. Thus, A must be sure that B is unsure of victory; this is of paramount importance in a head-to-head military dispute between democracy A and another democracy. Besides the asymmetric conflicts that characterize imperialism and wars of colonial expansion, war—that is, reciprocal violence—between democracies is unlikely, though disputes are not.

At a superficial level, many autocracies, particularly military dictatorships, appear to have the upper hand over democracies in terms of the military balance. On the whole, military states invest in their armed forces at a higher rate than democracies. Yet this misunderstands the purpose of their military spending. As demonstrated in chapter 5, democratic leaders spend resources on effective public policy. In contrast, spending in autocracies is focused on the provision of private goods. Although dictators might invest vast proportions of their resources in the military, this is often to reward their supporters rather than as a policy to provide effective defense of their society. During the Falklands War between Argentina and Britain, for instance, the Argentine military junta neither garrisoned the Falklands with their best troops nor put the main elements of their fleet to sea. It was raw recruits, not seasoned soldiers, who faced the British forces. The junta was dominated by army and navy officers. Recall also that the use of raw recruits was a problem for the Spartans at Leuctra.

It is worth emphasizing here a distinction made in chapter 1 when we introduced our use of public and private goods. National security policy, if oriented toward providing actual security for the residents in a state, is consumed as a public good, though its production is a private benefit to manufacturers, soldiers, and so on. Weapons manufacturers benefit privately from the production of systems required to protect national security. So do generals. In general, the production of military capabilities is private; in small-coalition systems the private production or acquisition of military capabilities is also distorted, so that the quality of these capabilities may be such that little by way of the public good of security consumption is achieved. This is a central problem in autocracies when they find themselves in disputes likely to escalate to violence against more democratic, larger-coalition rivals. Some of the details of this problem—and some of its solutions for autocrats—are discussed in chapter 9, when we address war aims and when we assess postwar prospects of nation building.

We have now established theoretically that autocracies fight one another provided either one believes it has a consequential advantage: Autocracies are more reluctant to initiate wars against democracies because of the difference in levels of effort, though they are not precluded from doing so when the conditions in the model are right. Finally, democracies target autocratic states just under those circumstances when the democracy expects to win, although this is more often than we might naively suppose because of the effort advantage induced by democratic institutions. The latter two results suggest an explanation for Benoit's (1996) finding that overall, democracies are more pacific than other systems.

The institutional arrangements within democracies mean that the survival of democratic leaders depends more on policy success than on the provision of private goods to supporters. Given this, once engaged in a war, democratic leaders typically make every effort to win. Should a war break out between two democracies, it is likely to be a bloody and hard-fought affair, both sides utilizing every available resource. As we have already shown, democratic leaders, not wanting to risk their political tenure in office, are reluctant to engage in a war unless they are extremely confident of winning. As we saw above, democratic leaders can often almost assure themselves of victory against autocracies by their willingness to try hard. Yet, when matched against a democracy, democratic leaders find it harder to overwhelm their opponents, who, given the institutional arrangements they face, are also prepared to go the extra mile for policy success. Since victory has to be a near certainty in order for a large-coalition democracy to fight rather than negotiate, it is extremely difficult for either democracy to have a sufficiently large advantage so that it prefers fighting to negotiation. Consequently, democracies are highly likely to negotiate a resolution of their mutual disputes rather than fight. Only democratic leaders who do not strongly value holding onto office are willing to fight when the perceived odds of victory are not extremely high.[12]

The dyadic selectorate model supports the claims that democracies tend not to fight one another, but do tend to fight wars against autocracies provided the democratic state has a substantial probability of victory. We also saw that our logic indicates that autocracies can readily fight one another and that autocrats are less inclined to negotiate than are democrats. Thus, while we began with seven observed empirical regularities of interest, we have shown how institutional arrangements explain four empirical patterns. While the remaining three regularities have not been explicitly discussed so far, the model can readily be directed to address these questions too.

It is commonly assumed, and has been demonstrated empirically, that the costs a nation endures in war and the length of time it takes a nation to win are inversely related to its military dominance (Bennett and Stam 1998; Bueno de Mesquita 1983). If this is so, nations that overwhelm their opponents are likely to win quickly and suffer fewer casualties in the process. As we have shown theoretically, democracies tend to make greater effort. Therefore, on average we should expect them to win quickly and to have lower casualties, as has been observed (Siverson 1995). Although the relationship between costs and relative military dominance is outside the formal framework of our model, it further reinforces our findings. Democracies find it hard to overwhelm other democracies because both sides are prepared to make an all-out effort during the war. Hence, a war between democracies is likely to be a long and costly struggle. Since the survival of democratic leaders depends on public policy success, they typically want to avoid long and costly wars.

Edward Mansfield and Jack Snyder (1995) suggest that transitional democracies are not bound by the democratic peace. Rather, unstable, transitional democracies are more war prone than are either democracies or autocracies, according to them. Our model may shed some light on the regularity they have advanced. Later we report on preferences over the selection of institutions. We find a larger set of theoretical conditions under which there are incentives to expand the size of the selectorate than there are to expand the size of the winning coalition.

If states in transition from autocracy to democracy expand their selectorate faster than they expand their winning coalition, reducing W/S, the willingness to risk war increases. By expanding the selectorate first or faster than the winning coalition, the transitional regime temporarily mimics the structure of a more autocratic system (W is getting smaller relative to S). In that case, the model suggests that the government is more willing to risk war than it will be when W expands enough to increase the ratio of W/S. These suggestive implications seem compatible with the regularity advanced by Mansfield and Snyder (1995). This explanation is reinforced by Ward and Gleditsch's (1998) result that shows that rather than all transitional democracies being war prone, it is those undergoing reversal in the democratization process that are most apt to fight.

We now turn to the empirical regularity uncovered by Morgan and Campbell (1991), namely, that large democracies appear particularly constrained to avoid war. To do so, we return to the debate between Madison and Montesquieu regarding the relative advantages of large republics and small republics. Major-power democracies typically have a significant advantage over their opponents in terms of the military balance. This enhances their bargaining position relative to smaller, less powerful democracies. Powerful democracies can use their advantageous bargaining position to obtain nearly everything they want anyway through negotiations. Even if certain of victory, the small additional gains made through military victory are likely to be offset by the costs of fighting. Therefore, powerful democracies should strongly manifest the expected behavior of democracies in a manner consistent with the Morgan-and-Campbell results.

Diversionary War and Compromise Agreements

Although we present a general model of war, for clarity of exposition, we have focused on particular cases. These stylized cases suggest that democracies are only aggressive if they are nearly certain of victory. When the outcome of the war is less certain, democracies prefer negotiated settlements. Because this conclusion drives the democratic peace predictions, it is worthwhile exploring its robustness, especially since there are legitimate, identifiable conditions under which it breaks down.

For mathematical convenience we assumed the distribution of challenger types was exponential. Our arguments about effort levels are grounded on how institutions shape the rewards supporters receive and not specifically on the marginal impact of these benefits. So, with respect to effort level, our assumption that challenger types are distributed exponentially is benign. However, with respect to the decision to fight, our assumption is less benign. For example, in examining the limiting case ($W \to \infty$), we utilized the concavity of the exponential distribution. While it certainly seems reasonable to assume there are diminishing marginal returns from additional rewards for supporters when a leader is already likely to remain in office, such an assumption is less tenable when a leader's initial prospects of survival are low. We might, for example, prefer to assume challengers are distributed normally, making the reselection decision appear as a probit model. Of course, provided a leader had reasonable prospects of survival, the logic behind our stylized case holds. Unfortunately, for leaders who, ex ante, have little hope of remaining in office, the rationale for our stylized case diminishes and may even be reversed. Democratic leaders with failed domestic policies may be extremely belligerent.

Given her institutional incentives, a democratic leader with failed public policies is unlikely to retain office unless she has an astonishing change in performance. If we think of reselection as modeled in a probit setting, then the leader is believed to have little prospect of remaining in office. Given the increasingly marginal returns on additional rewards when starting from such a low base, a leader with failed policies has an incentive to gamble everything on the outcome of conflict. It is perhaps only through a successful war that she has any significant chance of remaining in office. If a leader is in a position where accepting the negotiated settlement leaves her with little chance of domestic survival, then, counter to our earlier argument, she faces no downside from fighting. If she loses, she will be deposed, but she would have been removed anyway. Yet victory holds the prospects (although not necessarily high, significantly greater than with negotiations) of remaining in office. Hence, a democratic leader with failed policies is potentially bellicose. This, of course, is the gambling-for-resurrection idea inherent in the diversionary-war-theory literature (Downs and Rocke 1995; Levy 1989; Smith 1998b; Werner 1996; Goemans 2000; Richards et al. 1993).

These diversionary hypotheses might appear to undermine our earlier conclusions, but this is not so. Indeed, quite the contrary, these diversionary results are satisfying on several dimensions. The selectorate theory does not simply state that democracies are either more cautious or more bellicose. It states the conditions under which each of these eventualities occurs. This distinction is important. Our theory does not state that a war between democracies is impossible. Rather we show that the conditions under which a democrat would attack another democrat are more restrictive than the conditions under which a democrat would attack an autocrat. This constraint, which occurs because democrats are less attractive targets due to their high war effort, holds even in diversionary circumstances. While autocrats always remain more attractive targets, war between democracies is most likely when both democratic leaders have failed domestic policies, as we elaborate below.

In terms of theory building, the diversionary hypotheses above are pleasing. A new theoretical model is convincing when it accounts for the predictions of extant models. The fact that our model simultaneously accounts for findings in both the diversionary-war and democratic peace literature strengthens our arguments.

Negotiations are complex, and for convenience we have not modeled their details. However, the objectives of leaders during negotiations differ depending on their institutional arrangements. Since autocratic leaders survive whatever the policy outcome, provided they do not squander their resources, they simply seek to maximize their gains from the process. Democratic leaders face different pressures. It is harder for them to keep their jobs if they perform poorly on policy. They would like to get a good deal for their nation through negotiations, but they only need a deal good enough for them to be reselected. If the negotiations break down, the democrat must be militarily successful to satisfy domestic policy wants and to survive politically. Hence, a democratic leader might be prepared to accept a modest negotiated settlement rather than allowing the negotiations to break down and risk being removed by failure during war. This is particularly true if the democrat is faced with a democratic rival, because the rival will try hard in any war. Again, then, we see that democrats are unlikely to fight one another; they are likely to look for ways to succeed through negotiations even if it means that one makes additional concessions to avoid a breakdown.

For autocrats, the story is different. Autocrats survive domestically by providing private goods. Unless the international outcome is really horrendous, as examined in chapter 9, it is unlikely to influence their reselection prospects. So they do not have a great incentive to avoid the breakdown of negotiations. They have a smaller incentive than democrats to make additional concessions in negotiations to avoid a war against a belligerent foe. While domestic policy failures make domestic leaders belligerent, autocrats find it less important to keep negotiating than do democrats. Democratic leaders are destined to fight each other only when neither is able to make additional concessions. This circumstance arises only when both have domestically failed policies. The same motivations exist for autocrats, but these incentives are not as strong, since autocrats are surer of reselection whatever the international outcome.[13]

Empirical Assessments

The selectorate model explains the known regularities of the so-called democratic peace. The explanation also includes novel hypotheses that indicate, for instance, that (1) because of their selection criteria for fighting, leaders of large-coalition systems show no reluctance to engage in wars of colonial or imperial expansion, contrary to normative accounts of the democratic peace; (2) democrats are willing to make larger concessions in negotiations than are autocrats; (3) leaders who rely on a large coalition try harder in interstate wars than leaders who rely on a small coalition; (4) but leaders who rely on a large coalition do not try harder in wars with near certainty of victory (i.e., colonial or imperial wars) than leaders who rely on small coalitions or in wars where political survival is known to be at stake from the outset. We test the first, third, and fourth hypotheses now. We lack the information necessary to test the second. The third and fourth are most important, because they speak directly to a heretofore unexamined and undetected aspect of behavior during military disputes.

The selectorate model indicates that large-coalition systems are prepared to fight wars against especially weak adversaries, like prospective colonies, all else being equal. The theory does not suggest any reluctance by small-coalition systems to engage in similar wars, or in wars with poorer odds. Normative accounts of the democratic peace argue that democracies favor compromise and avoid violence, using it only defensively when confronting nondemocratic regimes in disputes. Consequently, the normative account of the democratic peace appears to suggest that democracies should be disproportionately unlikely to engage in wars of colonial and imperial expansion, because the adversaries are especially unlikely to represent threats to the security of the stronger democratic state. The selectorate model parts from such normative accounts in suggesting no hesitation by large-coalition systems, including democracies, to engage in such wars. Large-coalition systems, according to the selectorate theory, have no basis for behaving differently from their small-coalition counterparts as aggressors in imperial or colonial wars. To test the competing claims we construct a dummy variable called *Colonial/ImperialWar*. We code this variable 1 in any year a leader entered a colonial or imperial war—that is, a war categorized by the Correlates of War Project as extrasystemic. Otherwise it is coded 0.

Normative vs. Selectorate Account

The test of the normative democratic peace account and the selectorate account is straightforward. We examine two logit analyses. The first is between *Colonial/ImperialWar*, the standard region and year fixed effects we have used throughout, and *Democracy*. The second also includes the regional/year fixed effects and substitutes *W* for *Democracy*. If the normative account is correct, there will be a significant inverse relationship between a country's degree of democracy as measured on the POLITY scale and participation in *Colonial/ImperialWar*. If the selectorate account is supported, there will not be a negative association

Table 6.1
Colonial/imperial war, democracy, and coalition size

	Coef., (std. error), prob.	Coef., (std. error), prob.	Coef., (std. error), prob.
W	1.21, (0.231), 0.000		1.35, (0.269), 0.000
Democracy		1.34, (0.224), 0.000	
WB:DemRes			−0.13, (0.442), 0.772
Summary statistics	$N = 4,870$, F.E. = 171, $\chi^2 = 27.79$	$N = 3,577$, F.E. = 165, $\chi^2 = 36.92$	$N = 2,618$, F.E. = 160, $\chi^2 = 25.64$

between coalition size and *Colonial/ImperialWar*. Three logit analyses, reported in table 6.1 (and available for replication through our website, along with all other statistical results), report the findings.

Democracy has a significant impact on the likelihood of extrasystemic war in the opposite direction from that anticipated by those who advocate a normative explanation of the democratic peace. That is, democracies are more likely to engage in wars of colonial and imperial expansion than are nondemocracies. The logit analysis based on coalition size, like the analysis with regard to *Democracy*, shows that large-coalition systems are especially likely to be involved in colonial and imperial wars. The third analysis evaluates the impact of coalition size and the residual, independent impact of other characteristics of democracy on the likelihood of colonial and imperials wars. We fail to find support for the normative account. The characteristics of governance independent of coalition size neither make democracies more nor less likely than autocracies to engage in colonial and imperial wars. Polities that depend on a large winning coalition—a key characteristic of democracy—continue to be significantly more inclined than autocrats to be colonial or imperial powers.

Who Tries Harder in War?

Perhaps the most important and surprising deduction regarding the "selectorate peace" is that leaders who depend on large coalitions try harder in war, committing proportionately more extra resources to their war efforts than do leaders who depend on small coalitions. We offer a variety of tests of this proposition. The analysis of this question uses three dependent variables. The first is the logarithm of national military expenditures (referred to as *Log(MilEx)*) on a year-by-year basis, with expenditures drawn from the Correlates of War data. The second is the logarithm of the number of soldiers (*Log(MilPers)*) in each country on a year-by-year basis. These data are also drawn from the Correlates of War database. The third, referred to as *Log(MilEx/Soldier)*, is the logarithm of military expenditures per soldier on a year-to-year basis. The correlation between *Log(MilEx)* and *Log(MilPers)* is 0.63; between *Log(MilEx)* and *Log(MilEx/Soldier)* it is 0.78; and between *Log(MilPers)* and *Log(MilEx/Soldier)* it is 0.01. Each of these correlations is based on 9,196 observations. The observations are nation-years spanning the period from 1816 to 1993.

It will help in the explanation of our reasons for choosing the three dependent variables if we first explain part of the structure of the tests we conduct. Each test includes the one-year lagged value of the dependent variable. This means that the variance not explained by the prior year's military expenditures or military personnel or expenditures per solider represents the change in the society's budgetary or personnel commitment to the military from one year to the next. That is, the variance not explained by the lagged dependent variable is the difference in military effort from one year to the next. Our hypothesis says that a significant portion of this change—the portion of the dependent variable not explained by its lagged value—is expected to be accounted for by the advent of war in the case of large-coalition political systems. To assess this factor, we must first control for several additional considerations. Polities whose leaders depend on a large coalition probably already make considerable effort to ensure national security against foreign threats. Thus it might be the case that democracies or large-coalition systems just spend more or have more soldiers on average than do more autocratic or smaller-coalition systems (Reiter and Stam 2002). To assess this possibility, we control for the one-year lagged value of *W* or of *Democracy*, depending on the test.

The heart of our tests consists of a comparison of two variables. One, called *IS_War*, is coded 1 each year that a state participated in an interstate war in which it was an initial belligerent and 0 otherwise. We exclude third-party joiners; many were the victims of invasion and had little choice in the matter, and others may have engaged in bandwagoning while placing themselves at relatively little risk. The theory does not explicitly address the effort level of these states. The second key variable is *IS_War*Lagged W*. The first of these two variables evaluates the effect entering a war has on the level of military effort for all war participants separate from what their country was doing on military spending or personnel commitments prior to the war. The second, *IS_War*Lagged W*, evaluates the difference in military effort between all states and states with increasingly large coalition structures. The hypothesis being tested is that *IS_War + IS_War*Lagged W > IS_War* so that *IS_War*Lagged W* is significantly larger than zero. The hypothesis is refuted if *IS_War*Lagged W* is insignificant or is negatively signed. We construct an equivalent interaction term, called *IS_War*Lagged D*, which evaluates the marginal effect of *Democracy* on military spending, number of soldiers, or spending per soldier.

Each of the dependent variables we have chosen in conjunction with a control for the variable's lagged value allows us to evaluate the impact of war and political institutions on military effort. A positive effect associated with war involvement—that is, an increase in spending, in spending per soldier, or in the number of soldiers—reflects an increase of effort committed to the war. Having said that, each variable has limitations. We believe *Log(MilEx)* is the best of the three indicators and that *Log(MilPers)* is the weakest.

It seems straightforward that the more a government spends above its steady-state level on the military, the more likely the nation is to put forward a more effective effort to advance or protect its interests as defined by the leadership. Military spending per soldier is chosen as a basis for evaluating effort in an attempt to distinguish expenditures that effectively improve military capabilities from expenditures that do not. We have already suggested that military expenditures may go to improving a nation's prospects of military success, or they may take the form of private benefits for generals and other critical officers while leaving national defense in the hands of poorly trained and inadequately equipped soldiers. Societies that spend little per soldier are unlikely to train and equip their soldiers well. Rather, in the event of a war such societies are likely to treat ordinary soldiers as so much cannon fodder. In such a case, total military expenditures could be sizable, but the amount per soldier is likely to be small. This specification places a heavy burden on the selectorate theory. Large-coalition societies, being oriented toward public goods, are more likely than small-coalition polities to provide well for national defense. Therefore, they are likely to spend a large amount per capita on their military at all times. If this is so, then extra effort in wartime represents a substantial sacrifice, because they are already spending large amounts to protect their nation. When we turn to empirical tests, we will evaluate a model that controls for the previous year's spending per soldier and for the institutional arrangements in the state to assess whether the preexisting level of spending per soldier has a different effect on subsequent total military spending depending on whether the regime relies on a large or a small coalition.

Log(MilPers) evaluates how many soldiers a country has mobilized. By controlling for the previous year's value we assess the change in the number of mobilized soldiers. Naturally, newly recruited soldiers are likely to be less effective fighters than those who have had adequate opportunity to be trained and equipped. Still, having more soldiers at the margin improves the chances for victory. More well-trained and well-equipped soldiers (that is, those for whom military expenditure per soldier is high) are especially likely to improve a country's prospects of victory. Presumably, the baseline number of soldiers—as evaluated by the lagged logarithm of military personnel—can be higher in an autocracy because soldiers cost little. But then there is likely to be less incentive to divert resources toward putting more soldiers in the field should the country find itself at war in such societies than is expected to be true for large-coalition societies. We use the logarithm of expenditures, of soldiers, and of expenditures per soldier under the supposition that for each there are marginally decreasing gains as the magnitude of these factors increases.

We test each dependent variable against the lagged version of that variable, *Lagged W* (or *Lagged Democracy*), *IS_War*, and *IS_War* times *Lagged W* or *Lagged Democracy*. We also control for region-year fixed effects. We then replicate the tests, adding controls for the size of the state and for the wealth of the citizenry. More populous polities clearly are more likely to spend absolutely more on the military and to have more soldiers than are smaller polities. To take this scale factor into account, we control for the logarithm of the nation's population. This variable is called *Log(Pop)*. Wealthier societies are better able to afford the expense of a large military and higher costs per soldier. Data on per capita income are not available for a broad array of countries prior to the Cold War, so as a proxy for per capita income, we control for the logarithm of energy consumption per capita in each state. This variable is estimated by using the Correlates of War energy consumption indicator divided by the country's total population. Wealthier societies probably consume more energy per person than do poorer societies.

The models tested are

War model 1: $Log(MilEx) = f(Lagged(LogMilEx), Lagged\ W, IS\_War,$ $IS\_War*Lagged\ W,$ fixed effects)

War model 2: $Log(MilPer) = f(Lagged(LogMilPer), Lagged\ W, IS\_War,$ $IS\_War*Lagged\ W,$ fixed effects)

War model 3: $Log(MilEx/Soldier) = f(Lagged(LogMilEx/Soldier),$ $Lagged\ W, IS\_War, IS\_War*Lagged\ W,$ fixed effects)

War model 4: $Log(MilEx) = f(Lagged(LogMilEx), Lagged\ W, IS\_War,$ $IS\_War*Lagged,\ W, Log(Pop), Log(Energy/Capita),$ fixed effects)

War model 5: $Log(MilPer) = f(Lagged(LogMilPer), Lagged\ W,$ $IS\_War, IS\_War*Lagged,\ W, Log(Pop), Log(Energy/Capita),$ fixed effects)

War model 6: $Log(MilEx/Soldier) = f(Lagged(LogMilEx/Soldier),$ $Lagged\ W, IS\_War, IS\_War*Lagged\ W, Log(Pop),$ $Log(Energy/Capita),$ fixed effects)

We also utilize a duplicate set in which the lagged POLITY *Democracy-Autocracy* scores are substituted for *Lagged W* both on its own and in the relevant interaction, for a total of twelve tests related to effort levels during interstate war. An additional set of tests replicate the above models, but this time substituting *EX_War for IS_War, EX_War*Lagged W for IS_War*Lagged W, and EX_War*Lagged Democracy* for *IS_War*Lagged Democracy. Ex_War* is a dummy variable coded 1 when the country in question was involved in a colonial or imperial war—that is, a war referred to by the Correlates of War Project as extrasystemic.

The selectorate theory specifically predicts that each test will show a significant positive coefficient associated with *IS_War*Lagged W* and that the coefficient will be so large that the sum of the coefficients associated with *IS_War* and *IS_War*Lagged W* will also be significant and positive. Although we expect a similar pattern when *Democracy* is substituted for *W*, the selectorate theory does not specifically predict this. Rather, the expectation arises because democracies tend to be large-coalition systems. When *EX_War* is substituted for *IS_War*, the selectorate theory does not expect significant coefficients associated with *EX_War*Lagged W* (or *EX_War*Lagged Democracy*). Leaders generally do not need to try harder when fighting such wars because these wars involve a near certainty of victory from the start.

Table 6.2 presents the results for the first three models, which assess the relationship between *IS_War*, coalition size (*W*), and the three measures of military effort without controls for population size or per capita wealth. The findings are consistent with the prediction derived from the dyadic selectorate model. In each test, *IS_War*Lagged W* is positive and significant. Furthermore, the sum of *IS_War* + *IS_War*Lagged W* is significantly larger than 0 in each case, indicating that large-*W* systems increase their military effort during wartime and that they do so at a greater level than do smaller-coalition systems. In fact, table 6.2 offers a perhaps surprising, interesting additional perspective on warfare. The fact that a country finds itself enmeshed in a war does not imply that it increases its military expenditure. The regression analysis when the dependent variable is *Log(MilEx/Soldier)* shows that *IS_War* in this case is not significant (and has a negative sign). That is, spending per soldier does not increase in small-coalition polities when they find themselves at war. Presumably the leaders in these societies were spending the optimal amount all along as private goods oriented toward maintaining the loyalty of key officers and other cronies. Not wanting to place their

Table 6.2
Military effort in interstate war and coalition size

β, σ, prob.	Model 1: *Log(MilEx)*	Model 2: *Log(MilPers)*	Model 3: *Log(MilEx/Soldier)*
Lagged dependent variable	0.974, 0.002, 0.000	0.982, 0.002, 0.000	0.904, 0.004, 0.000
Lagged W	0.023, 0.024, 0.112	−0.017, 0.010, 0.100	0.087, 0.025, 0.001
IS_War	0.136, 0.034, 0.000	0.068, 0.024, 0.004	−0.050, 0.061, 0.419
*IS_War*Lagged W*	0.114, 0.055, 0.040	0.132, 0.041, 0.001	0.233, 0.099, 0.019
Constant	0.324, 0.022, 0.000	0.086, 0.009, 0.000	0.660, 0.029, 0.000
*Prob(IS_War + IS_War*Lagged W > 0)*	$F = 55.62, p = 0.000$	$F = 62.43, p = 0.000$	$F = 9.85, p = 0.002$
Summary statistics	$N = 8,896$, F.E. = 853 $R^2 = 0.98, F = 60,580$	$N = 10,879$, F.E.= 948 $R^2 = 0.98, F = 93,036$	$N = 8,910$, F.E. = 836 $R^2 = 0.94, F = 13,739$

Table 6.3
Military effort in war and coalition size, with controls for population and wealth

β, σ, Prob.	Model 1: *Log(MilEx)*	Model 2: *Log(MilPers)*	Model 3: *Log(MilEx/Soldier)*
Lagged dependent variable	0.911, 0.005, 0.000	0.935, 0.004, 0.000	0.876, 0.005, 0.000
Lagged W	−0.020, 0.016, 0.196	−0.059, 0.013, 0.000	0.033, 0.028, 0.231
IS_War	0.165, 0.036, 0.000	0.064, 0.029, 0.027	−0.035, 0.065, 0.595
*IS_War*Lagged W*	0.092, 0.057, 0.104	0.107, 0.047, 0.023	0.162, 0.103, 0.116
Log(Pop)	0.034, 0.005, 0.000	0.051, 0.004, 0.000	−0.031, 0.007, 0.000
Log(Energy/Capita)	0.048, 0.004, 0.000	0.006, 0.002, 0.011	0.058, 0.006, 0.000
Constant	0.121, 0.055, 0.028	−0.573, 0.055, 0.000	0.944, 0.095, 0.000
Prob(IS_War + IS_War Lagged W > 0)*	$F = 58.77, p = 0.000$	$F = 37.36, p = 0.000$	$F = 4.53, p = 0.033$
Summary statistics	$N = 7{,}587$, F.E. = 757 $R^2 = 0.98$, $F = 38{,}429$	$N = 8{,}198$, F.E. = 773 $R^2 = 0.98$, $F = 48{,}031$	$N = 7{,}698$, F.E. = 745 $R^2 = 0.93$, $F = 8{,}015$

own political survival at risk for the good of the state, they do not boost spending per soldier even when they are at war.[14]

Table 6.3 displays the results when we add controls for population size and per capita wealth. Despite absorbing virtually all of the variance in the dependent variables with the lagged effect of the dependent variable, the strong scaling effects of population and wealth, and the numerous fixed effects in each regression, it still remains true that coalition size increases the military effort made by states at war.[15]

The tests that replicate the above results while substituting *Democracy* for coalition size reinforce the view that the specific feature of democracy that encourages the democratic peace is large coalition size. The result based on *Lagged Democracy* times *IS_War* is significant ($p = 0.039$, one-tailed) and positive when the dependent variable is *Log(MilEx)*, but the result is not significant when effort is assessed with *Log(MilPers)* ($p = 0.208$, one-tailed) or *Log(MilEx/Soldier)* ($p = 0.116$, one-tailed).

Rome in the Punic Wars: An Illustration of Extra Effort

Before turning our attention to the special case in which large-coalition systems are predicted to try no harder than their small-coalition counterparts, we pause to consider an illustrative example of the extra effort in war that arises as *W* gets bigger. Here we compare Rome and Carthage in the Second Punic War. We set the stage by reflecting on the gradual expansion in Rome's winning-coalition requirements during the period of the Republic.

Rome's political institutions underwent significant changes during the period of the Republic, changes that necessitated dependence on an enlarged winning coalition at the time of the Punic Wars. The early political history of the Republic is replete with competition between the wealthy patrician families who achieved domination through the *Comitia Centuriata* and the Senate, and the ordinary citizens, the plebs. The plebs extracted substantial concessions, including the formation of their own assembly, the *Concilium Plebis*, and an increase in the power of the Tribunes. Initially, the *Concilium Plebis* was nothing more than an opportunity for the people of Rome to express an opinion; however, over time its legal authority grew, climaxing in the *Lex Hortensia* of 271 BC. These laws are often seen as the high point of democracy in Rome, with the importance of the *Concilium Plebis* subsequently declining as the tribunes were co-opted.

The plebs gained political concessions through their use of protests, riots, and their threat to withdraw from the polity at a time when a Greek confederation was challenging Rome from southern Italy. According to the theory, such actions have the effect of expanding public-goods provision by increasing the size required for a winning coalition. The concessions granted to the plebs resulted in a shift of votes away from the class-dominated *Comitia Centuriata* to the tribal-based *Comitia Tributa*. Such reforms meant that a winning coalition could no longer be created from only the wealthiest classes. As the selectorate theory suggests, these reforms heralded Rome's economic development and its supremacy in Italy. The ascendancy of the tribunes and the shift to voting by tribes effectively increased winning-coalition size. This in turn forced leaders to shift their policies away from favoring the patrician class and toward the general interests of the public as a whole. These shifts improved the prospects of foreign policy success in the manner described by the dyadic selectorate model.

By around 270 BC, with the subjugation of Bruttium and Calabria, Rome dominated the whole of Italy south of the Po River, with subsequently even greater military achievements made in the first Punic War, 261–241 BC. In this conflict against the Carthaginians, despite numerous catastrophes and no history of seamanship, the Romans won largely through naval conquest. Rome's spoils included Sicily and subsequently Sardinia, providing enormous impetus to Roman trade (Caven 1980; Lazenby 1996).

No better example of the difference between how large- and small-*W* systems fight wars can be found than in the second Punic War, which started in 219 BC when Hannibal marched a Carthaginian army out of Spain and crossed the Alps into Italy. Before his eventual defeat at the hands of Scipio at the battle of Zama in 202 BC, Hannibal crushed numerous Roman armies and terrorized the Italian peninsula. Yet despite winning practically every battle for five years, he never defeated the Romans. They simply tried harder than the Carthaginians.

Carthage was an oligarchy of wealthy traders. As the dyadic selectorate model suggests, Carthage, being a small-*W* system, pursued policies aimed at helping the few rather than the many. Despite repeated calls by Hannibal for men and materials—in particular for siege equipment, without which he was almost powerless to take the major Roman strongholds—the leadership in Carthage never diverted resources away from promoting the trading interests of the winning coalition and toward fighting the war. After years of conflict, Hannibal's resources, men, and allies whittled away. He had continually defeated Rome militarily, but Carthage never gave him the tools he needed to finish the task. Indeed, the fact that he thrived so long in Italy is a testimony to his genius and brutality.

In contrast to Carthage's miserable effort, Rome's effort was enormous. Despite losing nearly entire armies at the battles of Trebia (218 BC), Lake Trasimene (217 BC), and Cannae (216 BC), Rome continued to raise, equip, and train large armies.[16] Following its defeat of Carthage, Roman success continued with the defeat of the Gauls in 200 BC and the conquest of much of Greece by 168 BC.

Unfortunately, Rome's successes combined with the dislocations of the Punic Wars and changed economic circumstances undermined the size of Rome's *W*, which eventually led to the collapse of the Republic and the succession of Empire, a small-*W* , large-*S* system.

Colonial Wars: An Exception to Trying Harder

The dyadic selectorate model identifies two circumstances when large coalition size does not imply greater effort than small coalition size during foreign conflict. These arise when leaders anticipate that their survival is at risk regardless of regime type, or when the leader's survival is not at risk regardless of regime type.

Wars of colonial and imperial expansion, as noted earlier, have a very low ex ante probability of ending in defeat for the aggressive state. They also have a low ex ante probability of bringing down the leader of the aggressor state. Therefore, in looking at our three dependent variables, controlling for *EX_War* and its relevant interaction terms, we expect that the interaction term for coalition size will not be statistically significant. That is, we do not believe leaders alter military expenditures in response to their participation in colonial or imperial wars regardless of the structure of their political system. Using the same models as were used to test effort levels when a state is embroiled in an interstate war, but substituting *EX_War* and *EX_War*Lagged W* or *Lagged Democracy*, we find that the hypothesis is consistent with the evidence. Table 6.4 summarizes the results.

The results in table 6.4 are reinforced when we introduce controls for population size and energy consumption per capita. In each case it remains true that no extra effort is made regardless of regime type. *EX_War* and *EX_War*Lagged W* are both indistinguishable from zero in each case. Substituting *Democracy* for coalition size does not alter the results. Again, in the basic analysis and in the analysis with controls for population and energy use per capita, regime type does not significantly alter military effort in extrasystemic wars.

Table 6.4
Military effort in colonial/imperial war and coalition size

β, σ, prob.	Model 1: *Log(MilEx)*	Model 2: *Log(MilPers)*	Model 3: *Log(MilEx/Soldier)*
Lagged dependent Variable	0.978, 0.002, 0.000	0.985, 0.002, 0.000	0.905, 0.004, 0.000
Lagged W	0.028, 0.014, 0.052	−0.006, 0.010, 0.553	0.097, 0.025, 0.000
EX_War	0.018, 0.048, 0.709	0.040, 0.037, 0.272	−0.013, 0.083, 0.877
*EX_War*Lagged W*	0.020, 0.075, 0.789	−0.028, 0.058, 0.629	0.066, 0.129, 0.612
Constant	0.293, 0.023, 0.000	0.077, 0.009, 0.000	0.654, 0.029, 0.000
*Prob(EX_War + EX_War*Lagged W > 0)*	$F = 0.95, p = 0.329$	$F = 0.16, p = 0.686$	$F = 0.63, p = 0.426$
Summary statistics	$N = 8,896$, F.E. $= 853$ $R^2 = 0.98$, $F = 59,810$	$N = 10,879$, F.E. $= 948$ $R^2 = 0.98$, $F = 92,098$	$N = 8,910$, F.E. $= 836$ $R^2 = 0.94$, $F = 13,721$

The second exception to the prediction that large-coalition polities try harder in war arises when leaders believe ex ante that there is an elevated risk of their being deposed following a military defeat. This is a harder proposition to test because it is difficult to know what leaders believe their risks are at the outset of hostilities. Nevertheless, the selectorate theory provides guidance as to a reasonable test. In chapter 9 we will argue (and test empirically) that the selectorate theory implies that when the victor in a war relies on a large coalition, she is more likely to depose the incumbent in the defeated state and impose a puppet government than when the victor relies on a small coalition. Simply put, democratic victors are more likely to remove the leader of a state they have vanquished than are autocrats. Our reasoning is that incumbent leaders, being rational and being highly motivated with regard to risks to their political survival, know that the risk of deposition is heightened if they are defeated militarily by a democratic rival. One consequence of this risk is that disputes with democratic, large-coalition rivals are more likely to be resolved through negotiation than through war. But if a war ensues, it also follows that autocrats, like democrats, should try hard to win in order to forestall the threat of their removal by a victorious democratic opponent. Thus, we use the regime type of the primary rival in an interstate war as a way to identify disputes for which there is a heightened ex ante belief that political survival is at stake. We replicate our earlier analyses for interstate war, but now looking at all nation-years when there is no war and only those war years when the primary rival's coalition size was at least as large as 0.75 on our scale (recall that W varies between 0 and 1). The hypothesis is that *IS_War* will be positive and *IS_War*Lagged W* will be insignificantly different from zero. Table 6.5 summarizes the findings.

The results regarding effort, as assessed by *Log(MilEx/Soldier)*, are not consistent with the hypothesis. Large-coalition systems continue to try harder than do small-coalition polities in this case, and this remains true when we add controls for population and energy consumption. However, when effort is evaluated in terms of military expenditures or in terms of the number of soldiers mustered, the proposition is supported in detail. That is, *IS_War* is significant and positive, indicating that all regimes increase effort when they find themselves at war against rivals who depend on a large coalition. Yet *IS_War*Lagged W* is insignificant, indicating that larger-coalition systems do not produce greater military

Table 6.5
Military effort in interstate war against rivals with large coalitions

β, σ, prob.	Model 1: *Log(MilEx)*	Model 2: *Log(MilPers)*	Model 3: *Log(MilEx/Soldier)*
Lagged dependent variable	0.974, 0.002, 0.000	0.982, 0.002, 0.000	0.905, 0.004, 0.000
Lagged W	0.022, 0.014, 0.116	−0.022, 0.010, 0.026	0.087, 0.025, 0.000
IS_War	0.161, 0.087, 0.065	0.089, 0.052, 0.091	−0.296, 0.162, 0.069
*IS_War*Lagged W*	0.169, 0.165, 0.306	−0.004, 0.102, 0.970	1.022, 0.302, 0.001
Constant	0.323, 0.023, 0.000	0.085, 0.008, 0.000	0.657, 0.292, 0.000
Summary statistics	$N = 8{,}474$, F.E. = 825 $R^2 = 0.99$, $F = 57{,}284$	$N = 10{,}399$, F.E. = 945 $R^2 = 0.98$, $F = 100{,}025$	$N = 8{,}508$, F.E. = 812 $R^2 = 0.94$, $F = 13{,}371$

effort than smaller-coalition systems under these conditions. This pattern is even more strongly reflected in the analyses that control for population size and energy consumption per capita. Thus, while the findings are mixed, the preponderance of the evidence supports the contention that all states try hard in wars in which leaders anticipate an elevated risk of deposition if they lose. Large-coalition polities generally try hard in interstate wars (but not in colonial wars), and small-coalition autocracies generally try less hard.

Conclusion

We have posed a dyadic extension of the selectorate model. In it, leaders must decide how much effort to put into winning a war versus reserving resources to be spent as private benefits for their key backers. They also have the option of seeking a negotiated resolution of international disputes. We demonstrated that large-coalition leaders, when faced with a war, are more inclined to shift extra resources into the war effort than are small-coalition leaders. This was shown to follow because as the winning coalition gets larger, the prospects of political survival increasingly hinge on successful policy performance. The extra effort made by large-*W* leaders gives them a military advantage over small-coalition rivals in war. Additionally, we have shown that large-coalition leaders are prone to fight when they are very confident of military victory, a restriction not observed by small-coalition leaders. Otherwise, those who head a large coalition prefer to negotiate.

We have shown that democrats, because of their large coalitions, make relatively unattractive targets. Domestic reselection pressures cause leaders to mobilize resources toward the war effort. This makes it harder for other states to target them for aggression. In addition to trying harder, democrats are also more selective in their choice of targets. Since defeat typically leads to domestic replacement for those who rely on a large coalition, these leaders only initiate wars when they expect to win. These two factors lead to the interactions between polities that are often referred to collectively as the democratic peace, a set of interactions that might better be called the "selectorate peace." Small-coalition leaders (like many autocrats), while needing a slight expected advantage over other small-coalition adversaries to initiate conflict, need more overwhelming odds against large-coalition (usually democratic) foes. This is true because those who depend on a large coalition compensate for any initial military disadvantage by devoting additional resources to the war effort. To initiate war, democrats generally need overwhelming odds of victory. However, this does not mean that they are passive. Because democrats utilize their resources for the war effort rather than reserving them to reward their backers, they are generally able, given their war-fighting selection criteria, to overwhelm small-coalition autocracies, resulting in short and relatively low cost wars. Yet democracies find it hard to overwhelm other democracies because they also try hard due to their large coalitions. In general, democracies make unattractive targets if the conditions make it likely that they will fight rather that seek to negotiate. They are particularly unattractive to other democracies. Hence, democratic states rarely attack other democratic states.

One concern about what is termed the democratic peace is that it has lacked a comprehensive explanation. Explanations based on norms or on constraints account for some of the democratic peace regularities, but they do not explain all. The model here appears to offer a more comprehensive account. Several novel hypotheses follow: large-coalition systems (democracies) try harder; political incentives in systems with a large W (democracies) do not make them immune from wars of imperial expansion; they do not try harder during such wars; and they offer more concessions in negotiations that do autocracies. Additionally, autocrats try as hard as democrats when they face a rival who heightens the risk that they will be deposed if they lose the war, a fate more likely to confront an autocrat if she is defeated by a democratic rival than if she loses to another autocrat. We provided evidence for all but the proposition regarding concessions during negotiations (for which we lack appropriate data). The hypothesis about willingness to fight colonial or imperial wars seem to contradict the core of the norms-based explanations of the democratic peace. The model we propose offers an explanation for these diverse phenomena without attributing better motives or greater civic-mindedness to one kind of leader over another. The explanation is driven purely by self-interested leaders seeking to hold office and facing alternative institutional arrangements.

Appendix

The game starts with two nations A and B in dispute. The structure of the game is as follows:

1. The leader in nation A chooses between war and negotiations. If she selects war she also chooses how hard to fight, $g_A \in [0,1]$.

2. If war occurs, then, having observed A's effort level, the leader of B chooses how hard to fight, $g_B \in [0,1]$.

3. Nature determines the outcome of the war.

4. In each nation, the members of the winning coalition, having observed the international outcome and the level of private goods allocated to them, decide whether to retain their leader or defect to a domestic political rival, thereby removing the current leader from office.

International Outcomes

We model war as a costly lottery. The values of victory and defeat are normalized to 1 and 0, respectively. In addition, players pay a per capita cost, k, associated with the war's destruction and the risks of fighting. Therefore, the utility of victory equals $1 - k$ and the utility for defeat is $-k$.

The probability of victory depends on the observable military balance, M, and the proportion of additional national resources committed to the war effort, g_i. The subscript refers to nation A or B, as appropriate. The military balance, which takes values between 0 and 1, represents the ratio of observable military assets of the two sides. Additional resources dedicated to the war effort by either country are drawn from the R_i

resources each leader has at her disposal. By choosing to devote the proportion g_i of R_i to the war effort, she generates an additional $g_i r$ military assets, where r represents the exchange rate between resources and military capability.

The probability that A wins in a war, denoted $p_A = p_A(g_A, g_B, M)$, is increasing in military balance, M, and in A's effort, g_A, and is decreasing in B's effort, g_B. Obviously, the probability B wins is $p_B = 1 - p_A$. A general method of modeling this process is to treat p_A as the probability that a random variable ε, with distribution $\Phi(\varepsilon)$, is less than a function of the variables $h(g_A, g_B, M)$, a common example of which is the probit model, where $\Phi(\varepsilon)$ is the standard normal distribution, and $h(g_A, g_B, M) = M - (\frac{1}{2}) + g_A r - g_B r$.[17]

A and B's expected rewards from a negotiated settlement are χ and $1 - \chi$, respectively. We assume that all international outcomes are public goods that benefit all residents of a state equally. We let z represent the generic outcome. Everybody in nation A receives the policy payoff $V_A(z)$ associated with the outcome z, and all members of polity B receive the payoff $V_B(z)$.

In addition to these international payoffs, members of the winning coalition receive private goods. If the incumbent survives, each member of her coalition receives a $1/W$ share of any resources not used in the war effort. Thus if the crisis ends in a negotiation, or if the leader uses no extra resources in a war, each member of the coalition (including the leader) receives a payoff of R_i/W_i. If the leader allocates g_i resources to the war effort, each member of the coalition receives a private-goods payment of $(1 - g_i)R_i/W_i$.

Incumbents are deposed when they can no longer convince W members of the selectorate to support them. If the package of benefits an incumbent offers to her supporters is better than the rewards any challenger can credibly offer, the incumbent can find W members of the selectorate who will retain her in office. If, however, the incumbent fails to provide benefits to the winning coalition in excess of what a challenger can credibly promise to provide, the incumbent can no longer garner enough support to form a winning coalition. At this point, supporters defect and the incumbent is ousted.

Defection is risky. For simplicity's sake, we treat the probability of being a member of the successor winning coalition in nation A as (W_A/S_A). As discussed earlier at length, the selectorate theory requires that the probability of a current member of the winning coalition remaining in the coalition is higher than the probability of the individual being included in the challenger's coalition. The term W/S reflects this condition and provides mathematical convenience. Given that the challenger has R resources to distribute, the expected utility from private goods in a new coalition if one defects to a challenger is $(R_A/W_A)(W_A/S_A) = R_A/S_A$. We denote the competence, strength, or ability of the challenger in nation A as c_A and use comparable notation for B's challenger in his nation. Though the selectorate is uncertain of the ability of the challenger, its members learn something about the challenger's ability through the process of mounting a campaign. At the time the incumbent leader makes her choices about fighting or negotiating and about how to allocate resources, she is uncertain of the qualities of a prospective domestic rival. We represent the distribution of the possible challengers the incumbent may face by using the cumulative density function $F_A(x)$, where $F_A(x) = Pr(c_A \leq x)$. For technical convenience, we assume the distribution of challengers is exponential: $F_A(x) = 1 - \exp(-x/\sigma)$.

The challenger cannot make credible promises regarding how he will perform during a dispute or on other policy questions. Knowing this, the selectorate's members focus on the reservation value they expect if they choose a new leader. We assume that the reservation value for picking the challenger is $c_A + R_A/S_A$.

Incumbents can anticipate what they must give to supporters in order to defeat challengers. They simply must provide more utility for their coalition members than that offered by the challenger. Incumbents provide $(1 - g_A)R_A/W_A + \mu_A + V_A(z)$, where μ represents the performance of the leader on all policy dimensions other than the international dispute. This utility term is quite intuitive. $V_A(z)$ is the utility supporters derive from the outcome of the policy of the leader in the international dispute. $(1 - g_A)$ is the proportion of resources reserved for distribution as private goods to the winning coalition after spending g_A on the war effort. Of course, if there is no war, $g_A = 0$. The total pool of resources R_A is diminished by whatever portion has gone to the war effort, if any. What remains is distributed evenly to the members of the winning coalition, so that each member receives $(1 - g_A)R_A/W_A$.

The incumbent survives if she offers her supporters more than a challenger can credibly offer: $(1 - g_A)R_A/W_A + V_A(z) + \mu_A \geq c_A + R_A/S_A$. Hence the incumbent survives with probability $Pr((1 - g_A)R_A/W_A + V_A(z) + \mu_A$

$\geq c_A + R_A/S_A) = Pr((1 - g_A)R_A/W_A - R_A/S_A + V_A(z) + \mu_A \geq c_A) = F((1 - g_A)R_A/W_A - R_A/S_A + V_A(z) + \mu_A).$

Given international outcome z and effort level g_A, the incumbent in A receives a payoff of $U_A(z,g_A) = V_A(z) + \Psi F_A(V_A(z) + (1 - g_A)R_A/W_A + \mu - R_A/S_A) + (1 - g_A)R_A/W_A$, where Ψ is the leader's utility for remaining in office and $(1 - g_A)R_A/W_A$ refers to her private-goods reward as a member of the coalition. $F_A()$, recall, is the distribution of challenger types, and hence $F_A(V_A(z) + (1 - g_A)R_A/W_A + \mu - R_A/S_A)$ is the probability that A retains power given the international outcome z and effort g_A.

Subgame Perfect Equilibria

We now characterize the properties of subgame perfect equilibria to the game. Using the backward induction logic inherent in SPE, we start with the last decision and work backward through the tree.

Effort Level

Once engaged in conflict, leaders decide how hard to try. The effort level is increasing in the size of the winning coalition. We start with B's effort decision. B, having observed A's effort, g_A, decides what proportion of available resources to dedicate to the war effort.

PROPOSITION 1   B's optimal effort level, g_B^*, is weakly increasing in the size of B's winning coalition W_B.

Proof   Suppressing all subscripts, B's effort level, g, influences the probability that it wins the war, $p(g) = p_B(g_A,g_B)$. B's expected payoff from the war is $Y(g,W)$, given effort level g. Furthermore $Y(g,W) = p(g) - k + (1 - g)(R/W) + \Psi(p(g)F(v + (1 - g)(R/W)) + (1 - p(g))F(1 + (1 - g)(R/W)))$, where $v = 1 - k + \mu - (R/S)$, $1 = -k + \mu - (R/S)$, and $F(.)$ represents the distribution of challengers, which we assume is exponential $F(x) = 1 - \exp(-x/\sigma)$.

Let $g^* = g^*(W)$ be the effort level that maximizes B's expected payoff, given a winning coalition of size W: $g^*(W) = \mathrm{argmax}_{g \in [0,1]} Y(g,W)$. For what follows, we assume that this optimal effort is unique.[18]

There are two cases to consider: B's optimal effort lies on a boundary (i.e., $g^* = 0$ or $g^* = 1$) and B's optimal effort is interior ($g^* \in (0,1)$). In the former case, B strictly prefers to spend either nothing ($g^* = 0$) or all her available resources ($g^* = 1$) on the war effort. Straightforwardly, under these contingencies an infinitesimal change in W has no impact on B's optimal effort: $dg^*(W)/dW = 0$. Hence, we focus on the latter case, where B's optimal-effort decision is interior. Under this contingency, the first- and second-order conditions imply $\partial Y(g,W)/\partial g = 0$ and $\partial^2 Y(g,W)/\partial g^2 < 0$. The first-order condition implies that $H(W) = \partial Y(g,W)/\partial g = (p'(g)W - R + \Psi W p'(g)(F(x) - F(y)) - \Psi R(p(g)F'(x) + (1 - p(g))F'(y)))/W = 0$, where $x = v + (1 - g)(R/W)$, $y = l + (1 - g)(R/W)$, $p'(g) = dp(g)/dg$, and $F'(x) = dF(x)/dx$. Defining the numerator of $H(W)$ as $G(W)$, $\partial H/\partial W = (W(\partial G/\partial W) - G(\partial W/\partial W))/W^2$, which given the first-order condition $G(W) = 0$, reduces to $\partial H/\partial W = (\partial G/\partial W)/W$. By the implicit-differentiation rule, $dg^*(W)/dW = -(\partial H/\partial W)/(\partial H/\partial g)$. Since, by the second-order condition, $\partial H/\partial g < 0$, $\partial G/\partial W > 0$ implies $dg^*/dW > 0$.[19]

Evaluating $\partial G/\partial W$ yields $\partial G/\partial W = p'(g) + \Psi p'(g)(F(x) - F(y)) - (R/W)\Psi p'(g)(1 - g)(F'(x) - F'(y)) + ((R^2)/(W^2))\Psi(1 - g)(p(g)F''(x) + (1 - p(g))F''(y))$. Given that $F(x) = 1 - \exp(-x/\sigma)$, $F'(x) = (1/\sigma)\exp(-x/\sigma)$, and $F''(x) = -(1/\sigma^2)\exp(-x/\sigma)$, $\partial G/\partial W > 0$. Hence, $dg^*(W)/dW > 0$, so optimal effort levels increase as the winning coalition grows. QED.

A's Effort Decision

The analysis of A's effort decision is analogous to B's decision above. Hence we omit a proof.

PROPOSITION 2   A's effort level, g_A^*, is weakly increasing in the size of A's winning coalition, W_A.

In general, the interaction between the effort levels of A and B depends on the precise function mapping effort into probability of victory, $p(g_A, g_B)$. However, for the special case where $p(g_A, g_B)$ is the force ratio model, increased effort by one side elicits increased effort from the other.

The Decision to Fight or to Negotiate

If leader A initiates conflict, her payoff is $U_A(WAR|g_A^*, g_B^*) = p_A - k + (1 - g_A^*)R_A/W_A + \Psi(p_A F_A(v_A + (1 - g_A^*)R_A/W_A) + (1 - p_A)F_A(l_A + (1 - g_A^*)R_A/W_A))$, where p_A is the probability that A wins given effort levels g_A^* and g_B^*. If A chooses negotiation rather than conflict, her expected payoff is $U_A(\text{nego}) = \chi + \Psi F_A(n_A + R_A/W_A) + R_A/W_A$, where $n_A = \chi + \mu_A - R_A/S_A$.

A only initiates conflict when the benefit of doing so exceeds what she expects from a negotiated settlement: $U_A(WAR|g_A^*,g_B^*) \geq U_A(\text{nego})$.[20] The more likely A is to win, the more likely it is that this condition is met. We define P as the probability of victory that makes A indifferent between negotiations and war

$$P = \frac{\chi + k + g_A^* \dfrac{R_A}{W_A} + \Psi F_A\left(n_A + \dfrac{R_A}{W_A}\right) - \Psi F_A\left(l_A + (1 - g_A^*)\dfrac{R_A}{W_A}\right)}{\left(1 + \Psi\left(F_A\left(v_A + (1 - g_A^*)\dfrac{R_A}{W_A}\right) - F_A\left(l_A + (1 - g_A^*)\dfrac{R_A}{W_A}\right)\right)\right)}$$

A only initiates conflict if $p_A \geq P$. Although this expression is mathematically precise, it provides little substantive interpretation of the incentives that leaders face. Here we consider limiting cases. As the winning coalition expands, $W \to \infty$, each supporter's private-goods allocation becomes vanishingly small, $R/W \to 0$. Under this contingency, private goods have no value to leaders, either in terms of personal or reselection benefits. Hence leaders allocate all available resources to extra war effort, $g^* = 1$. Under this condition A only attacks if $p_A = \lim_{W \to \infty} P = (\chi + k + \Psi F(n) - \Psi F(l))/(1 + \Psi F(v) - \Psi F(l))$. Of course, if leaders care nothing about reselection ($\Psi = 0$), this again reduces to the unitary-actor solution. However, if, as we believe, the reselection motive is primary (large Ψ), then concavity in $F(.)$ is sufficient to ensure that $(\chi + k + \Psi F(n) - \Psi F(l))/(1 + \Psi F(v) - \Psi F(l)) > \chi + k$. Given our assumption that challenger types are exponentially distributed, this means that leaders in systems with large W must be more certain of winning before they would attack than is true for their autocratic counterparts.

In contrast as the winning coalition contracts, $W \to 0$, each supporter's private-goods allocation becomes massive, $R/W \to \infty$. Under this contingency, provided the leader retains resources, she faces no reselection threat. To maximize her payoff she retains all resources; thus A attacks only if $p_A = \lim_{W \to 0} P = \chi + k$.

Large-coalition leaders need to be more certain of victory than their small-coalition counterparts before choosing to fight. However, this does not necessarily make them more docile, as we now show. A only initiates conflict if the value of doing so exceeds the value of a negotiated settlement: $Z(W) = U_A(WAR|g_A^*(W),g_B^*(W)) - U_A(\text{nego}) = 0$. Writing the utility from war in terms of W only, $U_A(WAR|W) = p - k + (1 - g)(R/W) +$

$\Psi(pF(v + (1 - g)(R/W)) + (1 - p)F(1 + (1 - g)(R/W))$, where p is the probability that A wins given optimal effort levels g and $v = 1 - k + \mu - (R/S)$, and $1 = -k + \mu - (R/S)$. If A chooses negotiation rather than a conflict, her expected payoff is $U_A(\text{nego}) = \chi + \Psi F(n + (R/W)) + (R/W)$, where $n = \chi + \mu - (R/S)$.

Therefore, $Z(W) = p - k + (1 - g)(R/W) + \Psi(pF(v + (1 - g)(R/W)) + (1 - p)F(1 + (1 - g)(R/W))) - (\chi + \Psi F(n + (R/W)) + (R/W))$. This expression is the payoff difference between conflict and negotiations. Next, we examine how institutional features affect Z, by differentiating it with respect to W.

$$dZ/dW = (dp/dg)(dg/dW)(1 + \Psi(F(x) - F(y))) + Q + \Psi Q(pF'(x) + (1 - p) \\ F'(y)) + R/W^2 + (R/W^2)\Psi F'(n + R/W)$$

where $Q = -(dg/dW)(R/W) - (1 - g)(R/W^2)$, $x = v + (1 - g)(R/W)$, and $y = 1 + (1 - g)(R/W)$. Substituting the first-order condition from the effort decision

$$(1 + \Psi(F(x) - F(y))) = (R/W)[1 + pF'(x) + (1 - p)F'(y)]/(dp/dg)$$

this can alternatively be written as

$$dZ/dW = (R/W^2)[g - (1 - g)\Psi(pF'(v + (1 - g)(R/W)) + (1 - p)F'(1 + (1 - g) \\ (R/W))) + \Psi F'(n + (R/W))]$$

The sign of this expression determines whether an increase in the size of W makes A more-or-less aggressive. A positive sign means increases in W make A more likely to use force. Regrettably, this expression cannot be unambiguously signed, and whether an increase in W makes war more-or-less likely depends on the precise conditions. However, to get a handle on factors that influence the sign of this expression, suppose that bargaining strength approximately correlates with military strength (i.e., $n \approx p$). Under such circumstances concavity in $F(.)$ suggests $F'(n + (R/W)) < (pF'(x) + (1 - p)F'(y))$. Although dependent on precise conditions, this suggests that when effort levels are already high (g close to 1), an increase in W makes A more aggressive ($dZ/dW > 0$). Alternatively, when g is low, $dZ/dW < 0$.

There is no clear distinction between the use of force and coalition size. Similarly, as we will now show, the size of the negotiated settlement that is just sufficient to avoid a resort to arms is not a monotonic function of coalition size. Rather whether the size of a deal is sufficient to buy off an autocrat or a democrat depends on the particular conditions, not just on the size of the winning coalition. Suppose n_c is the value of negotiations that makes A indifferent between negotiation and conflict (i.e., if $\chi = n_c$ then $Z = 0$).

Dropping all inessential terms and subscripts, we let $N(n_c,W)$ define the identity of A being indifferent between conflict and negotiation: $N(n_c,W) = U_A(\text{attack}|W) - U_A(\text{nego}|n_c,W) = 0$. Since increasing n_c increases the value of negotiation relative to conflict, $\partial N/\partial n_c < 0$. Utilizing the implicit-differentiation rule, $dn_c/dW = -(\partial N/\partial W)/(\partial N/\partial n_c)$. Hence whether an increase in W results in a larger or small negotiated settlement being just sufficient to buy off A depends on the size of $\partial N/\partial W$, which is equivalent to dZ/dW.

Hence, in general we cannot unambiguously determine whether an increase in W increases or decreases the deal sufficiently to buy off A. Substantively this implies that increasing W may increase or decrease the prospects for a negotiated settlement depending on the precise conditions. Democrats need not be more dovish than autocrats.

7 Political Survival

As every sports fan knows, election to the Hall of Fame requires consistent, high-quality performance over many years. One good season is not enough. John F. Kennedy envisioned a different sort of leadership Hall of Fame. In *Profiles in Courage* (1956) he highlighted political leaders who sacrificed their own continuation in office in pursuit of a noble cause. These were individuals who, in our terms, produced public goods even when doing so meant losing their job. Few political leaders are profiles in courage.

If citizens were to choose leaders to belong to a Leadership Hall of Fame, they might emphasize individuals who consistently, over a long career in office, produced peace and prosperity for their country. Peace and prosperity, after all, are the cornerstones of a flourishing, successful government that does its utmost to promote the well-being of its citizens.

If a broad sample of national leaders were to select candidates for a Leadership Hall of Fame, their criteria might be different. They might forgo measures of peace and prosperity and just emphasize longevity in office. Long tenure is not necessarily the hallmark of a government that promotes social welfare, but it is the hallmark of a politically successful leader.

We construct two Halls of Fame—the citizens' pick and the leaders' pick—to illustrate several principles. Each membership list reflects the twenty-five leaders who, holding office beyond 1955, met the requisite performance criteria by the time they left office, or in the case of those still in power as of this writing (summer 2002), those who met the criteria by 1999, the last year for which we have data. The "citizens'-pick" list selects leaders who, over their tenure in office, produced a long-term growth rate that ranks at least in the top quartile for all heads of national governments during that period and whose nation experienced neither civil nor interstate war during their term in office. Additionally, to make the list, an incumbent's country had to have an average political-rights or civil liberties score of at least 4.5 or higher on the Freedom House seven-point scale during the leader's term in office. Finally, to be eligible for the list, a leader had to last at least three years in office and had to come from a country whose population was at least one million. The top twenty-five performers were those leaders who did best on all of these criteria over the past half century.

The second list, the "leaders'-pick" Hall of Fame, chooses individuals who were among the twenty-five longest-lasting leaders since 1955 in

Table 7.1
Citizens pick the Leadership Hall of Fame

Leader	Country	W	Tenure	Growth	CL	PR
Sato	Japan	1.00	7.7	9.8	7.0	6.0
Meir	Israel	0.75	5.2	9.3	5.0	6.0
Bin Onn	Malaysia	0.75	5.5	8.3	4.2	5.0
Castro	Honduras	0.00	3.3	8.3	5.0	2.0
Balaguer	Domnican Republic	0.52	12.0	8.1	5.9	4.6
Tae Woo	South Korea	0.75	5.0	7.9	5.2	6.0
Masire	Botswana	0.75	17.7	7.8	5.4	6.2
Razak	Malaysia	0.75	5.3	7.6	4.6	5.4
Azocar	Chile	0.75	4.0	7.3	6.0	6.0
Ferrer	Costa Rica	1.00	4.0	7.1	7.0	7.0
Shearer	Jamaica	1.00	4.9	7.0	6.0	7.0
Ibarra	Ecuador	0.60	3.5	6.9	5.0	1.0
Prem	Thailand	0.75	8.4	6.8	4.3	5.0
Borrero	Colombia	0.75	4.0	6.6	6.0	6.0
Osorio	Guatemala	0.70	4.0	6.4	5.3	5.3
Rabin	Israel	0.75	3.3	6.3	5.3	6.8
Portillo	Mexico	0.50	6.0	6.3	4.1	4.6
Echeverria	Mexico	0.50	6.0	6.0	4.8	3.8
Galimay	Panama	0.75	4.7	5.9	4.8	4.0
Gandhi, R.	India	0.75	5.1	5.8	5.0	6.0
Garcia	Guatemala	0.50	4.0	5.7	4.6	4.2
Quiros	Costa Rica	1.00	4.0	5.7	7.0	7.0
Jungnauth	Mauritius	1.00	13.5	5.7	6.0	6.3
Gandhi, I.	India	0.75	4.8	5.6	5.0	6.0
Rao	India	0.75	4.9	5.5	4.0	4.7

countries with a population of at least one million without regard for whether they performed well in producing peace, prosperity, and civil and political freedom for the average citizen. Not even one member of the citizens' list appears on the leaders' list. Just how different the lists produced by these two sets of criteria are is evident from a comparison of tables 7.1 and 7.2.[1]

We could have been more cynical and chosen members of the leaders list not only for their longevity in office, but for their success in creating opportunities to steal from the state. This list would be the "Haul of

Table 7.2
Leaders pick the Leadership Hall of Fame

Leader	Country	W	Tenure	Growth	CL	PR
Mwambutsa	Burundi	0.47	50.6	2.4	NA	NA
Ibn Talal	Jordan	0.25	46.5	6.2	2.9	2.9
Kim Il-Sung	North Korea	0.50	45.8	NA	1.0	1.0
Castro	Cuba	NA	43.0	NA	NA	NA
Hoxha	Albania	0.48	40.4	2.1	1.0	1.0
Reza	Iran	0.22	37.3	0.5	2.3	2.5
Franco	Spain	0.20	36.2	6.7	2.5	3.0
Salazar	Portugal	0.41	36.2	6.6	NA	NA
Tito	Yugoslavia	0.48	35.2	NA	2.4	2.0
Eyadema	Togo	NA	34.7	NA	NA	NA
Stroessner	Paraguay	0.50	34.6	5.4	2.8	3.1
Houphouet-Boigny	Ivory Coast	0.50	33.3	4.6	3.0	2.1
Selassie	Ethiopia	0.42	32.6	NA	2.3	2.7
Qaddafi	Libya	NA	32.3	NA	NA	NA
Tsendenbal	Mongolia	0.50	32.2	6.7	1.0	1.0
Suharto	Indonesia	0.27	32.2	6.5	2.8	2.5
Hassan II	Morocco	0.27	31.8	4.5	3.4	3.7
Mobutu	Zaire	0.41	31.5	−0.2	1.8	1.4
Bin Said	Oman	NA	31.4	NA	NA	NA
Kadar	Hungary	0.51	31.0	4.6	2.8	2.2
Bourguiba	Tunisia	0.52	30.3	5.7	2.9	2.4
An-Nahayan	UAR	NA	30.1	NA	NA	NA
Birendra	Nepal	NA	29.3	NA	NA	NA
Assad	Syria	NA	29.3	NA	NA	NA
Sihanouk	Cambodia	0.47	28.9	NA	NA	NA

Fame." Many on the leaders' list would remain in the Haul of Fame, but we prefer to believe that government officials are not so venal that they seek office just to aggrandize themselves and their cronies. Thus, the leaders' list simply reflects our basic assumption that incumbents want to keep their jobs.

The two Halls of Fame are strikingly different not only in their composition, but also in the characteristics of their members. The average long-term growth rate achieved by the citizens' list is 7.0 percent per annum; for the leaders' list the average growth rate is 4.4 percent among the bare majority of the latter list who report growth data (fourteen out of twenty-five as compared to all twenty-five for the citizens'-pick hall of fame). The tenure profiles of the leaders on the two lists are also dramatically different even though longevity in office was a selection criterion for both lists. Those in the citizens' Leadership Hall of Fame lasted, on average, about 6.0 years, while those on the leaders' list survived on average 35.1 years in office. It is improbable that this is a chance occurrence ($p = 0.000$). Also noteworthy is the difference in democraticness and the size of the coalition on which the leaders depended. The citizens' list, though not chosen by institutional criteria, favors more democratic, larger-coalition systems. The leaders on the citizens' list have an average democracy score of 0.75 and an average coalition score of 0.72. The leaders' list, though also not selected on institutional criteria, has an average democracy score of 0.12 and a coalition average of 0.41.

The differences between the two Leadership Halls of Fame encourage the belief that those who produce good performance also produce relatively short-lived terms of office. Those who enjoy persistence in power perform at a lower level. Those who do a good job tend to depend on large coalitions, while those who perform less well, in terms of public welfare, depend on smaller coalitions. The remainder of this chapter is devoted to a close and careful exploration of the theoretical and empirical relationship between institutions for selecting leaders, policy performance, and the effect these factors have on the risks leaders face of being deposed.

In this chapter we examine the survival of leaders. We reexamine the theory developed in chapters 2 and 3 and derive predictions as to how institutions and policy performance influence persistence in office. After developing modifications to our basic model designed to account for leadership deposition, we examine the empirical evidence regarding predictions we derive and then discuss the effects of mortality and term limits in the context of the selectorate logic.

Survival as Explained by the Selectorate Theory

In the model in chapter 3 all leaders survive. Consequently, that model cannot predict how leader tenure varies with the sizes of the winning coalition and selectorate. We present four extensions of that model to provide different reasons why challengers can and do replace incumbent leaders. We discuss each of these reasons informally, rather than through formal models, because each adds substantial complexity to the model. All of these extensions are straightforward.

The world of the model presented in chapter 3 is very certain and regular, allowing leaders to calculate exactly what policies will keep them in office. The real political world is not so certain and regular. The real world is buffeted with changes of economic fortune; when the followers of a leader judge her on economic performance, such changes can bring her down. Additionally, there is no effective variation between leaders and challengers in the basic model; real-world leaders vary substantially in their ability to manage the organs of their government to produce benefits for their followers. In the basic model, affinities between the leader and her followers are known perfectly, yet the affinities between followers and the challenger are a complete mystery. In reality, leaders, challengers, and members of the selectorate have some sense of their affinities for each other, but experience helps to clarify those beliefs. Changes in economic fortunes, particularly competent challengers, and more equal information in the hands of challengers and incumbents about affinities all create chances for leaders to be removed from office and so can explain leader tenure. All of these approaches lead to similar conclusions about patterns of leader tenure across selection institutions. The common conclusions give us confidence that our underlying argument about how selection institutions drive the provision of public and private goods also reflects the dynamics of leader tenure in office.

The first argument focuses on how the vagaries of the economy cause variations in the amount of resources available to the leader. These variations in available resources change the level of goods that the leader can produce. Changes in the level of goods would not matter if the leader's followers could determine the precise economic conditions and hence the available resources. If they cannot observe the available resources, the leader has an incentive to divert resources to her own use and claim that the economy prevents her from producing the level of goods normally expected. This argument then shows how economic downturns lead to leader removals and why some leaders in some systems seem immune to this threat. Incidentally, it also helps explain why some governments simply do not report data on how the state is doing.

The second argument begins with the assumption that politicians, leaders, and challengers differ in their competence. More competent leaders are able to produce higher levels of goods from a given level of resources. Contests for leadership then focus on competence, because more competent leaders will produce more goods in the future for members of their winning coalition. Of course, the importance of competence varies with selection institutions because of the nature of the goods the leader provides.

The third and fourth arguments loosen our restrictive assumptions about affinities between leaders and followers. Our original model favors the incumbent by assuming that affinities between her and the selectors are common knowledge and that affinities between the challenger and the selectors are completely unknown. These assumptions create a situation in which the members of the leader's winning coalition are certain that they will always receive private goods in the future if they remain loyal and in which they have no idea whether the challenger will include them in his winning coalition if he is chosen as leader. The risk of exclusion in the original model is, then, $1 - W/S$, because every selector has an equal chance of being in the challenger's winning coalition in the future.

We loosen these assumptions in two ways. The third argument assumes that affinities are never fully known but are revealed through interaction over time. Because selectors have more experience with the incumbent than with the challenger, they can more accurately predict whether they will be included in the winning coalition in the future if the leader is retained. The risk of exclusion from private goods continues to operate for members of the current winning coalition.

Our fourth argument assumes that all affinities are known to all, thereby relaxing the incumbency advantage assumed in the basic model of chapter 3. Selectors then know whether the challenger will include them in his winning coalition should he come to power. Members of the winning coalition are willing to defect to the challenger when they have stronger affinity with him than with the current leader. The leader counters the possibility of such defections by oversizing her coalition so that she can suffer some defections from her winning coalition and still have a sufficient number of loyal members to retain power. The defectors can then be excluded from the leader's winning coalition as a punishment for their defection. Thus the risk for defectors from the winning coalition changes from the risk of exclusion in the challenger's winning coalition to the risk of exclusion from the leader's winning coalition if the challenger fails to come to power.

All four of these arguments rely on some basic principles of the logic of the model. We briefly review these principles to highlight their key role in shedding light on how selection institutions affect leader tenure.

To survive in office, leaders need to offer a level of benefits to their supporters at least as large as the greatest possible offer that can credibly be made by a potential challenger. The institutions under which they operate influence how much leaders need to spend to offer the requisite benefits. When the winning coalition is large, and so as a consequence leaders rely on public goods to reward supporters, the incumbent has little advantage over the challenger. In this case the incumbent must spend practically all available resources if she wishes to keep her supporters loyal. There is little slack in the system for the incumbent. Thus, although in the original model leaders always have enough resources to survive, we can see that for a leader in a system with a large winning coalition, even a small exogenous shock can be enough to leave her without sufficient resources to match the challenger's best offer. As a consequence, leaders in systems with large winning coalitions find it hard to retain office.

When the winning coalition is small, private goods predominate in the package of rewards leaders offer. As described in chapter 3, incumbents are advantaged in their ability to provide future private goods. Hence when political competition is primarily based on such rewards, incumbents find it easy to match the best possible offer that challengers can make. This leaves lots of slack in the system and allows such leaders to redirect resources toward discretionary projects. These excess resources can also be redirected to providing additional benefits to compensate for any deficiency in rewards caused by an economic or other shock. This ability to reserve resources for a rainy day is particularly strong when the selectorate is large. Leaders in small winning-coalition systems find it easier to survive shocks or the introduction of incomplete information.

Although all leaders survive in the model presented in chapter 3, with the addition of incomplete information or exogenous shocks to the system, survival becomes uncertain. Yet the greater the difference between a leader's available resources, R, and the amount the leader actually needs to spend, M, the more slack there is in the system and the easier it is for leaders to compensate supporters in response to an exogenous shock or in the face of an unusually attractive challenger. The gap between available and required resources $(R - M)$ provides a metric to measure the ease with which leaders survive. The smaller W is, the greater the difference between R and M and, therefore, the easier it is for small-coalition leaders to survive. Large selectorates also make it easier for leaders to survive since large S increases the risk of exclusion from future coalitions, thereby enhancing the loyalty norm. The influence of S is most important when W is small.

We now turn to an elaboration of each of the four arguments set out above, because each can help explain leader tenure. We do not give any one argument priority over the others because we believe all of them capture some elements in political competition that lead to the removal of leaders. Slack resources and the loyalty norm play a central role in the implications that follow from each of the four arguments.

Leader Competence

Leaders vary in their competence. While there are many dimensions of political competence, we focus on the leader's ability to induce the government to run efficiently. More competent political leaders, in our view, are able to produce more goods, both public and private, from the same pool of resources. Competence then helps a leader retain office, and a challenger gains office because each is capable of doing more for the selectorate (or their coalition of supporters) than are less competent others. For convenience, we will think of leader competence as a factor that divides the prices the leader pays to produce public and private goods.[2] The higher this factor, the more competent the leader. A leader of average competence has a factor of 1, incompetent leaders have factors less than 1, and highly competent leaders have factors above 1. In essence, the competence of a leader increases the resources available to her; if a leader's competence is K and the pool of resources available is R, she has KR resources to allocate.[3]

Competence influences the value of the challenger's offer of goods to the selectorate. More competent challengers offer more public and private goods because their prices for both are lower. Recall that challengers commit all available resources to public and private goods in order to produce the most attractive offer they can to the selectorate. The exact mix of goods the challenger offers depends on the values the selectorate attaches to public versus private goods at the level of the offer. In equilibrium, the challenger's offer equates marginal utility divided by price for both goods. Because competence divides the price of both goods by the same factor, any shift in the ratio of public and private goods offered depends solely on which good the selectors value more highly at the margin. A more competent challenger offers both more public goods and more private goods than a lesser challenger does.

The competence of the challenger affects how many resources the leader commits to public and private goods. Against a highly competent challenger, the leader may not be able to produce enough to retain power, even given the advantages of the loyalty norm. In order for the challenger to make a more attractive offer to the current winning coalition than can the incumbent, there must be either a vast difference in competence or the winning coalition must be large enough to force the leader to produce predominantly public goods. This follows because coalition members discount the value of any future benefits from private goods by their risk of exclusion if the challenger wins. In most cases, the incumbent could produce enough to hold the loyalty of her winning coalition *if* she knew the challenger's competence. The incumbent would offer enough so that every member of her winning coalition remained loyal. The amount the leader needs to offer to beat a challenger of a given competence K increases with K because more competent challengers can offer more to members of the winning coalition. The winning amount also rises with the size of the winning coalition, W, because increases in W drive leaders to produce more public goods and reduce the amount of the private goods that each individual member of the winning coalition receives. The reduction in private goods also reduces the consequences of the risk of exclusion for members of the winning coalition. The winning amount declines with increases in the size of the selectorate because the risk of exclusion rises. As before, the size of the selectorate has its greatest effect when the winning coalition is small, so that the incumbent relies on private goods to retain her position. We expect, therefore, that introducing a known level of competence for the challenger creates a chance that a highly competent challenger will replace the leader, and that this possibility is more likely in systems with large winning coalitions.

The picture changes dramatically if the leader does not know the challenger's competence when she sets policy. This uncertainty creates a risk-return trade-off for the leader. The more resources she commits to public and private goods, the less the chance that her challenger will be competent enough to offer the winning coalition more than she offers. However, those additional resources come at the expense of the resources she could otherwise retain for her own use. Reducing her allocation of goods raises her own pool of resources but also increases her risk of removal. Exactly where the leader strikes this balance depends on her own competence and on the selection institutions. The more competent the leader, the more public and private goods she produces, and so the risk of removal decreases. Part of the reason for this shift is that more competent leaders use fewer resources to produce a given level of goods. Consequently, they retain more resources and their expectation from holding office is greater than that of less competent leaders. The greater value of holding office leads them to insure their position by producing more goods, reducing their risk of removal. Length of leader tenure should—unsurprisingly—increase with competence.

The larger the winning coalition, the more risk of deposition the leader can accept. As the winning coalition increases, the leader commits more resources to satisfying the winning coalition, thereby reducing her own pool of resources and the value of holding office. A leader compensates by reducing her commitment to goods, raising both her risk of removal and her payoff in this round. Increasing the size of the selectorate induces the leader to reduce her risk of removal by committing more resources to goods for her winning coalition *when* the winning coalition is small.

What pattern of leader tenure does this argument imply? Over time, all systems select leaders on the basis of competence; less competent leaders are more likely to be removed than highly competent leaders. This selection pressure is higher in systems with large winning coalitions. Democratic elections are contests of competence, as judged by the voters both retrospectively and prospectively. The risk of removal is greater in systems with large winning coalitions than in those with smaller coalitions. Systems with small winning coalitions allow relatively incompetent leaders to retain power by providing their winning coalition with private goods, and this effect should be more pronounced as the size of the selectorate grows (holding the size of the winning coalition fixed). Still, highly competent leaders should be extremely difficult to remove in systems with small winning coalitions. They can easily ward off challengers, allowing them to retain a greater proportion of resources for their own use. Consequently, they work hard to retain office because it is so valuable to them.

Economic Shocks

The basic model assumes that the resources of the state are unaffected by external circumstances. In reality, the resources the state extracts from the population depend on the condition of its economy, and the condition of the economy is partially dependent on external factors. State revenues go up and down as the economy fluctuates. Industrial economies have business cycles; economies dependent on exports of primary products suffer from shifts in the world price of the goods they export. These changes in economic fortunes can be thought of as "shocks," random occurrences outside the control of the leader. The idea of economic shocks is common in much of macroeconomics. These shocks are generally modeled as a random walk around the underlying economic trend, which, as we saw in chapter 4, the leader does influence. Fluctuations in resources should be reflected in the level of public and private goods that the leader can provide to her winning coalition. Fewer resources available in a period should mean a lower level of public and private goods.

At first blush, economic shocks should not matter. The challenger's offer cannot exceed what can be produced with the currently available resources. The same strategic dynamics of the risk of exclusion and the loyalty norm should operate no matter what level of resources are available in the current round. *If* the members of the winning coalition know what resources are available in this round, economic shocks should have no effect on the logic of leader survival. Because the leader's abilities are irrelevant to the occurrence of exogenous economic shocks, followers should not draw inferences about future benefits from the occurrence of a temporary economic downturn.[4]

The argument above, like the model in chapter 3, assumes that members of the selectorate have a great deal of information about economic conditions. Two limitations on their information could explain how economic shocks influence the removal of leaders. First, members of the selectorate may not know precisely what current economic conditions are. Instead, they can only observe the public and private goods the leader produces and compare them to their limited knowledge of the current state of the economy. Second, selectors may not know the leader's competence and so are forced to use current economic conditions to infer the leader's ability to produce the goods they want. This argument also requires that selectors not know the precise current state of the economy; otherwise they could sort out the effects of economic shocks to determine the leader's competence.

These uncertainties present a problem in judging the leader's performance because the leader also has an incentive to reduce the level of public and private goods provided in order to divert resources to her own purposes. When individual members of the winning coalition do not know the state of the economy, the leader could attempt to reduce the goods she provides for them and blame the shortfall on a bad economic shock. Alternatively, an incompetent leader could blame her inability to produce the expected level of goods on a temporary economic downturn outside of her control. When the selectors do not know the state of the economy, they cannot tell whether such excuses for poor leader performance are valid. Consequently, they cannot believe such accounts from the leader. Otherwise the leader will take advantage of them, either to divert resources to herself or to enable her to hold office even when she could be defeated by a more competent challenger.

Members of the winning coalition can protect themselves from such exploitation by adopting a simple strategy of removing the leader whenever her performance falls below a fixed level (Ferejohn 1987). This threat induces the leader to produce the necessary level of goods whenever she can—that is, when economic conditions are good enough to allow her to do so, subject to her competence. What level of goods should the winning coalition demand to retain the leader? A higher demand will force the leader to produce more when she can. However, there are limits to how high the level should be pushed. It should not exceed the value of the challenger's best offer, assuming a normal economy (the shock equals 0) and a challenger of average competence (if uncertainty about competence exists). Otherwise, the winning coalition sometimes will remove the leader when she can outperform what they expect from the challenger.

The greater the slack resources that the leader would retain for her own uses under average conditions, the better her chances of being able to meet the demands of the winning coalition, and so retain office. First, she can allocate some of the slack to compensate for a bad economic shock. Second, she can stockpile slack resources over time to provide an emergency fund for bad economic times.[5] As before, slack resources $(R - M)$ that the leader can use for her own purposes decrease as the size of the winning coalition increases and increase as the size of the selectorate increases. If leader competence is included, more competent leaders are more likely to survive an economic downturn. Modern, mass democracies then are most likely to replace their leaders because of a decline in the economy. These leaders have the fewest slack resources. Unlike the earlier argument about leader competence, it does not take a more competent challenger to remove the incumbent. Even highly competent leaders face the prospect of economic times so bad that they cannot please their winning coalition.

In the long run, leaders answering to a small winning coalition should become more entrenched in office as their tenure extends. Not only is there a smaller chance of a shock big enough to remove them than in large winning-coalition systems, but also they can draw on their reserves to fend off a challenge when the economy is weak. Leaders who answer to a large winning coalition can attempt to stockpile resources when the economy is strong. However, they do not have as much slack to stockpile as authoritarian leaders do and are more likely to be called to use their stockpile to hold office in response to small downturns in the economy.

Partial Knowledge of Affinities

The basic model assumes that all affinities between leaders and selectors were fully revealed as soon as the leader came to office. In reality, learning about these idiosyncratic factors is gradual. Selectors and leaders continue to learn about each other over time. The least is known about challengers because the affinities between them and prospective followers have not been put to the test. One's closest supporters in the climb to power may seek power for themselves once they are close to the leader. Should the challenger come to power, the affinities between leaders and their followers will be tested by the competition to hold power. The learning curve between leaders and their supporters should be steepest at the beginning of the leader's term. Yet affinities will not be completely revealed on assuming office, so leaders and selectors continue to learn about each other as long as the incumbent is in office, although presumably at a decreasing rate.

Once affinities are completely revealed, incumbents can fully and credibly commit to maintaining members of their current coalition in all future coalitions. This creates the loyalty norm. The incumbent can promise future private goods to her coalition with certainty, while the challenger can promise them only probabilistically since, on learning about affinities, he will realign his coalition. This ensures that the loyalty norm favors the incumbent. The strength of the loyalty norm depends on the relative value of inclusion versus exclusion from the coalition, and on the probability of inclusion versus exclusion. When W is small, the majority of rewards are in the form of private goods, so the cost of exclusion is high. When the ratio W/S is small, the risk of exclusion is high. Therefore, the loyalty norm, as well as the resulting incumbency advantage, are strongest in small-W, large-S systems.

The loyalty norm only functions when learning has taken place. Prior to learning that their place in future coalitions is secure, members of a leader's current coalition are reluctant to commit to her. This implies that in small-W, large-S systems, once affinities are known leaders find it easy to survive in office. In the language of survival analysis, their hazard rate drops as they learn about affinities. Since learning occurs over time, leaders find it easier and easier to survive politically as their tenure in office progresses. The longer they have been in office, the more growth they experience in the loyalty norm that is induced by their ability to credibly promise future private goods or to exclude supporters from them. Consequently, we should expect the risk of political deposition to drop over time for leaders who depend on a small coalition for their survival.

In contrast, in large-coalition systems the majority of rewards are provided via public goods. As a result, the cost of exclusion from future coalitions is low, and the risk of exclusion is also low since W/S is large. The loyalty norm is weak in such large-coalition systems. Moreover, the incumbent is little advantaged relative to her challengers since political competition is based on the quality of public policy. While in such systems, the risk of political deposition also falls over time as affinities are learned, the reduction in risk is small. Leaders who depend on a large coalition almost always find it difficult to survive in office.

The pattern of survival is radically different during the early period in office, which we termed the transition period in chapters 2 and 3. Unfortunately for a new incumbent early in her term—when there is still considerable uncertainty about affinity—the new leader has little incumbency advantage in the supply of private goods. This lack of advantage is especially telling for small-coalition leaders, because they are most dependent on private-goods allocations to keep them in office. Members of the current coalition who suspect they will not be included in the incumbent's long-run coalition want to depose the new leader before she can learn affinities and realign her coalition, dropping those in the transition coalition who are believed to be least loyal. For leaders in small-W systems, the early years in office are especially treacherous. Should they survive the early years, however, their risk of political deposition becomes remote.

Defection and Oversized Coalitions

In the basic model, the leader can always hold the loyalty of her winning coalition, in part because coalition members have no expectation beyond random chance about whether they will receive private goods if the challenger comes to power. In the real world, selectors have some knowledge of their affinity for the challenger and so the challenger can attempt to recruit members of the current winning coalition who are close to her. As a contrast to the model where selectors know nothing about their affinity with the challenger, we discuss a model where they know their affinity for the challenger when they must select between the leader and the challenger.

Selectors prefer a leader with whom they have a closer affinity. Consequently, members of the winning coalition will defect to the challenger if they have a higher affinity for the challenger than for the current leader. These opportunistic defections create a risk for the leader that she will lose enough members of her winning coalition to force her from office. This risk increases with the size of the winning coalition as a proportion of the selectorate. When the winning coalition is a small proportion of the selectorate, the leader chooses a winning coalition with whom she has a strong affinity. It is unlikely that the members of this small coalition will have higher affinity for the challenger than for the leader, and so they are likely to remain loyal to the leader. As the size of the winning coalition grows relative to the selectorate, the leader must include selectors with whom she has lower affinities. These members of her winning coalition are more likely to defect simply because the chance that they have a higher affinity for the challenger is substantial. So the probability of defections from the winning coalition grows with the size of the winning coalition relative to the selectorate.

The leader can compensate for these possible defections by oversizing her coalition. Because she needs at least W members to hold power, adding extra members to her winning coalition increases the chance that she will still hold the loyalty of W members after defections. The value of oversizing the winning coalition decreases as W increases relative to S. When W/S is small, the members of the winning coalition have high affinity with the leader and so are unlikely to defect. The leader then needs to add only a few extra members to her winning coalition to significantly increase her chances of continuing to hold power. When W/S is large, the chance of some defections is large, forcing the leader to oversize her coalition substantially to provide insurance against deposition. Oversizing the coalition means both bringing in members of dubious loyalty to the leader and spreading private goods across more members of the expanded winning coalition. Because the private goods committed to the oversized coalition come out of the resources the leader retains for her own use, she always faces a decision about whether she should add another member to her coalition, costing her resources, or live with a smaller winning coalition, raising her risk of removal.

As both W and S get larger—that is, as the selectorate expands while the selection ratio remains constant—the leader provides more public goods relative to private goods. Slack resources also decrease, since she must commit more resources to public and private goods in her efforts to retain office. This shift by itself increases the risk of removal because it reduces the difference between the offers of the challenger and leader, increasing the chance of defection. It also decreases the value of holding office because the resources the leader can use for her own purposes decrease. These two shifts oppose each other in their effect on the leader's interest in oversizing her coalition. The former pushes her toward adding more extra members in order to reduce the risk of removal, while the latter inclines her to cut back on extra members in order to retain more resources for her own use. If we separate the effects of the size of the winning coalition or selectorate while holding the other institution's size constant, we see that increases in the size of the winning coalition raise the chance that the leader will be removed, and increases in the selectorate size decrease the chance that the leader will be removed. This argument, like the three previous arguments, implies that autocratic leaders face the smallest risk of removal and democratic leaders the greatest risk.

All four arguments predict that the risk of removal decreases as the size of the winning coalition shrinks; leaders of large winning-coalition systems face the highest risk of losing office. All four arguments also predict that the risk of removal decreases as the selectorate increases. The slack resources available to the leader $(R - M)$ provide a gauge of the leader's ability to weather a challenge to her, and such resources are largest for small winning-coalition, large-selectorate systems, commonly referred to as *autocracies*. Finally, the model predicts how the risk of removal of authoritarian leaders changes with their tenure in office. The first three arguments predict authoritarian leaders become more entrenched in office over time. Such leaders are likely to be competent at producing goods for their supporters, have accumulated a stockpile of resources that allows them to weather an economic shock, and have loyal supporters because affinities are well known. The final argument predicts no variation in removal rate with tenure. Because all four arguments make almost identical predictions about how leader survival varies with selection institutions, we have confidence that these conclusions are robust with respect to the exact mechanism that leads to leader removal. We are agnostic about which of these four arguments is the "right argument." Instead, we believe that all four of them capture an aspect of the processes that cause followers to defect from their current leader to the challenger.

While we systematically test these predictions later, we first illustrate the pattern of survival for leaders in small-W systems by examining the Mamluks who ruled Egypt between 1250 and 1517.

Mamluk Egypt

The Mamluks, often referred to as slave soldiers, constituted a truly fascinating polity made up entirely of former slaves. They disenfranchised their own offspring, perpetuating their ranks by importing new slaves. The Mamluks attained power in 1250 in Egypt by deposing the Ayyubid dynasty of the caliphate. They did so by exploiting the opportunity created by a succession crisis within the then-ruling dynasty and by capitalizing on their victory over French King Louis IX's crusader armies at the battle of Mansura. Once in power, the Mamluks, who numbered only about 10,000, ruled through harsh means over the native Egyptian population until their defeat by the Ottoman Emperor Selim I in 1517.

The Mamluks were not native to Africa, or even Muslim by birth. They were slave boys typically brought from the Kipchuk steppe, and later from the Caucasus. They entered one of twelve special schools where, in addition to acquiring military skills, they learned to read and write and were taught the Muslim religion. When these students graduated they were freed and entered the army (becoming Mamluks), but they kept a bond with their former owner, who would typically be a senior emir (Mamluk army officer). Fidelity between the emir and his former slaves was extremely strong. The Mamluks disassociated themselves from the native Egyptians, whom they ruled ruthlessly. They spoke Turkish rather than Arabic, dressed distinctly, typically married either slave girls from their own region or the daughters of other Mamluks, and lived apart from the population in a citadel in Cairo, the Qal'at al-Jabal. Perhaps most interestingly, the descendants of these former slaves typically were disenfranchised because they were born to freed men and not as slaves.

The approximately 10,000 Mamluks alone were responsible for choosing the ruling sultan. There were no established or accepted rules of selection. Candidates for sultan needed the support of the emirs, each of whom had the personal loyalty of his former slaves. These ordinary soldiers worked to further the career of their benefactor, who, should he be made sultan, would place them in positions of power. The bond of fealty between an emir and his former slaves meant effectively that a system of bloc voting existed. Although voting per se did not actually occur, each emir controlled numerous soldiers so that, although there were 10,000 Mamluks, there were effectively only several hundred selectors.[6] A successful sultan needed to form a coalition of supporters from these emirs.

This truly was an exceptionally small-S and small-W system. As predicted, the Mamluks ruthlessly extracted resources from the native population, providing no public goods in return except for defense. We might question even the value of this defense since many Egyptians initially welcomed Ottoman rule when it removed the Mamluks. The average Mamluk soldier received wages for service. In addition, a senior officer would receive Iqta, or fief, a form of temporary land grant that entitled him to extract taxes. As an approximate gauge, Finer (1999) reports an estimate that in 1316 a private in the army received an annual salary of 24–52 dinars. In contrast, an emir of a Hundred received 109,000–126,000 dinars.[7] Kleptocracy also flourished. The Sultan was entitled to five-twelfths of the income of Egypt. The Mamluks seem to fit our predictions for a small-coalition system. We now turn to the question of survival under Mamluk rule.

Competition to be sultan was intense and few individuals managed to remain sultan for long.[8] The modal category was less than a year and the normal pattern of successors was continual turnover of the sultan, punctuated with the occasional long reign. Indeed, of the twenty-four sultans who comprised the Bahri dynasty, only three survived more than five years (seventeen, fourteen, and forty-one years), according to Finer (1999, 735). Eleven sultans were removed after a year or less, and nineteen of the twenty-four sultans were deposed by the end of three years. It appears that once a sultan survived beyond five years his reign would be long, but few ever achieved such tenure. The problem, as described by Ayalon (1977, 206–220), was that the incoming sultan would inherit a coalition of officeholders and generals from his predecessor. Unfortunately, while the new sultan needed these immediate supporters to maintain the continuance of government, he often had little connection with them and wanted to replace them with those who, in terms of our model, had a greater affinity for him. Maintaining the support of the officers that the sultan intended to replace was a difficult balancing act, because they surely were aware of the risks they faced and the benefits that could be gained by overturning him. If the sultan succeeded in surviving early threats, his tenure was assured.

This pattern of rapid turnover of leaders punctuated by an occasional long reign is a pattern common in many other small-coalition systems, such as Syria and most of the other republican states in the Middle East, at least from the 1950s through the 1970s (Van Dam 1996). Mexico prior to Porfiro Diaz's dictatorship, which started in 1876, also experienced the rapid turnover of leaders typified by the experience in Mamluk Egypt (Donghi 1993).

Summary of Survival Predictions

The selectorate theory predicts leaders in small-coalition systems have a greater incumbency advantage than their large-coalition counterparts if they survive past the initial, transition period. As such, leaders dependent on small coalitions survive in office longer than leaders who depend on large coalitions. The ability of small-coalition leaders to survive in office is further enhanced by a large selectorate. For leaders in large-coalition systems, political survival depends on the provision of public goods. Since a leader's incumbency advantage is derived from the ability to credibly promise future private goods, a large-coalition leader is readily deposed by a challenger offering better public policies. It is always hard for large-coalition leaders to survive, and their survival depends on the provision of effective public policy. For leaders in small-coalition systems, survival depends on their ability to credibly promise access to future private goods. This ability grows as a leader's tenure increases. Therefore, while it is initially difficult for small-coalition leaders to survive, it becomes easier the longer they remain in office. We turn now to a systematic assessment of these predictions.

Empirical Assessment of Political Survival

To evaluate leadership survival we must use data organized according to leadership rather than by country-year as in our previous analyses. The data on leadership survival has three main components: the identity of the leaders, their time of entry into office, and their time of departure.

Leaders' Data

Leaders were identified principally through the combined use of two previous enumerations by Bienen and van de Walle (1991) and Spuler, Allen, and Saunders (1977), but we also drew on other biographic sources, historical chronologies (Langer 1980; Dupuy and Dupuy 1986), a number of national histories, and—for the most recent cases—Zarate's Political Collection (<http://www.terra.es/personal2/monolith/>). We have used these main compilations previously, and we have found that when used with each other they give an excellent survey of who was in power for how long. The Bienen and van de Walle data do not include the exact dates of entry and departure from office, but that is a particular strength of the Spuler, Allen, and Saunders data from which we gathered that particular information. Additionally, we expanded the data set to include a large number of leaders who were not reported in the original Bienen and van de Walle data. For example, their data on European states do not begin until the early twentieth century and presidents of the United States begin with William McKinley in 1897. Once leaders were located, it was usually straightforward to ascertain the dates they entered and left office. However, in a small number of cases—mainly from Latin America in the nineteenth century—it was not possible with our resources to determine the exact day on which a leader entered office. In these cases we used the first day of the month. In an even smaller number of cases, it was not possible to determine either the day or the month a leader entered office, and so we chose July 1 as the entry day. It was, on the other hand, almost always possible to determine the day leaders left power. However, in an extremely small set of cases where this was not possible, we followed the same procedures we followed with unknown entries.

Our approach to the effect of crises on leadership survival principally involves the application of survival analysis, one variant of a general class of methods often alternatively referred to as either event-history or duration analysis. We explain the fundamental aspects of survival analysis as it pertains to our research in the next section. However, here we comment on one aspect of survival analysis that influences variable construction in the leadership data. One virtue of event-history analysis is that the associated methods allow us to include cases that otherwise would be excluded or treated improperly by other statistical techniques. For example, some leaders are still in office at the end of our data and we thus do not know how long they will remain in office. A glance at the Halls of Fame, particularly the leaders'-choice Hall of Fame, reveals, for instance, that at the time of this writing Fidel Castro still leads Cuba. We cannot know how long he will remain in office. What we actually know is that his tenure is at least forty-three years. This is an example of censored data. Fortunately, hazard analysis deals with such data appropriately, forcing us neither to drop the censored cases nor to assume that current tenure equates to final tenure.[9]

Benchmarks

Of the 2,960 leaders in our data, the mean survival time was 4.63 years, with a median survival time of 2.25 years. Approximately one-third of leaders fail to survive their first year, 27 percent survive five or more years, and only about 14 percent survive ten or more years.

Coalition size influences survival. Although conceptually W is a continuous variable, for purposes of presentation we sometimes dichotomize the data into small- and large-coalition systems. We define the variable *binaryW* to be 1 if $W \geq 0.75$ and 0 otherwise.

The survival of leaders differs drastically according to coalition size. The mean survival times for small-coalition and large-coalition system leaders are 5.69 years and 3.56 years, respectively. In comparison, the median survival times are 2.60 years and 2.03 years, respectively. While in terms of mean and median survival time, small-coalition leaders last longer, the proportionate difference is much greater in mean times. This suggests that while many leaders are removed early in office in both systems, as predicted, conditional on having survived a few years, small-coalition leaders survive much longer than larger-coalition leaders. This is borne out by examining the mean survival times for leaders of small and large coalitions conditional on surviving at least one year in office. Given this conditionality, the mean tenure in office in small-coalition systems is 8.06 years (median of 4.25 years), while in large-coalition systems the mean tenure in office conditional on surviving at least one year is 5.23 years (median of 4.00 years).

Figure 7.1a, which compares the survival of leaders from small- and large-coalition systems, also supports this conclusion. The vertical axis shows the proportion of leaders who survive. The horizontal axis is time in office. The graphs show the proportion of leaders who survive for a particular length of time in office. For small-coalition systems, approximately 70 percent of leaders survive their first year. Sixty-four percent of leaders in large-coalition polities survive in office beyond their first year. By the end of their second year, 56 percent of small-coalition leaders are still in office, while only 51 percent of leaders in large-coalition systems remain. By the end of five years, 28 percent of leaders with small coalitions and 20 percent of leaders with large coalitions remain in office. At the ten-year mark the comparative numbers are 16 percent and 6 percent. The difference between the survival curves for small- and large-coalition systems is statistically significant at the 0.000 level ($N = 2,706$). It would appear that leaders in small-coalition systems really do have an incumbency advantage over their large-coalition counterparts, but that this advantage takes time to become established.

Figure 7.1b show the survival curves for different-sized coalitions ($W = 0, 0.25, 0.5, 0.75, 1$). While more cluttered, this figure reveals the same

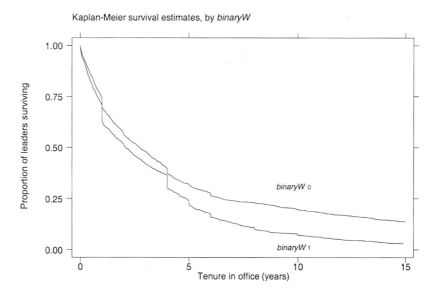

Figure 7.1a
Survival of political leaders in large- and small-coalition systems

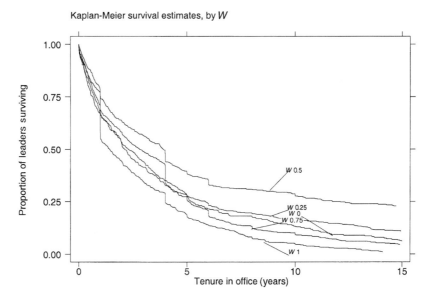

Figure 7.1b
Survival of political leaders by coalition size

general pattern. Leaders from small-coalition systems find it hard to survive the first few years in office but subsequently find it easier to survive than leaders from large-coalition systems. This high risk during early years is particularly noticeable for the smallest coalitions ($W = 0$), which, by the definition of W, primarily are military regimes. Figure 7.1b shows that the first-year drop-off in survival for leaders in this category is greater than for other categories. As we discussed with respect to the Mamluks, surviving the first year in such systems is difficult.

The preliminary comparisons of the survival functions support our prediction that small-coalition leaders have a significant incumbency advantage, but that this advantage takes time to be established. We now test these predictions systematically. To do so we utilize an aspect of econometrics typically referred to as *hazard* or *survival analysis* (Flemming and Harrington 1991; Greene 1993; Kalbfleisch and Prentice 1980).[10] The basic objective of these methods in this context is to estimate how long a leader is anticipated to survive in office under different conditions. Although the underlying problem is to assess length of tenure, it is typical to think of the estimation problem in terms of the hazard rate. In the current context, the hazard rate is the probability that a leader is removed from office. More specifically, since our data are organized by leader-year, in each year we ask, conditional on having survived thus far, what is the probability that a particular leader is removed in the current year? Further, to test our hypotheses, we want to know how the probability of removal from office (the hazard rate) varies with institutional details and performance. For instance, we want to know how the risk of removal for a large-coalition leader who is in her third year in office and who has achieved an average annual growth rate of 4 percent compares to the risk of removal for a small-coalition leader in her first year in office with no economic growth. Of course this comparison is just illustrative. Our analyses will focus on a variety of pertinent comparisons that help us discern the best strategies leaders can follow to enhance their prospects of survival given the selection institutions found in their polities.

The above illustrative comparison of leaders at different points in their tenure with different performances under different political-selection institutions indicates three aspects of the estimation problem. In particular, we want to know how (1) political-selection institutions, (2) performance, and (3) tenure in office to date affect the risk of removal in each year. In common with other statistical tests, measures of political-selection institutions and policy performance are included in our empirical assessments to determine their impact on leader survival. In addition to considering these standard factors, we also need to ask how a leader's risk of removal varies over time.

Over time does it become easier or harder for leaders to survive? As affinities are revealed, leaders can credibly promise future private goods. This makes it easier for them to survive in office, alternatively expressed as a decline in the hazard rate. To capture this effect, we need to include an additional parameter in our statistical analysis to assess how the hazard rate changes with prior time in office. We use Weibull regression, a parametric hazard technique. Technically the model specifies the risk of removal—the hazard rate—at time t, as $h(t) = pe^{X\beta}t^{(p-1)}$. In addition to the standard independent variable, X, and the associated coefficient vector, β, this technique includes the additional ancillary parameter p. This parameter p, which is sometimes also called a *shape parameter*, determines how the hazard rate changes over time. If p is greater than 1, then over time the risk of removal increases. In the context of leader survival, when p is greater than 1, each successive year a leader finds it harder to survive than was true in the previous year. In contrast, when p is less than 1, which is the situation the theory predicts, each successive year a leader finds it easier to survive in office than was true in the previous year. When p is less than 1, the hazard rate declines over time.

Weibull hazard analysis is a standard technique in studies of political survival and cabinet duration (Bueno de Mesquita and Siverson 1995; Bienen and van de Walle 1991; Browne, Frendreis, and Gleiber 1986; Diermeier and Stevenson 1999; Diermeier and Merlo 2000; King et al. 1990; Warwick 1992, 1995; Smith 2004). The selectorate theory, however, predicts that a standard Weibull model would be misspecified. The theory predicts that as affinities are revealed, leaders gain an incumbency advantage in that they can credibly promise future private goods, while their potential challengers can offer future private goods only probabilistically. The strength of this incumbency advantage depends on political-selection institutions. In large-coalition systems political competition is dominated by the provision of public goods, and the advantage of being able to promise future private goods does not provide the same incumbency advantage as it does in small-W systems. This presents an additional complication to the statistical tests, since we not only need to assess how the hazard rate changes over time. We also need to assess how W and S influence how the hazard rate changes over time, which is distinct from how these institutions influence the hazard rate at any time.[11]

The theory leads us to predict that the ancillary parameter p is smaller in small-W systems than in large-W systems, although we anticipate that p is less than 1 in both cases.[12] Substantively this means that for large-W systems the hazard rate is expected to decline modestly over time (p less than 1). In contrast, in small-W systems, the dominance of private goods means the progressive revelation of affinities creates a larger incumbency advantage. The large decline of the hazard rate over time that this creates means the ancillary parameter p should be smaller than it is for large-W systems.

To reflect how the hazard rate changes over time as a function of political-selection institutions, we model the ancillary parameter p as a linear function of either W or W and S. With regard to estimating p, we anticipate a negative coefficient on W and a positive coefficient on S, meaning p is smallest in small-W systems with a large loyalty norm (W/S small) and largest in large-W systems.

To reflect the theoretical expectations, the results in table 7.3 show that political-selection institutions, affect survival in two ways. First, W and S have their standard impact as independent variables, making deposition more or less likely. This is the $X\beta$ component. Second, they influence how the hazard changes *over time*. This is the ancillary parameter, p.[13] Table 7.3 reports four numbers in each cell for the $X\beta$ component. The first number is the parameter estimate, under which, in parentheses, is the standard error of this estimate. A positive parameter estimate indicates that an increase in the value of the independent variable increases the hazard rate, meaning deposition becomes more likely. The number reported in the top right of each cell is the hazard ratio. This alternative representation of the parameter estimate provides a convenient metric for estimating the impact of independent variables on the risk of deposition. For instance, a hazard ratio of 2 would mean that a unit increase in the independent variable would produce a doubling in the risk of deposition. A hazard ratio of 0.50 means that a unit increase in the independent variable halves the risk of removal. The final number reported, at the bottom right of each cell, is the significance level of a two-tailed test for which the null hypothesis is that the independent variable has no impact on the risk of removal from office (i.e., the hazard ratio equals

Table 7.3
Weibull and exponential analysis of how institutions influence leader survival

		Model 1	Model 2	Model 3
$X\beta$	W	−0.069, 0.94 (0.246), 0.80	−0.095, 0.929 (0.27), 0.75	0.02, 1.02 (0.10), 0.83
	S		−0.07, 0.93 (0.13), 0.57	
	ln (years + 1)			−0.61, 0.54 (0.04), 0.00
	W*ln (years + 1)			0.27, 1.31 (0.07), 0.00
	Constant	−1.01 (0.13), 0.00	−0.89 (0.12), 0.00	−0.92 (0.07), 0.00
Ancillary parameter, $\ln(p)$	W	0.36 (0.10), 0.00	0.36 (0.10), 0.00	Exponential regression: p fixed at $p = 1$
	S			
	Constant	−0.49 (0.05), 0.00	−0.49 (0.06), 0.00	
Summary statistics	*Observations*	$N = 16{,}004$ Leaders = 2,886	$N = 13{,}382$ Leaders = 2,690	$N = 16{,}004$ Leaders = 2,885
	Log Likelihood	−5,227.69	−4,631.36	−5,229.76

Note: In the $X\beta$ section the cell entries are parameter estimate, hazard ratio, standard error (in parentheses), and significance level, respectively. In the ancillary parameter section the cell entries are parameter estimate, standard error (in parentheses), and significance level, respectively.

1.00 in the null hypothesis). The lower portion of table 7.3 reports the impact of W and S on the logarithm of the ancillary parameter, p. That is, it indicates how W and S influence the underlying shape of the hazard function for different political institutions. The numbers reported are the parameter estimate, its standard error (in parentheses), and the level of significance in a two-tailed test. A positive parameter estimate means that a reduction in W reduces the value of the ancillary parameter such that it becomes increasingly easy for leaders to survive as their tenure increases.

In model 1, W is included as both a standard regressor and as a determinant of the ancillary parameter, p. While the negative coefficient for W in the $X\beta$ component indicates that leaders from large-coalition systems find it easier to survive, the effect is insignificant. The effect of W on the ancillary parameter, however, is large and significant. Model 1 indicates that the ancillary parameter for the smallest-coalition systems

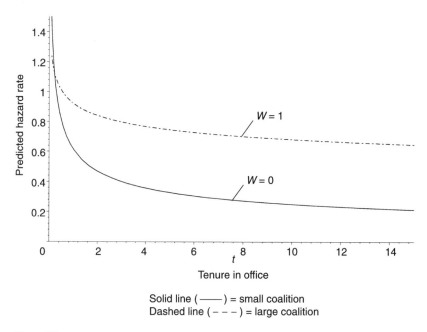

Figure 7.2
Predicted hazard rates for large- and small-coalition systems against years in office

$(W = 0)$ is 0.610, indicating the hazard for leaders in such systems declines rapidly over time. In contrast, for the largest-coalition systems $(W = 1)$ the ancillary parameter is $p = 0.870$.[14] The hazard rate for leaders of large-coalition systems declines more modestly over time. In model 2, which includes S as a regressor, the ancillary parameters for the smallest and largest systems are 0.611 and 0.873 respectively.

Figure 7.2 plots the predicted hazard rates generated from model 1 for $W = 1$ and $W = 0$. For the first six months of office, leaders from small-coalition systems are at greater risk of deposition than leaders from large-coalition systems. Beyond this short initial period, leaders from small-coalition systems find it much easier to survive. That is, the early transition period is especially risky for small-coalition leaders, whose survival depends on their reliable commitment to provide coalition members with private goods, a commitment they cannot make before learning more about affinities. Because private goods are less important to the survival of large-coalition leaders, these results are precisely what the selectorate theory leads us to expect.

Table 7.4
The effect of coalition size and tenure on government expenditure

	Model 4: *Ln(Per Capita Government Expenditure)*
Lagged Ln(Per Capita Government Expenditure)	0.909 (0.007), 0.000
ln(years + 1)	−0.010 (0.005), 0.049
ln(years + 1)*W	0.021 (0.006), 0.001
Constant	0.030 (0.024), 0.000 $N = 2{,}492$, F.E. = 198 $F(32{,}291) = 5{,}561.86$

Note: Cell entries are parameter estimate, significance level in two-tailed test, and standard error (in parentheses).

Since modeling the ancillary parameter as linearly dependent on regressors is relatively uncommon, we use a more conventional approach in model 3 to demonstrate how time in office radically reduces the risk of removal in small-coalition systems but not in large ones. Model 3 is the exponential model, which fixes the ancillary parameter at $p = 1$. Two additional regressors, *ln(years + 1)* and its interaction with *W*, are added. The variable *ln(years + 1)* is the logarithm of the number of years that a leader has been in office plus 1. The addition of 1 is to ensure that the logarithmic operation is possible. The negative coefficient on the *ln(years + 1)* variable indicates that the risk of deposition declines over time. The effect is strong and significant. However, the significant positive coefficient on *W*ln(years + 1)* means that the effect of tenure on reducing the risk of deposition is more moderate for large-coalition systems.

The growing incumbency advantage enjoyed by small-coalition leaders means that they can assure their supporters of access to future private goods. Consequently, they can reduce their expenditures and still match the best credible offers of challengers. In table 7.4 we provide a direct assessment of this claim by analyzing how coalition size and length of tenure influence government expenditure. The dependent variable is the logarithm of government expenditure as a percentage of *GDP* (*Log(Expenditure)*), as explained in chapter 4. The lagged logarithm of government expenditure (*Lag(LogExpenditure)*) is included in the analysis. Hence the effects of coalition size and length of tenure can be interpreted as proportional changes in expenditures. The analysis includes the region-year fixed effects.

The negative coefficient on the *ln(years + 1)* variable indicates that as a leader's tenure increases, she decreases expenditures. This reduction of spending is offset in large-coalition systems. The positive coefficient on the *ln(years + 1)*W* term indicates an increase in expenditures as tenure increases for those who rule with the support of a large coalition. It appears that leaders in small coalitions reduce their expenditures once they have established themselves in office, while large-coalition leaders continue working hard on behalf of their supporters. These results are consistent with expectations from the selectorate theory.

All of the analyses above support the same conclusion: leaders in small-coalition systems gain an incumbency advantage the longer they remain in office. While for these leaders surviving the initial few years in office is difficult, should they do so, the risk of deposition declines sharply. In contrast, leaders in large-coalition systems always find surviving in office difficult.

How Performance and Policy Provisions Affect Survival

In this section we ask how policy performance influences survival in office. The theory suggests that the basis of political competition in small-*W* systems is the provision of private goods, while in large-*W* systems political competition is based on the quality of public policy. This suggests that the political survival of leaders in small-*W* systems should be relatively more sensitive to the provision of private than of public goods as compared to the situation of leaders in large-*W* systems. We now assess these expectations.

While the theory predicts a public-goods focus in large-*W* systems, it does not specify which bundle of policies are emphasized in particular societies. With this in mind, we examine a single core public good, namely, economic growth. This good is always difficult to attain and its provision represents a serious and successful commitment to public policy. We use black market exchange-rate premiums as the measure of private-goods provision.

Table 7.5 examines the effect of economic growth on the survival of leaders in different institutional settings. The results strongly support the earlier analyses with respect to the growing incumbency advantage for leaders from small-coalition systems. As coalition size shrinks and selec-

Table 7.5
The effect of economic growth on survival in different institutional settings (Weibull analysis)

		Model 5	Model 6
$X\beta$	W	−0.378, 0.685 (0.162), 0.019	0.223, 1.249 (0.240), 0.354
	S		−0.601, 0.548 (0.194), 0.002
	Growth	−0.034, 0.967 (0.008), 0.000	−0.038, 0.963 (0.008), 0.000
	W*Growth	0.004, 1.004 (0.015), 0.802	0.009, 1.009 (0.015), 0.541
	Constant	−0.935 (0.111), 0.000	−0.843 (0.114), 0.000
Ancillary parameter, $\ln(p)$	W	0.494 (0.091), 0.000	0.553 (0.117), 0.000
	S		−0.243 (0.089), 0.006
	Constant	−0.525 (0.063), 0.000	−0.338 (0.062), 0.0000
Summary statistics	Observations	$N = 5{,}821$ Leaders = 1,084	$N = 5{,}694$ Leaders = 1,069
	Log Likelihood	−1,698.85	−1,640.82

Note: In the $X\beta$ section the cell entries are parameter estimate, hazard ratio, standard error (in parentheses), and significance level, respectively. In the ancillary parameter section the cell entries are parameter estimate, standard error (in parentheses), and significance level, respectively.

torate size grows (approaching the form of a rigged-election autocracy), the ancillary parameter p declines, meaning leaders in such systems find it increasingly easy to survive as their tenure progresses. The negative coefficient on the growth variable indicates that the higher the growth rate a leader achieves, the lower her risk of deposition. The positive effect of growth on tenure is common to all systems. Although the effect is statistically insignificant, the positive coefficient on the W*growth variable suggests that the beneficial effects of growth on tenure are less for leaders in large-coalition systems. The effective hazard ratio for a leader in a $W = 1$ system is 0.97, while for a leader in a $W = 0$ system it is 0.96. Hence a 1 percent increase in the growth rate reduces the risk of deposition by 3 percent and 4 percent for a large-coalition and a small-coalition leader, respectively.

On the surface it would appear that, in terms of survival, small-coalition leaders benefit more than large coalition leaders do from economic growth. Yet this straightforward interpretation neglects to consider the contingent circumstances and so is misleading.

Once they survive beyond the initial years in office, small-W leaders are relatively more immune to deposition, as we have seen. Although economic growth helps such leaders stay in office, their likelihood of deposition is already sufficiently small that the marginal reduction in risk due to economic growth is low. In contrast, large-coalition leaders face a much higher risk of removal because they are not advantaged the way their small-coalition counterparts are in the ability to promise future private goods. For such leaders the benefits of a 3 percent reduction in the risk of deposition produced by a 1 percent increase in economic growth has a larger marginal impact. Hence, notwithstanding the larger net coefficient on growth, beyond the initial years in office, the marginal effect of economic growth on survival is much higher for large-coalition leaders than for small-coalition leaders, the probability of deposition for small-coalition leaders already being small.

From the theoretical perspective we expect large-coalition leaders to be more sensitive to growth (i.e., a negative coefficient on the $W*Grow$ variable) than we observe. Overall, however, the results are generally consistent with expectations. While the theory is clear in its predictions, from a statistical perspective it is not surprising that it is difficult to differentiate how the marginal effect of policy varies across institutions for selecting leaders. The inability of statistical methods to determine how the marginal effects of the hazard rate vary in response to policy change across systems stems from measurement-error problems and from the nonrandom selection of policy implied by the selectorate theory.

Given that attempts to measure what we mean by coalition size are only just beginning, our measure of W is a crude five-point scale. Yet both conceptually and in reality, coalition size is on a continuum. Since we assign all coalitions to some place on a five-point scale, we *must* overestimate the size of some coalitions and underestimate others. This creates measurement error.

Leaders do not choose policy randomly. Rather they select policies they believe will enhance their survival in office. This strategic choice of policy makes it difficult to estimate how policy choices influence survival. According to the theory we should be able to tell which policies best enhance a leader's survival by simply observing which policies she chooses. The strategic selection of policy and the problem of measurement error in the assessment of coalition size diminish our ability to tell how policy choices affect survival across different regimes (Achen 1986).

Suppose for a moment that the theory is right and that the larger the coalition, the harder it is for a leader to survive in office and the more such a leader's survival depends on the provision of public goods. If we could do an experiment and randomly adjust the provision of public goods under different institutional circumstances, we could easily assess how institutions influence the extent to which the provision of public goods determines survival. Unfortunately, we cannot do such an experiment. Suppose we look at coalitions of a specific size as measured by our crude indicator, and in the data we observe a large-coalition leader who produces fewer public goods and more private goods than expected given her coalition size. The theory suggests that a leader who fails to produce the optimal mix of public and private goods jeopardizes her tenure and should be expected to survive for less time than her same-sized coalition counterparts who produce the optimal mix of goods. Measurement error in the assessment of coalition size suggests an alternative interpretation for these observations.

Assuming leaders want to survive, they produce the optimal mix of goods. When we encounter a leader who systematically underproduces public goods, we should infer that we have overestimated her coalition size and that her true coalition size is less than the crude score we assigned it. Given the incumbency advantage for small-coalition system leaders, we should expect her survival to be greater than for those leaders we categorized as her contemporaries. Unfortunately, from a statistical viewpoint, we observe a leader from a large coalition who provides too few public goods and yet survives longer.

While the theory provides a clear prediction, measurement error in the size of the coalition and the strategic selection of policy provisions undermine our ability to estimate how policy provisions influence survival for different-sized coalitions. The effects of policy provisions on the survival of leaders should be substantially greater than those estimated. Given this proviso, we now examine the effect of the public good—growth—and the private good—black market exchange-rate premiums —on the survival of leaders, recognizing that we are almost certainly *underestimating* the actual effects.

In the analyses in table 7.6 we examine how the provision of private
and public goods influences survival in small (*binaryW* = 0) and large
(*binaryW* = 1) coalition systems. The inclusion of both these private and
public measures of performance reduces the number of observations.
Small-*W* systems, as we know from chapter 4, discourage growth and
transparency. Consequently, they often fail to report GDP figures. Researchers who collect data on black market exchange-rate premiums
typically only investigate systems where they suspect disparity between
the official and unofficial exchange rates. Consequently, these data tend
not to be reported for large-coalition systems. These combined effects

Table 7.6
The effect of economic growth and black market exchange-rate premiums on survival in
different institutional settings (Weibull analysis)

		Model 7	Model 8	Model 9
*X*β	*BinaryW*	−0.172, 0.842 (0.190), 0.366	0.437, 1.548 (0.225), 0.052	0.176, 1.192 (0.251), 0.485
	S		−0.916, 0.400 (0.162), 0.000	−0.504, 0.604 (0.257), 0.049
	Growth	−0.026, 0.974 (0.012), 0.036	−0.024, 0.977 (0.012), 0.048	−0.025, 0.975 (0.012), 0.038
	BinaryW Growth*	−0.024, 0.976 (0.022), 0.270	−0.028, 0.973 (0.021), 0.197	−0.027, 0.974 (0.022), 0.216
	BlackMarket	−0.139, 0.870 (0.088), 0.117	−0.120, 0.887 (0.090), 0.181	−0.115, 0.892 (0.090), 0.200
	*BinaryW*Black Market*	0.055, 1.056 (0.172), 0.751	0.049, 1.050 (0.172), 0.776	0.042, 1.043 (0.172), 0.807
	Constant	−1.012 (0.126), 0.000	−0.716 (0.131), 0.000	−0.852 (0.153), 0.000
Ancillary parameter, ln(p)	*BinaryW*	0.274 (0.085), 0.001	0.179 (0.086), 0.036	0.307 (0.108), 0.005
	S			−0.234 (0.116), 0.044
	Constant	−0.274 (0.058), 0.000	−0.177 (0.059), 0.003	−0.079 (0.074), 0.286
Observations		1,771 Leaders = 396	1,764 Leaders = 395	1,764 Leaders = 395
Log Likelihood		−536.65	−520.04	−518.04

Note: In the *X*β section the cell entries are parameter estimate, hazard ratio, standard error
(in parentheses), and significance level, respectively. In the ancillary parameter section the
cell entries are parameter estimate, standard error (in parentheses), and significance level,
respectively.

reduce the number of observations to 1,771, with missing data on S reducing the sample further to 1,764. Despite these missing-data problems and measurement problems, the analysis supports the theory's predictions. In large-coalition systems survival is best enhanced by high growth. In small-coalition systems, although growth improves survival prospects, it does not do so to the same extent as it does in large-W systems. The sum of the coefficients for *BinaryW*Growth* and *Growth* is substantially more beneficial to survival than is the coefficient for just *Growth* in each of the three models tested in table 7.6. Black market premiums enhance survival most in small-coalition systems. Rather than explaining these effects in terms of the estimates reported in table 7.6, we use the estimates in model 7 to examine how growth and black markets influence survival time in both large- and small-coalition systems.

Economic growth improves the survival prospects of all leaders. However, good economic performance is particularly important for the survival of leaders who depend on large winning coalitions. Table 7.7 compares the survival of leaders in large and small winning coalitions at a high growth rate (6 percent annual increase in GDP) and a low growth rate (–2 percent annual change in GDP) when there is no black market exchange-rate premium. These growth rates represent unusually, but not unrealistically, high and low rates among common growth rates. For instance, since 1961 U.S. economic (annual) growth has only fallen to –2 percent or lower once (1982). At the other extreme, U.S. annual growth once reached 6 percent in 1984.

The table shows the elapsed time in office at which 50 percent, 25 percent, and 10 percent of leaders, given their coalition size, are expected to remain in office. The first row shows that if leaders in large-coalition

Table 7.7
Survival time for large and small coalitions at different growth rates (with no black market exchange-rate premium)

Survival probability	50%	25%	10%
Large coalition with 6% growth	2.9 years	5.8 years	9.6 years
Large coalition with –2% growth	1.9 years	3.9 years	6.4 years
Small coalition with 6% growth	2.6 years	6.4 years	12.4 years
Small coalition with –2% growth	1.9 years	4.8 years	9.4 years

systems maintain a 6 percent growth rate, then after 2.9 years 50 percent of the leaders are expected to still be in office. After 5.8 years 25 percent of leaders are anticipated to still be in office, and it takes until 9.6 years for only 10 percent of such leaders to remain in office. In comparison, 50 percent of large-coalition leaders who experience recession (–2 percent growth) are removed within 1.9 years. Thus moving from a low growth rate to a high one adds approximately one year (i.e., more than 52 percent) to the median survival time for a leader in a large-coalition system.

Likewise economic performance improves survival prospects for small-coalition leaders. Moving from low (–2 percent) to high growth (6 percent) increases the median survival time for small-coalition leaders by 0.7 years (i.e., 37 percent). While good economic performance clearly helps small-coalition leaders survive their difficult first few years, once established in office they survive much better than their large-coalition counterparts. Indeed, the results in table 7.7 suggest that the 10 percent survival time for small coalition leaders who inflict a sustained recession (–2 percent annual growth) on their nation for a decade is almost identical to the 10 percent survival time of a large-coalition leader who produces exceptional growth (6 percent) throughout her term in office. This striking difference supports the idea that doing a bad job is beneficial for those who run a state with the backing of a small coalition. While these results are staggering in and of themselves, the statistical problems of measurement error and strategic policy choice mean that the differences are probably far larger than those we report.

Economic performance matters for leaders in both types of systems, but its effect is different. In large-W systems, achieving growth is always important to leader survival. In small-W systems, growth retards the rate of deposition, but once established in office and having survived the initial years, small-coalition leaders' risks of deposition are relatively low whatever their economic performance. Apparently, given time in office, they can get away with economic disaster as long it does not preclude their making the requisite private-goods payments to their coalition members.

Private-goods provisions also influence survival, helping to reinforce the unhappy story suggested by the analysis of growth rates and survival. Table 7.8 fixes the growth rate at 2 percent, close to the sample average, and examines the impact of black market exchange-rate premiums in

Table 7.8
Survival time for large and small coalitions at different black market exchange-rate premiums (with growth fixed at 2 percent)

Survival probability	50%	25%	10%
Large coalition with no black market exchange-rate premium	2.4 years	4.7 years	7.9 years
Large coalition with a tenfold black market exchange-rate premium	3.4 years	6.9 years	11.5 years
Small coalition with no black market exchange-rate premium	2.2 years	5.5 years	10.8 years
Small coalition with a tenfold black market exchange-rate premium	5.1 years	12.6 years	24.6 years

large- and small-coalition systems. In particular, we compare survival times when leaders adopt policies that produce a tenfold exchange-rate premium over the official exchange rate. Although such large black market premiums are exceptional, they have occurred in Guinea in 1984, Nicaragua in the mid-1980s, Poland in the early 1980s, Uganda in 1978, Ghana in 1981, Sierra Leone in 1988, and Iran in the late 1980s.

In both large- and small-coalition systems, the introduction of a black market extends tenure, although the effect is larger in small-coalition system. The result for the large-coalition systems is contrary to the predictions of the selectorate theory. As we have already discussed, problems of restricted sample size, strategic reporting of data, measurement error in our calculation of W, and strategic policy choice mean that these tests are likely to underreport the impact of policy choice on survival. Table 7.8 is used for illustration rather than as a definitive test. There the evidence forces us to remember that the selectorate theory does not preclude corruption in large-W systems; rather the theory suggests such systems are relatively less corrupt than their small-coalition contemporaries. In small-coalition systems the corresponding change in black market premium *extends* the 25 percent survival time from 5.5 to 12.6 years. A vibrant black market is dramatically beneficial for small-coalition leaders.

The evidence in table 7.8 is striking. For those at the helm of a small-coalition government, bad policy clearly is good politics. An exceptional black market gives such leaders a 10 percent survival time that is approximately double what they could have expected had they produced extraordinary economic growth instead (12.4 vs. 24.6 years). It is 156 percent higher than the tenure time at which a large-coalition leader has a 10

Table 7.9
Survival time for large- and small-coalition leaders evaluated at the average behavior in large- and small-coalition systems

Survival probability	50%	25%	10%
Large coalition with growth and black market indicative of a *large* coalition	2.6 years	5.3 years	8.8 years
Large coalition with growth and black market indicative of a *small* coalition	2.7 years	5.5 years	9.1 years
Small coalition with growth and black market indicative of a *large* coalition	2.4 years	6.0 years	11.7 years
Small coalition with growth and black market indicative of a *small* coalition	2.7 years	6.8 years	13.2 years

percent chance of still being in office if she consistently produces 6 percent per annum economic growth. The story should by now be regrettably familiar: once again, for leaders who head small-coalition systems, bad policy is good politics. In table 7.9 we examine the effect of growth and black markets on survival evaluated at the mean values for each system. In our sample, large-coalition systems experience an average (mean) growth rate of 4.19 percent and the mean exchange-rate premium is 24 percent. The enormity of the latter figure should alert the reader than our data for exchange-rate premiums is an extremely biased sample. The median exchange-rate premium is zero. In small-coalition systems the corresponding mean performances are 3.75 percent and 51 percent respectively.

Leaders choose policies that enhance their survival. The first two rows of table 7.9 enable us to compare how the survival of an average-performing large-coalition leader would change if she adopted the policies of an average small-coalition leader. The latter two rows make the opposite comparison, showing how long a small-coalition leader survives if she behaves as an average small-coalition leader or as an average large-coalition leader.

Large-coalition leaders enhance their survival by behaving as large-coalition leaders, while small-coalition leaders enhance their survival by behaving as small-coalition leaders. The effects shown in table 7.9 that are of greatest interest compare how a typical large-coalition leader does and how a typical small-coalition leader does—that is, the first and last rows. A typical small-coalition leader does a relatively poor job on growth and a "good" job in fostering a black market. Such a leader has a 10 percent survival time that is 50 percent higher than that expected by a large-coalition leader. Yet the large-coalition leader does a better job, on average, in promoting economic growth and in avoiding black marketeering in her society. Differences in survival prospects earlier in each type's term are less striking. There are significant statistical problems associated with constructing these counterfactuals. We have explained that strategic selection of policy and measurement error in our crude assessments of W suppress the magnitude of coefficient estimates. The true effects of changes in policy provision are likely to be much higher. Therefore, we should not interpret the estimates in tables 7.5 through 7.9 too strongly since we present them only to illustrate the substantive point. More accurate estimates would, alas, almost certainly reveal that the true story is even more depressing for prospective leaders who come to office in small-coalition systems aspiring to achieve good governance.

The picture portrayed through tables 7.5 to 7.9 is depressing. Bad policy turns out to be good politics for autocrats, monarchs, and junta leaders. Just as surely, good policy is bad politics for these leaders. Government leaders and their economic advisors engaged in trying to help economically depressed states seem to conclude that the problem is that the leaders among these depressed states foolishly fail to implement what are patently good economic recommendations. They urge sensible changes in borrowing, taxing, and spending policies; shifts to a market economy; free trade; autonomous national banks; and so forth. All of these are patently good economic suggestions. Having given money to bail a country out of a financial crisis, they then watch in despair as the prescribed policy changes are ignored. Perhaps if more economic advisors and government leaders thought more about the political incentives of political leaders, rather than thinking that they are benign agents of the public's well-being, more energy would be put into thinking about how to change the political incentives that make bad policy good politics. This is a topic we return to in later chapters.

Extrapolitical Risks of Deposition

The theory provides clear predictions. For leaders in large-W systems, survival in office is always difficult and depends on their ability to produce good public policy. In contrast, in small-W systems, although survival is initially difficult, once established, leaders find it easy to remain in office. The theory, however, considers loss of power only as a result of direct political removal from office. In reality, leaders face other risks of deposition, not least of which is their own mortality. Term limits are also an increasingly common constraint on the survival of leaders. In this section we consider these extrapolitical risks and examine their consequences. We predict that these consequences differ radically by political system. We start by considering mortality and actuarial risk.

Mortality and Actuarial Risk

All leaders are mortal, so above and beyond political risks, they risk losing office through death or infirmity. On a simple actuarial basis the risk of losing office increases for aging leaders. While in chapter 5 we demonstrated a direct link between personal longevity and selection institutions for the population as a whole, we believe all leaders have access to quality health care, which should mitigate their personal actuarial risk. There is also a literature on the fate of leaders. For example, Goemans (2000) shows that autocrats are more likely to be harmed when they lose office than are democrats. Here we examine the causality in the opposite direction. Ill-health and infirmity increase the likelihood of political deposition, particularly in small-W systems.

Once leaders in small-coalition systems have survived sufficiently long to learn affinities, they have an incumbency advantage over their challengers in that they can credibly guarantee future private goods, while challengers can only offer such goods probabilistically. This enables them to survive in office from a political standpoint. Leaders, however, cannot promise to continue the flow of private goods to their supporters beyond their own death. Once it is known that a leader is terminally ill, supporters are aware that their access to private goods is about to dry up. This breaks the loyalty norm and ends the incumbency advantage. This means that political deposition is likely to precede anticipated death or infirmity, particularly in small-W systems, because the supply of future private goods determines survival. For example, the kleptocrats Ferdinand Marcos of the Philippines and Mobutu Sese Seko of Zaire were both deposed only when it was known that they were seriously ill. Since the ability of these large-S, small-W leaders to survive and steal stems from their capacity to promise future private goods, ill-health implies their political demise.

Given this prediction, it is not surprising that the health of small-coalition system leaders is often kept secret. For example, China's Mao Zedong and Deng Xiao Ping each had prolonged illnesses and probable incapacitation before their deaths, yet the details were carefully kept from public or international scrutiny and, perhaps, from their own internal backers as well, at least to the extent this was possible. Mao was not seen in public for nearly four months before his death was announced. The same pattern existed in North Korea during the period leading up to the announcement of the death of Kim Il Sung and succession by his son.

In contrast, when leaders depend on large coalitions, a terminal health diagnosis, while still politically serious, does not result in the rapid political deposition of the leader. In large-W systems political survival depends on effective public policy, not the ability to promise future private goods. Further, supporters in large-coalition systems have shorter horizons with respect to receiving private goods; they anticipate their leader is unlikely to last long anyway. Of course infirmity does reduce what little incumbency advantage large-coalition leaders have and so poor health is sometimes hidden. For example, during most of his presidency few people realized Franklin Delano Roosevelt was wheelchair bound. Today, few people still realize that John Kennedy was in perpetual pain and was treated with steroids that can make individuals tense and irritable. It is often rumored that Woodrow Wilson was incapacitated by a stroke and that his wife, keeping virtually everyone away from the president, actually made policy in his stead. Despite these and other examples, the health of the U.S. President, British prime minister, and other democratic leaders is generally common knowledge. The results of the American president's annual medical exam typically are made public. This is a far cry from the speculation in China as to whether Deng was actually functional or not in the last few years of his life.

Term Limits

Many democracies have implemented term limits. Autocracies almost never do, though we note that China under Jiang Zemin has made retirement mandatory at a stipulated age. Many rigged-election systems impose term limits, but these are routinely overturned when a leader's "legal" term is drawing to a close. We return to "term limits" in autocracies later.

Here we explore the relationship between the selectorate theory and restrictions on officeholding in the context of large-coalition democratic systems. We offer some conjectures and illustrative anecdotes, leaving systematic evidence for future research because we currently do not have the data necessary for rigorous tests regarding term limits.

Term limits prevent leaders from serving in office for more than some specified time. In the selectorate theory, leaders promote policies that enable them to persist in office. As the end of their legal term approaches, leaders know they will be removed whatever their policy performance. This undermines their incentive to generate effective policy.

In the context of the selectorate theory, term limits create cyclical incentives for leaders. Prior to the end of their term, term limits encourage leaders to work hard to provide benefits for their supporters. As the end of the term approaches, leaders—facing removal whatever their performance—have little incentive to provide benefits for their backers. From the perspective of the selectorate theory, the presence of terms limits means that during most of their term leaders work harder to provide benefits for supporters than they otherwise would, but toward the end they engage in kleptocratic behavior.

Term limits undermine the incumbency advantage by restricting the length of time for which leaders can credibly promise private benefits to their coalition. As the end of the term approaches, leaders must produce increasingly high levels of benefits for their coalition in order to maintain its support. Of course, the issue of term limits is only relevant when they are enforceable, which in practice means large-W systems. Since in these systems the focus of political competition is the provision of public goods, the loyalty norm is already weak and so the impact of adding term limits to further diminish the loyalty norm is marginal.

As the end of a leader's term approaches, the survival incentive that drove her policy provision is lifted. Whether she performs well and produces high levels of benefits for her supporters or engages in kleptocratic behavior, her political fate is the same: removal. With the incentives to behave well in office removed, we should expect leaders in the last moments of their term to shift their policy provisions away from effective public policy and toward a policy of skimming off resources for themselves.

We proceed by illustrating the effects of term limits in the Roman Republic. Term limits are an example of institutional arrangements that

decouple the selection and retention of leaders from their policy performance. To explore the safeguards required for the efficient functioning of such institutions, we discuss the safeguards incorporated into
the Athenian polity after 508 BC, when Cleisthenes' democratic reforms
strongly decoupled leader selection from policy performance, not only
by introducing one-year term limits but also by creating selection by lot.
After doing so, we review the overall effect of term limits and discuss
why term limits are only enforceable in large-W systems.

The Roman Republic illustrates how term limits shift the policy
focus at the end of a term (Livy 1965). Consuls were appointed to a
single-year term. In 218 BC during the Second Punic War, Hannibal led
Carthaginian forces across the Alps and into Italy. For the following
twelve years he wreaked devastation on Roman armies, but eventually
he was defeated by his inability to capture fortified cities. Fabius recognized that while Hannibal's genius made him a formidable enemy on
the battlefield, his lack of support from Carthage made him vulnerable
to a war of attrition. Hence, rather than fight Hannibal in pitched battle,
Fabius proposed containing Hannibal, whose lack of supplies and inability to recruit manpower meant his strength waned with inaction. During
his dictatorship of 217 BC. Fabius effectively implemented these policies.

Such a policy made good military sense, but it deprived consuls
of the personal glories that would accrue to the leader who defeated
Hannibal. While Fabius's policies exhibited public spiritedness, those of
his contemporaries did not. In particular, while they were happy to tie
Hannibal's forces down for most of the year, consuls often could not resist
the opportunity for personal glory and would fling their armies against
Hannibal as their term was about to expire (Livy 1965). Unfortunately for
the Romans, Hannibal became good at anticipating and exploiting these
rash military moves. Approaching term limits drove some consuls to place
their opportunity for personal glory over good military policy.

Term limits decouple policy performance and leader survival. They
are not the only institutional innovation to do so. In Athens in 508 BC
Isagoras became chief archon despite the greater popularity of
Cleisthenes. Cleisthenes revived his political fortunes by proposing
popular democratic reforms. Although Isagoras tried to strengthen his
position by inviting Spartan troops into Athens, the citizens rose up and
deposed him. After his recall, Cleisthenes implemented his proposed
democratic reforms, which increased the size of the winning coalition. In

this regard, perhaps his most important contribution was to reorganize the Athenian polity into a series of ten tribes, replacing the prior clan-like system through which chiefs gained enormous political influence by controlling the right to citizenship (Hignett 1952; Jones 1952; Rhodes 1986; Buckley 1996).

Cleisthenes also reformed the institutions of government. Most government positions had a one-year term limit and most appointments were by lot. While the motives for reforms are a fascinating topic, we do not focus on them. Instead we examine the extensive series of checks developed to restrain the kleptocratic tendencies created by decoupling officeholding and policy performance. We start with a brief overview of Athenian institutions after Cleisthenes' reforms.

The heart of political power in Athens was the assembly, or Ecclesia. All citizens over eighteen years old had the right to attend the Ecclesia. There was an advisory council called the Boule of 500 to which election was by lot and that took the lead in preparing the agenda and motions for the assembly. Cleisthenes' reforms also set up the Heliaea, or people's court, which elected 6,000 jurors by lot.

Election to the Boule, as a juror to the people's court, or to most of the other numerous government posts was by lot and there were strict term limits. For example, no one could serve on the Boule more than twice and not in successive years. These term limits and selection by lot meant that an individual's access to office was unrelated to performance. Although there were inevitably some rigged lotteries, in general all citizens had equal opportunity to get a position (Staveley 1972, 101–117).[15] Under such a random selection process, policy failure in the past was not an obstacle to holding office in the future. Combined with strict term limits, the selectorate theory suggests that the leaders chosen in this manner should be expected to engage in kleptocratic behavior. The Athenian constitution recognized this risk and did much to mitigate it. In particular, we examine four aspects by which Athens addressed the kleptocratic incentives created by term limits: (1) complex government structures that necessitated cooperation between leaders to implement policy; (2) legislative review of officials; (3) legal review of officials departing from office; and (4) growth in the importance of ranks, such as generals, which, though elected, had no term limits.

Athenian government was complex. Rather than having a hierarchical structure with a strong leader at the top, Athenian administration was devolved through many boards and committees whose members were chosen by lot. Since no one person could implement policy alone, the numerous boards served to monitor each other's conduct (Buckley 1996, 254–255). While redundancy and interboard competition might reduce efficiency, this structure avoided putting too much policy power in any one set of hands. As such it was difficult for any individual to steal from the state. Control of the assembly also shows this decentralized theme.

Modern political science has recognized the importance of agenda control (see, for instance, Romer and Rosenthal 1978). However, in Athens control over the agenda was difficult to maintain. Each year was divided into ten prytany, one for each tribe. During each prytany there were typically four meetings of the assembly. Prior to the start of each, a chair for the meeting was elected by lot. The Boule took responsibility for preparing the agenda for the assembly. The assembly would vote on each issue as it was read, with the issues that received unanimous support being immediately passed. Once the noncontentious and routine issues were dispensed with, the assembly would return to debate the more controversial issues. Each Athenian citizen had the right to speak, and once a citizen was recognized by the chair, any amendments or proposals made would be voted on. Since the identity of the chair was not known in advance of any meeting, leaders could not maintain control of the agenda and had to rely on their oratorical skill.

At the first meeting of each prytany, the assembly would vote on the performance of officials. Hence, although selected by lot, officials effectively received ten confidence votes during their term. In this context they had only their last thirty-six or so days in office free of reselection incentives. Further, officials were constrained by the threat of prosecution in the courts. The Areopagus, an aristocratic body consisting solely of former archons (senior officials), and the people's court monitored the performance of officials. In particular the Areopagus monitored officials in three ways.

First, it examined whether individuals were eligible to hold the office. Second, it monitored their performance during office. Third, it performed the ethuna, a post-officeholding review. This final review was particularly important for senior officials since it determined their admission to the Areopagus, a great honor. After (probably) 462 BC the Areopagus was dissolved and its responsibilities split between the Boule and the people's court. Athenian officials, like their modern-day democratic counterparts, risked investigation and prosecution if they were suspected of private-goods-oriented or kleptocratic policies during their term in office.

Not all Athenian offices were allocated by lot or subject to term limits. Some, particularly those requiring specialized skills, were directly elected. Generals constitute one key example. These ranks grew in importance during the fifth century, when Athens was almost continually involved in conflict (Rhodes 1986, 115).[16] This shift away from term limits helped mitigate the perverse incentives that term limits create at the end of a term.

The selectorate theory suggests term limits have two opposing effects. Knowing that a leader will be removed in the future reduces her incumbency advantage because she cannot guarantee private goods beyond her term in office. This makes a leader work harder on behalf of supporters. In contrast, at the very end of her term all reselection incentives are removed since policy performance and survival are decoupled. Figure 7.3 shows how term limits influence how hard a leader works on behalf of her supporters. Initially a leader works hard. However, as affinity is learned her incumbency advantage grows since she can promise

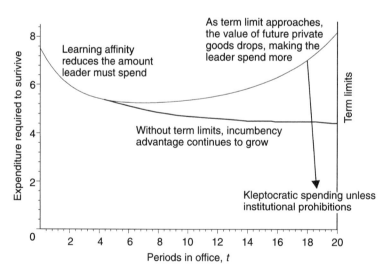

Figure 7.3
The effect of term limits on expenditures by incumbents

private goods to her coalition. As her term progresses, the length of time for which a leader can promise access to future private goods decreases, and with it, her incumbency advantage declines. This induces her to start working harder again for her supporters. At the very end of her term, performance and survival are decoupled, which makes leaders kleptocratic. Fortunately, as the Athenian example shows, there are several ways, such as post-officeholding judicial review, to keep leaders working hard and to prevent them from stealing from the state during their final moments in office.

Term limits are only enforceable in large-coalition systems. It was only with the contraction of coalition size in Rome, for instance, that consuls overcame the norm of term limits and served in successive years. The enforcement of term limits requires the active support of the winning coalition to remove the incumbent. In large-W systems private goods account for only a small proportion of the rewards. Coalition members are willing to risk exclusion from future coalitions in order to force the incumbent to work slightly harder. In contrast, when the coalition is small, the relative value of continued coalition membership is much higher, and so coalition members do not want to enforce term limits and risk exclusion from future coalitions. Indeed, as we will see in chapter 8, they are willing to support and take part in oppression of their fellow citizens to ensure their continued receipt of private benefits.

A Tale of Two Countries

The central finding of this chapter is easily summarized and has often been repeated: for those who depend on a small coalition, good policy is bad politics and bad policy is good politics. Having shown that this is a depressingly reliable statistical generalization, we illustrate this result by comparing policy performance and political longevity in two countries, Thailand and Cameroon. Each relied on small coalitions between 1960 and 1988, when Thailand seemed headed toward a more convincingly democratic form of government, perhaps as a result of a severe financial crisis. We discuss developments across these years, though our main emphasis is on 1970–1998, for which we have comparable data for the two countries.

Governance in Thailand and Cameroon between 1960 and 2000 had elements in common and elements that distinguish each from the other. In 1960, at the inception of independence from France, Cameroon institutionally required a fairly large-sized coalition drawn from a large selectorate but moved quickly, as we discuss below, to a small-coalition government, still drawn from a nominally large selectorate. That is, Cameroon switched quickly from a fairly democratic polity to a rigged-election autocracy, where it has remained institutionally. Thailand began the same period with a very small coalition government drawn primarily from a selectorate made up of the military and remained that way throughout the 1960s. Thus, both Cameroon and Thailand had small-coalition governments for most of the 1960s. The 1970s saw substantial vacillation in Thailand's institutional format, with the government sometimes being a military junta (small coalition and small selectorate), sometimes being dominated by the monarchy (again small coalition, small selectorate), and occasionally experimenting with a large-coalition, large-selectorate, fairly democratic form of government. The experimentation with more democratic forms, however, was frequently interrupted by intervention by the Thai military, a pattern that is itself predicted by the selectorate theory, as explained in chapter 8. Military intervention in governance has continued in Thailand, though with decreasing frequency in the 1990s and beyond.

Cameroon was led by its first president, Ahmadou Ahidjo, from 1960 until 1982, when he voluntarily stepped down, citing exhaustion and ill-health. He was replaced by his prime minister, Paul Biya, who continues in office as of this writing (2002). Ahidjo first won office in 1960 with a small majority in a closely contested election. However, using opposition violence as a justification, he suspended the constitution in 1962, dispensed with competitive elections, and presided over a one-party state, ruling through presidential emergency powers. He stood for reelection several times, but without any opportunity for meaningful electoral opposition. Paul Biya, himself inclined toward dictatorship, later indicted and tried Ahidjo in absentia for allegedly plotting a coup d'état, for which Ahidjo was sentenced to death. Ahidjo, exiled in France, died peacefully. Biya continues to rule over Cameroon, having been "reelected" several times by nearly 100 percent of the vote. Of course, it helps with reelection that the Cameroon government permits no opposition.

While Cameroon has only had two governments between 1960 and 2000, Thailand has been ruled by about twenty governments during the same period. Over this same span, the Thai government experienced at least twelve attempted (and many successful) coups d'état. Six governments were led by the military. The longest term in office for a prime minister—the military leader Thanom Kittikachorn—equaled nearly a decade. The shortest—the February 1975 government of Seni Pramoj—lasted less than two weeks. Although the Thai monarchy remains a bastion of stability, Thai administrations seem to come and go with alacrity, often deposed by coups reflecting significant military defections within the ruling circle. Some deposed leaders succeed in returning to office later, so that they at least live to fight another day. Between the many coups d'état, Thailand has also held numerous competitive elections and, more recently, gives the impression of reigning in the military's inclination to intervene in civil government. That is, Thailand appears on the path to democratic rule. Cameroon, thus far, does not.

During the years 1960–1998, Thailand enjoyed solid economic growth, generally running about 50 percent ahead of the global average. That rosy description, however, masks two rather distinct periods. Until about 1988, when Thailand's generally low *Democracy* score increased to 0.75, annual growth averaged around 4 percent. From 1988 onward, until the financial crisis of 1998, growth ran at about double that rate. For Cameroon, however, the picture is rather different. Although outperforming many African governments, its economic growth rate was about 50 percent below the global average. Cameroon's true growth may be even lower, because the country has the good fortune of having oil deposits, which helped ease its way through the oil shocks of the 1970s.

The comparison between Thailand and Cameroon is bleak for Cameroon. Figures 7.4a and 7.4b show the annual per capita GDP (based on World Bank data) and tenure in office for Cameroon and Thailand from 1970 to 1998. The comparison is revealing. Thailand and Cameroon performed comparably well at increasing per capita income during the early years for which we have data, but then drew sharply apart around 1988 when per capita prosperity shot up in Thailand and turned down in Cameroon. This coincided precisely with the time that Thailand shifted markedly—though not completely or finally—to a more democratic government with a significantly increased selectorate and coalition. Biya in

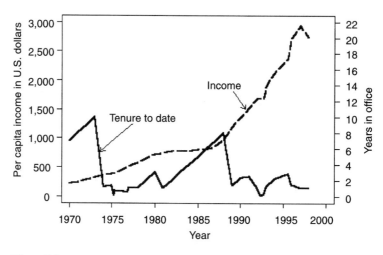

Figure 7.4a
Short-term growth and leadership tenure: Thailand

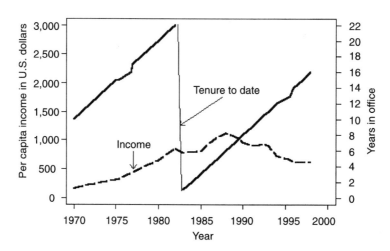

Figure 7.4b
Short-term growth and leadership tenure: Cameroon

Cameroon, in the meantime, was consolidating his one-party, small-coalition, autocratic rule. Clearly, despite its impressive economic performance, Thai leaders had poor prospects of surviving in office while, with less impressive economic credentials, Ahmadou Ahidjo and Paul Biya proved remarkably adept at holding onto power. The selectorate theory suggests an explanation for the discrepancy between tenure in office and public policy performance.

Thailand and Cameroon have been among the most corrupt states in the world. The 1999 Transparency International Corruption Index places Cameroon dead last among the ninty-nine countries evaluated in terms of curbing corruption. Thailand, still a very corrupt society, ranks sixty-eighth, a substantially better performance than Cameroon. The same relationship has held in the Transparency International ratings since 1996. Unfortunately, there are no comparable data for earlier years, although Transparency International has created retrospective estimates for the periods from 1980 to 1985 and 1988 to 1992. In those periods, Cameroon was less corrupt than Thailand, though still one of the more corrupt polities in the world. Perhaps it was a coincidence, perhaps not, but the great expansion in Thai prosperity substantially overlapped with its shift to a larger-coalition system and with its shift to a relatively less corrupt system. Cameroon's decline in per capita GDP, as seen in figure 7.4b, coincided substantially with Biya's consolidation of power and with the country's apparent increase in corruption. These are the patterns the selectorate theory suggests.

Good economic performance has failed to bolster survival time for Thai leaders, while relatively less good performance is strongly associated with longer terms of office in Cameroon. An institutional difference between the two may help account for this fact. As mentioned earlier, once Ahmadou Ahidjo abandoned competitive elections (in 1962), Cameroon has operated and continues to operate as a small-coalition, large-selectorate, rigged-election system. That is, in our terms, the loyalty norm for members of the winning coalition is strong in Cameroon since W/S is small. Because the coalition members enjoy the private benefits their support entails and because defection from the coalition is risky, they are content to stay with the incumbent through thick and thin. Thus, Ahidjo enjoyed and Biya is enjoying political longevity with growing corruption and declining prosperity.

Thai leaders have experienced much greater volatility in the loyalty norm. When Thailand has been more democratic, it has also had a weaker loyalty norm (i.e., relatively large W/S); when Thailand has been less democratic its loyalty norm has been stronger (i.e., smaller W/S). In fact, there is a significant negative correlation between Thailand's loyalty norm, measured of course as W/S, and the political survival of leaders. That is, the ratio W/S accurately tracks the consequences of weak or strong loyalty. This is precisely what the evidence presented in this chapter has shown for leaders in general. It appears that the differences between Cameroonian and Thai economic performance, shifting corruption, and incumbency tenure all fall into place if we follow the logic of the selectorate theory.

We close this comparison with a final observation. During part of its period of high growth, Thailand experienced repeated military coups. Cameroon did not "suffer" from such events. Coups, as we note in the next chapter, are associated with regimes that have a small coalition and a small selectorate and, as we will show, they tend logically and empirically to be precursors to greater democratization. The same is true of monarchy, another institutional arrangement found in Thailand but not in Cameroon. In Cameroon, W/S has almost always been small, indicating a strong loyalty norm. In Thailand, even in its less democratic periods, W/S often was large, with both coalition and selectorate size being small. Weak loyalty forces leaders to spend more and may thereby help contribute to economic growth through fiscal stimulus even when that stimulus is somewhat inefficient. That is, coup-ridden juntas appear preferable to rigged-election systems (Feng 2001; Londregan and Poole 1990; Jackman 1978).

Conclusion

Political leaders respond to the incentives created by their institutional setting. Those who must find broad support spend more, even correcting for national income, and focus their spending disproportionately on producing public goods. Those who lead a small coalition spend less and focus on providing private goods to their backers. Each type of leader improves the prospects of surviving in office by responding to the specific incentives identified through the selectorate theory. Good policy performance in the sense of enhancing national prosperity improves survivability for those who rely on a large coalition and who live with a weak loyalty norm. Poor policy in the sense of not enhancing citizen welfare through prosperity, but rather promoting corruption and black markets, most improves the survivability of those who rule with a small coalition. For them, it would be a strategic error to promote citizen welfare if they desire to stay in office as long as they can. In contrast, following the strategy of a small-coalition government has bad consequences for political survival if one heads a large coalition.

One of the primary puzzles that motivates this study is to explain why those who enjoy good governance turn their leaders out with alacrity and those who suffer under the misery of poverty, poor health, and poor opportunity in general do not. We now have provided a theoretical solution to this puzzle and have shown, albeit with crude and therefore preliminary indicators, that the record of history bears out our explanation. It is worth repeating the "mantra" of this chapter: good policy is bad politics and bad policy is good politics for small-coalition leaders. Good policy is good politics and bad policy is bad politics for those who head a large-coalition government, but even then, those at the helm of a large-coalition system suffer from an inherent institutional incumbency disadvantage. When combined, small coalitions and large selectorates promote incumbency, just as they promote misery. The evidence from thousands of leaders and decades of data, as well as from the illustrative case analyses of Cameroon and Thailand, unmistakably points to these distressing conclusions. With this evidence in mind, we now turn our attention in part III to an examination of the selection of and changes in institutions of governance.

III CHOOSING INSTITUTIONS

8 Institutional Preferences: Change from Within

Leaders survive longest when they depend on a small coalition and a large selectorate. They also do least under these conditions to promote the well-being of most people living under their control. It seems literally true that life, liberty, and the pursuit of happiness (or at least John Locke's earlier formulation of life, liberty, and the pursuit of property) are best advanced by political leaders who depend on a large coalition drawn from a large selectorate. Yet in the world today and the world of the past, an extraordinary variety of political arrangements have been tried. Big unitary states, small states, and big, federal states with smaller subunits can be found throughout the world. Parliamentary democracies, presidential democracies, inherited monarchies, elected monarchies, constitutional monarchies, military dictatorships, benign dictatorships, oligarchies, aristocracies, autocracies, tyrannies, juntas—the very plethora of words and phrases to describe regimes attests to the variety of institutional arrangements. The choice and variability of governing rules require explanation. Why do leaders or citizens choose such different political arrangements in different places and at different times? Is there not a best set of institutions? These issues are explored here and in the remaining chapters.

In addressing shifts in the institutions for selecting leaders we organize the chapter around three closely related themes. First, we investigate how, given free reign, different subsets of a country's domestic population would alter institutions. Second, we assess preferences over countermeasures to thwart efforts to change the polity's selection institutions. Third, we analyze the actions and counteractions different segments of a country's population resort to in order to keep institutions in line with their interests.

When we turn to actions designed to alter or preserve coalition size and selectorate size, we explore the empirical implications that follow from preferences for actions and counteractions. Our empirical analyses explore such phenomena as population migration, antigovernment activities (demonstrations, strikes, and riots), revolution, coups d'état, and other specific measures taken to change institutions to see if their occurrence and consequences match expectations from the selectorate theory.

In evaluating such actions we must also address the empirical aspects of countermeasures. Countermeasures take two broad forms: factors that create the *expectation* of government-led oppression and factors that assess the *realization* of oppressive measures. In analyzing countermeasures we show the extent to which oppressive measures are expected to occur and do occur under different institutional arrangements. In our discussion of government-led actions designed to frustrate efforts to change institutions or leaders, we elaborate on how and why some people (and not others) are mobilized to participate in oppression and who the most likely targets are of oppressive policies. By doing so we demonstrate that the same factors that explain authoritarian survival rates and the focus of autocrats on private goods (i.e., small W, large S) also account for their disproportionate tendency to engage in acts of oppression. Rather than seeing oppression as an alternative explanation for the success of small-coalition leaders at staying in office, we show that these actions are explained by the selectorate theory. Of course, war and international interventions can also change political arrangements, and we will deal with these in chapter 9.

The goals of this chapter are to establish theoretically derived preferences over institutions for the disenfranchised, the selectorate, the winning coalition, and incumbent leaders; to investigate whether institutional changes follow in the predicted manner from the actions available to different groups; and to assess the use of or avoidance of oppressive measures by leaders, their coalition members, and others. We will claim that antigovernment protests, revolutions, and civil war are the means by which members of the disenfranchised or the selectorate (not in the winning coalition) can change their polity's institutions to improve their lot. Additionally, when possible these groups can also improve their well-being by leaving their country and becoming immigrants in societies that better fulfill their interests. We will see why coalition members and leaders are likely and even willing to use extreme measures like oppression and terror to prevent people from opposing the institutions of government. And yet we will also come to understand how coalition members can and do use coups to benefit themselves, sometimes with the side effect of benefiting the whole of society (other than the incumbent) in the process. The selectorate theory will also be used to evaluate the institution-altering actions leaders take to improve their prospects of political survival. In the process, we will also show how this theory helps solve an important empirical puzzle that notes that democracies with high per capita incomes seem immune to institutional changes that otherwise would turn them into nondemocratic polities (Przeworski and Limongi 1997; Przeworski 2001).

The Selectorate Theory and Institutional Preferences

The selectorate theory links the institutions W and S to decisions about the allocation of resources and ties those choices to the political survival of leaders. We have shown substantial evidence, albeit based on crude estimates of coalition size and selectorate size, that the implications of the selectorate model are consistent with a broad body of historical evidence. At the same time, we recognize that the selectorate model is a simplification of reality. Now we investigate what the selectorate model has to say about the choice of institutions, but we also enrich the discussion with an examination of how factors outside the formal models we presented—but consistent with the sense of the general theory—may give shape to political arrangements.

The results reported thus far show how differences in institutions alter the mix and quantity of goods allocated by leaders. They also show how institutional arrangements influence the pool of discretionary resources at the incumbent's disposal and the implications these factors have for tenure in office. A bleak relationship between policy performance and political survival was uncovered earlier. Those who generate the most public welfare also get dropped from office rather quickly, even though they help produce high per capita incomes, solid growth rates, safe water, good educations, widespread access to medical care, little corruption, confident investors, civil liberties, transparent governance, and on and on.[1] Those who foster corruption among their backers, support flourishing black markets, enjoy ample opportunities to engage in kleptocracy, and keep people under the yoke of poverty thrive in office. We now pull these insights and observations together to discuss what the selectorate theory suggests about the preferences of four domestic groups regarding institutional arrangements. These four groups are: members of the selectorate outside the winning coalition; disenfranchised residents in the polity (that is, those who are not members of the selectorate); members of the winning coalition; and the incumbent leader. We characterize the welfare—or level of benefits—that members of each of these groups receive under different institutional arrangements. Implicitly we are asking the following question: If each group had unilateral control over institutional change, how would it modify institutions? This characterization of institutional preference is a necessary first step in a theory of endogenous institutional change. In chapter 9 we examine the effect of a fifth group on alterations in institutions. This fifth group consists of foreign rivals. Governments not only are changed from within, as discussed in this chapter, but also from without by external force.

The Selectorate and the Disenfranchised

According to the selectorate model, and as seen in the comparative static analysis in the technical appendix to chapter 3, the welfare of those outside the winning coalition strictly increases as the size of the winning coalition increases. The welfare of the disenfranchised and those in the selectorate but not in the winning coalition (i.e., outsiders) diminishes as the selectorate gets larger and as the value they attach to future returns increases. Given these implications of the selectorate theory, what can we say about institutional preferences among members of these two groups?

Those outside the winning coalition benefit from government only as a consequence of the public goods produced by their polity; they enjoy none of the private benefits doled out by the government. As such, the government's impact on their welfare depends on its choice of tax rate and on the value of the public goods it produces. Because leaders in small-coalition systems emphasize high tax rates and low public-goods production, such systems are unattractive to disenfranchised residents ($N - S$) and to members of the selectorate who are not in the current winning coalition ($S - W$). Therefore, if given their druthers, these groups have reasons to prefer to increase the size of the winning coalition. Doing so induces leaders to increase the provision of public goods. Consequently, those outside the winning coalition tend to prefer a government with a large winning coalition, such as a democracy, to other styles of government. We say "*tend to*" because how strongly this preference is held depends on whether one is disenfranchised or one is in the selectorate but not in the current winning coalition.

Reliance on a large coalition necessitates a weak loyalty norm (i.e., W/S is large). Those outside the coalition desire just such a political system. Recall that when the loyalty norm is weak, the leadership must spend more to keep the coalition happy. As the leadership spends more, some portion of the added spending can be expected to go toward providing additional public goods that spill over to benefit outsiders. How much more is spent on public goods depends on whether W and S are both small or both large. For the disenfranchised the preference is clear: they want the winning coalition to be large. For those in the selectorate but outside the coalition, their preference is less obvious. Here we diverge somewhat from the comparative statics derived in chapter 3. In the formal model, the incumbent always survived in office. Although those selectors outside W had some nominal chance of being in future coalitions, on the equilibrium path of the model these opportunities were never realized. Yet in reality, leadership turnover occurs, so members of S outside of W have more vested in the current system than do the disenfranchised.

When W is small and S is large, as in rigged electoral systems, the selector's preferences are very close to those of the disenfranchised. The small value of W/S in these forms of governance means selectors outside of W have little prospect of entering a future coalition when a new leader takes office. Additionally, since leader turnover is low, even these remote possibilities of future inclusion are rare.

In contrast, when W is small and S is also small, selectors outside of the coalition might have significant attachment to existing institutions. Given the weak loyalty norm of these systems, leaders must work hard to provide rewards for their supporters, meaning that supporters receive high levels of private goods. The high ratio of W/S means leadership turnover takes place relatively frequently. When it does, outsiders have a significant chance of becoming key supporters and hence of gaining access to the wealth of private goods. Selectors outside of W also like large-W systems for the same reasons the disenfranchised like them.

Thus, selectorate members prefer most alternative forms of government to autocracy, but depending on circumstances, they could go either way with regard to junta (or monarchy) and democracy. Indeed, selectorate members can also live with autocracy, provided the current leader is deposed and replaced with a new incumbent who includes them in the newly constituted winning coalition. This is a key difference between the institutional interests of the disenfranchised and selectorate members. When the loyalty norm is weak and the selectorate size is small, the prospects of gaining future access to private goods are improved for those in the selectorate but not for the disenfranchised. The disenfranchised have no chance of entering a future winning coalition under the existing political arrangements. Therefore, all residents who are not in the winning coalition prefer a large-coalition, large-selectorate system over a small-coalition, large-selectorate autocracy. The disenfranchised prefer a large-coalition, large-selectorate system over all other types. However, selectorate members have a stronger preference for junta or monarchy over autocracy than do those in the disenfranchised group and may or may not prefer democracy over monarchy or junta. Additionally, if the loyalty norm is weak and the selectorate size is small, the disenfranchised have a somewhat greater incentive to foster institutional change than do members of the selectorate. As we see later, this incentive translates into expectations regarding concrete actions—ranging from migration to antigovernment activities, the latter even going as far as civil war and revolution—that are expected to be more common among the disenfranchised than among the members of the selectorate.

The Winning Coalition

We discussed the welfare of coalition members in light of changes in W and S in chapters 3 and 4. Here we review and build on that earlier discussion. The welfare of the winning coalition decreases as selectorate size and patience—that is, the shadow of the future—increase. The relationship between the welfare of coalition members and changes in the size of the winning coalition is not simple, linear, or even monotonic.

Two forces operate in opposite directions on the interests of coalition members. Increasing the coalition's size weakens the loyalty norm, encouraging the incumbent to spend more in order to dissuade any members of the coalition from defecting. Naturally, this is good for members of the coalition. Increasing the coalition's size, however, also leads to a reduction in the value of private goods received by each member of the coalition. As the coalition gets bigger, the value of private goods diminishes for two reasons. First, these goods must be shared among more people, thereby spreading them more thinly. Second, as the coalition gets larger, leaders shift away from private-goods provision and toward public-goods provision, so that the advantage of membership in the coalition diminishes. Which of these forces dominates depends on the specific size of the selectorate, the coalition, tax rates, and so forth. The general impact of these two forces, however, is readily characterized.

The selectorate theory showed logically—and the evidence in chapter 4 supported empirically—the inference that the welfare of members of the coalition declines as the coalition gets bigger up to some turning point, after which further increases in coalition size lead to improvement

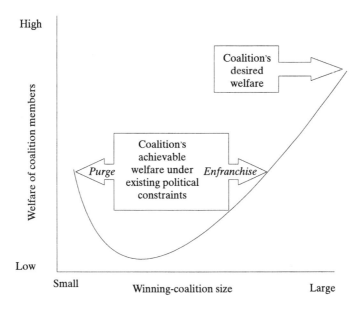

Figure 8.1
To purge or to enfranchise: alternative solutions to improving the coalition's welfare

in the members' welfare. A curve describing the expected association between the welfare of members of the winning coalition and increases in the size of that group was depicted earlier and is reproduced here, annotated with additional information, as figure 8.1. The curve shown in this figure looks very much like a check mark or a swoosh. Figure 4.2 provided evidence that the empirical record yields results very much in line with the shape of this curve.

What can we infer about institutional preferences among members of the winning coalition, given the above implications of the theory? Of course, no one in the winning coalition supports the idea that the coalition should get smaller at his or her expense, though each member might favor a reduction in its size as long as she or he continues to be a member. Obviously, the same holds true for any expansion of the coalition.

The coalition's interests can be broadly interpreted in terms of common regime types. Our results suggest that members of the coalition, like forward-looking members of the selectorate, prefer monarchy, junta, or democracy to autocracy because of differences in their typical coalition and selectorate size. In a monarchy or junta, both the coalition and the selectorate are small. When the winning coalition is sufficiently small—that is, to the left of the low point on the welfare function drawn in figure 8.1—it is contrary to the interests of its members to pursue a modest expansion of the coalition. A small expansion only dilutes each member's rewards. Hence in monarchies, we should expect, at least initially, that the court and the king share a common goal of restricting the size of the court. In a junta, the military officers in charge are loath to bring in new officers. Perhaps this is why common perception indicates that coups are more likely to be led by colonels than generals.

If the winning coalition can be expanded beyond a threshold size—that is, to the right of the low point on the welfare function in figure 8.1—its members prefer further coalition expansion, while the king or general does not. As a monarchy or junta becomes more inclusive, a wedge is driven between the leader and her supporters. The queen, king, colonel, or general continues to prefer a small winning coalition while the court, or lower-rank military, with its members' share of private goods already diluted, can prefer to push for additional expansion in the winning coalition to force the incumbent leader to work harder on their behalf. Numerous studies of economic history support the effects on transitions from monarchy to more democratic forms suggested here (Moore 1966; North and Weingast 1989; Tilly 1990; Root 1994; Bates et al. 1998). We examine empirically whether the details of the theoretical expectations are borne out in a later section of this chapter, when our focus turns from preferences to actions.

Leader's Institutional Preference

Recall that the incumbent leader receives a payoff equal to the value she attaches to holding office plus the difference between revenue and expenditure ($\Psi + R - M$) for each period she survives in office and she receives 0 if she is deposed. The incumbent's welfare improves as resources (R) increase and as nondiscretionary expenditures (M) decrease. Expenditures decrease when the coalition is small and the selectorate is large because of the strong loyalty norm. These factors reveal the institutional preferences held by leaders. Leaders prefer to have a small winning coalition and a large selectorate. The importance that such institutional arrangements place on private goods induces a strong loyalty norm. In common parlance, leaders most prefer autocratic regimes with universal suffrage (implying rigged elections). Universal suffrage is a way of signaling that almost anyone could, with a very low probability, make it into a winning coalition. Thus, among the obscure peasantry or laboring class of the old Soviet Union, a Stalin, a Khrushchev, a Brezhnev, and a Gorbachev were the very lucky few who could and did rise from their nondescript beginnings to elite status. They turned out to have the special proficiencies that warranted giving them membership in the Communist Party. From within that relatively small circle, they emerged not only to be in the winning coalition, but as figures capable of competing for and even winning the top leadership positions. The large selectorate, combined with a small coalition (and rigged elections), ensures that a small, elite group gets to share the valuable private goods that the leader dispenses. These two conditions increase the strength of the loyalty norm that keeps autocrats in office for long periods, as we saw in chapter 7. Thus, leaders do not want to rule over a large coalition if they can avoid it. Neither do they desire monarchy or junta, each of which has a weak loyalty norm as compared to a rigged-election autocracy.

Summary of Institutional Preferences

The disenfranchised strongly prefer a large-coalition, large-selectorate system such as is common in democracy. Members of the selectorate who are not currently in the winning coalition may share this preference, though probably not as strongly. How strongly depends on whether they are living in a system that already has a relatively weak loyalty norm, as in a monarchy, or in a system with a strong loyalty norm, as in an autocracy. If the loyalty norm is strong, selectorate members have a poor prospect of getting access to private goods and so more strongly favor a shift to a large-coalition system or a shift to a new leader, who will turn to them to participate in a new coalition. If, however, the existing loyalty norm is already fairly weak, members of the selectorate have a good chance of gaining access to private goods and so are less inclined to switch to a larger-coalition system. Those in the winning coalition would like to weaken the loyalty norm by increasing W/S. Decreasing the selectorate is always in the coalition's interest. Whether the members prefer to increase or decrease W depends on the current size of the coalition and other factors. Their preference is tied to increasing their welfare, and their welfare changes in a nonlinear, nonmonotonic fashion as coalition size increases. Leaders, like the disenfranchised, have a straightforward view of the world. The disenfranchised want to reduce S and increase W. The leadership wants to increase S and decrease W. That is, the leadership wants autocracy.

Now that we have identified what the selectorate theory suggests about endogenously induced preferences over institutional arrangements, we turn to how these preferences can be prevented from being put in place by countermeasures.

Oppression

The soldan of EGYPT, or the emperor of ROME, might drive his harmless subjects, like brute beasts, against their sentiments and inclination: But he must, at least, have led his mamalukes, or praetorian bands, like men, by their opinion.
—David Hume, "On the First Principles of Government"

Repression is . . . like making love—it is always easier the second time.
—Lee Kwan Yew, quoted in Minchin 1990, 285

There is no doubt that selection institutions change from time to time. There is also no doubt that these institutional conditions remain unaltered within a polity most of the time. Since different segments of any country's population have different preferences over selection institutions, we know that there are always people in a society who, given free reign, would rather change how leaders are chosen. This means that there also must always be others who would rather block such changes in order to preserve their personal benefits from current arrangements. Indeed, every society adopts methods of preventing the existence of free reign over institution selection. Such free reign is part of what Hobbes had in mind when he described the state of nature. Some societies erect orderly methods of change that revolve around the rule of law and focus specifically on amending constitutions. In other societies, a common means of preventing alterations in selection institutions is by oppressing those who are dissatisfied with current arrangements.

The oppression of political opposition is all too common in many political systems. The worst cases of violence by a government against its domestic opponents or prospective opponents—the crimes of Maximilien Robespierre, Idi Amin, Mobutu Sese Seko, Mao Zedong, Adolf Hitler, Pol Pot, Joseph Stalin, and so many others—are well known.

Stalin's use of torture against putative "enemies of the people" is described vividly by Nikita Khrushchev in his secret speech to the Twentieth Party Congress of the Communist Party of the Soviet Union:

> Stalin originated the concept "enemy of the people." This term automatically rendered it unnecessary that the ideological errors of a man or men engaged in a controversy be proven; this term made possible the usage of the most cruel repression, violating all norms of revolutionary legality, against anyone who in any way disagreed with Stalin, against those who were only suspected of hostile intent, against those who had bad reputations. This concept "enemy of the people" actually eliminated the possibility of any kind of ideological fight or the making of one's views known on this or that issue, even those of a practical character. In the main, and in actuality, the only proof of guilt used, against all norms of current legal science, was the "confession" of the accused himself; and, as subsequent probing proved, "confessions" were acquired through physical pressures against the accused. This led to glaring violations of revolutionary legality and to the fact that many entirely innocent persons, who in the past had defended the party line, became victims. We must assert that, in regard to those persons who in their time had opposed the party line, there were often no sufficiently serious reasons for their physical annihilation. The formula "enemy of the people" was specifically introduced for the purpose of physically annihilating such individuals. (Nikita Khrushchev, *Crimes of the Stalin Era*, Special Report to the Twentieth Congress of the Communist Party of the Soviet Union, Closed Session, February 24–25, 1956)

Opponents of the leader suffer punishments ranging from confiscation of their wealth and imprisonment, to torture and execution. Oppression need not be brutal to be effective. Sometimes the threat of exclusion from private benefits in the future is enough to deter defections from the winning coalition. The Soviet scholar and government advisor Georgi Arbatov (1992, 86) makes this point in plain terms: "Privileges have been an effective instrument for the maintenance of totalitarian rule ever since the revolution. The very existence of privileges brought along the fear that they could be lost and that your living standard could decline radically." Now we turn to what our theory says about the occurrence, magnitude, and intensity of oppression.

Leaders, of course, oppress opponents to deter threats to their leadership. Although political oppression is commonly thought of as a single phenomenon, there are three separate targets and reasons for oppression in our theory. First, leaders may seek to punish challengers. If successful, a leader would not face challenges to her rule because rivals would be unwilling to run the risk of suffering the punishment if their challenges failed to displace the current leader. Second, leaders may seek to punish members of the selectorate who support a challenger. If successful, challengers would be unable to garner sufficient support to unseat the leader. Third, leaders may seek to punish the disenfranchised who might be engaged in revolutionary action against the regime. If repression is successful, a revolution could not be organized, removing this threat to the leader from outside the selectorate.

Four Questions

We use our theory to explain each type of oppression and to explain when we should expect leaders to engage in each type. Our argument allows us to differentiate oppression against the disenfranchised from oppression of defectors within the selectorate. As with our discussion of leader tenure, we do not present a formal model of oppression. Instead, we use the results already derived from the theory to discuss the motivation behind oppression, who leaders target, and what systems make oppression a useful tool for leaders seeking to retain their position.

We ask four related questions. First, when is oppression useful in deterring challengers and their supporters? Second, when do leaders have the most interest in using oppression to hold onto power? Third, when can leaders recruit those who will carry out the oppressive measures against opponents? Fourth, when is oppression likely to succeed in deterring challenges? The answers to these four questions lay out how oppression should vary according to our theory.

Potential challengers consider the benefits of coming to power and weigh them against the risk and the consequences of failure. Oppression is intended to deter challengers by raising the costs of failure for unsuccessful opponents. To restore deterrence, the intensity of oppression should increase with the gains a challenger can expect if he succeeds in becoming a leader. By *intensity* we mean just how horrible the reprisals are that failed challengers must endure. The more benefits a leader receives compared to her winning coalition and selectorate, the more tempting it is for someone to challenge her for power. Similarly, the greater the difference between the leader's payoff and the payoff to her followers and selectors, the greater the *magnitude* of oppression—that is, the more widespread the terror is among the winning coalition and selectorate.

The answer to our first question focuses on what systems produce the greatest difference between the leader's payoff and the payoffs of the selectorate and winning coalition. As chapters 3 and 4 demonstrated, this difference declines as the size of the winning coalition grows and increases as the size of the selectorate expands. Small winning coalitions lead to a focus on the provision of private goods to the winning coalition, allowing the leader to retain more resources for her own purposes. Increasing the selectorate in a system with a small winning coalition strengthens the loyalty norm, allowing the leader to reduce the private goods provided to her winning coalition, thereby increasing her own resources. Authoritarian systems, those with small winning coalitions and large selectorates, should then engage in the most brutal and extensive oppression of prospective challengers.

Members of the leader's winning coalition pose a special case of the argument above. A successful challenge requires the defection of enough members from the incumbent's winning coalition to reduce it below W. A challenger drawn from within the current winning coalition is particularly dangerous because his coalition begins with one member of the winning coalition, himself. Leaders should more fiercely oppress members of their own winning coalition who lead challenges than other challengers. After all, those close to the throne are the biggest threat to the leader. As Machiavelli aptly advised in *The Prince*,

> Friendships that are obtained by payments, and not by greatness or nobility of mind, may indeed be earned, but they are not secured, and in time of need cannot be relied upon; and men have less scruple in offending one who is beloved than one who is feared, for love is preserved by the link of obligation which, owing to the baseness of men, is broken at every opportunity for their advantage; but fear preserved you by a dread of punishment which never fails. (*The Prince*; Machiavelli [1515] 1948, chap. 17, pp. 130–131).

Challengers need supporters to come to power, and so leaders may use oppression to deter selectors from joining the nascent coalition supporting a challenger. The model analyzed the incentives of members of the leader's winning coalition to defect to the challenger. Members of the selectorate outside the winning coalition are always willing to support the challenger in the model because his challenge offers some hope of entering the winning coalition. Leaders can use oppression to discourage this source of support for the challenger. The intensity and magnitude of oppression of the selectorate should rise as the prospect of joining the winning coalition becomes more attractive to selectors. That is, a leader has the greatest incentive to oppress selectors when the selectors stand to gain the most from unseating her. Since the difference in welfare between selectors inside and outside the coalition is equivalent to the value of private goods, the leader's incentive to oppress the selectorate is highest when institutions promote high levels of private goods, namely, small-W systems, particularly those with small S. Hence oppression of the selectorate should be more common in juntas and monarchies than in rigged-election autocracies and democracies.

Leaders also use oppression to stop revolutionary movements from arising within the ranks of the disenfranchised. As discussed later in this chapter, revolutions hold out the prospect that members of the disenfranchised can improve their lot by overthrowing the system. They have the promise of both increasing public goods through the expansion of the winning coalition and the possibility of joining the winning coalition in a new system. Often that promise is not realized even when the revolution succeeds, as we explain below. The disenfranchised have the greatest incentive to join a revolutionary movement when the system provides few public goods—that is, when the winning coalition is small regardless of the size of the selectorate. Autocracies and monarchies both have the motivation to suppress rebellion violently.

Our first question about when oppression is useful for deterrence is now answered. The motivation to mount or join a challenge to the leader increases as the size of the winning coalition shrinks and the size of the selectorate expands. The motivation to join a revolution increases as the size of the winning coalition shrinks. The value of oppression as a deterrent increases as these motivations increase.

The second question is the reverse of the first: When do leaders have the incentive to use any means to hold onto power? Political systems dispose of removed leaders in different ways. Democracies generally accept former leaders as revered figures, while autocracies often execute former leaders. Exile and imprisonment seem most common in monarchies and oligarchies. The leader of a large winning-coalition system returns to the selectorate or possibly even the winning coalition if her party continues to hold power after she leaves office. Because large winning-coalition systems provide primarily public goods and allow the leader to retain only a small amount of resources for her own use, the difference between being the leader and being ousted is small compared to other systems. Consequently, the motivation for democratic leaders to hold onto office through oppression is much weaker than in other systems.

Small winning-coalition systems create a substantial difference between the value of holding power and being ousted. An ousted leader in such systems will lose the resources she retains as leader and probably will lose any share of the private goods that the new leader will dispense. Even if a system with a small winning coalition allows a deposed leader to return to life as a member of the selectorate, the loss of resources is substantial and provides the leader with a strong motivation to hold office by all means available.

As noted above, small winning-coalition systems not only provide a strong incentive for leaders to oppress, they also strengthen this incentive by punishing removed leaders. In such systems, a deposed leader is a powerful prospective challenger to the new leader. The former leader has organized a winning coalition in the past and has proven her competence and affinity over time in office. The members of the former winning coalition constitute a natural base to launch a challenge against the new leader. Consequently, the new leader may see elimination, exile, or imprisonment of the old leader as a necessary step to defend his newly acquired position. In a large winning-coalition system, the loyalty norm is weak because leaders rely on their ability to provide public goods rather than private goods to hold office. Consequently, the removed leader has little advantage over other prospective challengers to the new leader, and the new leader has no particular reason to remove the former leader from the political scene. Our theory then also explains the fate of deposed leaders depending on the selection institutions of their system.

Successful oppression requires someone to carry it out. In 1979, Saddam Hussein personally participated in executions of purged members of the Ba'ath party and compelled his government ministers and top party members to join the firing squad by handing them pistols (Aburish 2000, 173; Makiya 1998, 72). In general, though, leaders do not carry out oppressive measures themselves. Nor could they when oppression is extensive, as it is expected to be in small winning-coalition systems. Widespread oppression requires the recruitment of a large number of people into the organs of repression. Kanan Makiya (1998, 32–39) estimates that in 1980, 677,000 Iraqis—about one in twenty—

were employed by the army, party militia, and the Ministry of the Interior in repression. Even a less extreme level of oppression requires a large number of people to carry it out; Fred Halliday (1979, 76–84) estimates that the regime of the Shah of Iran employed 100,000 to 130,000 people between SAVAK and the Imperial Iranian Gendarmerie in the 1970s.

The third question about oppression concerns the ability of the leader to recruit people to carry out repressive punishments. As with the answers to the first two questions, differences in payoffs drive the willingness to carry out oppression. The foot soldiers of oppression are more willing to do what it takes to protect the leader when they benefit from her rule. Members of the winning coalition are obvious recruits because they have an interest in protecting their position, so as to continue to collect private goods. Again, the incentive of the winning coalition to protect the leader is greatest in small winning-coalition, large-selectorate systems. Members of the winning coalition should be willing to oppress any source of opposition to the leader, whether it emanates from a challenger, the selectorate, or a revolution from among the disenfranchised. This observation suggests why the military and secret police—the main organs of oppression—are key members of winning coalitions in autocracies.

Members of the selectorate who benefit from the current system of selection institutions may be willing to participate in oppression against the disenfranchised even if they do not benefit specifically from the current leader. The system favors members of the selectorate in the long run if they have a good chance of inclusion in the future winning coalition of a new leader, and the system provides substantial private goods to members of the winning coalition. That is, selectorate members have heightened incentives to protect the selection institutions when W/S is large and W is small, as in monarchy or military junta.[2] Members of the selectorate are willing to assist in the suppression of revolution in systems with a small winning coalition and a small selectorate. Authoritarian systems, on the other hand, must rely on the winning coalition to suppress revolution because most members of the selectorate are unlikely to benefit from the current system, and so will not fight hard to preserve it.

Finding people who will punish challengers from within the winning coalition poses a particular problem for the leader. Members of the winning coalition have an interest in punishing would-be defectors, although they also benefit from the existence of credible challengers to the leader. The leader provides private goods to her followers to prevent them from defecting to a challenger. If oppression succeeds in deterring all possible challengers, the leader need not provide private goods to her coalition's members. A leader could remove this dilemma from the mind of the members of her winning coalition. She could recruit members of the selectorate who are outside the winning coalition to punish challengers from within the coalition. Participation by selectorate members in this oppression could be their ticket to promotion into the winning coalition. In systems with small winning coalitions and large selectorates, this tactic could remove any reluctance that members of the winning coalition would have in punishing their fellow members.

Democratic leaders should find it difficult to recruit individuals willing to oppress fellow citizens because the benefits of being an insider are slight compared to the benefits in other types of systems. Given the higher rates of turnover in systems with large winning coalitions, supporters of a defeated leader can look ahead to having a good chance of coming back into power later, further reducing the cost of losing power.

Our fourth and last question concerned the credibility of oppression. Oppression is a punishment strategy; it attempts to deter challenges by punishing those involved in them after they are discovered. The credibility of such threats depends in part on the leader's ability to retain office in the face of a challenge. The threat to punish challengers and defectors after they fail to take power is less effective when the targets of such threats know that they have a good chance of succeeding and, thereby, avoiding the punishment. As we saw in chapter 7, leaders in small winning-coalition systems are more likely to survive in office over time, and their security increases as the selectorate expands (holding the size of the winning coalition constant). Then oppression is attractive to authoritarian leaders because prospective challengers and their supporters find that the threat of oppression is more credible coming from them than from democratic leaders. As with the three previous questions, a small winning coalition and a large selectorate is the pattern most conducive to effective oppression.

Credible oppression also needs to be targeted at opponents of the leader. Random oppression cannot succeed in deterring challenges because there is no connection between opposing the government and suffering the punishment. Even massacres and other atrocities designed to intimidate a civilian population during a revolutionary movement target populations believed to favor the rebels. If government forces could separate the supporters of the rebels from the civilian population, they would not kill the local population that does not support the rebels. Unfortunately, one way a leader can enhance the credibility of her oppressive threats is to kill anyone suspected of opposing the leader, albeit at the cost of provoking further opposition.

Punishment strategies are most effective at deterring action when the acts to be deterred can be observed, so that the link between violation—here supporting a challenge—and the punishment is clear. Understandably, then, leaders seek to determine who is supporting a challenger even before the challenge occurs. However, not all challenges can be discovered before they come into play. Challenges to authoritarian leaders are typically secret precisely to avoid punishment before the challenge is made. Democracies use secret ballots in part to prevent politicians from identifying and punishing those who vote against them.[3] Attempts to suppress voting through violence in transitional democracies tend to concentrate on districts that vote heavily for one candidate.

In summary, systems with a small winning coalition and a large selectorate encourage oppression, both in intensity and magnitude. Such systems present a greater incentive to challenge the leader, a greater incentive for the leader to hang onto power by all possible means, a greater ability to recruit those who will carry out the threats, and greater credibility because of the longer tenure of their leaders. Frequency and intensity of oppressive measures should be strongest against members of the winning coalition because they pose the most direct threat to the leader. The oppressors are most likely to be members of the winning coalition or members of the selectorate seeking to be promoted into the winning coalition. Other members of the selectorate are also willing to join in the suppression of revolution in systems with a small winning coalition and small selectorate. Oppression is unattractive to democratic leaders because the benefits of holding leadership and the costs of losing leadership are not as great as in other systems. Furthermore, in these large-W, large-S systems, leaders cannot readily recruit followers to carry out the repression.

Some Suggestive Evidence

One death is a tragedy; a million deaths is a statistic.
—Joseph Stalin

Stalin clearly preferred statistics to tragedy. His regime killed millions of its own citizens, prominent and obscure. Soviet citizens were killed by starvation, by firing squad, and by being worked to death in the Gulag. Ukrainians were killed when they resisted the collectivization of agriculture, Tartars were killed for supporting the Nazis during World War II, and top party members and army leaders were killed for the slightest suspicion that they sought to overthrow Stalin himself. No one was above suspicion, although some lucky ones may have been below it.

Not all the mass murder of the Stalinist regime falls into oppression as we conceive it. Of the three great waves of death that crossed the Soviet Union under Stalin, only the Great Terror of 1936–1938—when those perceived to be disloyal in the party and army were liquidated— is a clear example of oppression to protect the leader. The Great Famine of 1930–1931 in the Ukraine sought to crack the power of small land-holders, and the mass killings of Soviet citizens by the Soviet state during the Second World War both punished elements believed to support the Nazi invaders and motivated soldiers to fight by presenting them with the horrible choice of the guns of Germans in front of them and the guns of the NKVD behind them. Our theory does not attempt to explain all mass murder committed by governments; the Holocaust for one lies outside the scope of our theory because the Jews, gypsies, homosexuals, and other minorities slaughtered posed no threat to the Nazi regime. This is not to suggest that genocide is somehow less objectionable than killing to oppress or vice versa, merely that our theory does not seek to explain nor can it explain genocide against those who pose no threat to the regime.[4]

Historians disagree about how many died during the Great Terror in 1936–1938. The "totalitarians" argue that the number was in the range of 5 to 20 million (Conquest 1990; Rummel 1990); the "revisionists" maintain that the death toll lay between 1.5 and 3 million (Thurston 1996).[5] Both sides do agree that the Terror fell hardest on the top levels of the party and the army, key components of Stalin's winning coalition:

"The most vulnerable groups were the party elite, former oppositionists, high-ranking economic officials, and military officers" (Freeze 1997, 315). In 1934, 139 new members were elected to the Central Committee of the Communist Party; by the Seventeenth Party Congress in 1939, 114 of those new members had been executed or sent to the Gulag (Thurston 1996, 68).[6] Similarly, of the 1,966 delegates who attended the party congress in 1934, only 59 were alive to attend the next party congress in 1939 (Rummel 1990). The purge eliminated 36 percent of party members (Rummel 1990) and 35 percent of the officer corps (Freeze 1997, 322). Still, the ranks of the Communist Party were quickly filled and even expanded after the purge; there were about 2.4 million members of the party before the purge and 3.8 million in 1941, three years after the end of the purge.[7] Individuals also moved up to high positions based on their willingness to kill others; Lavrenti Beria rose to the head of Internal Security because he carried out the orders to eliminate Nikolai Yezhov, who had led the purge up to that time. The Great Terror then conforms with our expectations of oppression within the winning coalition.

The Cultural Revolution purged the Chinese Communist Party to enable Mao to restore his own clear leadership over China and the party and to maintain control over the choice of his successor. Although the Cultural Revolution neither claimed as many victims as the Great Terror, nor were most killed, its toll too fell hardest on the highest ranks of the party. Of the twenty-three members of the Politburo before the Cultural Revolution, fourteen were dropped from it by the Ninth Congress of the Chinese Communist Party in 1969 (Harding 1997, 242–245).

These well-known cases of the most extreme physical oppression overshadow less widely noted but still effective means of suppressing opposition. By way of illustration, consider the case of Singapore under Lee Kwan Yew, generally and correctly regarded as a mostly progressive, even visionary leader.

Lee Kwan Yew's Singapore was in many ways a model society. There is no reason to believe that the leadership used its discretion to steal from the people. Rather, Singapore enjoys an exceptionally good reputation for low levels of corruption. The government seems to have actively pursued policies designed to promote broad welfare, such as public housing, as discussed in chapter 2. Yet Singapore stands out among the polities with low corruption and high per capita income for its poor respect for civil liberties. While virtually all of its economic equals score the maximum (7) on the Freedom House seven-point civil liberties scale discussed in chapter 5, Singapore has not earned more than a 4 or less than a 3, placing it squarely among societies that are not strongly committed to civil freedoms. Singapore's economic equals also tend to have strongly competitive democratic governments, while it typically operates as essentially a one-party state.

Singapore's government has used a combination of its Internal Security Act and the legal system to repress and intimidate political opponents. The Internal Security Act allows the government to detain individuals for up to two years without charges. Lawsuits for libel can be brought against opponents in Singapore's parliament because there is no legal protection for parliamentary debate. Under British law, on which Singapore's legal code is modeled, defendants have to prove their statements were true to successfully defend themselves against a libel suit (Perry, Kong, and Yeoh 1997, 62–67). Legal punishment of political opponents has occurred repeatedly in Singapore. The courts in Singapore disbarred J. B. Jeyaretam, leader of the Workers Party, on minor charges that were dismissed but later restored by a higher court. Lee Siew Choh and Francis Seow were banned from seats in Parliament because both faced charges of income tax fraud (Minchin 1990, 219, 339).[8] Seow was later detained for months under the Internal Security Act, and then published in exile a book about his detention (Seow 1994). Clearly this is a "better" form of oppression than the annihilation used by Stalin, but still it is a strong signal to keep opposition to oneself. Weak civil liberties allow governments to get away with such measures. When the press, speech, and assembly are free, government finds it much more difficult to use oppression to quash opposition.

Cross-National Evidence on Oppression

Actual governmental oppression of opponents is difficult to observe in a systematic way. Most people change their behavior in response to the expectation that they will be made to pay a heavy price for opposing the government. A few severe demonstrations of the government's willingness to use extreme punishment often are sufficient to deter opponents from giving voice to their discontent, resulting in a diminution in observed oppression as a result of rational expectations. Later we will see systematic evidence regarding the deterrent effects of the expectation of oppression. Now we turn to a systematic analysis of available data regarding the actual use of oppression by governments against their own citizens. This analysis allows us to test the hypotheses that follow from the selectorate theory regarding the association between selection institutions and the magnitude and intensity of oppression. The analysis presumably underestimates the true relationship between oppression and small-coalition/large-selectorate systems because of the deterrent effect of rational expectations.

Steven C. Poe, C. Neal Tate, and Linda Camp Keith (1999; also see Poe and Tate 1994) analyze a data set of government oppression from 1976 to 1993 (<http://www.psci.unt.edu/ihrsc/poetate.htm>). They collect data based on reports by Amnesty International and the U.S. Department of State on human rights abuses coded on a five-point scale. A score of 1 indicates a country in which political imprisonment, torture, and murders are extremely rare. These are countries in which the government almost never oppresses political opponents. Countries that score 2 infrequently imprison people for nonviolent political activity, with torture and beatings being exceptional and political murders being rare. A score of 3 indicates a country where political detention without trial or execution of political opponents is accepted and common; a score of 4 denotes countries in which the practices denoted for level 3 encompass a large number of people and in which murders and disappearances are a common part of life; a score of 5 indicates a country where such practices are imposed on the whole population for political reasons.[9] Examples of countries that score 1 in the data of Poe and colleagues are Costa Rica, Japan, and New Zealand. Examples of scores of 5 are Sri Lanka in 1989 and 1990, a particularly bloody period in the war against the Tamil Tigers, and Bosnia in 1992 and 1993. This data collection provides us with a means of testing hypotheses about oppression on a wide sample of countries.[10]

Poe, Tate, and Keith (1999) perform a time-series, cross-section analysis of the data including a range of variables. Briefly, they find that democracy reduces human rights abuses, larger population worsens them, higher per capita GNP reduces them, and war—both civil and international—exacerbates such oppression. Here we reanalyze their data with our measures of the size of the winning coalition and W/S to test our hypotheses on oppression. Table 8.1 presents the results of our analysis using the scores of human rights abuses drawn from reports by Amnesty International; table 8.2 gives the results using the scores from reports by the U.S. Department of State.

Table 8.1
How oppression varies with selection institutions: amnesty international scores of abuses of human rights

Variable	Model 1	Model 2	Model 3	Model 4
W	−1.41, −18.81, 0.000		−1.36, −17.08, 0.000	−1.30, −15.70, 0.000
W/S		−1.37, −17.01, 0.000		
Log(Pop)		0.20, 15.79, 0.000	0.20, 16.06, 0.000	0.20, 14.47, 0.000
WS: Income		−0.22, −10.51, 0.000	−0.22, −10.36, 0.000	−0.24, −11.02, 0.000
WS:DemRes				−0.78, −7.40, 0.000
Summary statistics	$N = 2{,}754$ F.E. = 126 $R^2 = 0.17$	$N = 1{,}851$ F.E. = 116 $R^2 = 0.33$	$N = 1{,}851$ F.E. = 116 $R^2 = 0.34$	$N = 1{,}726$ F.E. = 116 $R^2 = 0.32$

Note: All cell entries for the variables are estimated coefficient, *t*-statistic, and significance probability. The last row gives the summary statistics of each model.

Table 8.2
How oppression varies with selection institutions: U.S. State Department scores of abuses of human rights

Variable	Model 1	Model 2	Model 3	Model 4
W	−1.55, −21.11, 0.000		−1.36, −18.27, 0.000	−1.32, −17.43, 0.000
W/S		−1.36, −18.10, 0.000		
Log(Pop)		0.156, 13.48, 0.000	0.16, 13.75, 0.000	0.16, 12.67, 0.000
WS: Income		−0.23, −11.79, 0.000	−0.23, −11.57, 0.000	−0.25, −12.40, 0.000
WS:DemRes				−0.95, −9.85, 0.000
Summary statistics	$N = 2{,}754$ F.E. = 126 $R^2 = 0.18$	$N = 1{,}851$ F.E. = 116 $R^2 = 0.35$	$N = 1{,}851$ F.E. = 116 $R^2 = 0.35$	$N = 1{,}726$ F.E. = 116 $R^2 = 0.35$

Note: All cell entries for the variables are estimated coefficient, *t*-statistic, and significance probability. The last row gives the summary statistics of each model.

The results are consistent across all the models in tables 8.1 and 8.2. Systems with large winning coalitions engage in substantially less oppression than those with small winning coalitions. Respect for human rights is common in systems with large winning coalitions; oppression of political opponents is common in systems with small winning coalitions. It is interesting that the residual of democracy after removing the effects of selection institutions (*WS:DemRes*) reduces the level of human rights abuses. Recalling our discussion in chapter 4 of how our measure of *W* differs from common measures of democracy, the principal difference lies in the large role that executive constraints (*XCONST*) play in the

Table 8.3
How selection institutions change oppression over time: Amnesty International scores of abuses of human rights

Variable	Model 1	Model 2	Model 3	Model 4
W	−0.33, −6.45, 0.000		−0.47, −7.21, 0.000	−0.44, −6.45, 0.000
W/S		−0.47, −7.16, 0.000		
Log(Pop)		0.069, 7.01, 0.000	0.070, 7.11, 0.000	0.07, 6.48, 0.000
WS: Income		−0.09, −5.21, 0.000	−0.084, −5.16, 0.000	−0.087, −5.11, 0.000
WS:DemRes				−0.23, −2.88, 0.004
Lagged Abuse	0.77, 61.86, 0.000	0.67, 39.97, 0.000	0.66, 36.96, 0.000	0.665, 35.25, 0.000
Constant	0.74, 14.81, 0.000	0.50, 4.88, 0.000	0.48, 4.82, 0.000	0.44, 3.97, 0.000
Summary statistics	$N = 2,564$ F.E. = 119 $R^2 = 0.72$	$N = 1,736$ F.E. = 109 $R^2 = 0.71$	$N = 1,736$ F.E. = 109 $R^2 = 0.71$	$N = 1,620$ F.E. = 109 $R^2 = 0.71$

Note: All cell entries for the variables are estimated coefficient, *t*-statistic, and significance probability. The last row gives the summary statistics of each model.

latter but not in the former. Human rights is an area where constraints on the executive play an additional role beyond the size of the winning coalition in constraining oppression by the leader. Higher income helps reduce abuses and larger population increases them, as was the case in Poe, Tate, and Keith's (1999) analysis of human rights.

Our second analysis of human rights abuses parallels Poe and colleagues' (1999) analysis. It examines the dynamics of such abuses by including a lagged dependent variable. Patterns of abuse tend to persist over time; including a lagged dependent variable allows us to see how abuse persists over time and what factors cause it to increase or decrease.[11] We rerun our four models on the data collected from Amnesty International and the U.S. State Department reports to see how selection institutions change the level of oppression over time. Tables 8.3 and 8.4 present the results of these analyses.

Again, the size of the winning coalition leads to a substantial reduction in human rights abuses over time. States with the maximum measure of *W* have their level of abuses drop a full level about every two years, compared with states with small winning coalitions, *W* = 0. Oppression tends to rise over time in small winning-coalition systems, while declining over time in large winning-coalition systems. This effect can be seen in the steady-state level of oppression that can be calculated from the

Table 8.4
How selection institutions change oppression over time: U.S. State Department scores of abuses of human rights

Variable	Model 1	Model 2	Model 3	Model 4
W	−0.34, −6.78, 0.000		−0.46, −7.62, 0.000	−0.47, −7.52, 0.000
W/S		−0.56, −7.48, 0.000		
Log(Pop)		0.05, 5.92, 0.000	0.05, 6.02, 0.000	0.06, 5.63, 0.000
WS: Income		−0.08, −5.22, 0.000	−0.08, −5.19, 0.000	−0.09, −5.56, 0.000
WS:DemRes				−0.26, −3.46, 0.001
Lagged Abuse	0.67, 6.78, 0.000	0.68, 38.73, 0.000	0.69, 38.70, 0.000	0.67, 35.90, 0.000
Constant	0.67, 13.89, 0.000	0.51, 5.43, 0.000	0.51, 5.43, 0.000	0.51, 4.98, 0.000
Summary statistics	$N = 2,564$ F.E. = 119, $R^2 = 0.72$	$N = 1,736$ F.E. = 109 $R^2 = 0.72$	$N = 1,736$ F.E. = 109 $R^2 = 0.72$	$N = 1,620$ F.E. = 109 $R^2 = 0.72$

Note: All cell entries for the variables are estimated coefficient, *t*-statistic, and significance probability. The last row gives the summary statistics of each model.

estimates above for different values of W. When the level of oppression is higher than the steady-state level, it will tend to decline over time; when oppression is lower, it tends to rise over time. Using model 1 from tables 8.3 and 8.4, the steady-state level of oppression in a system with $W = 0$ is 3.72 for the Amnesty International scores and 3.62 for the U.S. State Department scores. For a system with $W = 1$, the steady-state levels of oppression are 1.92 for Amnesty International scores and 1.58 for U.S. State Department scores.[12] Again, large winning-coalition systems reduce oppression over time, while small winning coalitions increase it over time.

We have now laid out our argument regarding preferences over selection institutions and preferences over the use, targets, and agents of oppression. We have shown that the actions taken by regimes to oppress opposition are consistent with the predictions derived from the selectorate theory. The remainder of the investigation in this chapter focuses on specific actions taken by those who want to alter selection institutions. We associate those actions with the group or groups most likely to pursue them in search of fulfillment of their preferences and in search of the means to prevent changes in the institutions of leadership selection. In these analyses we turn from ex post measures of realized oppression (that is, the measures used by Poe and colleagues) to ex ante indicators of the degree to which oppression was expected as a means of countering efforts to change selection institutions. By investigating actions and expected counteractions we see what the expected endogenous institutional choices are likely to be.

Political Actions to Alter Institutions

People can act in one of three basic ways to improve the match between their institutional preferences and their institutional experience. They can try to alter the institutions where they live. This can be done through mechanisms ranging from the relatively benign to the extremely aggressive. For instance, institutions can be altered through such peaceful means as constitutional amendments on up through such aggressive measures as revolution, assassination, or coup d'état. Alternatively, people discontent with the institutional arrangements can migrate to another country with a winning coalition and selectorate more in line with their preferences. Finally, individuals can be disgruntled about their *institutions* but take no action, showing patience while they wait for circumstances to change and improve their lot. We begin this part of our empirical investigation by looking at who is most likely to follow an exit strategy, choosing to migrate. Then we discuss antigovernment activities, including demonstrations, strikes, riots and even revolutions and civil wars.

The sections that follow lay out the argument regarding specific actions and anticipated counteractions and then, where possible, provide systematic tests of the theory's implications. Before making our way through the details behind the actions and countermeasures of interest, we briefly summarize the linkage between our earlier discussion of institutional preferences and the action expected for each of the four sectors of the population: the disenfranchised, members of the selectorate, members of the winning coalition, and leaders.

The disenfranchised and to a lesser extent the selectorate are most likely to become immigrants in a new land. Failing that, they are also the groups most inclined to engage in antigovernment actions, including demonstrations, strikes, riots, civil war, and even revolution. The desired consequence of these actions is to increase the extent to which these groups gain access first to public goods and, with luck, later also to private benefits. Members of the existing winning coalition are unlikely to try to improve their lot through any of the means just mentioned. Instead, winning-coalition members can benefit institutionally through coups d'état.[13] For them, the desired consequence is to weaken the loyalty norm by increasing the ratio of W/S. This means that coups are expected to result in movement away from autocracy and toward either democracy or junta/monarchy, with the movement increasing the size of W relative to S. This can be achieved by shrinking the selectorate faster than the coalition or by increasing the coalition faster than the selectorate. Thus, when they follow coups, purges—by which we mean the removal of coalition members and/or selectorate members—are expected to fall disproportionately on the shoulders of selectorate members. Incumbent leaders are especially likely to favor purging members of their own winning coalition, using exogenous circumstances like financial crises or foreign threats and the like to justify a realignment of their government. We discuss purges at greater length below. Realignments instigated by leaders can be expected to shift the society toward a strong loyalty norm and a small coalition relative to the selectorate. Furthermore, leaders and coalition members in small-coalition systems are—as we have seen—particularly likely to engage in actions that oppress their opponents, as well as to engage in policies that signal the expectation that opposition to government will result in oppression. The latter policies, examined empirically later in this chapter, are intended to suppress opposition before it arises.

Population Migration: The Disenfranchised and the Selectorate

The preference for large-W, large-S systems among those outside the winning coalition carries implications concerning regime changes and political choices. It is one thing to prefer a large-coalition system and quite another to convert that preference into reality. What can the disenfranchised or those excluded from the winning coalition do to improve their welfare?

The selectorate theory leads directly to predictions about the behavior of members of these two groups, behavior designed to improve their welfare. What they do to improve their welfare depends on whether they adopt an exit strategy, give voice to their desires, or display loyalty to the existing regime.

Exit from a bad circumstance—that is, from a polity that produces private goods to which those outside the winning coalition have no access—can be achieved by migrating from resource-poor and public-goods-poor polities to resource-rich societies that produce many public goods. In other words, emigration is expected from poor societies to rich societies—no surprise there—and especially from small-coalition systems (autocracies) to large-coalition systems (democracies).

Immigration, of course, has consequences for the society receiving newcomers. Migration patterns, for instance, can help reinforce increases in coalition size once the new arrivals gain the franchise, helping to reinforce public-goods production. After all, as immigrants become enfranchised, they become members of the selectorate, thereby increasing its size by whatever their numbers are in the population. If the now-enfranchised former outsiders moved to a representative, large-coalition system, they also expand the size of the winning coalition because representativeness implies that the coalition's size is a proportion of the selectorate. Thus, in representative political systems with low barriers for enfranchising immigrants, like the United States, immigrants become a stimulus for greater public-goods provision. In large-coalition societies, like Japan, in which barriers to naturalization make acquiring citizenship difficult, this additional emphasis on more public-goods production is absent because immigrants rarely become members of the selectorate or the coalition. This suggests that, relative to their resource base, these societies are somewhat more likely to experience corruption or other forms of private-goods provision and less likely to experience large welfare payments to the disenfranchised than are their large-coalition counterparts who make enfranchisement easy.

Not everyone has the option of migrating to a new polity. The decision to emigrate is costly, and it can be made costlier if the polity does not permit emigration, as was true for many communist states between 1945 and the dissolution of the Soviet Union, and especially after the construction of the Berlin Wall, itself a remarkable symbol of barriers to emigration. Immigration is also made costly if the target country of the émigré's desires erects laws to keep newcomers out. Still, even in that case, the world consists of many countries, some of which are open to immigrants at any given time. Would-be émigrés with the requisite financial resources can generally find a suitable place that will take them in. Therefore, the barriers to emigration are harder to overcome than the barriers to immigration.

Personal financial costs are certainly an important impediment to emigration, as are emotional ties to one's home, family, and homeland. So too are some features of governance. These latter considerations involve government policies designed to restrict emigration. Although we cannot assess individual decisions, we can evaluate government policies that are indicative of high costs associated with emigration and that help sort out informational differences regarding emigration and immigration data. We begin the analysis of population migration, therefore, by considering biases in reporting these data. We then evaluate where émigrés go—that is, we examine patterns of immigration to see if exit strategies lead to entrance into polities that produce high volumes of public goods, as predicted by the selectorate theory. After completing the assessment of immigration, we turn to what people do when they do not have a viable option to become immigrants. At that point, we consider ways to estimate the political costs prospective émigrés might anticipate are associated with their efforts to leave their homeland. We also examine the actions people can take if they do not have the opportunity to leave their country for a polity with institutions closer to their preferred arrangement.

Biased Reporting

How does politics influence the decision to report population-migration data? Answering this question is important for two reasons. Evaluating reportage helps us gauge systematic bias in the data on immigration and emigration. Those biases reveal a great deal about how large-coalition and small-coalition polities differ. Additionally, we can extrapolate from such bias to think about means of measuring whether a given society is expected to impose high costs on emigration, perhaps with the hope that those costs will deter would-be emigrants. The latter factor is taken up at length when we discuss alternatives to emigration for those who seek to change the institutional conditions under which they live.

We construct two dummy variables that are coded 1 when data on immigration or emigration (Mitchell 1998a, 1998b) are reported by a government and 0 otherwise. These dummy variables are called *Immigration:Report* and *Emigration:Report*. The evidence strongly indicates that reportage on emigration and immigration is politically biased. As is seen in table 8.5, large-coalition systems are vastly more likely to report these data than are small-coalition systems, even after controlling for population size and real per capita income. The control variables take

Table 8.5
Biased reporting on immigration and emigration

	Immigration:Report Coefficient, (Std. Error), Prob.	Emigration:Report Coefficient, (Std. Error), Prob.
W	6.374, (1.759), 0.000	5.760, (1.498), 0.000
Log(Population)	1.911, (0.075), 0.000	1.491, (0.050), 0.000
Log(Income)	2.843, (0.171), 0.000	2.865, (0.167), 0.000
	$N = 4{,}245 \; x^2 = 1{,}478.30, p = 0.0000$	$N = 4{,}245 \; x^2 = 1{,}340.38, p = 0.0000$

into account two natural impediments to reporting population movement, namely, poverty and smallness of scale. In fact, an order-of-magnitude increase in population size makes a country nearly twice as likely to report immigration and about 50 percent more likely to report emigration. An order-of-magnitude increase in per capita income results in almost a threefold improvement in the odds of reporting population migration into and out of the country. These are significant effects, but their magnitude pales in comparison to the impact of coalition size on the likelihood of reporting population movement: the largest-coalition systems are more than five times more likely to report migration than are the smallest-coalition systems. Governments that depend on a small coalition appear to make a systematic choice to withhold information about people leaving or entering their society.

Also noteworthy with regard to the bias in reporting is that democracies are more likely to report population-migration data than are autocracies, but the difference is not as pronounced as it is for coalition size. Furthermore, the portion of democraticness not accounted for by W (i.e., $WS{:}DemRes$) manifests a reversal in the bias. That is, large-coalition systems are more likely to report population-migration data than are small-coalition systems, while those with a large democracy residual are somewhat less likely to report population migration.

The bias in reporting can be viewed still more carefully. We know large-coalition systems are especially likely to report emigration and immigration data. In fact, the mean coalition score (W) for those who report neither emigration nor immigration data is 0.43 ($N = 14{,}680$, standard deviation = 0.27), while for those who report both forms of population movement the average W is 0.69 ($N = 1{,}665$, standard deviation = 0.31). If immigration and emigration are reported more-or-less accurately, then on a global basis for every immigrant reported there should be an emigrant who also was reported. Yet the data do not show this.

For example, within the data reported in 1950 there is a huge discrepancy between those emigrating and those arriving. According to our data, within the set of countries who report immigration, about twice as many people arrived as new immigrants in 1950 as were reported to be emigrants in that year. This enormous discrepancy is not an isolated case.

To see the distortions in reportage, we focus on the post–World War II years. The mean and median global annual ratio of total reported emigrants to total reported immigrants in the post-1945 years equals only 0.65. That is, one-third of emigrants are unreported. Presumably, many of these are people who left their homeland illegally and so do not show up in normal reporting. The biases in the data must be kept in mind as we proceed to investigate migration patterns. Furthermore, biased reporting itself will prove useful as a means of evaluating some of the uglier behavior of governments toward their citizens.[14]

Immigration

The bias in reportage on population movement operates against our hypothesis that people become immigrants in countries that have a large winning-coalition. Because polities with a small coalition are much less likely to provide information on population immigration, the data suffer from truncation at the lower end of W. The very societies expected to receive the fewest immigrants fail to report on how many immigrants they do receive. Even with that truncation, however, and controlling for population, per capita income, and region-year fixed effects, still the impact of coalition size on the likelihood of attracting immigrants is significant ($t = 2.47$, $p = 0.014$, $N = 579$). The results show, as predicted, that immigration is greatest in countries with a large-coalition system— that is, polities that provide the most public goods. So robust is the attraction of a large-coalition system that the impact of W on immigration is undiminished by control for wealth. People are drawn to move when they can to regimes that are predisposed to produce public goods. This is seen still more clearly by exploring an alternative account of immigration.

People may move to gain the benefits of public goods, as we contend. Alternatively, they may move to gain access to private goods through their individual entrepreneurship. Black markets provide opportunities for people to become rich while avoiding taxation. If law enforcement is lax, the black market could be a great equalizer, giving anyone willing to take the associated risks the chance to become wealthy through trade in contraband. If, however, anti–black market laws are selectively enforced, as the selectorate theory suggests, so that they protect those in the winning coalition and punish others, a vibrant black market simply reinforces the disadvantages of such societies for the disenfranchised and for those in the selectorate but outside the coalition. If laws are selectively enforced, people will not want to be immigrants in these countries. As we have shown in chapters 4 and 5, large winning-coalition systems produce greater economic growth in part because they provide the rule of law, a public good essential to economic growth and opportunity. Additionally, they have lower tax rates, which allow successful entrepreneurs to retain more of the benefits of their success.

We argued in chapter 5 that black market exchange-rate premiums are selectively available to coalition members. Furthermore, we showed that these premiums are largest in small-coalition systems. Indeed, black markets are so small in large-coalition systems that data on exchange-rate premiums are rarely reported by monitoring agencies for these polities. If the selectorate theory is correct, immigrants would avoid systems that have high black market exchange-rate premiums. If, however, the theory is wrong and these benefits are accessible to anyone willing to take the risks associated with selling contraband, then immigrants should be especially attracted to societies that have a vibrant black market. We already know that immigrants do not choose small-coalition systems, but perhaps, controlling for coalition size, they favor places that offer entrepreneurs in the black market great opportunities.

The evidence rejects this alternative hypothesis strongly, albeit based on a small sample. With only 124 observations we must be cautious in rejecting the idea that immigrants seek out societies that offer substantial black market opportunities. Still, whether we look only at the bivariate relationship between *Immigration* and *BlackMarket* or we control for the logarithm of population, coalition size, the logarithm of real per capita income, and our standard fixed effects, *BlackMarket* is significantly and negatively associated with immigration. The larger the black market premium, the smaller the set of people migrating into the society. Immigrants apparently prefer societies without black market premiums but with a large winning coalition. That at least is how they vote with their feet. Thus it seems safe to say that one way people can improve their lot is to experience a change in institutions by moving to countries with institutions more in line with their preferences. Immigrants follow that pattern. They surely are among those outside a society's winning coalition and they choose to go to places with large coalitions and high production of public goods.

Protest, Civil War, and Revolution

For those for whom emigration is not feasible, an alternative is to give voice to their displeasure with the institutionally induced choices of their leaders. Some among the disenfranchised and those in the selectorate with little prospect of entering the winning coalition (i.e., W/S is small) protest governmental policy and structure. In extremis, they might even take such risky steps as supporting revolution or civil war (Skocpol 1998; Feng and Zak 2001). Revolution seems intended to overturn the existing institutions and establish new institutions within the state that encourage greater public-goods production. Civil war is apparently designed to allow those who believe themselves to be oppressed to break free from the institutions of the state by establishing a new polity with more favorable institutions. In that sense civil war is an extreme form of exit, one in which a portion of the homeland is seized and "liberated" rather than abandoned.

If our contentions are correct regarding "voice strategies," then at least one impetus for peaceful antigovernment protests, violent antigovernment demonstrations, civil war, and revolution is the same as an impetus for emigration. In all these cases, those excluded from the winning coalition are frustrated by the systematic effort their government makes to focus resources on private-goods production that does not benefit them. At least some among those excluded from the coalition seek to redress their frustration by escape or by trying to force a change in the mode of governance. Their economic well-being and their political circumstances are inextricably linked. By altering the institutions of governance, they seemingly hope to enhance their well-being by stimulating more governmental attentiveness to public goods. Thus, protest, civil war, and revolution are actions in the domain of the many who are deprived of private goods in small-coalition systems.

Members of the selectorate who are not in the winning coalition and who have poor odds of getting into the coalition (i.e., W/S is small) can increase their prospects of future coalition membership if they can succeed in throwing the rascals out. Disenfranchised residents, so long as they remain in that status, have no chance at all of entering a winning coalition under existing institutional arrangements. They need some fundamental change in the political rules to gain access to coalition membership. This means that members of the selectorate and members of the disenfranchised group are predicted to be the groups most likely to rebel against small-coalition, large-selectorate, autocratic regimes. Conversely, those enjoying the fruits of government-provided private goods are expected to take actions to thwart revolutionary efforts to change the institutional setup. Just as antigovernment activity is action in the domain of the disenfranchised so, as we argued earlier, are countermeasures primarily in the domain of actions of the winning coalition and the leadership. This discussion raises issues about antigovernment actions and their anticipated consequences.

The selectorate theory suggests that, in the absence of government countermeasures designed to deter antigovernment activities, polities with a strong loyalty norm and a small coalition would be the prime targets of vocal and intense domestic resistance. Large-coalition systems, if the theory is correct, tend to avoid severe antigovernment actions by the selectorate and the disenfranchised because in such systems those groups enjoy the benefits of ample public goods. Small-coalition systems avoid such antigovernment actions by adopting severe punishment strategies aimed at those who oppose government policies, as we saw earlier. Oppression, repression, and suppression of government opponents is an endogenous feature of polities with a small coalition. In a counterfactual world in which such strategies did not exist, autocrats would be expected to face an almost constant barrage of broad-based antigovernment actions by those excluded from the leader's circle of beneficiaries.

The Deterrent Impact of Oppression

We already know from chapter 5 that civil liberties are strongly associated with the size of a polity's winning coalition. Recall that for chapter 5 we transformed the civil liberties index (a seven-point scale) so that high values reflect high levels of civil liberties and low values reflect low degrees of such freedoms. Now we revert to the scale in its original order and divide its value by 7 so that the variable *CLCost* varies between 0 and 1, with 1 reflecting societies with the fewest civil liberties and presumably the highest expected costs imposed on citizens who oppose government policies.[15] We use this indicator to evaluate the costs citizens anticipate their government will impose on them if they oppose the government's policies. We also develop a second indicator of government's expected willingness to impose oppressive costs on citizens who express displeasure with its policies.

We have noted that many governments restrict the freedom of citizens to vote with their feet by emigrating. This is a subtler form of oppression. People who seek to leave are punished for doing so, and those who do not try to leave but are unhappy with their circumstances may be driven to more extreme forms of action. To approximate government-imposed costs of emigration—that is, government policies designed to take away people's exit option—we return to the variable *Emigration:Report*. We reverse the direction of the variable so that a 1 implies that no emigration data were reported, which we take as a signal that emigration is a risky and costly action, and a 0 indicates that emigration data were reported, which we use as an indication that emigration is not so politically costly. We call this variable *Emigration:Cost*. What is the intuition behind treating the failure to report emigration as an indicator that voting with one's feet can be expected to be politically costly?

There surely are benign reasons for governments failing to report emigration. Earlier we saw that the failure to report these numbers is significantly dependent on the society's level of per capita income. Countries with low incomes just may not have enough money to monitor emigration adequately. This might help explain inadequacies in reportage. Still, a legal emigrant normally must acquire a passport or other official documents and so come in contact with government agents. Because such contact is almost always mandatory, it is not especially costly for governments to keep track of departures. We also saw earlier that countries with a relatively small population, like their low-income counterparts, are more likely to fail to report emigration, though the impact of population scale was modest as compared to the effects of the polity's coalition requirements. As with low-income societies, small societies still require legal emigrants to come in contact with government officials.

While we do not discount the likelihood that some good reasons exist for not reporting emigration numbers, we are left with the conjecture that government failure to report emigration often is an effort to mask oppressive government measures designed to prevent people from leaving. Russia, for instance, provided emigration information at least from 1827 until the overthrow of the czarist regime. The Soviet regime, according to our information, never reported emigration data. That regime, of course, frequently punished those who sought to emigrate, a factor its citizens could anticipate and take into account in choosing their actions. Some innocent societies may be caught in the net of our dummy variable *Emigration:Cost*, but in the main we believe that those who do not report such information are also those who oppress citizens who try to leave on a permanent basis. Because *Emigration:Cost* is perfectly inversely correlated with *Emigration:Report*, we know that it is small-coalition polities that appear to be most oppressive by this measure as well as by the *CLCost* variable.

Before turning to our tests of the relationship between actions, selection institutions, and anticipated costs, we should clarify the expected difference between the effects of these costs and realized costs. While realized costs—such as are estimated with Poe, Tate, and Keith's data—should increase with the occurrence of antigovernment actions, expected costs should lead to a decline in the incidence of such actions. Realized costs occur *after the fact* and so reflect the actual response a government makes to antigovernment activity. Of course, today's realized costs become part of tomorrow's expected costs. Our two indicators of anticipated costs evaluate choices governments make *before the fact*—that is, policies aimed at stifling citizens' inclinations to engage in actions opposed to the government, its leaders, and its policies. If these government choices are effective they should lead to a decrease in the realization of antigovernment activities.

Protesting Government Policies: Alternative Actions

Those precluded from leaving a country in quest of greater access to public goods may stoically stand by and hope for a better tomorrow, or they may take action to redress their grievances. We now test the option of giving voice to dissatisfaction by examining the relationship between three different forms of antigovernment activity and coalition size. Again it is our expectation that the use of protests to alter policies and regimes is least likely in large-coalition polities and most likely in small-coalition systems.

The first of the dependent variables for this analysis is called AGDEMONS (Banks 1996). We refer to the variable as *Demonstrations*. It is an annual count of any peaceful public gathering consisting of at least 100 people with the primary purpose of displaying or voicing opposition to government policies or authority, excluding demonstrations of a distinctly antiforeign nature. The second dependent variable, also from Banks 1996, is *Strikes*. This variable reports the number of strikes of 1,000 or more industrial or service workers that involve more than one employer and that are aimed at national government policies or authority. The third dependent variable designed to assess giving voice to disgruntlement is called *Riots* and is also taken from Banks 1996. *Riots* encompasses a higher level of antigovernment demonstration and reports the number of violent demonstrations or clashes of more than 100 citizens involving the use of physical force. When we complete our investigation of these forms of protest, we then turn to still more extreme actions, including civil war and revolution.

To test how institutions influence the willingness of people to engage in antigovernment activities like demonstrations, strikes, and riots, we must control for the expected costs associated with taking to the streets and the costs tied to efforts to emigrate. Our tests control for the two indicators of anticipated oppression—that is, *CLCost* and *Emigration:Cost*.

The first set of tests evaluate the impact of W, *CLCost*, and the interaction between W and *CLCost* on *Demonstrations*, *Strikes*, and *Riots*. We also include our standard fixed effects for region-year. The selectorate theory anticipates that antigovernment activities of the sort just described are means available to the disenfranchised to express their demands for changes in government policy. The controls for *CLCost* and *CLCost*W* are designed to evaluate antigovernment activity after correcting for the costs the political system can be expected to impose on antigovernment statements or activities.

The expectation of the theory is that large-W systems produce fewer antigovernment activities than do small-coalition systems, all else being equal, because the government is already providing the disenfranchised with ample public goods and with a relatively easy exit option through emigration. The disenfranchised have relatively little to protest about.

All things, however, are rarely equal. The anticipation of high government-imposed costs on citizens (*CLCost* approaches or equals 1) is expected to dampen enthusiasm for antigovernment activities, because people normally try to avoid costs, whether those involve voting with one's feet (i.e., emigration) or voicing dissatisfaction. Whether the impact of anticipated high costs or large coalition size has a greater impact on dampening antigovernment activities, we cannot say. The selectorate theory does not provide guidance regarding whether the institutional impact of a small coalition increases antigovernment activity more or less than the offsetting impact that expected high costs for protesting are anticipated to have in reducing such activity. With this in mind, the selectorate theory leads us to predict that in the cases of *Demonstrations*, *Strikes*, and *Riots*: (1) the coefficient for $W < 0$, (2) the coefficient for $CLCost < 0$, and (3) the sum of the coefficients for $W + CLCost + CLCost*W < 0$. Table 8.6 summarizes the results of these tests.

The tests in table 8.6 are rather demanding and complex. We anticipate a relationship in which large-W systems that are expected to impose few costs on antigovernment activity also experience little by way of antigovernment demonstrations, while small-coalition systems diminish such activities by creating environments in which citizens anticipate high costs for protesting. Both of these are true according to the evidence. On balance, anticipated oppression is more effective at quashing protests of government policies than is high public-goods production (i.e., the interaction term $CLCost*W$ is positive). People can be more unhappy with government policy in an autocracy than in a democracy, but feel freer to object to the specific policies of a large-coalition government than they

Table 8.6
Antigovernment activity and coalition size

	Demonstrations Coef., (*t*-stat), prob.	*Strikes* Coef., (*t*-stat), prob.	*Riots* Coef., (*t*-stat), prob.
W	−2.845, (0.313), 0.000	−0.565, (0.098), 0.000	−2.035, (0.286), 0.000
CLCost	−2.864, (0.337), 0.000	−0.729, (0.106), 0.000	−2.463, (0.308), 0.000
*CLCost*W*	4.069, (0.437), 0.000	0.745, (0.137), 0.000	3.164, (0.400), 0.000
Constant	2.824, (0.270), 0.000	0.712, (0.085), 0.000	2.177, (0.247), 0.000
$W + CLCost + CLCost*W < 0$	$F = 28.12, p = 0.000$	$F = 32.02, p = 0.000$	$F = 22.28, p = 0.001$
$N = 3,998$, F.E. = 194	$F = 30.11, p = 0.000$	$F = 17.00, p = 0.000$	$F = 23.41, p = 0.000$

do to the policies of a small-coalition system. Large-coalition systems are designed to tolerate protest. That is a feature of civil liberties. Small-coalition systems are designed to suppress protest. That is a feature of permitting few civil liberties.

We have argued that such antigovernment activities as demonstrations, strikes, and riots are specific alternative responses to emigration by the disenfranchised or those in the selectorate but outside the coalition in autocratic-style governments. Our first set of tests showed that these activities respond in the way expected when a general indicator of anticipated government oppression is taken into account. Now we undertake a more focused test. Here we substitute *Emigration:Cost* and *Emigration:Cost*W* for *CLCost* and *CLCost*W*. One specific reason to take to the streets in protest against government policy is that the alternative of exiting the society is restricted. Where one has difficulty becoming an emigrant, there are heightened incentives to protest. Our expectations are identical to those reported in table 8.6, though the correlation between *CLCost* and *Emigration:Cost* is only 0.42, suggesting that these are two quite different indexes of expected governmental oppression.

Table 8.7 displays the results of the analyses that control for *Emigration:Cost*. Like table 8.6, this table tells the story of diminished motives to protest when the society is dependent on a large coalition and diminished willingness to protest when costs are expected to be high. The costliness of exit is almost certainly manifested through government policies aimed at signaling preparedness to punish those who try to leave. We can

Table 8.7
Antigovernment activity, coalition size, and emigration: cost

	Demonstrations Coef., (*t*-stat.), prob.	Strikes Coef., (*t*-stat.), prob.	Riots Coef., (*t*-stat.), prob.
W	−1.056, (0.180), 0.000	−0.215, (0.056), 0.000	−1.425, (0.206), 0.000
Emigration:Cost	−1.206, (0.168), 0.000	−0.317, (0.052), 0.000	−1.913, (0.192), 0.000
Emigration:Cost*W	1.232, (0.198), 0.000	0.234, (0.062), 0.000	1.790, (0.226), 0.000
Constant	1.525, (0.158), 0.000	0.415, (0.049), 0.000	2.169, (0.180), 0.000
W + Emigration:Cost + Emigration:Cost*W < 0	$F = 39.00, p = 0.000$	$F = 33.47, p = 0.000$	$F = 67.35, p = 0.000$
Summary statistics	$F = 17.54, p = 0.000$, $N = 7,296$, F.E. = 439	$F = 19.53, p = 0.0003$, $N = 7,296$, F.E. = 439	$F = 38.44, p = 0.000$, $N = 7,296$, F.E. = 439

only observe this obliquely, but still we see its effects strongly in the light of the statistical results.

Civil War, Guerilla War, and Revolution: The Disenfranchised vs. the Selectorate

Members of a society's winning coalition or its leadership generally have little reason to engage in antigovernment activities. They are not the people one expects to find demonstrating, striking, or rioting against the government. They are even less likely to be behind the instigation of more extreme forms of violent antigovernment behavior. Civil war, guerilla warfare, and revolution reflect perhaps the most extreme actions that dissatisfied people can take against their state.

Revolutions and civil wars have much in common. Civil wars come in two main varieties. The American Civil War and the Biafra Civil War are examples of the type intended to sunder political relations between two territories within a state. The Spanish Civil War illustrates the other type, when people seek to replace one selectorate with another. Revolutions often exemplify successful civil wars, especially those in the second category. The American Revolution, for example, severed the political dependence of the American colonies on the British government. Before the war, the British Crown and Parliament determined the central leadership in the colonies, while local citizens determined who their local leaders were. Following the revolution, the local citizenry fully replaced the British selectorate in determining its leadership at every level of government. The French Revolution, Russian Revolution, Chinese Revolution, and so on all fulfill this criterion. In each case, not only were the rulers deposed; so was the prerevolutionary selectorate. What is more, in each instance the new selectorate was larger than the one that came before it.

We will, for clarity, refer to attempts by the disenfranchised to overthrow the system as revolutions. As the group that does not and can never receive private goods under the existing selection institutions, they have the greatest interest in overthrowing them. The selectorate forms the pool of those who may fight to defend the current system. They either receive private benefits or hold the possibility of receiving them in the future and so have an interest in keeping the current system.

The selectorate theory suggests that revolutionaries are motivated by the intention to overthrow the existing political order so that the excluded (i.e., the revolutionaries and their followers) become the included (Moore 1966; Migdal 1974; Tilly 1975; Goldstone 1995). We think of revolutionary struggle as a contest between disenfranchised individuals rallied by a revolutionary leader to fight the system against members of the selectorate who fight to retain the system. In essence, both sides count up how many people or how much strength they can rally to their side, and the side with the most wins.

The selectorate has two advantages in a revolutionary struggle. First, those defending the current institutions possess an advantage in the tools and skills of violence. As we discussed in chapter 2, military skill has often been a critical qualification for membership in the selectorate, and now we see why. Those favored by current institutions want to monopolize military ability to increase their ability to defeat a revolutionary challenge. If the military was disenfranchised, they could overthrow that system. We represent the advantage in military skills by assuming that in the comparison of strength, each member of the selectorate is multiplied by a factor that represents this advantage. For instance, if the military advantage factor was 10, the revolution would have to recruit ten times as many active participants from the disenfranchised as the regime does from the selectorate to overthrow the system. The military advantage of the selectorate has varied over time with changes in military technology and the ways of war. In the Middle Ages, for example, the nobles held a large advantage over the peasants through their monopoly of armor, weapons, and training in their use. The spread of cheap automatic weapons after the Second World War reduced this advantage.

The second advantage of the selectorate lies in its greater ability to mobilize forces from its members because of an asymmetry of motivation. The leader of each side must recruit people to fight for its side; we do not assume that all members of the disenfranchised fight against the system, nor that all members of the selectorate fight for it. Each individual's decision whether to fight depends on the benefits and costs he faces. One who is disenfranchised may gain the benefits of a selector in a new system if the revolution succeeds, but he also faces the likelihood of oppression or even death if it should fail. Passivity is safe for the disenfranchised. The opposite is true for the selectorate. If the revolution succeeds, the members of the selectorate will lose the privileges they hold and may be killed as well. Inaction is dangerous for them. Still, the risk of injury or death in the fighting may be sufficient to deter members of the selectorate from fighting for the system that favors them.

The benefits from fighting for the disenfranchised depend on the system that the revolutionary leadership promises to install on coming to power. Ideology, in the sense of a description of the new selection institutions and the affinity of the new leader for her followers, is critical for mobilizing a revolutionary coalition. It explains the benefits of a successful revolution to recruits from the disenfranchised. The larger the difference in expected benefits between the current and the proposed new system, the easier it will be for the revolutionary leader to recruit supporters.

The willingness of the selectorate to fight for the current system depends on their benefits under that system against those in a new system. The better they do under the current system, the more willing they are to fight for it. The more attractive the alternative proposed by the revolutionaries, the less they are inclined to fight for it.

Large-coalition systems, then, are relatively invulnerable to revolution. Although the selectorate receives relatively few private benefits in such a system, a revolutionary leader cannot improve on their current situation. A new system with a large winning coalition does not improve the lot of the current selectorate. If the revolutionary leader proposes a small winning coalition, she will place her followers, not the members of the current selectorate, in that winning coalition. The current selectorate would lose any hope of receiving private benefits as well as any hope of receiving the public goods produced by the current large winning-coalition system. A revolutionary leader will find it difficult to recruit supporters because the disenfranchised receive public goods in a large winning-coalition system even though they have no hope of receiving private benefits. Finally, the selectorate probably has as many members as or more members than the disenfranchised in such a system, making it almost impossible for a revolutionary leader to recruit more supporters than there are defenders of the current system.

Small-coalition systems are doubly vulnerable to revolution. First, when coalition size is small, there are many outsiders from which to draw revolutionaries. Second, small-coalition systems produce few rewards for outsiders, giving these potential revolutionaries cause to rebel. The selectorate, and especially the winning coalition, is greatly favored by such a system, and so should be very willing to fight for it.

Arguments about the role of selectorate size are more complex. When the selectorate is small, such as in a junta or monarchy, there are a vast number of disenfranchised. The outsiders want to change the system such that they might one day have the requisite abilities to enter the winning coalition.

When S is large, the disenfranchised make up a smaller proportion of the population. However, these residents are generally worse off than their contemporaries in a small-S system, assuming a comparable size W in each case. Further, when S is large and W is small, selectors outside of the winning coalition have little reason to defend the current system. Although these selectors have some nominal chance of entering the coalition in the future, the expected value associated with this chance is low. First, given the high loyalty norm, leaders provide fewer goods in toto, reserving more for themselves. Second, the lengthy tenure of leaders in such systems means selectors have few opportunities to enter future coalitions. Thus, selectorate members, although better off than the disenfranchised, are unlikely to fight for such a system and might even support a rebellion when S is large. Given these competing influences, we cannot be certain whether revolutions will be more common in small- or large-selectorate systems. We are certain however, that in either case it is in small-coalition systems where outsiders have little chance of becoming insiders and where public-goods production is low that revolution is most likely.

Systems with small winning coalitions and large selectorates are unlikely to survive a revolutionary movement. Consequently, they focus their efforts on making the recruitment and organization of a revolutionary coalition difficult through oppression and suppression of rights to organize. The communist regimes in Eastern Europe are an excellent example of this principle. Once they allowed mass demonstrations against the regime, their systems collapsed rapidly because opponents could now coordinate (Lohmann 1994). Change promised large winning coalitions, and so it was not even in the interest of most Communist Party members to fight for their system.

Successful revolutions should expand the size of the selectorate. Membership in the new selectorate is a minimal incentive for the disenfranchised; why fight if you are still disenfranchised after the revolution? If the revolutionary leader must amass a coalition larger than the current selectorate and overcome their military advantage, she has to promise to expand the selectorate to be able to recruit enough supporters to win. Later, we will expand on this point when we examine the evidence.

This argument about revolution also solves the collective-action problem often said to lie at the heart of rebellion (Tullock 1971; Lichbach 1995). This view sees revolutionary success as a public good, and consequently, the classic free-rider problem should hinder building a revolutionary coalition. Our view agrees that building a revolutionary coalition is difficult and critical to a successful revolution. However, to recruit supporters, our revolutionaries can promise private benefits as well as membership in the future selectorate and winning coalition. They can exclude those who do not fight from the benefits of the new system.

We also observe that our argument about revolution leads to an important observation about civil-military relations. In small winning-coalition systems, the military must be part of the selectorate to protect the system against revolutionary threats. Consequently, the military cannot be separated from politics in such systems. In large winning coalitions, though, the military is not needed to protect the system against revolutionary threats, and so can be professionalized and removed from politics.

Evidence

Arthur Banks has amassed data on revolutions and guerrilla warfare from 1919 to 1999. The Correlates of War Project assembled data on civil wars from 1816 to 1997. These data reflect each year that a country experienced the relevant event. We construct an additional set of variables that are coded 1 for the first year of civil war, guerrilla war, or revolution respectively and coded 0 otherwise. These variables are called *CL_War_Start*, *Guerrilla_Start*, and *Revolution_Start* respectively.

The selectorate theory predicts that the disenfranchised are most likely to resort to revolutions, guerrilla wars, and civil wars when their lot is worst. That suggests these violent forms of protest are most likely when the winning coalition is small, and when the loyalty norm is high. It is under these circumstances that leaders expropriate resources and provide few public goods in return. The data overwhelmingly support this prediction. Whether we look at revolution, guerrilla wars, civil wars, or the onset of these event, coalition size and the loyalty norm strongly influence these violent events.[16] Tables 8.8 and 8.9 summarize the results of logit analyses.

The results shown control only for our standard region-year effects. However, the impact of institutional variables is robust to the inclusion

Table 8.8
How institutions influence violent protest

	Revolution	Guerrilla War	CivilWar
W	−3.04, (0.097), 0.000	−2.18, (0.09), 0.000	−1.23, (0.14), 0.000
Summary statistics	N = 11,281, F.E. = 464, Log Likelihood = −5,257.40	N = 11,276, F.E. = 463, Log Likelihood = −5,256.45	N = 10,106, F.E. = 427 Log Likelihood = −2,394.19

Table 8.9
How the loyalty norm influences violent protest

	Revolution	Guerrilla War	CivilWar
W/S	−1.976, (0.117), 0.000	−0.685, (0.113), 0.000	−1.53, (0.14), 0.000
Summary statistics	N = 7,604, F.E. = 358, Log Likelihood = −2,888.37	N = 7,863, F.E. = 355, Log Likelihood = −2,886.43	N = 7,401, F.E. = 407 Log Likelihood = −1,985.62

of control variables. The impacts of the control variables are themselves interesting. For instance, *CLCost*, our measure of lack of civil rights, makes revolution, guerrilla conflict, and civil war more likely. Wealth (per capita GDP) and economic growth both retard the probability of civil strife. When leaders do a poor job of providing public goods, such as civil liberties, prosperity, and growth, residents are most likely to protest. Violent protest is also more likely in countries with large populations. The linkage between coalition size and civil war, guerrilla war, and revolution remains robust even after we control for the significant exacerbating impact that riots, antigovernment demonstrations, and strikes have on the risk of more serious efforts to topple the government and its institutional composition. When these somewhat less violent means fail to prompt institutional improvement, more extreme actions become vastly more likely. These factors together seem necessary, though they may not be sufficient for revolution. Certainly they should markedly increase the risk of revolution. This claim stipulates that societies with small winning coalitions, poor civil liberties (as assessed by *CLCost*), and poor economic performance (as assessed by the economic growth rate and the residual per capita income that is independent of coalition and selectorate size) are especially likely to experience revolution. The results in table 8.10, reported in odds-ratio terms for ease of interpretation, strongly support the hypothesis.

Table 8.10
Revolutions, institutions, and public goods

Variable	Odds ratio, (std. error), prob.
W	0.203, (0.073), 0.000
S	0.506, (0.094), 0.000
$CLCost$	4.371, (1.546), 0.000
$WS:IncomeRes$	0.630, (0.041), 0.000
$Growth$	0.957, (0.008), 0.000
Summary statistics	$N = 2{,}934$, F.E. $= 135$, $\chi^2(5) = 282.93$

The cause of or impetus for revolution is one thing. The consequences of such events are an entirely separate matter. One question that frequently arises with successful revolutions is whether the leaders will abide by their previctory promises. Before a revolution succeeds, its leaders almost always promise to create a freer, fairer society that protects and improves the welfare of its poorest people. After the revolution, fulfillment of these promises turns out to be much less certain.

The selectorate theory offers an explanation for the frequently heard declarations of support for democracy among revolutionary leaders. It also offers ideas about why some revolutionaries fulfill their promises for more inclusive government and others do not. Whether one reflects on Fidel Castro, Nelson Mandela, Jomo Kenyatta, George Washington, Maximilien Robespierre, Mao Zedong, or a host of other revolutionaries, the call for a government broadly representative of the downtrodden and disenfranchised is a hallmark of revolution. The Chinese communists, for instance, declared the formation of a Chinese Soviet Republic on November 7, 1931, saying:

From today onward, within Chinese territory, there are two totally different states: one is the Republic of China which is an instrument of the imperialist powers; it is a state used by the warlords, landlords, and the capitalists to suppress the workers, farmers, and soldiers; the Nationalist Government under Chiang Kai-shek and Wang Ching-Wei is the anti-revolutionary political machine of this state. Another state is the Chinese Soviet Republic; it is the state of the suppressed workers, farmers, soldiers, and working masses. Its flag calls for the downfall of imperialism, the liquidation of landlords, the overthrow of the warlord government of the Nationalists. We shall establish a soviet government over the whole of China; we shall struggle for the interests of thousands of deprived workers, farmers, and soldiers and other suppressed masses; and to endeavor for peaceful unification of the whole of China.[17]

A comparable sentiment in favor of a government reflective of the interests of the disenfranchised was articulated by Jomo Kenyatta at a meeting of the Kenya African Union (K.A.U.) on July 26, 1952:

If we unite now, each and every one of us, and each tribe to another, we will cause the implementation in this country of that which the European calls democracy. True democracy has no colour distinction. It does not choose between black and white. We are here in this tremendous gathering under the K.A.U. flag to find which road leads us from darkness into democracy. In order to find it we Africans must first achieve the right to elect our own representatives. That is surely the first principle of democracy. We are the only race in Kenya which does not elect its own representatives in the Legislature and we are going to set about to rectify this situation. . . . It has never been known in history that a country prospers without equality. We despise bribery and corruption, those two words that the European repeatedly refers to. Bribery and corruption is prevalent in this country, but I am not surprised. As long as a people are held down, corruption is sure to rise and the only answer to this is a policy of equality. (Cornfield 1960, 301–308)

It is noteworthy that Mao Zedong and Jomo Kenyatta each ruled his country for a long time—in each case, in fact, until dying of natural causes. Neither brought the equality, fairness, democracy, and liberty he promised. Kenyatta railed against corruption in his 1952 speech, a decade before Kenya became independent. Yet, as long as Transparency International has measured corruption, Kenya has consistently been counted among the most corrupt states. In recent rankings Kenya shows every sign of continuing this unhappy record. In 1999, Kenya was 90th out of 99 states ranked; in 2000, it placed 82nd out of 90 ranked states. In each instance, a ranking near the bottom means high levels of corruption. Based on available data, China seems to have an equally dismal record of protecting its people against corruption and other abuses against the poor and downtrodden. China too consistently ranks among the most corrupt states. In 1995 it ranked 40th out of 41 evaluated states; in 1996, 50th out of 54; in 1999 it still was in the bottom half at 58th out of 99; and in 2000 it began to backslide, sinking to 63rd out of 90 states, placing it in a tie with Egypt.

Mao, Kenyatta, and innumerable other revolutionary leaders promise democracy, freedom, and equality. They offer peace and prosperity, but they all too often deliver corruption, poverty, and despair. Are their promises hollow and cynical or sincere? Are their subsequent records of poor performance compatible or incompatible with the institutionally induced incentives identified by the selectorate theory?

The selectorate theory suggests that when revolutionaries promise to improve public welfare *at the time before victory*, they are sincere. Revolutionary leaders normally arise outside the elite who constitute the winning coalition in their societies. Their societies usually are ruled by autocrats or petty dictators who retain power by transferring wealth or rent-seeking opportunities to their essential cronies and to themselves, often making these transfers at the direct expense of the poor. Indeed, whether we control for per capita income and population size or not, coalition size proves to be a powerful predictor of revolution. Societies whose leaders depend on a large coalition appear to be immune to revolution. Polities run with a small coalition seem especially prone to revolution. The promotion of public well-being is not the means by which such leaders retain office.

Before victory, revolutionaries and their followers are far removed from opportunities for personal gain enjoyed by members of the winning coalition. Being so removed, their preferred form of government is one that delivers public goods, and so they declare themselves in favor of just such political systems. That is, they declare themselves in favor of a political system with a large winning coalition and a large selectorate. The rub is that when revolutionaries defeat their oppressors, the victorious revolutionaries become the new leaders or members of the new winning coalition. Having shifted from being outsiders to being those privileged with access to private benefits, they respond to their new incentives. The institutional preferences of outsiders are not the same as the institutional preferences of leaders, and only sometimes are they the same as those held by members of a winning coalition. Thus, before victory, it is *always* incentive compatible for revolutionaries to favor democratic, large-coalition, large-selectorate government. Those who are victorious and who become leaders or members of the winning coalition continue to do what is in their interest, though what defines that interest can be changed by their new role. If their institutional role changes, their incentives shift and so does their behavior. When revolutionaries become leaders, their institutional preferences shift in favor of a small-coalition, large-selectorate arrangement. They may be constrained to implement democracy, as we discuss shortly, but absent such constraints they can be expected to favor a rigged electoral system. Thus, the promises of revolutionaries imply two institutional changes: expansion of the selectorate and expansion of the winning coalition. The interests—as distinct from the promises—of relatively unconstrained successful revolutionaries favor implementing an expansion in the selectorate but not in the winning coalition.

We examine the change in the size of the selectorate over a three-year period moving forward from the year of observation. We examine the impact that the start of a revolution (*Revolution_Start*) and the end of a revolution (*Revolution_End*) have on the subsequent size of the selectorate. Revolutions lead, as predicted, to an increase in selectorate size. The effects both at the start of a revolution and at its end are significant. Table 8.11 summarizes the findings. The substantive impact is most readily understood by conditioning our test just to look at societies that change their selectorate size. We find that those that experienced revolution are about three times more likely to increase the selectorate than are those that do not experience revolution. In fact, the sum of the effects of a start and an end to a revolution is to increase the size of the selectorate by about 0.60 units on our scale of 0 to 1.

One might wonder why the start of a revolution should produce an increase in the size of the selectorate independent of the effect at the end of the revolution. The incumbent leadership can strengthen the loyalty norm by increasing S. This is most beneficial if W is small. This implies that the smaller W is at the outset of the revolution, the more attractive it is to increase the selectorate's size as a means of enhancing the incumbent's prospects of survival. At the end of a revolution, whoever wins, the incentive is the same. That is, the smaller the coalition is at any stage during a revolution, the greater the incentive the incumbent has to increase the selectorate size to promote her own political

Table 8.11
Three-year change in selectorate size as explained by prior coalition size and revolution

Variables	Coef., (std. error), prob.	Coef., (std. error), prob.
Revolution_Start	0.054, (0.014), 0.000	0.108, (0.024), 0.000
Revolution_End	0.045, (0.014), 0.001	0.124, (0.026), 0.000
*Revolution_Start*W*		−0.189, (0.047), 0.000
*Revolution_End*W*		−0.221, (0.047), 0.000
W		−0.156, (0.015), 0.000
Constant	−0.004, (0.004), 0.270	0.091, (0.010), 0.000
Summary statistics	$N = 7{,}343$, F.E. = 428, $F = 10.96$	$N = 7{,}343$, F.E. = 428, $F = 49.08$

survival. Of course, if the incumbent loses the revolution, the new leaders share the interest in increasing the size of the selectorate. Table 8.11 tests the hypothesis that the selectorate's size is especially likely to increase during a revolution if the polity operates with a small coalition.

The results in table 8.11 show a strong link between involvement in revolution and a subsequent increase in selectorate size. At the same time, the results highlight the fact that a larger coalition at the outset of a revolution (W + $Revolution\_Start*W$), during the revolution (W), and at the end of the revolution (W + $Revolution\_End*W$) discourages an increase in selectorate size, while a small coalition at each stage of the revolution strongly encourages subsequent expansion of the selectorate. That is, those who head a small-coalition government, or those who come to head such a government following revolution, alter institutions to strengthen their loyalty norm and, thereby, their prospective future tenure in office.

Some revolutionaries, like Nelson Mandela in South Africa, Jawaharlal Nehru in India, or George Washington in the United States, maintain or adopt democratic inclinations even after the revolution is over. The selectorate theory offers an explanation that distinguishes these leaders from those who become autocrats or self-appointed monarchs or dictators. To understand the difference between these leaders we must reflect on the institutional preferences of coalition members and leaders. Leaders always want a small coalition drawn from a large selectorate. Coalition members prefer that the ratio of W/S be large, compelling leaders to spend more to keep the coalition's loyalty.

Because small-coalition, large-selectorate systems are most attractive to leaders, we can expect that any time an incumbent has a fairly unconstrained opportunity to choose institutions, the choice will be an autocracy with a strong loyalty norm. It is little surprise that this was the choice made by Fidel Castro, Mao Zedong, Ho Chi Minh, and many other victorious revolutionary leaders despite their earlier declarations of support for democracy. The selectorate theory leads us to infer, as intimated earlier, that the pro-democracy declarations were sincere when these revolutionary leaders were outsiders, but their incentives shifted once they became insiders.

There are at least two puzzling facts associated with the institutional preferences of leaders. One concerns their general failure to make a deal with revolutionary leaders to co-opt them. The other, perhaps more puzzling fact is that not all leaders adopt an autocratic political con-figuration. To be sure, many postcolonial or revolutionary leaders did, but there are compelling exceptions, a few of whom include Nelson Mandela, Robert Mugabe (for nearly two decades), Jawaharlal Nehru, and George Washington. The selectorate theory suggests a solution to these puzzles.

Why autocrats do not often co-opt revolutionaries is readily explained. Revolutionaries, before victory, are interested in creating a system that relies on a large coalition and has a weak loyalty norm. They favor changes that will bring their followers into the mainstream of politics and that emphasize the production of public goods. Incumbent autocrats, before defeat at the hands of revolutionaries, want a small-coalition, large-selectorate system with a strong loyalty norm. The grounds for a compromise are severely limited. A deal with revolutionaries either makes them members of the winning coalition, or replaces the autocratic leader with the leader of the revolutionaries. In the latter case, the old incumbent loses power, clearly a nonstarter from her perspective, thereby preventing a negotiated deal.

Furthermore, to the extent that co-opting revolutionaries requires bringing them into the winning coalition, there is also an issue of credible commitment. After all, once a new coalition is formed that includes former revolutionaries, the leader wishes to replace these revolutionaries with selectors who share greater affinity with the incumbent. Once the revolutionary exposes himself and joins the coalition, he risks being purged from or replaced in the coalition with a more trustworthy backer of the leader.

Compromise with revolutionaries is further exacerbated by members of the already-existing coalition. Expansion of the winning coalition to include co-opted revolutionaries shifts the political focus away from private-goods production toward more public-goods production. In doing so, the old members of the incumbent's coalition are likely to defect, provoking a coup d'état that prevents the "compromise" with the revolutionaries. Cutting a deal with people pushing for an expansion of the winning coalition is simply incredible and contrary to the interests of the incumbent autocrat. Such a deal is feasible if the incumbent already rules a system dominated by public-goods production, but in that case, there is little incentive for the excluded to engage in revolutionary behavior.

The second puzzle is more interesting, though its solution is related to the analysis of the previous puzzle. Sometimes deals are made, though not generally by autocrats and revolutionaries. Consider the cases of South Africa, Zimbabwe, America, and India.

Neither Nelson Mandela in South Africa nor Robert Mugabe in Zimbabwe won outright victories over their foes. They were not ousting a foreign colonial master who could or would simply retreat to the homeland. Instead, in each case, the transition to a new form of government was worked out as a negotiated compromise between warring factions. Most of the members of each warring side were long-term residents with no place to run or to return to. They were in their homeland. The negotiated compromise in these cases was designed to protect the interests of the rival groups even as power was transferred from one side to the other. That is, the new rules of governance were dictated by a coalition agreement that insured participation in the future winning coalition by at least some members of each competing side. The rules were not dictated by a single, more-or-less unitary victor. Such was not the case in many instances of African decolonization.

It is noteworthy that Zimbabwe's Mugabe in recent years has switched from the fair electoral system put into place decades ago to a rigged electoral system. With the passage of time, he has shored up his position sufficiently that he no longer needs to respect the compromise agreement he reached with the Ian Smith government in the 1980s. As we saw in the discussion of Ahidjo in Cameroon, the choice was to abandon broadly representative arrangements when possible and substitute a small-coalition, large-selectorate, rigged-election political system.

Nehru and Washington reflect a somewhat different set of circumstances from Mandela or Mugabe (at least between 1980 and about 1999). Unlike Mandela and Mugabe, the colonial American forces and the Indian nationalists did, in essence, win victory on the ground. The Americans defeated the British militarily, while the Indians defeated Britain morally. In either case, the former colonial master withdrew back to the homeland. But, unlike the pattern of victory manifested by Mao, Castro, or Ho, there was not a single, unitary organization and leader that could take exclusive credit for victory. The thirteen American colonies had divergent interests, as was manifestly evident in the framing of the American constitution, itself a highly contentious coalitional process (Riker 1996; Beard 1986).

When victory is achieved by and attributed to a coalition rather than a single individual or cohesive leadership, it is more likely that the coalition rather than any single decision maker gets to choose the new institutions of government. Each American colony mustered its own militia to fight the British, and each colony and each colonial leader had views on how best to govern in the postcolonial period. Victory was a federalized, coalitional accomplishment. When the victorious coalition chooses institutions, its members are least inclined to select or agree to an authoritarian structure. Rather, the coalition is likely to lean toward monarchy, military government, or representative democracy. This was the case for the Americans. During the debate over the Constitution, anti-federalists claimed George Washington was being duped into becoming a king. He vehemently and correctly denied this charge. He accepted the idea of competing for the presidency in a new republic.

The situation in India was much the same as it had been in the American colonies. To be sure, the Indian nationalists had not won a military victory that ousted their colonial masters. The moral advantage gained by Mohandas Karamchand Gandhi's Satyagraha campaigns, combined with effective terrorist actions against the British raj by the political heirs of Bal Gangadhar Tilak, and the economic realities of post–World War II Britain, all helped convince Britain, in Gandhi's famous phrase, to "Quit India." As in the American colonies, however, India's nationalists had been divided along regional, ethnic, linguistic, cultural, and political party lines.

Though the Congress Party was the preeminent force for independence, it was itself highly fractionalized, and there also was a strong independence push by the Muslim League and by a host of smaller political parties (e.g., Samyukta Socialists, Republican Party, Hindu Maha Sabha) and interest groups (e.g., the Rashtriya Swayamasewak Sangh). In the wake of Britain's departure, it was necessary to form a government from among some of these contending interests and factions. The one Indian leader who might have had the clout to impose institutions—Gandhi—held no official position in the Indian National Congress, had no such inclinations, and in any event was assassinated by a Hindu extremist who feared the influence he might exert.

With Gandhi gone, Nehru was but one of several important independence leaders given the task of forging a new government. A group of such leaders, reflecting diverse interests, assembled in a constitutional convention and hammered out a democratic, federal political system. To be sure, the winning coalition designed rules that disproportionately benefited the strongest among its members, namely the Congress Party. The Congress-dominated constitutional convention erected primarily single-member districts with first-past-the-post elections. These election rules practically guaranteed the Congress coalition members legislative majorities in the absence of popular electoral majorities. Indeed, the Congress Party dominated the national parliament, often with around two-thirds of the membership, despite not winning a majority in the popular vote (Park and Bueno de Mesquita 1979). The choice of voting rules was surprising since India had a multiparty system at independence. Furthermore, India had prior experience under the British raj with quasi-proportional representation electoral rules. The so-called rules of weightage introduced in 1909 that reserved seats through separate electorates for key ethnic groups provided a quasi-proportional representation structure. The dyarchy system introduced in 1919 created a two-tiered governance system in which powers were shared between British and Indian interests, especially at the provincial level again reinforcing a form of proportional representation.

When leaders win clean-cut victories over opponents, they tend to erect autocratic regimes. When leaders must rely on a coalition to erect institutions, as in the case of the American Revolution or Indian independence, the institutions are more likely to be democratic. The puzzle of why Mandela, Mugabe, Washington, Nehru, and others deviated from the patterns of Ho Chi Minh, Fidel Castro, and so forth apparently has a plausible solution embedded within the logic of the selectorate theory.

Purges and Coups d'état: Actions by Coalition Members

When, for whatever reasons, a polity reaches the point (in figure 8.1) around which the welfare of coalition members is near bottom, disputes are likely to arise regarding who is and who is not enfranchised. Some in the winning coalition will prefer to reduce the coalition's size, purging individuals (other than themselves, of course) from coalition membership. Doing so can improve the welfare of those who remain in the coalition. Others in the existing coalition will prefer to expand membership because a larger coalition can also improve the welfare of all members. Indeed, even if there were no political or economic constraints, like a recalcitrant monarch, anti-immigrant factions, or declining resources, coalition members could still be conflicted over changes in coalition size that are best for them. Figure 8.1 depicts the conflict between expanded and contracted coalition size. At the same time, figure 8.1 also hints at reasons that societies experience a limited franchise and suggests a solution to a puzzle identified by Adam Przeworski regarding the point at which democracy appears to be stable. We address each of these issues.

The low point on the coalition's welfare curve can be politically paralytic. The incumbent, always favoring a smaller coalition, will not support the idea of expanding the coalition. The disenfranchised always want to improve their welfare by expanding coalition size. Coalition members will be torn between factions favoring expansion of the franchise and others favoring its contraction. If they decide to move to the right in figure 8.1, there are natural pressures to shift from a limited franchise to a move way up the curve—that is, toward universal suffrage. If, however, the coalition shifts to the left in the figure, there is likely to be strong resistance to an expanded franchise. Only a crisis large enough to push the coalition's welfare back to its approximate low point would rekindle that group's interest in expanding the franchise.

Members of the winning coalition like certain styles of autocratic polities least of all. Although autocracies have a small coalition, which can be beneficial to members of the coalition, rigged-election autocracies have a large selectorate. The larger the selectorate, the stronger the loyalty norm, and the stronger the loyalty norm, the less the incumbent must spend to keep coalition members from defecting. We showed that this is true logically in chapter 3, and we showed that it is true empirically in chapter 4. This suggests an important difference between what coalition members might do if they overthrow the incumbent regime as compared to what those outside the winning coalition might do. Those outside the coalition, as we have now seen, prefer to expand the coalition, which often requires expanding the selectorate as well. Those in the coalition can now have incentives to shrink the size of the selectorate, the size of the coalition, or both. This means that purges, at least in the way we use the term, can take three different forms.

Purges

In conventional or journalistic usage, a purge consists of the elimination of members of a ruling elite. When we speak of a purge we refer specifically to the elimination from membership of some in the winning coalition or the selectorate or both. Thus, we denote three forms of purges.

Coalition members can be purged, reducing the size of the coalition while maintaining the size of the selectorate. This form of purge is not appealing to coalition members because it reduces how much the leader must spend on those who remain in the winning coalition. It is a more appealing form of purge from the perspective of incumbent leaders. This may explain why autocrats like Saddam Hussein seem frequently to resort to purges of their own inner circle as a means of retaining their hold on power during periods of economic decline. Stalin and Hitler also made frequent use of purges within their own ranks.

By way of example, consider Hitler's decisions to purge supporters as a means of securing his hold over power. From the time Hitler joined the precursor to the National Socialist Workers Party, the German Workers Party, he worked assiduously to remove any who might be in his way. Following his failed Putsch of 1923, Hitler vowed to rise to power through legal means. In 1925 he quickly displaced Anton Dexler, founder of the German Workers Party, doing so primarily on the strength of his fiery oratory. In 1934, however, having succeeded in coming to power through the ballot box, Hitler resorted to murder to gain full control over the future of the Nazi movement.

Hitler secured his control over the party by ordering the executions of Ernst Röhm and his supporters, in the process ensuring that in the future he would have complete control over the SA. In this way he purged the winning coalition of those whose "affinity" for him was questionable. The timing of these purges is interesting. The Nazi Party became a major political force during the first elections of 1932, when the party garnered 14 million votes out of an electorate of approximately 37 million, slipping back in November 1932 to 12 million or about one-third of the total votes cast. In March 1933 the Nazis gained 44 percent of the vote in the mass electorate and Hitler maneuvered his way to the chancellorship. As soon as he was granted extraordinary powers, in July 1933, Hitler, the newly entrenched incumbent, banned all political parties other than the Nazi Party. This effectively reduced the winning coalition to a very small fraction of the German population.

Several criteria were required for party membership, including "pure" German blood, freedom from "Jewish or colored racial admixture," no hereditary illness fitting the law of July 14, 1933 (that would increase the risk of producing congenitally deformed children), nonmembership in the Freemasons or other secret societies, no clergy or others with strong denominational connections, having attained the age of twenty-one (though exceptions could be made for eighteen-year-olds), completion of military service (for males), subordination of the self for the good of national socialism, and so forth. The ideal size of the Nazi Party was stipulated to be 10 percent of racial comrades in the Greater German Reich (<http://web.jjay.cuny.edu/~jobrien/reference/ob79.html>).

By banning all political parties except the Nazi Party and by establishing criteria based on lineage, age, beliefs, and small party membership, Hitler ensured that his coalition would be a tiny fraction of the selectorate he inherited on coming to power in March 1933. The support of millions was required to hold office in the Weimar regime. Hitler came to power initially on the strength of the votes of millions. Once in office, he promoted changes in the rules so that support was needed from a tiny fraction of the population. He effectively pruned the winning coalition until it was vanishingly small. And then he murdered those within the party who might become rivals for control, leaving himself with a small winning coalition with high affinity and strong loyalty to him.

A second variety of purge calls for maintaining coalition size, while members of the selectorate are removed from that status. Doing so weakens the loyalty norm by making W a larger proportion of S. A weakened loyalty norm translates into greater expenditures by the incumbent on the coalition membership to ensure that none of the members defect. Since the coalition size was maintained, the private goods produced by the incumbent continue to be spread over the same number of people as before, so that only the quantity of total goods has changed. The quantity has gone up. Clearly such a change in institutional arrangements is attractive for members of the coalition, though not for the incumbent. Such a shift is an improvement over a rigged electoral system with a large selectorate, but it is not optimal for members of the selectorate outside the coalition, or the disenfranchised. The incumbent is forced to spend more and so has less in reserve for her own discretionary use. The outsiders see a shift in resources away from the incumbent, but the shift primarily benefits the coalition members and not those excluded from that group. Such purges of the selectorate are commonplace following military coups and the erection of a military junta or the creation of a quasi-hereditary "monarchy."

Pakistan's history has been punctuated by just such coups that shift the country away from nascent experiments with democracy and toward junta. Thailand also went through a period that favored this second type of purge, though it seems to have escaped the cycle of democratization followed by military coup and contraction of the selectorate in recent years. Syria seems to be following the path of quasi-hereditary monarchy as Hafiz al-Assad's son succeeded to the presidency on his father's death, a pattern also observed in North Korea and elsewhere. These societies increasingly make familial ties essential for coalition membership, removing the semblances of their former rigged-election autocratic structure.

A third form of purge reduces both the size of the coalition and the size of the selectorate. If there is to be a purge, this is the optimal form for coalition members who remain in the winning coalition, but, of course, any time members of the coalition are purged, each individual member runs the risk that he will be among the newly excluded. For those who survive such a purge, the benefits can be twofold. If the selectorate is reduced by a larger proportion than the coalition, increasing the value of W/S, the loyalty norm is weakened and so the incumbent must spend more. If the coalition is made smaller, albeit at a slower rate than the selectorate, the incumbent finds it more gratifying to increase private-goods production rather than public-goods production while she increases total spending. Remember, smaller-coalition systems provide proportionately more private goods than larger-coalition systems. Thus, if there is to be a purge and if it is controlled by coalition members, as in a "palace" coup d'état, the ideal purge reduces the coalition's size and the selectorate's size, thereby weakening the loyalty norm.

Although these developments were not strictly a purge, but rather a gradual alteration of institutions, we illustrate the idea of shrinking both the selectorate and the coalition by examining the history of the preconquest English monarchy. Specifically, we focus on the shift from selection of the king by a relatively broad assembly of all the people to selection in the *witenagemot*, the council of wise men and women.

Prior to the kingship of Eadgar (944–975), what today we think of as England was divided among distinct small kingdoms. The heptarchic monarchies first came broadly to be dominated by Wessex in 829 and then led to consolidation into a single English crown. In that sense, Eadgar the Peaceful was the first king of all of the English. As the seven kingdoms became consolidated into a larger kingdom, it proved all but impossible to hold a folkmoot, a general assembly of the people to which the people came bearing arms and granted or withheld consent for the policies of their king. It was also through these general assemblies that kings were chosen.

As power became consolidated, so too did the king consolidate his holdings of land. He and his thegns—backers who agreed to fight on behalf of the king in exchange for their rights to lands—emerged as a landed nobility, the precursors to the earls of King John's day. In this process of transition, the land held in common by all the people became—first in essence and then in fact—the king's land. Because general assemblies could no longer be convened over the large distances implied by a united kingdom, the witenagemot emerged as the mechanism by which kings were constrained politically and chosen on the death of the prior king. As Hannis Taylor (1889, 183–184) notes,

In the absence of the principle of representation, it is quite possible to understand how an originally democratic assembly, into which the magnates of the land entered as the great factors, would naturally shrink up into a narrow aristocratic body composed of the magnates only, wherever the extent of territory to be traversed rendered it difficult for the mass of the people to attend. . . . Furthermore, each advance in the process of aggregation was attended by a corresponding increase in the power of the king and thegnhood, and with a consequent depression of the popular power.

As the witenagemot replaced the general assembly of the people, the selectorate contracted from all adult residents to generally fewer than 100 magnates. The witenagemot held in 966, for instance, and regarded as typical, consisted of King Eadgar, his mother, two archbishops, seventeen bishops, five ealdormen, and fifteen thegns (Taylor 1889, 185).

The last gasp of "popular sovereignty" through a relatively large selectorate used for choosing the king is seen in the competition between Edmund II (also known as Edmund Ironside, about 993–1016) and Canute the Great (994–1035). Edmund was chosen king by the citizens of London, while Canute was chosen by the witan. A war ensued, ending with an agreement to divide the land between Canute and Edmund and with the further agreement that whichever survived the other would inherit the whole of the kingdom. Edmund died a few months later and the will of the witan thereafter prevailed.

With membership in the selectorate and in the winning coalition now restricted to those in the witenagemot, policy shifted notably toward use of public lands as rewards to loyal supporters of the king. For the first time a fairly general tax was levied, used to fight the Danes and to provide opportunities for redistribution from the poor to the rich thegns. The gradual "purge" of the selectorate and the winning coalition, eliminating the general assemblies, resulted in improved welfare for the coalition's members—that is, the thegns loyal to the king in the witenagemot. The agreement by Edward I in 1297 to accept the confirmation charter represented, as indicated earlier, an important step toward reestablishing the expanded coalition and selectorate of the prewitenagemot period.

Referring again to figure 8.1, we note that coalition members do not necessarily pursue purges if they gain control of government institutions. If these members are to the left of the low point in their welfare function, purges are a way to improve their welfare. But substantial expansion of the coalition, so that their welfare is catapulted to the long, upward slope on the right-hand side of the welfare function's low point, also is an attractive alternative. Indeed, if they expand coalition membership sufficiently, the greater representativeness of the government deprives them of private goods, but it can more than compensate with the greater production of public goods. The upward slope on the right-hand side of the low point is not as steep as the upward slope on the left-hand side, but it is sustained longer. In fact, these qualities of the coalition's welfare function provide clues to the solution of an important empirical puzzle and provide a way out of the cyclical trap of nascent democratization followed by purges and coups d'état.

Persistent Survival of High-Income Democracies

Adam Przeworski (2001) reports that no democracy whose per capita income exceeds $6,055 in 1985 purchasing-power parity dollars has ever ceased being a democracy. He notes further that the probability that democracy will survive in a state increases as per capita income goes up. Przeworski proposes an elegant model to explain these empirical regularities. His model leads also to the conclusion that democracy is sustained in affluent societies because citizens face too high a cost in personal welfare in turning against democracy. He demonstrates that redistributive policies face endogenously arising limitations so that a norm emerges in equilibrium that protects against excessively inefficient policies that would erode individual welfare in democracies.

Przeworski's theoretical results and empirical observations are consistent with deductions from the selectorate theory. We have already seen that large-coalition systems—like most democracies—foster policies that lead to high and growing per capita incomes and that norms arise that lead to low tax rates in large-coalition systems and to equilibration between spending on public goods and private goods. These effects are equivalent to finding a limit on redistribution. Particularly, as coalition size grows, tax rates drop, leaving less and less revenue available to the government to redistribute through its spending policies.

We saw in chapter 7 that the survival time for leaders decreases as coalition size increases. One might think that this contradicts the observation that democracies with high incomes seemingly persist forever. Przeworski's observation, however, is with regard to the survival of the political institutions of democracy and not the survival of individual leaders. We now offer an account that follows from the selectorate theory and that provides an explanation of the general characteristics of Przeworski's puzzle—that is, why democracies with high per capita incomes seem to persist indefinitely, even though their leaders are frequently turned out of office.

Figure 8.2 displays the welfare function for members of the winning coalition as deduced from the selectorate theory. The figure reproduces the function in figure 8.1, but now displays a dashed horizontal line that bifurcates the welfare function into two areas of interest. When the coalition's welfare is below the dashed line, coalition members can improve their well-being by increasing or decreasing coalition size, depending on where they are on the horizontal axis and depending on how far to the left or to the right they can shift the institutional arrangements. For instance, the two arrows in the bottom part of the figure (below the dashed line) both emanate from a point of low coalition welfare. Each arrow shows a path to improved coalition welfare by changing the size of the coalition. The left-pointing arrow clearly indicates how the remaining coalition's utility can be improved by purging some members of the group. The right-pointing arrow demonstrates how the coalition's welfare could be improved by increasing access to coalition membership. So, from below the dashed line, political systems can evolve away from, oscillate, or move toward more democracy, indexed here as a larger-coalition

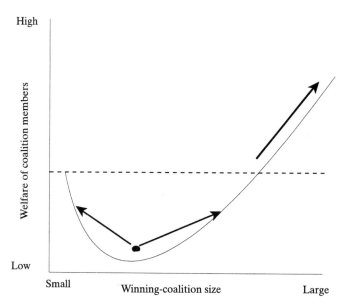

Figure 8.2
Survival of institutions: why high-income democracies persist

system. Movement toward a larger coalition, as we know from the selectorate theory and evidence, leads to improvements in per capita income and a host of other factors that enhance not only the well-being of coalition members, but also of all in the selectorate and among the disenfranchised. That is, high per capita income—such as Przeworski points to as immunizing democracy from being overthrown—is a consequence of large coalition size to a substantial degree. Reducing the coalition's size, as we also know, harms the disenfranchised and those in the selectorate but not in the coalition. It may or may not improve the lot of the leadership. All points below the dashed line provide a domain in which we might observe institutional change brought on by such actions as coups d'état, antigovernment protests, civil war, revolution, and so forth. These actions, when occurring below the dashed line, might reduce the degree of openness of the political system or they might increase it. In fact, as long as coalition welfare remains below the dashed line, the society has real prospects of swinging back and forth between different institutional arrangements, producing an unstable, volatile form of government.

Once a winning coalition's welfare is above the dashed line, the option of purging coalition members as the path to improving the remaining members' lot is no longer a rational choice. Instead, as the arrow above the dashed line indicates, coalition members can only enhance their well-being above the dashed line by expanding the size of the winning coalition essentially to its upper bound. This means, in the common parlance of categorical regime types, that once a society gets above the dashed line—itself an indicator of a welfare threshold—*everyone* except for the leader can improve welfare only by maintaining or expanding the degree of democracy in the polity. *Once the welfare threshold is crossed, no reduction in coalition size can make anyone except the leader better off.*

The selectorate and the disenfranchised prefer more public goods. Expanding coalition size fosters the provision of more public goods. Coalition members prefer a weaker loyalty norm, which prompts greater government spending. Once the threshold welfare value of the dashed line is reached, the loyalty norm, can only be weakened *and the welfare of coalition members improved* if the coalition's size expands.

Where the dashed line falls depends on the exact values of all of the parameters in the model, so we cannot say that it is precisely at a per capita income of $6,055 or at any other single income level. Having said that, we know that per capita income increases with coalition size and that, therefore, the more "democratic" the state is, the higher per capita income is according to the selectorate theory, exactly as reported by Przeworski. What is more, we know theoretically from figure 8.2 that a point always exists beyond which only leaders have a motivation to do away with a large-coalition—read democratic—political system. That point is where the dashed line crosses the coalition's welfare function, moving from left to right in the figure. Thus, democracies that are above the dashed line will never devolve to any other form of government through coups d'état, antigovernment protests, civil war, revolution, or any other mechanism favored by the disenfranchised, the selectorate, or the members of the winning coalition. Only a leader could alter the regime type to become more autocratic, but in polities above the dashed line this will prove extremely difficult, because such a leader (or challenger) will find it impossible (without an exogenous shock to the political system) to muster sufficient support to implement her wishes. No prospective coalition members can credibly be assured of payoffs sufficiently large to make them better off backing a shift to autocracy once coalition members (and the polity) have achieved a welfare level above the dashed line. Thus, when a polity is above the dashed line, its coalition size is sufficient to immunize it against the abandonment of democracy, thereby offering a theoretical explanation of the enduring quality of democracies with high per capita incomes.

The claims we just made regarding actions oriented toward changing institutions are testable. To start, we consider the incentives of those outside the winning coalition. We supplement earlier tests of antigovernment actions with the inclusion of income. Again we will find that, despite the ease with which they can protest (in terms of civil liberties), residents in large, wealthy systems protest less than residents in smaller-coalition systems. The institutions are already to their liking. To further test this logic we examine the consequences of antigovernment action to show that when residents in large-coalition systems protest, they do so to preserve or expand the size of the coalition yet further.

After showing that in large-W systems outsiders do not wish to change institutions, we explore the possible actions of insiders. To understand the incentives and aims of those within the winning coalition, we examine when they orchestrate coups and the consequences of coups for institutional arrangements. However, we start by considering the actions of those outside the winning coalition.

Antigovernment Actions and Their Consequences

As already discussed, antigovernment protests are the mechanism through which the disenfrachised, and sometimes those selectors outside of W, attempt to alter institutional arrangements. We classify methods of protest with two new dummy variables. The first, *Action*, is coded 1 if any of the following occur: *Demonstrations, Strikes, Riots, CivilWars, Guerrilla Wars,* or *Revolts*. It is coded 0 otherwise. The variable *BigAction* focuses only on the more extreme forms of protest: civil war, revolution, or guerrilla war. This variable is coded 1 if any of these actions occur in a particular year and 0 otherwise.

We examine how institutions affect the occurrence of protest, as measured by *Action* and *BigAction*, using logit analysis. Since Przeworski's claim surrounds wealth, as well as institutional configuration, we add the *WS:Income* variable, the residual effect of income (logged per capita GDP in 1995 U.S. dollars) not explained by institutional arrangements, and its interaction with W. We also include our standard region-year fixed effects. The expectation is that the likelihood of *Action* or *BigAction* is greatly diminished as *W* increases and as *W*WS:Income* increases.

The selectorate theory anticipates that when *W* is small *and income is high* (so that *W*WS:Income* is small while *WS:Income* is large), *Action* and *BigAction* are especially likely because so many in the polity find their welfare out of line with their expectations. They have the resources with which to resist government policy and they have the desire to generate greater public goods. The overall expectation is that the combined impact of the three independent variables is to reduce the likelihood of action, so that when per capita income and coalition size are both large, efforts to overturn the regime or the political system are especially unlikely.

Table 8.12 shows the results of the analysis of the likelihood of antigovernment action as coalition size increases, income increases, and both coalition and income rise. As predicted, larger coalition size leads to a substantial reduction in the likelihood of *Action* or *BigAction*, as does the interaction of income and coalition size. Polities with a high per capita income and a small coalition, in contrast, are more likely to experience antigovernment activities because people seemingly feel dissatisfaction with the balance between their possibilities (produced by high income) and their reality, produced by a small coalition. The overall impact of the independent variables is, as expected, to reduce the likelihood of *Action* or *BigAction* significantly, especially *BigAction*.

The first test establishes that those outside the coalition are unlikely to take actions designed to change the form of government when the

Table 8.12
Antigovernment action, income, and coalition size

	Action Coef., (std. error), prob.	*BigAction* Coef., (std. error), prob.
W	−0.907, (0.131), 0.000	−1.402, (0.154), 0.000
WS:Income	−0.313, (0.069), 0.000	−0.263, (0.078), 0.000
W*WS:Income	0.224, (0.098), 0.000	−0.100, (0.116), 0.000
P(W + W*WS:Income + WS:Income) < 0	$\chi^2(1) = 50.83, p = 0.000$	$\chi^2(1) = 99.49, p = 0.000$
Summary statistics	$N = 4{,}798$, F.E. $= 246$, $\chi^2(3) = 65.85, p = 0.000$	$N = 4{,}587$, F.E. $= 223$, $\chi^2(3) = 119.47, p = 0.000$

coalition is already large and per capita income is high, though they are likely to engage in such measures when the coalition is small and income is high. Income, then, by itself cannot be the explanation for the seeming immunity of wealthy democracies from fundamental institutional change. These facts must be true if the theory's account squares with Przeworski's observations, but they are not sufficient.

To further examine the incentive of groups outside the winning coalition, we examine the consequences of their protest. To do so we ask how antigovernment actions influence institutional change conditional on existing institutions. Do people protest to move toward democracy or away from it?

To examine this issue we construct a binary dependent variable, *UpDown*, based on how the winning coalition changes over the following three years. In particular, ΔW_{t3-t0} is W measured three years in the future minus the current coalition size. We ask whether, following events today, institutions change over the next several years. For ease of presentation, we examine the variable *UpDown*, which is coded 1 if the coalition size increases or remains the same ($\Delta W_{t3-t0} \geq 0$) and coded 0 if the coalition size contracts ($\Delta W_{t3-t0} < 0$). We have also carried out the analysis looking at a trichotomous version of the variable, looking directly at ΔW_{t3-t0}, and looking at the sum of the number of antigovernment actions rather than just at whether any government action took place. These analyses give similar answers, but for ease of presentation we examine the simple dichotomous *UpDown* variable.

We now consider the effect of *Action* (or *BigAction*), its interaction with W, and with $(Action*W)^2$ on institutional change. We include the squared term since the theory leads us to expect nonmonotonic effects. We cannot of course include the term *Action* squared without its interaction with W because *Action* is a dummy variable. The results of the logit analysis, including our standard fixed effects for region-year, are shown in table 8.13.

Since the coefficients are similar in both analyses, we focus on the case of the *Action* variable only. Rather than attempt the difficult job of interpreting the coefficients directly, figure 8.3 shows the predicted probability that coalition size will enlarge or stay the same. The predicted probability that coalition size contracts is 1 minus the probability graphed in figure 8.3.

Table 8.13
Retrenchment or sustainment of democracy

	Based on *Action* Coef., (std. error), prob.	Based on *BigAction* Coef., (std. error), prob.
*(Big)Action*W*	−7.204, (1.260), 0.000	−5.420, (1.371), 0.000
*((Big)Action*W)²*	5.411, (1.010), 0.000	3.337, (1.178), 0.005
(Big)Action	2.273, (0.395), 0.000	2.062, (0.158), 0.000
W	−1.754, (0.168), 0.000	−1.694, (0.158), 0.000
N = 10,514, F.E. = 461	χ^2 = 275.37, *p* = 0.000	χ^2 = 263.90, *p* = 0.000

Figure 8.3 reveals an interesting pattern. When W is very small ($W = 0$), the analysis predicts that the probability the coalition size will either expand or remain the same is close to 1, whether or not outsiders take action. This result should come as no surprise. When coalition size is at its lowest possible value it cannot be reduced further. Hence the result for small-coalition systems is largely an artifact of our coding of coalition size. At the other end of the scale, when $W = 1$, coalition size cannot increase further; thus the comparison is between whether coalition size remains the same or is reduced. The graph reveals a large difference in the probability that the coalition size will be reduced depending on whether outsiders take antigovernment actions. When they do—the solid line in the graph—they markedly reduce the probability of contraction in the coalition. When they do not—the dashed line in the figure—the odds of coalition contraction are substantially higher. This stands in marked contrast to smaller coalition size, where the effect of antigovernment action on the change in coalition size is much smaller.

As coalition size increases from the bottom, the difference antigovernment actions make in terms of predicted probabilities for changes in W becomes small. Indeed, for coalitions of size $W = 0.5$ and $W = 0.75$, the probability that the coalition contracts appears unaffected by antigovernment actions. When coalition size is at its largest, the impact of antigovernment protest is at its greatest, as is witnessed by the divergent lines in figure 8.3. When those outside the coalition do not protest the coalition is significantly more likely to contract. When residents take antigovernment actions they do so for the purpose of enlarging the

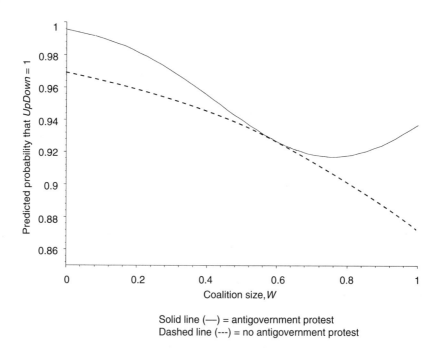

Solid line (—) = antigovernment protest
Dashed line (---) = no antigovernment protest

Figure 8.3
How prior institutional arrangements influence the effect of antigovernment actions

coalition. As the selectorate theory predicts, those outside the winning coalition want to preserve a large coalition size rather than contract it.

The data support the selectorate theory's predictions. Residents outside the winning coalition most prefer large-coalition systems. If they achieve this institutional configuration, they are least likely to partake in antigovernment actions, and if they do so it would appear to be with the motive to maintain the leader's dependence on a large coalition. In a moment we return to this analysis to discuss how leaders change institutions when they are unconstrained. However, before that we explain the motives and actions of members of the winning coalition.

Weaken the Loyalty Norm: Coups d'État

How might coalition members achieve institutional changes that enhance their welfare? The answer depends, in part, on whether they prefer to reduce coalition size and pursue purges, as indicated by the left-pointing arrow in figure 8.2, or whether they prefer to expand the coalition, as indicated by the right-pointing arrows in figure 8.2. In either case, however, weakening the loyalty norm by increasing W/S serves their interests. Although both the leader and the coalition might gain from a contraction in W, the incentives of the coalition and the leader diverge with respect to both enlarging the coalition and weakening the loyalty norm. Thus, to enhance their own welfare, members of the winning coalition may find it necessary to displace the incumbent. Several means of doing so are available. Terrorism and revolution make little sense for coalition members. After all, the current arrangement is giving them access to private benefits. Zorro or the Scarlet Pimpernel are the fancies of fiction and rarely a reality of politics.

Coup d'état is an appealing strategy for members of the winning coalition who want to give voice to their discontent. In a coup, they can displace the incumbent with someone from their own ranks in the hope that the newly installed leader will promote their interests. Much as revolutionaries can have a change in incentives once they succeed, so too may a coup leader once he is ensconced in power. Still, if dominated by a coalition rather than one individual, coups d'état can advance the coalition's interests. Those interests call for the political system to shift away from a rigged-election, large-selectorate, small-coalition system toward either a smaller-coalition, smaller-selectorate polity or toward a larger-coalition, larger-selectorate system. Thus, coups can be an avenue for creating juntas, monarchic-style systems, or democracy and for doing away with rigged-election autocracy. A key institutional purpose of a coup, according to the selectorate theory, is to weaken the loyalty norm by increasing the ratio of coalition size to selectorate size, although, provided the welfare of the coalition is below the dashed line in figure 8.2, the size of W could be either expanded or contracted. Once the coalition's welfare rises above the dashed line in figure 8.2, the coalition members are expected to only support further expansion of W.

The theoretical discussion of coups suggests some testable hypotheses. First, we investigate the incentives for members of the winning coalition to orchestrate coups. Second, we examine the consequences of coups for institutional arrangements. In carrying out these empirical investigations, we finish testing our explanation of Przeworski's claim about the reversal of democracy by showing that once a coalition expands sufficiently, members of the coalition no longer wish to perpetrate coups.

Under what conditions do coups start? First, we examine the likelihood of a coup as a function of the size of the winning coalition and as a function of the strength of the loyalty norm. In these tests we include controls for population size, residual per capita income, and residual democracy. Second, we examine the data to observe both the institutional conditions under which coups occur and, when they do happen, their consequences for the size of W. Consistent with the selectorate theory, we find that coups do not occur in the largest-coalition political systems ($W = 1$), but when they occur in smaller-coalition systems ($W < 1$), they can either increase or decrease subsequent coalition size. Third, we examine the effect of coups on the loyalty norm. Although coups can either increase or decrease W, in both cases coalition members make themselves even better off if, during their realignment of the coalition, they also increase the ratio W/S. The data suggest they do.

As with our previous analyses, we control for the fixed effects of region-year to ensure that we are not simply measuring some global trend or regional characteristic. Through the fixed effects we correct for the fact, for instance, that coups seem more common in Latin America or Africa than in Europe or North America. Tests of the relationship between the likelihood of a coup and coalition size are persistently significant and in the predicted direction, as seen in table 8.14. What is more, population and democraticness all fail to show a significant association with the risk of coup d'état once the effects of coalition size are taken into account. Coups are likely in polities with small winning coalitions and large selectorates.

Before moving on to examine the consequences of coups, we pause for a more direct examination of the coup data. Theoretically, once the welfare of the coalition has moved above the dashed line in figure 8.2, members of the winning coalition no longer wish to alter institutions since a contraction in W harms their welfare. Hence in large-coalition systems we should see no coups. Below the coalition size associated with the dashed line in figure 8.2 coups occur, and these coups can either increase or decrease W. Table 8.15 examines the number of coups that occur for each of our five measures of coalition size. We also record whether three years after the coup, W had contracted, stayed the same, or expanded. Obviously, given our crude coding of coalition size, coalitions recorded as $W = 0$ cannot contract further, nor can the largest category of coalitions ($W = 1$) expand.

Table 8.14
The prospects of a coup d'état

	Coef., (std. error), P	Coef., (std. error), P	Coef., (std. error), P	Coef., (std. error), P
W	−4.198, (0.233), 0.000		−7.146, (0.588), 0.000	−6.909, (0.796), 0.000
W/S		−3.738, (0.222), 0.000		
$Log(Pop)$			−0.143, (0.092), 0.082	−0.092, (0.095), 0.334
$WS:IncomeRes$			−0.710, (0.142), 0.000	−0.738, (0.164), 0.000
$WS:DemRes$				0.691, (0.770), 0.370
Summary statistics	$N = 5,901$, $\chi^2 = 427.76$, F.E. = 320, $p = 0.000$	$N = 5,654$ $\chi^2 = 356.40$, F.E. = 308, $p = 0.000$	$N = 2,088$ $\chi^2 = 273.36$, F.E. = 88, $p = 0.000$	$N = 1,701$ $\chi^2 = 221.28$, F.E. = 77, $p = 0.000$

Table 8.15
How institutional arrangements affect the occurrence and consequences of coups

W	Number of observations: nation-years	Number of coups	Subsequent enlargement of W (3 years later)	Size of W unaltered (3 years later)	Subsequent contraction of W (3 years later)
$W = 0$	690	140	49	91	NA
$W = 0.25$	3,413	167	46	108	13
$W = 0.5$	2,784	109	14	79	16
$W = 0.75$	3,276	46	2	36	8
$W = 1$	1,794	2	NA	2	0

Table 8.15 is constructed from all nation-years for which we have data, provided that an interstate war was not in progress. The data unmistakably support the predictions of the selectorate theory. First, coups are extremely unlikely in the largest-coalition systems. Second, in terms of coalition size, the consequences of coups vary, sometimes leading to an increase in W and at other times leading to a contraction in W.

Our data contain only three coups in our largest category of W. These occurred in Costa Rica in 1892 and 1919 and in Cyprus in 1974. The Cyprus case is eliminated from table 8.15 because Cyprus was involved in an interstate war. What is more, the coup was initiated by the Greek military junta, not Cypriot coalition members, making this event fit better within the discussion of our next chapter. If we restrict attention to a time frame for which we have economic data on wealth and hence consider the set of cases pertinent to Przeworski's claim, there are no cases of coups in the largest-coalition systems.

The winning coalition's motivation for a coup is to improve their welfare. The theory suggest that below the dashed line in figure 8.2, this can be achieved by either contractions or expansions of the coalition. Table 8.15 supports this prediction. Some coups enlarge the coalition and others contract it. The selectorate theory provides additional predictions on the consequences of coups. Whether members of W plot to increase or decrease coalition size, they enhance their welfare by reducing the loyalty norm. When a coup results in an increase in the ratio W/S, leaders need to work harder for their supporters and spend more on them.

We now investigate how coups affect the loyalty norm by regressing the change in the ratio W/S against coups, existing institutional arrangements, and a host of other controls, including of course our standard region-year fixed effects. Our analysis examines how the ratio W/S ($\Delta(W/S)_{(t+3)-t0}$) changes over a three-year period. In particular, the dependent variable is constructed by looking at W/S three years in the future and subtracting the current value for this variable. The analysis reveals that when a coup occurs, on average the ratio W/S will increase by 0.12 over the next three years ($N = 4383$, 249 F.E., $F(3,4131) = 25.19$). Controls for wealth and population size have no significant impact on change in the W/S ratio. Although coups can both expand and contract the winning coalition, they do so in a manner than reduces the loyalty norm. This is both the expectation from the theory and what we observe in the data.

Actions by Leaders: Constructing Autocracy

We know from the theory that, given their druthers, leaders would like to reduce coalition size and strengthen the loyalty norm. The latter requires either reducing coalition size and/or increasing selectorate size whenever possible. It is difficult to know across thousands of observations when changes in institutions are motivated specifically by actions taken by the incumbent leader. However, we can make sensible approximations. With those approximations we can test the theory's expectations. We examine only cases for which the variable *Action* = 0. This selects just those years in which the polity experienced no antigovernment demonstrations or strikes or riots or civil war or revolution or guerrilla war or coups d'état. The list of actions that lead observations to be excluded is the set of acts that coalition members, selectorate members, or the disenfranchised are likely to choose in their efforts to realign domestic institutions to be more in keeping with their preferences. We have, of course, already demonstrated that the frequency and consequences of these actions are consistent with the theory's predictions regarding institutional change.

When an incumbent leader faces no pressure from other sectors of the domestic population, there may be an opportunity to shift institutions more to her liking. She wants to reduce both W and W/S.

To assess the leader's ability to influence coalition size, we return briefly to figure 8.3. This figure plots the predicted probability that the winning coalition's size will either expand or remain the same as a function of initial coalition size and the actions taken by those outside of the coalition. Remember that the solid line indicates the probability that the coalition size does not contract if the antigovernment action takes place and the dashed line corresponds to the probability of noncontraction in the absence of antigovernment action. The graph shows that when residents do not protest, and hence we conjecture the leader gets the opportunity to assert her preferences, coalition size is more likely to contract as predicted. If coups, the actions of those inside the winning coalitions, are included in the analysis the results are similar.

We now supplement this earlier analysis by examining how the loyalty norm changes in the absence of antigovernment actions and coups. That is, when neither outsiders nor coalition members attempt to alter institutions, how does the loyalty norm (W/S) change? The expectation consistent with an incumbent's institutional preferences is that the dependent variable $\Delta(W/S)_{(t+3)-t0}$ will become smaller, reflecting a stronger loyalty norm that enhances leadership survival in office. The independent variables are W, S, and *Action* in the current year. We know that when actions are taken by those other than the incumbent, these actions tend to weaken the loyalty norm, so we expect that the marginal impact of *Action* = 1 is to offset some otherwise leadership-induced decline in W/S. This mitigating effect is not expected to be present when *Action* = 0. In those cases we should see a sharp decrease in W/S associated with larger values of W or S. This should be true across the board and even if we eliminate the cases in which $W/S = 1$ at the outset. Those

Table 8.16
Institutional change controlled by leaders

	$\Delta(W/S)_{(t+3)-t0}$ Coef., (std. error), prob.	If $W/S < 1$ $\Delta(W/S)_{(t+3)-t0}$ Coef., (std. error), prob.
W	−0.152, (0.006), 0.000	−0.222, (0.008), 0.000
S	−0.010, (0.005), 0.033	−0.003, (0.005), 0.530
Action	0.010, (0.003), 0.003	0.012, (0.004), 0.002
Constant	0.089, (0.005), 0.000	0.105, (0.005), 0.000
Summary statistics	$N = 11{,}460$, F.E. = 1,021, $F = 293.39, p = 0.000$	$N = 9{,}674$, F.E. = 1,016, $F = 337.64, p = 0.000$

cases, of course, can only produce a decline in W/S if there is any change at all.

The evidence from this suggestive test offers support for the hypothesis, especially with regard to the effort of autocrats to strengthen the loyalty norm when their current dependence is on a large-coalition. The larger W is initially, the greater the drop in W/S within three years. Table 8.16 displays the findings.[18] They are consistent with expectations.

Conclusion

Whatever the political arrangements in a society, some individual or group has an interest in changing the institutions of governance. When the government is not already autocratic, incumbent leaders have an interest in making the system more autocratic. They want to strengthen loyalty to them. This is achieved by reducing the size of the winning coalition and expanding the size of the selectorate. If the polity is autocratic, excluded groups want to make the coalition bigger, and, to the extent possible, they also want to make the selectorate smaller. Of course, they are constrained not to make the coalition bigger than the selectorate, so they might be happiest if the coalition includes a majority of the selectorate. Those in the winning coalition have somewhat different interests. They are best off when the coalition and selectorate converge in size, which means they can be content with monarchy, junta, or democracy. The members of a winning coalition do not particularly like autocracy. For them, the problem is that autocrats do not have to spend very much to maintain the coalition's loyalty.

We showed that institutional change is predictable and occurs in specified directions, depending on who gets to initiate the change. When coalitions have a choice in altering selection institutions, they weaken the loyalty norm, improving their own welfare to boot. When leaders change institutions, they strengthen the loyalty norm to enhance their prospects of surviving in office. When the disenfranchised or the selectorate protest government policies, they often succeed in improving their welfare. Once coalition size is expanded beyond a critical point, well-being for all reaches a level such that the inclusive institutions of government stay that way. That is, beyond a predictable threshold, democracy or at least a large coalition is relatively secure, at least from internal threat.

We also saw that when the disenfranchised do not find it overly costly, they can and do move to polities that provide lots of public goods—that is, large-coalition societies. In response to this threat to expropriation and rent seeking and in response to other threats to a leader's hold on power, we saw that oppressive policies adopted by leaders and coalition members are an endogenous feature of small-coalition systems. When the private benefits of office or coalition membership are large, people are more prepared to engage in horrendous acts of cruelty against others to ensure that their personal privileges are not lost. The selectorate theory helps us see why this is so and history makes abundantly clear that it is so. Our account suggests that many of the same factors that motivate revolutionaries also motivate emigrants. We also offered an account that explains why revolutionary leaders can be sincere in their declarations in favor of democracy before they come to power and yet can be expected to renege once they achieve victory. And we explained why some victorious revolutionaries adopt public-goods-producing governments that are broadly representative.

Our effort to explain changes in institutions is a beginning. Much remains to be done to refine theorizing about endogenous institution selection. One other piece of this puzzle is investigated in the next chapter, where we study how international disputes can give shape to institutional change.

9 The Enemy Outside and Within: War and Changes of Leaders and Regimes

Absolute monarchs will often make war when their nations are to get nothing by it, but for purposes and objects merely personal, such as thirst for military glory, revenge for personal affronts, ambition, or private compacts to aggrandize or support their particular families or partisans.
—The Federalist Papers, No. 4 (by John Jay)

The United States covets no one else's land, certainly not Afghanistan.
—Secretary of Defense Donald Rumsfeld (quoted in the New York Times, November 29, 2001)

On July 25, 1943, the Italian army arrested and imprisoned Benito Mussolini as the Western Allies were completing the conquest of Sicily and preparing to invade the Italian peninsula. The removal of Il Duce ended his fascist regime. Mussolini's quest for a new Roman empire around the Mediterranean had ended in failure. The new Italian government opened negotiations with the Western Allies to end Italy's participation in the Second World War. Unfortunately, German troops reacted before those negotiations could be concluded, seizing key points in Italy and disarming Italian troops. As a consequence, Italy became a battleground until the collapse of German forces and the end of the war in Europe in 1945. Mussolini met his fate at the hands of Italian Communist partisans. His body was hung on a meat hook and displayed in Milan.

In contrast, General Francisco Franco kept Spain out of the Second World War and continued to hold power until his death in bed in 1976. His fascist regime ended with his death as Spain became a democracy with a constitutional monarch. Unlike Mussolini, Franco did not join Nazi Germany in its war against the Allies and so avoided Mussolini's fate.[1]

War has the power to break leaders and regimes. This chapter considers war and the fate of regimes. The last chapter discussed internal changes of selection institutions; this chapter analyzes changes imposed from outside the state. We begin with a discussion of how selection institutions affect state goals in war. The politics anticipated after a war affect the aims a leader seeks for her state in wartime. We classify war aims into two broad categories, territory and policy. Territorial aims seek to increase the resource base of the state from which the leader extracts resources; policy aims cover all other war aims that involve changing the policies of the defeated state. We show that leaders who rely on small winning coalitions have a greater incentive to pursue territorial aims than those who require a large winning coalition. The central intuition here, as before, is twofold. First, more resources increase the advantage in the provision of private goods that leaders with small winning coalitions hold over possible challengers, increasing their hold on office. Second, such leaders retain a larger fraction of resources for their own use. More resources for the state means more resources for the leader personally.

Policy aims pose a commitment problem that can give the victor a reason to overthrow the regime of its opponent and replace the leader with one more favorable to the leader's interests. Victory may allow the victor to impose its policy aims on the defeated state at the end of a war; however, the victorious leader must also worry about whether her state can sustain the peace settlement in the face of attempts to revise it by the defeated state. The problem of winning the peace creates an incentive for a victorious leader to seek to replace the defeated leader with another less likely to challenge the postwar status quo. Further, the victorious leader may try to overthrow the regime of the defeated state and build new institutions there that will be conducive to her own interests. War also creates opportunities for internal challengers to overthrow a leader because defeat makes the failure of her foreign policy clear to all. The enemy outside the state empowers the leader's enemies within to end her rule.

Below we analyze why states may seek to overthrow foreign leaders and regimes through war and the likely consequences when they do. We also analyze how selection institutions affect territorial changes in states. We conclude the chapter by comparing the internal and external risks that leaders face in war.

Selection Institutions and War Aims

The ends state leaders seek in war depend on their domestic political situation. Victory in war allows the winning leader to impose conditions on the loser that benefit her winning coalition. As in chapter 6 on the democratic peace, the size and composition of a leader's winning coalition affect her foreign policy. Leaders see international politics through a lens of their own domestic politics. As the two quotations that open this chapter illustrate, a leader's war aims depend crucially on her winning coalition. The absolute monarch that Jay refers to answers to a small winning coalition and so seeks goods and glory for himself. Presidents answer to a large coalition and so seek security and policy support through war.

Public and Private Goods in War Aims

Foreign affairs opens up a range of goods that leaders can provide to their followers. We have discussed some of these goods, such as the benefits of openness to trade, earlier. Victory in war can secure the populace from an external threat, add territory to the state, and realize values that the winning coalition sees as important to pursue through changes in the defeated state's policies. In earlier days, war could also lead directly to material wealth for the winning coalition and the leader in the form of booty and tribute. To begin our discussion of the consequences of war for regimes, we classify war aims into public and private goods, which parallel, respectively, policy and territory.

Security is the essential public good of foreign policy. Although the days of roving bands of armed men raiding the populace of other polities are gone,[2] the twentieth century saw the depredations that the Nazis and Japanese, for example, inflicted on the civilian populations of the Soviet Union and China, respectively. Security from such foreign threats benefits all in society, and successful deterrence or defense protects all, even the disenfranchised. Even the most predatory leader does not wish for others to steal the wealth of her subjects; it means less for her to extract from them. We conceive of security in the narrowest of terms—the protection of the members of society from death, from wanton injury, and from theft by those who are armed.

The field of international relations has had great difficulty defining what it means by security.[3] We deliberately separate out many policies and outcomes often described as goals of national security, such as secure supplies of natural resources, because we believe those goals can be more accurately described within our framework of private and public goods. For instance, the use of military force to secure natural resources from foreign sources could produce a public good if those resources benefit the economy generally, or it could produce a private good if particular individuals alone benefit from the use of the state's military power to protect their foreign enterprises.

The determination of which war ends produce private goods depends on who receives the benefits. Territory can produce the public good of security if the occupation of strategic territory helps the state defend its citizens from external attack, or it can produce private goods if it contains natural resources or population that generate revenue with which the leader can reward her supporters. Some territorial demands combine elements of both public and private goods. Examples include France's claim for the return of Alsace-Lorraine before the First World War, since both the symbolic national value and the resources of those lost provinces were important to the French. Financial demands, such as tribute or reparations, generally operate as private goods because the wealth goes to the state to be allocated by the leader. Changes in the policy of the defeated state can be either public or private goods. The use of gunboat diplomacy, in the literal sense, by European states against Latin American states that did not pay their debts benefited creditors, generally nationals of the state sending the gunboats. The use of force by NATO against Yugoslavia in 1999 forced an end to atrocities by Serbian paramilitary forces against Kosovars; these benefits were public goods because the motivation for the populace of NATO states was moral rather than material.

The distinction between public and private goods in war aims is clear in theory. However, because it is novel, our distinction differs from common concepts of how war aims should be classified. Standard data collections do not correspond to our notion of the public and private goods sought in war. Further, because one concrete war aim can produce both public and private goods, as in the case of France's recovery of Alsace-Lorraine, exact classification of war aims into public and private goods can be difficult. We raise this issue here to alert the reader that the fit between our classification of war aims and those available from standard data sets is far from perfect. We discuss the fit between the two at greater length when we turn to an empirical examination of hypotheses about war aims. Given the difficulties of finding a single measure that captures the public- and private-goods elements of war aims, we perform a range of tests using different collections of data.

Our central point about war aims should be obvious to the reader now. Systems with small winning coalitions predispose their leaders to pursue private goods in war; systems with large winning coalitions motivate leaders to fight for public goods. As in earlier chapters, leaders of all systems provide a mix of both types of goods for their supporters, so war aims are almost never purely public or private goods. Instead, the size of the winning coalition shifts the mix in favor of one good rather than the other in a state's war aims.

Winning the Peace and War Aims

Regardless of the specific goals of a victorious state, the leaders of the defeated state often seek to undo the outcome of the war after it is over.[4] A well-known case of such revisionism was the German drive in the 1920s and 1930s to remove provisions of the Versailles Treaty that many Germans found burdensome and unacceptable. The desire to revise a peace settlement after a war is over creates a problem for the victor: having won the war, it now needs to win the peace as well. Failure to sustain the benefits won through war can be used by a challenger in his efforts to unseat the leader of the victorious state. Similarly, challengers in the defeated state may advocate revision as a way to replace their leader. This incentive to revise the postwar status quo exists in the defeated state even if the wartime leader is removed as a consequence of losing the war. The requirements for holding power in both the winning and losing states create the incentives for the issues fought over in war to continue to be in dispute.

The defeated state can most easily revise the outcome of a war when the victor's terms require the cooperation of the defeated. For example, the United Nations coalition that fought the Gulf War repeatedly demanded and received legal obligations that Iraq would cooperate with inspections to determine the extent, state, and destruction of its chemical and biological weapons after the war. In practice, the UN inspectors found Iraqi compliance with the inspections difficult to obtain at best. Direct obstruction of inspections by Iraqis was not unusual. Even when faced with a renewed risk of war, the Iraqi government resisted providing clear and open evidence of its alleged disarmament.

Territorial changes require the defeated state to challenge the postwar status quo openly through either diplomatic or military means. In either case, a change in the terms that ended the war requires the acquiescence of the victor even if that agreement is obtained under threat of war. We will refer to these two types of war aims as requiring *active* or *passive compliance* by the defeated state. War aims requiring active compliance are more difficult to enforce.

This distinction between active and passive compliance is important during war because leaders consider the stability of the peace when they form their war aims. Ends requiring the active compliance of the defeated force the victorious state to take measures to sustain the gains of its victory. Such efforts may be easy or difficult. War aims requiring the active compliance of the defeated lead to a long-term commitment by the victor to enforce compliance with the agreement that led to the end of the war. Such a commitment is likely to be a long-term issue in domestic politics, particularly if such efforts prove costly or ineffective over time.

Leaders may seek other ways to enforce their war aims that require active compliance. One way to enhance compliance by the defeated state is to replace its regime with a puppet regime. The puppet, owing his hold on power to the victor, should be willing to comply with the victor's terms. In essence, placing a puppet in power minimizes the need to enforce the peace. As Werner (1999, 927) concludes, "The evidence strongly indicates . . . that an imposed settlement that deposes the loser's government does enhance the durability of peace." Despite these attractions, it is costly for the victor to overthrow the regime of the losing state and replace it with a puppet. Removal of the old regime requires not just defeat, but conquest. Placing the puppet in power requires a military occupation to establish the new regime and possibly a willingness to provide it with military support to enable it to hold power in the face of violent domestic challenges in the future.

Most wars do not end with the total conquest of the loser. A decision by the winning side to make replacement of the regime of the losing state a war aim prolongs the war, imposing further costs on the victor. The choice is whether the added cost of continuing the war to put a puppet in place is justified by the gains from ensuring the compliance of the defeated state with any goals that require its active compliance.

Napoleon Bonaparte faced these problems with puppets. He could not annex all the territory he conquered, so he created new kingdoms and chose members of his family to rule them. His brother Louis became king of Holland, his brother Joseph first became king of Naples and then king of Spain, his brother Jerome king of Westphalia, his stepson Eugene de Beauharnais viceroy of Italy (Napoleon himself was king of Italy), and his sister, Caroline, queen of Naples when Joseph became king of Spain.

To be sure, the politics of puppets is not straightforward. In addition to the victor's decision to impose a puppet, the puppet makes decisions about whether to continue to comply with the victor's policy wishes. The puppet may have ideas of his own about how his country should be run and may implement such ideas in his own political interest. The puppet may wish to prolong his own rule by eliminating dependence on the victor or may face domestic challenges that compel him to break with the state that placed him in power to prevent his own downfall.

Marshal Joachim Murat, Caroline's husband and hence king of Naples, faced the problem of a puppet most directly. The allied powers allowed Murat to retain his position at the Congress of Vienna. When Napoleon first returned from Elba, Murat declared against him and for the allies. Unfortunately for Murat, he changed his mind and switched to supporting Napoleon before Waterloo. The allies defeated the Neapolitan army under Murat and removed him as king of Naples; they later executed him after he returned to his kingdom in an effort to regain power. Murat had to choose the winning side to survive as king, and he allowed his personal ties to Napoleon and promises of additional territory to overrule his initial sound judgment of the military situation. That is, first he defected from Napoleon's coalition when he thought that was politically wise, and then he defected from the allied coalition only to discover later—at the cost of his life—that this was a mistake.

Our model of war aims reflects the above considerations. Placing a puppet in power improves the prospects of compliance of the defeated state with the terms of the agreement. However, the victor will have to pay an extra cost to carry the war out to the point where it can replace the regime of the defeated state with a puppet. Further, the puppet must survive domestically if he is to pursue the goals of the victor. Unfortunately "King Louis proved rather too 'Dutch' for his brother's [Napoleon's] liking" (McKay and Scott 1983, 322). While puppets might be beholden to the victor, their domestic circumstances do not always allow them to carry out the policies prescribed for them. In particular, once the coalition in the defeated state is beyond a certain size, the puppet is sufficiently disadvantaged in the provision of international public goods relative to a domestic challenger that she cannot survive. As we will see, this often forces the victor to rearrange the institutions in the defeated state if she wants a leader to carry out her bidding.

We deduce hypotheses about the circumstances under which the removal of the regime of the opponent is a war aim and what type of regime victors install when they overthrow foreign leaders, thereby engaging in what today is called *nation building*.

Territorial Revision

The defeated state may attempt to reverse any territorial gains that the victor made at its expense. Territorial revision requires action by the defeated state, so territory is a war aim that only requires the passive compliance of the defeated. The ability of the victor to sustain its newly acquired territory in the face of a demand by the defeated state depends in large part on the balance of capabilities between the two (Powell 1996b, 1999). Territorial gains are generally easier to sustain than policy gains. The defeated state may alter the policy-based aspects of a settlement unilaterally by refusing to continue to honor the terms of the agreement. In contrast, to reorganize a territorial settlement typically means actively reverting to war.

Territorial expansion, like replacing the regime of the defeated state, is likely to require added effort and a longer war. Greater expansion means prolonging the war to seize the extra territory or to impose sufficient cost on the losing side that it cedes the territory to end the war.

The different ways that territory can produce public and private goods in our theory complicate the argument. When the territory gained through war contains substantial resources, the shift in those resources from the losing state to the victor also shifts the balance of resources between the two in favor of the victor. However, the chance each side has to win a war depends on the resources mobilized for a possible conflict over the territory in dispute. As we saw in chapter 6, large winning-coalition systems mobilize a greater additional portion of their resources in war than small winning-coalition systems when national survival is not in question. Both the war aims of leaders and their willingness to defend their gains from war vary with the size of the coalition to which they answer.

The stability of a territorial settlement that ends a war should depend on the systems of both the winning and losing states. Leaders of systems with large winning coalitions are less concerned about the possession of territory for the resources contained in them. A larger pool of state resources neither substantially increases their ability to hold office nor increases the resources available for their own discretionary projects. Consequently, such leaders should not seek territory for its resources nor strongly resist demands for revision in such territories. In contrast, leaders of small winning-coalition systems benefit from increases in state resources; a larger resource pool increases their ability to hold power as well as increasing their personal resources. They should seek territorial acquisitions for more resources and be willing to fend off demands to reverse their territorial acquisitions through war.

Strategic territory—militarily valuable territory containing few resources—should be of greater interest to leaders responsible to a large winning coalition. For instance, during the Suez crisis Britain and France showed no reluctance in using force against Egypt to secure open access to the Suez canal, the strategic lifeline of their oil supply and, for the United Kingdom, the link to the area "east of Suez." Similarly, having defeated Syria's forces, Israel undertook the additional step of capturing the Golan Heights. While these mountains give Israel valuable water resources, the primary benefit of controlling them is that it makes future Syrian attacks more difficult. Strategic territory increases the ability of large-coalition systems to provide the public good of security for the residents of their state. It also raises their ability to defend their other gains from a victorious war. Leaders of systems with small winning coalitions value strategic territory because it may allow them to reduce resources committed to defending other territory.

We qualify our arguments about territory and differing interests in territorial expansion in two ways. First, all leaders benefit by increasing the resources of their state through territorial expansion and through the acquisition of strategic territory. However, the winning coalition to which a leader answers inclines her toward one form of territorial expansion over the other. Just as all leaders provide a mixture of public and private goods, the difference across selection institutions is seen in the mix of policies pursued. Second, territory can contain resources from many sources: population, industry, or natural resources. The resource value of a territory depends on what the regime can extract for its own uses or direct to its supporters.

Territorial expansion, then, is of most interest to leaders with small winning coalitions when they can add to their state's resources through such expansion. Leaders of large winning coalitions are more likely to seek territorial expansion for strategic purposes. Overall, we expect that leaders of small winning-coalition systems are more inclined to seek territorial expansion.

Modeling War Aims

We elaborate the basic model presented in chapter 3 to include foreign policy as a source of public or private goods. Using this model as a platform, we analyze the possibility of territorial expansion, the removal of foreign leaders, and nation building. Our analysis focuses on the period after the end of a war to see how different war aims assist the leader of the victorious state in her efforts to retain power. This focus on the period after the war also allows us to examine the problem of revision discussed above.

Our model of war aims includes two states (A and B), with political competition in each. Suppose nation A has defeated nation B in a war. We consider actions the leader in nation A (who we will also refer to as A) might undertake to enhance her domestic survival, by altering the nature of the future international competition between A and B. In particular, A might take resources from nation B, she might install a puppet in B, or she might alter B's institutional arrangements. Institutional arrangements in both A and B affect the attractiveness of each of these options.

Although the leader in each state faces the reselection process, to cope with the additional complexity of two nations, we simplify the model of domestic competition from that used in chapter 3. In particular, we assume leaders have fixed levels of resources, R_A and R_B respectively, rather than modeling the taxation process explicitly. We also dispense with domestic public goods. Hence, leaders compete domestically over the provision of private goods and the provision of public goods through foreign policy.

Following any postwar settlement, nations A and B engage in ongoing competition over international affairs in which each side wants to secure its most desired international policy. As in chapter 3, we model this as an infinitely repeated game, in each round of which the leader and domestic challenger in each state propose a level of private goods for their coalition members and a level of foreign policy effort. Nations A and B compete over international outcomes, and the extent to which each nation prevails depends on the effort each side makes.

Our use of noncooperative game theory captures the credibility problem of maintaining any postwar settlement. Although leader B might have promised a particular foreign policy as part of a peace settlement, such an agreement requires active compliance and international outcomes depend on what both sides do. Further, even if leader B wanted to honor the terms of an agreement, domestic competition often forces him from this position. If his domestic rival proposes abrogating the agreement and offering a foreign policy more attractive to selectors, it becomes hard for leader B to survive, particularly in a large-coalition system, unless he is also prepared to abrogate the agreement. Following World War I, German leaders found it hard to stick to the terms of the Treaty of Versailles for precisely this reason. Political opponents gained great mileage from criticizing the terms of peace.

Individuals in both A and B care about foreign policy, and we assume that their interests are opposed. We represent the issue at hand on the unit interval *[0,1]*, where *1* represents A's preferred outcome, and *0* B's preferred outcome. For instance, suppose the issue in question is the amount of water A receives from a river that begins in B and then flows through A. The outcome *1* represents A receiving all the water it wants from their common watershed, with *0* representing A receiving only the water that B is willing to give it. Numbers between *0* and *1* represent intermediate resolutions of the division of the water. Everyone in A wants higher numbers; everyone in B lower numbers. In this sense, their interests are opposed, and foreign policy is a public good in both states.

The outcome of the issue at hand depends on the resources each side commits to it. The commitment of more resources by a state moves the outcome in its favor. Formally, the outcome f is a function of the resources both sides commit to foreign policy; $f = f(q_A, q_B) = q_A/(q_A + q_B)$, where q_A and q_B denote the resources each side commits to foreign policy. As A spends more on foreign policy, f increases. As B spends more on foreign policy, f declines.

Individuals in both A and B would like the international outcome to favor them as much as possible; they would also like more private goods. We model individual preferences with the following linear utility function: $V_A(g, f(q_A, q_B)) = g + q_A/(q_A + q_B)$ and $V_B(g, f(q_A, q_B)) = g + q_B/(q_A + q_B)$, where g is the level of private goods they receive.

As in chapter 3, we can characterize the level of resources leaders must spend on each type of good if they are to survive in office. Although the formal demonstration is relegated to the appendix, the underlying logic is the same as that used throughout this book. The challenger makes his best possible offer. However, he cannot promise more that the available resources allow. Neither can he promise long-term access to private goods. Should he come to power and learn his affinity for selectors, he will reorganize his coalition accordingly. The incumbent's promised benefits only need to match the expected value of the challenger's immediate offer plus the probabilistic access to future private goods if the challenger comes to power. Since the incumbent can guarantee future private goods to her coalition, she need not spend all available resources to survive.

How many resources A must spend and the mix of private goods and foreign policy effort depend on institutional arrangements in both A and B. As we have seen before, when coalition size is large, political competition revolves around the production of public goods, in this case, foreign policy. When coalition size is small, political competition revolves around private goods. Particularly when S is large, leaders can exploit their advantage in being able to credibly promise future private goods by skimming off societal resources for their own purposes.

Yet, unlike the production of domestic public goods considered earlier, the success of foreign policy depends not just on what one nations does, but on the relative effort of both nations. Indeed, in equilibrium, incumbent A produces $q_{AL}^* = W_B W_A^2 / (W_A + W_B)^2$ foreign policy effort. As is readily seen, A's attempts to influence foreign policy depend on institutional arrangements in both countries. The larger the winning coalition in nation A, the more effort A places on achieving international public policy success. But the greater effort her international rival makes, the harder it is for her to achieve foreign policy success. In equilibrium the outcome of international policy is $f(q_A^*, q_B^*) = W_A / (W_A + W_B)$. The smaller the coalition size in B, and hence the less inclined its leader is to focus on the public-goods aspects of foreign policy, the greater A's success in foreign policy. This result provides much of the intuition for what is to come.

When incumbent A's coalition is large, she wants the foreign rival to make little foreign policy effort. She can obtain this outcomes either by installing a puppet who does her bidding on the foreign policy dimension or by altering B's institutions to discourage foreign policy effort.

The above analysis of the postwar interactions between nations provides a platform from which to consider postwar settlements. We have seen that leaders in defeated states cannot commit to settlements that require their active compliance. Future international outcomes and the maintenance of agreements depend on the effort each side puts into foreign policy. How then should victorious leaders structure the postwar environment to their benefit, and how do institutions affect these choices?

We consider three actions a victorious leader might choose to shape postwar interactions. Leader A might take resources from B; she might install a puppet in B; or she might alter the institutional arrangements in B. Each of these actions requires additional effort and hence additional costs for A. At high enough costs, A might prefer not to undertake any of them. However, institutional arrangements in both A and B determine the relative benefits of each course of action.

When to Take Territory

The victor can seek to take territory from the defeated state in order to increase its own resource base. Recall that we consider strategic territory as a different war aim from adding resources through territorial expansion. The former seeks territory for the public policy benefit of security that strategic territory may help to provide. Here we examine when a victorious leader prefers to expand her resource base. (We refer to the victorious leader as she and the defeated leader as he.)

Seizing territory requires the victorious state to continue the war beyond the point when it could end the war with a favorable settlement. Hence territorial expansion imposes costs on the victorious leader. She must assess when the benefits of such expansion are expected to outweigh its immediate costs.[5] We examine the decision by a leader to take some piece of territory of fixed size. It would of course be interesting to consider how much territory A takes from B, but such an analysis requires assumptions about how the marginal cost of taking additional land changes as more land is taken. The selectorate theory provides no guide here. Therefore, we consider the question of whether at the additional cost of C_R, leader A wants to transfer ρ resources from B to A.

Territorial gain shifts resources from the defeated state to the victor. There are two effects from territorial gain. The resources of the victor increase and the resources of the defeated are reduced. We will assume that all of the reduction in the defeated state's resources go to the victor; there is no destruction of resources during war.[6] If A takes no resources, the postwar competition takes place with A having R_A and B having R_B resources. If A takes resources from B, postwar competition shifts because A has $R_A + \rho$ and B has $R_B - \rho$ resources. Of course, absent the cost, increasing resources is always attractive for all leaders. The interesting question is how institutions alter the relative value of taking resources. If costs are sufficiently large, it can be the case that no nation wants to take resources. Similarly, if costs are small enough, it could be the case that regardless of institutional arrangements, A always wants to take resources. However, between these extremes, the smaller A's coalition size the more attractive taking resources becomes.

When the victor's coalition, W_A, is small, political competition focuses on the provision of private goods and the incumbent is able to skim resources for her own discretionary projects. The greater the available resources, the easier it becomes for her to buy off her supporters and the easier it is for her to survive. Additionally, she can skim off more resources for herself. In contrast, political competition in large-coalition systems focuses on the provision of public policy. The challenger has no inherent disadvantage in the provision of public goods, and the increase in resources improves the best offer the challenger can make. This forces the incumbent to also spend her new additional resources on public policy. The public-goods focus makes it hard for leaders to skim off resources for themselves. Additional resources do not help large-W leaders as much as they do small-coalition leaders.

A victorious leader will always gain a share of those added resources for her own purposes because the leader does not allocate all incremental resources to her coalition. The greater the share of resources that the leader can retain for her own purposes, the greater her interest in territorial expansion for resources.

The size of the selectorate of the winning leader's state also influences her willingness to take territory. As S_A increases, the loyalty norm grows and leaders are able to skim off a greater proportion of available resources. Leaders with a small coalition and a large selectorate have the greatest incentive to take resources from defeated states.

The selection institutions of the defeated state can play a role in the victorious leader's decision whether to take territory. Although these predictions are beyond our simple model, B's selection institutions affect how B allocates resources. The larger W_B and the smaller S_A, the greater B's foreign policy effort and spending in general. Consequently, A has a bigger incentive to take resources when her foreign rival heads a large-coalition system; this helps reduce her rival's future foreign policy effort. We suspect the impact of the rival institutions will be secondary in magnitude compared to the effect of A's institutions. Large-coalition systems are the ones that care about their foreign rival's foreign policy effort, and these large-coalition states are the least disposed to taking territory.

Pulling the arguments of this section together, we have confidence in the following hypotheses about when states should seek territory:

1. The larger the winning coalition of a warring state, the less likely it is to seek to take territory from the opposing side.

2. The larger the size of the selectorate in a warring state, the more likely it is to seek territory as a war aim. The impact of selectorate size (S_A) should be most pronounced when W_A is small.

When to Install a Puppet

Overthrowing the regime of the losing state in favor of a puppet solves the problem of "winning the peace." The puppet, by definition, will do as the victorious leader asks, understanding that he serves at her pleasure. One might think, then, that victors would always attempt to put a puppet in power as a condition of ending the war. However, two obstacles face the imposition of a puppet.

First, the victor needs extensive political control over the defeated state to put her person in power. The defeated government must be removed or forced to flee the country. A total victory is required to install a puppet, and total victories generally require extensive fighting. The victor may be able to get the defeated leader to agree to make the policy concessions it seeks short of such a total victory. For example, the U.S.-led coalition in the Gulf War did not need to defeat Iraq completely to secure the agreement of the Iraqi government to Security Council Resolution 686, which specified the war aims of the coalition (Freedman and Karsh 1993, 407). The question is whether the added value of the assurance the puppet provides is worth the additional cost necessary to impose a puppet regime.

The second obstacle to installing a puppet lies in the puppet's ability to hold power against domestic challengers. It does the victor little good to install her person in the defeated state if he—the puppet—is then thrown out. When puppets adopt the victor's chosen foreign policy, they disadvantage themselves relative to an unconstrained domestic challenger. In terms of modeling, we assume a puppet makes minimal foreign policy effort, thus allowing the victorious leader to achieve a successful international outcome with little expenditure of resources. As we will subsequently show, this is particularly advantageous from the perspective of large-coalition leaders.

By restricting himself to minimal foreign policy effort, the puppet reduces the value he can produce for his winning coalition because he cannot allocate any resources to foreign policy, even when such allocations are in the interest of his winning coalition. Domestic political rivals are not so constrained. To survive, the puppet must offer his coalition benefits that at least match the expected value of the challenger's best offer. If the puppet cannot match the challenger's offer despite spending all available resources, he is deposed.

The difference between what the puppet and the challenger can produce for the puppet's winning coalition depends on how important foreign policy is in an unconstrained setting. The more resources an unconstrained leader would commit to foreign policy, the greater the disadvantage the puppet faces by his inability to commit any resources to foreign policy.

Relative to an unconstrained challenger, a puppet is disadvantaged in the provision of foreign policy, but like all incumbents, he is advantaged in the provision of private goods. When the focus of political competition is private goods, as it is in small-coalition systems (particularly those that also have a large selectorate), the puppet survives easily. However, as coalition size grows, and public goods become increasingly important, puppets can no longer overcome their disadvantage in the provision of foreign policy and they are deposed domestically. Once B's coalition is beyond a certain size, because of its foreign policy constraints a puppet cannot survive. Yet puppets survive when coalitions are small.

Having established the conditions when a puppet can be installed, we move to the question of who wants to install them. The comparative statics of when the leader of A will overthrow the regime in B in favor of a puppet are straightforward. The larger the role that foreign policy public goods play in the victorious leader's efforts to retain power, the more she must commit to foreign policy, and hence the greater the benefit of installing a puppet. Resources committed to foreign policy increase with the size of the winning coalition in A and decrease with the size of the selectorate in A. The leaders of mass democracies, then, have the greatest incentive to install puppets, all else being equal.

The existing selection institutions in B also give the leader of A incentives to install a puppet. The more resources B commits to foreign policy, the more the leader of A will have to allocate herself. The leader of B allocates more resources to foreign policy as the size of his winning coalition increases. Therefore, as the coalition size of a democracy's rival increases, the more likely it becomes that the democracy will install a puppet should it win. This is of course subject to the constraint that B's coalition is not too large; otherwise the installation of a puppet becomes impossible without modification to B's institutions.

Drawing these predictions together yields several hypotheses:

3. Puppets are not installed in large-coalition systems.

4. The larger the coalition in the victorious state (W_A), the more likely the victorious leader is to replace the defeated leader with a puppet.

5. Subject to puppets not being installed in the largest-coalition systems, the greater B's coalition, the greater the prospects that a puppet will be imposed on B.

Taken together, hypotheses 3 and 5 suggest that puppets become more likely as W_B increase up to some maximum size beyond which no puppets are installed. The discussion of puppets foreshadows our next section. Rather than simply replacing the existing leader, the victor might replace the entire regime, thus creating institutional arrangements under which her puppet might survive. More generally, institutional change might accompany a leadership change, or the two might be separate. Whether or not the leader is changed, changing B's institutions changes the leader's incentives and hence policy choices.

When to Change Institutions

Although a puppet who is beholden to leader A might carry out A's bidding, unless A remains in a position where she can remove the puppet, it is contrary to the puppet's interests to continue to do exactly what A wants once the threat of external deposition is gone. The recognition of this creates incentives for victors to alter the institutional arrangements in the defeated state, rather than just changing the individual in power. By doing such nation building, the victor will alter the motivations of leaders in rival foreign states as long as the new institutions of governance remain in place.

As we saw above, it is leaders from large-coalition systems who benefit most by reducing subsequent foreign policy effort in defeated states. Such leaders rely on public goods for their own survival. Reducing B's foreign policy effort through either a puppet or institutional reform improves their survival and allows them to skim off a few additional resources.

When leader A is from a large-coalition system, such as a democracy, her domestic survival depends on public-goods provision, which, in the current context, means foreign policy success. The larger W_B and the smaller S_B, the greater B's foreign policy effort and the harder it is for A to prevail. By reducing B's coalition size and increasing B's selectorate, by, for example, pushing for a rigged electoral system, A reduces B's foreign policy effort and hence helps herself retain office. Autocratic puppets are less likely to attempt to overturn the postwar status quo and so help to ensure that the victor wins the peace as well as the war. Further, autocratic leaders have longer tenures in office than leaders who answer to a large winning coalition, as we have shown in chapter 7. An autocratic puppet, then, has the additional advantage of reducing the risk that he or she will be replaced by another leader less willing to do as the victor wishes. It should also be noted that leader B, whether a puppet installed by A or not, supports A in her choice of institutional revisions. All unencumbered leaders prefer political systems with a small coalition drawn from a large selectorate.

For those who think of the benefits of democracy in normative or moral terms, the inclination of large-coalition victors to install rigged electoral systems or dictators is a sad implication. In the selectorate theory, democratic leaders do not inherently wish to improve the quality of governance in foreign states. Indeed, neither do democratic winning coalitions, selectorates, or disenfranchised residents. Maintaining autocracy abroad provides democratic residents with the policy outcomes they want: proselytizing democracy throughout the world harms their welfare. The only exception arises if it happens that the policy preferences among the defeated state's citizens coincide with those in the victorious state.[7]

We close this section with a list of hypotheses to be tested. We state the hypotheses in terms of general war aims, although we will test them on state goals in disputes short of war, the outcomes of wars, and the outcomes of violent disputes. Our argument leads to the following hypotheses:

6. The larger the winning coalition in the victorious state, the more likely it is to alter institutions by reducing coalition size and increasing selectorate size in the defeated state.

7. The larger the winning coalition in the losing state, the more likely a large-coalition victor is to seek institutional changes.

Three Caveats

There are three important caveats to the seven hypotheses we have advanced. The first caveat is that the hypotheses assume that all else is equal. Other factors, such as the importance of the issues in dispute between the two states, also affect postwar politics. When the issue at hand is critical for the defeated state, even an autocrat will devote more resources to efforts to overturn the outcome of the war. When the issue at hand is peripheral to the victorious state, it is less interested in over-throwing the defeated leader even if it anticipates that the latter will challenge the postwar status quo. We expect, therefore, that individual cases at variance with our hypotheses can be found.

The second caveat addresses some hypotheses we do not draw out of our model. The arguments above also suggest that the more powerful the defeated state, the more willing the victor should be to replace the defeated leader. The more resources B has, the more its leader will devote to foreign policy. This observation suggests that leaders of powerful states are more likely to be replaced when they lose a war. However, such a conclusion depends on the assumption that the cost of replacing the defeated leader is the same no matter what the size and degree of power of the defeated state are. It seems plausible that the cost of replacing the leader grows with the power of the defeated state; over-throwing the leader of a small state should be much easier than removing by force the leader of a major power. Because the victor compares the cost of removing the defeated leader against the benefit of installing a puppet, the willingness of the victor to install a puppet could increase or decrease with the power of the defeated state. The hypothesis depends on how fast the cost of removal grows relative to the benefit of removal. Our argument describes the latter but not the former, and so we cannot draw a clear conclusion about whether the leaders of more powerful states are more likely to be removed after a defeat.

The third caveat concerns another assumption of the model: that the interests of the victor and the defeated state will continue to be opposed after the war. That continued conflict of interest is why the members of the selectorate of the defeated state want to overturn the postwar status quo. However, there are cases in which the conflict of interest between the two sides disappears after the war. Without that conflict, the victor need not fear a challenge to the status quo from the defeated state, and the commitment problem of winning the peace disappears with the conflict of interest. Consequently, the victor no longer gains by imposing a puppet regime on the loser. Further, if the two sides now possess common interests, the victor may prefer installing a system with a large winning coalition and selectorate in the defeated state. Such systems induce their leaders to allocate more resources to foreign policy. These added resources from the defeated state now advance the common interests between the victor and the vanquished. Thus, the installation of democratic regimes in West Germany and Japan by the United States and its allies several years after World War II are consistent with our broader argument, although not with our specific model in which we examine cases of persistent conflict of interest.

We have considered the questions of when leaders take territory, when they install puppets, and when they alter institutional arrangements. Victorious leaders can, of course, do all of them. Stalin pushed the borders of the Soviet Union westward and installed puppet regimes in Eastern Europe in the wake of the Second World War. However, should a leader be forced to choose between one end or the other, our argument clearly predicts that leaders with large winning coalitions prefer puppets and institutional changes to territory and vice versa for those with small winning coalitions. Because the incentives produced by selection institutions are opposite for the two war aims, it is clear how such institutions should drive leaders toward puppets or territory.

The Anglo-Soviet Invasion of Iran

We have argued that leaders seek to remove the leaders of other states to control the future policies of the latter. The joint British-Soviet invasion of Iran during the Second World War is a good example of our logic.

The war was not going well for either Great Britain or the Soviet Union in the summer of 1941. Nazi forces had pushed British forces out of Greece and Libya and were overrunning the western territories of the Soviet Union. The prospect that the Germans might vault into the Middle East through the use of compliant minor powers was frightening to both states. Such a move would undermine the British position in Egypt and lay bare the oil supplies of the Persian Gulf to German attack and occupation. The British invaded Iraq in May 1941 to overthrow the new government of Rashid Ali and then invaded the Vichy French territory of Syria to prevent the Germans from using these countries as bases in the Middle East. For the Soviet Union, Nazi forces in the Middle East would outflank them to the south and expose their own oil wells at Baku to attack. Additionally, Iran provided the opportunity for the Western Allies to ship military material to support the Soviet war effort on a path that would not be icebound during the winter. Hence, both were interested in the policies of the Shah's government, particularly with respect to Nazi agents and sympathizers in Iran.

Having seen the British invade Iraq and overthrow Rashid Ali, the Shah of Iran understood that to survive he had to change his policies sufficiently to forestall British and Soviet military action. The problem the Shah faced was how to delay taking sides between Germany on the one hand and Britain and the Soviet Union on the other. A Nazi victory seemed a distinct possibility in August 1941. He ordered some German nationals expelled from Iran. Still, the British and Soviets demanded further actions and began to build up their forces on the borders of Iran. On August 25, they launched a simultaneous invasion of Iran, with Soviet forces entering from the north and British forces from the south. Fighting broke out between Iranian forces and the invaders and continued for several days, until the Shah ordered his army to cease resistance. He then resigned in favor of his son and fled the country. The new Shah followed the Allies' directions for the remainder of the war, while his country was under partial occupation by Soviet and British forces (primarily in the northwest on the Soviet border and in the southwest around the oil wells near the Persian Gulf). The Shah's last words to his son, the new Shah, before leaving Iran forever reflect exactly the position of a defeated leader: "Don't resist. We and the whole world are facing a storm that is bigger than any of us. Bow your head until the storm passes" (Stewart, 1988, 211).

Testing the War-Aims Argument

The logic of the argument is now clear, but does the evidence match the conclusions of that logic? We examine this question using a number of different data sets. Regrettably, several interesting hypotheses cannot be tested because of selection effects and selection bias in the data.

The theory suggests that large-coalition victors are particularly likely to depose defeated foreign rivals and impose puppets to ensure that their policy objectives are fulfilled. The likelihood of intending to depose the rival state's leader is heightened if that state has a large-coalition structure. That is, the most likely circumstance (barring a coincidence of policy preferences) under which a state has as an interstate war aim the deposition of its rival and the imposition of a puppet is when the two parties to the dispute are both large-coalition, democratic states. Yet we know from chapter 6 that war—and therefore the opportunity to depose the rival—is extremely unlikely between two democratic states. The theory suggests that the very cases most likely to be candidates for the installation of a puppet regime are cases that hardly ever occur in equilibrium. This means that the variance in observed events is truncated for the most relevant cases, making a multivariate assessment of the impact of selection institutions on the choice between policy goals and regime change virtually impossible.

Additional selection problems arise because of another endogenous effect discussed in chapter 6. Recall that large-coalition regimes tend to negotiate rather than fight unless their leaders value office highly and they are overwhelmingly confident of victory. As we saw in chapter 6, this means that such polities are particularly prone to engage in wars of colonial and imperial expansion against weak "nonstate" actors. Unfortunately, these wars have not been coded with regard to war aims in the data available to us. Consequently, although colonial and imperial wars almost always result in the overthrow of the defeated side's government, we cannot know the extent to which the war was motivated by a desire for extractable resources, to impose policy change, or to install a colonial government that would do the host government's bidding. Thus, we cannot evaluate the other category of cases in which large-coalition states are disproportionately likely to participate.

With these selection problems in mind, we undertake multivariate analyses of the quest for territory versus policy or regime change and then examine a series of simpler cross-tabulations to evaluate some subtleties in our predictions.

Militarized Interstate Disputes

Our first test examines the goals of states that engaged in violent conflict with one another. The Correlates of War Project (COW) provides data on militarized interstate disputes from 1815 to 1992 (Gochman and Maoz 1984; Jones, Bremer, and Singer 1996). These events vary from minor threats by one state that do not provoke a response all the way to events as severe as the World Wars, but exclude extrasystemic conflicts. We decompose disputes into pairs of states in conflict, and then break these dyads into individual disputant states.[8] Our analysis seeks to account for the motivations of these disputing states as coded by COW.

The disputants in this set include all states that minimally either threatened to use force or were the targets of such threats or of the use of force. Because this set includes some states that had very little involvement in a given dispute, we examine some subsets of the disputing states to focus on those whose motivations are clearest, and therefore likely to provide the fairest test of our argument. The first cut is whether the state in question escalated to violence during the dispute (i.e., had a hostility-level score of 4 or 5 in the Gochman and Maoz militarized interstate disputes data set). There is no question that such states were willing to pursue their interests to the utmost. We also differentiate between "joiners"—states that enter the dispute later in response to developments in the dispute—and original disputants. The motivations of the joiners are colored by those later developments. Consequently, we expect that the original disputants should provide a clearer test of our theory. We did run our analyses including both nonviolent disputants and joiners in order to test the robustness of our results with respect to these decisions and discuss the consequences of these judgments.

The COW project coded the motivations of disputing states in terms first of whether the state sought any revisions in the status quo, and if so, whether those revisions primarily had to do with territory, policy, or regime change. The territory category includes cases where the state sought to add territory; the policy category, cases where the state sought to change a policy of the opposing state; and the regime category, cases where the state sought to change the government of its opponent. In cases where a state had multiple goals, COW judged which was the principal objective of that state in the dispute. In some cases, a state's objective was ambiguous; COW coded these cases as "other." The COW trichotomy of territory, policy, and regime fits well with our theory. These codes, however, lump together territorial objectives that seek resources within the territory with those that seek strategic territory that does not provide resources to the controlling state. The latter aims are considered policy goals in our argument. So these categories are not a perfect fit with the concepts of our theory.

States that did not seek revisions in the status quo were coded by COW as not having a goal in the dispute. According to our theory, these nonrevisionist states pursued the policy goal of preserving the status quo. Consequently, we include the nonrevisionist disputants and consider them to have policy goals.

We perform four initial tests, reported in table 9.1, in which the dependent variable is coded 1 if the state's war aim was coded as territorial. The dependent variable is coded 0 if the war aim was reported to be either policy or regime change, with the latter motivated, according to our theory, by a desire to impose policy changes.

These tests require measures of the sizes of the winning coalition of both sides, because this selection institution of the target as well as of the state in question affects war aims according to our argument. Our second hypothesis indicates that the selectorate size of the victor state also is expected to exert an influence on the victor's prospects of pursuing territorial gain or policy/regime change. W indicates the size of the victor's coalition and $OppW$ the size of the loser's coalition. To capture the idea that the size of the victor's selectorate should matter only when the winning coalition is small, we create the variable *Effective S*, which equals $S(1 - W)$. Recall that W and S are both measured on the scale of 0 to 1. This construction then makes the size of the selectorate matter only when the winning coalition is small, and the smaller the winning coalition, the greater the range of possible effects the size of the selectorate can have. We assess the power of the state in question relative to its opponent by calculating the proportion the state in question possesses of the composite capabilities of the two states together:

$$\frac{cap_A}{cap_A + cap_B}$$

The higher this proportion, the stronger the state in question is relative to its opponent. We call this variable *PowerRatio*.

To distinguish between our argument and conjectures about normative differences between democracies and other political systems, we control for nominal regime type with the variables *WS:DemRes*. Controlling for nominal regime types helps us demonstrate that selection institutions separate from the normative properties of different types of regimes influence war aims.

We also include additional control variables. It is possible that any association between the indicators of institutional constraints and the motive for fighting may be spurious. For instance, today there are far fewer monarchies than in the nineteenth century, while there are many more democracies. Perhaps the changing distribution of institutional arrangements in the world and tastes over what to fight about have shifted together across time. For example, Zacher (2001) argues that a norm of territorial integrity has arisen in the international system in the wake of the Second World War. We introduce two control variables, the year the dispute began and whether the dispute occurred after 1945, for these possibilities.[9]

Alternatively, one could argue that the changing nature of production from traditional to industrial societies has altered the importance states place on controlling territory. Traditional societies extract resources from agricultural and craft production of the local population; without control of the territory, their leaders cannot extract resources from that population. Industrial societies, on the other hand, can trade their finished goods for the primary products of less developed societies and so do not need to control territory to extract resources from its population. According to this argument, then, economic development leads states to shy away from territorial expansion. We use two variables to control for this possibility. The composite capabilities index developed by the COW project uses two measures of industrialization: iron and steel production and energy consumption. We divide each of these production figures by the total population of a state (also found in the COW composite capabilities data) to get iron and steel production per capita and energy consumption per capita. However, economic development is correlated with the sizes of the winning coalition and selectorate of their societies, as we have shown earlier. Consequently, we construct instruments for both of these variables by regressing them on the state's selection institutions, the log of the population of the state, and year. We then use the residual from this regression as a measure of the added effect of economic development beyond these other variables. We include both of these instruments as controls and refer to them as the instruments for *energy per capita* and *steel per capita* respectively.

Additional control variables are *Log(Pop)*, introduced in chapter 4, and *Contiguity*. We control for total population, using the logarithm of population, to make sure that the effect of W is not purely driven by scale. We also control for geographic contiguity to help separate national security motivations and private-goods motivations behind the pursuit of territorial gain. Especially when states with shared borders fight, territorial acquisition may be about the promotion of national security, a public good. A control variable for contiguity helps to reduce the problem that the dispute-aims data do not distinguish efforts to control strategic territory from the pursuit of added resources. Additionally, territorial issues are more likely to be contested between contiguous states (Vasquez 1995). We code *Contiguity* in two ways. We present the results for the disputants being contiguous on land—that is, they share a land border. We also coded *Contiguity* as typically done in the literature: 1 if the states share a common border or are separated by less than 150 miles of water and 0 otherwise (Siverson and Starr 1991).

Our first analysis tries to separate disputing states seeking territorial gains from those with policy or regime goals. Our argument predicts that it is less likely that a state should have territorial goals as the size of its winning coalition increases and as the size of its selectorate decreases. Although not derived strictly from our model, we also conjecture that territorial conquest is most likely when the opposing state has a large winning coalition.

Table 9.1 presents the results of our main analysis on territorial aims versus policy aims, including regime aims as policy aims. We conduct a logit analysis to separate the cases where a disputing state ·had territorial aims (coded 1 in the dependent variable) from the cases in which maintenance of the status quo policy, policy change, or regime change were the stated goals (coded 0 in the dependent variable, with all other

Table 9.1
Separating territorial war aims from policy aims

Variable	All violent disputants	All violent disputants	Original violent combatants	Original violent combatants
W	−1.04	−1.96	−0.96	−2.09
	0.22	0.29	0.23	0.33
	0.00	0.00	0.00	0.00
$EFFS$	0.18	−0.18	0.02	−0.41
	0.20	0.24	0.23	0.27
	0.38	0.43	0.92	0.12
$OPPW$	0.73	0.99	0.46	0.80
	0.18	0.21	0.20	0.24
	0.00	0.00	0.02	0.00
$Powerratio$	0.21	0.38	0.17	0.34
	0.17	0.23	0.19	0.26
	0.22	0.11	0.37	0.19
$Log(Pop)$		−0.22		−0.15
		0.11		0.12
		0.04		0.20
$Year\ of\ dispute$		−0.003		−0.007
		0.003		0.004
		0.33		0.03
$Dispute\ after\ 1945?$		−0.93		−0.77
		0.24		0.28
		0.00		0.01
$Disputants\ share\ land\ border?$	1.05	0.95	1.16	1.16
	0.11	0.14	0.13	0.18
	0.00	0.00	0.00	0.00
$WS:DemRes$		−0.07		0.17
		0.28		0.31
		0.81		0.58
$Instrument\ for\ energy\ consumption\ per\ capita$		−0.24		−0.27
		0.07		0.09
		0.00		0.00
$Instrument\ for\ iron/steel\ production\ per\ capita$		−0.11		−0.20
		0.50		0.65
		0.82		0.76
N	2,189	1,730	1,754	1,393
Summary statistics	$\chi^2 = 137.1$	$\chi^2 = 173.8$	$\chi^2 = 112.6$	$\chi^2 = 153.9$
	$p = 0.000$	$p = 0.000$	$p = 0.000$	$p = 0.000$

categories of cases treated as missing data) using the variables of our argument and the control variables. We present four combinations of specifications and case selections and discuss the effects that alternative decisions have on the results. The full range of specifications and case selections can be reproduced from our website.

The results are strongest, as expected, for the size of the coalition of the disputing states. As predicted, states are more likely to fight for territorial aims when their own coalition is small. As we conjectured, states are also more likely to fight for territory when the coalition of their opponent is large. The disputing state's selectorate size is insignificant. The residual aspects of governing institutions not explained by coalition and selectorate size do not influence the choice of war aims, according to the results in table 9.1.

Postwar Treaties

The consequences of wars provide other, perhaps better tests of our argument. The model addresses decisions at or near the end of a war, and so the terms victors impose should be the best test. We begin by examining the terms of the sixteen peace treaties ending a number of wars in modern history that are found in Israel's (1967–1980) *Major Peace Treaties of Modern History*, 1648–1967.[10] Over time, the sizes of winning coalitions have grown, and so we expect that the terms of these treaties should shift from emphasizing private goods, particularly territory, in favor of policy ends.

Our count concerns the division of these treaties toward public versus private goods. We classify each article of each of the treaties we consider by its primary focus, dividing them into private goods, policy, regime goals, procedural articles, or articles concerned with the implementation of the treaty. Articles that covered private goods either shifted territory from one polity to another or provided tangible benefits to one party. Policy changes introduced through these treaties included such things as the toleration of religious freedom, amnesty for rebels, and the return of prisoners of war. We classified articles as addressing regime only when they legitimated the nature of a regime or prescribed the nature of the regime of one of the formerly warring parties. For instance, the fourth article of the Treaty of Utrecht (1713) recognizes the Protestant succession in Great Britain. Procedural articles include, for example, those that make reference to other treaties or agreements; articles addressing

Table 9.2
List of major treaties and the breakdown of their articles

Treaty	Year signed	Articles about policy	Articles about private goods	Articles about regime	Procedural articles	Articles of imple- mentation	Total articles
Westphalia	1648	36	56	1	18	17	128
Aix-la-Chapelle	1668	3	4	0	2	0	9
Utrecht	1713	23	14	1	12	8	58
Third Partition of Poland	1794	2	5	0	1	0	8
First Peace of Paris	1814	9	25	0	2	5	41
Frankfort	1871	10	9	0	2	0	21
Treaty of Paris	1898	10	8	0	0	5	23
Athens	1913	25	4	0	1	3	33
Versailles	1919	253	84	0	9	94	440
Chaco	1938	4	1	0	0	7	12
Japanese	1951	11	8	1	6	1	27
Korean Armistice	1953	23	0	0	4	36	63
Geneva Accord	1954	22	0	0	0	24	46
Austrian Peace Treaty	1955	25	12	1	1	12	51
Tashkent Declaration	1966	9	0	0	1	0	10
Paris Peace	1973	17	0	0	2	4	23

implementation cover the manner in which the terms of the treaty will be applied. Table 9.2 lists each of the treaties we examined and gives the breakdown of each into the five types of articles.

To evaluate whether policy has risen in importance compared to private goods in these treaties over time, we calculate the relative proportion of these two classes of war aims in each treaty. We include articles addressing regimes as policy aims as our argument assumes and then drop all other articles, because we have no hypotheses about how the use of such articles has changed over time. We then regress the variable *Year* on the relative percentage of policy and regime articles (out of the three classes of articles) and present the results in table 9.3. We cannot include the selection institutions of the victors for lack of data before 1800. Additionally, these multilateral treaties involve many victorious

Table 9.3
Tracing the growth of policy ends over private goods in major peace treaties

Variable	Estimated effect on percent of articles addressing policy or regime: unweighted regression	Estimated effect on percent of articles addressing policy or regime: weighted regression
Year	0.0017	0.0014
	0.0004	0.0003
	0.002	0.001
Constant	−2.44	−1.89
	0.81	0.59
	0.01	0.007
Summary statistics	$F = 14.64\ (1, 14)$	$F = 18.91\ (1, 14)$
	$p = 0.0018$, $R^2 = 0.51$	$p = 0.0007$, $R^2 = 0.57$

states, requiring us to look at average selection institutions of the victors. Because the number of articles varies widely across the treaties, the cases where the percentage is based on a small number of articles have a higher error variance than those based on many articles. Consequently, we run the analysis with and without weights to account for the different number of articles in each observation.[11]

The results in table 9.3 show clearly that articles addressing policy have risen in importance over time relative to those that address private goods in the treaties we examine. The effect is both statistically and substantively significant. According to our unweighted estimates, the percentage of articles devoted to policy and regimes—that is, public goods—relative to private goods has risen from 36 percent in 1648 to 91 percent in 1973 (the figures are 42 percent to 87 percent using the weighted estimates). Of course, the data and estimates are rough, but they do provide a picture of how policy ends have risen in importance while terms providing private goods have shrunk over time.

The Outcomes of Wars

The treaty analysis suggests that policy aims have risen in importance over time. We now turn to the outcomes of wars since 1815 to see if selection institutions have played a role in this change. Over this period of time, the sizes of winning coalitions and selectorates have risen. If these changes in selection institutions are related to war aims, the outcomes of wars should have changed along with these changes.

We begin with the widely used Correlates of War collection of inter-state wars (Singer and Small 1972; Small and Singer 1982; Sarkees 2000). As described in chapter 5, COW defined states as those with a recognized government and at least one million residents. Interstate wars occur when both sides use force and the total battle deaths are at least 1,000.[12] A state is considered an active combatant if it fields 1,000 combatants or suffers 100 battle fatalities. All active participants are grouped into two sides.

COW coded which side won the war, allowing for the possibility of draws when neither side won clearly. The Korean War is an example of the latter. We examine every pair of states where one side defeated the other. To construct this set, we pair every state on the winning side with every state on the losing side. For bilateral wars, this process produces only one dyad between the victor and vanquished. For multilateral wars, it can produce a large number of dyads, particularly for the World Wars. Of course, not all of these pairs of states actually fought one another. For instance, this procedure gives us China defeating Finland as part of the Second World War even though these two states never fielded armies on the same continent, much less actually fought one another. We have examined the set of all "warring" dyads to determine which pairs actually fought. We drop all dyads where the two states did not fight during the war in question.[13]

Because warring dyads are our observation here, we eliminate a warring dyad when the two reached a peace treaty ending the conflict between them or one side's forces surrendered to the other. Unlike COW, which considers the World Wars as a single event with eventual victors and losers, our process creates dyadic wars that end before the end of those general wars. Like Stam (1996), we code the victor of these wars based on which side surrendered to the other, even if that state ended up on the winning side when the complete war was over. Germany's defeat of the Netherlands in 1940 is an example of such a warring dyad. Some states, then, fought on both sides during the Second World War. France was an active combatant three times: as the Third Republic, which Germany defeated in 1940; Vichy France, which fought the Allies to retain control of Syria and Lebanon but whose active role ended with the Nazi occupation of Vichy territory; and Free France, which reentered the war with the liberation of Paris.[14] We exclude states that reentered the war after they were liberated by Allied forces unless they fielded substantial forces in combat after their liberation. Finally, we also repeated tests against data that excluded dyads where one state suffered 100 or fewer battle fatalities during the war. These minor war participants could contaminate our results because they were unlikely to secure either territory or remove an enemy leader as a consequence of their low level of commitment to the war.

These warring dyads give the set of victories in war where the victor could have taken territory or replaced the losing leader if it chose to do so (at the possible expense of additional fighting to accomplish those ends). We determine for each of these pairs whether the victor expanded into territory of the defeated state or replaced the defeated leader. For the former, we use the Territorial Change data set collected for use with Correlates of War data (see Goertz and Diehl 1992 and Tir et al. 1998 for discussions of this data set). This data set lists all territorial changes for states in the Correlates of War system since 1815. It includes the state adding the territory, the date of the change, the amount and character of the territory transferred, the state or nonstate entity losing the territory, and how the transfer was accomplished. Of all these transfers, we used those coded as occupations, annexations, or cessions, and we dropped secessions, creation of independent states, unifications, and new mandates because our interest is in when the victor expands, not when the territory of the loser shrinks. We matched the warring dyads with any transfer of territory from the losing state to the victor in the three years after the war ended. Each match was investigated to determine whether the territory in question was transferred as a consequence of the war, with the matches dropped if the transfer was unrelated to the war.[15]

The Territorial Change data set, like most Correlates of War data sets, does not collect territorial changes during the World Wars unless those changes were in force after the entire war ended. Consequently, gains in territory by the Central Powers in the First World War and the Axis in the Second World War are not included in that data set. Because we include warring dyads that ended during these wars, we have collected intrawar territorial changes by the victors at the expense of the states they defeated, using Gilbert 1994 for the First World War and Keegan 1989 for the Second World War.[16] These changes only incorporate cases where the victor expanded the borders of its own state through annexation or if it treated the territory in question the same as its homeland. We do not include puppet states carved out of the defeated states, such as Manchukuo by Japan in 1933 or Ukraine by Germany in 1918. Although the victor in both cases has control of the territory, it has not chosen to add it directly to its own territory. We do not include military occupations in these changes because such occupations are temporary, both practically and under international law. They reflect situations where the victor has not finalized its plans for the defeated state, so we cannot judge what they would have done had their side won the general war. Finally, we also include any transfers of these territories back to the loser after the war is over to restore the prewar borders. We test the robustness of our results by dropping these cases as gains of territory in some analyses.

We use our data on leaders and the POLITY data on political systems to collect leader changes imposed by the victor on the defeated. We begin with a similar matching process of leader changes in the defeated state in the three years after the war ends. We investigate whether these changes were imposed by the victor, either by placing the new leader in power or by forcing the defeated state to adopt a new political system that leads to a peaceful selection of a new leader after the removal of the defeated leader. To help identify the latter cases, the POLITY data set has a code for states undergoing a transitional system imposed by another state. Again, we investigate these cases to determine if the victor imposed institutions on the defeated state; military occupation alone is excluded.[17] In these cases, we also go past the three-year postwar period to look for new selection institutions. For instance, POLITY does not code the constitution that the United States imposed on Japan after the Second World War as a stable set of institutions until 1952, well past the three-year period. Our search into the future in cases where POLITY codes a change of regime imposed from outside captures these cases. Within the set of warring dyads, we only include the victors who actually were involved in the imposition of the new leader or the creation of the new institutions in the defeated state. Australia, for instance, helped defeat Japan in the Second World War, but we do not consider it as replacing the wartime leader of Japan as a consequence of its contribution to victory.

We conduct a pair of analyses, one to predict whether the victor took territory and a second whether it removed the leader of the loser. Unlike our analysis in table 9.1, here we do not use multivariate techniques. Two issues lead to our use of simpler analyses.

First, as discussed earlier, data on war victors reflects a set of states with strong selection effects, so we cannot consider this set as a random sample. Several factors affect the selection process. As we saw in chapter 6, the size of the winning coalition plays an important role in determining which side wins a war. States with large winning coalitions almost never lose wars, and they almost never fight one another. Further, the relative power of the warring parties also affects which side wins. Finally, states that expect to lose are unlikely to fight to begin with.

Second, the small number of cases, particularly of victories in major wars other than the World Wars, limits the amount of information that sophisticated multivariate techniques use in their estimation. Consequently, we present contingency tables and statistical tests of differences in means to show the relationships between selection institutions and the outcomes of wars.[18]

We hypothesized that states with larger winning coalitions were less likely to take territory after they won a war. Table 9.4 breaks down how often large and small winning-coalition states added territory after they won a war in our data. We distinguish small from large winning coalitions in the same way we have done in chapter 7. Large winning coalitions have values of W greater than or equal to 0.75; those smaller than 0.75 are judged to have small winning coalitions. Victors with small winning coalitions added territory after 42 percent of their victories, while victors with large winning coalitions did so only 25 percent of the time. This difference is statistically significant based on a one-tailed test ($\chi^2 = 5.56$, $p = 0.018$).[19]

The power relationship also affects the victor's interest in taking territory, although there are two effects that generally work against one

Table 9.4
Victorious states with large winning coalitions are less likely to take territory

	Do not add territory	Add territory
Small winning coalition	66 58%	48 42%
Large winning coalition	56 75%	19 25%

Note: $\chi^2 = 5.56$, $p = 0.018$.

Table 9.5
Victorious states with small winning coalitions are more likely to take territory when they are stronger than the defeated state

	Do not add territory	Add territory
Victor equal to or weaker than loser	40	21
	66%	34%
Victor stronger than loser	26	27
	49%	51%

Note: $\chi^2 = 3.17, p = 0.075$.

another. The stronger the loser relative to the winner, the more resources the winner will have to devote to foreign policy in the future, which reduces the value of taking territory to increase state resources. Conversely, taking territory from a stronger loser reduces the threat the loser poses in the future. The first effect makes taking territory from weaker losers more attractive for victors with small winning coalitions; the second effect makes taking territory from stronger losers more attractive for any victor. Table 9.5 tests the one clear prediction from these two effects: victors with small winning coalitions should be more likely to take territory when they are stronger than the loser. We classify the victor as stronger than the losing state when it has at least 50 percent more composite capabilities. Victors with small winning coalitions are more likely to take territory when they are stronger than the vanquished, and the difference approaches the conventional 0.05 level of statistical significance. We do not present results for victors with large winning coalitions because we have no clear prediction from these two arguments. Similarly, we cannot judge whether differences in power lead victors with small winning coalitions to take more valuable territory; the first argument suggests that stronger victors take more resources, the second that weaker victors should take more.

Leadership Removal

Now we turn to when the victor removes the leader of the defeated state. Again we present tables because the data are inadequate for more sophisticated techniques. Our argument leads to the hypothesis that victorious states should be more likely to remove the enemy leader as the size of their winning coalition increases. The results presented in table

Table 9.6
Victorious states with large winning coalitions are more likely to remove the defeated leader

	Do not remove leader	Remove leader
Small winning coalition	101	13
	89%	11%
Large winning coalition	64	11
	85%	15%

Note: $\chi^2 = 0.43$, p = not significant.

9.6 are consistent with this hypothesis; victors with large winning coalitions are more likely to replace the enemy leader (15 percent of the time to 11 percent), but the difference is not statistically significant. However, victors with very small winning coalitions (those with $W \leq 0.25$) are much less likely to remove defeated leaders. Only 5 percent do, a difference that is significant at the 0.016 level. States with larger winning coalitions are roughly equally likely to remove the enemy leader when they win a war. The systems with small but not very small winning coalitions are generally one-party dictatorships; the installation of Nazi governments by Germany during the Second World War and communist governments afterward by the Soviet Union account for six of the ten cases of such systems removing enemy leaders after victory.[20] Such one-party systems, however, typically have large selectorates, which contradicts our hypothesis that victors with small winning coalitions should be less likely to overthrow the enemy leader as the size of their selectorate expands. Still, the chance that the victor removes the defeated leader increases with the size of the winning coalition he or she must answer to.

Defeated leaders will put more effort into challenging the postwar status quo as the size of their winning coalition increases. Consequently, leaders with large winning coalitions are more likely to be removed if they lose a war. Tables 9.7a and 9.7b address this hypothesis. Table 9.7a distinguishes between defeated leaders with large or small winning coalitions and table 9.7b between defeated leaders with very small or other-sized winning coalitions. We drop cases where the victor had a very small winning coalition itself because such victors almost never depose the defeated leader in fact or according to the theory. Again, the difference lies between losers with very small winning coalitions and those with larger ones. The removal of leaders of one-party states is substantial, but

Table 9.7a
Victorious states are more likely to remove a defeated leader with a larger winning coalition

Defeated states	Do not remove leader	Remove leader
Small winning coalition	90 84%	17 16%
Large winning coalition	16 80%	4 20%

Note: $\chi^2 = 0.21$, p = not significant.

Table 9.7b
Victorious states are more likely to remove a defeated leader with a larger winning coalition: a second view

Defeated states	Do not remove leader	Remove leader
Very small winning coalition	65 88%	9 12%
Larger winning coalition	41 77%	12 23%

Note: $\chi^2 = 2.45$, $p = 0.12$. Victors with very small winning coalitions are dropped from both tables.

the number of cases here is somewhat misleading. When we break wars into warring dyads, the removal of Nazi Germany turns into five cases because the United States, Canada, Great Britain, France, and the Soviet Union are all considered to have overthrown the Nazi government.

War and Domestic Change

As we mentioned at the beginning of the chapter, war has the power to make and break leaders. The outcomes of war reflect the general patterns predicted by our argument, although the rarity of wars allows us to test our theory only in the most general terms. Selection institutions shape the incentives of leaders to seek territory or to overthrow their opponent in war. The consequences of international conflict extend further for leaders than just to the possibility of external overthrow; success and failure provide opportunities for domestic challenges to their power. These consequences begin during a crisis and extend beyond its resolution into the peace that follows. We now turn to examining how conflict, whether it escalates to war or not, affects the ability of leaders to hold power. We begin with the case of Vichy France to illustrate these points before turning to analysis of the broad patterns.

Germany's Creature: Vichy France

A defeated state faces pressure to conform to the foreign policy wishes of the victor, even when the victor cannot or does not impose a new regime on it. To do so, it may be necessary for the leader of the defeated state to change his or her state's selection institutions in order to carry out a foreign policy opposed by the existing selectorate. Vichy France is an example of this process.[21]

In June 1940, the Third Republic of France was disintegrating militarily and politically. France in its hour of need turned to Marshal Philippe Pétain, the hero of Verdun and the general who rallied the French army after the mutinies of 1917. On June 16, Prime Minister Paul Reynaud resigned and Pétain formed a new government set on peace with the Nazis. Hitler offered the new French government terms that would allow the continuation of an independent but subservient France in order to prevent the remains of the French forces, in particular the French navy, from fighting on from France's colonies in Africa and the Middle East. Hitler's terms, which became more demanding with every hour that his panzers plunged deeper into France, were quickly accepted by the Pétain government.

The terms were harsh for France. Germany occupied the north and west of the country, annexed Alsace-Lorraine, and imposed massive reparations on France. Those terms did, however, allow the new government to continue to rule the unoccupied south from the city of Vichy.

Pétain and his vice premier Pierre Laval changed France from a representative, if chaotic, democracy into an autocracy. Laval persuaded the Senate and Chamber of Deputies to give Pétain, as head of state, the power to rule by decree. Further, those legislative bodies gave Pétain discretion over when they could meet. He had no interest in convening them while he was in power. Pétain used these powers to purge the national and local governments of those who might be disloyal and then, taking no chances, compelled the remaining officials to take an oath of personal loyalty to himself. Trade unions and political parties were disbanded. The judiciary was corrupted and new laws, including the power to arrest anyone believed to be a danger to the state, were passed, giving the Vichy government the power to suppress opposition.[22] In December 1940, Pétain dismissed Laval himself when he suspected that Laval sought Pétain's position.

The costs of Vichy France's acquiescence with Nazi policies were high for the French people. In addition to the crushing financial costs imposed as part of the peace, Germany continued to hold French soldiers taken prisoner during the fighting. These prisoners were eventually used as pawns to force more skilled French workers to be transferred to war production inside Germany itself at an average exchange rate of one prisoner for six laborers. Vichy forces fought to prevent British and Commonwealth troops from occupying Syria and Lebanon. The occupying German forces also engaged in harsh reprisals against civilians for resistance attacks on German military personnel. In addition, Vichy France had to agree to deport French Jews to Germany, although it adopted its own harsh anti-Semitic laws beginning in October 1940. Finally, the ration level of food was about half of what an adult required, and infant mortality rose dramatically during the Vichy administration.

Even with its general compliance with Germany, Vichy France could not survive the increasing demands of the Nazis. When United States, British, and Free French forces invaded French Morocco and Algeria in November 1942, Vichy forces based there resisted at first. Hitler demanded further cooperation and inserted German and Italian troops in Tunisia and Algeria without seeking the consent of Vichy. This led Vichy military leaders in North Africa to switch sides and begin to fight the Axis. In response, the Nazis occupied all of France, and Vichy lost what little freedom of policy it had.

Dispute Outcomes and the Fate of Leaders

The analysis of war outcomes suffers from an important limitation for analyzing the question of how international conflict affects political leaders' hold on power. The Correlates of War Project only codes the mutual use of force between two states as a war if at least 1,000 people are killed in the fighting. According to our theory, the cost of replacing an enemy leader plays a large role in determining whether to do so. A victorious leader is more likely to overthrow the enemy leader when it is easy, generally because the former is vastly stronger than the latter. These cases do not produce enough fighting and loss of life to qualify as wars according to COW. For instance, the Anglo-Soviet invasion of Iran discussed earlier does not appear in the COW list of wars; Iran is not even considered a participant in the Second World War. The fighting was significant enough to kill hundreds of soldiers, but the reality of the situation was that resistance by the Iranian army would not save the Shah. If we omit this event and others like it, we omit a substantial number of cases of foreign overthrow of a state's leader. The first reason for looking at the outcome of disputes is to include these cases and others where foreign removal of a leader could have occurred.

The set of disputes also allows us to examine how the outcomes of disputes affect the ability of leaders to retain office. The members of the winning coalition and selectorate care about how their state fares in international politics, both for material and policy concerns. Militarized disputes are the most signal international events a nation and its leader face, so we expect that the outcomes of disputes should have a large effect on the ability of leaders to hold office. Even if the enemy cannot remove a leader, her failure to best that enemy may lead her own winning coalition to abandon her in favor of a new leader. We draw attention to this claim as we explore the question suggested by the title of this chapter: Is the enemy outside more dangerous than the enemy within? Are leaders more worried about being overthrown by another state or by their own supporters? This question returns us to a central problem in the theory of international relations. Realists (e.g., Waltz 1979) claim that the external threat to a state's existence is so great that its leaders must always attend to the external security of the state. We and others (e.g., Lamborn 1991) contend that leaders see international politics through a lens of domestic politics. How a state fares in international politics is important for a leader, but she perceives success through the eyes of her winning coalition. Personal security in office looms larger for leaders than does national security. The latter matters to the extent that compromising national security displeases the winning coalition and so threatens the leader's hold on power.

We return to the Militarized Interstate Disputes data to explore these questions of how crises affect internal and external replacement of leaders. We construct the set of all directed dyads in the dispute data (one member from each side of the dispute). The Cuban Missile Crisis with three participants becomes four directed dyads: the United States ⇒ Soviet Union, United States ⇒ Cuba, Soviet Union ⇒ United States,

and Cuba $\Rightarrow$ United States. We match the dates of each state's participation with any leader changes in that country. We look for changes both
during the dispute and in the year after the dispute ends for that state
to capture any change that may have been caused by the state's fortunes
in the dispute. Disputes sometimes end when the leader of the losing
state falls from power, allowing that state to accept a less-than-favorable
outcome. The Fashoda Crisis, for one, ended when the fall of Prime
Minister Delcasse, allowing France to withdraw Marchand's expedition
to the upper Nile and accept British control of the Sudan.

For each disputing dyad, we identified characteristics of the dispute for
each participant. The COW coding provides for each dispute information on the level of hostile actions that each state took, the outcome, how
it was settled, whether and how each state sought to revise the status quo
(we used these codes in our analysis of aims in disputes), and the dates
of each state's participation. From the level of hostile actions, we determine whether a state and its opponent used violence in the dispute. Those
assigned a hostility code of 4 or 5 by COW used force. From the outcome
variable, we code a state as winning if COW coded the dispute as a
victory for its side or if the other side yielded, with the other member of
the dyad losing. A majority of disputes do not end with a clear victory;
both sides are considered to reach a draw in these cases.

To determine cases where the victor removed the leader of the
defeated state, we separated out all the cases where a state was defeated,
where a state had a leader change, and where the outcome of the dispute
was imposed. Historical sources were consulted to determine in which
cases the winning side had removed the losing leader. There are cases
where both internal and external removal of leaders in one state occurs.
Japan in the Second World War had both types of changes: a domestic
removal of Prime Minister Hideki Tojo in 1944, followed by the fall of
his successor Koiso in April 1945 and the removal of his successor by the
Allies at the end of the war. We matched these dyads with our data on
selection institutions and national capabilities for each state in the year
before the dispute began.

There are two parts to our analysis, separately focusing on internal and
external removal of leaders. However, before we get to the analyses of
the two sources of change separately, we observe that internal leader
changes are much more common than external leader changes. Among
the 831 cases of losses that we have, the losing leader is removed by the

other side 37 times (4 percent) and by domestic forces 295 times (36 percent). Even victory does not protect the leader from removal; 253 of 831 (30 percent) victorious leaders were removed during or after the dispute.

The analysis of internal removals in and after disputes faces the issue of selection. Whether a state wins or loses a dispute should have a large impact on the leader's fate, and we certainly wish to examine the effects of the outcome. However, many of the factors that influence the leader's hold on power, such as selection institutions, also affect whether that state wins or loses. Leaders with large winning coalitions are both more likely to be removed and more likely to win should the dispute escalate to war. Consequently, we have to control for possible selection effects to discern the true consequences of dispute outcomes for leader removal.

We use a Heckman selection model to deal with the selection issue. These models estimate two equations simultaneously, one for the outcome of the dispute and a second for the leader's removal given the outcome. Disputes have three possible outcomes, so we run separate analyses for each outcome. The first expresses the likelihood of the leader being removed by domestic forces if his state wins the dispute, the second if the dispute is a draw, and the third if his state loses. The selection model is appropriate because we believe the outcome of the dispute drives the removal of the leader in at least some of the cases. Even if the removal occurs during the dispute, the outcome is often clear when the leader loses power.

For this analysis, we drop all cases where a monarch was the state leader before the dispute began. These monarchs held power solely without a responsible prime minister and succession was hereditary, according to POLITY's coding rules. They left office only from natural death, revolution, or external replacement; they were practically impossible to remove by a normal procedure. Consequently, these leaders were barely susceptible if at all to the consequences of disputes and so should not fit our argument. We also drop the disputes that COW codes with an outcome of "Released." These cases cover incidents where one state seizes the citizens of another state or their property, commonly for violation of borders or territorial waters. The seizure counts as a use of force and so as a militarized dispute. If the seizure ends with the release of the property or people but no further use of force, the incident is unlikely to have much consequence for the leader of either side.

We are interested in how the likelihood of removal from office varies with selection institutions and the outcome of the dispute. In particular, we care about the interaction between outcome and selection institutions. We will see that leaders with large winning coalitions are always more likely to be removed than those with small winning coalitions, as we should expect. The question of interest is how important the outcome is under different selection institutions. Consequently, we focus on these patterns across all three analyses, rather than emphasizing the statistical significance in any one equation.

We constructed variables to pull out cases of particular interest in our theory. The theory argues that leaders with small winning coalitions seek territory for its resources because added resources make them more difficult to remove from office. We identify cases where a leader answering to a small winning coalition ($W \leq 0.5$) sought territory and test whether those leaders were less likely to be removed if they won. We also identify when leaders with large winning coalitions ($W \geq 0.75$) used violence to see if such leaders were punished more heavily for using violence. In addition, we identify when such leaders used violence to defend the status quo instead of trying to change it under the argument that the use of violence may be less objectionable in the face of a challenge to the status quo.

Table 9.8 presents the results of the three Heckman analyses. All three equations include all variables of interest, so that we can compare how the estimated likelihood of internal removal changes with these variables. Although we report the estimated standard errors of these coefficients, we remind the reader that our real interest lies in the full pattern of predicted probabilities from these estimates.

Table 9.9 presents the estimated probabilities of removal for the three basic combinations of selection institutions: a large winning-coalition system ($W = 1$, by definition *Effective S* = 0), a small winning coalition and selectorate ($W = 0$, *Effective S* = 0), and a small winning-coalition system with a large selectorate ($W = 0$, *Effective S* = 1). For each combination, we give the estimated probability of removal if they win, draw, and lose a dispute and also those probabilities under the other conditions listed. These estimates give the probabilities of internal removal if the outcomes of win, draw, and lose did not censor the data.

Table 9.9 illustrates the conclusions of our analysis of internal leader removal during and after disputes. First, the outcome of crises has a

Table 9.8
Selection analyses of the domestic removal of leaders during and after disputes

Coef., (std. error)	Win	Draw	Lose
Size of winning coalition	0.30, (0.76)	0.14, (0.13)	0.54, (0.44)
Effective size of selectorate	0.67, (0.53)	−0.16, (0.16)	−0.64, (0.46)
Used violence?	0.37, (0.26)	−0.10, (0.09)	0.33, (0.20)
Use of violence by large winning coalition	0.04, (0.36)	0.30, (0.12)	−0.06, (0.51)
Use of violence by large w in defense of the status quo	0.28, (0.28)	0.14, (0.11)	−0.15, (0.45)
Territorial aims by small winning coalition	−0.46, (0.27)	0.16, (0.11)	0.10, (0.29)
Constant	−1.79	−0.69	0.80
Selection equation			
Size of winning coalition	0.80, (0.23)	−0.07, (0.17)	−0.57, (0.44)
Effective size of selectorate	0.74, (0.21)	−0.37, (0.19)	0.03, (0.26)
Size of opponent's winning coalition	−1.01, (0.15)	0.43, (0.12)	0.52, (0.15)
Effective size of opponent's selectorate	−0.16, (0.22)	−0.02, (0.16)	0.48, (0.18)
Power ratio	0.17, (0.22)	−0.03, (0.04)	−0.15, (0.20)
Summary statistics	Wald $\chi^2(6) = 12.76$ $p = 0.047$	Wald $\chi^2(6) = 26.37$ $P = 0.0002$	Wald $\chi^2(6) = 16.48$ $P = 0.011$

Table 9.9
Estimated probabilities of removal during and after disputes

	Win	Draw	Lose
Large winning coalition ($W = 1$)	0.068	0.294	0.910
Uses violence	0.142	0.368	0.947
Uses violence to defend status quo	0.213	0.421	0.928
Small winning coalition and selectorate ($W = 0, S = 0$)	0.037	0.247	0.789
Uses violence	0.078	0.217	0.872
Seeks territory	0.012	0.299	0.816
Small winning coalition and large selectorate ($W = 0, S = 1$)	0.131	0.198	0.565
Uses violence	0.227	0.172	0.691
Seeks territory	0.057	0.246	0.603

substantial effect on the risk of removal. Winning disputes helps keep leaders in power; losing makes domestic removal very likely. Second, leaders with large winning coalitions are always at greater risk of removal. Their likelihood of removal is higher no matter what the outcome with one exception, winning a crisis without the use of violence. Losing a dispute as a leader with a large winning coalition sharply increases the chance of losing office. As we argued in chapter 6, leaders with large winning coalitions choose their fights carefully. Here we see why. Third, among the leaders with small winning coalitions, a large selectorate helps to insulate the leader from challenges when his state does not win the dispute. Such leaders are unlikely to face personal consequences if they engage in international ventures that turn out poorly for their state.

These three general conclusions about selection institutions, leader removal, and crisis outcomes are complemented by two more specific conclusions. First, leaders with small winning coalitions benefit from gaining territory. Regardless of whether their selectorate is small or large, the risk of removal drops dramatically when such a leader wins a dispute in which she seeks territory. As our theory contends, leaders with small winning coalitions should seek territorial expansion; they reduce their risk of replacement if they succeed but face a small added risk of removal if they fail. Second, leaders with large winning coalitions must be careful about using force. All leaders face a higher risk of removal when they use force, but the added risk is much greater for leaders with large winning coalitions.

Turning to our second analysis, that of external leader changes, we again use a Heckman selection model to control for selection effects. The selection criterion here is just losing, because a state must lose a dispute for its leader to be removed by the other side. The selection institutions of both sides should affect whether an external removal occurs. Our theory predicts that states with large winning coalitions should be more likely to remove the enemy leader if victorious. However, the effect of both sides' selection institutions on the likelihood of losing a dispute and also on the likelihood of the losing state's leader being removed by the victor creates issues for the estimation of a selection model. Further, there are very few external leader removals, as we noted earlier. Consequently, we include only the sizes of the winning coalitions of both sides in the leader-removal equation and add the other side's use of violence to the selection equation to aid in the identification of that equation.[23] As with the model for internal leader removals, we drop the disputes that end in a "Released" outcome. Unlike that analysis, though, we include the true monarchies as cases because heredity did not prevent the victor from overthrowing a monarch, even if it did stop his subjects from doing so.

Table 9.10 presents the results of our selection analysis of external leader removal. Systems with large winning coalitions are much more likely to have their leaders removed by the enemy if they lose a dispute. According to the estimates of the underlying removal relationship, a leader with a small winning coalition ($W = 0$) has a 65 percent chance of being removed by the victor, while a leader with a large winning coalition has an 88 percent chance (assume opponent's $W = 0$ in both cases).[24] The leaders of disputing states would like to remove their opponent more often than not, particularly when their opponent answers to a large winning coalition. In reality, they rarely secure a large enough victory to do so, especially against states with large winning coalitions.

Summarizing this section, the internal threat of removal after a dispute is much greater than the external threat. Although leaders would often like to remove the opposing leader, they rarely win clear enough victories to be able to do so. In other words, they rarely pursue the total victory needed to remove their opponent. Internal opponents, however,

Table 9.10
Selection analyses of the foreign removal of leaders during and after disputes

	Lose
Size of winning coalition	0.80*, (0.23)
Size of opponent's winning coalition	0.062, (0.22)
Constant	0.39
Selection equation	
Size of winning coalition	−0.91*, (0.16)
Effective size of selectorate	−0.10, (0.18)
Size of opponent's winning coalition	0.55*, (0.15)
Effective size of opponent's selectorate	0.52*, (0.18)
Power ratio	−0.22, (0.16)
Opponent used violence?	0.41*, (0.10)
Summary statistics	Wald $\chi^2(2) = 16.99$, $p = 0.0002$

*Coefficients statistically significant at the 0.001 level.

can use the conflict as the pretext for removing their leader, even when their state wins in the dispute. Indeed, it might be precisely for this reason that leaders desiring regime change do not push for additional victories. Selection institutions have important effects for internal and external leader removals, as our theory has predicted. Leaders with large winning coalitions are more vulnerable to internal replacement, and external opponents would like to remove them more often. These incentives produce another result that we have not commented on yet: the difficulty of defeating states with large winning coalitions. The selection equations concerning whether a state wins or loses in these analyses clearly show that states with large winning coalitions are more likely to win and are very difficult to defeat in a dispute. Leaders who answer to a large winning coalition apparently understand the insecurity of their position and how failure in international conflict jeopardizes their hold on power. Consequently, they choose their conflicts carefully and make the effort to win when they do fight, just as we argued in chapter 6.[25]

Nation Building After Disputes

Finally, we turn to changes in selection institutions following international conflicts, commonly referred to as nation building. Our theory contends that a victor will impose a small winning coalition and a large selectorate when it installs a new leader in order to ensure the compliance of the vanquished state. Of course, the victor may not need to make any changes if the institutions of the defeated state already give the new leader the latitude to ignore domestic pressures to revise the status quo. Moreover, the case of Vichy France suggests that leaders of losing states who are not removed also wish to change domestic institutions to give themselves the latitude to ignore domestic pressures to revise the outcome of the conflict. How do selection institutions change after conflict?

For all the parties in the dispute data, including those that joined disputes, we compare their selection institutions in the year before they became involved in the dispute with those three years after their role in the dispute ended. We look at institutions three years afterward to avoid any immediate disruption of domestic politics after the dispute. Even with this three-year interval, there are systems that have not returned to normal politics in this analysis. For instance, the United States and its allies did not allow free elections in Japan or West Germany until the early 1950s, well past our three-year interval. These cases help to make our point that victors are unwilling to allow political competition in vanquished states until they know that the winners of that competition will not seek to overturn the postwar status quo.

Victors who remove the leader of the defeated state should want to impose the selection institutions that insulate their puppet from the pressures of domestic political competition—a small winning coalition and a large selectorate. Table 9.11 presents the prewar and postwar breakdown of whether the winning coalition in these defeated states was large or small ($W \leq 0.5$ defines a small winning coalition). When the defeated state had a small winning coalition, it changed to a large winning coalition in only 15 percent of the cases. When the defeated state had a large winning coalition, it changed to a small winning-coalition system 75 percent of the time. Admittedly, there are very few cases of leaders with large winning coalitions being externally removed after losing a dispute. Such leaders rarely lose, perhaps because—as the selectorate theory predicts—they pick their fights carefully. Nevertheless, the pattern of changes from prewar institutions is clear. The chance that large winning-coalition systems are shrunk is much higher than that for small winning coalitions expanding, and the difference is statistically significant at the 0.026 level using the Fisher exact test.

The victor should also want to expand the size of the selectorate if it imposes a small winning coalition on the defeated state. Because of missing data on our measure of the size of the selectorate, we have only nine cases with the size of the selectorate for small winning-coalition

Table 9.11
Change in postwar selection institutions when the victor removes the defeated leader

		Size of postwar winning coalition	
		Small winning coalition	Large winning coalition
Size of prewar winning coalition	Small winning coalition	28 85%	5 15%
	Large winning coalition	3 75%	1 25%

systems after their defeated leader is removed. Eight of these nine cases have large selectorates ($S = 1$) three years later, which accords with our theory.

International conflict can induce a leader to change domestic institutions even if the other side does not force such changes. The outcome of the dispute should play a large role in such changes. A leader in charge when her state loses a dispute is likely to face challenges and so may wish to reduce the size of her winning coalition to increase her security in office. In contrast, the leader who supplants such a losing leader can blame the failure on his predecessor and will not feel as strong a push to shrink the size of the winning coalition. Tables 9.12a and 9.12b break down changes in the size of the winning coalition in states that lost a dispute by whether the leader in power during the dispute is replaced during or within one year of the end of the dispute. Defeated leaders still in power are less likely to expand their winning coalition from small to

Table 9.12a
Change in postwar selection institutions in defeated states with small winning coalitions before dispute

	Size of postdispute winning coalition	
	Small winning coalition	Large winning coalition
Defeated leader remains in power	405 91%	41 9%
Defeated leader removed domestically	179 80%	46 20%

Note: $\chi^2 = 16.78, p = 0.000$.

Table 9.12b
Change in postwar selection institutions in defeated states with large winning coalitions before dispute

	Size of postdispute winning coalition	
	Small winning coalition	Large winning coalition
Defeated leader remains in power	34 38%	56 62%
Defeated leader removed domestically	17 24%	53 76%

Note: $\chi^2 = 3.30, p = 0.070$.

large (table 9.12a) and more likely to shrink it from large to small (table 9.12b) than are leaders who replace a loser. The results are statistically significant and consistent with the theory.

Franco, Mussolini, and the Enemy Within

We conclude the chapter by returning to where we began, with the fates of Mussolini and Franco as a consequence of the Second World War. Mussolini jumped into the war when the defeat of France was assured; he then expanded the war by invading Egypt and Greece. His territorial objective was the establishment of a new Roman empire around the Mediterranean. The domestic groups on whose support Mussolini relied did not push for war or territorial expansion, but he saw those goals as a way to change his own political system to eliminate the constraints such groups placed on him. According to MacGregor Knox (1982, 286), "Internally, expansion would consolidate Fascist power, eliminate all competing authorities and unwelcome restraints, and mold the Italians into a people 'worthy' of the imperial mission Mussolini claimed for them." The military disasters in Greece and at Sidi Barrani shattered that scheme; the eventual downfall of Mussolini came with the approach of Allied forces to Italy.

Franco, unlike Mussolini, did not join the Axis powers during the Second World War. Franco negotiated with Hitler in the summer of 1940 over Spain's possible entry into the war. Like Mussolini, Franco sought territorial gains in North Africa as Spain's reward if it joined the war. But the territories in question were colonies of Vichy France, which Hitler could not alienate at that time. As negotiations between Nazi Germany and Franco's Spain dragged out, Franco began to see that German victory was not inevitable and so demanded greater economic aid in addition to territory as the price for Spanish participation. He needed that aid not just to fight the war and to feed his population, but to placate his supporters.[26]

The two dictators met in Hendaye, France, on October 23, 1940, for the critical face-to-face negotiation where they could weigh one another's willingness to fulfill their respective goals. The negotiations did not go well. Franco afterward summarized the negotiations for Ramon Serrano Suñer, his brother-in-law and minister of foreign affairs: "These people [the Nazis] are intolerable. They want us to come into the war in exchange for nothing. We cannot trust them if they do not undertake, in whatever we sign, a binding, formal contract to grant to us now those territories which I have explained to them are ours by right. Otherwise, we will not enter the war now" (quoted in Preston 1993, 397–398).

Hitler was also displeased with the negotiations. He complained to Mussolini afterward that "rather than go through that [negotiating with Franco] again, I would prefer to have three or four teeth taken out" (Preston, 1993, 399). From this point on, Spanish participation in the Second World War receded as a real possibility.

Franco and Mussolini are just two examples of leaders who must weigh the threat they face internally from supporters against the external threat posed by other states and their leaders. Success and failure in foreign policy enter into calculations about both threats because domestic supporters care about foreign policy. Supporters, however, have a greater opportunity to remove their leader. The enemy within is more dangerous than the enemy outside.

Conclusion

We proposed an extension of our theory that provides an explanation of how selection institutions influence war aims. The theory and the evidence both support the central claims. Governments that depend on a large coalition are more likely to fight for policy goals and to depose foreign rivals than are regimes ruled with a small coalition. Small coalitions lead to disputes over the acquisition of resources, measured here in terms of various aspects of territorial gains following war.

Defeat in war increases the odds that a leader will be deposed. This risk is much higher if the defeated leader heads a large-coalition polity. When leaders are deposed, internal challengers are the immediate culprits more often than foreign victors are, though a foreigner's victory paves the way for deposition. Following the deposition of a leader after military defeat, there is a substantial probability that the regime's selection institutions will be changed. Victorious large-coalition states disproportionately tend to engage in nation building that results in the establishment of autocratic regimes with small coalitions and large selectorates. That institutional configuration, while antidemocratic, does best at solving a defeated state's problem in committing to sustain the postwar settlement. Given the logic and the evidence behind postconflict nation building, we are not optimistic about the prospects that victorious democracies will help vanquished states become democratic as well. That pattern of nation building is only likely when the vanquished state's policy interests coincide with the interests of the winning coalition in the victor state. We are reminded that neither Germany nor Japan enjoyed democratic rule for at least seven years after the end of World War II. In the first postwar decade, these countries were administered by governments imposed by the Allies and then by leaders chosen under constitutions designed by the war's victors. Naturally, in each case, the constitution reflected the interests of the victors as much as those of the people subject to the constitution.

Appendix

This appendix presents a formal model of the international policy competition between states. It builds on the model in chapter 3, although to deal with the added complication of two nations we have simplified the structure of domestic political competition. For instance, we drop the choice of a domestic public good, and instead consider competition over a foreign policy public good. In chapter 3 we analyzed the choice of coalition size. Here, rather than further complicate the model, we build the results on endogenous coalition choice directly into the game form by assuming leaders always pick the W members of S for whom they have the highest affinity. For ease of presentation, we also use specific functional forms.

We proceed as follows. First, we consider foreign policy competition between nations A and B. Each nation chooses how much effort to make in the international policy struggle. In this regard we model "winning the peace." Second, we consider the situation that nation A has defeated nation B in a war. From this perspective, we ask whether leader A, at additional cost, wishes to take resources from B, replace the leader in B with a puppet, or alter the institutions in B. In particular, the model addresses how selection institutions shape these choices.

In addition to referring to leaders as A and B, we will sometimes explicitly subscript variables with AL and BL for incumbents and Ac and

Bc for domestic challengers. We assume each leader has a fixed quantity of resources available, hence we ignore the taxation decisions of chapter 3. From these resources, leaders and challengers propose a level of private goods, g_i, and a level of foreign policy effort, $q_i \in [q_m, R]$, subject to the budget constraint: $W_i g_i + q_i \leq R_i$. The outcome of foreign policy, f, depends on the relative effort of each side. In particular, we assume the outcome is the ratio of inputs: $f(q_a, q_b) = q_a/(q_a + q_b)$. To ensure this function is well defined, we insist that each side make some minimal foreign policy effort (i.e., $q_m > 0$); however, for much of the analysis we examine the case where $q_m \rightarrow 0$.

We consider specific utility functions, $V_A(g, f) = g + q_a/(q_a + q_b)$ and $V_B(g, f) = g + q_b/(q_a + q_b)$. Hence individuals' payoffs are linear in foreign policy and private goods.

The game, like that in chapter 3, is infinitely repeated where a representative round is as follows:

1. The leader and a randomly chosen challenger in each state (*AL*, *BL*, *Ac*, and *Bc*) simultaneously propose allocations of private and foreign policy goods (*g,q*) subject to the budget constraint. The incumbents choose the coalition of the *W* selectors for whom they have the highest affinity. Challengers choose a coalition of size *W* that includes at least one member of the incumbent's coalition.

2. The selectors in A observe the leader's and challenger's allocations and simultaneously choose between them. They make this decision without observation of B's allocations. The selectors in B make parallel decisions. The incumbent retains her job unless she receives support from less than *W* members of her coalition and the challenger receives support from at least *W* members of his coalition.

3. The chosen leaders implement their allocations, and affinities are revealed.

Equilibrium Policies

Paralleling the results in chapter 3, we describe a Markov perfect equilibrium in which incumbents survive in every period. Equilibrium behavior implies an incumbency condition that (1) the incumbent matches the best possible offer of the challenger, (2) the challenger makes his best possible offer by spending all available resources (the budget constraint) with (3) the optimal mix of private and foreign policy goods, and (4) the incumbent spends resources optimally over private and foreign policy goods. The optimal mix of private goods versus foreign policy goods implies that the marginal impact of additional spending on each good for the welfare of a coalition member is equal. These four conditions for each nation imply that eight identities hold in equilibrium. Given the large number of subscripts, we use the notation D_x to denote a derivative with respect to x.

Nation A

1A. Incumbency condition (incumbent matches the challenger's best possible offer):

$$IA1 = V_A(g_{Ac}, f(g_{Ac}, g_{BL})) - V_A(g_{AL}, f(g_{AL}, q_{BL})) + (\delta/(1-\delta))$$
$$((W_A/S_A)V_A(g_{AL}, f(q_{AL}, q_{BL})) + (1 - (W_A/S_A))V_A(0, f(q_{AL}, q_{BL})))$$
$$- (\delta/(1-\delta))V_A(g_{AL}, f(q_{AL}, q_{BL})) = 0$$

2A. Budget constraint:

$$IA2 = R_A - W_A g_{Ac} - q_{Ac} = 0$$

3A. Incumbent's optimal policy choice:

$$IA3 = D_g V_A(g_{AL}, f(g_{AL}, q_{BL})) - W_A D_q V_A(g_{AL}, f(g_{AL}, q_{BL})) = 0$$

4A. Challenger's optimal policy choice:

$$IA4 = D_g V_A(g_{Ac}, f(g_{Ac}, q_{BL})) - W_A D_q V_A(g_{Ac}, f(g_{Ac}, q_{BL})) = 0$$

There are four analogous conditions for nation B. This produces a total of eight equations in eight unknowns ($g_{AL}, g_{Ac}, g_{BL}, g_{Bc}, q_{AL}, q_{Ac}, q_{BL}, q_{Bc}$). Fortunately, given the specific functional forms, we can solve these equations. In particular, on the equilibrium path,

$$g_{AL}^* = \left(R_A(W_A + W_B)^2 - W_A^2 W_B\right)(1-\delta)S_A \Big/ \left((W_A + W_B)^2 W_A(S_A - \delta W_A)\right)$$

$$q_{AL}^* = W_B W_A^2 \Big/ (W_A + W_B)^2$$

$$g_{BL}^* = \left(R_B(W_A + W_B)^2 - W_B^2 W_A\right)(1-\delta)S_B \Big/ \left((W_A + W_B)^2 W_B(S_B - \delta W_B)\right)$$

$$q_{BL}^* = W_A W_B^2 \Big/ (W_A + W_B)^2$$

This implies the foreign policy outcome of $f(q_A, q_B) = W_A/(W_A + W_B)$; thus the state with the largest coalition tries hardest and gets the more favorable foreign policy outcome. We use the asterisk to represent equilibrium outcomes in the basic game.

Given that the incumbent retains unspent resources, her payoff Y^* equals $\Psi + R_A - W_A g^*_{AL} - q^*_{AL}$, where Ψ is the inherent value of office-holding. Consequently $Y^* = \Psi + \delta(S_A - W_A)(R_A(W_A + W_B)^2 - W_A^2 W_B)/((W_A + W_B)^2(S_A - \delta W_A))$. The winning coalition's payoff is $V_A(g^*_{AL}, f(q^*_{AL}, q^*_{BL})) = (R_A(W_A + W_B)^2 - W_A^2 W_B)(1 - \delta)S_A/((W_A + W_B)^2 W_A(S_A - \delta W_A)) + W_A/(W_A + W_B)$. The selectorate's payoff is $V_A(0, f(q^*_{AL}, q^*_{BL}{}^*)) = W_A/(W_A + W_B)$.

How the Victor Disposes of the Vanquished

We now suppose nation A has defeated nation B in a war. Nation A at additional costs might take resources, install a puppet regime, or alter the institutional arrangements in B. Following these decisions the nations will engage in the infinitely repeated game described above. The question we address is how domestic political institutions affect the desirability of taking resources, installing puppets, or changing institutional arrangements.

At an additional cost of C_R, A can take ρ resources from B, thus shifting resources from R_A and R_B to $R_A + \rho$ and $R_B - \rho$. Such an action simultaneously increases A's resources and decreases B's resources in the subsequent game. How does regime type affect the desirability of this decision? To indicate the change in resources we use the superscript r.

If leader A takes resources from B, her payoff improves by $Y^r - Y^* = \rho\delta(S_A - W_A)/(S_A - \delta W_A)$. This change is beneficial to all leaders, but our question is which institutional arrangements make this shift most attractive for leaders. Since $d(Y^r - Y^*)/dW_A = -\delta\rho(1 - \delta)S_A/(S_A - \delta W_A)^2 < 0$ and $d(Y^r - Y^*)/dS_A = \delta\rho(1 - \delta)W_A/(S_A - \delta W_A)^2 > 0$, from the leader's perspective taking resources becomes more attractive as the selectorate size increases and as the winning coalition decreases.

At the additional cost of C_p, nation A might replace leader B with a puppet who will do her bidding. By definition, a puppet makes minimal foreign policy effort—that is, $q_{BL} = q_m$. We use the superscript p to indicate the puppet scenario.

First we examine the conditions under which a puppet can survive in office. Since the puppet is constrained to minimal foreign policy effort but her domestic challenger is not, she is disadvantaged in the provision of foreign policy goods. Given that puppet B can spend no more than all available resources, we characterize the conditions under which she can match the best credible offer a challenger can make. In particular, puppet B can only survive domestically if $W_B \leq W_B^p$, where $W_B^p = S_B \delta R_B / (S_B(1 - \delta) + \delta R_B)$ when $q_m \to 0$. When the focus of political competition is on private goods, a puppet can survive. When political competition revolves around public policy, a puppet cannot adopt the puppet master's policies and survive. Hence A can only effectively establish a puppet in nation B if the winning-coalition size in nation B is sufficiently small.

Next, conditional on the installation of a puppet being possible, we assess for which leaders such an option is most attractive. In particular, the additional value of installing a puppet for leader A is $Y^p - Y^* = \delta(S_A - W_A)W_A^2 W_B / (W_A + W_B)^2 (S_A - \delta W_A)$. $d(Y^p - Y^*)/dW_A = (2S_A^2 W_B + 2\delta W_A^2 W_B + S_A(\delta W_A^2 - \delta W_A W_B - W_A^2 - 3W_A W_B))\delta W_A W_B / ((W_A + W_B)^3 (S_A - \delta W_A)^2)$. Although $d(Y^p - Y^*)/dW_A$ is difficult to sign analytically, all our simulations suggest it is positive: $d(Y^p - Y^*)/dS_A = -(1 - \delta)\delta dW_A^3 W_B / (W_A + W_B)^2 (S_A - \delta W_A)^2 < 0$. Hence the larger the winning coalition and the smaller the selectorate, the greater A's incentive to install a puppet where possible: $d(Y^p - Y^*)/dW_B = -(W_B - W_A)(S_A - W_A)\delta W_A^2 / ((S_A - \delta W_A)(WA + WB)^3)$. When W_A is large, the benefit of installing a puppet increases as B's coalition size increases, although remember that B's coalition can not be beyond a certain size or the puppet cannot survive.

Finally, having defeated B, A might engage in nation building and alter institutional arrangements in nation B. We have already seen that large-coalition leaders benefit most from the installation of a puppet, but that successfully installing a puppet requires that nation B not have a large winning coalition. Hence if A is a large-coalition system, A might want to reduce the size of W_B to ensure her puppet survives. We now consider the more general question of institutional choice.

Leader A's payoff is $Y^* = \delta(S_A - W_A)(R_A(W_A + W_B)^2 - W_A^2 W_B) / ((W_A + W_B)^2 (S_A - \delta W_A))$. The derivative of A's payoff with respect to B's coalition size is $dY^*/dW_B = \delta(S_A - W_A)W_A^2 (W_B - W_A) / (W_A + W_B)^3 (S_A - \delta W_A)$. Hence when A governs a large-coalition system ($W_A > W_B$), she wishes to reduce the size of her international rival's coalition. Conversely, when W_A is small, A wants to increase her foreign rival's coalition, since the increase in foreign policy efforts makes it harder for her domestic political rivals to promise foreign policy goods. It should be noted that the intensity of this latter preference is not as strong as the former, since public policy competition is relatively unimportant when W_A is small.

Promoting Peace and Prosperity

When Hobbes wrote about government, he concluded that the best path away from his litany of miseries in the hypothetical state of nature is rule by Leviathan, an enlightened dictator. Beyond the developments in the arts, economics, the physical sciences, and medicine that have improved life, the invention of representative government based on a large winning coalition that is a substantial proportion of the selectorate has also contributed mightily to improving life's good qualities. Hobbes's hopes notwithstanding, a Leviathan proves to be possibly the worst political system for promoting peace, prosperity, and human dignity, while representative democracy, especially with direct election of the head of government, appears to be the best yet invented to achieve those ends. We have demonstrated that social welfare is enhanced when leaders depend on a large coalition rooted in a large-selectorate system. In this chapter we explore what the selectorate theory suggests about how to engineer politics so as to enhance the prospects that everyone can live with dignity, peace, and prosperity.

The Hobbes Index

Social welfare is a difficult concept since it is inevitably subjective. Hobbes proposed one broad view of social welfare that seems to have withstood the test of time. He codified life's miseries in the state of nature by emphasizing how short, nasty, solitary, poor, and brutish life can be. Presumably, the more a society manages to move away from the condition in the state of nature, the better off are its people. With that in mind, we construct the Hobbes Index, by which we evaluate how far nations have come from the state of nature.[1]

The shortness of life is directly measurable. In fact, we assessed expected longevity at birth in chapter 5. In building the Hobbes Index, we first thought to use the variable *Lives* to assess shortness. However, we chose instead to use *Death*, the measure of deaths per 1,000 population. The reason is straightforward. Doing so greatly expands the number of countries for which we can construct the Hobbes Index simply because we have more complete data on death rates than on life expectancy at birth. For the cases where we have data on both variables, the correlation between these two indicators of the shortness of life is -0.88 ($N = 3,131$). Of course, the direction of *Death* is opposite that for *Lives*. We correct for this as follows. We first rank all country-year observations since 1972 in terms of death rates.[2] Then we subtract the minimum rank from each country's rank, and divide by the difference between the maximum rank and minimum rank, multiplying the result by 100. This gives us a scale that has a lower bound of 0 and an upper bound of 100. In the case of *Death*, however, the variable increases as life becomes shorter rather than longer. To correct this we subtract 100 from the previous calculation and multiply the answer by −1. This gives us again a score that can vary between 0 and 100, but now lower values are indicative of higher death rates (which is very strongly correlated with a shorter life expectancy). The above procedure is followed for each indicator we construct, although, of course, we do not carry out the final steps that reverse the direction of the scale when the index already moves from poorer performance to better performance as the value increases.

In chapter 4 we examined a variable that measures whether life is poor, at least in a material sense. The logarithm of per capita income is used in the Hobbes Index to assess poverty, normalized as above. Life is also nasty for citizens if they live without civil liberties. The *CivilLiberties* variable, recall, is a seven-point scale we have reassembled so that low scores reflect the fewest civil liberties and high score the greatest amount of civil liberties. This too is normalized as above from 0 to 100. As to brutishness, we build a composite index based on three indicators of a brutish existence. The components of the index assess the country's annual experience with civil war, revolution, and international war. We rank each component, normalize the component from 0 to 100, and reverse the direction so that low numbers mean high amounts of brutishness and high values mean low amounts of brutishness. The result is a scale of brutishness that varies between 0 for countries with the most such events in a given year to 100 for those with the fewest such events in a given year.

Solitariness is viewed from the perspective of the openness of the society. To assess how solitary life is we look at the number of radios per capita. Radios are sufficiently inexpensive that just about any village— and many individuals even in the poorest countries—can afford to own one to provide collective access to information, popular culture, and a window on the world beyond one's immediate surroundings. The data on radios per capita are drawn from Banks's (1996) collection. As with the other components, the data are ranked and then transformed to a 0-to-100 scale using the same procedure as for the other factors.

The Hobbes Index is the sum of the indicators for solitary, poor, nasty, brutish, and short, divided by 5, so that the Hobbes Index can vary between 0 and 100.[3] A country that outperforms all of the world in producing high incomes, low death rates, no war, civil war, or revolution, and that guarantees maximum civil liberties and in which information, popular culture, and so forth are readily available so that people form a community, would be a state that ensures a peaceful, prosperous, and dignified life for its citizens and resident aliens. It would achieve a score of 100 on the Hobbes Index.

Alas, the world has yet to produce a country that meets this ideal. In fact, only four countries in our data have an average annual Hobbes Index above 90: Iceland, Canada, Japan, and Australia. As for the worst, Burundi, Ethiopia, and Mozambique manage the worst single-year scores (a Hobbes Index of less than 10), while Angola, Cambodia, and Mozambique have the dubious distinction of having the worst national averages, with mean Hobbes Index values below 20.

Table 10.1 displays the ten best and the ten worst average performers on the Hobbes Index over the span of years 1972 to 1997, the years for which we have data. Several characteristics of these few countries are striking. First, the best performers span much of the globe, including North America, Oceania, Asia, and Europe; the worst performers, with the single exception of Cambodia, are all from Africa. Second, the best performers all also achieve the highest score on our variables *Democracy*, *W*, and *W/S* in every year for which the Hobbes Index is available. The worst performers almost always have very low *Democracy* values (mean = 0.22), small coalitions (mean = 0.29), and a strong loyalty norm (i.e., *W/S* is small; mean = 0.30). The bottom in performance remains disturbingly homogeneous if we expand our horizon to identify the bottom twenty states rather than just the bottom ten. Still, the polities are overwhelmingly dominated by rigged-election systems that emphasize a large selectorate and a small winning coalition and that are mostly found in Africa.

The best and the worst are, of course, extreme cases. Among the 1,865 country-years for which we were able to estimate the Hobbes Index, the average country earns a value of 62.13 with a standard deviation of 21.50.[4] Sad to say, the Hobbes Index shows only a weak general tendency

Table 10.1
The Hobbes Index: the best and the worst

The best		The worst	
Country	Hobbes Index	Country	Hobbes Index
Japan	92.7	Angola	13.0
Iceland	92.2	Mozambique	15.5
Australia	90.6	Cambodia	19.1
Canada	90.1	Burundi	22.8
New Zealand	88.8	Rwanda	23.6
Switzerland	88.7	Ethiopia	23.8
Netherlands	88.4	Chad	24.2
USA	86.8	Uganda	24.4
Norway	84.6	Zaire	26.6
Denmark	84.5	Guinea-Bissau	26.8

to improve over time, creeping up about 0.24 points each year. At that pace it would take the global community over forty years just to move another ten points farther away from the solitary, nasty, short, poor, and brutish life in the state of nature. Such a ten-point move would make the average country resemble the recent performance of Peru or the Dominican Republic. Neither the mean, median, nor variance is changing markedly over time.

Of course, global averages are a blunt instrument to tell us about the true state of the world. We can look at the Index more closely country by country or region by region. The worst performers, as noted, are overwhelmingly found on the African continent: twenty-five of the bottom thirty-six (the bottom quartile). Outside Africa, Laos, Haiti, Pakistan, Azerbaijan, Comoro Islands, and Nepal are among the few states to fall within the bottom quartile on the Hobbes Index.[5] Conversely, the top quartile is filled out with mostly Western European states (nineteen out of thirty-six), though Mauritius, Fiji, Singapore, Costa Rica, Jamaica, Chile, South Korea, and others also make this top group.

How do the leaders of the best- and worst-led states fare? The leaders of countries in the top quartile on the Hobbes Index survive in office for a substantially shorter time, on average, than do those in the bottom quartile. Bad performance seems to go hand-in-hand with political success.

The Hobbes Index provides a convenient shorthand for addressing relations between social welfare and the institutions of government. As we turn to policy implications of the selectorate theory, we will rely in part on the Hobbes Index to analyze the means by which peace and prosperity can be promoted in every corner of the earth. The Hobbes Index provides a broad view of public well-being. We share the conviction of most economists that sound fiscal and monetary policy, coupled with market forces and appropriate government intervention to manage externalities brought on by market failure, is a path to prosperity. But it is patently obvious that many governments have failed to adopt critical policies known to be economically beneficial. A central concern of this study has been to see the circumstances under which the pursuit of good policies represents bad politics.

With the knowledge that individual prospects of remaining in office can be enhanced through bad policy, we have offered an explanation for such policy choices without having to appeal to ignorance on the part of decision makers. Instead, we have shown that under the "right" institutional arrangements, it is politically irrational for government officials to follow the recommendations of knowledgeable economists who see a path to improving living conditions in a society, but whose vision of this path does not consider its harmful political consequences for the incumbent leader.[6] Any strategy for improving social welfare must look at both the policies required and the means of making the implementaton of those policies politically feasible for the incumbent leadership. The first issue to examine in institutional development is the question of what institutions are commensurate with a high value on the Hobbes Index. Then we can focus on how to make the adoption of those policies compatible with the incentive incumbents have to keep their jobs.

Explaining the Hobbes Index

Glancing at who is at the top and the bottom of the Hobbes Index suggests that large-coalition, democratic governments are especially helpful in moving people beyond the state of nature to a condition in which they can enjoy long, peaceful, prosperous, dignified lives. But looking at the extremes is not a fruitful way of estimating a central tendency, so we turn to a more exacting method to tease out further details about the exact impact that different institutions have on good governance.

We begin with four regression analyses, using the Hobbes Index as the variable to be explained. We use it as an index of fundamental public goods produced by the state. The independent variables in the first two regressions are W, $WS:DemRes$, $Log(Population)$, and $Parl\_Pres$. To ease interpretation, we also break the variable $Parl\_Pres$—introduced in chapter 4—into the three constituent democratic parts of relevance to the selectorate theory. *Parliamentary* is a dummy variable coded 1 if $Parl\_Pres$ has a score of 1, indicating a parliamentary system, as in the United Kingdom. *Mixed* is a dummy variable coded 1 when $Parl\_Pres = 2$, indicating a mixed parliamentary-presidential system, as in France. When $Parl\_Pres = 3$, the dummy variable *Presidential* is coded 1 to indicate a presidential system, as in the United States. We use these three factors in the second pair of regressions to analyze differences within democratic systems on performance on the Hobbes Index. When we examine these constituent parts of democracy, which we believe reflect increasingly larger coalition size, we look only at cases for which our crude coalition indicator, W, is as large as 0.75 or greater. In each pair of regression analyses we control first for our standard fixed effects (region-year) and then replicate the results, controlling for fixed effects for each country. These latter tests eliminate any state that has had constant selection institutions over the years 1972–1997, thereby "fixing" out virtually all of the impact of Western Europe, the United States, Canada, Australia, and so forth. These tests assess temporal change within countries. The former tests based on region-year evaluate cross-sectional variation in institutions and in performance on the Hobbes Index.

The variables in these tests are chosen specifically to speak to the impact that political-selection institutions have on the quality of life. If the selectorate theory is useful in thinking about how to "engineer" governments, we should find substantial positive associations between the Hobbes Index, W, and $Parl\_Pres$. If the coefficient for any one of the institutional factors (parliamentary, mixed, or presidential) in the separate "democratic" assessments points to especially beneficial effects on Hobbes, then that helps to focus attention on one form of democratic arrangement over another as a way to help engineer a better quality of life. The selectorate theory leaves us agnostic with regard to the impact that $WS:DemRes$ will have on the Hobbes Index, though it would be encouraging from an engineering point of view if $WS:DemRes$ proves to have a significant positive effect. That would mean, in conjunction with the direct effects of *W* and *Parl_Pres*, that if the sum of the coefficients of *W*, *Parl_Pres*, and *WS:DemRes* were strongly positive, democracy fosters improved quality of life. Democracy is so much more commonly and easily observed a characteristic than is *W* or *S* that this would facilitate efforts by policymakers to promote social welfare. Our conjecture about coalition size within different forms of democracy leads to the expectation that the variable *Presidential* will have a stronger positive effect than will *Parliamentary*, while *Mixed* is an insufficiently precise variable for us to predict an ordering of impact relative to *Presidential* and *Parliamentary*.[7] The expectation is that within democracies, directly elected presidents are more likely to lift the Hobbes Index than are prime ministers in parliamentary systems, because among democracies the former rely on a larger coalition than do the latter.[8]

Table 10.2 summarizes the regression results for all polities. The table tells an important story. The quality of life is clearly substantially enhanced by having a large-coalition democracy that relies on a presidential system (note that *Parl_Pres* is strongly positive). Even after removing the cross-sectional variation by switching to country fixed effects, coalition size and democraticness all remain profoundly important factors contributing to the quality of life. Larger population, which may attend the overall size of the winning coalition, also seems to help within the context of this test.

The results within democratic polities are reported in table 10.3. Here we see that more detailed work, especially on distinguishing among coalition sizes within democracies, needs to be done to understand the best

Table 10.2
The Hobbes Index and political institutions

Variable	Region-year fixed effects Coef., (std. error), prob.	Country fixed effects Coef., (std. error), prob.
W	28.57, (1.533), 0.000	14.593, (1.284), 0.000
WS:DemRes	13.083, (1.865), 0.000	5.676, (2.038), 0.005
Parl_Pres	3.643, (0.589), 0.000	1.664, (0.955), 0.082
Log(Population)	−1.896, (0.228), 0.000	16.607, (1.551), 0.000
Constant	70.817, (3.906), 0.000	−215.362, (24.747), 0.000
Summary statistics	$N = 1{,}127$, F.E. = 106, $F = 221.70$, $R^2 = 0.63$, $p = 0.000$	$N = 1{,}127$, F.E. = 110, $F = 83.91$, $R^2 = 0.02$, $p = 0.000$

Table 10.3
The Hobbes Index and political-selection institutions within democracies

Variable	Region-year fixed effects Coef., (std. error), prob	Country fixed effects Coef., (std. error), prob
Parliamentary	14.987, (1.212), 0.000	2.791, (1.500), 0.063
Mixed	13.677, (2.110), 0.000	4.367, (2.378), 0.067
Presidential	18.234, (1.970), 0.000	0.495, (5.522), 0.929
Log(Pop)	−1.816, (0.293), 0.000	20.592, (2.296), 0.000
Constant	94.830, (4.894), 0.000	−256.665, (36.750), 0.000
Summary statistics	$N = 656$, F.E. = 105, $R^2 = 0.41$, $F = 60.04, p = 0.000$	$N = 656$, F.E. = 70, $R^2 = 0.01$, $F = 23.08, p = 0.000$

institutional configuration for improvement in a country's performance on the Hobbes Index. The country fixed-effects model (which, among other things, ensures that results are not due to the effect of the United States or any other individual country) suggests that growing population promotes improvement in the Hobbes Index, while the region-year fixed-effects, cross-sectional analysis bolsters the expectation that smaller democracies on average do better on the Hobbes Index. Presidential systems do best cross-sectionally, though other democratic institutional arrangements also perform well. Looking at temporal variation lends greatest support to mixed or parliamentary systems. However it is sliced, democracies with their dependence on a large coalition outperform other institutional setups in promoting a high score on the Hobbes Index. In such polities life is least solitary, nasty, poor, brutish, or short.

The first column of results in table 10.4 shows the effects of changes in the value of W ($\Delta W30$) and the lagged (three years earlier) values of W and S to assess whether *changing* institutions has the desired impact on the Hobbes Index after controlling also for the following variables: the independent impact of economic growth, the residual effects of political rights (after removing the influence exerted by coalition size and selectorate size), the influence of transparency as evaluated by the variable *TaxYN* introduced in chapter 4, and the residual impact of trade openness (*Trade Residual*) and of human capital (*LaborEd Residual*) after removing the impact that W and S have on these economic factors. The second set of results replicates the first set, but substitutes country fixed effects for region-year fixed effects.

Table 10.4
Institutions, the Hobbes Index, and the economy

Variable	Region-year fixed effects Coef., (std. error), prob	Country fixed effects Coef., (std error), prob
$\Delta W30$	35.505, (2.770), 0.000	38.421, (7.915), 0.000
LagW3	40.666, (2.555), 0.000	41.710, (8.260), 0.000
LagS3	−8.700, (1.944), 0.000	−4.184, (1.432), 0.004
WS:DemRes	−4.580, (3.319), 0.168	−6.978, (3.278), 0.034
Parl_Pres	3.421, (0.659), 0.000	0.904, (1.632), 0.580
Growth	−0.032, (0.104), 0.757	−0.042, (0.058), 0.470
PRRes	2.125, (0.690), 0.002	3.300, (0.564), 0.000
TaxYN	1.932, (1.214), 0.112	1.411, (1.066), 0.186
LaborEd Residual	2.283, (0.177), 0.000	3.715, (1.675), 0.027
Trade Residual	0.052, (0.008), 0.000	0.058, (0.018), 0.001
Constant	39.246, (1.644), 0.000	35.467, (6.607), 0.000
Summary statistics	$N = 572$, F.E. = 76, $R^2 = 0.76$, $F = 79.18$, $p = 0.000$	$N = 572$, F.E. = 72, $R^2 = 0.73$, $F = 20.30$, $p = 0.000$

Table 10.4 tells a critical story for those in a position to exert influence over economic policy and political institutions. Policies that protect political rights, provide openness to trade, and produce a well-educated labor force sharply improve the Hobbes Index. Even when controlling for temporal change—thereby eliminating the impact of virtually all high-scoring societies—political rights and trade policy still jump out as critical areas in which improved policy can increase the quality of life. In a sense, there is no news in this. It has long been understood that these policy choices are good for a society. Still, our results reinforce the view that countries can succeed even if they are not democratic, provided they foster rule of law, the very factor most strongly associated with political rights and open trade policies. But as strongly as these programs improve the quality of life, they clearly take a second seat to promotion of a government that depends on a large winning coalition. Increasing the coalition from say 0 to 1 on our indicator W over a three-year period yields a Hobbes Index that is 35–40 points higher than if coalition size had remained at 0. The other trappings of democracy apparently do not improve the quality of life: coalition size is where the institutional action is.

It is also noteworthy that high economic growth rates do not rescue countries from oppressive governments that keep life solitary, nasty, poor, brutish, and short. Those who believe that countries—like China—that have enjoyed significant economic expansion will develop their way into more pleasant places for their citizenry may wish to reconsider (Bueno de Mesquita 2002). The evidence here at least does not support that view. Economic reform, as we showed in chapter 4, does not produce political change, but political change does lead to economic improvement. Apparently political change of this type leads to an overall improvement in life's circumstances. Are there more general ways in which the selectorate theory can help advance the quality of life through better governance?

Creating Better Governance and a Better Life

In this section we address four issues that have been the object of considerable contemporary discussion and analysis: democratization, governmental stability, international financial support for ailing economies, and military intervention. In doing so we attempt to show how the selectorate theory can lead to an understanding of each in a new way that will, we think, improve the related policies.

When Democracy Only Appears to Have a Large Coalition

One often-expressed hope is that the wave of democratization that has taken place since the demise of the Soviet Union will produce better governance. Perhaps so, but sometimes democracies utterly fail to provide the very items that seem to characterize a high quality of life. Here we address why the nominal label *democracy* does not necessarily imply dependence on a large coalition and the importance of what this means. We intimated in chapter 2 that the gap between democracy and a large-coalition might be due to "lumpiness" or correlated affinities that convert apparently large-coalition systems into functionally small-coalition governments. India's problems are indicative of policy failure in many seemingly democratic polities. The selectorate theory treats coalition members and selectorate members as independent agents, each making choices in the political arena. In our theory, these agents differ in their affinity for the incumbent sufficiently that new leaders must learn who their key, pivotal supporter is. But what happens when selectorate members do not act as individual agents?

Bloc voting can turn a large selectorate into a much smaller group. It can also convert a large-coalition requirement into an actual need to attract support from a small coalition. Two of the poorest states in India—Bihar and Orissa—illustrate this point.

Voting in many parts of India, but especially in old princely strongholds like Bihar and Orissa, is characterized by patron-client relations. Many poor villagers—and India even today is 60 percent rural—depend on an influential, usually upper-caste, patron for their livelihood, especially during difficult times. When crops fail or other economic problems beset villagers, the hierarchical patron-client system acts as social insurance against starvation. Patrons look after their clients and clients look out for their patrons. This system assures patrons of loyal political support among dependent villagers. Village patrons, in turn, often have their own patrons higher up the ladder. This turns out to imply that one individual selectorate member (a high-up patron) chooses a candidate to back and "delivers" his or her clients' votes. The delivery of votes works its way down the patron-client hierarchy, ensuring that by purchasing the backing of a few key clients, a candidate can assemble a winning coalition without having to appeal to a broader segment of the electorate.

Local political parties grounded in personal loyalties often dominate elections in Bihar and Orissa, as well as other parts of India (Park and Bueno de Mesquita 1979). The resulting governments do not actually need a large coalition to hold power. They need a small coalition of patrons who signal their clients how to vote. The patrons get rewarded for delivering their vote, and they in turn provide modest rewards for their clients while continuing to do what they can to provide "social security" if dire circumstances arise.

Tammany Hall did much the same for New York's large immigrant Irish-American population in the late nineteenth and early twentieth centuries. A few individuals—Al Smith was a good example—were identified who had the special skills needed to deliver the vote. These helpful patrons of the Irish-American poor could be counted on to find a job for an out-of-work constituent or to smooth things over with the parish priest and so forth. In exchange, the Irish-Americans voted as they were told and the patron rose in influence within the Tammany machine. The signals coming from ward bosses, like Al Smith, were sufficient to determine how individuals voted. Rather than producing independent votes, this system of "machine politics" produced correlated affinities and, therefore, interdependent voting. Labor unions today operate in much the same way in many countries. They deliver a large bloc of votes; their leaders gain privileged access and influence in the government; and the individual members get smaller benefits for their loyalty.

When support is aggregated through a hierarchical mechanism, such as bloc voting, the effective number of supporters required to form a coalition is often substantially lower than the nominal rule suggests. The more directly people's votes are aggregated into support for the leader or the challenger, the greater their influence on the selection process. Throughout this book we have illustrated numerous instances of hierarchical aggregation. For example, in chapter 2 we saw that although King John needed the support of a majority of knights fees, he could achieve this support from a small number of barons. Knights were not free to give their support. Rather their vote was effectively in the hands of the baron with whom they had a patron-client relationship. The king passed benefits to his baronial supporters, who in turn passed benefits on to their knights. Since a coalition of barons was substantially smaller than a majority coalition of knights, the king's policies were more private in nature and he could survive more easily, expropriating more resources for his pet projects (such as supporting crusades) than would have been the case had the knights directly chosen the king.

The Mamluks provide another powerful demonstration of how hierarchical aggregation of support through bloc voting creates small coalitions from a nominally larger coalition. As we detailed in chapter 6, to survive the sultan required the support of the preponderance of military power within the army of 10,000 Mamluks. Yet, strong, almost familial relations between master and former slaves (remember that the Mamluks were former slaves, who had been released by their master when they completed their training) created strict voting blocs. Emirs (senior military officers) controlled the support of the soldiers they had released from slavery. Hence control of the military power of the Mamluks only required support from within the several hundred emirs.

The basis of military power lies in control of most of the army's might. Yet individual soldiers typically have no say. Support is aggregated through military units, and leaders only need the support of the officers at the top of the military hierarchy to gain the requisite military might to remain in power. These are of course extreme examples, but even the most democratic of societies contain hierarchical practices that retard the required coalition size. For instance, in the United States, the president is chosen by the electoral-college. This system, in which most states give all their electoral-college votes to the candidate with the plurality of votes within the state, makes leaders beholden to a smaller coalition than would be the case under direct election of the president. In parallel to the case of single-member district parliamentary systems, the president only needs a little more than half the support in half the states, which is significantly less than a direct plurality of the U.S. electorate.[9] The selectorate theory suggests that a constitutional amendment doing away with the electoral college would promote a greater focus on effective public policy, encourage the president to work harder, and reduce presidential tenure. Of course the impact of such an amendment would be marginal, since the United States is already a large-coalition system.

In many democracies certain organizations, such as unions and business associations, have bloc voting rights within political parties. When individual trade union members are unable to exercise their choice of leader independently, the coalition size is reduced, increasing leader tenure and corruption, and reducing the promotion of effective public policy. Within democracies, removing hierarchical aggregation in favor of direct choice of those at the top increases coalition size, which further enhances the lives of residents. Although once coalition size is already large, further increases in W will produce only modest improvement in the quality of policies, these gains should not go unrealized.

For nations where bloc voting and other forms of hierarchical aggregation are endemic, increasing the independence of voters' choices offers a path to move citizens further from Hobbes's state of nature and closer to a long, peaceful, and prosperous life. If the independence of voters is violated, leaders are more likely to face the political incentives inherent in a small-coalition, large-selectorate system even though the trappings of government suggest that the system is democratic. This means that such governments will encourage corruption rather than public-goods production.

Breaking the hold of powerful political blocs is extremely difficult. Where they exist, international agencies should anticipate problems in converting economic assistance into social improvement. For instance, a measure of national ethnolinguistic fractionalization (Easterly and Levine 1997) probably provides a good estimate of the likelihood that a society experiences bloc voting, if it has voting at all. Ethnolinguistic fractionalization over the years for which data are available (1951–1990) shares a significant positive association with black marketeering, a strong indication of its tie to corruption. Ethnolinguistic fractionalization is significantly *reduced* as W or W/S increases, but it is unaffected by other aspects of democraticness. The selectorate theory suggests it is in the interest of political leaders—but not most citizens—to enhance ethnic, racial, religious, linguistic, and other social cleavages.

World Bank and other officials focused on problems in governance could contribute significantly to an improved understanding of how to reduce the socially harmful consequences of bloc voting by studying how bloc voting relates to political-unit size and to the prospects of a hierarchy of patrons who deliver bloc votes. Taking democracy at face value in assessing governance can only lead to serious errors. The degree of bloc voting is an area little investigated in this context but of significant concern. Identifying what, if anything, can be done through policy reform or legislation to diminish the hold of bloc voting in otherwise seemingly large coalition systems requires case-by-case country assessments. Elsewhere one of us has presented a model appropriate for such uses (Bueno de Mesquita 1997, 2002). The selectorate theory offers clear guidance as to the policies required, and for some problems also suggests concrete actions to be taken, but not regarding the microlevel political efforts needed to convince relevant interests to accept an alteration in bloc voting.

Stable Government: Leaders or Institution?

During the 1990s the Congressional Budget Office (CBO) conducted a study on the relationship between prosperity and stable political leadership. The CBO claimed that stable government is a necessary, if not sufficient, condition for economic growth. The CBO points to examples of such stability as China, Egypt, and others. The view expressed by the CBO is dangerous for public policy. If it were followed, the United States and such major international organizations concerned with economic growth as the IMF and the World Bank would place much greater attention on the factors that produce stable leadership than on the factors that actually produce growth or improvement on the Hobbes Index. If the CBO and others are right, a cure for instability would be a major step on the way to a cure for poverty.

Chapter 7 demonstrates that autocracies—because of their dependence on a small coalition—have more stable leadership than do democracies that depend on a large coalition. In fact, over the past forty years the most autocratic governments of the world have averaged only six leaders, one every seven years. Some countries have managed only one or two leaders in that time span. Fidel Castro, for instance, has led the Cuban government for more than forty years. Since the Chinese Communist Revolution in 1949, that country has only had five leaders; the Soviet Union during the approximately sixty-five years following the death of Lenin, only nine. The British and Americans have had vastly more just since the end of World War II, and these are both highly stable democratic leadership systems. The average number of leaders in each of the most democratic countries since 1961 is twenty-eight!

Small coalitions foster stable, long-lasting leadership, low growth, and poor performance on the Hobbes Index. Autocrats do not grow more efficient at improving their society over time. In fact, how long a leader has been in office is inversely correlated with changes in the Hobbes Index, while leader tenure to date multiplied by W is positively associated with changes in the Hobbes Index. That is, long-surviving, large-coalition democrats seem to continually improve the quality of life for their country's residents. Long-surviving, small-coalition autocrats, in contrast, seem not to improve the quality of life for the average resident.

We can understand why some believe that stable leadership is good for economic performance. The uncertainty provoked by instability might be thought to scare investors, but those effects—if they exist at all—are offset by the advantages inherent in political competition. In both autocracies and democracies, leadership *turnover* is positively associated with growth, though more weakly in autocracies than in democracies. Additionally, the average growth rate in large-coalition democracies is higher than in small-coalition autocracies for any given level of leadership turnover. Competition over leadership is not the only thing that gives democracies an advantage, but that competition is certainly an important element contributing to improved public welfare. Because large coalitions force leaders to be attentive to producing public goods, political competition gets turned into an "arms race" over policy ideas. In small-coalition systems, leaders and rivals compete over the provision of private goods. That is a competition designed to drain an economy and impoverish its citizenry through rent seeking.

Not only do leaders come and go, but so too do political regimes or institutional arrangements. Societies are vulnerable to institutional change under specific circumstances. As we saw in chapter 8, once a large-coalition system or democracy passes beyond a particular welfare threshold, no incentives exist among coalition members, those in the selectorate, or those among the disenfranchised to alter the institutions so as to terminate democracy. Leaders still have that incentive but are kept in check by the difficulty they face in putting together a coalition to support such an effort. This means that once a democracy has established the right configuration of coalition size and selectorate size to provoke low taxes, high labor effort, and public-goods production within the framework of a balanced budget, the problems associated with maintaining effective governance and social welfare have largely been solved. The difficulty lies in societies that have not reached this "take-off" stage (Rostow 1990; Organski 1965; Przeworski 2001), as explained in chapter 8.

To Bail Out or Not to Bail Out?

Autocrats are unusually advantaged in their efforts to stay in power. Exhortations from outside are unlikely to move them to change their behavior. Their survival in office is only made worse by shifting from policies that hamper public well-being to policies that improve their country's Hobbes score. Therefore, urging such regimes to accept the norms of democracy, transparency, civil liberties, and the like is shouting into the wind. Just about no one is likely to act on such exhortations. But there are moments of opportunity when the promises of autocrats to reform their ways can be made into more than so much cheap talk. These moments arise infrequently, but they could be seized on when they do arise. These are the moments when organizations like the World Bank, the IMF, or regional development banks could have a tremendously salutary impact on governance and on social welfare.

We have demonstrated that autocrats are likely to be threatened with the loss of power when they no longer provide adequate private goods to their key supporters. That is why, as shown in chapter 6, autocrats do not try as hard as democrats in wartime. Democrats need policy successes to survive politically. Autocrats need money to pay off their coalition. The rent-seeking incentives created by small-coalition systems erode economic efficiency. They prompt people to pursue leisure at the expense of productive labor, stymying growth. Eventually the inefficiencies catch up and there is not enough money to maintain loyalty. These circumstances—almost never recognized as such—are generally portrayed by the autocrat as a financial crisis needing international assistance to rescue the most severely deprived among the citizenry.

It is commonly argued by international agencies that countries facing a financial crisis first need to deal with reforming their economy and only later need to address their political problems. This is the general policy of the World Bank, for instance, as of this writing (2002). Such arguments are understandable. During financial crises regimes face the risk of defaulting on bank loans. Bank default can only make it harder to borrow in the future. Without loans, the government may not be able to provide the essential services designed to protect the population from privation and worse. And yet the evidence we presented suggests that autocrats spend precious little on staying the hand of want for their citizenry. Accumulated debt is sovereign, but the recipients of financial assistance are flesh-and-blood autocratic rulers. Given their penchant for distributing private goods to their backers and for engaging in kleptocracy themselves, can we take seriously their claims that they seek financial relief for the welfare of their people? The evidence tells us otherwise. Economic assistance relieves the autocrat's need for funds with which to maintain the loyalty of coalition members. Aid given in advance of political reform is more likely to prevent such reforms than to stimulate them.

Foreign aid per capita is either insignificantly or inversely related to changes over a three-year period in a country's subsequent score on the Hobbes Index, its economic growth rate, educational attainment, or a host of other indicators of quality of life. Aid per capita, however, does seem to contribute significantly to increased life expectancy. Viewed from the perspective of aid as a percentage of GDP, the picture is equally gloomy. Aid in GDP terms does not have a meaningful impact on many indicators of improved quality of life. It does foster some improvement in growth and some increase in life expectancy over a three-year period. However, it does nothing to promote real improvement in the Hobbes Index, or in equal opportunity in schools, and it is associated with a significant decline in the society's human capital as measured by the education of the labor force. The median aid recipient gets about $13.50 per capita per year in constant 1995 U.S. dollars, or about 3 percent of its GDP. With a coefficient of 0.035 for aid per capita (using World Bank data), it will take more than twenty years for the median recipient to improve its Hobbes score by ten points. The impact is negligible when viewed in terms of aid as a percentage of GDP.

Aid has failed to promote the welfare benefits for which it is generally thought to be designed (Easterly 2001). But economic assistance does have an effect in an area of great importance to national leaders. It improves their prospects of political survival. To see how aid influences political survival, we examine survival prospects of leaders as a function of aid received, measured as a percentage of GDP (and labeled *Aid/GDP*), controlling for economic growth rates, the magnitude of the recipient country's black market exchange-rate premium, and the size of the selectorate. Whether we define subjects in terms of their region-year or based on individual country effects, the results are the same. For larger-coalition polities (i.e., $W \geq 0.75$) aid has an insignificant effect on political survival, while economic growth promotes leadership longevity in office, as we saw in chapter 8. The magnitude of the black market exchange-rate premium is inconsequential in influencing survival prospects for large-W leaders, as is selectorate size. But when a leader depends on a small coalition ($W < 0.75$), aid markedly reduces the risk of losing office (coefficient = -6.851, standard error = 2.921, and $p = 0.019$ based on 796 cases with 188 individual country effects). If we add further control for the indebtedness of the government, the political-survival benefits from foreign aid are even more dramatic. The hazard of being deposed drops sharply (the coefficient for $Aid/GDP = -30.1015$, standard error = 7.636, with a probability of 0.000 based on 217 observation for 59 countries) if the government depends on a small coalition. There is not a significant impact on survival prospects for more democratic aid recipients (those with $W \geq 0.75$). There seems to be little doubt that aid benefits less democratic recipients in their quest to hold onto office.

Aid may also be beneficial to donors. To see how, let us consider what the selectorate theory suggests about the motivation of donors. Donors of foreign economic assistance are overwhelmingly governments dependent on a large winning coalition. Though many other democratic countries contribute more than the United States as a proportion of their GDP, the lion's share of aid still comes from the United States. Leaders in large-coalition polities, as we have seen, enhance their prospects of staying in office by delivering public policies that are attractive to their core constituents, their winning coalition. Though few constituents pay attention to foreign policy except under dire circumstances, still there are always some important constituents who at the margin respond electorally to foreign policy choices. Leaders in democratic donor countries, then, would like governments in other states to adopt policies commensurate with the policy goals of the would-be donor.

Donors face a problem. If they give substantial aid to democratic recipients, those recipients cannot credibly commit to adjust their policies to be in line with what the other state wants, as we saw in chapter 9. Prospective recipients who are democratic must satisfy their own constituents' policy wants. Thus, unless the policy preference profile of winning-coalition members in the prospective recipient state matches that in the prospective donor state, the would-be donor will be reluctant to give aid. But if the prospective recipient rules over a small-coalition system, the recipient can credibly commit to policy changes—provided they are not too extreme—toward the desires of the potential donor. The donor gains a domestic political advantage by extracting policy concessions, and the recipient gains money with which to satisfy backers through private-goods transfers.

Among prospective nondemocratic recipients of aid, the ones most likely theoretically to gain assistance from a democratic donor are those who rule with a small coalition and who have a weak loyalty norm. If their loyalty norm is weak (so that W/S is large), they will be especially eager for extra funds with which to enhance their prospects of political survival. Recall that leaders have to spend more on their coalition when their loyalty norm is weak. Consequently, such leaders will be more susceptible to making policy concessions in exchange for foreign economic assistance. Small-coalition polities with a weak loyalty norm typically are military juntas, monarchies, and petty, personalist dictatorships that do not bother with rigged elections or with a strong political party. If the selectorate account of incentives is correct, aid should go disproportionately to small-W, large-W/S regimes, with rigged-election autocracies next in line. Of course, if there are democratic states in need of aid with policy preferences aligned with those of prospective donors, they will head the list, but such conditions are likely to be relatively rare.

Table 10.5 reports the results of a Heckman selection model that allows us to answer two critical questions tied to the above discussion. The first phase of the Heckman estimation procedure provides an equation than answers the question "Who gets aid?" The second phase, the

Table 10.5
Who gets aid and how much do they get?

Variable	Who gets aid? Coef., (std. error), prob.	How much aid? Coef., (std. error), prob.
W	−1.0873, (0.422), 0.010	−269.082, (90.604), 0.003
S (*Effective S* in last column)	−1.533, (0.564), 0.007	−38.071, (11.023), 0.001
W/S		243.808, (94.773), 0.010
Log(Income/Capita)	−2.188, (0.149), 0.000	15.804, (1.853), 0.000
Government Debt	0.016, (0.002), 0.000	0.382, (0.039), 0.000
Constant	21.948, (1.419), 0.000	−60.965, (14.843), 0.000
Summary statistics	N = 1225 uncensored, 420 censored, LogLikelihood = −7,109.28	N = 1225 uncensored Wald χ^2 = 189.03, p = 0.000

regression phase, then addresses the question "Among those receiving aid, how much does each recipient get?"

We believe that the first question is answered by examining the size of W, S, the logarithm of per capita income, and government debt as a percentage of GDP. We expect that the likelihood of receiving aid increases as W decreases, as S decreases, as income decreases, and as debt increases. That is, aid goes to poor, small-coalition, small-selectorate, indebted societies. These are the polities whose leaders are most in need of resources to avoid political deposition.

Conditional on receiving aid, those with a weak loyalty norm, small W, small *Effective S*, high income, and high debt should receive more.[10] That is, heavily indebted, relatively well-off, juntas, monarchies, and petty, personalist dictators get more foreign aid on a per capita basis. The relatively well off do better because they are typically the nondemocratic polities with a weak loyalty norm—that is, juntas and monarchies, rather than the more extensively rent-seeking rigged-election autocracies. The evidence strongly supports these expectations. Every coefficient in table 10.5 is in the predicted direction and is statistically and substantively significant. Meeting the theory's criteria greatly improves the prospects of getting aid and of getting a lot of it.

Well-intentioned people urge economic relief to ward off starvation, mass population dislocations, and the like. The world community has responded generously to just such terrible circumstances in Somalia, Ethiopia, North Korea, and so many other places. In each of these cases, famine, mass dislocations, disease, and suffering are to a significant degree the consequence of political choices. None of these governments has reformed its ways following receipt of bailout money and goods. Their leaders have been sustained in office even as they have brought war, famine, and misery on their people. Funds, food, and materiel designed as humanitarian aid too often end up as black market contraband or as cash in the coffers of government officials. And still refugee camps fill with hapless people seeking to escape the consequences of their own government's disastrous policies.

The purposes actually served by economic assistance, especially during a fiscal crisis, should be crucial to determining whether aid is given. Good motives by donors do not alter the pernicious incentives of recipient officials. If aid is divorced from political reform, or if political reform is assumed to follow after economic relief, then a cycle of financial crises, economic stabilization, and subsequent crises can be expected. Each bailout may restore economic stability temporarily, but rent seeking will continue, so that gross inefficiency will swing the economy back into a tailspin. The persistent effect of economic relief will be in the survival of kleptocrats at the head of corrupt regimes. This is the sad and continuing history of economic bailouts by international agencies to date.

The selectorate theory provides the rationale for a different approach to economic crises. Such crises are an opportunity for governance reform, but only if financial or material assistance is made contingent on *prior* political reform, particularly institutional changes that explicitly put the tenure of the incumbent leadership at risk. During a financial crisis, autocratic leaders may be amenable to change simply because the crisis has already placed their prospects of political survival in jeopardy. With little to lose, they may be persuaded to make changes that can set their country on a more productive path for the future.

Debt relief, financial assistance, food aid, and the like should come with clear and explicit strings. Prior to meaningful political changes, emergency relief funds should be administered directly and completely by the outside granting agency or by local, nongovernmental organizations, without interference by the recipient country's government. Many government leaders will object, declaring such external control to be a violation of their sovereignty and interference in their internal affairs. They are right; it *is* interference in their internal affairs. They are not obligated to accept these conditions, and granting agencies are not obligated to spend other people's money to relieve the financial *and political* crisis faced by kleptocratic rulers. Those who refuse such interference have signaled that they are not prepared to sublimate their own personal interests to the good of their citizenry. They have signaled, as well, that they do not believe their political survival is so threatened by the crisis that they are better off making sacrifices in order to improve their chances of remaining in office. Consequently, we can be confident that aid controlled by them is unlikely to find its way into the hands of the poor people who need it most. Aid should not be given to those who refuse to subject themselves to this condition.

Some will object to attaching such strings to foreign assistance on the grounds that no one knows better than the local officials—as distinct from local nongovernmental agencies—how to administer the aid, where it is most needed, and how best to get it there. No doubt there is truth to these claims, but the local officials apparently were not skilled enough administrators to be able to avert the crisis they find themselves in. Of course, one must be careful not to blame officials when circumstances beyond their control are the source of the crisis. It is crucial to note whether the crisis is the result of an extraordinary event—a severe drought, a flood, an earthquake—or the result of government policies. Droughts are not produced by governments, but poor soil-management policies help turn droughts into famines. Earthquakes are not the consequence of bad policy choices, but collapsed buildings often are the product of shoddy construction, where too much money went into bribes rather than into efforts to meet proper building standards.

When aid is given, the recipients, whether they are governments or nongovernmental agencies, should be held accountable. Too often, accountability takes the form of evaluating inputs rather than output. Donors, not recipients, should provide the evaluation of performance. Those who demonstrate that aid has been used effectively to advance the goals for which the aid was given are the best candidates for renewed support. Consequently, continued support should depend on demonstrated effectiveness in using funds and on concrete steps to improve the institutional incentives of the government's leaders to improve their own political well-being by improving the well-being of their citizenry. We leave the details for other discussions (see Bueno de Mesquita and Root 2002), but note that these recommended steps are rarely followed by donor nations and donor organizations.

What Can Be Done?

Direct and indirect military intervention provide mechanisms through which institutions can be improved. Unfortunately, the political incentives of leaders from large-coalition interventionist systems do not promote the establishment of large-coalition systems abroad. Unless the foreign policy goals of the foreign state coincide with those of the nation-building state—as was the case in the two great exceptions, opposition to communism for Japan and West Germany—military intervention will not fulfill its potential for institutional reform.

Events in Afghanistan reinforce this point. The United States intervened militarily in Afghanistan in 2002 to support the rebels of the North Alliance in removing the Taliban regime because of the Taliban's support for international terrorism. Although the United States relied heavily on the troops of the North Alliance to defeat the Taliban, the United States still took a dominant role in shaping Afghanistan's new government. The United States chose to support an interim government led by Hamid Karzai. These arrangements paid lip service to greater inclusiveness, because the government requires the support of tribal leaders and offers the prospect of future elections. Yet, rather than having the leader rely directly on the independent support of members of a mass electorate, the reliance on tribal leaders created a hierarchical aggregation of support. The chosen institutions required the leader to retain the support of a small number of people from the small pool of tribal leaders. Even if elections are held, they are likely to be dominated by bloc voting. While such a small-W, small-S system does not encourage the promotion of public welfare, it does require the leader to spend considerable resources to reward supporters. The low loyalty norm created by small-S, small-W systems makes leaders most ready to trade policy for aid, and hence most likely to do the bidding of the United States.

Migration offers a mechanism to improve the lot of the world's people. As we established in chapter 8, people migrate from small winning coalitions (which promote misery and poverty), to large-coalition systems that promote the production of public goods. The selectorate theory suggests that with the right immigration policy, migration helps both migrants and recipient countries.

The logic as to why moving from a small- to a large-coalition system improves the welfare of an average resident should by now be obvious. Emigration also harms the welfare of small-coalition incumbent leaders, but not so much the welfare of large-coalition incumbents. Leaders of small-coalition systems can expropriate resources from their citizens. When W is small, leaders need not spend all they collect in order to reward their supporters. Since leaders make a profit from the economic activity of each resident, the more residents a leader has the greater her rents. This is precisely why leaders of small-coalition systems erect barriers to emigration. One way to tame such leaders is to take away their subjects. To encourage this to happen, large-coalition systems should adopt open immigration policies.

The effects of immigration on the welfare of the recipient nation's citizens depend on immigration rules. If immigration policy makes enfranchisement easy, migration further enlarges the coalition, promoting still further the production of public goods and still further improvements in welfare for all groups of society except the leader: a win-win situation. However, if new residents are not enfranchised, then immigration increases the population but not the size of the winning coalition. This is the case in Germany, where immigration policy makes it easy for people to enter Germany, but unless these people can demonstrate German ancestry they cannot join the franchise. Under these circumstances, migration makes the winning coalition a smaller proportion of the population. As the population swells with new immigrants, the cost of public-goods provision climbs. For instance, the provision of law and order requires more police officers and courts as the number of people increases. Since some public goods become more expensive, the government produces fewer of them. Further, since the government's supporters account for a smaller proportion of economic activity, the government increases its expropriations. The increase in tax rates and the decline in public-goods production harms all groups in society, except leaders. In contrast, states like the United Kingdom and the United States make it harder for immigrants to enter, but once in, these states make enfranchisement easy. Under such rules, immigration increases the absolute size of the winning coalition, pushing governments toward still greater public-goods production while holding government expropriations in check.

These differences in immigration rules provide a partial explanation for the rise in right-wing xenophobic movements in Germany and

France, but their relative absence in the United Kingdom and United States. When immigrants are denied entry to the selectorate and hence the winning coalition, the effect is to reduce the size of W as a proportion of the population. As our analyses in chapter 8 showed, this harms the welfare of everyone in society except the leader, and citizens should protest. While unfortunately the protest manifests itself in the ugliness of racism, the underlying motivation stems from how immigration without enfranchisement shapes institutional arrangements.

For a large-W system, an open immigration policy with easy enfranchisement promotes the welfare of both the migrants and the citizens of the recipient state. The arguments of the selectorate theory are further reinforced by an examination of who migrates. People willing to undertake the risks and costs of migration from small-coalition countries tend to be more enterprising and entrepreneurial than those unwilling to undertake actions to improve their lot. Such driven individuals are likely to contribute to the vitality of the country they enter.

Conclusion

The crucial element behind reform in governance and economic assistance is that policy changes need to address the political incentives for venal, greedy, corrupt, rent-seeking governance as they have been uncovered here. The political transition from a society ruled by an exclusive group to one with a broad, inclusive coalition structure appears to be fundamental for sustained improvement in the quality of life for the world's economically, socially, or politically oppressed peoples. We have seen theoretically and empirically that inclusive, large-coalition polities tend to produce the most public benefits. These public benefits can be seen in the strong impact such regimes have on per capita income (chapter 4), growth (chapter 4), civil liberties and political rights (chapter 5), quality health care and quality education (chapter 5), social equality (chapter 5), peace and security (chapters 6, 8, and 9), and the Hobbes Index. Accepting such institutional changes signals the commitment of previously corrupt rulers to alter their ways, because these institutions place their political survival at risk (chapter 7). Those who reform in favor of an inclusive form of governance will have ensured that life will not be solitary, nasty, poor, brutish, and short.

Notes

Chapter 1

1. Later we document these claims statistically and provide a theoretical explanation for why this should be so. In the process of doing so, we suggest that aspects of politics commonly thought to ensure longevity in office for dictators—such as the use of oppression—and short terms for democrats—such as competitive elections—are themselves endogenous to the political incentives induced by specific institutional arrangements.

2. Robinson (1998) provides an excellent summary of the economics literature concerned with politics and policy.

3. In chapter 8 we offer an explanation of the fate of deposed or retired leaders based on the theory we present.

4. It is worth noting that government policies often are public goods to the extent that no one can be excluded from consuming the policy's benefits, even if the production of the policy yields divisible benefits, as is true in our theory in that leaders provide public goods for their private benefit in retaining power. Many policies that yield public goods—perhaps all—also provide private benefits to some. For instance, a policy of openness to trade, if fairly enforced, provides a benefit to all in the efficiencies achieved through a competitive market, but the production of imports and exports necessarily creates divisible and excludable benefits in that some people are manufacturers, some are importers, some are exporters, and most are neither (Conybeare 1984; see also Marsh 1999; Destler 1995; Gowa 1994). Spending on the military provides another example of how goods are mixed in their value. To the extent that military spending purchases national security, it is a public good. Nevertheless, for defense contractors, military officers, and ordinary soldiers, defense spending also provides valuable private goods. Focusing on the mixture of goods is important in this context to help distinguish private-production benefits from public-consumption benefits.

5. In fact, our theory does not require that goods be distinctly public or private. They can be club goods with different degrees of "publicness" or "privateness." For a good summary of the relevant literature, see Cornes and Sandler 2001.

Chapter 2

1. We provide more precise definitions of *private goods* and *public goods* below. Throughout we use the terms *goods*, *benefits*, and *rewards* interchangeably. They are treated as meaning the same thing unless we state otherwise or unless the context makes a distinction obvious.

2. For clarity, throughout we refer to incumbents using the feminine gender and challengers using the masculine gender.

3. Machiavelli maintained that there were two forms of government: principality and republic. Hobbes contended that only three forms of government are possible no matter how diverse their names. He identified the three as monarchy, aristocracy, and democracy. Aristotle identified six, which included not only Hobbes's later set but also tyranny, oligarchy, and mob rule. For a sweeping historical account of variation in political systems, see Finer 1999.

4. One of our simplifying conditions that departs from the details of reality for some monarchies is that we treat leaders as members of the selectorate, whereas women who could succeed to the throne nevertheless sometimes had no formal say in selecting the monarch. Eleanor of Aquitaine, for example, could have had a legitimate claim to the English crown following the death of Richard I, but she was not among the English barons

endowed with the formal right to elect the monarch. This was not because she was a woman—there were women with a real say in the choice of king—but because she, being French, failed to have the requisite baronial landholdings to qualify as a selector.

5. From time to time, of course, many "universal suffrage" voting systems in fact invoke restrictions based on special proficiency or on personal characteristics. Portions of the United States for a time, for instance, identified certain skills—such as the ability to read technical material—as a selectively enforced requirement for enfranchising African-American citizens, thereby restricting the actual universality of the selectorate.

6. See our discussion in chapter 7 of the Mamluks in Egypt for a further illustration of this point.

7. Although the purges initiated during the Stalinist period have been the most noteworthy, they were not the first. There was a purge in 1921–1922 in which about one-fifth of the party members were expelled, and there were other smaller intermittent purges before the purges that began in 1934 (Shapiro 1959, 231–251, 435–451). Chapter 8 provides an explanation of three different types of purges in the context of the selectorate theory.

8. These characterizations are stylized. Although the American president is actually elected by electors chosen in each state, those electors are normally bound to follow the vote of the voters and the successful candidate needs a majority of electors. The number of electors per state roughly approximates the size of the state's population, so that usually the candidate winning a majority of the electors is the candidate who won the popular vote as well—Rutherford B. Hayes and George W. Bush being notable exceptions.

9. Actually, the picture can be even more complicated in democracy. In some democracies, people vote in large blocs, looking to a handful of bloc leaders for cues as to how to vote. Bloc voting undermines the true size of the winning coalition, making the actual size considerably smaller than the number of voters. India and Mexico both provide good examples of this sort of bloc voting, as did New York's Tammany Hall at the end of the nineteenth century or Richard Daly's Chicago in the 1960s and 1970s. When we elaborate our theory, we will return to the issue of bloc voting.

10. We can think of the distribution of public goods and private benefits as layered so that a given essential backer, like an earl, might in turn have his own set of essential backers and so forth. This layering of institutional constraints is certainly one way of thinking about federalism, committees and subcommittees, and so on.

11. In particular, we assume the incumbent has lexicographic preferences over who she includes in her coalition. That is, only when the costs of forming coalitions are identical will she choose between coalitions on the basis of affinity. In other formulations of the theory (Bueno de Mesquita et al. 2002) we consider selectors' affinity for leaders.

12. We call this rule a constructive vote of no confidence because of its similarity to the German parliamentary rules, which require no-confidence votes in the government to explicitly lead to a successor government.

13. We deal with the prospects of revolution in chapter 8. In that context, some attention must be paid to the policy preferences of all citizens. Clearly, it must be subgame perfect—so that choices are always best replies to all anticipated future actions—always to pay some attention to all citizens, because the possibility of revolution is always present. For now, we assume that probability is small enough that it does not materially alter the calculations on which we are focused. Later, we integrate expectations about foreign overthrow, revolution, and routine politics.

14. This group was later enlarged to nine.

15. The Freedom House rules for categorizing states are different from the rules used, for instance, by Ted Gurr and his colleagues in the POLITY categorization scheme (Gastil 1978–present; Bollen 1990; Gurr, Jaggers, and Moore 1990; see also the POLITY website at <http://www.bsos.umb.edu/cidcm/polity/> as well as Inkeles 1991). Although highly cor-

related with one another, these rules are far from identical. *Civil Liberties* as measured by Freedom House is correlated with *DEMOCRACY* as estimated by POLITY IV, for instance, at the level of 0.86, $N = 3,876$. In specific instances the difference in scores can be quite substantial. Cyprus in the late 1970s and Turkey in the early 1990s, for example, receive the highest *DEMOCRACY* score granted by the POLITY method. Yet these two countries each receive the third-worst rating out of seven possible ratings on Freedom House's *Civil Liberties* scale.

Chapter 3

1. Initially the game form restricts the incumbent's choice of coalition size to W. In the appendix, when we prove proposition 2, we relax this assumption and show that there is no utility-improving defection for the incumbent, who consequently always prefers the minimal winning coalition of $|W_L| = W$. In chapter 7 we relax a number of conditions from the basic model developed here. When we do so, we show conditions under which incumbents have incentives to oversize their winning coalition, and we explore the implications that follow from doing so.

2. Purely for technical convenience, we assume that if a leader's policies are not feasible (they promised to spend more than revenue), a caretaker policy is implemented. We might instead have assumed that leaders' strategies are restricted to feasible policies, or that if a promised resource allocation cannot be implemented, the "nearest" allocation that could be implemented would be implemented.

3. Intuitively, δ can be thought of as the proportion of a dollar that an individual would not consider important enough to take now rather than waiting to receive a whole dollar tomorrow.

4. Specifically, each individual's utility function is $V(x,g,y,l)$, and, given that individual i chooses leisure l_i, then i's payoff for that period is $V(x,(l_{WL,i})g_L,(1 - r_L)(1 - l_i), l_i)$, where $(l_{WL,i})$ is an indicator function that takes the value of 1 if i is a member of W_L and takes the value of 0 otherwise. To avoid corner solutions we focus on interior solutions. The sufficient, though not necessary, conditions for interior solutions are: $\lim_{x \to 0} V_x(x_L,\cdot) = -\infty$, $\lim_{g \to 0} V_x(g,\cdot) = -\infty$, $\lim_{y \to 0} V_y(y,\cdot) = -\infty$, and $\lim_{l \to 0} V_l(l_i,\cdot) = -\infty$.

5. One might argue that government-provided private goods and personally generated private economic rewards are similar in nature and that the citizen's utility function might be better specified as a three-good model—for example, $V(x,g,y,l) = x^{1/2} + (g + y)^{1/2} + l^{1/2}$. With the exception that members of the winning coalition choose lower effort levels than other citizens, the characterization of equilibria is similar. This might be an interesting way to think about the eighteenth-century French or British aristocrats, who routinely did not work. We leave this speculative idea for future research.

6. We also believe it is true in real politics that challengers, when they first gain power, are more likely to juggle the composition of their coalition, looking for a stable arrangement, than are those who are already secure in power. In fact, based on 3,904 observations, using data explained in the next chapter, we find a very strong inverse relationship ($t = -6.54$) between whether a leader's cabinet is changed (as a preliminary surrogate for change in coalition membership) and how long a leader has been in office. This means that members of the current winning coalition are assured of a flow of future private benefits as long as their leader remains the incumbent. Without a defection by at least one of the members of the incumbent's coalition, it is not possible for the challenger to depose the incumbent and replace her. Thus, the incumbent can credibly promise members of her coalition private goods in every future period, while the challenger can only offer future private goods probabilistically, credibly committing only to private payoffs during the initial, transition period.

7. The game leads to two types of equilibria, one in which $W \leq (S + 1)/2$ and one in which $W > (S + 1)/2$. The latter deals with political systems that require the incumbent to maintain more than a simple majority to stay in power. Because this is a rare form of government, we focus our discussion on what we consider to be the politically relevant type of equilibrium, when $W \leq (S + 1)/2$—that is, the winning coalition is equal to or smaller than a simple majority of the selectorate.

8. On the equilibrium path, members of the incumbent's current coalition will be members of her future coalition, and the identities of the individuals in W_L who the challenger tries to attract do not matter. However, off the equilibrium path if the incumbent includes individuals in her current coalition who will not be members of future coalitions, then which individuals the challenger attempts to attract is more complex. These issues are dealt with in the appendix. Here we stick to actions on the equilibrium path.

9. Later we will discuss implications of this theory for leadership tenure. At that time we will show the implications for political tenure that follow from the loyalty norm. In particular, we will show that the smaller the winning coalition and the larger the selectorate, the easier it is for incumbents to maintain the loyalty of their backers and, therefore, the easier it is for them to survive. In contrast, leaders in large-W and relatively small S systems find it hardest to survive in office and can skim off the fewest resources.

10. The budget constraint established by tax revenue can also be expanded through the receipt of foreign aid. For now we leave out consideration of the role of foreign aid. However, we discuss foreign policy implications of the selectorate theory with regard to decisions to give and to accept foreign aid in chapters 9 and 10. In particular, we examine the impact of foreign aid on political-survival prospects in the last chapter.

11. We add a bit more detail here. Although in the model the leader announces a single flat tax rate, the model predicts the equivalent of three tax levels within a polity. Those not in the winning coalition pay the announced rate. Those in the coalition pay the same flat rate but then receive private benefits that are equivalent to a reduction in their tax rate. In small-coalition systems, coalition members effectively pay, therefore, a much lower tax rate than do those excluded from the coalition. In large-coalition systems, the difference in tax rates between "insiders" and "outsiders" is smaller. Finally, leaders retain at their discretion any tax revenues not paid out in the form of public goods and private rewards to coalition members. In small-coalition systems this is equivalent to a substantial reduction in the leader's tax rate. In large-coalition systems leaders pay taxes that are essentially equal to those paid by the selectorate in general. Leaders in such systems tend toward a balanced budget as W increases in size and so have almost no opportunity to keep extra resources for themselves.

12. There is too large a literature on the controversial topic of the precise relationship between democracy and economic performance to cite comprehensively. Some influential works include Lipset 1959; Jackman 1974; Bollen and Jackman 1985; North and Weingast 1989; North 1990; Przeworski and Limongi 1993; Helliwell 1994; Knack and Keefer 1995; Roemer 1995; Barro 1997; Engerman and Sokoloff 1997; Weingast 1997; Przeworski et al. 2000.

13. For convenience, we assume there is an infinite pool of challengers such that once deposed, any leader's probability of reentering office is 0.

14. The reservation payoff is assumed to be "low."

15. To avoid corner solutions, we focus on interior solutions: sufficient, although not necessary, conditions for which are $\lim_{x \to 0} V_x(x_L, \cdot) = -\infty$; $\lim_{g \to 0} V_g(g_L, \cdot) = -\infty$; $\lim_{y \to 0} V_y(y, \cdot) = -\infty$; and $\lim_{l \to 0} V_l(l, \cdot) = -\infty$.

16. One might argue that government-provided private goods and private economic rewards are similar in nature and that the citizens' utility function might be better specified as a three-good model—for example, $V(x, g, y, l) = \sqrt{x} + \sqrt{(g + y)} + \sqrt{l}$. In such a setup members of the winning coalition choose lower effort levels than other citizens do.

17. The SOC is

$$(1-r_L)^2 V_{yy}(x_L,(1-\{W_L,i\})g_L,(1-r_L)(1-l_i),l_i)+V_{11}(x_L,(1_{\{WL,i\}})g_L,(1-r_L)(1-l_i),l_i)<0$$

18. Again the SOC are straightforward and omitted.

19. In addition to these equations, under the nonconstructive deposition rule we require other conditions to ensure that L does not want to add additional coalition members. In light of the results in the next section on oversized coalitions, the incumbent wants to increase her coalition, provided these additional members force the challenger to alter his coalition or policies to attract the support of these individuals.

20. There is a simple economic argument for $dK(w, (v(w - W + 1, 0) + k))/dw > 0$. The challenger has a smaller coalition ($w - W + 1 < w$) and spends more on his policy provision than the incumbent, hence the marginal impact of a private-goods price increase (an enlargement of coalition size) is larger for the challenger than for the incumbent.

Chapter 4

1. Stanislav Andreski (1968) has been credited with the first modern use of *kleptocracy*, though this term has been traced back to 1819.

2. POLITY data can be found at <http://www.cidcm.umd.edu/inscr/polity/>.

3. We will identify variables with italics.

4. The correlation between S and the transformed S for computing W/S is 0.9989, $N = 12,462$.

5. These regions were coded from the Correlates of War Project country codes.

6. Sample sizes differ due to missing data.

7. For instance, controlling for *Log(Pop)*, *WS:IncomeRes*, *WS:DemRes*, and fixed effects, a logit analysis of the likelihood that a country reports its tax revenue as a percentage of GDP yields a z-score for W of 12.97, with the coefficient associated with W being 2.89 based on 2,168 observations and 120 fixed effects. The impact of W with no control variables other than fixed effects is comparable (coefficient = 2.28, z-score = 11.82, $N = 2,491$).

8. In this test *WS:IncomeRes* is perfectly correlated with *LogIncome* since W and S both take the value 1 for all polities included in the test.

9. These results are particularly tentative, because we only have fifty-seven observations of tax as a percentage of GDP for democratic presidential systems, and one-third of those cases are data from the United States. However, see note 11 for a test that separates the influence of the United States from the effect of other presidential systems in our data.

10. Geddes 1999 provides an excellent review of the relevant literature.

11. We construct five dummy variables: *USA*, *Parliamentary*, *Mixed*, *Presidential*, and *Presidential*USA*. Each scores a 1 if its condition is met (e.g., if a system is parliamentary then *Parliamentary* = 1, otherwise it equals 0). The interaction between *USA* and *Presidential* is designed to separate the effect of presidentialism in the United States from its effect elsewhere in democracies. The regression analysis is performed on all countries that score 1.0 on W. Comparable results are found if we substitute *Democracy* = 1.0 for W. With *LogIncome* as the dependent variable, we find the following coefficients, standard errors, and significance levels:

Parliamentary:	1.41 0.16 0.00
Mixed:	1.34 0.18 0.00

Presidential:	2.19	0.21	0.00
USA:	0.92	0.33	0.01
*Presidential*USA*:	−0.29	0.40	0.47
Constant:	8.37	0.11	0.00

Clearly, the beneficial effects of presidential systems are not just a reflection of America's economic success.

12. Freedom House has devised a widely used seven-point scale to assess civil liberties and another seven-point scale to assess political rights. These data are available for about 140 countries spanning the years since 1972. They are updated annually and can be downloaded from the Freedom House website at <http://www.freedomhouse.org/>. In the Freedom House data, higher values are associated with lower levels of civil liberties or political rights. To avoid confusion, we reverse the direction of these variables by subtracting their scores from 8. This ensures that higher scores are associated with higher levels of political rights and civil liberties. The variables are identified, respectively, as *Civil Liberties* and *Political Rights*. In the next chapter we examine the association between selection institutions and these two factors. Here we use their residual values after regressing W and S on them.

13. The effect of using ΔW_{t0-t-2}, rather than $\Delta W/S_{t0-t-2}$, is very similar.

14. The third model in table 4.5 uncovers additional information that, though outside the framework of the selectorate theory, is interesting. Not surprisingly, savings and investment—beyond that influenced by coalition size and selectorate size—promote growth. Perhaps more surprisingly, neither the effect of civil liberties nor of political rights that is independent of the governing institutions W and S has a consequential impact on economic growth rates. The aspect of these factors that influences growth is already absorbed by the size of the system's winning coalition.

15. The effect that selection institutions have on economic growth remains robust if we add still other control variables, most notably foreign direct investment, a factor that itself significantly improves the prospects of growth. These and other results not detailed here are reported in the statistical analyses generated by the .do files on our website <http://www.nyu.edu/gsas/dept/politics/data.shtml>.

16. There are exceptions. Since 1789 France has had eleven constitutions. In only two was the size of S reduced. There are other states where instability is so high that it appears change is taking place. What is happening there, however, is that leaders are changing while the underlying character of the institutions remains the same.

17. We test these claims about political survival in chapter 7.

18. We find largely similar results when examining the deficit and surplus spending scenarios separately.

19. Using a Heckman selection model, we combine these analyses. Controlling for either W or W and S as determinants of whether expenditure data are reported, we find that W has a strong positive effect on expenditures, while S has a strong negative effect on expenditures.

Chapter 5

1. The private benefits that went to the Spartiate resemble club goods, public within a selective group, but excludable to others.

2. The syssitia has been characterized as "a perfect symbol, down to the mid third century BC of the Spartan roots as a conservative, totalitarian and militaristic city-state" (Fornis and Casillas 1997, 38).

3. The syssitia also seems to have served as a way to redistribute food beyond citizens to the lower classes (Figueira 1984).

4. In chapter 9 we use the selectorate theory to deduce how institutions influence the war aims of states, including an explanation of the conditions under which leaders seek to extract wealth from vanquished foes or, instead, pursue policy goals and/or the deposition of rival leaders.

5. We take up the subject of revolution in chapter 8 when we examine incentives to choose some institutional arrangements over others.

6. We show in chapter 6 that the selectorate theory indicates that leaders of small-coalition systems reserve resources for use as private goods to reward their followers rather than putting extra resources into war efforts, even when failing to do so significantly increases the risk of military defeat. This is just what appears to have happened in the case of the Spartan cavalry at Leuctra.

7. We select these two because of their prominence as summary indicators of how a state is performing. Our results on transparency, reported later, look the same if we substitute alternative economic indicators.

8. As indicated earlier, the body of the text only reports details about the fifth model, including control for parliamentary or presidential structure, for the core public goods. The analyses for this model can, however, be found on our website <http://www.nyu.edu/gsas/dept/politics/data.shtml>.

9. The data are available at <http://www.worldbank.org/html/prdmg/grthweb/ddfische.htm>.

10. The data, as presented by Stanley Fischer (1993), are found at <http://www.worldbank.org/html/prdmg/grthweb/ddfische.htm>.

11. A paper by Kauffman and Wei (1999) offers an empirical analysis of the supposed benefits of corruption for those who pay "grease money" to achieve ends they would not otherwise gain. Their evidence, however, indicates the contrary.

12. For an overview, see Bardhan's (1997) survey of the literature.

Chapter 6

1. Some studies suggest that democracies are, on the whole, more pacific than autocracies (Benoit 1996; Ray 1995). Yet such general war avoidance cannot account for the relative propensity to fight with different regime types.

2. Without some specification of war aims and mobilization costs, such as are found in the Weinberger Doctrine, the last phrase of this statement appears to allow anything with respect to democratic war behavior.

3. Benoit (1996) suggests that on average, democracies are slightly less war prone than other systems.

4. Although democracies do not fight wars with one another, they often become engaged in militarized disputes (Bueno de Mesquita and Lalman 1992; Oneal and Russett 1997). Indeed, the Militarized Interstate Disputes data for Europe even include twenty-two cases in which democracies became embroiled in violent disputes that fail to reach the definitional threshold for war. These twenty-two events will prove important later when we discuss implications of the selectorate model. See Senese 1997 for an alternative viewpoint.

5. Intangible or unobservable military capabilities may be important additional factors influencing the outcome of war. Introducing uncertainty into the model in this way, however, does not fundamentally alter any of our results, while needlessly increasing complexity.

6. When we say democrats "try harder," we mean that the change in the level of effort for democrats at war compared to their military or defensive effort at peace will be larger than it is for autocrats. We do not claim (or disclaim) that in the aggregate leaders dependent on a larger coalition will necessarily devote more resources to a war than those dependent on a smaller coalition, although this may certainly happen.

7. It is likely, however, that leaders did not recognize these risks to personal survival or to sovereignty at the outset of either World War. Indeed, if prospective war participants recognized that they were about to embark on an extremely costly and risky war, it is likely that they would choose to negotiate a resolution of differences rather than fight. Thus, it is unlikely that leaders hold ex ante beliefs that are consistent with the ex post revelation of a high political risk following defeat in a world war. Speer (1970, 287) illustrates this point when he writes that "it remains one of the oddities of this war [World War II] that Hitler demanded far less from his people than Churchill and Roosevelt did from their respective nations." As the war progressed and spread, the risks became more evident and German effort increased.

8. One might argue that the value of remaining in office is a function of regime type. As Goemans (2000) points out, being ousted is more often fatal for autocrats than democrats. This reinforces our conclusion. Our assumption is that the primary goal of all leaders is to keep their jobs. Given this, the principal component in every leader's set of goals is reselection. It may be true, conditional on being ousted, that autocrats are more likely to be killed or exiled than are democrats, but it is also true that the risk of being ousted is most effectively diminished for autocrats by spending less on the war effort and reserving more for their domestic coalition. Chapters 7 and 10 offer explanations of the variation in the fate of deposed leaders based on the selectorate theory.

9. Equally, any spoils won in the war are as available to be distributed by the challenger as by the incumbent in the event the incumbent is deposed.

10. Chapters 9 and 10 evaluate external threats to deposition in greater detail.

11. We use the approximation here to keep the presentation unencumbered by lots of notation. Of course, the appendix contains the full, precise mathematical statement.

12. Term limits in democratic systems presumably reduce a leader's value for office, at least in the final stages of the incumbent's last term. In chapter 7 we discuss term limits, exploring the subtle and perhaps surprising implications that term limits have for a host of policy areas, including issues related to the democratic or selectorate peace.

13. Chapter 9 presents a model that ties war aims to the size of the selectorate and the winning coalition. There we show how the extraction of resources from defeated foes, the deposition of vanquished leaders by the victors, and the imposition of policy changes on defeated adversaries relates to selection institutions in the victorious state and in the vanquished state.

14. The results that substitute *Lagged Democracy* for *Lagged W* also show that democracies try harder, as can be seen by examining the statistical details on our website at <http://www.nyu.edu/gsas/dept/politics/data.shtml>.

15. The table reports two-tailed significance levels while the hypothesis is directional so that, for instance, a significance probability of 0.116 actually reflects significance of 0.058. It is noteworthy that the results also hold when we evaluate military expenditure while adding additional controls for lagged spending per soldier and lagged spending per soldier interacted with lagged coalition size. In this case we see hints of the private-goods use of military spending in smaller-coalition polities. The details of this analysis can be found on our website.

16. As Livy points out, two aspects of Roman institutions hurt the Roman effort. First, the presence of two consuls, often leading the army on alternate days, led to a lack of coherence. Second, as the end of the consular year approached, consuls gave battle when pru-

dence would have been a better course of action. This was particularly the case for those who had achieved some level of numerical superiority or tactical advantage and feared having the honor of defeating Hannibal grabbed by their successor.

17. Other common examples used in international relations include the model of Bueno de Mesquita, Morrow, and Zorick (1997), who set $\Phi(\varepsilon) = 0$ if $\varepsilon < 0$ and $\Phi(\varepsilon) = 1$ if $\varepsilon \geq 0$, where $(\varepsilon) = 0$ and $h(M, m_A, m_B, g_A, g_B) = m_A + 2(M - 1) - m_B + g_A r - g_B r$, where m_A and m_B are intangible military capabilities, and the standard ratio-of-forces model (see for example Bueno de Mesquita 1981), which sets $\Phi(\varepsilon) = 0$ if $\varepsilon < 0$, $\Phi(\varepsilon) = \varepsilon$ if $\varepsilon \in [0,1]$, and $\Phi(\varepsilon) = 1$ if $\varepsilon > 1$ and $h(M, g_A, g_B) = ((M + rg_A)/(1 + rg_A + rg_B))$. Hirshleifer (1989) examines the implications of variation in these functions.

18. While given the nonlinearity of these equations flat spots or identical maxima are unlikely, deterrence offers a straightforward equilibrium selection refinement if there are. The higher B's effort level, the less attractive a target B becomes. Since higher effort levels deter A, and such effort levels are credible, we use the refinement that B picks the larger effort level.

19. Evaluating the SOC at the turning point, $\partial G/\partial g = W \, \partial H/\partial g = p''(g)W + W\Psi p''(g)(F(x) - F(y)) + (2/p(g))p'(g)(R - W) - (2/p(g))Wp'^2 g^\Psi (F(x) - F(y)) + (2/p(g))p'(g)R\Psi(F'(y) - p(g)F'(x)) + (R^2/W)\Psi(p(g)F''(x) + (1 - p(g))F''(y))$. The signs of the first two terms depend on $p''(g)$, and the sign of the third term is determined by $(R - W)$. Everything else is negative.

20. If $\chi < -k$, war is inevitable, since A would prefer losing to a negotiated settlement. At the other extreme, if A's expected deal through negotiations is greater that the best possible outcome from war, A always negotiates: $\chi \geq 1 - k$. Since we are primarily thinking of χ as a division between 0 and 1, the first extreme is generally impossible. To restrict ourselves to substantively interesting cases, we assume $-k \leq \chi \leq 1 - k$.

Chapter 7

1. Missing data may result in the exclusion of some leaders on either list who otherwise would have ranked in the top twenty-five on the relevant criteria. As is evident in several empirical chapters, missing data itself often indicates problems in governance in the societies that withhold pertinent information.

2. We model competence as influencing the price paid to create goods without distinguishing among different goals so competence does not affect the relative price of different goods. Changes in competence could produce different allocations to private and public goods through income effects, though.

3. To be more precise, higher competence does not exactly increase resources by a fixed factor because it does not change the price of resources the leader retains for her own uses.

4. The term for declines in economic growth has changed over time as politicians have attempted to downplay their consequences. What were once panics became depressions, depressions became recessions, and finally recessions have become downturns. When will politicians discover the term *economic shocks* in their quest to avoid responsibility for economic contractions?

5. Because this discussion is informal, we do not go into the exact questions of stockpiling resources, either how much is enough or the trade-offs involved in setting the size of the stockpile.

6. Ayalon (1977) provides estimates of the number of officeholders and emirs of various ranks. Although the precise numbers vary, there were typically between 100 and 300, which fits with estimates of one officer per 50 men in the army. The arrangement between emirs,

soldiers, and the selection of the sultan is reminiscent of the "election" process by which English kings were chosen. Recall that John Lackland needed support from a subset of 236 barons, each of whom controlled knights fees with which to hire and ensure fealty among knights.

7. The emirs were ranked as Emir of the Hundred, Forty, or Ten (and sometimes also Five) according to their wealth.

8. Average tenure was 5.5 years, compared with 17 years in the caliphate and 12 in Byzantium. All figures are taken from Finer 1999, 734–735.

9. Our theory concerns political deposition. Some leaders, however, die of natural causes while still in office. Unfortunately, our data do not contain reliable coding for natural death. Consequently, in some cases we are falsely attributing removal to political action. Such coding works against our hypotheses since the data are most likely to incorrectly code long-serving (and hence small-W) leaders. Regrettably, even reliable coding of "died in office" would not completely solve the problem. As we will discuss in the section on extrapolitical deposition, ill-health often prompts deposition. So even though death by natural causes follows political deposition, the expectation of impending death caused political removal.

10. In other social science areas, this is referred to as either *duration* or *event analysis* (Allison 1984).

11. This relationship violates a basic assumption of the Cox proportionate hazard model since the underlying hazard for large- and small-coalition systems differs.

12. Later we discuss actuarial or mortality risk. This factor predicts the contrary. All else being equal, elderly leaders are more likely to die (of natural causes) or become infirm.

13. We use the maximum-likelihood routines in Stata version 7 throughout.

14. The coefficients reported in the tables are for the log of p. Hence, for model 1, $p = \exp(-0.494 + 0.355W)$.

15. Although in principle open to all, prior to the reforms of Ephialtes and Pericles (from 462 BC onward) access to government was effectively restricted to the wealthy. The reforms just mentioned made government positions salaried, so that those without personal means could afford to serve.

16. Interestingly, much of this conflict involved Athens's attempt to dominate smaller Greek states—for example, its Delian League allies. While such behavior is consistent with the selectorate theory, it is inconsistent with normative explanations for the democratic peace.

Chapter 8

1. We hasten to add what should be obvious from chapter 7. Those who produce lots of public goods and who lead a large-coalition government enhance their political survival relative to those who produce fewer such goods and also lead a large-coalition system. The problem for leaders is that small-coalition systems provide a larger incumbency advantage than do large-coalition systems, and small-coalition systems reward leaders with longer periods in office if they produce mostly private goods. That is, producing public goods is not disadvantageous within large-coalition systems, but leaders in these systems are inherently disadvantaged relative to those who head small-coalition governments.

2. Recall the discussion in chapter 5 about King Leopold's Force Publique in the Congo Free State. Those who profited or stood to profit in the future from the regime engaged in wholesale atrocities to protect their—and Leopold's—access to wealth.

3. The secret ballot, of course, also makes the voter's compliance with a contract to buy his vote unobservable, and hence difficult to enforce. Otherwise, bribes—private goods in our model—can be targeted to those who vote for a leader.

4. Our theory could be used to explain the Turkish genocide against the Armenians from 1915 to 1918. During World War I, many Armenians fought with the Russian army in the Caucasus against Turkey, and so could be perceived as a threat to Turkey, although not one that called for the mass killing of the Armenian population. Historical evidence suggests that Turkish oppression of the Armenians led them to fight back, rather than Armenian support of the Russians leading to the oppression. It is clear that the genocide got worse, and more Armenians joined Russia against Turkey, as the war went on.

5. Revisionists argue that the Terror did not reach as deeply into Soviet society as the "totalitarians" (so named because they view the Great Terror as clear evidence of the totalitarian nature of the Soviet State, not because they advocate totalitarianism) do. Hence the death toll was lower.

6. Two other members were not purged because they died of natural causes.

7. The former figure comes from Rummel's (1990) estimate that 850,000 party members died in the purge, which was 36 percent of the total party membership. The latter figure is from Freeze 1997, 337.

8. Neither Lee nor Seow received sufficient votes to be elected, but Singapore's constitution requires that at least three opposition members be seated in Parliament. If an insufficient number are elected, the opposition candidates with the highest vote totals are awarded seats to bring the total up to three.

9. Further details of the coding scale and of how the data collection was carried out can be found in Poe, Tate, and Keith 1999, 297–299. Cingranelli and Richards (1999) use Mokkan scaling analysis to show that repressive measures can be captured by a single dimension, contrary to the claims of McCormick and Mitchell (1997). Unfortunately, Cingranelli and Richards provide the scaled values for only seventy-nine countries at three-year intervals from 1981 to 1996. We chose to use Poe, Tate, and Keith's data instead because of its wider coverage of states.

10. Neither Amnesty International nor the State Department provides reports for all countries for all years in their sample, although the range of country reports expands over time for both sources. Poe, Tate, and Keith (1999) fill missing data in one set of scores with the score of the other source when it is available for that country-year. This technique avoids possible bias from underreporting on countries with good records on human rights. Amnesty International tended to focus on the worst abusers and the State Department on recipients of U.S. aid in the early years of their time period. The scores seem roughly comparable across the two sources.

11. In methodological terms, we are correcting for serial correlation in the data by including a lagged dependent variable.

12. The steady state can be calculated by solving for the level of oppression that equals the sum of itself times the estimate of the lagged effect of oppression plus the constant plus W times its estimated effect.

13. The selectorate theory necessitates thinking about political actions in terms somewhat different from those in common usage. For instance, common parlance does not speak of coups in the context of winning coalitions and the selectorate. Still, if we think about what is usually meant when journalists and others speak of palace coups, it is clear that they mean a change in leadership designed to make the government's insiders—the winning coalition—better off. We use *coups* to mean exactly that. A coup in this context is an action intended to improve the welfare of members of the winning coalition.

14. We focus on the post–World War II years because of the availability of data with which to control for per capita income.

15. Of course, the correlation between the scale used in chapter 5 and the scale used here to assess costs is −1.

16. By onset, we mean that the variable for the onset of a civil war is coded 1 in the first year of a civil war, and 0 otherwise.

17. Translated by Yung Wei in personal correspondence, drawn from *Hong-she Zhong-gui* (Red China), December 1, 1931. We are most grateful to Yung Wei for bringing this quotation to our attention.

18. We have also replicated these results in analyses in which we look only at cases for which *Action* = 0, dropping, of course, *Action* as a variable in the regression. The results are comparable.

Chapter 9

1. Spain did raise a division of volunteers, which fought with the Nazis against the Soviet Union. However, Spain remained neutral.

2. Unfortunately, such depredations still occur in civil wars and domestic chaos.

3. For example, David Lake (1999, 20–24) defines two faces of security: one, freedom from the risk of death or impairment from violence by those external to the state, and two, the ability to accumulate and allocate wealth free from external coercion. This definition strikes us as too broad; even the Nazi invasion of Poland in 1939 could be described as increasing German security according to Lake's definition. Still, we commend Lake for making a serious effort to pin down the concept of security.
   Our definition of security here is narrower than one offered by Morrow (1987, 1991) in his earlier research. He defined security as the ability to defend the status quo on issues where the state did not pursue change. This definition includes private-goods ends, which are excluded from our definition of security here.

4. Our notion of changing the status quo covers both the enforcement and renegotiation problems that Werner (1999) discusses.

5. We do not consider arguments about how the efficiency of collecting resources from territory is related to the size of polities (Friedman 1977). Nor do we consider voluntary changes in the size of states for reasons of efficiency (Wittman 1991; Casella 1994). We are not opposed to such arguments; we merely wish to focus on the incentives that selection institutions present for territorial expansion for resources.

6. If the reader feels uncomfortable with this assumption, think of the long-term effects of war on societal resources rather than the short-term loss of life and destruction of property.

7. When W_A is small, the victor wants to increase the size of W_B. By doing so she increases the foreign policy effort of nation A. This increased effort reduces the ability of B's domestic rivals to promise foreign public goods. Reducing the ability of leaders in nation B to produce international public goods forces political competition toward private goods, a dimension that vastly favors the incumbent. Empirically we do not expect to obtain evidence for this latter finding, since the effect of public goods in small-W systems is small and such small-coalition systems are far more interested in securing additional resources.

8. EUGene (Expected Utility Generator), a program created by D. Scott Bennett and Allan Stam and available at <www.eugenesoftware.org>, was used in the construction of our dispute data and the decomposition into dyads. See Bennett and Stam 2000 for further details on EUGene.

9. We cannot of course use our standard region-year fixed effects, since virtually every disputing state would have a unique region-year.

10. The text of the Paris Peace Treaty that ended the Vietnam War was obtained through the Internet at the following address: <gopher://gopher.lib.muohio.edu/00/subject/history/vietnam/paris_peace_1973.txt>.

11. The weights are simply the inverse of the square root of the number of policy, regime, and private-goods articles in each treaty to account for the lesser variance of percentages based on more observations, that is, treaty articles in this analysis.

12. Give or take cases like the Falklands War in 1982, which falls slightly under the 1,000-death threshold but is included anyway.

13. Our decisions here are similar but not identical to those made by Zeev Maoz in his dyadic militarized dispute data. He appears to have coded two states as actually fighting only if they engaged in land or naval combat. We include dyads with other forms of military action. For example, we include the United States as fighting and defeating Hungary in the Second World War because the U.S. Army Air Corps bombed targets in Hungary during the war. A complete list of the changes we have made can be found at <http://www.nyu.edu/gsas/dept/politics/data.shtml/>.

14. We consider Great Britain and the United States to have defeated Vichy France as a consequence of Operation Torch in French North Africa and as a result of British military operations against Vichy forces in Syria, Lebanon, and Madagascar.

15. An example of a transfer in a postwar period that was not a consequence of the war is the Rann of Kutch arbitration between India and Pakistan in 1966, a year after their Second Kashmir War.

16. We do not include peaceful intrawar changes such as the Vienna Award in 1941 because these changes were not imposed by a victorious state on another state it has defeated.

17. This coding is an important difference between our analysis and that of Werner (1996), who includes such military occupations as impositions of regimes.

18. We did run Heckman selection analyses where first the set of victors is predicted from all warring dyads and then the determination of outcome—territory was taken or the losing leader was replaced—is predicted. This technique tries to control for effects of selection introduced when unmeasured factors that lead states to win also affect what terms they demand to end the war. These analyses were unstable and varied significantly with the specifications and set of cases used. Hence, we present contingency tables instead.

19. Adding the cases of minor war participation—where at least one side suffers 100 combat fatalities or less—makes this result stronger; 40 percent of the small winning-coalition systems take territory, and only 20 percent of the victors with large winning coalitions do so.

20. Two other cases here are the overthrow of the Khmer Rouge by the communist government of Vietnam and that of Idi Amin by Julius Nyerere's Tanzania, both in 1978.

21. The phrase "Germany's Creature: Vichy France" comes from Calvocoressi, Wint, and Pritchard 1989, vol. 1, 317–344, on which this section is based.

22. We point out to the reader that this is another case where the change in selection institutions by granting Pétain the power to ignore Parliament and rule by decree preceded the growth of laws used to repress political opposition.

23. Estimations that included the effective size of both sides' selectorates showed clear evidence of identification problems in the selection equation. The likelihood function was often not concave during the iterations of the maximum-likelihood algorithm, and Stata's routine for Heckman probability models did not return estimates for the standard errors of the coefficients in the removal model. Faced with the Scylla of dropping both sides' effective selectorate size and the Charybdis of unstable estimates, we, like Ulysses, chose Scylla

and so present estimates using just the sizes of the winning coalitions of both sides in the removal equation.

24. The reader may be puzzled why these estimated probabilities are so different from the actual frequency of external leader removal after defeats (around 5 percent). The probabilities we report here are those of the underlying model of leader removal. We only observe leader removal in the event of defeat, censoring the cases where one might observe leader removal. Further, the error term of the "lose" equation is highly and negatively correlated with the error term of the "removal" equation in our estimates. As the lose equation shows, systems with large winning coalitions rarely lose, meaning the factors outside the model (included in the error term) are large and positive. Then the error term of the removal equation must be large and negative in the cases we observe, and removal probabilities in the cases we observe are much lower than these probabilities taken from the estimate of the underlying process of removal.

25. In some extreme cases, leaders might choose internal institutional reforms to respond to an external threat. Reforms in Taiwan might fit this category. Although internally leaders prefer small-W, large-S systems, such systems produce few resources and fight poorly. When threatened by a powerful neighbor, a leader might increase W or reduce S to make her nation stronger. Although such reforms increase a leader's risk of internal deposition, they reduce the risk of international defeat.

26. See Preston 1993 on Franco's skill at placating supporters (p. 275) and on his disastrous economic policies (pp. 344–345, 347–348), particularly those of import substitution and an overvalued currency.

Chapter 10

1. Numerous quality-of-life indexes have been constructed over the years. Each is aimed at finding an alternative to a measure just of personal material well-being. Such indexes are usually motivated by the idea that material well-being—assessed through income and/or growth indicators—fails to capture important aspects of the quality of life. We neither agree nor disagree with these claims. Chapter 4 has already demonstrated strong relationships between coalition size, the loyalty norm, and measures of income and growth. Therefore, the Hobbes Index or any other measure of the quality of life is, for us, just another—neither preferred nor inferior—way of evaluating the linkage between social welfare and political-selection institutions.

2. We have chosen 1972 as the baseline year although we have data on death rates from 1960 to 1999. The choice of 1972 is made because some of the indicators for the Hobbes Index, notably *Civil Liberties*, are available only since 1972. Thus, 1972 is the earliest year for which we have information on all of the variables used in the Hobbes Index.

3. The correlations among the five components of the Hobbes Index are as follows ($N = 918$):

	Solitary	Nasty	Poor	Brutish	Short
Solitary	1.000				
Nasty	0.609	1.000			
Poor	0.808	0.682	1.000		
Brutish	0.220	0.230	0.241	1.000	
Short	0.375	0.245	0.412	0.098	1.000

4. Given full reporting of all data, we would expect a mean of 50. However, not all nations report all data for each year. Indeed, as the mean of 62.13 suggests, it is nations that score poorly on one or another component of the Hobbes Index that do not report data on other components.

5. The bottom quartile includes 36 out of 144 nations that are rated.

6. We are reminded of a story related by a colleague, a Nobel Laureate in economics. He reports being engaged as an advisor to the head of a Third World government. At the request of the government's leader, he produced a list of economic reforms that could help jump-start the economy. The country's leader agreed that the proposed reforms would work. Yet when the colleague returned months later he found that not a single recommendation had been followed. The leader of the government explained that while the policies were good economics, they were bad politics. If he followed them, the labor unions, teachers, military, and civil service would abandon him, and pretty soon he would not be the country's leader anymore. That was the end of his endorsement of economic reform. We hasten to add that the political ramifications of reform were not lost on our colleague. It is just that economic theory did not give him an adequate means of addressing the problem.

7. To the extent that *Mixed* indicates the existence of a meaningful presidency it should look more like *Presidential*, but we cannot be sure exactly what the correct weighting is between the balance of influence of a prime minister and a president in a mixed system as coded here.

8. Also recall from chapter 3 that we expect list-voting parliamentary systems to behave in a manner similar to direct-election presidential systems, but we anticipate that winner-take-all, single-member district parliamentary systems behave in a manner consistent with regimes that have a smaller winning coalition than do presidential systems or list systems. Our data do not distinguish among types of parliamentary regimes, so that we expect the impact of *Parliamentary* to be somewhat inflated, because it includes list systems that "look like" presidential systems in terms of coalition requirements.

9. The situation is more complex than the straightforward majoritarian parliament, since each state has electoral-college votes based loosely on its size. Each state receives one electoral-college vote for each congressional representative, plus one for each of its senators.

10. By *Effective S* we mean, as in the previous chapter, $S * (1 - W)$. This is appropriate here because the only circumstance under which S can independently influence policy choices is when W is small, allowing S to vary in size. When W is large, S must be large.

References

Aburish, Said K. 2000. *Saddam Hussein: The Politics of Revenge*. London: Bloomsbury.

Acemoglu, Daron, Simon Johnson, and James Robinson. 2001. "The Colonial Origins of Comparative Development: An Empirical Assessment." *American Economic Review* 91 (December): 1369–1401.

Acemoglu, Daron, and James Robinson. 2000. "Why Did the West Extend the Franchise? Democracy, Inequality and Growth in Historical Perspective." *Quarterly Journal of Economics* 115: 1167–1199.

Acemoglu, Daron, and James Robinson. 2001. "A Theory of Political Transitions." *American Economic Review* 91: 938–963.

Achen, Christopher H. 1986. *The Statistical Analysis of Quasi-experiments*. Berkeley: University of California Press.

Ades, Alberto, and Rafael Di Tella. 1997a. "National Champions and Corruption: Some Unpleasant Interventionist Arithmetic." *Economic Journal* 107: 1023–1042.

Ades, Alberto, and Rafael Di Tella. 1997b. "The New Economics of Corruption: A Survey and Some New Results." *Political Studies* 97: 496–515.

Ades, Alberto, and Rafael Di Tella. 1999. "Rents, Competition, and Corruption." *American Economic Review* 89: 982–993.

"After Mobutu" *Economist*, 340(7985): 53.

Alesina, Alberto, Sule Ozler, Nouriel Roubini, and Phillip Swagel. 1996. "Political Instability and Economic Growth." *Journal of Economic Growth* 1: 189–211.

Alesina, Alberto, and Howard Rosenthal. 1995. *Partisan Politics, Divided Government, and the Economy*. New York: Cambridge University Press.

Allison, Paul. 1984. *Event History Analysis: Regression for Longitudinal Event Data*. Quantitative Applications in the Social Sciences Series. Beverly Hills, CA: Sage.

Alvares, Michael, José Antonio Cheibub, Fernando Limongi, and Adam Przeworski. 1997. "Classifying Political Regimes." *Studies in Comparative International Development* 31: 3–36.

Andreski, Stanislav. 1968. *The African Predicament*. London: Joseph.

Aranson, Peter H., and Peter C. Ordeshook. 1985. "Public Interest, Private Interest, and the Democratic Polity." In Roger Benjamin and Stephen Elkin, eds., *The Democratic State*, 87–177. Lawrence: University Press of Kansas.

Arbatov, Georgi. 1992. *The System: An Insider's Life in Soviet Politics*. New York: Random House.

Arendt, Hannah. 1951. *The Origins of Totalitarianism*. New York: Harcourt, Brace.

Arrow, Kenneth. 1951. *Social Choice and Individual Values*. New York: Wiley.

Axelrod, Robert. 1984. *The Evolution of Cooperation*. New York: Basic Books.

Axelrod, Robert. 1986. "An Evolutionary Approach to Norms." *American Political Science Review* 80(4): 1095–1111.

Ayalon, David. 1977. *Studies on the Mamluks of Egypt (1250–1517)*. London: Variorum Reprint.

Baldwin, John W. 1986. *The Government of Philip Augustus: Foundations of French Royal Power in the Middle Ages*. Berkeley: University of California Press.

Banks, Arthur S. 1996. *Political Handbook of the World*. New York: CSA Publications.

Bardhan, Pranab. 1997. "Corruption and Development: A Review of the Issues." *Journal of Economic Literature* 35: 1320–1346.

Barro, Robert J. 1991. "Economic Growth in a Cross Section of Countries." *Quarterly Journal of Economics* 106: 407–444.

Barro, Robert J. 1996. "Democracy and Growth." *Journal of Economic Growth* 1(4): 449–486.

Barro, Robert J. 1997. *Determinants of Economic Growth: A Cross-Country Empirical Study*. Cambridge, MA: MIT Press.

Barro, Robert J. 2000. "Democracy and the Rule of Law." In Bruce Bueno de Mesquita and Hilton L. Root, eds., *Governing for Prosperity*, 209–231. New Haven, CT: Yale University Press.

Barzel, Yoram. 1989. *The Economic Analysis of Property Rights*. New York: Cambridge University Press.

Bates, Robert H., Avner Greif, Margaret Levi, Jean-Laurent Rosenthal, and Barry Weingast. 1998. *Analytic Narratives*. Princeton, NJ: Princeton University Press.

Beard, Charles A. 1986. *An Economic Interpretation of the Constitution of the United States*. New York: Free Press.

Benhabib, Jess, and Michael Spiegel. 1994. "The Role of Human Capital and Political Instability in Economic Development." In Mario Baldassari, Luigi Paganetto, and Edmund S. Phelps, eds., *International Differences in Growth Rates*, 55–94 New York: St. Martin's Press.

Bennett, D. Scott, and Allan C. Stam III. 1998. "The Declining Advantages of Democracy: A Combined Model of War Outcomes and Duration." *Journal of Conflict Resolution* 42(3): 344–366.

Bennett, D. Scott, and Allan C. Stam III. 2000. "*EUGene*: A Conceptual Manual." *International Interactions* 26: 179–204.

Benoit, Kenneth. 1996. "Democracies Really Are More Pacific (in General)." *Journal of Conflict Resolution* 40(4): 636–657.

Bergstrom, Theodore, and Robert P. Goodman. 1973. "Private Demands for Public Goods." *American Economic Review* 63: 280–296.

Bienen, Henry S., and Nicolas van de Walle. 1991. *Of Time and Power: Leadership Duration in the Modern World*. Stanford, CA: Stanford University Press.

Black, Duncan. 1958. *The Theory of Committees and Elections*. Cambridge: Cambridge University Press.

Bollen, Kenneth A. 1990. "Political Democracy: Conceptual and Measurement Traps." *Studies in Comparative International Development* 25(1): 7–24.

Bollen, Kenneth A., and Robert Jackman. 1985. "Political Democracy and the Size Distribution of Income." *American Sociological Review* 50: 438–457.

Brecher, Michael, and Jonathan Wilkenfeld. 1997. *A Study of Crisis*. Ann Arbor: University of Michigan Press.

Bremer, Stuart. 1992. "Dangerous Dyads: Conditions Affecting the Likelihood of Interstate War, 1816–1965." *Journal of Conflict Resolution* 26(2): 309–341.

Browne, Eric C., John P. Frendreis, and Dennis W. Gleiber. 1986. "The Process of Cabinet Dissolution: An Exponential Model of Duration and Stability in Western Democracies." *American Journal of Political Science* 30: 628–650.

Buchanan, James M. 1985. *Liberty, Market and State*. London: Wheatsheaf Books.

Buchanan, James M., Robert D. Tollison, and Gordon Tullock, eds. 1980. *Toward a Theory of the Rent-Seeking Society*. College Station: Texas A&M Press.

Buckley, Terry. 1996. *Aspects of Greek History 750–323 BC: A Source-Based Approach*. New York: Routledge.

Bueno de Mesquita, Bruce. 1974. "Need for Achievement and Competitiveness as Determinants of Political Success in Elections and Coalitions." *American Political Science Review* 68: 1207–1220.

Bueno de Mesquita, Bruce. 1981. *The War Trap*. New Haven: Yale University Press.

Bueno de Mesquita, Bruce. 1983. "The Costs of War: A Rational Expectations Approach." *American Political Science Review* 77: 347–357.

Bueno de Mesquita, Bruce. 1997. "A Decision Making Model: Its Structure and Form." *International Interactions* 23: 235–266.

Bueno de Mesquita, Bruce. 2002. *Foreign Policy Futures*. Columbus: Ohio State University Press.

Bueno de Mesquita, Bruce, and David Lalman. 1992. *War and Reason*. New Haven, CT: Yale University Press.

Bueno de Mesquita, Bruce, James D. Morrow, Randolph Siverson, and Alastair Smith. 1999. "An Institutional Explanation of the Democratic Peace." *American Political Science Review* 93: 791–807.

Bueno de Mesquita, Bruce, James D. Morrow, Randolph Siverson, and Alastair Smith. 2002. "Political Institutions, Policy Choice and the Survival of Leaders." *British Journal of Political Science* 32: 559–590.

Bueno de Mesquita, Bruce, James D. Morrow, and Ethan Zorick. 1997. "Capabilities, Perception and Escalation." *American Political Science Review* 91(1): 15–27.

Bueno de Mesquita, Bruce, and Hilton L. Root. 2002. "The Political Roots of Poverty." *National Interest* 68: 27–38.

Bueno de Mesquita, Bruce, and Hilton L. Root, eds. 2000. *Governing for Prosperity*. New Haven, CT: Yale University Press.

Bueno de Mesquita, Bruce, and Randolph Siverson. 1995. "War and the Survival of Political Leaders: A Comparative Study of Regime Types and Political Accountability." *American Political Science Review* 89: 841–855.

Bueno de Mesquita, Bruce, and Randolph Siverson. 1997. "Nasty or Nice?: Political Systems, Endogenous Norms, and the Treatment of Adversaries." *Journal of Conflict Resolution* 41(1): 175–199.

Bueno de Mesquita, Ethan. 2000. "Strategic and Non-Policy Voting: A Coalitional Analysis of Israeli Electoral Reform." *Comparative Politics* 33(1): 63–80.

Burkhart, R. E., and Lewis-Beck, Michael. 1994. "Comparative Democracy: The Economic Development Thesis." *American Political Science Review* 88(4): 903–910.

Calvocoressi, Peter, Guy Wint, and John Pritchard. 1989. *Total War: Causes and Courses of the Second World War, Vol. 1: The Western Hemisphere*. 2nd ed. New York: Pantheon.

Campos, Jose Edgardo, and Hilton L. Root. 1996. *The Key to the Asian Miracle: Making Shared Growth Credible*. Washington, DC: Brookings Institution.

Caplow, Theodore. 1968. *Two Against One: Coalition in Triads*. Englewood Cliffs, NJ: Prentice Hall.

Casella, Alessandra. 1994. "Trade as an Engine of Political Change: A Parable." *Economica*. New series, 61: 267–284.

Caven, Brian. 1980. *The Punic Wars*. London: Weidenfeld and Nicolson.

Chengze, Simon Fan, and Herschel I. Grossman. 2001. "Incentives and Corruption in Chinese Economic Reform." *Journal of Policy Reform* 4(3): 195–206.

Cingranelli, David L., and David L. Richards. 1999. "Measuring the Level, Pattern, and Sequence of Government Respect for Physical Integrity Rights." *International Studies Quarterly* 43: 407–417.

Conquest, Robert. 1990. *The Great Terror*. 2nd ed. Oxford: Oxford University Press.

Conrad, Joseph. 1903. *Youth, and Two Other Stories*. New York: McClure, Phillips.

Conybeare, John A. C. 1984. "Public Goods, Prisoner's Dilemmas, and the International Economy." *International Studies Quarterly* 28: 5–22.

Cornes, Richard, and Todd Sandler. 2001. *The Theory of Externalities, Public Goods, and Club Goods*. New York: Cambridge University Press.

Cornfield, F. D. 1960. "The Origins and Growth of Mau Mau." Sessional Paper No. 5 of 1959–1960 (Nairobi) at

Cox, Gary. 1987. *The Efficient Secret: The Cabinet and the Development of Political Parties in Victorian England*. Cambridge: Cambridge University Press.

Cox, Gary. 1997. *Making Votes Count*. New York: Cambridge University Press.

Dahl, Robert A. 1999. *On Democracy*. New Haven, CT: Yale University Press.

Destler, I. M. 1995. *American Trade Politics*. 3rd ed. Washington, DC: Institute for International Economics.

de Swaan, Abram. 1973. *Coalition Theories and Cabinet Formations*. Amsterdam: Elsevier Scientific.

de Tocqueville, Alexis. 2000. *Democracy in America*. Trans. and ed. Harvey C. Mansfield and Delba Winthrop. Chicago: University of Chicago Press.

Diamond, Jared M. 1997. *Guns, Germs, and Steel: The Fates of Human Societies*. New York: Norton.

Diermeier, Daniel, and Timothy J. Feddersen. 1998. "Cohesion in Legislatures and the Vote of Confidence Procedure." *American Political Science Review* 92(3): 611–621.

Diermeier, Daniel, and Antonio Merlo. 2000. "Government Turnover in Parliamentary Democracies." *Journal of Economic Theory* 94: 46–79.

Diermeier, Daniel, and Randy T. Stevenson. 1999. "Cabinet Survival and Competing Risks." *American Journal of Political Science* 43: 1051–1068.

Dixon, William. 1994. "Democracy and the Peaceful Settlement of International Conflict." *American Political Science Review* 88(1): 14–32.

Dodd, Lawrence C. 1976. *Coalitions in Parliamentary Government*. Princeton, NJ: Princeton University Press.

Donghi, Tulio H. 1993. *The Contemporary History of Latin America*. Ed. and trans. John Charles Chasteen. Durham, NC: Duke University Press.

Downs, Anthony. 1957. *An Economic Theory of Democracy*. New York: Harper.

Downs, George W., and David M. Rocke. 1995. *Optimal Imperfection?: Domestic Uncertainty and Institutions in International Relations*. Princeton, NJ: Princeton University Press.

Dupuy, E. Ernest, and Trevor N. Dupuy. 1986. *The Encyclopedia of Military History from 3500 BC to the Present*. 2nd ed. New York: Harper and Row.

Easterly, William R. 2001. *The Elusive Quest for Growth*. Cambridge, MA: MIT Press.

Easterly, William R., and Levine, Ross. 1997. "Africa's Growth Tragedy: Policies and Ethnic Divisions." *Quarterly Journal of Economics* 112: 1203–1250.

Emerson, Barbara. 1979. *Leopold II of the Belgians: King of Colonialism*. London: Weidenfeld and Nicolson.

Enelow, James, and Melvin J. Hinich. 1984. *The Spatial Theory of Voting*. New York: Cambridge University Press.

Engerman, Stanley, and Kenneth Sokoloff. 1997. "Factor Endowments, Institutions, and Differential Paths of Growth among New World Economies: A View from Economic Historians of the United States." In Steven Haber, ed., *Economic Growth and Latin American Economic Historiography*, Cambridge, MA: MIT Press 260–304.

Eulau, Heinz F. 1941. "Theories of Federalism under the Holy Roman Empire." *American Political Science Review* 35(4): 643–664.

Farber, Henry S., and Joanne Gowa. 1995. "Polities and Peace." *International Security* 20: 123–146.

Fearon, James. 1994. "Domestic Political Audiences and the Escalation of International Disputes." *American Political Science Review* 88(3): 577–592.

Fearon, James. 1995. "Rationalist Explanations for War." *International Organization* 49: 379–414.

Feldstein, Martin. 1974. "Social Security, Induced Retirement, and Aggregate Capital Accumulation." *Journal of Political Economy* 82(5): 905–926.

Feng, Yi. 1997. "Democracy, Political Stability and Economic Growth." *British Journal of Political Science* 27: 391–418.

Feng, Yi. 2001. "Political Freedom, Political Instability, and Policy Uncertainty: A Study of Political Institutions and Private Investment in Developing Countries." *International Studies Quarterly* 45: 271–294.

Feng, Yi, and Paul J. Zak. 1999. "Determinants of Democratic Transitions." *Journal of Conflict Resolution* 42(2): 162–177.

Feng, Yi, and Paul J. Zak. 2001. "A Theory of Democracy." Claremont Graduate University Working Paper, Claremont, CA.

Feng, Yi, and Paul J. Zak. 2003. "A Dynamic Theory of the Transition to Democracy." *Journal of Economic Organization and Behavor*. Forthcoming.

Ferejohn, John A. 1974. *Pork Barrel Politics: Rivers and Harbors Legislation, 1947–1968*. Stanford, CA: Stanford University Press.

Ferejohn, John A. 1987. *The Personal Vote*. Cambridge, MA: Harvard University Press.

Ferejohn, John A., and Barry R. Weingast, eds. 1997. *The New Federalism: Can the States Be Trusted?* Stanford, CA: Hoover Institution Press.

Figueira, Thomas J. 1984. "Mess Contributions and Subsistence at Sparta." *Transactions and Proceedings of the American Philological Association* 55: 87–109.

Fine, John V. A. 1983. *The Ancient Greeks*. Cambridge MA: Harvard University Press.

Finer, Samuel E. 1999. *The History of Government from the Earliest Times*. New York: Oxford University Press.

Fischer, Stanley. 1993. "The Role of Macroeconomic Factors in Growth." *Journal of Monetary Economics* 485–512.

Flemming, T. R., and D. P. Harrington. 1991. *Counting Processes and Survival Analysis*. New York: Wiley.

Forbath, Peter. 1977. *The River Congo*. New York: Harper and Row.

Fornis, César, and Juan-Miguel Casillas. 1997. "The Social Function of the Spartan Syssitia." Universidad Complutense, Madrid, *Ancient History Bulletin* 11(2–3): 37–46.

Forsythe, David P. 1992. "Democracy, War, and Covert Action." *Journal of Peace Research* 29: 385–395.

Freedman, Lawrence, and Efraim Karsh. 1993. *The Gulf Conflict, 1990–1991: Diplomacy and War in the New World Order*. Princeton, NJ: Princeton University Press.

Freeze, Gregory, ed. 1997. *Russia: A History*. Oxford: Oxford University Press.

Friedman, David. 1977. "A Theory of the Size and Shape of Nations." *Journal of Political Economy* 85(1): 59–77.

Fudenberg, Drew, and Jean Tirole. 1991. *Game Theory*. Cambridge, MA: MIT Press.

Gallego, Maria. 1999. "Endogenous Election Timing and Strategic Voting." Paper presented at the annual meetings of the American Political Science Association.

Gallego, Maria. 2001. "Election Timing and Intergovernmental Bargaining in a Two-Tier Three-Party Parliamentary System." Paper presented at the annual meetings of the American Political Science Association.

Gallenkamp, Charles. 1985. *Maya, the Riddle and Rediscovery of a Lost Civilization*. 3rd ed. New York: Viking.

Gamson, William. 1961. "A Theory of Coalition Formation." *American Sociological Review* 26: 373–382.

Gastil, Raymond D. 1978–present. *Freedom in the World: Political Rights and Civil Liberties*. New York: Freedom House.

Geddes, Barbara. 1999. "What Do We Know about Democratization After Twenty Years?" *Annual Review of Political Science* 2: 115–143.

Gilbert, Martin. 1994. *The First World War: A History*. New York: Holt.

Gleditsch, Kristian S., and Michael D. Ward. 1997. "Double Take: A Re-Examinination of Democracy and Autocracy in Modern Polities." *Journal of Conflict Resolution* 41: 361–383.

Gochman, Charles S., and Zeev Maoz. 1984. "Militarized Interstate Disputes, 1816–1976: Procedures, Patterns, and Insights." *Journal of Conflict Resolution* 28: 585–615.

Goemans, Hein. 2000. *War and Punishment: The Causes of War Termination and the First World War*. Princeton, NJ: Princeton University Press.

Goertz, Gary, and Paul Diehl. 1992. *Territorial Changes and International Conflict*. London: Routledge.

Goldstone, Jack A. 1991. *Revolution and Rebellion in the Early Modern World*. Berkeley: University of California Press.

Goldstone, Jack A. 1995. "Predicting Revolutions." In Nikki R. Keddie, ed., *Debating Revolutions*, 178–200. New York: New York University Press.

Gowa, Joanne S. 1994. *Allies, Adversaries, and International Trade*. Princeton, NJ: Princeton University Press.

Grant, Michael. 1999. *The Collapse and Recovery of the Roman Empire*. New York: Routledge.

Greene, William H. 1993. *Econometric Analysis*. 2nd ed. Englewood Cliffs, NJ: Prentice Hall.

Groennings, Sven, E. W. Kelly, and Michael Leiserson, eds. 1970. *The Study of Coalition Behavior*. New York: Holt, Rinehart and Winston.

Grossman, Herschel I. 1999. "Kleptocracy and Revolutions." *Oxford Economic Papers* 51: 267–283.

Guinness Book of Records 1999. 1998. London: Guinness Publishing.

Gupta, Sanjeev, Hamid Davoodi, and Rosa Alonso-Terme. 1998. "Does Corruption Affect Income Inequality and Poverty?" IMF Working Paper No. WP/98/76. International Monetary Fund.

Gurr, Ted Robert. 1990. "Polity II: Political Structures and Regime Change, 1800–1986." Ann Arbor, MI: Inter-University Consortium for Political and Social Research.

Gurr, Ted Robert, Keith Jaggers, and Will Moore. 1990. "The Transformation of the Western State: The Growth of Democracy, Autocracy, and State Power Since 1800." *Studies in Comparative International Development* 25: 73–108.

Haber, Stephen, and Armando Razo. 2000. "Industrial Prosperity under Political Instability: An Analysis of Revolutionary Mexico." In Bruce Bueno de Mesquita and Hilton L. Root, eds., *Governing for Prosperity*, 106–152. New Haven, CT: Yale University Press.

Haggard, Stephan, and R. R. Kaufman. 1995. *The Political Economy of Democratic Transitions*. Princeton, NJ: Princeton University Press.

Halliday, Fred. 1979. *Iran: Dictatorship and Development*. London: Penguin.

Hanushek, Eric, and Dennis D. Kimko. 2000. "Schooling, Labor Force Quality, and the Growth of Nations." *American Economic Review*. 90(5): 1184–1208.

Harding, Harry. 1997. "The Chinese State in Crisis, 1966–9." In Roderick MacFarquhar, ed., *The Politics of China: The Eras of Mao and Deng*, 2nd ed. Cambridge: Cambridge University Press.

Helliwell, J. F. 1994. "Empirical Linkages between Democracy and Economic Growth." *British Journal of Political Science* 24: 225–248.

Hignett, Charles. 1952. *A History of the Athenian Constitution to the End of the Fifth Century BC*. Oxford: Clarendon Press.

Hinich, Melvin J., and Michael Munger. 1994. *Ideology and the Theory of Political Choice*. Ann Arbor: University of Michigan Press.

Hirshleifer, Jack. 1989. "Conflict and Rent-Seeking Success Functions: Ratio vs. Difference Models of Relative Success." *Public Choice* 63: 101–112.

Hobbes, Thomas. [1651] 1996. *Leviathan*. Ed. Richard Tuck. New York: Cambridge University Press.

Hobson, John A. [1902] 1945. *Imperialism: A Study*. Ann Arbor: University of Michigan Press.

Hochschild, Adam. 1999. *King Leopold's Ghost*. Boston: Mariner Books.

Hodkinson, Stephen. 2000. *Property and Wealth in Classical Sparta*. London: Duckworth.

Huber, John. 1996. "The Vote of Confidence in Parliamentary Democracies." *American Political Science Review* 90: 269–282.

Hume, David. [1742] 1985. *Essays Moral, Political and Literary*. Ed. Eugene F. Miller. Indianapolis, IN: Liberty Classics.

Huntington, Samuel P. 1965. "Political Development and Political Decay." *World Politics* 17(3): 386–430.

Huntington, Samuel P. 1968. *Political Order in Changing Societies*. New Haven, CT: Yale University Press.

Huth, Paul K. 1996. *Standing Your Ground: Territorial Disputes and International Conflict*. Ann Arbor: University of Michigan press.

Ibrahim, Youssef M. 1995. "Iraq Said to Sell Oil in Secret Plan to Skirt U.N. Ban." *New York Times*, February 16, sec. A, p. 1.

Inkeles, Alex, ed. 1991. *On Measuring Democracy: Its Consequences and Concomitants*. New Brunswick, NJ: Transaction.

Israel, Fred L., ed. 1967–1980. *Major Peace Treaties of Modern History*, 1648–1967. 5 vols. New York: Chelsea House.

Jackman, Robert W. 1974. "Political Democracy and Social Equality: A Comparative Analysis." *American Sociological Review* 39(1): 29–45.

Jackman, Robert W. 1978. "The Predictability of Coups d'Etat: A Model with African Data." *American Political Science Review* 72: 1262–1275.

Jaggers, Keith, and Ted Robert Gurr. 1995. "Tracking Democracy's Third Wave with the Polity III Data." *Journal of Peace Research* 32: 469–482.

James, Patrick, and Glenn E. Mitchell, II. 1995. "Targets of Covert Pressure: The Hidden Victims of the Democratic Peace." *International Interactions* 21(1): 85–107.

Jervis, Robert. 1978. "Cooperation under the Security Dilemma." *World Politics* 30: 167–214.

Jones, A. H. M. 1952. *The Athens of Demosthenes*. Cambridge: Cambridge University Press.

Jones, Daniel M., Stuart A. Bremer, and J. David Singer. 1996. "Militarized Interstate Disputes, 1816–1992: Rationale, Coding Rules, and Empirical Patterns." *Conflict Management and Peace Science* 15: 163–213.

Judd, Kenneth. 1985. "Redistributive Taxation in a Perfect Foresight Model." *Journal of Public Economics* 28: 59–84.

Kalbfleisch, John D., and Ross Prentice. 1980. *The Statistical Analysis of Failure Time Data*. New York: Wiley.

Kauffman, Daniel, and Shang-Jin Wei. 1999. "Does 'Grease Money' Speed Up the Wheels of Commerce?" NBER Working Paper No. 7093. Cambridge, MA: NBER.

Keegan, John, ed. 1989. *The Times Atlas of the Second World War*. London: Times Books.

Kennedy, John F. 1956. *Profiles in Courage*. New York: Harper.

Kim, Woosang, and James D. Morrow. 1992. "When Do Power Shifts Lead to War?" *American Journal of Political Science* 36: 896–922.

King, Gary, James Alt, Nancy Burns, and Michael Laver. 1990. "A Unified Model of Cabinet Dissolution in Parliamentary Democracies." *American Journal of Political Science* 34: 846–871.

King, Gary, Michael Tomz, and J. Wittenberg. 2000. "Making the Most of Statistical Analyses: Improving Interpretation and Presentation." *American Journal of Political Science* 44(2): 347–361.

Knack, Stephen, and Philip Keefer. 1995. "Institutions and Economic Performance: Cross-Country Tests Using Alternative Institutional Measures." *Economics and Politics* 7: 207–227.

Knox, MacGregor. 1982. *Mussolini Unleashed 1939–1941: Politics and Strategy in Fascist's Italy's Last War*. New York: Cambridge University Press.

Krueger, Anne. 1974. "Political Economy of Rent-Seeking Society." *American Economic Review* 64: 291–303.

Kunicova, Jana. 2002. "Are Presidential Systems Predisposed to Political Corruption?" Unpublished ms., Yale University.

Lake, David A. 1992. "Powerful Pacifists: Democratic States and War." *American Political Science Review* 86(1): 24–37.

Lake, David A. 1999. *Entangling Relations*. Princeton, NJ: Princeton University Press.

Lake, David A., and Matthew A. Baum. 2001. "The Invisible Hand of Democracy: Political Control and the Provision of Public Service." *Comparative Political Studies* 34(6): 587–621.

Lam, Ricky, and Leonard Wantchekon. 1999. "Dictatorships as a Political Dutch Disease." In Center Discussion Papers from Yale University, Economic Growth Center.

Lamborn, Alan C. 1991. *The Price of Power: Risk and Foreign Policy in Britain, France, and Germany*. London: Unwin Hyman.

Langer, William. 1980. *An Encyclopedia of World History*. 5th ed. Boston: Houghton Mifflin.

Laver, Michael, and Norman Schofield. 1990. *Multiparty Government: The Politics of Coalition in Europe*. Oxford: Oxford University Press.

Laver, Michael, and Kenneth Shepsle. 1996. *Making and Breaking Governments*. Cambridge: Cambridge University Press.

Layne, Christopher. 1994. "Kant or Cant: The Myth of the Democratic Peace." *International Security* 19: 5–49.

Lazenby, John F. 1996. *The First Punic War: A Military History*. Stanford, CA: Stanford University Press.

Leff, Nathaniel. 1964. "Economic Development through Bureaucratic Corruption." *American Behavioral Scientist* 8(2): 8–14.

Leite, Carlos, and Jens Weidmann. 1999. "Does Mother Nature Corrupt? Natural Resources, Corruption, and Economic Growth." IMF Working Paper No. WP/99/85. International Monetary Fund.

Lenin, Vladimir Illyich. 1902. *What Is to Be Done?* <http://www.fordham.edu/halsall/mod/1902lenin.html>.

Levi, Margaret. 1998. "Conscription: The Price of Citizenship." In Robert H. Bates, Avner Greif, Margaret Levi, Jean-Lavrent Rosenthal, and Barry R. Weingast, eds., *Analytic Narratives*, 109–147. Princeton, NJ: Princeton University Press.

Levy, Jack. 1988. "Domestic Politics and War." *Journal of Interdisciplinary History* 18: 653–673.

Levy, Jack. 1989. "The Diversionary Theory of War: A Critique." In Manus Midlarsky, ed., *Handbook of War Studies*. 259–288. Boston: Unwin Hyman.

Lichbach, Mark Irving. 1995. *The Rebel's Dilemma*. Ann Arbor: University of Michigan Press.

Lincoln, Abraham. 1991. *Great Speeches,* "Annual Message to Congress, December 1, 1862," p. 79. New York: Dover.

Lindert, Peter H. 2001. "Democracy, Decentralization, and Mass Schooling Before 1914." Agricultural History Center, University of California, Davis, Working Paper Series No. 104.

Linz, Juan, and A. Stepan, eds. 1991. *The Breakdown of Democratic Regimes*. Baltimore: Johns Hopkins University Press.

Lipset, Seymour M. 1959. "Some Social Requisites of Democracy: Economic Development and Political Development." *American Political Science Review* 53: 69–105.

Livy. 1965. *The War with Hannibal: Books xxi–xxx of the History of Rome from Its Foundation*. Trans. Aubrey de Sélincourt; ed. Betty Radice. Baltimore: Penguin Books.

Lohmann, Susanne. 1994. "The Dynamics of Informational Cascades: The Monday Demonstrations in Leipzig, East Germany, 1989–91." *World Politics* 47: 42–101.

Lohmann, Susanne, and Sharyn O'Halloran. 1994. "Divided Government and U.S. Trade Policy: Theory and Evidence." *International Organization* 48: 595–632.

Londregan, John B., and Keith Poole. 1992. "The Coup Trap." *World Politics* 42: 151–183.

Lyon, Margot. 1971. *Belgium*. London: Thames and Hudson.

Machiavelli, Niccolo. [1515] 1948. *The Prince*, Trans. W.K. Marriott. New York: E.P. Dutton.

Machiavelli, Niccolo. 1950. *The Prince and the Discourses*. Ed. Max learner. New York: The Modern Library

Madison, James. 1961. "Federalist No. 10. "In Jacob Cooke, ed., *The Federalist*, pp. 56–65. Middletown: Wesleyan University Press.

Makiya, Kanan. 1998. *Republic of Fear*. 2nd ed. Berkeley: University of California Press.

Mansfield, Edward D., Helen V. Milner, and B. Peter Rosendorff. 1998. "Why Democracies Cooperate More: Electoral Control and International Trade Agreements." Paper presented at the annual meeting of the American Political Science Association, Boston.

Mansfield, Edward D., and Jack Snyder. 1995. "Democratization and War." *Foreign Affairs* 74: 79–97.

Maoz, Zeev. 1998. "Realist and Cultural Critiques of the Democratic Peace: A Theoretical and Empirical Re-assessment." *International Interactions* 24(1): 3–89.

Maoz, Zeev, and Nazrin Abdolali. 1989. "Regime Types and International Conflict, 1816–1976." *Journal of Conflict Resolution* 33(2): 3–36.

Maoz, Zeev, and Bruce M. Russett. 1993. "Normative and Structural Causes of the Democratic Peace." *American Political Science Review* 87: 624–638.

Marsh, Peter T. 1999. *Bargaining on Europe: Britain and the First Common Market, 1860–1892*. New Haven, CT: Yale University Press.

Mather, P. English translator of the French translation by J. C. Mardrus. 1947. *The Book of a Thousand Nights and One Night*. London: Routledge.

Mauro, Palo. 1995. "Corruption and Growth." *Quarterly Journal of Economics* 110: 681–712.

McCormick, James M., and Neal J. Mitchell. 1997. "Human Rights Violations, Umbrella Concepts, and Empirical Analysis." *World Politics* 49: 510–525.

McGillivray, Fiona. 1997. "Party Discipline as a Determinant of the Endogenous Formation of Tariffs." *American Journal of Political Science* 41: 584–607.

McGillivray, Fiona. 2003. *Targeting the Marginals*. Princeton, NJ: Princeton University Press.

McGillivray, Fiona, and Alastair Smith. 2000. "Trust and Cooperation through Agent-Specific Punishments." *International Organization* 51: 809–824.

McGuire, Martin, and Mancur Olson. 1996. "The Economics of Autocracy and Majority Rule." *Journal of Economic Literature* 34: 72–96.

McKay, Derek, and H. M. Scott. 1983. *The Rise of the Great Powers 1648–1815*. London: Longman.

McKelvey, Richard. 1976. "Intransitivities in Multidimensional Voting Models and Some Implications for Agenda Control." *Journal of Economic Theory* 12: 472–482.

McKelvey, Richard. 1979. "General Conditions for Global Intransitivities in Formal Voting Models." *Econometrics* 47: 1085–1112.

Migdal, Joel. 1974. *Peasants, Politics, and Revolutions*. Princeton, NJ: Princeton University Press.

Miller, Nicholas. 1983. "Pluralism and Social Choice." *American Political Science Review* 77: 734–747.

Minchin, James. 1990. *No Man Is an Island: A Portrait of Singapore's Lee Kuan Yew*. 2nd ed. North Sydney: Allen and Unwin.

Mitchell, B. R. 1998a. *International Historical Statistics: Africa, Asia & Oceania, 1750–1993*. 3rd ed. London: Macmillan Reference.

Mitchell, B. R. 1998b. *International Historical Statistics: Europe, 1750–1993*. 4th ed. London: Macmillan Reference.

Montesquieu, Charles de Secondat. [1748] 1977. *The Spirit of Laws*. Ed. David Wallace Carrithers. Berkeley: University of California Press.

Montinola, Gabriella, Yingyi Qian, and Barry R. Weingast. 1995. "Federalism, Chinese Style: The Political Basis for Economic Success in China." *World Politics* 48(1): 50–81.

Moore, Barrington. 1966. *The Social Origins of Dictatorship and Democracy*. Boston: Beacon Press.

Morgan, T. Clifton, and Sally Howard Campbell. 1991. "Domestic Structure, Decisional Constraints, and War: So Why Kant Democracies Fight?" *Journal of Conflict Resolution* 35(2): 187–211.

Morrow, James D. 1985. "A Continuous-Outcome Expected Utility Theory of War." *Journal of Conflict Resolution*, 29: 473–502.

Morrow, James D. 1987. "On the Theoretical Basis of a Measure of National Risk Attitudes." *International Studies Quarterly*, 31: 423–438.

Morrow, James D. 1991. "Alliances and Asymmetry: An Alternative to the Capability Aggregation Model of Alliances." *American Journal of Political Science* 35: 904–933.

Morrow, James D. 1993. "Arms Versus Allies." *International Organization* 47: 207–233.

Mousseau, Michael. 1998. "Democracy and Compromise in Militarized Interstate Conflicts, 1816–1992." *Journal of Conflict Resolution* 42(2): 210–230.

Mueller, John D. 1973. *War, Presidents, and Public Opinion*. New York: Wiley.

Muller, Edward N., and Mitchell A. Seligson. 1987. "Insurgency and Inequality." *American Political Science Review* 81: 425–451.

Niskanen, William A. 1997. "Autocratic, Democratic, and Optimal Government." *Economic Inquiry* 35(3): 464–479.

Norpoth, Helmut. 1987. "Guns and Butter and Governmental Popularity in Britain." *American Political Science Review* 81(3): 949–959.

North, Douglass C. 1988. *Structure and Change in Economic History*. New York: Norton.

North, Douglass C. 1990. *Institutions, Institutional Change, and Economic Performance*. New York: Cambridge University Press.

North, Douglass C., William Summerhill, and Barry R. Weingast. 2000. "Order, Disorder, and Economic Change: Latin America versus North America." In Bruce Bueno de Mesquita and Hilton L. Root, eds., *Governing for Prosperity*. New Haven, CT: Yale University Press.

North, Douglass C., and Barry R. Weingast. 1989. "Constitutions and Commitment: The Institutions Governing Public Choice in Seventeenth Century England." *Journal of Economic History* 44: 803–832.

O'Callaghan, Joseph. 1989. *The Cortes of Castile-León, 1188–1350*. Philadelphia: University of Pennsylvania Press.

Olmstead, Albert T. [1875] 1923. *History of Assyria*. New York: Charles Scribner's Sons.

Olson, Mancur. 1965. *The Logic of Collective Action*. Cambridge, MA: Harvard University Press.

Olson, Mancur. 1982. *The Rise and Decline of Nations*. New Haven, CT: Yale University Press.

Olson, Mancur. 1993. "Dictatorship, Democracy and Development." *American Political Science Review* 87: 567–576.

Olson, Mancur. 2000. *Power and Prosperity*. New York: Basic Books.

Oneal, John R., and Bruce M. Russett. 1997. "The Classical Liberals Were Right: Democracy, Interdependence, and Conflict, 1950–1985." *International Studies Quarterly* 4: 267–293.

Organski, A. F. K. 1958. *World Politics*. New York: Knopf.

Organski, A. F. K. 1965. *Stages of Political Development*. New York: Knopf.

Organski, A. F. K., and Jacek Kugler. 1980. *The War Ledger*. Chicago: University of Chicago Press.

Painter, Sidney. 1949. *The Reign of King John*. Baltimore: Johns Hopkins Press.

Park, Richard L., and Bruce Bueno de Mesquita. 1979. *India's Political System*, 2nd edition, Englewood Cliffs, NJ: Prentice Hall.

Perry, Martin, Lily Kong, and Brenda Yeoh. 1997. *Singapore: A Developmental City State*. Chichester: Wiley.

Persson, Torsten, and Guido Tabellini. 1999. "The Size and Scope of Government: Comparative Politics with Rational Politicians." *European Economic Review* 43: 699–735.

Persson, Torsten, and Guido Tabellini. 2000. *Political Economics*. Cambridge: MIT Press.

Persson, Torsten, Guido Tabellini, and Francesco Trebbi. 2000. "Electoral Rules and Corruption." Paper presented at the Hoover Institution Public Choice Seminar, November 2000.

Plutarch. N.d. *Plutarch's Lives: The Lives of Noble Grecians and Romans*. Trans. John Dryden. New York: Modern Library.

Poe, Steven C., and C. Neal Tate. 1994. "Repression of Rights to Personal Integrity in the 1980s: A Global Analysis." *American Political Science Review* 88: 853–872.

Poe, Steven C., C. Neal Tate, and Linda Camp Keith. 1999. "Repression of the Human Right to Personal Integrity Revisited: A Global Cross-National Study Covering the Years 1976–1993." *International Studies Quarterly* 43: 291–313.

Powell, Robert. 1996a. "Stability and the Distribution of Power." *World Politics* 48: 239–267.

Powell, Robert. 1996b. "Uncertainty, Shifting Power, and Appeasement." *American Political Science Review* 90: 749–764.

Powell, Robert. 1999. *In the Shadow of Power: States and Strategies in International Politics*. Princeton, NJ: Princeton University Press.

Preston, Paul. 1993. *Franco: A Biography*. London: HarperCollins.

Przeworski, Adam. 2001. "Why Democracy Survives in Affluent Societies?" Paper presented in the New York University Department of Politics Political Economy Seminar.

Przeworski, Adam, Michael Alvares, José Antonio Cheibub, and Fernando Limongi. 2000. *Democracy and Development: Political Institutions and Material Well-Being in the World, 1950–1990*. Cambridge: Cambridge University Press.

Przeworski, Adam, and Fernando Limongi. 1993. "Political Regimes and Economic Growth." *Journal of Economic Perspectives* 7(3): 51–69.

Przeworski, Adam, and Fernando Limongi. 1997. "Modernization: Theories and Facts." *World Politics* 49: 155–183.

Putnam, Robert D. 1988. "Diplomacy and Domestic Politics: The Logic of Two-Level Games." *International Organization* 42(3): 427–460.

Qian, Yingyi, and Barry R. Weingast. 1996. "China's Transition to Markets: Market-Preserving Federalism, Chinese Style." *Journal of Policy Reform* 1(2): 149–185.

Rabushka, Alvin. 1985. *From Adam Smith to the Wealth of America*. New Brunswick, NJ: Transaction Books.

Ray, James Lee. 1995. *Democracies in International Conflict*. Columbia: University of South Carolina Press.

Raymond, Gregory A. 1994. "Democracies, Disputes, and Third-Party Intermediaries." *Journal of Conflict Resolution* 38(1): 24–42.

Rebelo, Sergio. 1991. "Long-Run Policy Analysis and Long-Run Growth." *Journal of Political Economy* 99: 500–521.

Reiter, Dan, and Allan Stam III. 1998. "Democracy and Battlefield Military Effectiveness." *Journal of Conflict Resolution* 42(3): 259–277.

Reiter, Dan, and Allan Stam. 2002. *Democracies at War*. Princeton: Princeton University Press.

Rhodes, Peter J. 1986. *The Greek City States: A Sourcebook*. London: Croom Helm.

Richards, Diana, T. Clifton Morgan, Rick Wilson, Valerie Schwebach, and Garry Young. 1993. "Good Times, Bad Times and the Diversionary Use of Force: A Tale of Some Not-So-Free Agents." *Journal of Conflict Resolution* 37: 504–535.

Riker, William H. 1962. *The Theory of Political Coalitions*. New Haven, CT: Yale University Press.

Riker, William H. 1982. *Liberalism against Populism*. San Francisco: Freeman.

Riker, William H. 1996. *The Strategy of Rhetoric: Campaigning for the American Constitution*. New Haven, CT: Yale University Press.

Robinson, James A. 1998. "Theories of 'Bad Policy.'" *Policy Reform* 1: 1–46.

Roemer, John. 1995. *General Theory of Exploitation and Class*. Cambridge, MA: Harvard University Press.

Roemer, John. 2001. *Political Competition: Theory and Applications*. Cambridge, MA: Harvard University Press.

Romer, Thomas, and Rosenthal, Howard. 1978. "Political Resource Allocation, Controlled Agendas, and the Status Quo." *Public Choice* 33: 27–43.

Root, Hilton. 1989. "Tying the King's Hands: Credible Commitments and Royal Fiscal Policy During the Old Regime." *Rationality and Society* 1: 240–258.

Root, Hilton. 1994. *The Fountain of Privilege: Political Foundations of Economic Markets in Old Regime France and England*. Berkeley: University of California Press.

Root, Hilton. 1995. *Managing Development through Institution Building*. Manila: Asian Development Bank.

Root, Hilton, and Nahalel Nellis. 2000. "The Compulsion of Patronage: Political Sources of Information Asymmetry and Risk in Developing Country Economies." In Bruce Bueno de Mesquita and Hilton Root, eds., *Governing for Prosperity*, 85–105. New Haven, CT: Yale University Press.

Rosenthal, Jean-Laurent. 1998. "The Political Economy of Absolutism Reconsidered." In Robert H. Bates, Avner Greif, Margaret Levi, Jean-Laurent Rosenthal, and Barry R. Weingast, eds., *Analytic Narratives*, 64–108. Princeton, NJ: Princeton University Press.

Rostow, W. W. 1990. *History, Policy, and Economic Theory: Essays in Interaction*. Boulder, CO: Westview Press.

Rummel, Rudolph J. 1990. *Lethal Politics: Soviet Genocide and Mass Murder Since 1917*. New Brunswick, NJ: Transaction.

Russett, Bruce M. 1995. *Grasping the Democratic Peace*. Princeton, NJ: Princeton University Press.

Sachs, Jeffrey D., and Andrew M. Warner. 1995 "Natural Resource Abundance and Economic Growth." Unpublished ms., Harvard Institute for International Development.

Sachs, Jeffrey D., and Andrew M. Warner. 1999. "Natural Resource Intensity and Economic Growth." In Jörg Mayer, Brian Chambers, and Ayisha Farooq, eds., *Development Policies in Natural Resource Economie*s, 13–38. Cheltenham, UK: Edward Elgar.

Sarkees, Meredith Reid. 2000. "The Correlates of War Data on War: An Update to 1997." *Conflict Management and Peace Science*, 18: 123–144.

Schimmelpfennig, Bernhard. 1992. *The Papacy*. New York: Columbia University Press.

Schofield, Norman. 1978. "Instability of Simple Dynamic Games." *Review of Economic Studies* 45: 575–594.

Schroeder, Paul. 1994. *The Transformation of European Politics, 1763–1848.* Oxford: Oxford University Press.

Schultz, Kenneth. 1998. "Domestic Opposition and Signaling in International Crises." *American Political Science Review* 92(4): 829–844.

Schultz, Kenneth. 2001. *Democracy and Coercive Diplomacy.* Cambridge: Cambridge University Press.

Schultz, Kenneth, and Barry Weingast. 1998. "Limited Governments, Powerful States." In Randolph Siverson, ed., *Strategic Politicians, Institutions, and Foreign Policy,* 15–49. Ann Arbor: University of Michigan Press.

Schumpeter, Joseph A. 1942. *Capitalism, Socialism, and Democracy.* New York: Harper.

Schwartz, Thomas, and Kiron Skinner. 1997. "Democracy and the Paradox of Perpetual Peace." Paper presented at the annual meeting of the American Political Science Association, Washington, DC.

Senese, Paul D. 1997. "Between Dispute and War: The Effect of Joint Democracy on Interstate Conflict Escalation." *Journal of Politics* 59(1): 1–27.

Seow, Francis T. 1994. *To Catch a Tartar: A Dissident in Lee Kuan Yew's Prison.* New Haven, CT: Yale Center for International and Area Studies.

Shapiro, Leonard. 1959. *The Communist Party of the Soviet Union.* New York: Random House.

Shepsle, Kenneth, and Barry Weingast. 1981. "Political Preferences for the Pork Barrel." *American Journal of Political Science* 25: 96–111.

Shirk, Susan. 1993. *The Political Logic of Economic Reform in China.* Berkeley: University of California Press.

Singer, J. David, and Melvin Small. 1972. *The Wages of War, 1816–1965: A Statistical Handbook.* New York: Wiley.

Singer, J. David, and Melvin Small. 1994. *Correlates of War Project: International and Civil War Data, 1816–1992.* Interuniversity Consortium for Political and Social Research publication 9905. Ann Arbor: University of Michigan.

Sirowy, L., and Alex Inkeles. 1990. "The Effects of Democracy on Economic Growth and Income Inequality." *Studies in Comparative Economic Development* 25: 126–157.

Siverson, Randolph M. 1995. "Democracies and War Participation: In Defense of the Institutional Constraints Argument." *European Journal of International Relations* 1: 481–490.

Siverson, Randolph M., and Harvey Starr. 1991. *The Diffusion of War: A Study of Opportunity and Willingness.* Ann Arbor: University of Michigan Press.

Skocpol, Theda, ed. 1998. *Democracy, Revolution, and History.* Ithaca, NY: Cornell University Press.

Small, Melvin, and J. David Singer. 1982. *Resort to Arms: International and Civil Wars, 1816–1980.* Beverly Hills, CA: Sage.

Smith, Alastair. 1996. "Endogenous Election Timing in Majoritarian Parliamentary Systems." *Economics and Politics* 8(2): 85–110.

Smith, Alastair. 1998a. "Fighting Battles, Winning Wars." *Journal of Conflict Resolution* 42(3): 301–320.

Smith, Alastair. 1998b. "International Crises and Domestic Politics." *American Political Science Review* 92(3): 623–638.

Smith, Alastair. 2000. "Election Timing in Majoritarian Parliamentary Systems." Paper presented at the annual meeting of the American Political Science Association.

Smith, Alastair. 2004. *Election Timing*. New York: Cambridge University Press.

Smith, Hedrick. 1983. *The Russians*. New York: Times Books.

Sobel, Dava. 1999. *Galileo's Daughter*. New York: Walker.

Speer, Albert. 1970. *Inside the Third Reich*. New York: Macmillan.

Spiro, David. 1994. "The Insignificance of the Liberal Peace." *International Security* 19: 50–86.

Spuler, Bertold, C. G. Allen, and Neil Saunders. 1977. *Rulers and Governments of the World*. Vol. 3. London: Bowker.

Stam, Allan C. III. 1996. *Win, Lose, or Draw: Domestic Politics and the Crucible of War*. Ann Arbor: University of Michigan Press.

Staveley, E. S. 1972. *Greek and Roman Voting and Elections*. Ithaca, NY: Cornell University Press.

Stewart, Richard A. 1988. *Sunrise at Abadan: The British and Soviet Invasion of Iran, 1941*. New York: Praeger.

Strom, Kaare. 1990. *Minority Government and Majority Rule*. New York: Cambridge University Press.

Summers, Robert, and Alan Heston. 1991. "The Penn World Table: An Expanded Set of International Comparisons, 1950–88." *Quarterly Journal of Economics* 106: 327–368.

Sun Tzu. 1983. *The Art of War*. Ed. James Clavell. New York: Delacorte Press.

Tanzi, Vito. 1998. "Corruption around the World: Causes, Consequences, Scope and Cures." IMF Working Paper No. WP/98/63. International Monetary Fund.

Taylor, Alan. 1996. *William Cooper's Town*. New York: Vintage Books.

Taylor, Hannis. 1889. *The Origin and Growth of the English Constitution: An Historical Treatise. Part I*. New York: Houghton Mifflin.

Throup, David W., and Charles Hornsby. 1998. *Multi-Party Politics in Kenya*. Athens, OH: Ohio University Press.

Thurston, Robert W. 1996. *Life and Terror in Stalin's Russia, 1934–1941*. New Haven, CT: Yale University Press.

Tilly, Charles. 1975. "Revolutions and Collective Violence." In Fred I. Greenstein and Nelson W. Polsby, eds., *Handbook of Political Science*, vol 3. Reading, MA: Addison-Wesley.

Tilly, Charles. 1978. *From Mobilization to Revolution*. Reading, MA: Addison-Wesley.

Tilly, Charles. 1990. *Coercion, Capital, and European States, AD 990–1990*. New York: Blackwell.

Tir, Jaroslav, Philip Schafer, Paul F. Diehl, and Gary Goertz. 1998. "Territorial Changes, 1816–1996." *Conflict Management and Peace Science* 16: 89–97.

Triesman, Daniel. 2000. "The Causes of Corruption: A Cross-National Study." *Journal of Political Economy* 76(3): 399–457.

Tsebelis, George. 1990. *Nested Games: Rational Choice in Comparative Politics*. Berkeley: University of California Press.

Tullock, Gordon. 1971. "The Paradox of Revolution." *Public Choice* 11: 89–99.

Tullock, Gordon. 1986. *The Economics of Wealth and Poverty*. London: Wheatsheaf.

Van Dam, Nikolaos. 1996. *The Struggle for Power in Syria: Politics and Society Under Asad and the Ba'th Party*. New York: Tauris.

Vasquez, John A. 1995. "Why Do Neighbors Fight—Proximity, Interaction, or Territoriality?" *Journal of Peace Research* 32(3): 277–293.

Vasquez, John A. 2000. "What Do We Know about War?" In John A. Vasquez, ed., *What Do We Know about War?*, 335–370. Lanham, MD: Rowan and Littlefield.

Wagner, R. Harrison. 2000. "Bargaining and War." *American Journal of Political Science* 44: 469–484.

Waltz, Kenneth N. 1979. *Theory of International Politics*. New York: Random House.

Ward, Michael D., and Kristian S. Gleditsch. 1998. "Democratizing for Peace." *American Political Science Review* 92(1): 51–62.

Warwick, Paul V. 1992. "Economic Trends and Government Survival in West European Parliamentary Democracies." *American Political Science Review* 86: 875–887.

Warwick, Paul V. 1995. *Government Survival in Parliamentary Democracies*. New York: Cambridge University Press.

Weinberger, Caspar. 1984. "The Uses of Military Power." Remarks prepared for delivery to the National Press Club, Washington, D.C., November 28, 1984. <http://www.pbs.org/wgbh/pages/frontline/shows/military/force/weinberger.html/>

Weingast, Barry R. 1997. "The Political Foundations of Democracy and the Rule of Law." *American Political Science Review* 91: 245–263.

Weingast, Barry R., Kenneth Shepsle, and Christopher Johnsen. 1981. "The Political Economy of Benefits and Costs: A Neoclassical Approach to Distributive Politics." *Journal of Political Economy* 89: 642–669.

Werner, Suzanne. 1996. "Absolute and Limited War: The Possibilities of Foreign Imposed Regime Change." *International Interactions* 22: 67–88.

Werner, Suzanne. 1999. "The Precarious Nature of Peace: Resolving the Issues, Enforcing the Settlement, and Renegotiating the Terms." *American Journal of Political Science* 43: 912–934.

Wintrobe, Ronald. 1990. "The Tinpot and the Totalitarian: An Economic Analysis of Dictatorship." *American Political Science Review* 84: 849–872.

Wintrobe, Ronald. 1998. *The Political Economy of Dictatorship*. New York: Cambridge University Press.

Wittman, Donald. 1989. "Why Democracies Produce Efficient Results." *Journal of Political Economy* 97: 1395–1424.

Wittman, Donald. 1991. "Nations and States: Mergers and Acquisitions; Dissolutions and Divorce." *American Economic Review* 81(2): 126–129.

Xenophon. [c.360BC]. *Hellenica*. Book VI, chap. IV. Available at <http://www.fordham.edu/halsall/ancient/3711euctra.html>.

Zacher, Mark W. 2001. "The Territorial Integrity Norm: International Boundaries and the Use of Force." *International Organization* 55: 215–250.

"Zairian President Mobutu Steps Down, Flees." *Facts on File*, 57, no. 2946 (May 27, 1997): 351.

Zak, Paul J. 2000. "Socio-Political Instability and the Problem of Development." In Bruce Bueno de Mesquita and Hilton L. Root, eds., *Governing for Prosperity*. New Haven, CT: Yale University Press.

Index